ACCA

STUDY TEXT

Foundation Paper 3

Management information

New in this June 2000 edition

- New exam focus points which reflect the way in which this paper has been examined in recent sittings

- The text has been fully updated to reflect the ACCA Official Teaching Guide

FOR DECEMBER 2000 AND JUNE 2001 EXAMS

BPP Publishing
June 2000

First edition 1993
Eighth edition June 2000

ISBN 0 7517 0187 4 (Previous edition 0 7517 0157 2)

British Library Cataloguing-in-Publication Data
A catalogue record for this book is available from the British Library

Published by

BPP Publishing Limited
Aldine House, Aldine Place
London W12 8AW

www.bpp.com

Printed in Great Britain by Ashford Colour Press,
Gosport, Hants

We are grateful to the Association of Chartered Certified Accountants for permission to reproduce in this text the syllabus and teaching guide of which the Association holds the copyright.

We are also grateful to the Association of Chartered Certified Accountants for permission to reproduce past examination questions in our Exam Question Bank. The Exam Answer Bank has been prepared by BPP Publishing Limited.

Contents

Page

(iii)

BPP
PUBLISHING

Contents

HOW TO USE THIS STUDY TEXT

Aims of this Study Text

To provide you with the knowledge and understanding, skills and applied techniques required for passing the exam

The Study Text has been written around the ACCA's Official Syllabus and the ACCA's Official Teaching Guide (reproduced below, and cross-referenced to where in the text each topic is covered).

- It is **comprehensive**. We do not omit sections of the syllabus as the examiner is liable to examine any angle of any part of the syllabus - and you do not want to be left high and dry.

- It is **up-to-date as at 1 June 2000,** which means that it fulfils the requirement for the December 2000 exams that students should be up-to-date as at 1 June 2000.

- And it is **on-target**. We do not include any material which is not examinable. You can therefore rely on the BPP Study Text as the stand-alone source of all your information for the exam, without worrying that any of the material is irrelevant.

To allow you to study in the way that best suits your learning style and the time you have available, by following your personal Study Plan (see below)

You may be studying at home on your own until the date of the exam, or you may be attending a full-time course. You may like to (and have time to) read every word, or you may prefer to (or only have time to) skim-read and devote the remainder of your time to question practice. Wherever you fall in the spectrum, you will find the BPP Study Text meets your needs in designing and following your personal Study Plan.

To tie in with the other components of the BPP Effective Study Package to ensure you have the best possible chance of passing the exam

BPP PUBLISHING

Recommended period of use	Elements of the BPP Effective Study Package
3-12 months before exam	**Study Text** Acquisition of knowledge, understanding, skills and applied techniques.
1-6 months before exam	**Practice & Revision Kit** Tutorial questions and helpful checklists of the key points lead you into each area. There are then numerous Examination questions to try, graded by topic area, along with realistic suggested solutions prepared by BPP's own authors in the light of the Examiner's Reports. June 2001 examinees will find the 2001 edition of the Kit invaluable for bringing them up-to-date as at 1 December 2000, the cut-off date for the June 2001 examinable material.
last minute - 3 months before exam	**Passcards** Short, memorable notes focused on what is most likely to come up in the exam you will be sitting.
1-6 months before exam	**Success Tapes** Audio cassettes covering the vital elements of your syllabus in less than 90 minutes per subject. Each tape also contains exam hints to help you fine tune your strategy.
3-12 months before exam	**Breakthrough Videos** These supplement your Study Text, by giving you clear tuition on key exam subjects. They allow you the luxury of being able to pause or repeat sections until you have fully grasped the topic.
3-12 months before exam	**Master CD** Interactive CD-ROM containing questions on all aspects of the syllabus, cross referenced to help topics.

Settling down to study

By this stage in your career you are probably a very experienced learner and taker of exams. But have you ever thought about *how* you learn? Let's have a quick look at the key elements required for effective learning. You can then identify your learning style and go on to design your own approach to how you are going to study this text - your personal Study Plan.

Key element of learning	Using the BPP Study Text
Motivation	You can rely on the comprehensiveness and technical quality of BPP. You've chosen the right Study Text - so you're in pole position to pass your exam!
Clear objectives and standards	Do you want to be a prizewinner or simply achieve a moderate pass? Decide.
Feedback	Follow through the examples in this text and do the questions and the Quick Quizzes. Evaluate your efforts critically - how are you doing?
Study plan	You need to be honest about your progress to yourself - do not be over-confident, but don't be negative either. Make your Study Plan (see below) and try to stick to it. Focus on the short-term objectives - completing two chapters a night, say - but beware of losing sight of your study objectives
Practice	Use the Quick Quizzes and Chapter Roundups to refresh your memory regularly after you have completed your initial study of each chapter

These introductory pages let you see exactly what you are up against. However you study, you should:

- **read through the syllabus and teaching guide** - this will help you to identify areas you have already covered, perhaps at a lower level of detail, and areas that are totally new to you

- **study the examination paper section**, where we show you the format of the exam (how many and what kind of questions etc) and analyse all the papers set so far under the syllabus.

Key study steps

The following steps are, in our experience, the ideal way to study for professional exams. You can of course adapt it for your particular learning style (see below). Tackle the chapters in the order you find them in the Study Text. Taking into account your individual learning style, follow these key study steps for each chapter.

Key study steps	Activity
Step 1 *Chapter topic list*	Study the list. Each numbered topic denotes a numbered section in the chapter
Step 2 *Introduction*	Read it through. It is designed to show you *why* the topics in the chapter need to be studied - how they lead on from previous topics, and how they lead into subsequent ones
Step 3 *Knowledge brought forward boxes*	Not applicable to this Study Text
Step 4 *Explanations*	Proceed methodically through the chapter, reading each section thoroughly and making sure you understand. Where a topic has been examined, we state the month and year of examination against the appropriate heading. You should pay particular attention to these topics.
Step 5 *Key terms* and *Exam focus points*	• **Key terms** can often earn you *easy marks* if you state them clearly and correctly in an appropriate exam answer (and they are indexed at the back of the text so you can check easily that you are on top of all of them when you come to revise) • **Exam focus points** give you a good idea of how the examiner tends to examine certain topics - and also pinpoint *easy marks*
Step 6 *Note taking*	Take brief notes if you wish, avoiding the temptation to copy out too much
Step 7 *Examples*	Follow each through to its solution very carefully
Step 8 *Case examples*	Not applicable to this Study Text.
Step 9 *Questions*	Make a very good attempt at each one
Step 10 *Answers*	Check yours against ours, and make sure you understand any discrepancies
Step 11 *Chapter roundup*	Check through it very carefully, to make sure you have grasped the major points it is highlighting

Key study steps	Activity
Step 12 *Quick quiz*	When you are happy that you have covered the chapter, use the **Quick quiz** to check your recall of the topics covered. The answers are in the paragraphs in the chapter that we refer you to
Step 13 *Examination question(s)*	Either at this point, or later when you are thinking about revising, make a full attempt at the **Examination question(s)** suggested at the very end of the chapter. You can find these at the end of the Study Text, along with the **Answers** so you can see how you did. We highlight for you which ones are introductory, and which are of the full standard you would expect to find in an exam

Developing your personal Study Plan

Preparing a Study Plan (and sticking closely to it) is one of the key elements in learning success.

First you need to be aware of your style of learning. There are four typical learning styles. Consider yourself in the light of the following descriptions. and work out which you fit most closely. You can then plan to follow the key study steps in the sequence suggested.

Learning styles	Characteristics	Sequence of key study steps in the BPP Study Text
Theorist	Seeks to understand principles before applying them in practice	1, 2, 3, 4, 7, 5, 9/10, 11, 12, 13 (6 continuous)
Reflector	Seeks to observe phenomena, thinks about them and then chooses to act	
Activist	Prefers to deal with practical, active problems; does not have much patience with theory	1, 2, 9/10 (read through), 7, 5, 11, 3, 4, 9/10 (full attempt), 12, 13 (6 continuous)
Pragmatist	Prefers to study only if a direct link to practical problems can be seen; not interested in theory for its own sake	9/10 (read through), 2, 5, 7, 11, 1, 3, 4, 9/10 (full attempt), 12, 13 (6 continuous)

Next you should complete the following checklist.

Am I motivated? (a) [ ]

Do I have an objective and a standard that I want to achieve? (b) [ ]

Am I a theorist, a reflector, an activist or a pragmatist? (c) [ ]

How much time do I have available per week, given: (d) [ ]

- the standard I have set myself

- the time I need to set aside later for work on the Practice and Revision Kit and Passcards

- the other exam(s) I am sitting, and (of course)

- practical matters such as work, travel, exercise, sleep and social life?

BPP PUBLISHING

Now:

- take the time you have available per week for this Study Text (d), and multiply it by the number of weeks available to give (e).

- divide (e) by the number of chapters to give (f)

- set about studying each chapter in the time represented by (f), following the key study steps in the order suggested by your particular learning style.

This is your personal **Study Plan**.

Short of time?

Whatever your objectives, standards or style, you may find you simply do not have the time available to follow all the key study steps for each chapter, however you adapt them for your particular learning style. If this is the case, follow the Skim Study technique below (the icons in the Study Text will help you to do this).

Skim Study technique

Study the chapters in the order you find them in the Study Text. For each chapter, follow the key study steps 1-3, and then skim-read through step 4. Jump to step 11, and then go back to step 5. Follow through step 7, and prepare outline Answers to Questions (steps 9/10). Try the Quick Quiz (step 12), following up any items you can't answer, then do a plan for the Examination Question (step 13), comparing it against our answers. You should probably still follow step 6 (note-taking), although you may decide simply to rely on the BPP Passcards for this.

Moving on...

However you study, when you are ready to embark on the practice and revision phase of the BPP Effective Study Package, you should still refer back to this study text:

- as a source of **reference** (you should find the list of key terms and the index particularly helpful for this)

- as a **refresher** (the Chapter Roundups and Quick Quizzes help you here)

And remember to keep careful hold of this Study Text when you move onto the next level of your exams - you will find it invaluable.

ACCA OFFICIAL SYLLABUS

Aim of Paper 3

To provide a solid foundation in quantitative techniques and costing methods relevant to business and accounting.

Management Information is a broad-based syllabus which seeks to provide a foundation in cost and management accounting and quantitative analysis within business. This includes an appreciation of the part that information technology plays in facilitating the provision, analysis and presentation of financial and other quantitative data.

On completion of this paper, students should be able to:

- discuss the role of cost and management accounting and quantitative analysis within the organisation
- describe the role of computers in information analysis
- use various classifications to analyse costs within the organisation
- describe and apply the principles relating to the costing of the different resource inputs to a business
- demonstrate output costing methods appropriate to a variety of businesses
- illustrate and evaluate absorption and marginal costing methods
- formulate a problem in mathematical terms, solve the problem and be able to interpret the results
- understand and apply statistical techniques, including methods of presentation, which are appropriate in a business environment
- demonstrate the skills expected at the Foundation Stage.

The Examiner will test basic knowledge and skills. Students may be required to perform a variety of functions, for example, to:

- identify and sort related data or to process that data where necessary to produce information
- use formulae and solve problems
- present and communicate information in a logical format
- analyse results
- describe and appraise concepts and techniques

The Examiner will test not only recall but understanding and application.

Prerequisite knowledge

Understanding of accounting principles and practices from paper 1 Accounting Framework and a basic competence in numeracy.

Development of paper 3 topics to subsequent papers

Students need a sound understanding of the techniques covered in paper 3 for the more advanced study in subsequent papers.

The cost accounting aspects in paper 3 are built upon in paper 8 Managerial Finance and paper 9 Information for Control and Decision Making.

The quantitative techniques are integrated with their application in paper 6 Audit Framework, paper 8 Managerial Finance, paper 9 Information for Control and Decision Making, paper 10 Accounting and Audit Practice, paper 12 Management and Strategy and paper 14 Financial Strategy as shown below:

BPP PUBLISHING

CORE SUBJECT	SUPPORT SUBJECT
	Quantitative Techniques
Management Accounting	Papers 8 and 9
Financial Management	Papers 8 and 14
Auditing	Papers 6 and 10
Management	Paper 12

The coverage of computers and computer software is necessary background to paper 5 Information Analysis.

Key areas of the syllabus

The major features of the costing element of the syllabus are as follows.

- Cost classification
- Material, labour and overhead cost
- Cost bookkeeping
- Absorption and marginal costing
- Job/batch and contract costing
- Process costing; service costing
- Cost behaviour; CVP analysis

The main features of the quantitative techniques element of the syllabus are as follows.

- Data collection and presentation
- Measures of centrality and spread
- Index numbers
- Introduction to probability
- Normal distribution
- Estimation and testing
- Linear equations and linear programming
- Non-linear equations and differential calculus
- Interest and discounting

General notes

Students are advised to read the 'Exam Notes' published in the Students' Newsletter as these contain details of examinable legislation, changes in the syllabuses and other useful information for each examination session.

A normal distribution table, present value table and formulae sheet will be provided in the exam.

Quantitative Techniques Content (50%)

Introduction

This section introduces the quantitative techniques that are relevant to economics, business and accounting. Throughout, students should meet the material within a business context using real-life business data, where possible, so that they understand how the techniques can be used by accountants. An important aim of this section is to enhance the students' reasoning and analytical skills and to develop their problem-solving skills. With the advent of off-the-shelf packages employing quantitative techniques it is important that students understand the scope and limitations of a specific technique rather than the intricacies of the mathematics underlying the technique.

		Covered in Chapter
1	**Background information**	

This section looks at the role of quantitative techniques within business and, in particular, the accounting function. The role of quantitative techniques is to clarify and quantify the uncertainty in the decision making process. However such techniques will rarely be the only source of information that the accountant will use before reaching a decision.

(a)	The role of quantitative techniques in problem solving situations.	2
(b)	The value of qualitative and quantitative information in decision-making.	1
(c)	Interpretation of results and evaluation of the impact of optimum decisions.	16,21,26,27
(d)	The benefit of computer software (eg spreadsheets and statistics packages) in handling numerical information.	3

2 Arithmetic operations

This section provides an introduction to advanced arithmetic procedures within an accounting context. It applies some of the basic arithmetic operations to financial problems involving the way that the value of money varies with time.

(a)	Arithmetic procedures; powers and roots; logarithms.	2
(b)	Percentages and ratios.	2
(c)	Simple and compound interest; nominal and effective interest rates.	29
(d)	Discounted cash flow; net present value; internal rate of return.	29
(e)	Use of spreadsheets to carry out arithmetic operations.	3

3 Basic mathematical techniques

This section provides an introduction to the use of mathematics as a tool in economics and business. It should illustrate the use of mathematical solutions to define and describe relationships within an economic and accounting context.

(a)	Graphical representation of functions.	23-28
(b)	Solution of linear, simultaneous and quadratic equations.	2,23-26
(c)	Linear programming, graphical solution; application to business problems.	26
(d)	Gradients of curves; differentiation; maxima and minima; application to economics and management accounting problems.	27,28

4 Measurement of uncertainty

This section describes the measurement of uncertainty with an awareness of general applications to investment decisions, auditing, budgeting and other areas of business.

(a)	Probability: addition and multiplication laws, tree diagrams.	20,21
(b)	Normal distribution.	22
(c)	Expectation: application to decision problems.	21

5   Statistical presentation

This section describes those techniques useful in the collection and description of numerical business data.

6   Statistical measures

This section introduces techniques useful for summarising large data sets - commonly occurring within many business functions.

Cost Accounting Content (50%)

Introduction

This section covers the methods and systems of cost accounting. It provides both an extension of the financial accounting covered in paper 1 and also a basis for the study of management accounting in subsequent papers.

1   Cost and management accounting framework

This section provides an introduction to cost and management accounting including comparison with financial accounting and the classification and recording of cost information.

(a)   Cost and management accounting versus financial accounting:

		Covered in Chapter
(ii)	describe cost accounting's part in a management information system;	1
(iii)	appreciate the importance of non-financial information as well as financial information;	1
(iv)	appreciate the potential applications of information technology.	3

(b) Cost book-keeping:

(i)	understand and apply the principles of double-entry including the use of journal and control accounts;	5,7,10
(ii)	use integrated and inter-locking systems.	10

(c) Key cost classifications, concepts and terminology:

(i)	understand the nature and purpose of cost classifications/ definitions such as: - direct/indirect - fixed/variable - period/product - controllable/uncontrollable - avoidable/unavoidable - budget/standard/actual;	4,7,24
(ii)	use linear, curvi-linear and step functions and describe factors which influence cost behaviour;	7,24
(iii)	explain the concept of cost units, cost centres and profit centres;	4
(iv)	outline the difference between absorption and marginal costing systems.	9

2 Cost determination: costing of resource inputs

This section covers the principles and practice of costing the different resource inputs to a business viz materials, labour, other expenses.

(a) Materials:

(i)	account for stock movements;	5
(ii)	determine optimum purchase quantities;	5,28
(iii)	price material issues;	6
(iv)	identify and account for stock losses.	5

(b) Labour:

(i)	demonstrate understanding of direct and indirect labour;	7
(ii)	use and contrast different remuneration methods;	7
(iii)	calculate and explain labour efficiency;	7
(iv)	record labour costs;	7
(v)	calculate and appreciate the cost of labour turnover.	7

(c) Overheads:

(i)	describe the principles and process of overhead cost analysis;	8
(ii)	apportion and absorb overhead costs (including reciprocal service situations);	8,23

ACCA OFFICIAL TEACHING GUIDE

This is the Official Teaching Guide for the December 2000 and June 2001 exams.

**Syllabus
reference**
CA
Cost Accounting
QT
Quantitative
Techniques

Session 1   Introduction

QT 1a, b
QT 2a, b
QT 5a

- distinguish between 'data' and 'information'
- discuss the management of both financial and non-financial information requirements
- describe the role of quantitative techniques in the analysis of business information
- contrast financial and cost and management accounting
- outline the managerial processes of planning, decision-making and control
- describe cost and management accounting's part in a management information system
- understand basic arithmetic principles and calculations, including significant digits, percentages, ratios, symbols and equations
- evaluate expressions involving powers and roots
- identify relationships using logarithms

CA 1a(i), (ii), (iii)

Session 2   The role of information technology in management information

QT 1d,
QT 2e
QT 5c

- identify the characteristics and different types of computer hardware and software
- describe the potential value of computer systems in handling and processing business data
- describe methods of capturing and processing data by computer
- describe how data is grouped, tabulated, stored and output
- explain the role and features of spreadsheet systems
- explain the role and features of statistical packages

QT 6e,CA 1a(iv)

Session 3   Cost classification and processing

CA 1c(i), (iii) CA 3

- explain and illustrate classifications used in the analysis of product/service costs, including by function, direct and indirect, product and period, fixed and variable, avoidable and unavoidable, controllable and uncontrollable
- describe the nature of control achieved through the comparison of actual costs against plan
- explain and illustrate the concept of cost objects, cost units, cost centres and profit centres
- explain, in outline, the process of accounting for input costs and relating them to work done
- describe briefly the different methods of costing final outputs and their appropriateness to different types of business organisation/situation

Session 4   Material costs

CA 1b(i)
CA 2a(i),(iii),(iv)

- describe the different procedures and documents necessary for ordering, receiving and issuing materials from stock
- produce and interpret calculations to enable efficient stock control
- describe the control procedures used to monitor physical and 'book' stock and to minimise discrepancies and losses
- explain, illustrate and evaluate the alternative methods used to price raw material stock issues
- prepare journal and ledger entries for the receipt and issue of raw material stock
- interpret the entries and balances in the material stock accounts

- complete cost records and accounts in job, batch and contract cost accounting situations
- discuss, and illustrate, the treatment of direct, indirect and abnormal costs
- explain, and illustrate, measures of profit on uncompleted contracts

Session 11 Process costing: an introduction

CA 3b(i),(ii),(iii),
(iv)

- describe situations where the use of process costing is appropriate
- calculate the cost per unit of process outputs, and prepare simple work-in-process accounts, in absorption and marginal costing systems
- distinguish between by-products and joint products
- value by-products and joint products at the point of separation
- prepare process accounts in situations where by-products and/or joint products occur
- describe the key areas of complexity in process costing

Session 12 Process costing: work-in-process
and process losses/gains

CA 3b(ii),(iii),(iv)

- calculate equivalent units
- allocate process costs between work remaining in process and transfers out of a process using the average cost and first-in-first-out methods
- prepare process accounts in situations where work remains incomplete
- define 'normal' losses and 'abnormal' gains and losses
- state and justify the treatment of normal losses and abnormal gains and losses in process accounts
- account for process scrap
- prepare process accounts in situations where losses and gains are identified at different stages of the process (where no work remains in process)

Session 13 Service costing

CA 3c(i),(ii),(iii)

- describe situations where the use of operation costing or service costing is appropriate
- illustrate suitable unit cost measures that may be used in a variety of different operations and services
- carry out service cost analysis in internal service situations
- carry out service cost analysis in service industry situations

Session 14 Data collection

QT 5a, b

- describe types of data and information, both quantitative and qualitative, and their uses
- explain the differences between discrete and continuous data, primary and secondary data, raw and aggregated data, sample and population data, descriptive and inferential statistics
- describe the stages in sample data collection
- differentiate between random, quasi-random, and non-random sampling
- describe and appraise the different sampling techniques
- discuss sampling methods appropriate to auditing

Section 15 Data presentation

QT 1c
QT 5d, e

- demonstrate, and evaluate, the use of tables, bar charts and pie charts
- aggregate raw data into a frequency table, and construct and evaluate histograms, pictograms and polygons
- construct cumulative frequency tables and ogives
- identify percentiles, deciles and quartiles on the ogive
- construct a Lorenz curve from cumulative percentage frequency data
- extract and interpret key information from tables and charts

Session 16 Measures of centrality

- calculate the mean for both raw and grouped data
- explain the meaning of the arithmetic mean
- determine the median and the mode for both raw and grouped data
- explain the meaning of the median and the mode
- explain the basis for the difference between the averages from raw and those from grouped data
- explain the basis for the differences between, and uses of, the three measures of centrality in a business context

Session 17 Measures of spread

- explain why measures of spread are needed
- calculate the standard deviation and the coefficient of variation for both raw and grouped data
- explain the meaning of the standard deviation and the coefficient of variation
- calculate the interquartile range, the quartile deviation and the coefficient of skewness
- explain the meaning of the quartile deviation and the coefficient of skewness

Session 18 Index numbers

- state the purposes of index numbers, and calculate and interpret simple index numbers for one or more variables
- deflate time related data using an index
- construct a chained index series
- explain the term 'average index', distinguishing between simple and weighted averages
- calculate Laspeyres and Paasche price and quantity indices
- discuss the relative utility of the Laspeyres and Paasche indices

Session 19 Introduction to probability

- explain the concepts of uncertainty and probability
- calculate the probability of independent, mutually exclusive and conditional events
- use the multiplication and addition rules in their correct context
- calculate expected value from information supplied
- construct and interpret decision trees including probabilities and expected outcomes and values
- apply the concepts of probability and expected value to business decision problems

Session 20 The normal distribution

- describe the features of a continuous probability distribution
- explain the features of a normal distribution
- use normal distribution tables
- explain what is meant by statistical inference
- describe the features of a sampling distribution
- explain the meaning of the standard error and its relationship to the standard deviation of the population
- describe the properties of the Central Limit Theorem

Session 21 Estimation and testing

- explain the meaning of a confidence interval
- estimate a population mean using confidence intervals and sample data
- estimate a population proportion using confidence intervals and sample data
- calculate the sample size required to estimate a population mean or proportion with stated error and given level of confidence
- explain the meaning of the null and alternative hypotheses
- carry out, and interpret, one and two tailed tests for a population mean and a population proportion

	Syllabus reference
Session 22 Linear equations	QT 3a, b CA 2c(ii)

- explain the structure of linear functions and equations
- show a linear equation on a graph and explain the terms 'intercept' and 'slope'
- determine the intercept and slope from an equation
- solve a two equation problem using graphs
- solve a two equation problem using an algebraic method
- use simultaneous equations to apportion service department overheads

Session 23 Cost behaviour	QT 3(a),(b) CA 1(c)(ii)

- explain the importance of cost behaviour in relation to business decision-making
- describe factors which influence cost behaviour
- use linear, curvi-linear, and step functions
- provide examples of costs which contain both fixed and variable elements
- use high/low analysis to separate the elements

Session 24 Cost-volume-profit analysis	QT 3a, b CA 4c(i), (ii)

- explain the concept of break-even
- construct break-even, contribution, and profit/volume charts from given selling price, costs and volume data
- construct a cost/volume/profit (CVP) model representing the data in a marginal costing profit and loss account
- apply the CVP model in multi-product situations
- calculate, and explain, the margin of safety

Session 25 Linear programming	QT 1c QT 3a, b, c

- recognise what causes optimisation problems
- formulate a linear programming problem involving two variables
- determine the optimal solution to a linear programming problem using a graph
- determine the optimal solution to a linear programming problem using equations

Session 26 Non-linear equations and differential calculus	QT 3a, b, d

- explain the structure of non-linear functions and equations and represent on a graph
- recognise and draw a graph of a quadratic equation
- determine and interpret the solutions to a quadratic equation and use them to find the turning point of the function
- explain the purpose of differentiation and differentiate common functions
- use differentiation to find the turning point of a quadratic equation and to establish whether the turning point is a maximum or minimum value

Session 27 Applying differential calculus	QT 1c QT 3b,d CA 2a(ii)

- use differentiation in a business context
- calculate and interpret the maximum/minimum for a given business situation
- explain the elements of stock ordering costs and stock holding costs and their behaviour according to order quantity
- use the Economic Order Quantity (EOQ) model to calculate the optimum order size
- determine the number of orders to be placed and the frequency of orders
- explain the limitations of the EOQ model
- tabulate and graph costs to establish the EOQ

BPP PUBLISHING

Session 28 Interest

- explain the difference between simple and compound interest and calculate future values
- explain the difference between nominal and effective interest rates and calculate effective interest rates
- explain what is meant by discounting and calculate present values
- apply discounting principles to calculate the net present value of an investment project
- explain what is meant by, and calculate, the internal rate of return

THE EXAMINATION PAPER

Format of the paper

Paper 3 is a combined paper - quantitative techniques and cost accounting will each account for approximately 50% of the paper.

	Number of marks
5 (out of 6) questions of 20 marks each	100

The paper was examined in the above format for the first time in June 1997. The examiner has indicated that questions will be of a similar style and approach to questions asked since June 1994. Questions will however be longer and therefore have a wider syllabus coverage. Cost accounting and quantitative techniques elements may be examined in the same question. The overall weighting will remain 50:50 cost accounting and quantitative techniques. Approximately 25% of the paper will continue to require narrative rather than computational answers.

Analysis of past papers

The analysis below shows the topics which have been examined in Paper 3 *Management Information* since June 1996.

December 1999

5 (out of 6) questions of 20 marks each

1   Cost bookkeeping and process costing
2   Cost determination, forecasting, breakeven analysis
3   Arithmetic mean, standard deviation, data presentation
4   Stock control
5   Overhead apportionment, profitability calculations and commentary
6   Probability, confidence limits, sample sizes

June 1999

5 (out of 6) questions of 20 marks each

1   Contract costing, overhead apportionment and service costing
2   Computerised data processing systems, ogives and probability
3   Stocktaking, confidence intervals and sample sizes
4   Cost bookkeeping and labour costs
5   Interest, discounting, and probability
6   Breakeven analysis, marginal costing and absorption costing

December 1998

5 (out of 6) questions of 20 marks each

1   Arithmetic mean; data presentation; standard deviation and sampling
2   Stock control and cost bookkeeping
3   Job costing; absorption costing and joint products
4   Service costing and breakeven analysis
5   Index numbers
6   Linear programming

June 1998

5 (out of 6) questions of 20 marks each

1   Absorption costing
2   Process costing
3   Discounting, index numbers and probability
4   Averages, measures of spread and normal distribution calculations
5   CVP (breakeven) analysis
6   Calculus and stock control (with graphical presentation)

December 1997

5 (out of 6) questions of 20 marks each

1   Labour costs, cost classification
2   Decision making, NPV
3   Marginal costing and absorption costing
4   Job, batch and contract costing systems, stock valuation
5   Averages and measures of spread
6   Determination of maximum profit using graph, quadratic equations, differentiation

June 1997

5 (out of 6) questions of 20 marks each

1   Absorption costing and job costing
2   Sampling methods, grouped frequency distributions and frequency polygons
3   Linear programming, marginal costing and decision-making
4   Process costing, and standard deviation calculation
5   Break-even arithmetic and calculus
6   Coefficient of skewness, marginal and absorption costing

December 1996

Section A (30 marks)

20 multiple choice questions covering cost accounting and quantitative techniques

Section B (5 out of 6, 70 marks)

1   Probability and the normal distribution
2   Laspeyre and Paasche indices
3   Computer terminology and DCF calculations
4   Process costing, material documentation
5   Marginal costing, sales mix
6   Stock control

June 1996

Section A (30 marks)

20 multiple choice questions covering cost accounting and quantitative techniques

Section B (5 out of 6, 70 marks)

1   Stratified sampling and a sample size calculation
2   Bar charts and ogives
3   Quadratic equations, profit maximisation using differentiation, interest calculations, contract costing
4   Profit maximisation, marginal costing, scarce resources
5   Absorption rates, over/under absorption of overheads, job costing
6   Differences between cost and financial accounting, cost bookkeeping

Part A

Introduction to cost accounting and quantitative techniques

Chapter 1

MANAGEMENT INFORMATION AND COST ACCOUNTING

Chapter topic list	Syllabus reference
1 Information	QT 1(b); CA 1(a)(iii)
2 Planning, control and decision making	CA 1
3 Types of information	QT1(b); CA1(a)(iii)
4 Information systems and management information systems	CA 1 (a)(ii)
5 Financial accounting and cost and management accounting	CA 1(a)(i)

Introduction

Welcome to Management Information and hence to cost accounting and quantitative techniques. You are going to be tackling cost accounting first, moving on to quantitative techniques in the second part of this Study Text.

This and the following four chapters provide an introduction to both subjects. This chapter looks at **information** and introduces **cost accounting**, thereby providing a basis for the cost accounting chapters of this Study Text. Many cost accounting procedures require the application of mathematical techniques and so in Chapter 2 a brief revision of basic mathematics is provided.

1   INFORMATION

KEY TERMS

- **Data** is the raw material for data processing. Data relates to facts, events and transactions and so forth.

- **Information** is data that has been processed in such a way as to be **meaningful** to the person who receives it. **Information** is anything that is communicated.

1.1   Information is sometimes referred to as processed data. The terms 'information' and 'data' are often used interchangeably. It is important to understand the difference between these two terms.

1.2   Researchers who conduct market research surveys might ask members of the public to complete questionnaires about a product or a service. These completed questionnaires are **data**; they are processed and analysed in order to prepare a report on the survey. This resulting report is **information** and may be used by management for decision-making purposes.

BPP PUBLISHING

1.3   The qualities of good information are as follows.

- It should be **relevant** for its purpose.
- It should be **complete** for its purpose.
- It should be sufficiently **accurate** for its purpose.
- It should be **clear** to the user.
- The user should have **confidence** in it.
- It should be **communicated** to the right person.
- It should not be excessive - its **volume** should be manageable.
- It should be **timely** - in other words communicated at the most appropriate time.
- It should be communicated by an appropriate **channel** of communication.
- It should be provided at a **cost** which is less than the value of its benefits.

1.4   Let us look at those qualities in more detail.

(a)   **Relevance**. Information must be relevant to the purpose for which a manager wants to use it. In practice, far too many reports fail to 'keep to the point' and contain purposeless, irritating paragraphs which only serve to vex the managers reading them.

(b)   **Completeness**. An information user should have all the information he needs to do his job properly. If he does not have a complete picture of the situation, he might well make bad decisions.

(c)   **Accuracy**. Information should obviously be accurate because using incorrect information could have serious and damaging consequences. However, information should only be accurate enough for its purpose and there is no need to go into unnecessary detail for pointless accuracy.

(d)   **Clarity**. Information must be clear to the user. If the user does not understand it properly he cannot use it properly. Lack of clarity is one of the causes of a breakdown in communication. It is therefore important to choose the most appropriate presentation medium or channel of communication.

(e)   **Confidence**. Information must be trusted by the managers who are expected to use it. However not all information is certain. Some information has to be certain, especially operating information, for example, related to a production process. Strategic information, especially relating to the environment, is uncertain. However, if the assumptions underlying it are clearly stated, this might enhance the confidence with which the information is perceived.

(f)   **Communication**. Within any organisation, individuals are given the authority to do certain tasks, and they must be given the information they need to do them. An office manager might be made responsible for controlling expenditures in his office, and given a budget expenditure limit for the year. As the year progresses, he might try to keep expenditure in check but unless he is told throughout the year what is his current total expenditure to date, he will find it difficult to judge whether he is keeping within budget or not.

(g)   **Volume**. There are physical and mental limitations to what a person can read, absorb and understand properly before taking action. An enormous mountain of information, even if it is all relevant, cannot be handled. Reports to management must therefore be **clear** and **concise** and in many systems, control action works basically on the 'exception' principle.

(h)   **Timing**. Information which is not available until after a decision is made will be useful only for comparisons and longer-term control, and may serve no purpose even then. Information prepared too frequently can be a serious disadvantage. If, for example, a decision is taken at a monthly meeting about a certain aspect of a company's operations, information to make the decision is only required once a month, and weekly reports would be a time-consuming waste of effort.

(i) **Channel of communication.** There are occasions when using one particular method of communication will be better than others. For example, job vacancies should be announced in a medium where they will be brought to the attention of the people most likely to be interested. The channel of communication might be the company's in-house journal, a national or local newspaper, a professional magazine, a job centre or school careers office. Some internal memoranda may be better sent by 'electronic mail'. Some information is best communicated informally by telephone or word-of-mouth, whereas other information ought to be formally communicated in writing or figures.

(j) **Cost.** Information should have some value, otherwise it would not be worth the cost of collecting and filing it. The benefits obtainable from the information must also exceed the costs of acquiring it, and whenever management is trying to decide whether or not to produce information for a particular purpose (for example whether to computerise an operation or to build a financial planning model) a cost/benefit study ought to be made.

Question 1

The value of information lies in the action taken as a result of receiving it. What questions might you ask in order to make an assessment of the value of information?

Answer

(a) What information is provided?
(b) What is it used for?
(c) Who uses it?
(d) How often is it used?
(e) Does the frequency with which it is used coincide with the frequency with which it is provided?
(f) What is achieved by using it?
(g) What other relevant information is available which could be used instead?

An assessment of the value of information can be derived in this way, and the cost of obtaining it should then be compared against this value. On the basis of this comparison, it can be decided whether certain items of information are worth having. It should be remembered that there may also be intangible benefits which may be harder to quantify.

Why is information important?

1.5 Consider the following problems and what management needs to solve these problems.

(a) A company wishes to launch a new product. The company's pricing policy is to charge cost plus 20%. What should the price of the product be?

(b) An organisation's widget-making machine has a fault. The organisation has to decide whether to repair the machine, buy a new machine or hire a machine. What does the organisation do if its aim is to control costs?

(c) A firm is considering offering a discount of 2% to those customers who pay an invoice within seven days of the invoice date and a discount of 1% to those customers who pay an invoice within eight to 14 days of the invoice date. How much will this discount offer cost the firm?

1.6 In solving these and a wide variety of other problems, **management need information.**

(a) In problem (a) of Paragraph 1.5, management would need information about the **cost of the new product**.

(b) Faced with problem (b), management would need information on the **cost of repairing, buying and hiring the machine**.

(c) To calculate the cost of the discount offer described in (c), information would be required about **current sales settlement patterns** and **expected changes to the pattern** if discounts were offered.

1.7 The successful management of *any* organisation depends on information: non-profit making organisations such as charities, clubs and local authorities need information for decision making and for reporting the results of their activities just as multi-nationals do. For example a tennis club needs to know the cost of undertaking its various activity so that it can determine the amount of annual subscription it should charge its members.

What type of information is needed?

1.8 Having ascertained that all organisations require information we now need to consider what type of information is needed.

Question 2

You are a member of Dimbledon Tennis Club Committee. At the annual general meeting each year the treasurer of the club presents to members a statement of receipts and payments of cash during the last year. This is the only accounting information produced for the club's members and committee. The club has twelve courts and a club house in which there is a large bar. The club organises a large number of excursions each year to Wimbledon and other tennis tournaments, holds social events in the club house, runs coaching sessions for children during the school holidays and holds tennis tournaments throughout the year. Considerable revenue and expenditure is involved in all of these activities.

Required

List the other information that you think the committee and others ought to have during the year to ensure that Dimbledon Tennis Club's affairs are being run properly.

Answer

The following list is not a complete one. You will, more than likely, have other items on your list and will possibly not have included everything on this list.

(a) Information for planning

Long term plans

(i) Knowledge of the existing or changing age-range mix in the local population
(ii) Information on activities requested by members

Short term (for 12 months)

(i) Proposed activities and their organisers during the coming year
(ii) Estimates of expected receipts and payments for each activity
(iii) Estimates of the general costs of running the club
(iv) A forecast of membership and the proposed level of subscription
(v) Proposed equipment and other capital items which need to be bought
(vi) A summary of total expected cash receipts and payments

(b) Information for control

The following information relating to completed and continuing activities would be required throughout the year.

(i) Periodically updated cash forecast for the twelve months ahead

(ii) Receipts, payments, bookings and so on relating to each activity

      (iii)   Reports upon completed activities. Were they well supported? Who won the tournaments?

      (iv)   Reports on continuing activities such as the bar

      (v)   Comparisons of actual and planned costs, both on an activity by activity basis and on an overall basis

  (c)   Information for decision making

      (i)   Details of changes in membership

      (ii)   Progress and financial reports from organisers of planned activities, including any difficulties being encountered

      (iii)   Details on the current cash position of the club

      (iv)   All of the information necessary for planning and controlling the club

---

1.9   As you can see, we divided the list into the information requirements for **planning** the club's activities, **controlling** those activities and **making any decisions**. We will go on to look at these processes later in this chapter.

1.10   What should be clear to you is that the information required is not just of a **financial nature** (such as the receipts and payments relating to each activity) but also of a **non-financial nature** (membership details, activities required by members, local community population and so on). Business organisations go through much the same process of planning and controlling as a sports club (though on a larger scale) and therefore require both **financial** and **non-financial information**.

1.11   Financial and non-financial information may be combined to produce a significant third measurement. Suppose that the management of ABC Ltd have decided to provide a canteen for their employees.

  (a)   The **financial information** required by management might include canteen staff costs, costs of subsidising meals, capital costs, costs of heat and light and so on.

  (b)   The **non-financial information** might include management comment on the effect on employee morale of the provision of canteen facilities, details of the number of meals served each day, meter readings for gas and electricity and attendance records for canteen employees.

1.12   ABC Ltd could now **combine financial and non-financial information** to calculate the average cost to the company of each meal served, thereby enabling them to predict total costs depending on the number of employees in the work force.

1.13   Most people probably consider that management accounting is only concerned with financial information and that people do not matter. This is, nowadays, a long way from the truth. Just as the committee of Dimbledon Tennis Club would want to know whether their members enjoyed the trips to Wimbledon in order to help them to decide whether to run another similar trip, managers of business organisations need to know whether employee morale has increased due to introducing a canteen, whether the bread from particular suppliers is fresh and the reason why the canteen staff are demanding a new dishwasher. This type of non-financial information will play its part in **planning, controlling** and **decision making** and is therefore just as important to management as financial information is.

1.14   **Non-financial information** must therefore be **monitored** as carefully, **recorded** as accurately and **taken into account** as fully as financial information. There is little point in a careful and accurate recording of total canteen costs if the recording of the information on the number of meals eaten in the canteen is uncontrolled and therefore produces inaccurate information.

1.15 While management accounting is mainly concerned with the provision of **financial information** to aid planning, control and decision making, the management accountant cannot ignore **non-financial influences** and should qualify the information he provides with non-financial matters as appropriate.

2 PLANNING, CONTROL AND DECISION MAKING

2.1 When we defined the difference between data and information earlier in this chapter, we said that information is data processed into a form meaningful to the person who receives it. In terms of management accounting, the information is most likely to be for **planning**, **control** or **decision making**.

Planning

2.2 An organisation should never be surprised by developments which occur gradually over an extended period of time because the organisation should have **implemented a planning process**. Planning involves the following.

- Establishing objectives
- Selecting appropriate strategies to achieve those objectives

Planning therefore forces management to think ahead systematically in both the **short term** and the **long term**.

Long-term strategic planning

> **KEY TERM**
>
> **Long-term planning**, also known as **corporate planning**, involves selecting appropriate strategies so as to prepare a long-term plan to attain the objectives.

2.3 The time span covered by a long-term plan depends on the **organisation**, the **industry** in which it operates and the particular **environment** involved. Typical periods are 2, 5, 7 or 10 years although longer periods are frequently encountered.

2.4 **Long-term strategic planning** is a **detailed, lengthy process**, essentially incorporating three stages and ending with a **corporate plan**. The diagram on the next page provides an overview of the process and shows the link between short-term and long-term planning.

Short-term tactical planning

2.5 The **long-term corporate plan** serves as the **long-term framework** for the organisation as a whole but for operational purposes it is necessary to convert the corporate plan into a series of **short-term plans**, usually covering **one year**, which relate to **sections, functions** or **departments**. The annual process of short-term planning should be seen as stages in the progressive fulfilment of the corporate plan as each short-term plan steers the organisation towards its long-term objectives. It is therefore vital that, to obtain the maximum advantage from short-term planning, some sort of long-term plan exists.

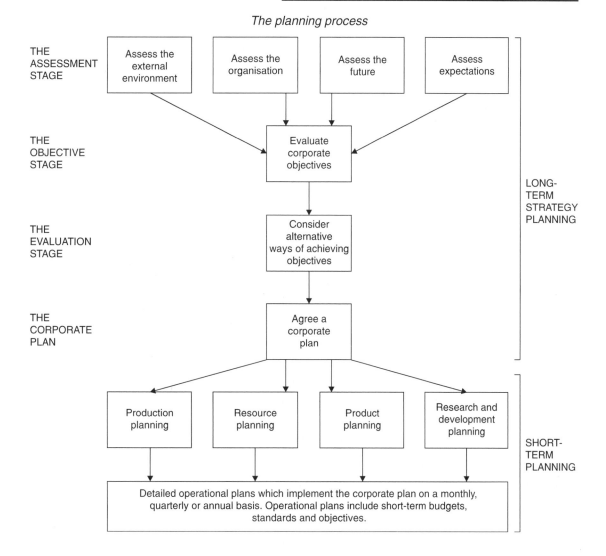

The planning process

Control

2.6   There are two stages in the **control process**.

(a)   The **performance of the organisation** as set out in the detailed operational plans is compared with the actual performance of the organisation on a regular and continuous basis. Any deviations from the plans can then be identified and corrective action taken.

(b)   **The corporate plan** is reviewed in the light of the comparisons made and any changes in the parameters on which the plan was based (such as new competitors, government instructions and so on) to assess whether the objectives of the plan can be achieved. The plan is modified as necessary before any serious damage to the organisation's future success occurs.

Effective control is therefore not practical without planning, and planning without control is pointless.

Decision making

2.7   **Management is decision taking.** Managers of all levels within an organisation take decisions. Decision making always involves a **choice between alternatives** and it is the role of the management accountant to provide information so that management can reach an informed decision. It is therefore vital that the management accountant understands the decision making process so that he can supply the appropriate type of information.

Decision making process

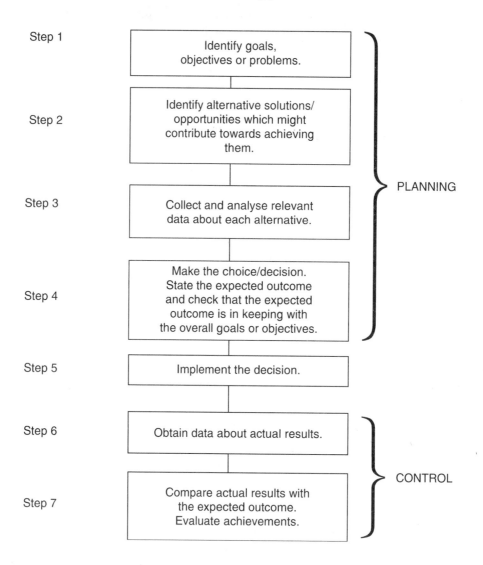

Decision-making process

Anthony's view of management activity

2.8 R N Anthony, a leading writer on organisational control, has suggested that the activities of **planning, control and decision making should not be separated** since all managers make planning and control decisions. He has identified three types of management activity.

(a) **Strategic planning:** 'the process of deciding on objectives of the organisation, on changes in these objectives, on the resources used to attain these objectives, and on the policies that are to govern the acquisition, use and disposition of these resources'.

(b) **Management control:** 'the process by which managers assure that resources are obtained and used effectively and efficiently in the accomplishment of the organisation's objectives'.

(c) **Operational control:** 'the process of assuring that specific tasks are carried out effectively and efficiently'.

Strategic planning

2.9 **Strategic plans** are those which **set or change the objectives,** or strategic targets of an organisation. They would include such matters as the selection of products and markets, the required levels of company profitability, the purchase and disposal of subsidiary companies or major fixed assets and so on.

Management control

2.10 Whilst strategic planning is concerned with setting objectives and strategic targets, **management control** is concerned with **decisions about the efficient and effective use of an organisation's resources** to achieve these objectives or targets.

 (a) **Resources**, often referred to as the '**4 Ms**' (men, materials, machines and money).

 (b) **Efficiency** in the use of resources means that optimum **output** is achieved from the **input** resources used. It relates to the combinations of men, land and capital (for example how much production work should be automated) and to the productivity of labour, or material usage.

 (c) **Effectiveness** in the use of resources means that the **outputs** obtained are in line with the intended **objectives** or targets.

Operational control

2.11 The third, and lowest tier, in Anthony's hierarchy of decision making, consists of **operational control decisions**. As we have seen, operational control is the task of ensuring that **specific tasks** are carried out effectively and efficiently. Just as 'management control' plans are set within the guidelines of strategic plans, so too are 'operational control' plans set within the guidelines of both strategic planning and management control. Consider the following.

 (a) Senior management may decide that the company should increase sales by 5% per annum for at least five years - **a strategic plan**.

 (b) The sales director and senior sales managers will make plans to increase sales by 5% in the next year, with some provisional planning for future years. This involves planning direct sales resources, advertising, sales promotion and so on. Sales quotas are assigned to each sales territory - **a tactical plan** (management control).

 (c) The manager of a sales territory specifies the weekly sales targets for each sales representative. This is **operational planning**: individuals are given tasks which they are expected to achieve.

Although we have used an example of selling tasks to describe operational control, it is important to remember that this level of planning occurs in all aspects of an organisation's activities, even when the activities cannot be scheduled nor properly estimated because they are non-standard activities (such as repair work, answering customer complaints).

2.12 The scheduling of unexpected or 'ad hoc' work must be done at short notice, which is a feature of much **operational planning**. In the repairs department, for example, routine preventive maintenance can be scheduled, but breakdowns occur unexpectedly and repair work must be scheduled and controlled 'on the spot' by a repairs department supervisor.

3 TYPES OF INFORMATION

3.1 Information within an organisation can be analysed into the three levels assumed in Anthony's hierarchy.

3.2 **Strategic information is used by senior managers** to plan the objectives of their organisation, and to assess whether the objectives are being met in practice. Such information includes **overall** profitability, the profitability of different segments of the business, capital equipment needs and so on.

Strategic information therefore has the following features.

- It is derived from both **internal** and **external** sources.
- It is summarised at a **high level**.
- It is relevant to the **long term**.
- It deals with the **whole organisation** (although it might go into some detail).
- It is often prepared on an 'ad hoc' basis.
- It is both **quantitative** and **qualitative** (see below).
- It cannot provide complete certainty, given that the future cannot be predicted.

3.3 **Tactical information is used by middle management** to decide how the resources of the business should be employed, and to monitor how they are being and have been employed. Such information includes **productivity measurements** (output per man hour or per machine hour), **budgetary control** or **variance analysis reports**, and **cash flow forecasts** and so on.

3.4 **Tactical information** therefore has the following features.

- It is primarily generated internally.
- It is summarised at a lower level.
- It is relevant to the short and medium term.
- It describes or analyses activities or departments.
- It is prepared routinely and regularly.
- It is based on quantitative measures.

3.5 **Operational information is used by 'front-line' managers** such as foremen or head clerks to ensure that specific tasks are planned and carried out properly within a factory or office and so on. In the payroll office, for example, information at this level will relate to day-rate labour and will include the hours worked each week by each employee, his rate of pay per hour, details of his deductions, and for the purpose of wages analysis, details of the time each man spent on individual jobs during the week. In this example, the information is required weekly, but more urgent operational information, such as the amount of raw materials being input to a production process, may be required daily, hourly, or in the case of automated production, second by second.

Operational information has the following features.

- It is derived almost entirely from internal sources.
- It is highly detailed, being the processing of raw data.
- It relates to the immediate term.
- It is task-specific.
- It is prepared constantly, or very frequently.
- It is largely quantitative.

4 INFORMATION SYSTEMS AND MANAGEMENT INFORMATION SYSTEMS

4.1 An organisation is made up of a series of **information systems**. It is difficult to define an information system since it is really a series of activities or processes.

- Identification of data requirements
- Collection and transcription of data (data capture)

- Data processing
- Communication of processed data to users
- Use of processed data (as information) by users

4.2 Sometimes there are separate information systems for sales, production, personnel, financial and other matters, sometimes there is integration of these sub-systems.

4.3 Information systems can be divided into two broad categories.

- Transaction (or data) processing systems
- Management information systems

Transaction processing systems

4.4 **Transaction processing systems** could be said to represent the **lowest level** in a company's use of information systems. They are used for routine tasks in which data items or transactions must be recorded and processed so that operations can continue. Handling sales orders, purchase orders and stock records are typical examples.

Management information systems

> **KEY TERM**
>
> A **management information system** (MIS) is defined as 'A collective term for the hardware and software used to drive a database system with the outputs, both to screen and print, being designed to provide easily assimilated information for management'.
>
> (CIMA *Computing Terminology*)

4.5 Management information is by no means confined to accounting information, but until relatively recently accounting information systems have been the most formally-constructed and well-developed part of the overall information system of a business enterprise.

4.6 An alternative definition of a management information system is 'an information system making use of available resources to provide managers at all levels in all functions with the information from all relevant sources to enable them to make timely and effective decisions for planning, directing and controlling the activities for which they are responsible.'

4.7 A management information system is therefore **a system of disseminating information which will enable managers to do their job.** Since managers must have information, there will always be a management information system in any organisation.

4.8 Most management information systems are not designed, but grow up informally, with each manager making sure that he or she gets all the information considered necessary to do the job. It is virtually taken for granted that the necessary information flows to the job, and to a certain extent this is so. Much accounting information, for example, is easily obtained, and managers can often get along with frequent face-to-face contact and co-operation with each other. Such an informal system works best in small organisations.

4.9 However, some information systems are specially designed, often because the introduction of computers has forced management to consider its information needs in detail. This is especially the case in large companies.

4.10 Management should try to develop/implement a management information system for their enterprise with care. If they allow the MIS to develop without any formal planning, it will almost certainly be inefficient because data will be obtained and processed in a random and disorganised way and the communication of information will also be random and hit-and-miss.

(a) Some managers will prefer to keep data in their heads and will not commit information to paper. When the manager is absent from work, or is moved to another job, his stand-in or successor will not know as much as he could and should about the work because no information has been recorded to help him.

(b) The organisation will not collect and process all the information that it should, and so valuable information that ought to be available to management will be missing from neglect.

(c) Information may be available but not disseminated to the managers who are in a position of authority and so ought to be given it. The information would go to waste because it would not be used. In other words, the wrong people would have the information.

(d) Information is communicated late because the need to communicate it earlier is not understood and appreciated by the data processors.

4.11 The consequences of a poor MIS might be dissatisfaction amongst employees who believe they should be told more, a lack of understanding about what the targets for achievement are and a lack of information about how well the work is being done. Whether a management information system is formally or informally constructed, it should therefore have certain essential characteristics.

(a) The functions of individuals and their areas of responsibility in achieving company objectives should be defined.

(b) Areas of control within the company (eg cost centres, investment centres) should also be clearly defined.

(c) Information required for an area of control should flow to the manager who is responsible for it.

Cost accounting systems

4.12 **An organisation's cost accounting system will be part of the overall management information system** and, as we shall see in the next section, it will both provide information to assist management with planning, control and decision making as well as accumulating historical costs to establish stock valuations, profits and balance sheet items.

Question 3

Briefly explain the meaning of the term *management information system*.

Answer

A management information system (MIS) is a system of providing and communicating information which will enable managers and administrators in an organisation to perform their roles (for example planning, decision making) properly. As managers and administrators must always have such information, there will be a management information system in any organisation. The quality of an MIS varies between (and within) organisations.

A system should be effective in providing good quality information at an acceptable cost, and at no time should the cost of providing it exceed the potential benefits of using the information. For information to be good it must be communicated to the right people, at the right time and as clearly and accurately as is possible. In other words, good management information is relevant, accurate and timely, allowing management to base decisions upon the information given, in complete confidence as to its reliability.

5 FINANCIAL ACCOUNTING AND COST AND MANAGEMENT ACCOUNTING

Financial accounts and management accounts

5.1 Management information provides a common source from which is drawn information for two groups of people.

(a) **Financial accounts** are prepared for individuals **external** to an organisation: shareholders, customers, suppliers, the Inland Revenue, employees.

(b) **Management accounts** are prepared for **internal** managers of an organisation.

5.2 The data used to prepare financial accounts and management accounts are the same. The differences between the financial accounts and the management accounts arise because the data is analysed differently.

Financial accounts	Management accounts
Financial accounts detail the performance of an organisation over a defined period and the state of affairs at the end of that period.	Management accounts are used to aid management record, plan and control the organisation's activities and to help the decision-making process.
Limited companies must, by law, prepare financial accounts.	There is no legal requirement to prepare management accounts.
The format of published financial accounts is determined by law (mainly the Companies Acts), by Statements of Standard Accounting Practice and by Financial Reporting Standards. In principle the accounts of different organisations can therefore be easily compared.	The format of management accounts is entirely at management discretion: no strict rules govern the way they are prepared or presented. Each organisation can devise its own management accounting system and format of reports.
Financial accounts concentrate on the business as a whole, aggregating revenues and costs from different operations, and are an end in themselves.	Management accounts can focus on specific areas of an organisation's activities. Information may be produced to aid a decision rather than to be an end product of a decision.
Most financial accounting information is of a monetary nature.	Management accounts incorporate non-monetary measures. Management may need to know, for example, tons of aluminium produced, monthly machine hours, or miles travelled by salesmen.
Financial accounts present an essentially historic picture of past operations.	Management accounts are both a historical record and a future planning tool.

BPP PUBLISHING

Cost accounts

5.3 Cost accounting and management accounting are terms which are often used interchangeably. It is *not* correct to do so.

Cost accounting is concerned with the following.

- Preparing statements (eg budgets, costing)
- Cost data collection
- Applying cots to inventory, products and services

Management accounting is concerned with the following.

- Using financial data and communicating it as information to users

5.4 **Cost accounting is part of management accounting. Cost accounting provides a bank of data for the management accountant to use.** Cost accounts aim to establish the following.

(a) The **cost** of goods produced or services provided.

(b) The **cost** of a department or work section.

(c) What **revenues** have been.

(d) The **profitability** of a product, a service, a department, or the organisation in total.

(e) **Selling prices** with some regard for the costs of sale.

(f) The **value of stocks of goods** (raw materials, work in progress, finished goods) that are still held in store at the end of a period, thereby aiding the preparation of a balance sheet of the company's assets and liabilities.

(g) **Future costs** of goods and services (costing is an integral part of budgeting (planning) for the future).

(h) **How actual costs compare with budgeted costs** (If an organisation plans for its revenues and costs to be a certain amount, but they actually turn out differently, the differences can be measured and reported. Management can use these reports as a guide to whether corrective action (or 'control' action) is needed to sort out a problem revealed by these differences between budgeted and actual results. This system of control is often referred to as budgetary control).

(i) **What information management needs** in order to make sensible decisions about profits and costs.

5.5 It would be wrong to suppose that cost accounting systems are restricted to manufacturing operations, although they are probably more fully developed in this area of work. **Service industries, government departments** and **welfare activities** can all make use of cost accounting information. Within a manufacturing organisation, the cost accounting system should be applied not only to **manufacturing** but also to **administration, selling and distribution, research and development** and all other departments.

Chapter roundup

- **Data** ('raw material') and **information** (data which has been processed into a form meaningful to the recipient and which is of real or perceived value for the intended purpose) and that you are aware of how to manage both financial and non-financial information.

- Good information should be **relevant**, **complete**, **accurate**, **clear**, it should **inspire confidence**, it should be **appropriately communicated**, its **volume** should be manageable, it should be **timely** and its **cost** should be less than the benefits it provides.

- Information for management accounting is likely to be used for **planning**, **control** and **decision making**.

- Anthony divides management activities into **strategic planning**, **management control** and **operational control**.

- Information within an organisation can be analysed into the three levels assumed in Anthony's hierarchy: strategic; tactical; and operational.

- An **MIS** is a system of providing and communicating information which will enable managers to do their jobs and as such an MIS is vital to the role of the cost and management accountant.

- **Financial accounting systems** ensure that the assets and liabilities of a business are properly accounted for, and provide information about profits and so on to shareholders and to other interested parties.

- **Management accounting systems** provide information specifically for the use of managers within the organisation.

- The relationship between cost accounting and management accounting maybe summarised as follows: **cost accounting provides a bank of data for the management accountant to use.**

Quick quiz

1 What is the difference between data and information? (see para 1.1 and key terms)

2 What are the three types of management activity identified by Anthony? (2.8)

3 What are the features of tactical information? (3.4)

4 What is an MIS? (key terms and 4.5-4.7)

5 List six differences between financial accounts and management accounts. (5.2)

Question to try	Level	Marks	Time
1	Introductory	n/a	15 mins

Chapter 2

BASIC MATHEMATICS

Chapter topic list	Syllabus reference
1 Integers, fractions and decimals	QT 2(a)
2 Mathematical notation	QT 2(a)
3 Percentages and ratios	QT 2(b)
4 Approximation and accuracy	QT 2(a)
5 Roots and powers	QT 2(a)
6 Equations	QT 3(b)
7 Logarithms	QT 2(a)

Introduction

Many students do not have a mathematical background. The purpose of this chapter is to cover the basic mathematics that you will need in the remainder of the Study Text. It is unlikely that a whole question will be based on the topics covered in this chapter, but many questions will draw on these skills.

Even if you have done mathematics in the past, don't ignore this chapter. Skim through it to make sure that you are aware of all the concepts and techniques covered. Since it provides the foundation for much of what is to follow it is an extremely important chapter.

Note that we have not given examination date references in this chapter since **the concepts and techniques covered underpin the majority of examination questions.**

1 INTEGERS, FRACTIONS AND DECIMALS

KEY TERM

An **integer** is a whole number and can be either positive or negative.

1.1 Examples of integers are ...,–5, –4, –3, –2, –1, 0, 1, 2, 3, 4, 5,...

1.2 **Fractions** (such as $^1/_2$, $^1/_4$, $^{19}/_{35}$, $^{101}/_{377}$, ...) and **decimals** (0.1, 0.25, 0.3135 ...) are both ways of showing parts of a whole. Fractions can be turned into decimals by dividing the numerator by the denominator (in other words, the top line by the bottom line). To turn decimals into fractions, all you have to do is remember that places after the decimal point stand for tenths, hundredths, thousandths and so on.

Addition, subtraction, multiplication and division of fractions

1.3 Fractions can be added, subtracted, multiplied and divided using the following rules.

(a) $\dfrac{x}{y} + \dfrac{a}{b} = \dfrac{xb}{yb} + \dfrac{ay}{yb}$ (c) $\dfrac{x}{y} \times \dfrac{a}{b} = \dfrac{xa}{yb}$

(b) $\dfrac{x}{y} - \dfrac{a}{b} = \dfrac{xb}{yb} - \dfrac{ay}{yb}$ (d) $\dfrac{x}{y} \div \dfrac{a}{b} = \dfrac{x}{y} \times \dfrac{b}{a}$

Question 1

Calculate the following

(a) $\dfrac{7}{10} + \dfrac{1}{3}$ (c) $\dfrac{7}{10} \times \dfrac{1}{3}$

(b) $\dfrac{7}{10} - \dfrac{1}{3}$ (d) $\dfrac{7}{10} \div \dfrac{1}{3}$

Answer

(a) $\dfrac{(7 \times 3) + (1 \times 10)}{(10 \times 3)} = \dfrac{31}{30}$ (c) $\dfrac{(7 \times 1)}{(10 \times 3)} = \dfrac{7}{30}$

(b) $\dfrac{(7 \times 3) - (1 \times 10)}{(10 \times 3)} = \dfrac{11}{30}$ (d) $\dfrac{7}{10} \times \dfrac{3}{1} = \dfrac{21}{10}$

Significant digits

1.4 Sometimes a decimal number has too many digits in it for practical use. This problem can be overcome by rounding the decimal number to a specific number of **significant digits** by discarding digits using the following rule.

If the first digit to be discarded is greater than or equal to five then add one to the previous digit. Otherwise the previous digit is unchanged.

1.5 EXAMPLE: SIGNIFICANT DIGITS

(a) 187.392 correct to four significant digits is 187.4
Discarding the 9 causes one to be added to the 3.

(b) 187.392 correct to three significant digits is 187
Discarding a 3 causes nothing to be added to the 7.

2 MATHEMATICAL NOTATION

Brackets

2.1 **Brackets** are commonly used to indicate which parts of a mathematical expression should be grouped together, and calculated before other parts. In other words, brackets can indicate a **priority**, or an **order** in which calculations should be made. The rule is as follows.

(a) Do things in brackets before doing things outside them.

(b) Subject to rule (a), do things in this order.

    (i)   Powers and roots

    (ii)   Multiplications and divisions, working from left to right

    (iii) Additions and subtractions, working from left to right

2.2 Thus brackets are used for the sake of clarity. Here are some examples.

(a) $3 + 6 \times 8 = 51$. This is the same as writing $3 + (6 \times 8) = 51$.
(b) $(3 + 6) \times 8 = 72$. The brackets indicate that we wish to multiply the sum of 3 and 6 by 8.
(c) $12 - 4 \div 2 = 10$. This is the same as writing $12 - (4 \div 2) = 10$ or $12 - (4/2) = 10$.
(d) $(12 - 4) \div 2 = 4$. The brackets tell us to do the subtraction first.

2.3 A figure outside a bracket may be multiplied by two or more figures inside a bracket, linked by addition or subtraction signs. Here is an example.

$$5(6 + 8) = 5 \times (6 + 8) = 5 \times 6 + 5 \times 8 = 70$$

This is the same as $5(14) = 5 \times 14 = 70$

The multiplication sign after the 5 can be omitted, as shown here $(5(6 + 8))$, but there is no harm in putting it in $(5 \times (6 + 8))$ if you want to.

2.4 When two sets of figures linked by addition or subtraction signs within brackets are multiplied together, each figure in one bracket is multiplied in turn by every figure in the second bracket. Thus:

$$(8 + 4)(7 + 2) = (12)(9) = 108 \text{ or}$$
$$8 \times 7 + 8 \times 2 + 4 \times 7 + 4 \times 2 = 56 + 16 + 28 + 8 = 108$$

Negative numbers

2.5 When a negative number (–p) is added to another number (q), the net effect is to subtract p from q.

(a) $10 + (-6) = 10 - 6 = 4$ 　　　　(b) $-10 + (-6) = -10 - 6 = -16$

2.6 When a negative number (–p) is subtracted from another number (q), the net effect is to add p to q.

(a) $12 - (-8) = 12 + 8 = 20$ 　　　　(b) $-12 - (-8) = -12 + 8 = -4$

2.7 When a negative number is multiplied or divided by another negative number, the result is a positive number.

(a) $-8 \times (-4) = +32$ 　　　　(b) $-18/(-3) = +6$

2.8 If there is only one negative number in a multiplication or division, the result is negative.

(a) $-8 \times 4 = -32$ 　　　　(c) $12/(-4) = -3$
(b) $3 \times (-2) = -6$ 　　　　(d) $-20/5 = -4$

Question 2

Work out the following.

(a) $(72 - 8) - (-3 + 1)$ 　　　　(c) $8(2 - 5) - (4 - (-8))$

(b) $\dfrac{88 + 8}{12} + \dfrac{(29 - 11)}{-2}$ 　　　　(d) $\dfrac{-36}{9 - 3} - \dfrac{84}{3 - 10} - \dfrac{-81}{3}$

Answer

(a) $64 - (-2) = 64 + 2 = 66$ 　　　　(c) $-24 - (12) = -36$
(b) $8 + (-9) = -1$ 　　　　(d) $-6 - (-12) - (-27) = -6 + 12 + 27 = 33$

Reciprocals

> **KEY TERM**
>
> The **reciprocal** of a number is just 1 divided by that number.

2.9 For example, the reciprocal of 2 is 1 divided by 2, in other words ¹/₂.

Extra symbols

2.10 We will come across several other mathematical signs in this book but there are five which you should learn right away.

- \> means **'greater than'**. So 46 > 29 is true, but 40 > 86 is false.
- ≥ means **'is greater than or equal to'**. So 4 ≥ 3 and 4 ≥ 4.
- < means **'is less than'**. So 29 < 46 < 57 is true, but 86 < 40 is false.
- ≤ means **'is less than or equal to'**. So 7 ≤ 8 and 7 ≤ 7.
- ≠ means **'is not equal to'**. So we could write 100.004 ≠ 100.
- ≈ means **approximately equal to**. So 44.779999 ≈ 44.78

2.11 To ensure that you have understood how to deal with brackets and negative numbers and to check that you are able to use your calculator to perform addition, subtraction, multiplication and division, try the following question.

Question 3

Work out all answers to four decimal places, using a calculator.

(a) $(43 + 26.705) \times 9.3$

(b) $(844.2 \div 26) - 2.45$

(c) $\dfrac{45.6 - 13.92 + 823.1}{14.3 \times 112.5}$

(d) $\dfrac{303.3 + 7.06 \times 42.11}{1.03 \times 111.03}$

(e) $\dfrac{7.6 \times 1{,}010}{10.1 \times 76{,}000}$

(f) $(43.756 + 26.321) \div 171.036$

(g) $(43.756 + 26.321) \times 171.036$

(h) $171.45 + (-221.36) + 143.22$

(i) $66 - (-43.57) + (-212.36)$

(j) $\dfrac{10.1 \times 76{,}000}{7.6 \times 1{,}010}$

(k) $\dfrac{21.032 + (-31.476)}{3.27 \times 41.201}$

(l) $\dfrac{-33.33 - (-41.37)}{11.21 + (-24.32)}$

(m) $\dfrac{-10.75 \times (-15.44)}{-14.25 \times 17.15} + \left(\dfrac{16.23}{8.4 + 3.002} \right)$

(n) $\dfrac{-7.366 \times 921.3}{10{,}493 - 2{,}422.8} - \left(\dfrac{8.4 + 3.002}{16.23} \right)$

Answer

(a) 648.2565

(b) 30.0192

(c) 0.5313

(d) 5.2518

(e) 0.01

(f) 0.4097

(g) 11,985.69

(h) 93.31

(i) −102.79

(j) 100 (Note that this question is the reciprocal of part (e), and so the answer is the reciprocal of the answer to part (e).)

(k) −0.0775

(l) −0.6133

(m) 0.7443

(n) −1.5434

3 PERCENTAGES AND RATIOS

3.1 **Percentages** are used to indicate the **relative size** or **proportion** of items, rather than their absolute size. For example, if one office employs ten accountants, six secretaries and four supervisors, the absolute values of staff numbers and the percentage of the total work force in each type would be as follows.

	Accountants	*Secretaries*	*Supervisors*	*Total*
Absolute numbers	10	6	4	20
Percentages	50%	30%	20%	100%

3.2 The idea of percentages is that the whole of something can be thought of as 100%. The whole of a cake, for example, is 100%. If you share it out equally with a friend, you will get half each, or $^{100\%}/_2$ = 50% each.

3.3 To turn a percentage into a fraction or decimal you divide by 100. To turn a fraction or decimal back into a percentage you multiply by 100%. Consider the following.

 (a) $0.16 = 0.16 \times 100\% = 16\%$
 (b) $^4/_5 = ^4/_5 \times 100\% = ^{400}/_5\% = 80\%$
 (c) $40\% = ^{40}/_{100} = ^2/_5 = 0.4$

3.4 There are four main types of situations involving percentages.

 (a) You may be required to calculate a percentage of a figure, having been given the percentage.

 Question: What is 40% of £64?

 Answer: 40% of £64 = 0.4 × £64 = £25.60.

 (b) You may be required to state what percentage one figures is of another, so that you have to work out the percentage yourself.

 Question: What is £16 as a percentage of £64?

 Answer: £16 as a percentage of £64 $= \dfrac{16}{64} \times 100\% = \dfrac{1}{4} \times 100\% = 25\%$

 In other words, put the £16 as a fraction of the £64, and then multiply by 100%.

 (c) You may be required to determine the percentage change between two figures.

 Question: What is the percentage increase/(decrease) between sales of £50,000 in Quarter 1 and sales of £84,000/(£35,000) in Quarter 2?

 Answer: Increase $= \dfrac{(84,000 - 50,000)}{50,000} \times 100\% = \dfrac{34,000}{50,000} \times 100\% = 68\%$

 Decrease $= \dfrac{(50,000 - 35,000)}{50,000} \times 100\% = \dfrac{15,000}{50,000} \times 100\% = 30\%$

 (d) You may be required to decrease/increase a figure by a certain percentage.

 Question: Selling prices were 10% higher in 20X1 than in 20X0. Sales revenue in 20X0 was £375,000 and in 20X1 £489,500. What is the percentage increase in sales volume in 20X1 compared with 20X0?

 Answer: 20X1 sales volume in 20X0 terms $= \dfrac{£489,500}{1.10} = £445,000$

 Percentage increase $= \dfrac{£(445,000 - 375,000)}{£375,000} \times 100\% = 18.67\%$

Question 4

In August raw material X cost £12.50 per tonne, a 25% decrease on the cost in July. Given that the cost of raw material X used by ABC Ltd was £10,000 in July and £12,000 in August, what is the percentage increase or decrease in purchase quantities in August compared with July?

Answer

August purchases in July terms $= \dfrac{£12,000}{0.75} = £16,000$

Percentages increase $= \dfrac{(16,000 - 10,000)}{10,000} \times 100\% = 60\%$

Profits

3.5 You may be required in your examination to calculate **profit, selling price** or **cost of sale** of an item or number of items from certain information. To do this you need to remember the following crucial formula.

	Example
	%
Cost of sales	100
Plus Profit	25
Equals Sales	125

Profit may be expressed either as a percentage of cost of sales (such as 25% ($^{25}/_{100}$) **mark-up**) or as a percentage of sales (such as 20% ($^{25}/_{125}$) **margin**).

3.6 EXAMPLE: PROFITS AND PERCENTAGES

Delilah's Dresses sells a dress at a 10% margin. The dress cost the shop £100.

Required

Calculate the profit made by Delilah's Dresses.

3.7 SOLUTION

The margin is 10% (ie ($^{10}/_{100}$))

∴ Let selling price   = 100%
∴ Profit   = 10%
∴ Cost   = 90% = £100
∴ 1%   = (£100/90)
∴ 10% = profit = £100/90 × 10 = £11.11

3.8 EXAMPLE: PERCENTAGES AND PROFITS

Trevor's Trousers sells a pair of trousers for £80 at a 15% mark-up.

Required

Calculate the profit made by Trevor's Trousers.

3.9 SOLUTION

The markup is 15%.

∴ Let cost of sales   = 100%
∴ Profit   = 15%
∴ Selling price   = 115% = £80
∴ 1% = $(^{£80}/_{115})$
∴ 15% = profit = $(^{£80}/_{115}) \times 15$ = £10.43

Proportions

3.10   A **proportion** means writing a percentage as a proportion of 1 (that is, as a decimal).

100% can be thought of as the whole, or 1. 50% is half of that, or 0.5. Consider the following.

Question: There are 14 women in an audience of 70. What proportion of the audience are men?

Answer: Number of men   =   70 − 14 = 56

               Proportion of men = $\dfrac{56}{70} = \dfrac{8}{10}$ = 80% = 0.8

(a) $^8/_{10}$ or $^4/_5$ is the **fraction** of the audience made up by men.
(b)   80% is the **percentage** of the audience made up by men.
(c)   0.8 is the **proportion** of the audience made up by men.

Ratios

3.11   Suppose Tom has £12 and Dick has £8. The **ratio** of Tom's cash to Dick's cash is 12:8. This can be cancelled down, just like a fraction, to 3:2.

3.12   Usually an examination question will pose the problem the other way around: Tom and Dick wish to share £20 out in the ratio 3:2. How much will each receive?

3.13   Because 3 + 2 = 5, we must divide the whole up into five equal parts, then give Tom three parts and Dick two parts.

(a)   £20 ÷ 5 = £4 (so each part is £4)

(b)   Tom's share = 3 × £4 = £12

(c)   Dick's share = 2 × £4 = £8

(d)   *Check:* £12 + £8 = £20 (adding up the two shares in the answer gets us back to the £20 in the question).

3.14   This method of calculating ratios as amounts works no matter how many ratios are involved. Here is another example.

Question: A, B, C and D wish to share £600 in the ratio 6:1:2:3. How much will each receive?

Answer: (a)   Number of parts   =   6 + 1 + 2 + 3 = 12.

           (b)   Value of each part   =   £600 ÷ 12 = £50

(c) A: $6 \times £50$ $=$ £300
    B: $1 \times £50$ $=$ £50
    C: $2 \times £50$ $=$ £100
    D $3 \times £50$ $=$ £150

(d) *Check:* £300 + £50 + £100 + £150 = £600.

Question 5

(a) Tom, Dick and Harry wish to share out £800. Calculate how much each would receive if the ratio used was:

(i)   3 : 2 : 5;
(ii)   5 : 3 : 2;
(iii) 3 : 1 : 1.

(b) Lynn and Laura share out a certain sum of money in the ratio 4 : 5, and Laura ends up with £6.

(i)   How much was shared out in the first place?

(ii)   How much would have been shared out if Laura had got £6 and the ratio had been 5 : 4 instead of 4 : 5?

Answer

(a) (i)   Total parts = 10
        Each part is worth £800 ÷ 10 = £80
        Tom gets $3 \times £80 = £240$
        Dick gets $2 \times £80 = £160$
        Harry gets $5 \times £80 = £400$

    (ii)   Same parts as (i) but in a different order.
        Tom gets   £400
        Dick gets   £240
        Harry gets   £160

    (iii) Total parts = 5
        Each part is worth £800 ÷ 5 = £160
        Therefore Tom gets £480
        Dick and Harry each get £160

(b) (i)   Laura's share = £6 = 5 parts
        Therefore one part is worth £6 ÷ 5 = £1.20
        Total of 9 parts shared out originally
        Therefore total was $9 \times £1.20 = £10.80$

    (ii)   Laura's share = £6 = 4 parts
        Therefore one part is worth £6 ÷ 4 = £1.50
        Therefore original total was $9 \times £1.50 = £13.50$

4   APPROXIMATION AND ACCURACY

Why does approximation arise?

4.1   **Approximation** arises because it is often not possible to obtain an accurate value for a large number (such as the population of a town) and some figures may only be easily measurable to the nearest whole number (for example the speed of a car). Sometimes, on the other hand, it may not be necessary or desirable to express data as accurately as they can be measured. In such circumstances numbers are rounded.

Rounding

4.2 We shall illustrate three methods of **rounding** using the figure 18,600.

(a) **Rounding up**: 18,600 would be expressed as 19,000 to the nearest thousand above.

(b) **Rounding down**: 18,600 would be expressed as 18,000 to the nearest thousand below.

(c) **Rounding to the nearest round amount**: 18,600 would be expressed as 19,000 to the nearest thousand. This is the most common method.

In rounding to the nearest unit, a value ending in 0.5 is usually rounded up. Thus, 3.5 rounded to the nearest unit, would be 4.

4.3 Rounding can be specified as follows.

- To the **nearest whole unit** (as above).
- By the **number of decimal places** (3.94712 to 2 decimal places in 3.95).
- By the **number of significant digits** (as covered earlier in this chapter).

Question 6

(a) What is £482,365.15 to the nearest:

    (i)   £1
    (ii) £100
    (iii) £1,000
    (iv) £10,000?

(b) What is 843.668 correct to:

    (i)   one decimal place
    (ii) two decimal places?

(c) What is 628.0273 to:

    (i)   five significant figures
    (ii) four significant figures?

Answer

(a) (i) £482,365   (b) (i) 843.7   (c) (i) 628.03
    (ii) £482,400   (ii) 843.67   (ii) 628.0
    (iii) £482,000
    (iv) £480,000

4.4 **Spurious accuracy** arises when a statistic gives the impression that it is more accurate than it really is. For example we might see stated '24.68% of women over the age of 30 are smokers'. This result is probably based on a sample and so we know that it cannot be as accurate as it seems: the two decimal places have arisen simply because of the arithmetic of the calculations. It would be less misleading to state 'approximately 25% of women over the age of 30 are smokers'. This removes the spurious accuracy implied by the decimal places.

Maximum errors

Absolute errors

4.5 Suppose that the population of a country is stated as 40 million. It is quite likely that this figure has been rounded to the nearest million. We could therefore say that the country's population is 40 million ± 500,000, where 40 million is the **estimate** of the population and 500,000 is the **maximum absolute error**.

4.6 In general terms an estimate with a maximum absolute error can be expressed as a ± b.

Relative errors

4.7 The error in the population of the country could also be expressed as 40 million ± 1.25%, where 500,000 is 1.25% of 40 million. In this instance the maximum error is a **maximum relative error.**

> ### FORMULA TO LEARN
>
> The **maximum relative error** is calculated as $\dfrac{\text{maximum absolute error}}{\text{estimate}} \times 100\%$.

Errors and calculations

4.8 If calculations are made using values that have been rounded then the results of such calculations will only be **approximate**. However, provided that we are aware of the maximum errors that can occur, we can still draw conclusions from the results of the calculations.

4.9 There are two rules to remember when performing calculations involving rounded or approximate numbers.

   (a) **Addition/subtraction**

   When two or more rounded or approximate numbers are added or subtracted the **maximum absolute error** in the result equals the sum of the individual maximum absolute errors.

   (b) **Multiplication/division**

   When two or more rounded or approximate numbers are multiplied or divided, the **approximate maximum relative error** in the result is obtained by adding the individual maximum relative errors.

4.10 EXAMPLE: ERRORS

A chemical producer plans to sell 50,000 litres (to the nearest 1,000 litres) of a particular chemical at a price of £10 (to the nearest pound) per litre.

The cost of materials used to produce the chemicals is expected to be £100,000 but depending on wastage levels this is subject to an error of ± 5%. Labour costs are estimated to be £300,000 ± 10%, depending on overtime working and pay negotiations.

Required

Calculate the maximum absolute error and the maximum relative error in revenue and costs of production.

4.11 SOLUTION

	Estimate	Maximum absolute error	Maximum relative error %
Quantity sold	50,000 litres	500 litres	1
Price	£10	£0.50	5
Materials	£100,000	£5,000	5
Labour	£300,000	£30,000	10

(a) Revenue = quantity sold × price
$$= (50,000 \pm 1\%) \times (£10 \pm 5\%)$$
$$= (50,000 \times £10) \pm (1\% + 5\%)$$
$$= £500,000 \pm 6\%$$
$$= £500,000 \pm £30,000$$

∴ Approximate maximum absolute error = £30,000

Approximate maximum relative error = 6%

Note that we need to use relative errors when doing multiplication/division calculations.

(b) Costs of production = material + labour
$$= (£100,000 \pm £5,000) + (£300,000 \pm £30,000)$$
$$= (£100,000 + £300,000) \pm (£5,000 + £30,000)$$
$$= £400,000 \pm £35,000$$
$$= £400,000 \pm 8.75\,\%$$

∴ Maximum absolute error = £35,000

Maximum relative error = 8.75%

Note that we need to use absolute errors when doing addition/subtraction calculations.

4.12 The rule in Paragraph 4.9(b) above only gives an approximate maximum relative error. Let's see what the actual error would have been in Paragraph 4.11(a) above.

Maximum revenue = maximum quantity × maximum price
$$= (50,000 + 1\%) \times (£10 + 5\%) = 50,500 \times £10.50 = £530,250$$

∴ Our approximation of the maximum absolute error was correct to within £(530,250 – 530,000) = £250.

Question 7

Suppose that $A = \dfrac{J \times B}{M}$

where J and B are subject to a maximum relative error of 10% and M to a maximum relative error of 20%.

Required

(a) Calculate the approximate maximum relative error in A (using the rule in Paragraph 5.9).
(b) Calculate the actual maximum relative error.

Answer

(a) Approximate maximum relative error = 10% + 10% + 20%
                                          = 40%

(b) A is at a maximum when the numerator is big and the denominator small, that is when J and B are at a maximum and M at a minimum.

$$\text{Maximum A} = \frac{1.1J \times 1.1B}{0.8M} = \frac{1.5125JB}{M}$$

∴ Actual maximum positive relative error = 51.25%.

A is at a minimum when the numerator is small and the denominator big, that is when J and B are at a minimum and M at a maximum.

$$\text{Minimum A} = \frac{0.9J \times 0.9B}{1.2M} = \frac{0.675JB}{M}$$

∴ Actual maximum negative relative error = 32.5%

5   ROOTS AND POWERS

KEY TERMS

- The **square root** $(\sqrt{\ })$ of a number is the value which, when multiplied by itself, equals the original number.

- The **cube root** $(\sqrt[3]{\ })$ of a number is the value which, when multiplied by itself twice, equals the original number.

- The **nth root** $(\sqrt[n]{\ })$ of a number is a value which, when multiplied by itself $(n-1)$ times, equals the original number.

5.1 $\sqrt{9} = 3$, since $3 \times 3 = 9$

5.2 $\sqrt[3]{64} = 4$, since $4 \times 4 \times 4 = 64$

5.3   **Powers** work the other way round.
        Thus the 6th power of $2 = 2^6 = 2 \times 2 \times 2 \times 2 \times 2 \times 2 = 64$.

        Similarly, $3^4 = 3 \times 3 \times 3 \times 3 = 81$.

        Since $\sqrt{9} = 3$, it also follows that $3^2 = 9$, and since $\sqrt[3]{64} = 4$, $4^3 = 64$.

FORMULAE TO LEARN

- When a number with an index (a 'to the power of' value) is multiplied by the *same* number with the same or a different index, the result is that number to the power of the **sum** of the indices.

- When a number with an index is divided by the *same* number with the same or a different index, the result is that number to the power of the first index **minus** the second index.

- Any figure to the power of zero equals one.

 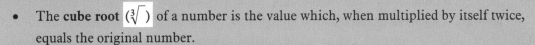

5.4 These rules can be demonstrated as follows.

(a) $5^2 \times 5 = 5^2 \times 5^1 = 5^{(2+1)} = 5^3 = 125$

(b) $4^3 \times 4^3 = 4^{(3+3)} = 4^6 = 4,096$

(c) $6^4 \div 6^3 = 6^{(4-3)} = 6^1 = 6$

(d) $7^8 \div 7^6 = 7^{(8-6)} = 7^2 = 49$

5.5 The product of two or more numbers to a certain power $((abc)^3)$ equals the product of the numbers, each of which has been raised to that power $(a^3 b^3 c^3)$. So $(7 \times 5 \times 3)^2 = 7^2 \times 5^2 \times 3^2$.

5.6 $1^0 = 1, 2^0 = 1, 3^0 = 1, 4^0 = 1$ and so on.

Similarly, $8^2 \div 8^2 = 8^{(2-2)} = 8^0 = 1$

5.7 An **index** can be a **fraction**, as in $16^{\frac{1}{2}}$. What $16^{\frac{1}{2}}$ means is the square root of 16 ($\sqrt{16}$ or 4). If we multiply $16^{\frac{1}{2}}$ by $16^{\frac{1}{2}}$ we get $16^{(\frac{1}{2}+\frac{1}{2})}$ which equals 16^1 and thus 16.

Similarly, $216^{\frac{1}{3}}$ is the cube root of 216 (which is 6) because $216^{\frac{1}{3}} \times 216^{\frac{1}{3}} \times 216^{\frac{1}{3}} = 216^{(\frac{1}{3}+\frac{1}{3}+\frac{1}{3})}$ $= 216^1 = 216$.

5.8 An **index** can be a **negative** value. The negative sign represents a reciprocal. Thus 2^{-1} is the reciprocal of, or one over, 2^1

$$= \frac{1}{2^1} = \frac{1}{2}$$

Here are some more examples.

(a) $2^{-2} = \frac{1}{2^2} = \frac{1}{4}$ and $2^{-3} = \frac{1}{2^3} = \frac{1}{8}$

(b) $4^5 \times 4^{-2} = 4^5 \times \frac{1}{4^2} = 4^{5-2} = 4^3 = 64$

5.9 When we multiply or divide by a number with a negative index, the rules previously stated still apply.

(a) $9^2 \times 9^{-2} = 9^{(2+(-2))} = 9^0 = 1$ (That is, $9^2 \times \frac{1}{9^2} = 1$)

(b) $4^5 \div 4^{-2} = 4^{(5-(-2))} = 4^7 = 16,384$

(c) $3^8 \times 3^{-5} = 3^{(8-5)} = 3^3 = 27$

(d) $3^{-5} \div 3^{-2} = 3^{-5-(-2)} = 3^{-3} = \frac{1}{3^3} = \frac{1}{27}$. (This could be re-expressed as $\frac{1}{3^5} \div \frac{1}{3^2} = \frac{1}{3^5} \times 3^2 = \frac{1}{3^3}$.)

Question 8

Work out the following, using your calculator as necessary.

(a) $(18.6)^{2.6}$

(b) $(18.6)^{-2.6}$

(c) $\sqrt[2.6]{18.6}$

(d) $(14.2)^4 \times (14.2)^{\frac{1}{4}}$

(e) $(14.2)^4 + (14.2)^{\frac{1}{4}}$

Answer

(a) $(18.6)^{2.6} = 1{,}998.64$

(b) $(18.6)^{-2.6} = \left(\dfrac{1}{18.6}\right)^{2.6} = 0.0005$

(c) $= \sqrt[2.6]{18.6} = 3.078$

(d) $(14.2)^{4} \times (14.2)^{\frac{1}{4}} = (14.2)^{4.25} = 78{,}926.98$

(e) $(14.2)^{4} + (14.2)^{\frac{1}{4}} = 40{,}658.69 + 1.9412 = 40{,}660.6312$

---

6   EQUATIONS

6.1   So far all our problems have been formulated entirely in terms of specific numbers. However, think back to when you were calculating powers with your calculator earlier in this chapter. You probably used the x^y key on your calculator. x and y stood for whichever numbers we happened to have in our problem, for example, 3 and 4 if we wanted to work out 3^4. When we use letters like this to stand for any numbers we call them variables. Today when we work out 3^4, x stands for 3. Tomorrow, when we work out 7^2, x will stand for 7: its value can vary.

6.2   The use of **variables** enables us to state general truths about mathematics.

For example:

$$x = x$$
$$x^2 = x \times x$$

If $y = 0.5 \times x$, then $x = 2 \times y$

These will be true *whatever* values x and y have. For example, let $y = 0.5 \times x$

If $y = 3, x = 2 \times y = 6$
If $y = 7, x = 2 \times y = 14$
If $y = 1, x = 2 \times y = 2$, and so on for any other choice of a value for y.

6.3   We can use variables to build up useful **formulae**. We can then put in values for the variables, and get out a value for something we are interested in.

6.4   Let us consider an example. For a business, profit = revenue – costs.

Since revenue = selling price $\times$ units sold, we can say that

profit = selling price $\times$ units sold – costs.

'Selling price $\times$ units sold – costs' is a formula for profit.

We can then use single letters to make the formula quicker to write.

Let   x   =   profit
      p   =   selling price
      u   =   units sold
      c   =   cost

Then $x = p \times u - c$.

If we are then told that in a particular month, p = £5, u = 30 and c = £118, we can find out the month's profit.

$$\text{Profit} = x = p \times u - c = £5 \times 30 - £118$$
$$= £150 - £118 = £32.$$

6.5 It is usual when writing formulae to leave out multiplication signs between letters. Thus $p \times u - c$ can be written as $pu - c$. We will also write (for example) $2x$ instead of $2 \times x$.

Equations

6.6 In the above example, $pu - c$ was a formula for profit. If we write $x = pu - c$, we have written an **equation**. It says that one thing (profit, x) is equal to another ($pu - c$).

6.7 Sometimes, we are given an equation with numbers filled in for all but one of the variables. The problem is then to find the number which should be filled in for the last variable. This is called **solving the equation**.

6.8 (a) Returning to $x = pu - c$, we could be told that for a particular month $p = £4$, $u = 60$ and $c = £208$. We would then have the equation $x = £4 \times 60 - £208$. We can solve this easily by working out $£4 \times 60 - £208 = £240 - £208 = £32$. Thus $x = £32$.

(b) On the other hand, we might have been told that in a month when profits were £172, 50 units were sold and the selling price was £7. The thing we have not been told is the month's costs, c. We can work out c by writing out the equation.

$$£172 = £7 \times 50 - c$$

$$£172 = £350 - c$$

We need c to be such that when it is taken away from £350 we have £172 left. With a bit of trial and error, we can get to $c = £178$.

6.9 Trial and error takes far too long in more complicated cases, however, and we will now go on to look at a rule for solving equations, which will take us directly to the answers we want.

The rule for solving equations

6.10 To solve an equation, we need to get it into the form:

Unknown variable = something with just numbers in it, which we can work out.

We therefore want to get the unknown variable on one side of the = sign, and everything else on the other side.

6.11 The rule is that **you can do what you like to one side of an equation, so long as you do the same thing to the other side straightaway.** The two sides are equal, and they will stay equal so long as you treat them in the same way.

6.12 For example, you can do any of the following.

Add 37 to both sides.   Take the reciprocal of both sides.
Subtract $3x$ from both sides.   Square both sides.
Multiply both sides by -4.329.   Take the cube root of both sides.
Divide both sides by $(x + 2)$.

6.13 We can do any of these things to an equation either before or after filling in numbers for the variables for which we have values.

6.14 (a) In Paragraph 6.8 above, we had

$$£172 = £350 - c.$$

We can then get

$£172 + c = £350$	(add c to each side)
$c = £350 - £172$	(subtract £172 from each side)
$c = £178$	(work out the right hand side).

(b)
$450 = 3x + 72$	(initial equation: x unknown)
$450 - 72 = 3x$	(subtract 72 from each side)
$\dfrac{450 - 72}{3} = x$	(divide each side by 3)
$126 = x$	(work out the left hand side).

(c)
$3y + 2 = 5y - 7$	(initial equation: y unknown)
$3y + 9 = 5y$	(add 7 to each side)
$9 = 2y$	(subtract 3y from each side)
$4.5 = y$	(divide each side by 2).

(d)
$\dfrac{\sqrt{3x^2 + x}}{2\sqrt{x}} = 7$	(initial equation: x unknown)
$\dfrac{3x^2 + x}{4x} = 49$	(square each side)
$(3x + 1)/4 = 49$	(cancel x in the numerator and the denominator of the left hand side: this does not affect the value of the left hand side, so we do not need to change the right hand side)
$3x + 1 = 196$	(multiply each side by 4)
$3x = 195$	(subtract 1 from each side)
$x = 65$	(divide each side by 3).

(e) Our example in Paragraph 6.6 was $x = pu - c$. We could change this, so as to give a formula for p.

$x = pu - c$	
$x + c = pu$	(add c to each side)
$\dfrac{x + c}{u} = p$	(divide each side by u)
$p = \dfrac{x + c}{u}$	(swap the sides for ease of reading).

Given values for x, c and u we can now find p. We have rearranged the equation to give p in terms of x, c and u.

(f) Given that $y = \sqrt{3x + 7}$, we can get an equation giving x in terms of y.

$y = \sqrt{3x + 7}$	
$y^2 = 3x + 7$	(square each side)
$y^2 - 7 = 3x$	(subtract 7 from each side)
$x = \dfrac{y^2 - 7}{3}$	(divide each side by 3, and swap the sides for ease of reading).

6.15 In equations, you may come across expressions like $3(x + 4y - 2)$ (that is, $3 \times (x + 4y - 2)$). These can be re-written in separate bits without the brackets, simply by multiplying the number outside the brackets by each item inside them. Thus $3(x + 4y - 2) = 3x + 12y - 6$.

Question 9

Find the value of x in each of the following equations.

(a) $47x + 256 = 52x$

(b) $4\sqrt{x} + 32 = 40.6718$

(c) $\dfrac{1}{3x + 4} = \dfrac{5}{2.7x - 2}$

(d) $x^3 = 4.913$

(e) $34x - 7.6 = (17x - 3.8) \times (x + 12.5)$

Answer

(a)

$47x + 256$	$=$	$52x$
256	$=$	$5x$ (subtract 47x from each side)
51.2	$=$	x (divide each side by 5).

(b)

$4\sqrt{x} + 32$	$=$	40.6718
$4\sqrt{x}$	$=$	8.6718 (subtract 32 from each side)
$\sqrt{x}$	$=$	2.16795 (divide each side by 4)
x	$=$	4.7 (square each side).

(c) $\dfrac{1}{3x + 4} = \dfrac{5}{2.7x - 2}$

$3x + 4 = \dfrac{2.7x - 2}{5}$ (take the reciprocal of each side)

$15x + 20$	$=$	$2.7x - 2$ (multiply each side by 5)
$12.3x$	$=$	-22 (subtract 20 and subtract 2.7x from each side)
x	$=$	-1.789 (divide each side by 12.3).

(d)

x^3	$=$	4.913
x	$=$	1.7 (take the cube root of each side).

(e) $34x - 7.6 = (17x - 3.8) \times (x + 12.5)$

This one is easy if you realise that $17 \times 2 = 34$ and $3.8 \times 2 = 7.6$, so

$2 \times (17x - 3.8) = 34x - 7.6$.

We can then divide each side by $17x - 3.8$ to get

$2 \quad = \quad x + 12.5$

$-10.5 \quad = \quad x$ (subtract 12.5 from each side).

Question 10

(a) Rearrange $x = (3y - 20)^2$ to get an expression for y in terms of x.

(b) Rearrange $2(y - 4) - 4(x^2 + 3) = 0$ to get an expression for x in terms of y.

Answer

(a) $x = (3y - 20)^2$

   $\sqrt{x} = 3y - 20$ (take the square root of each side)

   $20 + \sqrt{x} = 3y$ (add 20 to each side)

   $y = \dfrac{20 + \sqrt{x}}{3}$ (divide each side by 3, and swap the sides for ease of reading).

(b) $2(y - 4) - 4(x^2 + 3) = 0$

   $2(y - 4) = 4(x^2 + 3)$ (add $4(x^2 + 3)$ to each side)

   $0.5(y - 4) = x^2 + 3$ (divide each side by 4)

   $0.5(y - 4) - 3 = x^2$ (subtract 3 from each side)

   $x = \sqrt{0.5(y - 4) - 3}$ (take the square root of each side, and swap the sides for ease of reading)

   $x = \sqrt{0.5y - 5}$

---

7   LOGARITHMS

7.1   Your calculator might well enable you to work out complex values with little difficulty. For example, if you want the value of 1.12^{15} it could be a simple matter of entering two values into your calculator to obtain an answer.

7.2   However, when sophisticated calculators are unavailable, **logarithms** are one way of doing **compounding arithmetic** relatively easily. Furthermore, knowledge of logarithms enables us to ascertain the rate of change of a variable over time. Let us start by seeing what logarithms actually are.

7.3   The figure 10 can be expressed as 10^1. Similarly,

   100   can be expressed as 10^2
   1,000   can be expressed as 10^3
   10,000   can be expressed as 10^4
   1   can be expressed as 10^0

and so on.

To multiply 100 by 1,000, one way of expressing the calculation is

   $100 \times 1,000 = 10^2 \times 10^3 = 10^{(2+3)} = 10^5 = 100,000$

7.4   Logarithms work on the same principle. Every number can be converted into 10 to a certain power. For example:

   $2 = 10^{0.3010}$
   $20 = 10^{1.3010}$
   $200 = 10^{2.3010}$

How do we know this?

(a)   Any value between 1 (10^0) and 10 (10^1) must have a **'to a certain power'** value between 0 and 1.

(b)   Similarly, any value between 10 (10^1) and 100 (10^2) must have a **'to a certain power'** value between 1 and 2.

(c) Again, any value between 100 (10^2) and 1,000 (10^3) must have a 'to a certain power' value between 2 and 3.

This explains the figures to the left of the decimal points.

The value to the right of the decimal points, for 2, 20, 200 and indeed for 2,000, 20,000, 0.2, 0.02 and so on, is the same, and it is found by looking it up in **logarithm tables**. Tables are shown in the Appendix at the back of the Study Text. For 2, we look at row 20, column 0 and find .3010.

7.5 Here are some more examples to illustrate the use of logarithm tables.

(a) (i) The logarithm of 2.4 is 0.3802.

The value to the left of the decimal point is 0 because we want the logarithm of a figure between 1 and 10.

The value to the right of the decimal point is found from the tables, row 24, column 0.

(ii) The logarithm of 24 is 1.3802.

(iii) The logarithm of 240 is 2.3802.

(b) The logarithm of 2.45 is 0.3892. The value to the right of the decimal point is found from the tables, row 24, column 5.

(c) The logarithm of 24.8 is 1.3945. The value to the right of the decimal point is found from the tables, row 24, column 8.

Multiplying with logarithms

7.6 If we multiply 10^x by 10^y, we get $10^{(x+y)}$. It follows that if $2 = 10^{0.3010}$ and $20 = 10^{1.3010}$ then $2 \times 20 = 10^{(0.3010 + 1.3010)} = 10^{(1.6020)}$.

This is how we multiply with logarithms.

- We find the logarithms of the figures we are multiplying.
- We then add them together to get the solution, also expressed as a logarithm.

7.7 To convert this logarithm answer back to a 'normal' number, we can again use tables.

(a) There are **antilogarithm tables**, similar to logarithm tables, but which are used to convert logarithms back to normal numbers.

(b) Alternatively, you can find the solution by looking for the logarithm within the logarithm tables. In our example of $2 \times 20 = 10^{1.6020}$, we look for 0.6020 in the log tables and find that this is the logarithm of 400 (approximately). Thus, converting logarithm 1.6020 to a 'normal' figure we get 40 and so logarithms tell us that $2 \times 20 = 40$.

Question 11

Use logarithms to calculate the following.

(a) 3×4

(b) 30×40

Answer

(a)

	Logarithm
3	0.4771
4	0.6021
3×4	1.0792

Looking in the tables for 0.0792 we find that this is the logarithm for row 12, column 0. 1.0792 is therefore the logarithm of 12 and $3 \times 4 = 12$.

(b)

	Logarithm
30	1.4771
40	1.6021
30×40	3.0792

Solution = 1,200

The figure on the left hand side of the decimal point in the logarithm value gives us the size of the answer: above $10^3 = 1,000$, but below $10^4 = 10,000$.

Logarithms of values between 0 and 1

7.8 We know that $10^0 = 1$ and $10^{-1} = 0.1$.

It follows that numbers between 0.1 and 1 ought to have logarithms between 0 and –1.

Similarly, since $10^{-2} = 0.01$, it follows that numbers between 0.01 and 0.1 ought to have logarithms between –1 and –2.

7.9 This is so. The logarithm of 0.2 is written $\overline{1}.3010$, pronounced 'bar one point 3010'.

The bar means minus and so $\overline{1} = -1$, $\overline{2} = -2$ and so on. So the logarithm of 0.2, which is $\overline{1}.3010$, is minus 1 **plus** 0.3010.

(a) Any figure from 0.1 up to just less than 1 has a logarithm with $\overline{1}$ to the left of the decimal point.

(b) Any figure from 0.01 up to just less than 0.1 has a logarithm with $\overline{2}$ to the left of the decimal point.

(c) Similarly, any figure from 0.001 up to just less than 0.01 has a logarithm with $\overline{3}$ to the left of the decimal point.

If we multiply 0.3 by 4, say, using logarithms, we get the following.

	Logarithm
0.3	$\overline{1}.4771$
4	0.6021
	0.0792

Remember that $\overline{1}.4771$ is minus 1 plus 0.4771. The 0.4771 is a positive value, and is not negative. Only the bar 1 is negative, being –1.

From the tables 0.0792 is the logarithm of 1.2, and so $0.3 \times 4 = 1.2$.

Dividing with logarithms

7.10 Just as $10^x \times 10^y = 10^{x+y}$, so $10^x \div 10^y = 10^{x-y}$. We can use logarithms to divide, but we subtract instead of add.

For example, $8 \div 16$ is computed as follows.

	Logarithm
8	0.9031
16	1.2041
8 ÷ 16	1.6990

$\overline{1}$.6990 is the logarithm of 0.5.

Compounding with logarithms

7.11 To calculate $8^4 (= 8 \times 8 \times 8 \times 8)$ we can use logarithms as follows.

	Logarithm
8	0.9031
8	0.9031
8	0.9031
8	0.9031
8^4	3.6124

3.6124 is the logarithm of 4,100 (approximately).

Logarithms and the examination

> **Exam focus point**
> In the examination you should ensure that you have a calculator that will give you logarithms and will convert logarithms to 'normal' numbers.

7.12 Although logarithm tables will not be provided in the examination we have worked through this section using tables since this provides a greater understanding of how logarithms are devised. Most calculators do not use the $\overline{1}$, $\overline{2}$ system but give you negative numbers where appropriate (−0.3979 for log 0.4).

Identifying relationships using logarithms.

7.13 Logarithms enable us to view the **relationship** between the rate of change of a variable and time. If we plot the logarithm of the variable against time we can see whether one of the following relationships is valid.

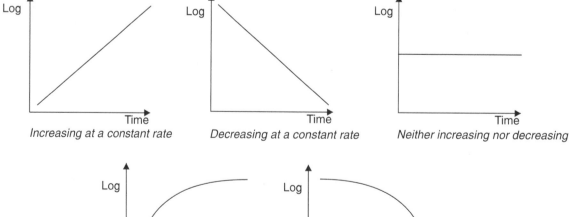

Increasing at a constant rate   *Decreasing at a constant rate*   *Neither increasing nor decreasing*

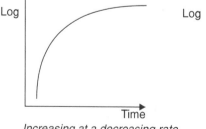

Increasing at a decreasing rate   *Decreasing at an increasing rate*

Chapter roundup

- **Brackets** indicate a **priority** or an **order** in which calculations should be made.

- The **negative number rules** are as follows.

$$-p + q = q - p \qquad\qquad -p \times -q = pq \text{ and } \frac{-p}{-q} = \frac{p}{q}$$

$$q - (-p) = q + p \qquad\qquad -p \times q = -pq$$

- The **reciprocal** of a number is 1 divided by that number.

- **Percentages** are used to indicate the **relative size** or **proportion** of items, rather than their absolute size. To turn a percentage into a fraction or decimal you divide by 100. To turn a fraction or decimal back into a percentage you multiply by 100%

- A **proportion** means writing a percentage as a proportion of 1 (that is, as a decimal).

- **Ratios** show relative shares of a whole.

- **Approximation** arises if it is not possible to obtain an accurate figure or if a number has been rounded. **Rounding** can be specified to the nearest whole unit, by the number of decimal places or by the number of significant figures.

- **Maximum errors** can be **absolute** or **relative**. When two or more rounded or approximate numbers are added or subtracted, the maximum absolute error in the result equals the sum of the individual maximum absolute errors. When two or more rounded or approximate numbers are multiplied or divided, the approximate maximum relative error in the result is obtained by adding the individual relative errors.

- The **n^{th} root** of a number is a value which, when multiplied by itself ($n-1$) times, equals the original number. Powers work the other way round.

- When we use letters to stand for any numbers we call them **variables**. The use of variables enables us to state general truths about mathematics.

- The general rule for solving equations is that you can do what you like to one side of an equation, so long as you do the same thing to the other side straightaway.

- A **logarithm** of a number is the power to which 10 has to be raised to produce that number. **Multiplication** with logarithms involves **adding** the logarithms of the numbers. We can use logarithms to **divide**, but we **subtract** instead of add. Logarithms enable us to view the **relationships between the rate of change of a variable and time** by plotting the logarithm of the variable against time.

Quick quiz

1. Is $3^{3}/_{4}$ an integer? (see key terms)

2. What is 1004.002955 to nine significant digits? (1.4, 1.5)

3. What is the product of a negative number and a negative number? (2.7)

4. $217 \leq 217$. True or false? (2.10)

5. How do you turn a fraction into a percentage? (3.3)

6. What is spurious accuracy? (4.4)

7. Define the nth root of a number. (key terms)

8. What is the difference between a formula and an equation? (6.6)

Question to try	Level	Marks	Time
2	Introductory	n/a	15 mins

BPP PUBLISHING

Chapter 3

THE ROLE OF INFORMATION TECHNOLOGY IN MANAGEMENT INFORMATION

Chapter topic list	Syllabus reference
1 The value of computer systems in handling and processing data	QT 1(d); CA 1(a)(iv)
2 Computer hardware	QT 6(e), CA 1(a)(iv)
3 Computer software	QT 1(d)
4 Capturing and processing data	QT 6(e), CA 1(a)(iv)
5 Data output	QT 6(e), CA 1(a)(iv)
6 Storage devices	QT 5(c)
7 Spreadsheet packages	QT 1(d)
8 Statistical packages	QT 1(d), 2(e), 6(e)

Introduction

This Study Text is about **information**. In the modern business environment the **storage**, **retrieval** and **analysis** of information frequently depends upon **information technology**. In fact, the majority of organisations would cease to function without the support offered by computers since information technology is used for stock control, payroll, sales and purchases, budgeting and a multitude of other tasks. It is therefore vital that you are aware of the terminology used to describe business **information technology**, the elements of a typical business computer system and the principal tasks performed by such a system. You will encounter the subject in far more detail at the Certificate Stage of your studies. Here we cover the basics.

1 THE VALUE OF COMPUTER SYSTEMS IN HANDLING AND PROCESSING DATA
6/99

1.1 Here is a very simple example of a data processing model.

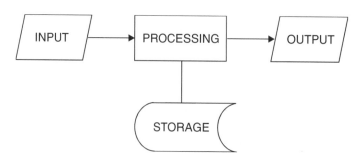

1.2 The processing of business data can be illustrated by a person working at his desk dealing with matters in his in-tray.

(a) A person receives **input from his in-tray**, which he must deal with.

(b) To help him, the person may have a procedures manual or have learned a set of rules telling him how to do the job. He may also use a **calculator** to do computations.

(c) To work on the data from his in-tray, he might need to retrieve some further data/ information from **filing** cabinets.

(d) As a result of doing the work, the person will:

(i) produce some **output**, perhaps a report or a completed routine task;

(ii) probably add to the information held on file in the filing cabinet, or change the information to bring it up to date.

1.3 **Data processing** is essentially the same, no matter whether it is done manually or by computer. Computers use **programs** instead of instruction books, and they store data on **disks** instead of in filing cabinets, but their work still follows the **input, process, output** storage pattern.

Advantages of computers

1.4 Computers are widely used for data processing because they have certain advantages over humans.

(a) **Speed.** Computers can process data much more quickly than a human. This means that a computer has a much higher productivity and so ought to be cheaper for large volumes of data processing than doing the work manually. As computer costs have fallen, this cost advantage of the computer has become more accentuated.

The ability to process data more quickly means that a computer can produce more timely information, when information is needed as soon as possible.

(b) **Accuracy.** Computers are generally accurate, whereas humans are prone to error. The errors in computer data processing are normally human errors (errors in the input of data) although there can be software errors (errors in the programs) and hardware errors (faults or breakdowns in the equipment itself).

(c) **Volume and complexity.** As businesses grow and become more complex, their data processing requirements increase in volume and complexity too. More managers need greater amounts of information. More transactions have to be processed. The volume of DP work is often beyond the capability of even the largest clerical workforce to do manually. Clearing banks, for example, would be unable to function without electronic data processing to ease the demands on their workforce.

(d) **Access to information.** The use of databases and the ability to link a number of users via some form of network improves the distribution of information within and beyond the organisation.

1.5 However the 'manual' or 'human' method of data processing is more suitable when human judgement is involved in the work. For example, the human brain stores a lifetime of experiences and emotions that influence decisions and it is capable of drawing on them and making connections between them at phenomenal speed.

2   COMPUTER HARDWARE

KEY TERM

A **computer** is 'A *device* which will accept input data, process it according to programmed logical and arithmetic rules, store and output data and/or calculate results. The ability to store programmed instructions and to take decisions which vary the way in which a program executes (although within the defined logic of the program) are the principal distinguishing features of a computer. ...'   (CIMA *Computing Terminology*)

2.1   Computer hardware components can be classified by their function.

(a)   **Input devices** accept input data for processing.

(b)   A **processing device**. The computer has a central processor, which performs the data processing, under the control of the stored program(s), by taking in data from input devices and external storage devices, processing them, and then transferring the processed data (information) to an output device or an external storage device. This processing device is called the **central processing unit** (CPU).

(c)   **Storage devices** hold data or information on file until they are needed for processing.

(d)   **Output devices** accept output from the processing device and convert it into a usable form. The most common output devices are **printers** (which print the output on paper) and **screens** (which display the output).

The input devices, external storage devices and output devices are collectively known as **peripheral devices**. Any unit connected to a computer is a **peripheral**.

The processor or CPU

KEY TERM

The **processor (CPU)** is 'The collection of circuitry and registers that performs the processing in a particular computer and provides that computer with its specific characteristics. In modern computers the CPU comprises a single (albeit increasingly sophisticated) chip device but this is supported by other chips performing specialist functions.'   (CIMA *Computing Terminology*)

2.2   The processor (or CPU) is divided into three areas.

- The arithmetic and logic unit
- The control unit
- The main store, or memory

The set of operations that the processor performs is known as the **instruction set**, or **repertoire**, and this determines in part the speed at which processing can be performed.

Exam focus point
A question in the December 1996 exam asked for a brief explanation of the meaning and role of the CPU and also of ROM and RAM.

Computer chips

2.3 In modern computer systems the processing unit may have all its elements - arithmetic and logic unit, control unit, and the input/output interface-on a single 'chip'. A **chip** is a small piece of silicon upon which is etched an integrated circuit, which consists of **transistors** and their interconnecting patterns on an extremely small scale.

2.4 The chip is mounted on a carrier unit which in turn is 'plugged' on to a circuit board - called the **motherboard** - with other chips, each with their own functions.

Arithmetic and logic unit

2.5 The **ALU** is the part of the central processor where the **arithmetic** and **logic** operations are carried out. The **arithmetic** element might be as simple as x + y = z. The **logic** will be something along the lines of '*if* x + y *does not* = z, *then* add 3 to x and try again'.

2.6 The operations are all simple but the significant feature of computer operations is the very rapid speed with which computers can perform vast numbers of simple-step instructions, which combine to represent quite complex processing.

Control unit

2.7 The **control unit** receives program instructions, one at a time, from the main store and decodes them. It then sends out **control signals** to the peripheral devices. The signals are co-ordinated by a clock which sends out a 'pulse' - a sort of tick-tock sequence called a 'cycle' - at regular intervals. The number of cycles produced per second is usually measured in Megahertz (MHz).

1 MHz = one **million** cycles per **second**.

2.8 A typical modern PC might have a specification of 266 MHz. Speeds are improving rapidly. A typical business PC with a specification of 450 MHz was available in Spring 1999 for around £1,000.

Memory

2.9 Just as humans can work more quickly if they can remember the rules for doing something rather than having to look them up, a computer's processing is much faster if it has the information it needs readily to hand. The computer's memory is also known as **main store**, **internal store** or **immediate access storage**. This is circuitry which is used to store data within the processing unit whilst the computer is operating.

Bits and bytes

2.10 Each individual storage element in the computer's memory consists of a simple circuit which can be switched on or off. These two states can be conveniently expressed by the numbers 1 and 0 respectively. Any piece of data or instruction must be coded in these symbols before processing can commence.

2.11 Each 1 or 0 is a **bit**. Bits are grouped together in groups of eight to form **bytes**. A byte may be used to represent a character, for example a letter, a number or another symbol. A byte coding system that is commonly used in microcomputers is ASCII.

BPP PUBLISHING

2.12 The processing capacity of a computer is in part dictated by the capacity of its memory. Capacity is calculated in **kilobytes** (1 kilobyte = 2^{10} (1,024) bytes) and **megabytes** (1 megabyte = 2^{20} bytes) and **gigabytes** (2^{30}). These are abbreviated to Kb, Mb and Gb.

RAM and ROM

> **KEY TERMS**
>
> * **RAM** (random access memory) is memory that is **directly available** to the processing unit. It holds the data and programs in current use. Data can be written on to or read from random access memory. RAM can be defined as memory with the ability to access any location in the memory in any order with the same speed.
>
> * **ROM** (read-only memory) is a memory chip into which fixed data is written permanently at the time of its manufacture. New data cannot be written into the memory, and so the data on the memory chip is unchangeable and irremovable.

2.13 Random access is an essential requirement for the main memory of a computer. RAM in microcomputers is '**volatile**' which means that the contents of the memory are erased when the computer's power is switched off.

2.14 The RAM on a typical business PC is likely to have a capacity of 32 to 128 megabytes. The size of the RAM is *extremely* important. A computer with a 450 MHz clock speed but only 32 Mb of RAM will not be as efficient as a 266 MHz PC with 128 Mb of RAM.

2.15 ROM is '**non-volatile**' memory, which means that its contents do not disappear when the computer's power source is switched off. A computer's start-up program, known as a 'bootstrap' program, is always held in a form of a ROM.

Types of computer

2.16 Computers can be classified as follows, although the differences between these categories are becoming increasingly vague.

* Supercomputers
* Mainframe computers, now sometimes called 'enterprise servers'
* Minicomputers, now often called 'mid-range' computers
* Microcomputers, now commonly called PCs

Supercomputers

2.17 **A supercomputer is used to process very large amounts of data very quickly**. They are particularly useful for occasions where high volumes of calculations need to be performed, for example in meteorological or astronomical applications. Manufacturers of supercomputers include Cray and Fujitsu. They are not used commercially.

Mainframes

2.18 **A mainframe computer system is one that has at its heart a very powerful central computer,** linked by cable or telecommunications to hundreds or thousands of terminals, and capable of accepting simultaneous input from all of them. A mainframe has many times more processing power than a PC and offers extensive data storage facilities.

2.19 Older systems are typically very large in terms of size and very sensitive to fluctuations in temperature and air quality, requiring them to be housed in a controlled environment. However, the main modern example (the IBM S/390) uses the same kind of components that are used in PCs, may not be much larger than a fridge-freezer, and has far less need for a specialised environment. The basic IBM S/390 costs around £50,000.

2.20 Mainframes are used by organisations such as banks that have very large volumes of processing to perform and have special security needs. Many organisations have now replaced their old mainframes with networked 'client/server' systems of mid-range computers and PCs because this approach (called **downsizing**) is thought to be cheaper and offer more flexibility.

2.21 Nevertheless, mainframes are considered to offer greater reliability, functionality and data security than networked systems. Proponents claim that for organisations with 200 or more users they are cheaper to run in the medium term than other alternatives.

Medium and small business computers

Minicomputers

2.22 **A minicomputer is a computer whose size, speed and capabilities lie somewhere between those of a mainframe and a PC**. The term was originally used before PCs were developed, to describe computers which were cheaper but less well-equipped than mainframe computers (which had until then been the only type of computer available). The advent of more powerful chips now means that some 'superminis', and even PCs linked in a network, can run more powerfully than some older mainframes.

2.23 With the advent of PCs, and with mainframes now being physically smaller than in the past, the definition of a minicomputer has become rather vague. There is really no definition which distinguishes adequately between a PC and a minicomputer. Price, power and number of users supported have been used to identify distinguishing features, but these differences have tended to erode as microchip technology has progressed. Manufacturers of minicomputers include IBM with its AS400, ICL and DEC.

PCs

2.24 **Personal computers or PCs are now the norm for small to medium-sized business computing and for home computing**. Often they are linked together in a network to enable sharing of information between users.

2.25 A typical PC comprises a keyboard, a screen, a base unit or tower unit (containing the processor and other circuitry and floppy disk drives and CD-ROM drives), a mouse, and sometimes a pair of speakers. A typical modern business PC might have 64Mb of RAM, a 266 Mhz 'Pentium' processor and a 5 Gb hard drive.

File servers

2.26 **A file server** is more powerful than the average desktop PC and it is dedicated to providing additional services for users of networked PCs.

BPP PUBLISHING

2.27 A very large network is likely to use a 'mainframe' computer as its server, and indeed mainframes are beginning to be referred to as **'enterprise servers'**.

Portables

2.28 The original portable computers were heavy, weighing around five kilograms, and could only be run from the mains electricity supply. Subsequent developments allow true portability.

(a) The **laptop** is powered either from the electricity supply or using a rechargeable battery. It has a hard drive and also uses 3½" floppy disks, CD-ROMs and DVDs, a liquid crystal or gas plasma screen and is fully compatible with desktop PCs.

(b) The **notebook** is about the size of an A4 pad of paper. Some portables are now marketed as **'sub-notebooks'**.

(c) The **pocket computer** or handheld, may or may not be compatible with true PCs. They range from machines which are little more than electronic organisers to relatively powerful processors running 'cut-down' versions of Windows 98 and communications features.

2.29 While portable PCs are becoming more popular (even in the office, as they save precious space on crowded desks), disadvantages include the following.

- **Keyboard ergonomics** (ie keys which are too close together for easy, quick typing).
- **Battery power** (although manufacturers are trying to reduce power consumption).
- The **relative expense** of having to use the telecommunications network to send data.

3   COMPUTER SOFTWARE

3.1 **Software refers to computer programs**. Hardware cannot operate without software and software is needed to make the hardware process data in the ways required.

3.2 **Software has to be 'written' by a programmer, and program writing is a labour-intensive operation,** so that although hardware costs have fallen in recent years with the development of integrated circuit technology, the costs of software have tended to rise (because salaries and wages have risen). Software costs can now be much higher than the costs of the hardware for a computer system. The two main categories of software are as follows.

- Operating software
- Application software

> **KEY TERM**
>
> **Operating software** is software that controls the basic operation of a computer system. It is software that makes the hardware perform its functions, such as bringing data input into store and outputting information to an output device.

3.3 An operating system will typically perform the following tasks.

- Initial set-up of the computer, when it is switched on.
- Checking that the hardware (including printers) is functioning properly.
- Calling up of program files and data files from external storage into memory.
- Opening and closing of files, checking of file labels etc.
- Maintenance of directories in external storage.
- Controlling input and output devices, including the interaction with the user.

- Controlling system security (for example monitoring the use of passwords).
- Handling of interruptions (for example program abnormalities or machine failure).
- Managing multitasking.

3.4 **Multi-tasking** means doing lots of tasks at once, eg printing out a document you have just finished while working on the next one.

3.5 The best-known operating system is Windows 98.

> **KEY TERM**
>
> **Applications** are ready made programs written to perform a particular job for the user rather than operate the computer. The job will be common to many potential users, so that the package could be adopted by all of them for their data processing operations.

3.6 Examples of **applications** for commercial users which are available in software packages include the following.

- Payroll
- Production control
- Sales accounting (sales ledger system)
- Purchase accounting (purchase ledger system)
- Nominal ledger system and cost book system
- General bookkeeping system
- Audit packages (for internal and external audit use)
- Network analysis (or critical path analysis) programs

3.7 A distinction is sometimes made between application packages and more general purpose packages. A **general purpose package** is an off-the-shelf program that can be used for processing of a general type, but the computer user can apply the package to a variety of specific uses of his own choice.

3.8 Examples of general purpose packages are as follows.

(a) **Database systems.** This is a package of programs that allows the user to work with a large collection of data held on file (that is, a data base). With most commercial database packages, the user will key the data on to file to create the database records, but with some packages the database is already provided. The data on file can then be extracted and processed in different ways, according to the nature of the information that the user wants to obtain.

(b) **Expert systems.** This is similar to a database package, in which the file holds a large amount of specialised data, eg legal, engineering or medical information. The user keys in certain facts and the program uses its information on file to produce a decision about something on which an expert's decision would normally be required - for example a user without a legal background can obtain guidance on the law without having to consult a solicitor; or a non-medical user can obtain a medical diagnosis about a patient without having to consult a doctor or surgeon.

(c) **Word processing packages.** These give the user the facility of altering and re-organising large blocks of text on a terminal screen (correcting errors, inserting extra text and so on), and keeping files of standard text for repetitive use.

 BPP PUBLISHING

(d) **Spreadsheet packages**. These are used extensively in financial planning for budgeting, forecasting and other financial modelling.

Integrated software

3.9 **Integrated software** refers to programs, or packages of programs, that perform a variety of different processing operations, using data which is compatible with whatever operation is being carried out.

3.10 Accounts packages often consist of program 'modules' that can be integrated into a larger accounting system. There will be a module each for the sales ledger, the purchase ledger, the nominal ledger, and so on. Output from one 'module' can be used as input to another. The master file in one module can also be used in another module. For example the purchase ledger and sales ledger files could be used to provide input to the nominal ledger system.

4 CAPTURING AND PROCESSING DATA

4.1 The collection of data and its subsequent input to the computer are often problematical areas of data processing. The computer will only accept data which is in machine-sensible form, and if data is captured on a source document that is not in machine-sensible form it must be transcribed into a different form for input to computer processing.

4.2 Because of this, data collection and preparation for input can be lengthy and expensive operations. **The stages of data input are as follows.**

(a) **Origination** of data (transactions giving rise to data which needs to be recorded and processed).

(b) **Transcription** of data into a machine-sensible form, if this is necessary.

(c) Data **input**.

4.3 The ideal methods of data collection and input are those which do the following.

(a) Minimise the time needed to record the original data, and transmit, prepare and input the data to the computer.

(b) Minimise costs.

(c) Minimise errors.

(d) Minimise the 'turnround time' between submitting data for input and getting the processed information back.

Direct data entry with VDU and keyboard

4.4 The principal method of direct data entry is by means of a terminal comprising a VDU with keyboard. **VDU** and **keyboard** can be used as media for **direct data entry** as terminals connected to a mainframe or minicomputer or as an integral part of a microcomputer installation.

Keyboard layout and functions

4.5 A basic keyboard includes the following.

- **Ordinary typing keys** used to enter data or text.
- A **numeric key pad** for use with the built-in calculator.

- **Cursor control keys** (basically up/down/left/right keys to move the cursor).
- A number of **function keys** for use by the system and application software.

4.6 In addition to the function keys, there are special keys that are used to communicate with the operating programs, to let the computer know that you have finished entering a command, that you wish to correct a command and so on. Nothing appears at the cursor point when these keys are used, but they affect operations on screen.

The VDU

4.7 A **VDU** (or monitor) **displays text** and **graphics** and serves a number of purposes.

- It allows the operator to carry out a visual check on what he or she has keyed in.
- It helps the operator to input data by providing 'forms' on the screen for filling in.
- It displays output such as answers to file enquiries.
- It gives messages to the operator.

Character-based systems

4.8 Older systems offer two ways of using a keyboard with VDU to input data. Screen displays typically show white characters on a black background.

(a) **By selecting options from a menu.** A menu is a display of a series of options, and the operator selects which option he or she wants by keying in an appropriate letter or number. A VDU screen might list a number of different options, from which the computer user must choose what he or she wants to do next. For example, a main menu for purchase and sales ledger functions might include:

A - Define codes
B - Set up standing orders
C - Purchase ledger entries
D - Sales ledger entries
E - Supplier details
F - Client details

By selecting D, the operator will be specifying that he or she wants to do some processing of sales ledger entries. When D has been keyed in, another menu may be displayed, calling for the operator to narrow down still further the specification of what he or she wants to do next. A menu-system is thus a hierarchical list of options.

(b) **Using commands.** Command codes or instructions are keyed in, to indicate to the program what it should do with the data that follow. The data are then keyed in and processed by the program.

Graphical user interfaces

4.9 Modern systems are more user-friendly than character-based ones, especially for people who have little experience of using computers and/or who have difficulty using a keyboard. They are based on divisions of the screen into sections and coloured images of various kinds: hence the name graphical user interface (**GUI**).

4.10 **Graphical user interfaces** have become the principal means by which humans communicate with machines. Features include the following.

(a) **Windows.** This basically means that the screen can be divided into sections or 'windows' of flexible size which can be opened and closed. This enables two or more documents to be viewed and edited together, and sections of one to be inserted into another. This is particularly useful for word processed documents and spreadsheets, which are too large for the VDU screen.

(b) **Icons**. An icon is an image of an object used to represent an abstract idea or process. In software design, icons may be used instead of numbers, letters or words to identify and describe the various functions available for selection, or files to access. A common icon is a waste paper bin to indicate the deletion of a document.

(c) **Mouse**. This is a device used with on-screen graphics and sometimes as an alternative to using the keyboard to input instructions. It can be used to pick out the appropriate icon (or other option), to mark out the area of a new window, mark the beginning and end of a block for deletion/insertion and so on. It also has a button to execute the current command.

(d) **Pull-down menu**. An initial menu (or 'menu-bar') will be shown across the top of the VDU screen. Using the mouse to move the pointer to the required item in the menu, the pointer 'pulls down' a subsidiary menu, somewhat similar to pulling down a window blind in a room of a house. The pointer and mouse can then be used to select the required item on the pulled-down menu.

(e) Many GUIs (such as Microsoft Windows) also display dialogue boxes, buttons, sliders, check boxes, and a plethora of other graphical widgets that let you tell the computer what to do and how to do it.

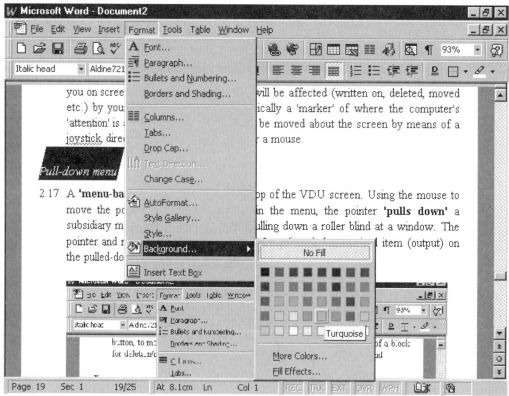

Document reading methods

4.11 Transcribing manually-prepared data into a computer-sensible form such as disk or tape is costly in manpower, time and accuracy. **Document reading methods of data collection involve the use of a source document that both humans and computers can read.** The data on the source document might be pre-printed, or added later by manual processing, but in either case the source document itself is fed in to the computer. Data transcription and verification become unnecessary.

Magnetic ink character recognition (MICR)

4.12 **MICR** is the **recognition of characters** by a machine that reads special formatted characters printed in magnetic ink. Using ink which contains a metallic powder, highly stylised characters are encoded on to documents by means of special typewriters. The document must be passed through a magnetic field before the characters can be detected by a suitable reading device.

4.13 The largest application of MICR is the banking system. Cheques are **pre-encoded** with the customer account number, branch code and cheque number and, after use, **post-encoded** with the amount of the cheque. The cheques are then passed through the reading device and details stored on magnetic disk or tape.

4.14 The main advantage of MICR is its accuracy, but MICR documents are expensive to produce, and so MICR has only limited application in practice.

Optical character recognition (OCR)

> **KEY TERM**
>
> **OCR** is 'a method of input which involves a machine that is able to read characters by optical detection of the shape of those characters'. *(CIMA Computing Terminology)*

4.15 Optical (or laser) scanners can read printed or typed documents at up to 300 pages per hour. They recognise the characters, convert them into machine code and record them on to the magnetic medium being used (or directly input the data to the CPU). The advantage of OCR over MICR is that the computer can read ordinary typed or printed text, provided that the quality of the input document is satisfactory.

Optical mark reading (OMR)

4.16 You use **optical mark reading** when you enter the National Lottery or do a multiple choice exam. Values are denoted by a line or cross in an appropriate box on a preprinted source document. The document is then read by a device which senses the mark in each box and translates it into machine code.

4.17 A business application in which OMR is used is the recording of gas and electricity meter readings by meter readers onto preprinted documents. Once the readings are made, the documents are input to the computer using an OMR reading system.

Bar coding

4.18 A **bar code reader** is a device which reads documents which contain bar codes. These are groups of marks which, by their spacing and thickness, indicate specific codes or values. Such devices are now commonly seen as an input medium for point of sale systems in supermarkets. Many products now carry bar coding on their labels.

Turnround documents

4.19 A **turnround document** is a document that is initially produced by computer. It is then used to collect more data and then re-input to the computer for processing. Examples of turnround documents are as follows.

(a) Credit card companies include a payment counterfoil with their computer- produced bill which will then be used for inputting payment data to a computer.

(b) An examining body that stores multiple choice questions on a computer file can produce examination papers by computer. Candidates are then asked to tick the correct answer, and the position of the answer mark will be detectable by OMR reader, and so the examination paper can be marked by computer.

Card reading devices

Magnetic stripe cards

4.20 **Magnetic stripe cards** have been widely distributed over the past decade, so that almost every person with a bank or building society account can use one. None of the information on the surface of the card is strictly necessary for data input to a computer system. All the machine-sensible data is contained on the back, on a magnetic stripe, which is a thin strip of typical magnetic recording tape, about 1.2cm wide stuck to the back of the card. The magnetic card reader converts the information on the tape into computer-sensible form.

Electronic point of sale (EPOS) devices

4.21 More and more large retail stores are introducing **electronic point of sale devices** which act both as cash registers and as terminals connected to a main computer. This enables the computer to produce useful management information such as sales details and analysis and stock control information very quickly. Many use bar coding, as described earlier, or direct keyboard entry. A fully itemised, accurate and descriptive receipt can be produced for the customer, who will also feel the benefit of faster moving queues at the checkout. Management will obtain more information more quickly than was ever possible before, in the following ways.

- Immediate updating of stock levels.
- Identification of fast-moving items for reordering, hence avoidance of stock-outs.
- Sales information.

4.22 The provision of immediate sales information (such as which products sell quickly), perhaps analysed on a branch basis, permits great speed and flexibility in decision-making (certainly of a short-term nature), as consumer wishes can be responded to quickly.

Question

As we have seen, there is a wide range of input methods, each one having its own advantages and disadvantages. From the descriptions given in this chapter you should be able to formulate your own ideas on the advantages and disadvantages of each method and you may be required in your examination to select the most suitable data input method in a particular situation. What factors should you consider in selecting an input method?

Answer

(a) **Suitability** for the application
(b) The **timing requirements** of the system (response times required)
(c) The **volume** of data
(d) The **accuracy** required
(e) The **cost** of the method chosen as compared with the benefits to be derived
(f) The use of **turnround** documents for data capture and the benefit of OCR methods

5 DATA OUTPUT

Printers

5.1 A **line printer** prints a complete line in a single operation, usually printing between 600 and 1,000 lines per minutes. They offer the operational speeds necessary for the **bulk printing requirements** of many systems.

5.2 **Character printers** print a single character at a time. Examples include daisy-wheel printers, dot matrix printers.

(a) Daisy wheel printers are **slow and noisy**, but produce print of a **high quality**. Companies are unlikely to buy new daisy wheel printers today because other types of printers are more versatile.

(b) Dot matrix printers are quite widely used in accounting departments. Their main drawback is the **low-resolution** of their printed characters, which is unsuitable for many forms of printed output. They are also relatively **slow** and rather **noisy.** Prices start at under £100.

5.3 **Bubblejet** and **inkjet** printers are small and prices start at under £100, making them popular where a 'private'; output device is required, for example in a director's office. They work by sending a jet of ink on to the paper to produce the required characters. They are fairly **quiet and fast**, but they may produce **smudged** output if the paper is not handled carefully.

5.4 **Laser printers** print a whole page at a time, rather than line by line. Unlike daisywheel and dot matrix printers, they print on to individual **sheets of paper** (in the same way as photocopiers do) and so they do not user 'tractor fed' continuous computer stationery.

5.5 The resolution of printed characters and diagrams with laser printers is **very high** - up to 600 dots per inch - and this high-quality resolution makes laser printing output good enough to be used for commercial printing.

5.6 Typically, a desk-top laser printer will print about 4 to 24 A4 pages per minute. **High speed** lasers print up to 500 pages per minute. Laser printers are a microprocessor in their own right, with **RAM memory for storing data prior to printing.**

5.7 Laser printers are **more expensive** than other types - a good one will cost about £700 - but it is quite possible that several users will be able to **share** a single laser printer.

The choice of output medium

5.8 As with choosing an input medium, choosing a suitable output medium depends on a number of factors, which you should bear in mind when we go on to consider each type of output in turn. These factors are as follows.

(a) **Is a 'hard' copy of the output required**; in other words, is a printed version of the output needed? If so, what quality must the output be?

(i) If the output includes documents that are going to be used as OCR turnround documents, the quality of printing must be good.

(ii) If the information will be used as a working document with a short life or limited use (eg a copy of text for type-checking) then a low quality output on a dot matrix printer might be sufficient.

(b) **The volume of information produced**. For example, a VDU screen can hold a certain amount of data, but it becomes more difficult to read when information goes 'off-screen' and can only be read a bit at a time.

(c) **The speed at which output is required**. For example, to print a large volume of data, a high speed printer might be most suitable to finish the work more quickly (and release the CPU for other jobs).

(d) **The suitability of the output medium to the application** - ie the purpose for which the output is needed.

    (i) A VDU is well-suited to interactive processing with a computer.

    (ii) A graph plotter would be well-suited to output in the form of graphs.

    (iii) Output on to a magnetic disk or tape would be well-suited if the data is for further processing.

    (iv) Large volumes of reference data for human users to hold in a library might be held on microfilm or microfiche, and so output in these forms would be appropriate.

(e) **Cost**: some output devices would not be worth having because their advantages would not justify their cost, and so another output medium should be chosen as 'second best'.

6 STORAGE DEVICES

Disks

6.1 **Disks** are the predominant form of backing storage medium nowadays because they offer direct access to data, an extremely important feature.

6.2 **Disks are covered on both sides with a magnetic material**. Data is held on a number of circular, concentric tracks on the surfaces of the disk, and is read or written by rotating the disk past read/write heads, which can write data from the CPU's memory on to disk, or can read data from the disk for input to the CPU's memory. The mechanism that causes the disk to rotate is called a **disk drive**. The data on a disk is located by its sector, as each track and sector has a unique identification number.

Hard disks

6.3 A modern business PC invariably has an **internal hard disk,** but external disks may be used too. External disks sit alongside the computer in an extra 'box', with its own power supply and plug socket. Internal disks are incorporated inside the microcomputer itself. At the time of writing the average new PC has a hard disk size of around 4 Gigabytes, but 15 Gb disks are not uncommon. The standard size has increased dramatically over recent years as ever more Windows-based software which is hungry for hard disk space is released.

6.4 In larger computer systems **removable disk packs** are commonly used. Several flat disks are mounted on a spindle. There is one read/write head for each surface, and the heads are moved in a synchronised manner across the disk surfaces. The disks rotate at about one thousandth of a millimetre from the heads; the disks need a very clean atmosphere to prevent dirt or dust coming between them. With the growth of minicomputer systems it became necessary to develop a magnetic disk storage medium which was less expensive than the exchangeable disk pack, but which still offered substantial storage capacity. The Winchester disk is a number of flat disks sealed into an airtight pack. They have a very high recording density.

Floppy disks

> ### KEY TERM
>
> A **floppy disk** is an exchangeable circular, flexible disk (typically $3^{1}/_{2}$ inches in diameter) which is held permanently in a plastic case. The case can bear an identification label for recognising the disk. A $3^{1}/_{2}$" disk can hold up to 1.44 Mb of data.

6.5 Modern PCs will also have one or two **floppy disk** drives. The floppy disk provides a cost-effective means of on-line storage for small business computer systems. Floppy disks are used in the smallest microcomputer systems as well as with minicomputers, and are particularly useful in providing a means of decentralised processing.

6.6 **Floppy disks do not require special storage conditions,** and indeed, they are often stored or filed in open trays. However, data on them can be easily corrupted. In particular, they are subject to physical wear, because the read/write head actually comes into contact with the disk surface during operation. This is not the case with other types of disk. Because they can be left lying around an office, they are also prone to physical damage, such as having cups of coffee spilled over them. As the disks tend to be less reliable than hard disks administrative procedures should be instituted to protect them (for example the use of steel filing cabinets and careful handling).

Tape storage

6.7 Like an audio or video cassette, data has to be recorded **along the length** of a computer tape and so it is more difficult to access. In using tapes, it is not practical to read from and then write on to a single piece of tape. Reading and writing are separate operations, using separate heads, and so two drives are necessary for the two operations.

6.8 It follows that magnetic tape as a file storage medium is only practical when every record on the file will be processed in turn. For example a supermarket's stock records might have movements in every item of stock every day, and so tape would be a suitable for backing up at the end of the day.

6.9 Tape cartridges have a **larger capacity** than floppy disks and they are still widely used as a **backing storage** medium.

6.10 Like any other storage medium tapes can get lost, or the data on them can get corrupted. Since tapes can only be updated by producing a completely new carried forward tape this provides an automatic means of data security. The brought forward tapes can be kept for two or three 'generations' to safeguard against the loss of data on a current file. This 'grandfather-father-son' technique allows for files to be reconstructed if a disaster should occur.

CD-ROM

6.11 **Optical disks,** which use similar technology to the laser-based compact disc audio system, are being used increasingly for data storage. Optical disks have very high capacity compared with other media and they are **more difficult to damage:** these advantages suggest that they are likely to develop into the main form of removable storage in the future. The latest PCs are now automatically supplied with a **CD-ROM** drive and some software packages are now only available on CD-ROM.

6.12 The initials **ROM** stand for **read-only memory**. This means that all data is implanted onto the disc when it is made, and subsequent users can only retrieve information, they cannot alter or overwrite or delete what is already on the disk. The **speed** of a CD-ROM drive is relevant to how fast data can be retrieved: an **eight speed** drive is quicker than a **four speed** drive.

6.13 **CD recorders** are now available for general business use with blank CDs (CD-R), but this does not alter the fact that until recently, CDs have not been reusable in the way that floppy disks are. This is why PCs invariably have floppy disk drives as well as CD-ROM drives. However, a **rewritable disk** (CD-RW) is now available. A CD-R can hold up to **650 Mb** of data.

DVD-ROM

6.14 The CD format has started to be superseded by DVD. CD-ROMs hold 650 megabytes of data, which only a few years ago was considered enough for any application. However, the advent of Multimedia files with video graphics and sound encouraged the development of a new storage technology.

6.15 **Digital Versatile Disk (DVD)** ROM technology can store almost 5 gigabytes of data. Access speed are improved as is sound and video quality.

6.16 DVD is some times referred to as **Digital Video Disk**. Many commentators believe DVD will not only replace CD-ROMs, but also VHS cassettes, audio CDs and laser discs.

7 SPREADSHEET PACKAGES

7.1 As you may already have realised, a large amount of accounting work entails drawing up tables and adding up rows and columns of numbers. A **spreadsheet** is a software package designed to do just that.

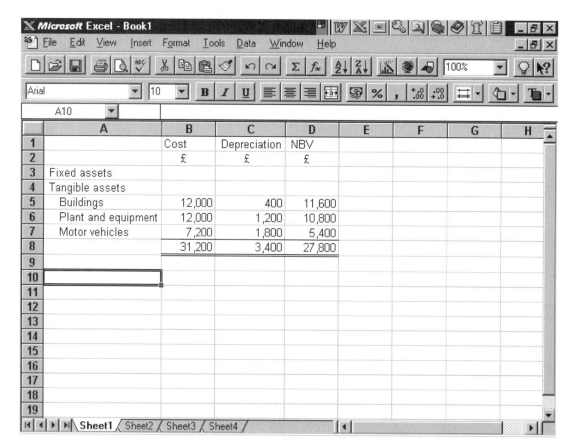

7.2 A **spreadsheet** consists of a large number of **boxes** or **cells**, each identified by a reference such as A4, D16, AA20 etc. AA20 is immediately to the right of Z20 and to the left of AB20. The screen cursor will highlight any particular cell - in the example above, it is placed over cell A10. At the top or bottom of the screen, the spreadsheet program will give you such information as:

(a) the **reference** of the cell where the cursor lies;
(b) the **width** of the column where the cursor lies;
(c) the **contents** of the cell where the cursor lies, if there is anything there.

7.3 The contents of the cell can be any one of the following.

(a) **Text**. Text contains words or numbers not used in computation.

(b) **Values**. A value is a number used in a computation, or a formula.

(c) **Formulae**. These refer to other cells in the spreadsheet and perform computations with them.

(d) **Automated commands** or **macros.**

How is a spreadsheet used?

7.4 The idea behind a spreadsheet is that the model builder should construct a model, in rows and columns format as follows.

(a) Identifying what data goes into each row and column, by inserting text - eg column headings and row identifications.

(b) Specifying how the numerical data in the model should be derived. Numerical data might be treated as follows.

(i) Inserted into the model via keyboard input.

(ii) Calculated from other data in the model by means of a formula specified within the model itself. The model builder must insert these formulae into the spreadsheet model when it is first constructed.

(iii) Occasionally, imported from data from another computer application program or module.

Commands and facilities

7.5 Spreadsheets are versatile tools. Different spreadsheets will offer different facilities, but some of the more basic ones which should feature in all spreadsheet programs are as follows.

(a) **Print commands**. You should be able to print the contents of the spreadsheet in total or in part, with or without the spreadsheet row and column labels.

(b) **File commands**. You should be able to save the spreadsheet data on your disk, so that you can use the data again, and so the facility to save data is an essential one. A spreadsheet is saved as a file of data.

(c) **Cell editing facilities**. The program should allow alteration of anything shown on the spreadsheet. This is particularly useful for 'what if?' calculations. For instance, suppose you had prepared a forecast balance sheet and you wanted to know what net current assets would be if taxation was £500,000 higher. Using editing facilities, you just have to change the taxation figure, then ask the computer to recalculate the entire spreadsheet on the basis of the new figures. This 'what if' manipulation of data is

BPP PUBLISHING

probably the most important facility in a spreadsheet package, and we shall return to it again later.

(d) **Facilities to rearrange the spreadsheet**. You can **insert** a column or row at a desired spot. The insert command facilitates this, and the formulae in the spreadsheet are adjusted automatically. You can **move** or **copy** a cell, row or column (or range of cells) elsewhere. You can **delete** a cell row or column.

(e) **Format**. This command controls the way in which headings and data are shown, for example by altering column widths, 'justifying' text and numbers (to indent or have a right-hand justification, etc), changing the number of decimal places displayed etc. You can format the whole spreadsheet, or, in certain cases, a specified **range** of cells.

(f) **Copy a formula**. For example, suppose you wanted to have a cumulative list of numbers as follows.

	A	B	C
1	Operation	Cost per operation	Cumulative cost
2	No.	£	£
3	1	9.00	9.00
4	2	10.00	19.00
5	3	14.00	33.00
6	4	3.00	36.00
7	5	86.00	122.00
8	6	9.00	131.00
9		131.00	

The cumulative numbers in the B column are calculated as follows.

	A	B	C
1	Operation	Cost per operation	Cumulative cost
2	No.	£	£
3	1	9	=B3
4	2	10	=C3+B4
5	3	14	=C4+B5
6	4	3	=C5+B6
7	5	86	=C6+B7
8	6	9	=C7+B8
9		=SUM(B3:B8)	

To save time it is possible to input = C3+B4 in the C4 cell and then to copy the formula down the column. The spreadsheet package will generate all the other formulae needed automatically, making the necessary changes each time. It is possible to 'replicate' formulae in this way, downwards or sideways throughout the spreadsheet.

(g) **Database** facility. A spreadsheet package will usually provide a facility for sorting data (alphabetically or numerically).

(h) Most spreadsheets also contain a **graphics** facility which enables the presentation of data as graphs or flowcharts for example.

(i) Some spreadsheets offer a **search and replace** facility to highlight and alter individual formulae.

(j) **Macros**. Many spreadsheet commands are provided as **options** in a menu. Some procedures require a number of commands to be executed. This is often time consuming. For example, if you wish to 'print' some or all of your spreadsheet, you will first execute the print command. You may then see a menu which asks you to specify:

(i) what **range** of the spreadsheet you wish to print;

(ii) what **print 'options'** you wish to use. This will lead to a submenu, which will ask you to specify the length of the pages you are using in the printer, what you wish the size of the margins to be and so forth.

Several commands must be executed before the spreadsheet is printed, and you will have to repeat them each time you wish to print your spreadsheet. Many spreadsheets provide a macro facility. This allows the user to automate a sequence of commands, executing them with the depression of two keys.

(k) Some spreadsheets offer a **'protect' facility** to ensure that the contents of a specified range of cells (for example the text titles, or a column of base data) cannot be tampered with.

Using spreadsheet models: sensitivity analysis

7.6 Whenever a forecast or budget is made, management should consider asking **'what if'** questions, and so carry out a form of **sensitivity analysis**. Suppose a forecast profit and loss account has been prepared using a spreadsheet. The accountant might ask a number of questions about it such as the following.

- What if sales were higher?
- What if administrative expenses were reduced by 25%?
- What if closing stock was reduced by £1 million?

7.7 Using the spreadsheet model, the answers to these questions, and others like them, can be obtained simply and quickly, using the editing facility in the program. A great number of such 'what if' questions can be asked and answered quickly, such as what if sales growth per month is nil, ½%, 1%, 1½%, 2½% or minus 1% etc? The information obtained should provide management with a better understanding of what the cash flow position in the future might be, and what factors are critical to ensuring that the cash position remains reasonable.

8   STATISTICAL PACKAGES

8.1 Before the widespread use of computers and microcomputers, accountants wishing to use certain statistical and mathematical techniques had to be arithmetic wizards. Often endless calculations had to be performed and then re-performed before a conclusion could be reached.

8.2 Fortunately computers have changed that. **Computers will perform any necessary calculations speedily and accurately,** leaving the accountant free to analyse and conclude. Familiarity with computers is therefore vital for any accountant wishing to use mathematical and statistical techniques.

8.3 Accountants could, of course, write their own programs each time they wished to use a mathematical or statistical technique. There are, however, a number of suitable packages on the market which, if used, leave the accountant free to analyse and conclude instead of being involved in computer technicalities.

Spreadsheets and statistics

8.4 Modern spreadsheet packages such as **Microsoft Excel** and **Lotus 1-2-3** include statistical functions that probably go well beyond the need of most accountants.

8.5 Besides financial maths techniques like Discounted Cash Flow and statistical techniques like Normal distributions, spreadsheets can calculate medians, modes, and so on, perform tests such as chi-squared tests, do linear programming, regression and so on. All of the techniques, in fact, that you will learn to do **manually** for Paper 3, and in your later studies, can be done easily with a spreadsheet.

Statistical software packages

8.6 There are also a variety of packages available that are dedicated to statistical work. Some of these are specially designed to make the work easy for people who are not adept at the techniques. Here are just two examples.

SPSS

8.7 SPSS is the market leader in statistical software for desktop computers. It offers an extensive set of statistics, graphs and reports and a user-friendly interface that enables the user to enter data in a spreadsheet like format (or import data directly from an existing spreadsheet, accounting package or database) and perform a large number of statistical tests. The results can then be exported into packages such as Word or Excel and incorporated into reports

8.8 It is designed to help with tasks like market research, sales forecasting, process control. It does so by identifying patterns in data, and visualising them in the form of bar charts , scattergraphs and so on. Over 60 statistical functions are offered: far more than you will learn about in this book.

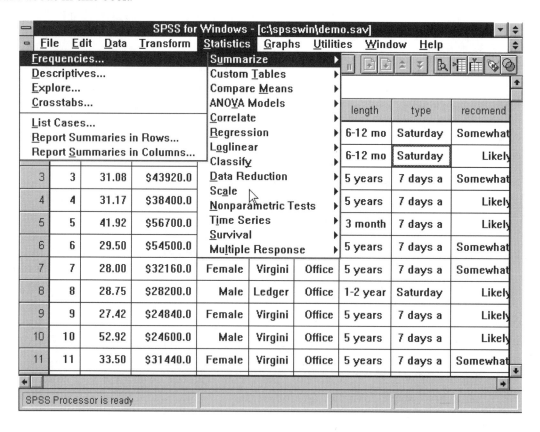

8.9 The **advantage** of statistical software packages is that they take all the agony out of analysing figures. Instead of hours of number-crunching an analysis can be obtained at the click of a button by selecting the rows and columns of data you want to analyse.

8.10 The **disadvantage** is that it is too easy: if users do not understand what the statistic calculated actually means in the first place, they will not be able to draw any conclusions from the results produced. Worse, they may set up the data wrongly and then draw incorrect conclusions because they cannot see that the results do not make sense.

WinForecast

8.11 In practice, more advanced statistical techniques are relatively little used by many businesses, not least because accountants that should be using them do not feel confident about them. More familiar will be simple management accounting techniques such as cash flow forecasting, and projected profit and loss accounts.

8.12 WinForecast is a package designed to help with this sort of work. Its manufacturer claims that it is 5 to 10 times faster than using a spreadsheet to produce a variety of familiar management accounting reports, because it is designed to remove as much of the mechanics of producing projections as possible.

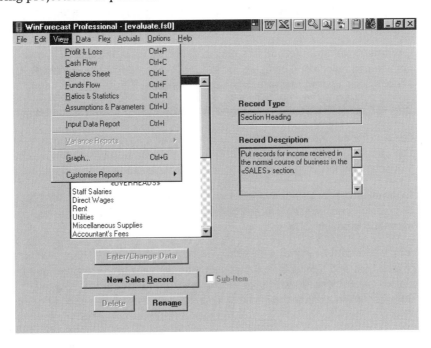

8.13 WinForecast offers What If? facilities to evaluate the effect of changes in variables such as price or demand. It can generate graphs and charts of various types for visual presentation and analysis of data, and it can incorporate formulae to manipulate or compare different scenarios.

BPP PUBLISHING

Chapter roundup

- Manual and electronic data processing are essentially the same. When compared with human beings, however, computers can process data much more **quickly**, are generally **accurate** (whereas human beings are prone to error) and can process both **larger volumes of data** and **more complex data.**

- Computers can be classified as mainframe computers, minicomputers or PCs.

- **Hardware** means the physical devices and components that make up a computer system, such as the CPU, disk drives, VDUs and so on. **Software** refers to the computer programs.

- **Operating software** controls the basic operation of a computer system. **Applications software** enables a computer to do the data processing for the various processing applications the user wishes to computerise (such as a sales ledger system or a payroll system).

- The principal method of direct data input to the computer is by means of a terminal comprising a **VDU** and **keyboard**.

- Instead of direct data entry, data may be copied from source documents and be written on to a magnetic disk or a magnetic tape from a keyboard or terminal. This process is called **encoding**.

- **Document reading methods** of data collection involve the use of a source document that both human beings and computers can read. Such method include **MICR**, **OCR**, **OMR**, **mark sensing**, **bar coding** and **turnround documents**.

- Data can also be collected by **card reading devices**, **magnetic stripe cards** and **EPOS devices**.

- **Output devices** include the **VDU** and **printers** such as **dot matrix** printers and **laser** printers. The choice of output medium will depend on factors such as the volume of information produced, whether a hard copy is required and the speed at which output is required.

- **External storage devices** are used to store data in computer-sensible form. The most commonly used backing storage medium is **magnetic disk**. Other storage media include **magnetic tape** and **CDs**.

- A **spreadsheet** is a software application which allows you to define a problem logically in terms of text, data and formulae, and then lets the computer bear the brunt of the complicated and tedious calculations. It can be used whenever the problem can be set out in logical stages. Spreadsheets are one of the principal means by which computers are used in cost accounting.

- Statistical packages are available to carry out a huge range of techniques. Modern spreadsheets incorporate a wider range of statistical functions than most accountants would ever need.

Quick quiz

1 What are the advantages of computerised data processing over manual data processing? (see para 1.4)

2 What is a CPU? (key terms)

3 What are the disadvantages of portable PCs? (2.29)

4 What is an operating system? (3.3)

5 What is an application? (key terms)

6 Explain the following terms.

GUI (4.9, 4.10)

MICR, OCR, OMR (4.12, 4.15, 4.16 and key terms)

7 Which gives better quality output: a dot matrix printer or a laser printer? (5.4, 5.5)

8 What is the disadvantage of tape storage? (6.8)

9 List five features of a spreadsheet package. (7.5)

10 What are the disadvantages of statistical packages? (8.10)

Question to try	Level	Marks	Time
3	Examination	14	25 mins

BPP PUBLISHING

Chapter 4

COST CLASSIFICATION

Chapter topic list	Syllabus reference
1 Total product/service costs	CA 1(c)(i)
2 Direct costs and indirect costs	CA 1(c)(i)
3 Functional costs	CA 1(c)(i)
4 Fixed costs and variable costs	CA 1(c)(i)
5 Product costs and period costs	CA 1(c)(i)
6 Other cost classifications	CA 1(c)(i)
7 Cost centres, cost units, cost objects and profit centres	CA 1(c)(iii)

Introduction

The **classification of costs** as either **direct** or **indirect**, for example, is essential in the costing method used by an organisation to determine the cost of a unit of product or service.

The **fixed** and **variable cost classifications**, on the other hand, are important in **absorption** and **marginal costing**, **cost behaviour** and **cost-volume-profit analysis**. You will meet all of these topics as we progress through the Study Text.

This chapter therefore acts as a foundation stone for a number of other chapters in the text and hence an understanding of the concepts covered in it is vital before you move on.

1 TOTAL PRODUCT/SERVICE COSTS

1.1 The total cost of making a product or providing a service consists of the following.

(a) Cost of **materials**

(b) Cost of the **wages** and **salaries** (labour costs)

(c) Cost of **other expenses**

- Rent and rates
- Electricity and gas bills
- Depreciation

2 DIRECT COSTS AND INDIRECT COSTS   6/94, 12/95, 12/97

2.1 Materials, labour costs and other expenses can be classified as either **direct costs** or **indirect costs**.

KEY TERMS

- A **direct cost** is a cost that can be traced in full to the product, service, or department that is being costed.

- An **indirect cost** or **overhead** is a cost that is incurred in the course of making a product, providing a service or running a department, but which cannot be traced directly and in full to the product, service or department.

2.2 (a) **Direct material costs** are the costs of materials that are known to have been used in making and selling a product (or even providing a service).

(b) **Direct labour costs** are the specific costs of the workforce used to make a product or provide a service. Direct labour costs are established by measuring the time taken for a job, or the time taken in 'direct production work'.

(c) **Other direct expenses** are those expenses that have been incurred in full as a direct consequence of making a product, or providing a service, or running a department.

2.3 Examples of indirect costs include supervisors' wages, cleaning materials and buildings insurance.

2.4 Total expenditure may therefore be analysed as follows.

Materials	=	Direct materials	+	Indirect materials
+		+		+
Labour	=	Direct labour	+	Indirect labour
+		+		+
Expenses	=	Direct expenses	+	Indirect expenses
Total cost	=	Direct cost		Overhead

Direct material

KEY TERM

Direct material is all material becoming part of the product (unless used in negligible amounts and/or having negligible cost).

2.5 Direct material costs are charged to the product as part of the **prime cost**. Examples of direct material are as follows.

(a) **Component parts**, specially purchased for a particular job, order or process.

(b) **Part-finished work** which is transferred from department 1 to department 2 becomes finished work of department 1 and a direct material cost in department 2.

(c) **Primary packing materials** like cartons and boxes.

Direct labour

Exam focus point

In the 12/95 exam, the examiner commented that many candidates had difficulty in analysing wages into direct and indirect components. Make sure that you are clear about the classification of labour costs.

KEY TERM

Direct wages are all wages paid for labour (either as basic hours or as overtime) expended on work on the product itself.

2.6 **Direct wages** costs are charged to the product as part of the **prime cost**.

Examples of groups of labour receiving payment as direct wages are as follows.

(a) Workers engaged in **altering** the condition or composition of the product.

(b) Inspectors, analysts and testers **specifically required** for such production.

(c) Foremen, shop clerks and anyone else whose wages are **specifically identified.**

2.7 Two **trends** may be identified in **direct labour costs.**

- The ratio of direct labour costs to total product cost is falling as the use of machinery increases, and hence depreciation charges increase.

- Skilled labour costs and sub-contractors' costs are increasing as direct labour costs decrease.

Question 1

Classify the following labour costs as either direct or indirect.

(a) The basic pay of direct workers (cash paid, tax and other deductions) *direct*

(b) The basic pay of indirect workers *indirect* *

(c) Overtime premium *indirect with exceptions*

(d) Bonus payments *indirect*

(e) Employer's National Insurance contributions *indirect*

(f) Idle time of direct workers *indirect*

(g) Work on installation of equipment *— capital cost of equipment*

Answer

(a) The basic pay of direct workers is a direct cost to the unit, job or process.

(b) The basic pay of indirect workers is an indirect cost, unless a customer asks for an order to be carried out which involves the dedicated use of indirect workers' time, when the cost of this time would be a direct labour cost of the order.

(c) Overtime premium paid to both direct and indirect workers is an indirect cost, except in two particular circumstances.

    (i) If overtime is worked at the specific request of a customer to get his order completed, the overtime premium paid is a direct cost of the order.

    (ii) If overtime is worked regularly by a production department in the normal course of operations, the overtime premium paid to direct workers could be incorporated into the (average) direct labour hourly rate.

(d) Bonus payments are generally an indirect cost.

(e) Employer's national insurance contributions (which are added to employees' total pay as a wages cost) are normally treated as an indirect labour cost.

(f) Idle time is an overhead cost, that is an indirect labour cost.

(g) The cost of work on capital equipment is incorporated into the capital cost of the equipment.

Direct expenses

> **KEY TERM**
>
> **Direct expenses** are any expenses which are incurred on a specific product other than direct material cost and direct wages

2.8 **Direct expenses** are charged to the product as part of the **prime** cost. Examples of direct expenses are as follows.

- The **hire of tools** or equipment for a particular job
- **Maintenance costs** of tools, jigs, fixtures and so on

Direct expenses are also referred to as **chargeable expenses.**

Production overhead

> **KEY TERM**
>
> **Production (or factory) overhead** includes all indirect material cost, indirect wages and indirect expenses incurred in the factory from receipt of the order until its completion.

2.9 Production overhead includes the following.

(a) **Indirect materials** which cannot be traced in the finished product.

- Consumable stores, eg material used in negligible amounts

(b) **Indirect wages,** meaning all wages not charged directly to a product.

- Wages of non-productive personnel in the production department, eg foremen

(c) **Indirect expenses** (other than material and labour) not charged directly to production.

- Rent, rates and insurance of a factory
- Depreciation, fuel, power, maintenance of plant, machinery and buildings

Administration overhead

> **KEY TERM**
>
> **Administration overhead** is all indirect material costs, wages and expenses incurred in the direction, control and administration of an undertaking.

2.10 Examples of administration overhead are as follows.

- **Depreciation** of office administration overhead, buildings and machinery.
- **Office salaries**, including salaries of directors, secretaries and accountants.
- Rent, rates, insurance, lighting, cleaning, telephone charges and so on.

Selling overhead

> **KEY TERM**
>
> **Selling overhead** is all indirect materials costs, wages and expenses incurred in promoting sales and retaining customers.

2.11 Examples of selling overhead are as follows.

- **Printing** and **stationery**, such as catalogues and price lists.
- **Salaries** and **commission** of salesmen, representatives and sales department staff.
- **Advertising** and **sales promotion**, market research.
- Rent, rates and insurance of sales offices and showrooms, bad debts and so on.

Distribution overhead

> **KEY TERM**
>
> **Distribution overhead** is all indirect material costs, wages and expenses incurred in making the packed product ready for despatch and delivering it to the customer.

2.12 Examples of distribution overhead are as follows.

- Cost of packing cases.
- Wages of packers, drivers and despatch clerks.
- Insurance charges, rent, rates, depreciation of warehouses and so on.

Costs which are both direct and indirect

2.13 A cost may be a **direct cost** in one part of a cost analysis and an **indirect cost** in another part. This point is perhaps best illustrated with a simple example.

2.14 The Donkey Oater Racing Stables trains and races two horses, Sancho Panza and Rosinante. Costs for the recent month are as follows.

		£
Salary of the stable manager		1,000
Wages:		
Special groom to Sancho Panza		80
General stable boy		80
Jockey for both horses:	retainer	200
	race fees	200
Race entrance fees:	Sancho Panza (three races)	150
	Rosinante (two races)	100
Hay, straw and so on		600
Depreciation on stable and riding equipment		200

	£
Rent and rates	300
Heating and lighting	100

2.15 All of the costs listed are direct costs of operating the training and racing stable, with the exception of the various race fees (which are only incurred as and when horses are entered for races).

The direct costs of keeping one of the horses, Sancho Panza, in the month are the costs of the special groom and race fees. All other costs are one of the following.

(a) Costs shared with Rosinante (stable manager's salary, wages of stable boy, jockey's retainer, hay and straw, depreciation, rent, rates, heating and lighting). Some of these costs could be charged directly (for example hay and straw consumed, stable boy's time) if a system for recording the material issued to each horse or time spent with each horse were in operation.

(b) Direct costs of the other horse (race fees).

The direct costs of a race are the entrance fee (£50) and the jockey's fees (£40). Indirect costs would be not only the jockey's retainer, but also the other costs of running the stable.

In conclusion, when classifying a cost as direct or indirect (an overhead), the cost accountant must consider the product or service whose cost is being established.

Question 2

A direct labour employee's wage in week 5 consists of the following.

		£
(a)	Basic pay for normal hours worked, 36 hours at £4 per hour =	144
(b)	Pay at the basic rate for overtime, 6 hours at £4 per hour =	24
(c)	Overtime shift premium, with overtime paid at time-and-a-quarter $\frac{1}{4} \times 6$ hours $\times$ £4 per hour =	6
(d)	A bonus payment under a group bonus (or 'incentive') scheme - bonus for the month =	30
	Total gross wages in week 5 for 42 hours of work	204

Required

Establish which costs are direct costs and which are indirect costs.

Answer

Items (a) and (b) are direct labour costs of the items produced in the 42 hours worked in week 5.

Overtime premium, item (c), is usually regarded as an overhead expense, because it is 'unfair' to charge the items produced in overtime hours with the premium. Why should an item made in overtime be more costly just because, by chance, it was made after the employee normally clocks off for the day?

Group bonus scheme payments, item (d), are usually overhead costs, because they cannot normally be traced directly to individual products or jobs.

In this example, the direct labour employee costs were £168 in direct costs and £36 in indirect costs.

3 FUNCTIONAL COSTS

Production, administration and marketing costs

3.1 In a 'traditional' costing system for a manufacturing organisation, costs are classified as follows.

(a) **Production** or **manufacturing costs.** These are costs associated with the factory.

(b) **Administration costs.** These are costs associated with general office departments.

(c) **Marketing,** or **selling** and **distribution costs.** These are costs associated with sales, marketing, warehousing and transport departments.

Classification in this way is known as **classification by function.** Expenses that do not fall fully into one of these classifications might be categorised as **general overheads** or even listed as a classification on their own (for example research and development costs).

3.2 In costing a small product made by a manufacturing organisation, direct costs are usually restricted to some of the production costs. A commonly found build-up of costs is therefore as follows.

	£
Production costs	
Direct materials	A
Direct wages	B
Direct expenses	C
Prime cost	A+B+C
Production overheads	D
Full factory cost	A+B+C+D
Administration costs	E
Selling and distribution costs	F
Full cost of sales	A+B+C+D+E+F

Classification by function in more detail

3.3 Functional costs include the following.

(a) **Production costs** are the costs which are incurred by the sequence of operations beginning with the supply of raw materials, and ending with the completion of the product ready for warehousing as a finished goods item. Packaging costs are production costs where they relate to 'primary' packing (boxes, wrappers and so on).

(b) **Administration costs** are the costs of managing an organisation, that is, planning and controlling its operations, but only insofar as such administration costs are not related to the production, sales, distribution or research and development functions.

(c) **Selling costs,** sometimes known as marketing costs, are the costs of creating demand for products and securing firm orders from customers.

(d) **Distribution costs** are the costs of the sequence of operations with the receipt of finished goods from the production department and making them ready for despatch and ending with the reconditioning for reuse of empty containers.

(e) **Research costs** are the costs of searching for new or improved products, whereas **development costs** are the costs incurred between the decision to produce a new or improved product and the commencement of full manufacture of the product.

(f) **Financing costs** are costs incurred to finance the business such as loan interest.

Question 3

Within the costing system of a manufacturing company the following types of expense are incurred.

Reference number

1	Cost of oils used to lubricate production machinery
2	Motor vehicle licences for lorries
3	Depreciation of factory plant and equipment
4	Cost of chemicals used in the laboratory
5	Commission paid to sales representatives
6	Salary of the secretary to the finance director
7	Trade discount given to customers
8	Holiday pay of machine operatives
9	Salary of security guard in raw material warehouse
10	Fees to advertising agency
11	Rent of finished goods warehouse
12	Salary of scientist in laboratory
13	Insurance of the company's premises
14	Salary of supervisor working in the factory
15	Cost of typewriter ribbons in the general office
16	Protective clothing for machine operatives

Required

Place each expense within the following classifications.

(a) Production costs
(b) Selling and distribution costs
(c) Administration costs
(d) Research and development costs

Each type of expense should appear only once in your answer. You may use the reference numbers in your answer.

Answer

The reference number for each expense can be classified as follows.

		Reference numbers
(a)	Production costs	1, 3, 8, 9, 14, 16
(b)	Selling and distribution costs	2, 5, 7, 10,11
(c)	Administration costs	6, 13, 15
(d)	Research and development costs	4, 12

4 FIXED COSTS AND VARIABLE COSTS   12/97

4.1 A different way of analysing and classifying costs is into **fixed costs** and **variable costs.** Some items of expenditure are part-fixed and part-variable or 'semi-fixed' costs but, in cost accounting, **semi-fixed** or **semi-variable costs** are divided into their fixed and variable elements.

> ### KEY TERMS
>
> - A **fixed cost** is a cost which is incurred for a particular period of time and which, within certain activity levels, is unaffected by changes in the level of activity.
>
> - A **variable cost** is a cost which tends to vary with the level of activity.

4.2 Some examples are as follows.

(a) Direct material costs are **variable costs** because they rise as more units of a product are manufactured.

(b)   Sales commission is often a fixed percentage of sales turnover, and so is a **variable cost** that varies with the level of sales.

(c)   Telephone call charges are likely to increase if the volume of business expands, and so they are a **variable overhead cost.**

(d)   The rental cost of business premises is a constant amount, at least within a stated time period, and so it is a **fixed cost.**

4.3   Costs can be classified as follows.

- Direct costs
- Indirect costs
- Fixed costs
- Variable costs

5   PRODUCT COSTS AND PERIOD COSTS

KEY TERMS

- **Product costs** are costs identified with a finished product. Such costs are initially identified as part of the value of stock. They become expenses (in the form of cost of goods sold) only when the stock is sold.

- **Period costs** are costs that are deducted as expenses during the current period without ever being included in the value of stock held.

5.1   When preparing financial statements (a profit and loss account and balance sheet), accountants frequently distinguish between **product costs** and **period costs.**

6   OTHER COST CLASSIFICATIONS   12/94, 12/97

KEY TERMS

- **Avoidable costs** are specific costs of an activity or business which would be avoided if the activity or business did not exist.

- **Unavoidable costs** are costs which would be incurred whether or not an activity or sector existed.

- A **controllable cost** is a cost which can be influenced by management decisions and actions.

- An **uncontrollable cost** is any cost that cannot be affected by management within a given time span.

- **Discretionary costs** are costs which are likely to arise from decisions made during the budgeting process. They are likely to be fixed amounts of money over fixed periods of time.

6.1   Examples of discretionary costs are as follows.

- Advertising
- Research and Development

- Training

7 COST CENTRES, COST UNITS, COST OBJECTS AND PROFIT CENTRES

12/94

Allocation of costs to cost centres

7.1 Costs consist of the costs of the following.

- Direct materials
- Direct labour
- Direct expenses
- Production overheads
- Administration overheads
- General overheads

7.2 When costs are incurred, they are generally allocated to a **cost centre.** A cost centre acts as a **collecting place** for certain costs before they are analysed further. Cost centres may include the following.

- A department
- A machine, or group of machines
- A project (eg the installation of a new computer system)
- Overhead costs eg rent, rates, electricity (which may then be allocated to departments or projects)

7.3 Cost centres are an essential 'building block' of a costing system. They are the starting point for the following.

(a) The classification of actual costs incurred.
(b) The preparation of budgets of planned costs.
(c) The comparison of actual costs and budgeted costs (management control).

Cost units

7.4 Once costs have been traced to cost centres, they can be further analysed in order to establish a **cost per cost unit.** Alternatively, some items of cost may be charged directly to a cost unit, for example direct materials and direct labour costs.

KEY TERM

A **cost unit** is a unit of product or service to which costs can be related. The cost unit is the basic control unit for costing purposes.

7.5 Examples of cost unit include the following.

- Patient episode (in a hospital)
- Barrel (in the brewing industry)
- Room (in a hotel)

Question 4

Suggest suitable cost units which could be used to aid control within the following organisations.

(a) A public transport authority
(b) A hotel with 50 double rooms and 10 single rooms
(c) A hospital
(d) A road haulage business

Answer

(a)   (i)   Passenger/mile
     (ii)   Mile travelled
     (iii)   Passenger journey
     (iv)   Ticket issued

(b)   (i)   Guest/night
     (ii)   Bed occupied/night
     (iii)   Meal supplied

(c)   (i)   Patient/night
     (ii)   Operation
     (iii)   Outpatient visit

(d)   (i)   Tonne/mile
     (ii)   Mile

Cost objects

> **KEY TERM**
>
> A **cost object (or objective)** is any activity for which a separate measurement of costs is desired.

7.6   If the users of management information wish to know the cost of something, this something is called a **cost object**. Examples include the following.

- The cost of a product
- The cost of a service
- The cost of operating a department

Profit centres

7.7   We have seen that a cost centre is where costs are collected. Some organisations, however, work on a profit centre basis. A **profit centre** is similar to a cost centre but is accountable for **costs** *and* **revenues**.

7.8   Profit centre managers should normally have control over how revenue is raised and how costs are incurred. Often, several cost centres will comprise one profit centre.

Chapter roundup

- A **direct cost** is a cost that can be traced in full to the product, service or department being costed. An **indirect cost** (or overhead) is a cost that is incurred in the course of making a product, providing a service or running a department, but which cannot be traced directly and in full to the product, service or department.

- **Classification by function** involves classifying costs as production/manufacturing costs, administration costs or marketing/selling and distribution costs.

- A different way of analysing and classifying costs is into **fixed costs** and **variable costs**. Many items of expenditure are part-fixed and part-variable and hence are termed **semi-fixed** or **semi-variable**.

- For the preparation of financial statements, costs are often classified as **product costs** and **period costs**. Product costs are costs identified with goods produced or purchased for resale. Period costs are costs deducted as expenses during the current period.

- **Cost centres** are collecting places for costs before they are further analysed. Costs are further analysed into cost units once they have been traced to cost centres.

Quick quiz

1   Give two examples of direct expenses. (see para 2.8)

2   Give an example of an administration overhead, a selling overhead and a distribution overhead. (2.10 - 2.12)

3   What are functional costs? (3.1, 3.3)

4   What is the distinction between fixed and variable costs? (key terms)

5   What are product costs and period costs? (key terms)

6   What is a cost centre? (7.2)

7   What is a cost unit? (key terms)

Question to try	Level	Marks	Time
4	Examination	14	25 mins

Part B

Cost determination: material, labour and overheads

Chapter 5

MATERIAL COSTS

Chapter topic list	Syllabus reference
1 What is stock control?	CA 2(a)(i)
2 The ordering, receipt and issue of raw materials	CA 2(a)(i)
3 The storage of raw materials	CA 2(a)(i), (iv)
4 Stock control levels	CA 2(a)(i), (ii)
5 Ledger entries relating to materials	CA 1(b)(i)

Introduction

The investment in stocks is a very important one for most businesses, both in terms of monetary value and relationships with customers (no stock, no sale, loss of customer goodwill). It is therefore vital that management establish and maintain an **effective stock control system** *and* are aware of the major costing problem relating to materials, that of pricing material issues and valuing stock at the end of each period.

This major costing problem (**stock valuation**) will be the subject of the next chapter. In this chapter we will concern ourselves with an examination of an effective stock control system, which covers ordering, receiving, issuing and storing stock, including the level at which stock should be held.

1   WHAT IS STOCK CONTROL?

1.1 The stocks held in any organisation can generally be classified under four main headings.

- Raw materials
- Work in progress
- Spare parts/consumables
- Finished goods

1.2 This chapter will concentrate on a **stock control system** for materials, but similar problems and considerations apply to all forms of stock. Controls should cover the following functions.

- The **ordering** of stock
- The **purchase** of stock
- The **receipt** of goods into store
- **Storage**
- The **issue** of stock and maintenance of stock at the most appropriate level

Qualitative aspects of stock control

1.3 We may wish to **control stock** for the following reasons.

- Holding costs of stock may be expensive.
- Production will be disrupted if we run out of raw materials.

- If stock with a short shelf life is not used it will go to waste.

1.4 If manufactured goods are made out of low quality materials, the end product will be of low quality also. It may therefore be necessary to control the **quality of stock**, in order to maintain a good reputation with consumers.

2 THE ORDERING, RECEIPT AND ISSUE OF RAW MATERIALS 12/96

Exam focus point
Stock documentation was part of a longer question in December 1996.

Ordering and receiving materials

2.1 Proper records must be kept of the physical procedures for ordering and receiving a consignment of materials to ensure the following.

- That enough stock is held
- That there is no duplication of ordering
- That quality is maintained
- That there is adequate record keeping for accounts purposes

(a) Current stocks run down to the level where a reorder is required. The stores department issues a **purchase requisition** which is sent to the purchasing department, authorising the department to order further stock. An example of a purchase requisition is shown below. Note the details that are shown on the requisition form.

PURCHASE REQUISITION Req. No.			
Department _____ Suggested Supplier:	Date Requested by: Latest date required:		
Quantity	**Description**	**Estimated Cost**	
		Unit	£
Authorised signature:			

(b) The purchasing department draws a **purchase order** which is sent to the supplier. (The supplier may be asked to return an acknowledgement copy as confirmation of his acceptance of the order.) Copies of the purchase order must be sent to the accounts department and the storekeeper (or receiving department).

Purchase Order/Confirmation

Our Order Ref: Date

To

⌐ *(Address)*   ⌐   Please deliver to the above address

                                  Ordered by:

                                  Passed and checked by:

⌊   ⌋   Total Order Value £

		Subtotal		
		VAT (@ 17.5%)		
		Total		

(c) The supplier delivers the consignment of materials, and the storekeeper signs a **delivery note** for the carrier. The packages must then be checked against the copy of the purchase order, to ensure that the supplier has delivered the types and quantities of materials which were ordered. (Discrepancies would be referred to the purchasing department.)

(d) If the delivery is acceptable, the storekeeper prepares a **goods received note (GRN)**. The GRN will show various items of information. An example is shown below.

ACCOUNTS COPY

GOODS RECEIVED NOTE WAREHOUSE COPY

DATE: _ _ _ _ _ _ _ _ _ _ _ _ _   TIME: _ _ _ _ _ _ _ _ _ _ _ _ _.   NO 5565

ORDER NO: _

SUPPLIER'S ADVICE NOTE NO: _ _ _ _ _ _ _ _ _ _ _ _ _ _ _ _   WAREHOUSE A

QUANTITY	CAT NO	DESCRIPTION

RECEIVED IN GOOD CONDITION: (INITIALS)

(e) A copy of the **GRN** is sent to the accounts department, where it is matched with the copy of the purchase order. The supplier's invoice is checked against the purchase order and GRN, and the necessary steps are taken to pay the supplier. The invoice may contain details relating to discounts such as trade discounts, quantity discounts (order in excess of a specified amount) and settlement discounts (payment received within a specified number of days).

Question 1

What are the possible consequences of a failure of control over ordering and receipt of materials?

Answer

(a) Incorrect materials being delivered, disrupting operations
(b) Incorrect prices being paid
(c) Deliveries other than at the specified time (causing disruption)
(d) Insufficient control over quality
(e) Invoiced amounts differing from quantities of goods actually received or prices agreed

You may, of course, have thought of equally valid consequences.

Issue of materials

2.2 Materials can only be issued against a **materials/stores requisition**. This document must record not only the quantity of goods issued, but also the cost centre or the job number for which the requisition is being made.

The materials requisition note may also have a column, to be filled in by the cost department, for recording the cost or value of the materials issued to the cost centre or job.

Materials requisition note

Date required _____		Cost centre No/ Job No _____	
Quantity	Item code	Description	£
Signature of requisitioning Manager/ Foreman _____			Date _____

Materials transfers and returns

2.3 Where materials, having been issued to one job or cost centre, are later transferred to a different job or cost centre, a **materials transfer note** should be raised. Such a note must show not only the job receiving the transfer, but also the job from which it is transferred. This enables the appropriate charges to be made to jobs or cost centres.

2.4 Material returns must also be documented on a **materials returned note**. This document is the reverse of a requisition note, and must contain similar information. The value of the materials returned will be entered by the cost department.

Materials returned note

Date returned _ _ _ _ _ _ _ _ _ _ _		Cost centre No/ Job No _ _ _ _ _ _ _ _ _ _ _	
Quantity	*Item code*	*Description*	*£*
Signature of receiving storekeeper _		Date _ _ _ _ _ _ _ _	

Impact of computerisation

2.5 Many stock control systems these days are computerised. Computerised stock control systems vary greatly, but most will have the features outlined as follows.

(a) **Data must be input into the system.** For example, details of goods received may simply be written onto a GRN for later entry into the computer system. Alternatively, this information may be keyed in directly to the computer: a GRN will be printed and then signed as evidence of the transaction.

Other types of transaction which will need to be recorded include the following.

(i) **Transfers** between different categories of stock (for example from work in progress to finished goods)

(ii) **Despatch,** resulting from a sale, of items of finished goods to customers

(iii) **Adjustments** to stock records if the amount of stock revealed in a physical stock count differs from the amount appearing on the stock records

Note that the input of data into the system may take place as the transaction is occurring, with hard copy records generated by the system as output, or after the transaction has happened, with data from manually prepared documents keyed in separately to the computer.

(b) **A stock master file is maintained.** This file will contain details for every category of stock and will be updated for new stock lines. A database file may be maintained.

Question 2

What type of information do you think should be held on a stock master file?

Answer

Here are some examples.

(a) Stock code number, for reference
(b) Brief description of stock item
(c) Reorder level
(d) Reorder quantity
(e) Cost per unit
(f) Selling price per unit (if finished goods)
(g) Amount in stock
(h) Frequency of usage

The file may also hold details of stock movements over a period, but this will depend on the type of system in operation. In a **batch system**, transactions will be grouped and input in one operation and details of the movements may be held in a separate transactions file, the master file updated in total only. In an **on-line system**, transactions may be input directly to the master file, where the record of movements is thus likely to be found. Such a system will mean that the stock records are constantly up to date, which will help in monitoring and controlling stock.

The system may generate orders automatically once the amount in stock has fallen to the reorder level.

(c) **The system will generate outputs**. These may include, depending on the type of system, any of the following.

    (i)   **Hard copy** records of transactions entered into the system.

    (ii)   Output on a **VDU** screen in response to an enquiry.

    (iii)   Various **printed reports**, devised to fit in with the needs of the organisation. These may include stock movement reports, detailing over a period the movements on all stock lines, listings of GRNs, despatch notes and so on, or listings of the physical amounts and values of stock lines at a particular time.

2.6   A computerised stock control system is usually able to give **more up to date information** and **more flexible reporting** than a manual system but remember that both manual and computer based stock control systems need the same types of data to function properly.

3   THE STORAGE OF RAW MATERIALS

6/95, 12/98, 6/99

Exam focus point

The 6/95 and the 6/99 exams tested candidates' ability to explain continuous stocktaking and perpetual inventory.

3.1   **Storekeeping** involves storing materials to achieve the following objectives.

- Speedy **issue** and **receipt** of materials
- Full **identification** of all materials at all times
- Correct **location** of all materials at all times
- Provision of suitable storage conditions to **protect** materials from damage
- Provision of **secure stores** to avoid pilferage, theft and fire
- **Efficient** use of storage space
- **Maintenance** of correct stocking levels
- Keeping correct and up-to-date **records** of receipts, issues and stock levels

Types of store

3.2   Materials may be kept in either a **central** (main) store or a **departmental** (sub) store. The advantages of a **central store** are as follows.

(a)   Smaller stocks are required.
(b)   A smaller overall staff is required; staff can also specialise.
(c)   Control of stock levels is simplified; only one set of stores records needs to be kept.
(d)   Paperwork is therefore reduced.
(e)   Stocktaking is facilitated.

Question 3

What do you see as possible disadvantages to centralised storekeeping?

Answer

(a)   Handling and transportation costs are increased; stores must be sent out over longer distances.
(b)   There may be delays in issuing to departments.
(c)   Fire risk is increased.
(d)   If the centralised system breaks down, all other departments will suffer disruption.

3.3   **Sub-stores** may be advantageous for storing the following.

- High value items
- Inflammable and corrosive materials
- Part-finished goods

Recording stock levels

3.4   One of the objectives of storekeeping is to maintain **accurate records of current stock levels**. This involves the accurate recording of stock movements (issues from and receipts into stores). Systems for recording stock movements are as follows.

- Bin cards
- Stores ledger accounts

Bin cards

3.5   A **bin card** shows the level of stock of an item at a particular stores location. It is kept with the actual stock and is updated by the storekeeper as stocks are received and issued. A typical bin card is shown below.

Bin card

Part code no_ _ _ _ _ _ _ _ _ _ _ _ _ _ _			Location _ .			
Bin number _ _ _ _ _ _ _ _ _ _ _ _ _ _ _ _			Stores ledger no _ _ _ _ _ _ _ _ _ _ _ _ _ _ _ _ _ .			
Receipts			*Issues*			Stock balance
Date	Quantity	G.R.N. No.	Date	Quantity	Req. No.	

Stores ledger accounts

3.6   A typical stores ledger account is shown as follows. Note that it shows the value of stock.

Stores ledger account

Material	....			Maximum Quantity	....					
Code	....			Minimum Quantity	....					

Date	Receipts				Issues				Stock		
	G.R.N. No.	Quantity	Unit Price £	Amount £	Stores Req. No.	Quantity	Unit Price £	Amount £	Quantity	Unit Price £	Amount £

3.7 The above illustration shows a card for a manual system. The same type of information is normally included in the computer file of computerised stock records.

Free stock

3.8 As well as knowing the physical stock balance, knowledge of the **free stock balance** is also necessary in order to obtain a full picture of the current stock position of an item. Free stock represents what is really **available for future use** and is calculated as follows.

	Materials in stock	X
+	Materials on order from suppliers	X
−	Materials requisitioned, not yet issued	(X)
	Free stock balance	X

3.9 Physical stock aids stock issuing, stocktaking and controlling maximum and minimum stock levels: free stock aids ordering.

Identification of materials: stock codes (materials codes)

3.10 Materials held in stores are **coded** and **classified**. Advantages of using code numbers to identify materials are as follows.

(a) Ambiguity is avoided.

(b) Time is saved, as narrative can be time-consuming.

(c) Production efficiency is improved if the correct material can be accurately identified from a code number.

(d) Computerised processing is made easier.

(e) Numbered code systems can be designed to be flexible, and can be expanded to include more stock items as necessary.

The digits in a code can stand for the type of stock, supplier, department and so forth.

Exam focus point
There were five marks available in the 12/98 exam for explaining the term 'materials coding system' and for listing the advantages of materials coding.

Stocktaking

3.11 Stocktaking involves counting the physical stock on hand at a certain date, and then checking this against the balance shown in the clerical records. There are two methods of carrying out this process, **periodic stocktaking** and **continuous stocktaking**.

Periodic stocktaking

3.12 **Periodic stocktaking is usually carried out annually and the objective is to count all items of stock on a specific date.** It is a very important exercise and the following steps would usually be taken.

(a) All staff involved should be issued with stocktaking instructions well before the date of the actual count. Often non-stores staff will be involved in the count.

(b) A 'cut-off' time should be set, after which no movement of stock is allowed until the count has been completed.

(c) A team of stock-checkers should be allocated to count all stock in one area, to ensure that all stock is counted once, and that no omissions or duplications occur.

(d) Stock checkers should enter amounts counted on pre-printed stock sheets.

(e) In the office, the completed stock sheets should be collated and totalled, and the quantities checked against the stock records.

(f) Any stocks showing discrepancies should be recounted, and if still not resolved should be reported to management.

(g) Senior staff or auditors should perform sample checks on a number of items.

Continuous stocktaking

3.13 **Continuous stocktaking involves a specialist team counting and checking a number of stock items each day, so that each item is checked at least once a year.** Valuable items could be checked more frequently. The advantages of this system compared to periodic stocktaking are as follows.

(a) The annual stocktaking is unnecessary and the disruption it causes is avoided.

(b) Regular skilled stocktakers can be employed, reducing likely errors.

(c) More time is available, reducing errors and allowing investigation.

(d) Deficiencies and losses are revealed sooner than they would be if stocktaking were limited to an annual check.

(e) Production hold-ups are eliminated because the stores staff are at no time so busy as to be unable to deal with material issues to production departments.

(f) Staff morale is improved and standards raised.

(g) Control over stock levels is improved, and there is less likelihood of overstocking or running out of stock.

Stock discrepancies

3.14 If stock checks disclose discrepancies between the physical count and the stock records, the cause of the discrepancy should be investigated, and appropriate action taken to ensure that it does not happen again.

Question 4

List as many possible causes of discrepancies between physical and book stock as you can think of.

Answer

Here are some ideas.

(a) Suppliers deliver a different quantity of goods than is shown on the goods received note. Since this note is used to update stock records, a discrepancy will arise. This can be avoided by ensuring that all stock is counted as it is received, and a responsible person should sign the document to verify the quantity.

(b) The quantity of stock issued to production is different from that shown on the materials requisition note. Careful counting of all issues will prevent this.

(c) Excess stock is returned from production without documentation. This can be avoided by ensuring that all movements of stock are accurately documented. In this case, a materials returned note should be raised.

(d) Clerical errors may occur in the stock records such as an entry having been made on the wrong bin card. Regular checks by independent staff should detect and correct mistakes.

(e) Breakages in stores may go unrecorded. All breakages should be documented and noted on the stock records.

(f) Employees may steal stock. Regular checks or continuous stocktaking will help to prevent this, and only authorised personnel should be allowed into the stores.

(g) Items may be placed in the wrong location.

(h) Arithmetical errors may have been made when calculating the balance on the bin card.

3.15 If the stock discrepancy is found to be caused by clerical error, then the records should be rectified immediately. If the discrepancy occurs because units of stock appear to be missing, the lost stock must be written off. The accounting transaction will be recorded by a stores credit note if items of stock have been lost, or a stores debit note if there is more actual stock than the amount recorded.

Perpetual inventory

3.16 **A perpetual inventory system involves recording every receipt and issue of stock as it occurs on bin cards and stores ledger accounts.** This means that there is a continuous clerical record of the balance of each item of stock. The balance on the stores ledger account therefore represents the stock on hand and this balance is used in the calculation of closing stock in monthly and annual accounts. In practice, physical stocks may not agree with recorded stocks and therefore continuous stocktaking is necessary to ensure that the perpetual inventory system is functioning correctly and that minor stock discrepancies are corrected.

Obsolete, deteriorating and slow-moving stocks and wastage

3.17 **Obsolete stocks are those items which have become out-of-date and are no longer required.** Obsolete items are written off to the profit and loss account and disposed of.

3.18 All **wasted stock** items should be noted on the stock records immediately so that physical stock equals book stock. The cost of the wastage should be **written off** to the profit and loss account.

3.19 **Slow-moving stocks are stock items which are likely to take a long time to be used up.** For example, 5,000 units are in stock, and only 20 are being used each year. This is often caused by **overstocking**. Managers should investigate such stock items and, if it is felt that the usage rate is unlikely to increase, excess stock should be written off as for obsolete stock, leaving perhaps four or five years' supply in stock.

4   STOCK CONTROL LEVELS   *12/96, 6/99, 12/99*

Why hold stock?

4.1   The costs of purchasing stock are usually one of the largest costs faced by an organisation and, once obtained, stock has to be carefully controlled and checked.

4.2   The main reasons for holding stocks can be summarised as follows.

- To ensure sufficient goods are available to meet expected demand
- To provide a buffer between processes
- To meet any future shortages
- To take advantage of bulk purchasing discounts
- To absorb seasonal fluctuations and any variations in usage and demand
- To allow production processes to flow smoothly and efficiently
- As a necessary part of the production process (such as when maturing cheese)
- As a deliberate investment policy, especially in times of inflation or possible shortages

Holding costs

4.3   **Holding costs** are associated with high stock levels. The reasons they occur are as follows.

(a)   **Costs of storage and stores operations**. Larger stocks require more storage space and possibly extra staff and equipment to control and handle them.

(b)   **Interest charges**. Holding stocks involves the tying up of capital (cash) on which interest must be paid.

(c)   **Insurance costs**. The larger the value of stocks held, the greater insurance premiums are likely to be.

(d)   **Risk of obsolescence**. When materials or components become out-of-date and are no longer required, existing stocks must be thrown away and written off to the profit and loss account.

(e)   **Deterioration**. When materials in store deteriorate to the extent that they are unusable, they must be thrown away (with the likelihood that disposal costs would be incurred) and again, the value written off stock plus the disposal costs will be a charge to the profit and loss account.

(f)   **Theft**.

> ### Exam focus point
> The 12/99 exam included a question that asked you to state two items that would be regarded as stockholding costs and to explain how they might be controlled effectively.

Costs of obtaining stock

4.4   **Ordering costs** are associated with low stock levels, and include the following.

- **Administrative costs** associated with accounting for goods
- **Transport costs**
- **Production run costs**

Stockout costs

4.5 If stocks are kept too low, costs associated with running out of stock may arise. These are known as **stockout** costs and are caused by the following.

- Lost contribution from lost sales
- Loss of future sales due to disgruntled customers
- Loss of customer goodwill
- Cost of production stoppages
- Labour frustration over stoppages
- Extra costs of urgent, small quantity, replenishment orders

Objective of stock control

4.6 The overall objective of stock control is, therefore, to maintain stock levels so that the following costs are minimised.

- Holding costs
- Ordering costs
- Stockout costs

Three stock control levels

4.7 By establishing **when to order** and **how many to order**, three critical control levels can be calculated and used to maintain stocks at their optimum level (in other words, a level which minimises costs).

(a) **Reorder level.** When stocks reach this level, action should be taken to replenish stocks. The reorder level is determined by consideration of the following.

    (i) The maximum rate of consumption

    (ii) The maximum lead time, which is the time between placing an order with a supplier, and the stock becoming available for use

FORMULA TO LEARN

Reorder level = maximum usage × maximum lead time

(b) **Minimum level.** This is also a warning level to draw management attention to the fact that stocks are approaching a dangerously low level and that stockouts are possible. It is essentially a buffer stock and is set by consideration of the following.

- The reorder level
- The average rate of consumption
- The average lead time

The minimum level is also known as the **safety stock level**.

FORMULA TO LEARN

Minimum level = reorder level – (average usage × average lead time)

(c) **Maximum level.** Stock levels must not exceed this uppermost limit. It acts as a warning to management that stocks are reaching a potentially wasteful level. The maximum level is set by consideration of the following.

- The reorder level
- The quantity ordered each time (the reorder quantity)
- The minimum rate of consumption
- The minimum lead time

FORMULA TO LEARN

Maximum level = reorder level + reorder quantity - (minimum usage × minimum lead time)

Question 5

A company uses a maximum of 1,000 units of component L each week. An order (which is always for 3,000 units) placed with the supplier of component L takes, at most, four weeks to arrive.

Required

At what level should the company reorder component L?

Answer

Reorder level   = maximum usage × maximum lead time
                             = 1,000 × 4 = 4,000 units

Reorder quantity

KEY TERM

The **reorder quantity** is the quantity of stock which is to be ordered when stock reaches the reorder level.

4.8   If the reorder quantity is set so as to minimise the total costs associated with **holding** and **ordering** stock, then it is known as the **economic order quantity (EOQ)**.

EXAM FORMULA

$$EOQ = \sqrt{\frac{2C_0 D}{C_H}}$$

where: C_H is the cost of holding one unit of stock for one year
          C_0 is the cost of ordering a consignment from a supplier
          D is the annual demand
          Q is the economic order quantity.

Question 6

The following data relate to an item of raw material used by S Khan and Co Ltd

Cost of raw material	£20
Usage per week	250 units
Cost of ordering material, per order	£400
Annual cost of holding stock, as a % of cost	10%

(handwritten annotations: D= 250 units × 48 wk = ; C= £400; C_H)

A year consists of 48 weeks and a week consists of 5 days.

Required

Calculate the EOQ.

Answer

$$EOQ = \sqrt{\frac{2C_oD}{C_H}} = \sqrt{\frac{2 \times 400 \times (250 \times 48)}{10\% \text{ of } £20}} = \sqrt{4,800,000} = 2,191 \text{ units}$$

Other systems of stores control and reordering

4.9 (a) **Under the order cycling method, quantities on hand of each stores item are reviewed periodically** (every 1, 2 or 3 months).

(b) **The two-bin system of stores control is one whereby each stores item is kept in two storage bins.** When the first bin is emptied, an order must be placed for re-supply; the second bin will contain sufficient quantities to last until the fresh delivery is received.

(c) **Materials items may be classified as expensive, inexpensive or in a middle-cost range.** Because of the practical advantages of simplifying stores control procedures without incurring unnecessary high costs, it may be possible to segregate materials for selective stores control.

(d) A similar selective approach to stores control is the **Pareto (80/20) distribution.** It is based on the finding that in many stores, 80% of the value of stores is accounted for by only 20% of the stores items, and stocks of these more expensive items should be controlled more closely.

Just-in-time stock control techniques

4.10 A recent innovation in the way in which companies control stocks has been the introduction of **Just-in-time (JIT)** techniques.

4.11 Briefly, an organisation using JIT seeks to minimise its holdings of stock by ensuring that an item of stock is only acquired from a supplier when it is actually needed for input to a production process. JIT works on the principle that it is better not to produce at all than to produce unnecessarily: unnecessary production adds to costs rather than profitability (in other words, it is better to have machines idle than produce goods which sit in a warehouse, incurring holding costs for several weeks).

4.12 JIT has the following aims.

(a) To **minimise warehousing** and **storage costs**.

(b) To **eliminate waste** by maintaining control over the quality of stocks input to a production process.

(c) To **reduce the amount of raw materials and work in progress stock** carried as working capital, through more efficient production planning thus saving on financing costs.

(d) To **reduce the amount of finished goods stock held as working capital**. If large volumes of stock are held, it is not always easy to identify which are slow moving or obsolete.

4.13 Proponents of JIT believe that in the EOQ model, the holding costs element is much higher than generally appreciated. Included in holding costs are the expenses of quality control (checking production for faulty items) and rectification.

4.14 JIT goes hand in hand therefore with a commitment to quality at each stage in the production process.

4.15 JIT has a number of limitations.

(a) It is costly to administer.

(b) It depends on very close relationships with suppliers in terms of production scheduling and quality control.

(c) Suppliers are more likely to be chosen because of the price that they can offer, rather than how close the relationship between the supplier and an organisation.

5 LEDGER ENTRIES RELATING TO MATERIALS 6/95

> **Exam focus point**
> The 6/95 exam required candidates to record a week's transactions in the materials store account (for a single item of material).

5.1 In cost accounting, we are concerned not only with the cost of individual items of stock, but with the total costs of all raw material stocks used, and the total costs of all finished goods sold during an accounting period. These total costs, which are the sum of all the costs on individual stores ledger records, are recorded as follows.

(a) In a **raw material stores account,** or stores ledger control account, for raw materials stocks.
(b) In a **finished goods stock (control) account,** for finished goods stocks.

The cost of stocks manufactured in the production department is recorded in the **work in progress control account.**

5.2 EXAMPLE: LEDGER ENTRIES FOR MATERIALS

At 1 July 20X6, the total value of items held in store was £50,000. During July the following transactions occurred.

	£
Materials purchased from suppliers, on credit	120,000
Materials returned to suppliers, because they were of unsatisfactory quality	3,000
Materials purchased for cash	8,000
Direct materials issued to the production department	110,000
Indirect materials issued as production overhead costs	25,000
Value of materials written off after a discrepancy was found in a stock check	1,000
Direct materials returned to store from production	4,000

Required

Draw up a stores ledger account and stock adjustment account for July 20X6.

5.3 SOLUTION

(a) The opening balance of stocks brought forward is a debit balance in the stores account.

(b) When materials are received which are bought on credit, the accounting entry is to:

DEBIT Stores account
CREDIT Trade creditor's (supplier's) account

(c) When materials are returned to suppliers, the reduction of items in stock and the reduction in the amounts owed to the suppliers is shown by the double entry:

CREDIT   Stores account
DEBIT   Creditor's account

(d) When materials are purchased for cash, the entry is:

DEBIT   Stores account
CREDIT   Cash (or bank) account

when the goods are received and the cash paid.

(e) When materials are issued from stores, the reduction in stocks is shown as a credit entry in the stores account. The corresponding debit entry is to work in progress account (for direct materials) or production overhead account (for indirect production materials).

CREDIT   Stores account
DEBIT   Work in progress account or production overhead account

(f) The entries are reversed when materials are returned to store unused by the department which requisitioned them.

(g) The accounting entries for stock credit notes or debit notes have already been described, ie for a loss of stocks:

CREDIT   Stores account
DEBIT   Stock adjustment account

(h) The balance on the account at the end of the period will be closing stocks, carried forward as opening stocks at 1 August 20X6.

In our example, the stores account for July 20X6 will be as follows.

STORES ACCOUNT

	£		£
Opening stock b/f	50,000	Returns to suppliers (creditors a/c)	3,000
Purchases (creditors a/c)	120,000		
Purchases (cash a/c)	8,000	Work in progress account - issues	110,000
Returns from WIP (WIP a/c)	4,000	Production overhead a/c -issues	25,000
		Loss of stock - adjustment a/c	1,000
		Closing stock c/f	43,000
	182,000		182,000
Opening stock b/f	43,000		

STOCK ADJUSTMENT ACCOUNT

	£		£
Stores account	1,000	Profit and loss account	1,000

Chapter roundup

- **Stock control** includes the functions of ordering, purchasing, receiving goods into store, storing, issuing and controlling the level of stocks.

- Every movement of material in a business should be documented using the following as appropriate: purchase requisition, purchase order, GRN, materials requisition note, materials transfer note and materials returned note.

- **Perpetual inventory** refers to a stock recording system whereby the records (bin cards and stores ledger accounts) are updated for each receipt and issue of stock as it occurs.

- Each material item should be identified by a unique code number.

- Stocktaking can be carried out on a **continuous** or **periodic** basis.

- **Free stock balance** calculations take account of stock on order from suppliers, and of stock which has been requisitioned but not yet delivered to cost centres.

- **Stock costs** include purchase costs, holding costs, ordering costs and stockout costs.

- **Stock control levels** can be calculated in order to maintain stocks at the optimum level. The four critical controls levels are reorder level, reorder quantity, minimum level and maximum level.

- The **economic order quantity** is the ordering quantity which minimises stock costs.

- **JIT** seeks to minimise storage costs, eliminate waste and reduce stock held as working capital. It involves a commitment to quality at each stage in the production process.

Quick quiz

1   List five steps in the ordering and receipt of raw materials. (see para 2.1)

2   List six objectives of storekeeping. (3.1)

3   List six elements in the cost of holding stock. (4.3)

4   What are the three stock control levels and how are they calculated? (4.7)

5   How is the EOQ calculated? (exam formulae)

6   What is JIT and what are its aims? (4.11, 4.12)

7   What is the double entry in the ledger accounts when materials are returned to suppliers? (5.3)

Question to try	Level	Marks	Time
5	Introductory	n/a	15 mins

Chapter 6

STOCK VALUATION

Chapter topic list	Syllabus reference
1 Why is stock valuation problematic?	CA 2(a)(iii)
2 FIFO (first in, first out)	CA 2(a)(iii)
3 LIFO (last in, first out)	CA 2(a)(iii)
4 Cumulative weighted average pricing	CA 2(a)(iii)
5 Periodic weighted average pricing	CA 2(a)(iii)
6 Standard cost pricing	CA 2(a)(iii)
7 Replacement cost pricing	CA 2(a)(iii)
8 The cost of a unit of stock	CA 2(a)(iii)
9 Stock valuation and profitability	CA 2(a)(iii)

Introduction

In this chapter we explain why stock valuation may be problematic. The various methods for stock valuation and materials issues pricing will be illustrated and their advantages and disadvantages explained. We will end the chapter with an assessment of how the valuation method used can affect profitability.

1   WHY IS STOCK VALUATION PROBLEMATIC?

1.1   There are three significant difficulties which may be encountered in stock valuation.

- The **valuation** of a stock item
- **Changing** units of stock to cost of production of cost of sales
- The **cost** of a unit of stock

The valuation of an item of stock

1.2   There are several ways in which stock might be valued.

   (a)   At their **selling price.** This would not be prudent, since it would be recognising profit **before** making a sale. Stock is therefore **not** valued in this way.

   (b)   At their **original cost.** This may be the purchase cost (eg raw materials) or production cost (eg finished goods). It is usual to value stock in this way.

   (c)   At their **net realisable value.** This is their selling price, less any costs associated with selling the goods. If the net realisable value is **less than** the original cost, then stock may be valued in this way.

(d) At their **current replacement cost.** In a conventional historical cost accounting system, this is not a method which is used for valuing stocks. (Stocks would be valued this way in a current cost accounting system.)

Stock in the balance sheet is valued at the lower of cost and net realisable value.

1.3 In practice, stocks will probably be valued at cost in the stores records. When the period ends the value of the stock in hand will be reconsidered. Items with a net realisable value below their original cost will be revalued downwards, and the stock records altered to reflect this.

Charging units of stock to cost of production or cost of sales

1.4 It is important to be able to distinguish between the way in which the physical items in stock are actually issued. In practice a storekeeper may issue goods in the following way.

- The oldest goods first
- The latest goods received first
- Randomly
- Those which are easiest to reach

1.5 The cost of the goods issued must be determined on a **consistently applied basis**, and must ignore the likelihood that the materials issued will be costed at a price different from the cash paid for them.

1.6 This may seem a little confusing at first, and it may be helpful to explain the point further. Suppose that there are three units of a material item in stock.

Units	Date received	Purchase cost
A	June 20X1	£100
B	July 20X1	£106
C	August 20X1	£109

In September, one unit is issued to production. As it happened, the physical unit actually issued was B. The accounting department must put a value or cost on the material issued, but the value would not be the cost of B, £106. The principles used to value the materials issued are not concerned with the actual unit issued, A, B, or C. The accountant may choose to make one of the following assumptions.

(a) The unit issued is valued as though it were the **earliest unit in stock,** (ie at the purchase cost of A, £100). This valuation principle is called **FIFO**, or first in, first out.

(b) The unit issued is valued as though it were the **most recent unit received into stock,** that is, at the purchase cost of C, £109. This method of valuation is **LIFO**, or last in, first out. It is used in particular where a company is concerned about inflation and the rising cost of replacing stocks used up in production, and the company wishes to charge a cost to production which most closely reflects the current replacement cost of the stock.

(c) The unit issued is valued at an **average price** of A, B and C, that is, £105.

1.7 In the following sections we will consider the various pricing methods, using the following transactions to illustrate the principles in each case.

BPP
PUBLISHING

TRANSACTIONS DURING MAY 20X3

	Quantity	Unit cost	Total cost	Material value per unit on date of transactions
	Units	£	£	£
Opening balance, 1 May	100	2.00	200	
Receipts, 3 May	400	2.10	840	2.11
Issues, 4 May	200			2.11
Receipts, 9 May	300	2.12	636	2.15
Issues, 11 May	400			2.20
Receipts, 18 May	100	2.40	240	2.35
Issues, 20 May	100			2.35
Closing balance, 31 May	200			2.38
			1,916	

2 FIFO (FIRST IN, FIRST OUT) 12/98

2.1 **FIFO assumes that materials are issued out of stock in the order in which they were delivered into stock**. Using FIFO, the cost of issues and the closing stock value in the example would be as follows.

Date of issue	Quantity issued	Value		
	Units		£	£
4 May	200	100 at £2.00	200	
		100 at £2.10	210	
				410
11 May	400	300 at £2.10	630	
		100 at £2.12	212	
				842
20 May	100	100 at £2.12		212
Cost of issues				1,464
Closing stock value	200	100 at £2.12	212	
		100 at £2.40	240	
				452
				1,916

Notes

(a) The cost of materials issued plus the value of closing stock equals the cost of purchases plus the value of opening stock (£1,916).

(b) The market price of purchased materials is rising dramatically. In a period of inflation, there is a tendency for materials to be issued at a cost lower than the current market value, although closing stocks tend to be valued at a cost approximating to current market value.

2.2 The advantages and disadvantages of the **FIFO** method are as follows.

(a) **Advantages**

   (i)   It is a logical pricing method (the oldest stock is likely to be used first).
   (ii)   It is easy to understand and explain to managers.
   (iii) It can be near to a valuation based on replacement cost.

(b) **Disadvantages**

   (i)   FIFO can be cumbersome to operate because of the need to identify each batch of material separately.

   (ii)   Managers may find it difficult to compare costs and make decisions when they are charged with varying prices for the same materials.

3 LIFO (LAST IN, FIRST OUT) 12/97

3.1 **LIFO assumes that materials are issued out of stock in the reverse order to which they were delivered.**

Using LIFO, the cost of issues and the closing stock value in the example above would be as follows.

Date of issue	*Quantity issued*	*Valuation*		
	Units		£	£
4 May	200	200 at £2.10		420
11 May	400	300 at £2.12	636	
		100 at £2.10	210	
				846
20 May	100	100 at £2.40		240
Cost of issues				1,506
Closing stock value	200	100 at £2.10	210	
		100 at £2.00	200	
				410
				1,916

Notes

(a) The cost of materials issued plus the value of closing stock equals the cost of purchases plus the value of opening stock (£1,916).

(b) In a period of inflation there is a tendency with LIFO for the following to occur.

   (i) Materials are issued at a price which approximates to current market value.
   (ii) Closing stocks become undervalued when compared to market value.

3.2 The advantages and disadvantages of the **LIFO** method are as follows.

(a) **Advantages**

   (i) Stocks are issued at a price which is close to current market value. This is not the case with FIFO when there is a high rate of inflation.

   (ii) Managers are continually aware of recent costs when making decisions, because the costs being charged to their department or products will be current costs.

(b) **Disadvantages**

   (i) The method can be cumbersome to operate because it sometimes results in several batches being only part-used in the stock records before another batch is received.

   (ii) LIFO is often the opposite to what is physically happening and can therefore be difficult to explain to managers.

   (iii) Decision making can be difficult because of the variations in prices.

4 CUMULATIVE WEIGHTED AVERAGE PRICING 6/95, 12/97, 12/98

4.1 The cumulative weighted average pricing method has the following features.

- It calculates a **weighted average price** for all units in stock.
- Issues are priced at the average unit cost. (Total cost ÷ total number of units).
- Stock held always has the same unit valuation.
- A new weighted average price is calculated each time materials are received.

4.2 In our example, issue costs and closing stock values would be as follows.

Date	Received Units	Issued Units	Balance Units	Total stock value £	Unit cost £	£
Opening stock			100	200	2.00	
3 May	400			840	2.10	
			* 500	1,040	2.08	
4 May		200		(416)	2.08	416
			300	624	2.08	
9 May	300			636	2.12	
			* 600	1,260	2.10	
11 May		400		(840)	2.10	840
			200	420	2.10	
18 May	100			240	2.40	
			* 300	660	2.20	
20 May		100		(220)	2.20	220
						1,476
Closing stock value			200	440	2.20	440
						1,916

* A new stock value per unit is calculated whenever a new receipt of materials occurs.

Notes

(a) The cost of materials issued plus the value of closing stock equals the cost of purchases plus the value of opening stock (£1,916).

(b) In a period of inflation, using the cumulative weighted average pricing system, the value of material issues will rise gradually, but will tend to lag a little behind the current market value at the date of issue. Closing stock values will also be a little below current market value.

Exam focus point

When stock valuation has been examined, candidates have been asked to tabulate stock movement over a period of time, showing changes in stock level, valuation per unit and total stock value.

4.3 The advantages and disadvantages of **average pricing** are these.

(a) **Advantages**

(i) Fluctuations in prices are smoothed out, making it easier to use the data for decision making.

(ii) It is easier to administer than FIFO and LIFO, because there is no need to identify each batch separately.

(b) **Disadvantages**

(i) The resulting issue price is rarely an actual price that has been paid, and can run to several decimal places.

(ii) Prices tend to lag behind a little behind current market values when there is gradual inflation.

Question 1

P Tsar Ltd, a company which makes Italian food, keeps the following account for their secret ingredient, x, which they use in their pizzas.

Date	Receipts Quantity Units	Receipts Value £	Issues Quantity Units	Issues Value £	Balance Quantity Units	Balance Value £
April 1					100	150
April 8	300	456			400	606
April 9	200	310			600	916
April 11			250			
April 12			150			

Required

Value the issues of April 11 and 12 using the following methods.

(a) FIFO
(b) LIFO
(c) Cumulative average weighted pricing

Answer

(a) *FIFO*

	Quantity Units	Issues price £	Issues value £
April 11	100	1.50	150
	150	1.52	228
	250		378
April 12	150	1.52	228

(b) *LIFO*

	Quantity Units	Issues price £	Issues value £
April 11	200	1.55	310
	50	1.52	76
	250		386
April 12	150	1.52	228

(c) *Weighted average*

The closing stock on April 9 can be analysed as follows.

Quantity	Price £	Value £
100	1.50	150
300	1.52	456
200	1.55	310
600		916

$$\text{Weighted average price} = \frac{£916}{600} = £1.5267$$

Quantity Units	Issues price £	Issues value £
250	1.5267	382
150	1.5267	229

5 PERIODIC WEIGHTED AVERAGE PRICING

5.1 Under the **periodic weighted average pricing**, a retrospective average price is calculated for all materials issued during the period.

FORMULA TO LEARN

The **average issue price** is calculated as follows.

$$\frac{\text{Cost of all receipts in the period } + \text{ Cost of opening stock}}{\text{Number of units received in the period } + \text{ Number of units of opening stock}}$$

Closing stock values are a balancing figure.

5.2 In our example, issue costs and closing stock values would be as follows.

$$\frac{\text{Cost of receipts in period} + \text{cost of opening stock}}{\text{Number of units received} + \text{number of units of opening stock}} = \frac{£1,716 + £200}{800 + 100}$$

$$= \frac{£1,916}{900}$$

Issue price = £2.129 per unit

Date of issue	Quantity issued Units	Valuation £
4 May	200 × £2.129	426
11 May	400 × £2.129	852
20 May	100 × £2.129	213
Cost of issues		1,491
Value of opening stock plus purchases		1,916
Value of 200 units of closing stock (at £2.129)		425

(*Note.* The periodic weighted average pricing method is easier to calculate than the cumulative weighted average method, and therefore requires less effort, but it must be applied retrospectively since the costs of materials used cannot be calculated until the end of the period.)

Question 2

Receipts and issues of part number 6288 for the month of August are as follows.

	Receipts Units	Total value £	Issues Units
3 August	2,000	6,000	
7 August	3,000	9,900	
11 August	2,000	8,000	
16 August			4,000
24 August	3,000	10,500	
30 August			5,000

Opening stocks of part number 6288 were 1,000 units, valued at £2,800.

Required

Calculate the value of closing stock on 31 August using periodic weighted average pricing.

Answer

$$\frac{\text{Cost of receipts in period} + \text{cost of opening stock}}{\text{Number of units received} + \text{number of units in opening stock}} = \frac{£(34,400 + 2,800)}{10,000 + 1,000} = \frac{£37,200}{11,000}$$

Average issue price = £3.38 per unit

Closing stock of 2,000 (10,000 + 1,000 - 9,000) units = 2,000 × £3.38 = + £6,760

6 STANDARD COST PRICING

6.1 **Under the standard costing method, all issues are at predetermined standard price**. SSAP 9 defines standard cost as 'the calculation of the cost of stocks on the basis of periodically predetermined costs calculated from management's estimates of expected levels of costs, and of operations and operational efficiency and related expenditure'.

(a) The predetermined standard price may not be the same as the actual price paid for materials delivered. Where this occurs there is a difference (variance) called a materials price variance, which is written off to the profit and loss account at the end of a period.

(b) There are serious problems, especially during a period of inflation, in deciding what the standard price should be. It is common (but by no means necessary) to estimate a mid-period price to be the standard price.

6.2 Let us assume in our example that the standard price applied is £2 per unit.

(a)

Date of issue	Quantity issued	Valuation
	Units	£
4 May	200 × £2	400
11 May	400 × £2	800
20 May	100 × £2	200
		1,400
Closing stock	200 × £2	400
		1,800

(b) There is a materials price variance as shown below.

Date of purchase	Quantity received	Expected cost	Actual cost	Price variance
	Units	£	£	£
3 May	400	800	840	40 (adverse)
9 May	300	600	636	36 (adverse)
18 May	100	200	240	40 (adverse)
	800	1,600	1,716	116 (adverse)

Note: The cost of the materials issued plus the value of closing stock (£1,800) differs from the combined value of opening stock plus purchases (£1,916) by the amount of the materials price variance (£116). At the end of an accounting period this variance will be taken as an adjustment to the profit and loss account to reconcile actual costs paid.

6.3 The advantages and disadvantages of **standard cost pricing** are as follows.

(a) **Advantages**

    (i) All issues are made at a constant price, therefore comparisons can be easily made.

    (ii) It is easy to use and administer.

    (iii) Standards of performance are set which can be used for management control reporting. (Price variances can be monitored by purchasing managers.)

(b) **Disadvantages**

    (i) Determination of standards can be difficult and time-consuming.

    (ii) Issues may not be at current market value.

    (iii) The price will not be an actual price paid and a variance will arise on issues.

    (iv) Problems of inflation are difficult to manage.

7   REPLACEMENT COST PRICING

> **KEY TERMS**
>
> •   **Replacement costing** is a method of pricing material issues and stock values at the current replacement cost of material.
>
> •   **Replacement cost** is 'the cost at which an identical asset could be purchased or manufactured' (SSAP 9).

7.1   Arguments for **replacement cost pricing** include the following.

(a)   The cost of issuing materials from store is the cost of replacing them. This is because generally issues will need to be replaced. The replacement cost will be the current cost.

(b)   Stocks in the balance sheet should be valued at replacement cost. This would show the true **current** value of the stock.

7.2   Suppose, for example, that a retail business buys and then sells an item of stock.

Opening stock	100 units (cost £300)
Sales	100 units, when the market price for replacing the units is £3.50 per unit
Sales revenue	£380

If the cost of sales is priced at £300 the profit would be £80. However, £350 is needed to replace the units sold, and the true profit margin for the business is only £(380 − 350) = £30. The remaining £350 cash (sales revenue less profit) could be used to replace the units sold.

7.3   In our example, the cost of issues and the value of closing stock would be as follows.

	Quantity issued	*Replacement cost*	*Valuation*
	Units	£ per unit	£
4 May	200	2.11	422
11 May	400	2.20	880
20 May	100	2.35	235
Closing stock	200	2.38	476
			2,013
Value of opening stock plus purchases			1,916
Difference			97

(*Note.* As with standard costing, there will be a difference between the cost of opening stock plus purchases and the value of materials issued plus closing stock (in this case £97). Unlike the materials price variance, however, this difference is not taken to the profit and loss account at the end of a period. It is a difference which must be kept away from the profit figure in order that a 'true profit' from operations may be calculated, and it is written instead to a 'stock revaluation reserve' which will appear in the balance sheet.)

7.4   The advantages and disadvantages of **replacement costing** are as follows.

(a)   **Advantages**

(i)   Issues are at up-to-date costs so that managers can take recent trends into account when making decisions based on their knowledge of the costs being incurred.

(ii)   Is it recommended as a method of accounting for inflation.

(iii)   It is easy to operate once the replacement cost has been determined.

(b) **Disadvantages**

(i) The price may not be an actual price paid, and a difference will then arise on issues.

(ii) It can be difficult to determine the replacement cost.

(iii) The method is not acceptable to the Inland Revenue or for SSAP 9.

7.5 **The most practicable alternative to replacement costing is LIFO**. LIFO is a reasonably accurate method of accounting for inflation provided that closing stock values are periodically reviewed and revalued.

Next in, first out (NIFO)

7.6 This method values issues at the price to be paid for the next delivery, which may or may not be the same as replacement cost. It does value issues at the most up-to-date price but it is administratively difficult.

8 THE COST OF A UNIT OF STOCK

8.1 The different methods of valuing stocks are applied to the different types of stock.

- Raw materials
- Work in progress
- Finished goods

Raw materials

8.2 The value of an item in stock, or the value of an item issued from stores, will depend on the valuation method used.

(a) **FIFO or LIFO.** These methods will produce different valuations, although they will be purchase costs.

(b) **Weighted average costing.** The valuation will be an **average** of past purchase costs. It will not be an actual unit price paid to suppliers for any particular order.

(c) **Standard cost.** The valuation will not be an actual purchase price, but a price that ought to have been paid.

(d) **Replacement cost.** The valuation will not be an actual purchase price, but instead the price that would be paid now to purchase replacement units.

Finished goods

8.3 The valuation of stocks of finished goods will depend on the valuation method used for raw materials issues. However, there are a number of other factors to consider.

(a) The **direct labour cost** of making the finished goods. A costing system must therefore provide a method of recording hours spent by the direct labour force on each job.

(b) The **production overhead costs** may or may not be included in the cost of making the finished goods.

- **Marginal costing** will **not** include any production overhead.
- **Full absorption costing** will include production overheads.

Work in progress

8.4 The valuation of **work in progress** will depend on the valuation method used for raw materials issues. Direct labour and production overhead costs (as for finished goods stock) will also need to be considered. For valuation of unfinished work in progress, the following additional factors will need to be considered.

(a) In a **continuous process** industry where there is a continuous flow of input raw materials and output finished goods, it may be impossible to determine the following.

- **Direct materials** attributable to the work in progress
- **Direct labour** attributable to the work in progress
- **Production overhead cost** attributable to the work in progress

(b) If it is impossible to determine how complete the work in progress is, it may be necessary to make **estimates**, eg if stocks are estimated to be 60% complete at year end, they would be valued at 60% of the cost of fully produced units.

8.5 **Stock valuations** are therefore **subjective**, and may be based on **estimates.**

9 STOCK VALUATION AND PROFITABILITY

9.1 Each method of stock valuation that we have looked at produces different costs of both **closing stocks** and also of **material issues**. Since production raw material costs affect the cost of production, and the cost of production works through eventually into the cost of sales, it follows that different methods of stock valuation will provide different **profit figures**.

Chapter roundup

- Several different methods of pricing materials issues and valuing closing stock can be used in practice. The pricing method selected for each item of stock must be the most appropriate for management purposes and must be consistently applied.

- **FIFO** assumes that materials are issued out of stock in the order in which they were delivered into stock: issues are priced at the cost of the earliest delivery remaining in stock.

- **LIFO** assumes that materials are issued out of stock in the reverse order to which they were delivered: the most recent deliveries are issued before earlier ones and issues are priced accordingly.

- There are two weighted average methods of pricing: **cumulative weighted average** and **periodic weighed average**.

- Under the **standard costing method**, all issues are at a predetermined standard price. Price variances will arise using this method.

- Although **replacement costing** is recommended as a method of accounting for inflation, in many instances it is impractical because of the difficulty of maintaining records of material replacement market values.

Quick quiz

1   Provide three reasons why stock valuation is problematic. (see para 1.1)

2   List five methods of charging materials issues to production. (2.1, 3.1, 4.1, 5.1, 6.1, 7.6, key terms)

3   What are the advantages and disadvantages of using LIFO in materials issues pricing? (3.2)

4   How would you calculate a periodic weighted average price? (formulae to learn)

5   What are the advantages and disadvantages of replacement cost pricing? (7.4)

Question to try	Level	Marks	Time
6	Examination	14	25 mins

Chapter 7

LABOUR COSTS

Chapter topic list	Syllabus reference
1 Measuring labour activity	CA 2(b)(iii)
2 Remuneration methods	CA 2(b)(ii)
3 Recording labour costs	CA 2(b)(iv)
4 Labour turnover	CA 2(b)(v)
5 Accounting for labour costs	CA 1(b)(i)

Introduction

Just as management need to control stocks and operate an appropriate valuation policy in an attempt to control material costs, so too must they be aware of the most suitable **remuneration policy** for their organisation. We will be looking at a number of methods of remuneration and will consider the various types of **incentive scheme** that exist. We will also examine the procedures and documents required for the accurate **recording of labour costs**. **Labour turnover** will be studied too.

1   MEASURING LABOUR ACTIVITY   12/94

KEY TERMS

- **Production** is the quantity or volume of output produced.

- **Standard hour of production** is a concept used in standard costing, and means the number of units that can be produced by one worker working in the standard way at the standard rate for one hour.

- **Productivity** is a measure of the efficiency with which output has been produced.

1.1   Suppose that an employee is expected to produce three units in every hour that he works. The standard rate of productivity is three units per hour, and one unit is valued at $1/3$ of a standard hour of output. If, during one week, the employee makes 126 units in 40 hours of work the following comments can be made.

(a)   **Production** in the week is 126 units.

(b)   **Productivity** is a relative measure of the hours actually taken and the hours that should have been taken to make the output.

     (i)   **Either,** 126 units should take   42 hours
                 But did take   40 hours
                 Productivity ratio = 42/40 × 100% =   105%

    (ii)   **Or alternatively,** in 40 hours, he should make (× 3)   120 units

           But did make   126 units

           Productivity ratio = 126/120 × 100% =   105%

A productivity ratio greater than 100% indicates that actual efficiency is better than the expected or 'standard' level of efficiency.

1.2   Management will wish to **plan** and **control** both production levels and labour productivity.

    (a)   **Production levels can be raised** as follows.

- Working overtime
- Hiring extra staff
- Sub-contracting some work to an outside firm
- Managing the work force so as to achieve more output.

    (b)   **Production levels can be reduced as follows.**

- Cancelling overtime
- Laying off staff

    (c)   **Productivity,** if improved, will enable a company to achieve its production targets in fewer hours of work, and therefore at a lower cost.

Productivity and its effect on cost

1.3   **Improved productivity** is an important means of reducing total unit costs. In order to make this point clear, a simple example will be used.

1.4   Clooney Ltd has a production department in its factory consisting of a work team of just two men, Doug and George. Doug and George each work a 40 hour week and refuse to do any overtime. They are each paid £100 per week and production overheads of £400 per week are charged to their work.

    (a)   In week one, they produce 160 units of output between them. Productivity is measured in units of output per man hour.

Production	160 units
Productivity (80 man hours)	2 units per man hour
Total cost	£600 (labour plus overhead)
Cost per man hour	£7.50
Cost per unit	£3.75

    (b)   In week two, management pressure is exerted on Doug and George to increase output and they produce 200 units in normal time.

Production	200 units (up by 25%)
Productivity	2.5 units per man hour (up by 25%)
Total cost	£600
Cost per man hour	£7.50 (no change)
Cost per unit	£3.00 (a saving of 20% on the previous cost; 25% on the new cost)

    (c)   In week three, Doug and George agree to work a total of 20 hours of overtime for an additional £50 wages. Output is again 200 units and overhead charges are increased by £100.

Production	200 units (up 25% on week one)
Productivity (100 man hours)	2 units per hour (no change on week one)
Total cost (£600 + £50 + £100)	£750
Cost per unit	£3.75

(d) Conclusions

    (i)   An increase in production without an increase in productivity will not reduce unit costs (week one compared with week three).

    (ii)   An **increase in productivity will reduce unit costs** (week one compared with week two).

1.5   **Labour cost control** is largely concerned with **productivity**. Rising wage rates have increased automation, which in turn has improved productivity and reduced costs.

1.6   Where **automation** is introduced, productivity is often, but misleadingly, measured in terms of **output per man-hour**.

Suppose, for example, that a work-team of six men (240 hours per week) is replaced by one machine (40 hours per week) and a team of four men (160 hours per week), and as a result output is increased from 1,200 units per week to 1,600 units.

	Production	*Man hours*	*Productivity*
Before the machine	1,200 units	240	5 units per man hour
After the machine	1,600 units	160	10 units per man hour

Labour productivity has doubled because of the machine, and employees would probably expect extra pay for this success. For control purposes, however, it is likely that a new measure of productivity is required, **output per machine hour**, which may then be measured against a standard output for performance reporting.

Efficiency, capacity and production volume ratios

1.7   Other measures of labour activity include the following.

- Production volume ratio, or activity ratio
- Efficiency ratio (or productivity ratio)
- Capacity ratio

Efficiency ratio	$\times$ **Capacity ratio**	= **Production volume ratio**
$\dfrac{\text{Expected hours to make output}}{\text{Actual hours taken}}$	$\times \dfrac{\text{Actual hours worked}}{\text{Hours budgeted}}$	$= \dfrac{\text{Output measured in expected or standard hours}}{\text{Hours budgeted}}$

These ratios are usually expressed as percentages.

1.8   EXAMPLE: RATIOS

Rush and Fluster Ltd budgets to make 25,000 standard units of output (in four hours each) during a budget period of 100,000 hours.

Actual output during the period was 27,000 units which took 120,000 hours to make.

Required

Calculate the efficiency, capacity and production volume ratios.

1.9   SOLUTION

(a) Efficiency ratio $\dfrac{(27,000 \times 4) \text{ hours}}{120,000} \times 100\% = 90\%$

(b) Capacity ratio $\dfrac{120{,}000 \text{ hours}}{100{,}000 \text{ hours}} \times 100\% = 120\%$

(c) Production volume ratio $\dfrac{(27{,}000 \times 4) \text{ hours}}{100{,}000} \times 100\% = 108\%$

(d) The production volume ratio of 108% (more output than budgeted) is explained by the 120% capacity working, offset to a certain extent by the poor efficiency (90% × 120% = 108%).

1.10 Where efficiency standards are associated with remuneration schemes they generally allow 'normal time' (that is, time required by the average person to do the work under normal conditions) plus an allowance for rest periods and possible delays. There should therefore be a readily achievable standard of efficiency (otherwise any remuneration scheme will fail to motivate employees), but without being so lax that it makes no difference to the rate at which work is done.

> **Exam focus point**
>
> Part of an exam question in 12/94 required candidates to demonstrate that they understood labour efficiency (4 marks). The examiner commented that many candidates made no attempt to answer this part of the question

2 REMUNERATION METHODS　　　　　　　　　6/94, 12/95, 12/97

2.1 Labour remuneration methods have an effect on the following.

- The cost of finished products and services.
- The morale and efficiency of employees.

2.2 There are three basic groups of remuneration method.

- Time work
- Piecework schemes
- Bonus/incentive schemes

Time work

> **FORMULA TO LEARN**
>
> The most common form of **time work** is a **day-rate system** in which wages are calculated by the following formula.
>
> Wages = Hours worked × rate of pay per hour

2.3 If an employee works for more hours than the basic daily requirement he may be entitled to an **overtime payment**. Hours of overtime are usually paid at a **premium rate**. For instance, if the basic day-rate is £4 per hour and overtime is paid at time-and-a-quarter, eight hours of overtime would be paid the following amount.

	£
Basic pay (8 × £4)	32
Overtime premium (8 × £1)	8
Total (8 × £5)	40

2.4 The **overtime premium** is the extra rate per hour which is paid, not the whole of the payment for the overtime hours.

2.5 If employees work unsocial hours, for instance overnight, they may be entitled to a **shift premium**. The extra amount paid per hour, above the basic hourly rate, is the **shift premium**.

2.6 **Day-rate systems** may be summarised as follows.

(a) They are easy to understand.

(b) They do not lead to very complex negotiations when they are being revised.

(c) They are most appropriate when the quality of output is more important than the quantity, or where there is no basis for payment by performance.

(d) There is no incentive for employees who are paid on a day-rate basis to improve their performance.

Piecework schemes

FORMULA TO LEARN

In a **piecework scheme**, wages are calculated by the following formula.

Wages = Units produced × Rate of pay per unit

2.7 Suppose for example, an employee is paid £1 for each unit produced and works a 40 hour week. Production overhead is added at the rate of £2 per direct labour hour.

Weekly production Units	Pay (40 hours) £	Overhead £	Conversion cost £	Conversion cost per unit £
40	40	80	120	3.00
50	50	80	130	2.60
60	60	80	140	2.33
70	70	80	150	2.14

As his output increases, his wage increases and at the same time unit costs of output are reduced.

2.8 It is normal for pieceworkers to be offered a **guaranteed minimum wage**, so that they do not suffer loss of earnings when production is low through no fault of their own.

Question 1

Penny Pincher is paid 50p for each towel she weaves, but she is guaranteed a minimum wage of £60 for a 40 hour week. In a series of four weeks, she makes 100, 120, 140 and 160 towels.

Required

Calculate her pay each week, and the conversion cost per towel if production overhead is added at the rate of £2.50 per direct labour hour.

Answer

Week	Output		Pay	Production overhead	Conversion cost	Unit conversion cost
	Units		£	£	£	£
1	100	(minimum)	60	100	160	1.60
2	120		60	100	160	1.33
3	140		70	100	170	1.21
4	160		80	100	180	1.13

There is no incentive to Penny Pincher to produce more output unless she can exceed 120 units in a week. The guaranteed minimum wage in this case is too high to provide an incentive.

2.9 If employee makes several different types of product, it may not be possible to add up the units for payment purposes. Instead, a **standard time allowance** is given for each unit to arrive at a total of piecework hours for payment.

2.10 EXAMPLE: PIECEWORK

An employee is paid £5 per piecework hour produced. In a 35 hour week he produces the following output.

	Piecework time allowed per unit
3 units of product A	2.5 hours
5 units of product B	8.0 hours

Required

Calculate the employee's pay for the week.

2.11 SOLUTION

Piecework hours produced are as follows.

Product A	3 × 2.5 hours	7.5 hours
Product B	5 × 8 hours	40.0 hours
Total piecework hours		47.5 hours

Therefore employee's pay = 47.5 × £5 = £237.50 for the week.

Differential piecework schemes

2.12 **Differential piecework schemes** offer an incentive to employees to increase their output by paying higher rates for increased levels of production. For example:

up to 80 units per week, rate of pay per unit	=	£1.00
80 to 90 units per week, rate of pay per unit	=	£1.20
above 90 units per week, rate of pay per unit	=	£1.30

Employers should obviously be careful to make it clear whether they intend to pay the increased rate on all units produced, or on the extra output only.

Piecework schemes generally

2.13 **Piecework schemes** may be summarised as follows.

- They enjoy fluctuating popularity.
- They are occasionally used by employers as a means of increasing pay levels.
- They are often seen to drive employees to work too hard to earn a satisfactory wage.

Careful inspection of output is necessary to ensure that quality doesn't fall as production increases.

Bonus/incentive schemes

2.14 In general, **bonus schemes** were introduced to compensate workers paid under a time-based system for their inability to increase earnings by working more efficiently. Various types of incentive and bonus schemes have been devised which encourage greater productivity. The characteristics of such schemes are as follows.

(a) Employees are paid more for their efficiency.

(b) The profits arising from productivity improvements are shared between employer and employee.

(c) Morale of employees is likely to improve since they are seen to receive extra reward for extra effort.

2.15 A bonus scheme must satisfy certain conditions to operate successfully.

(a) Its **objectives** should be **clearly stated** and **attainable** by the employees.

(b) The **rules** and conditions of the scheme should be **easy to understand**.

(c) It must **win** the full **acceptance** of everyone concerned.

(d) It should be seen to be **fair to employees and employers**..

(e) The bonus should ideally be **paid soon after the extra effort has been made** by the employees.

(f) **Allowances** should be made for external factors outside the employees' control which reduce their productivity (machine breakdowns, material shortages).

(g) Only those employees who make the extra effort should be rewarded.

(h) The scheme must be **properly communicated** to employees.

2.16 We shall be looking at the following types of incentive schemes in detail.

- High day rate system
- Individual bonus schemes
- Group bonus schemes
- Profit sharing schemes
- Incentive schemes involving shares
- Value added incentive schemes

Some organisations employ a variety of incentive schemes. A scheme for a production labour force may not necessarily be appropriate for white-collar workers. An organisation's incentive schemes may be regularly reviewed, and altered as circumstances dictate.

High day-rate system

KEY TERM

A **high day-rate system** is a system where employees are paid a high hourly wage rate in the expectation that they will work more efficiently than similar employees on a lower hourly rate in a different company.

2.17 For example if an employee would make 100 units in a 40 hour week if he were paid £2 per hour, but 120 units if he were paid £2.50 per hour, and if production overhead is added to cost at the rate of £2 per direct labour hour, costs per unit of output would be as follows.

(a) Costs per unit of output on the low day-rate scheme would be:

$$\frac{(40 \times £4)}{100} = £1.60 \text{ per unit}$$

(b) Costs per unit of output on the high day-rate scheme would be:

$$\frac{(40 \times £4.50)}{120} = £1.50 \text{ per unit}$$

(c) Note that in this example the labour cost per unit is lower in the first scheme (80p) than in the second (83.3p), but the unit conversion cost (labour plus production overhead) is higher because overhead costs per unit are higher at 80p than with the high day-rate scheme (66.7p).

(d) In this example, the high day-rate scheme would reward both employer (a lower unit cost by 10p) and employee (an extra 50p earned per hour).

2.18 There are two **advantages** of a high day-rate scheme over other incentive schemes.

(a) It is **simple** to calculate and **easy** to understand.

(b) It **guarantees** the employee a consistently **high wage**.

2.19 The **disadvantages** of such schemes are as follows.

(a) **Employees cannot earn more than the fixed hourly rate for their extra effort**. In the previous example, if the employee makes 180 units instead of 120 units in a 40 hour week on a high day-rate pay scheme, the cost per unit would fall to £1 but his wage would be the same - 40 hours at £4.50. All the savings would go to benefit the company and none would go to the employee.

(b) **There is no guarantee that the scheme will work consistently**. The high wages may become the accepted level of pay for normal working, and supervision may be necessary to ensure that a high level of productivity is maintained. Unit costs would rise.

(c) **Employees may prefer to work at a normal rate of output**, even if this entails accepting the lower wage paid by comparable employers.

Individual bonus schemes

> **KEY TERM**
>
> An **individual bonus scheme** is a remuneration scheme whereby **individual** employees qualify for a bonus on top of their basic wage, with each person's bonus being calculated separately.

2.20 (a) The bonus is **unique** to the individual. It is not a share of a group bonus.

(b) The individual can earn a bonus by working at an **above-target** standard of efficiency.

(c) The individual earns a **bigger bonus the greater his efficiency**, although the bonus scheme might incorporate quality safeguards, to prevent individuals from sacrificing quality standards for the sake of speed and more pay.

BPP PUBLISHING

2.21 To be successful, however, an **individual bonus scheme** must take account of the following factors.

(a) Each individual should be rewarded for the **work done by that individual**. This means that each person's output and time must be measured separately. Each person must therefore work without the assistance of anyone else.

(b) Work should be **fairly routine**, so that standard times can be set for jobs.

(c) The bonus should be **paid soon after the work is done**, to provide the individual with the incentive to try harder.

Group bonus schemes

> **KEY TERM**
>
> A **group bonus scheme** is an incentive plan which is related to the output performance of an entire group of workers, a department, or even the whole factory.

2.22 Where individual effort cannot be measured, and employees work as a team, an individual incentive scheme is impracticable but a **group bonus scheme** would be feasible.

2.23 The other **advantages** of group bonus schemes are as follows.

(a) They are **easier to administer** because they reduce the clerical effort required to measure output and calculate individual bonuses.

(b) They **increase co-operation** between fellow workers.

(c) They have been found to **reduce** accidents, spoilage, waste and absenteeism.

2.24 Serious **disadvantages** would occur in the following circumstances.

(a) The employee groups demand **low efficiency standards** as a condition of accepting the scheme.

(b) Individual employees are browbeaten by their fellow workers for working too slowly.

Profit-sharing schemes

> **KEY TERM**
>
> A **profit sharing scheme** is a scheme in which employees receive a certain proportion of their company's year-end profits (the size of their bonus being related to their position in the company and the length of their employment to date).

2.25 The advantage of these schemes is that the company will only pay what it can afford out of actual profits and the bonus can be paid also to non-production personnel.

The disadvantages of profit sharing are as follows.

(a) Employees must **wait until the year end** for a bonus. The company is therefore expecting a long-term commitment to greater efforts and productivity from its workers without the incentive of immediate reward.

(b) **Factors** affecting profit may be **outside the control** of employees, in spite of their greater efforts.

(c) **Too many employees** are involved in a single scheme for the scheme to have a great motivating effect on individuals.

Incentive schemes involving shares

2.26 It is becoming increasingly common for companies to use their shares, or the right to acquire them, as a form of incentive.

> **KEY TERMS**
>
> - A **share option scheme** is a scheme in which gives its members the right to buy shares in the company for which they work at a set date in the future and at a price usually determined when the scheme is set up.
>
> - An **employee share ownership plan (ESOP)** is a scheme which acquires shares on behalf of a number of employees, and it must distribute these shares within 20 years of acquisition.

The Government has encouraged companies to set up schemes of this nature in the hope that workers will feel they have a stake in the company which employs them. The **disadvantages** of these schemes are as follows.

(a) As the benefits are not certain, as the market value of shares at a future date cannot realistically be predicted in advance.

(b) The benefits are not immediate, as a scheme must be in existence for a number of years before members can exercise their rights.

Value added incentive schemes

2.27 **Value added is an alternative to profit as a business performance measure** and it can be used as the basis of an incentive scheme. It is calculated as follows.

> **KEY TERM**
>
> Value added = sales – cost of bought-in materials and services

The advantage of value added over profit as the basis for an incentive scheme is that it excludes any bought-in costs, and is affected only by costs incurred internally, such as labour.

A basic value added figure would be agreed as the target for a business, and some of any excess value added earned would be paid out as a bonus. For example, it could be agreed that value added should be, say, treble the payroll costs and a proportion of any excess earned, say one third, would be paid as bonus.

Payroll costs for month	£40,000
Therefore, value added target (× 3)	£120,000
Value added achieved	£150,000
Therefore, excess value added	£30,000
Employee share to be paid as bonus	£10,000

2.28 EXAMPLE: INCENTIVE SCHEMES

Swetton Tyres Ltd manufactures a single product. Its work force consists of 10 employees, who work a 36-hour week exclusive of lunch and tea breaks. The standard time required to make one unit of the product is two hours, but the current efficiency (or productivity) ratio being achieved is 80%. No overtime is worked, and the work force is paid £4 per attendance hour.

Because of agreements with the work force about work procedures, there is some unavoidable idle time due to bottlenecks in production, and about four hours per week per person are lost in this way.

The company can sell all the output it manufactures, and makes a 'cash profit' of £20 per unit sold, deducting currently achievable costs of production but *before* deducting labour costs.

An incentive scheme is proposed whereby the work force would be paid £5 per hour in exchange for agreeing to new work procedures that would reduce idle time per employee per week to two hours and also raise the efficiency ratio to 90%.

Required

Evaluate the incentive scheme from the point of view of profitability.

2.29 SOLUTION

The current situation

Hours in attendance	10×36	=	360 hours
Hours spent working	10×32	=	320 hours
Units produced, at 80% efficiency	$\dfrac{320}{2} \times \dfrac{80}{100}$	=	128 units

	£
Cash profits before deducting labour costs ($128 \times £20$)	2,560
Less labour costs ($£4 \times 360$ hours)	1,440
Net profit	1,120

The incentive scheme

Hours spent working	10×34	=	340 hours
Units produced, at 90% efficiency	$\dfrac{340}{2} \times \dfrac{90}{100}$	=	153 units

	£
Cash profits before deducting labour costs ($153 \times £20$)	3,060
Less labour costs ($£5 \times 360$)	1,800
Net profit	1,260

In spite of a 25% increase in labour costs, profits would rise by £140 per week. The company and the workforce would both benefit provided, of course, that management can hold the work force to their promise of work reorganisation and improved productivity.

Question 2

Ball and Chain Ltd is a company making a single product in a single production operation. There are 20 direct labour employees, each working a 36-hour week and paid at the rate of £4 per hour, with a guaranteed minimum wage of £144 per man. Overtime is paid at time-and-a-quarter, but the maximum overtime allowed is 9 hours per man per week. Additional direct labour employees cannot be recruited.

The average time required for one man to make one unit of output is 45 minutes.

Sales demand for the product fluctuates from week to week, but the company is unable to maintain a 'buffer' stock of goods, and must produce enough units each week to equal the immediate sales demand. The minimum weekly sales demand is 600 units, but the maximum demand is well in excess of the company's production capacity, in spite of overtime working.

The company's management has proposed a wages incentive scheme whereby the hourly wage rate would be increased to £4.50 per hour if the standard time to produce a unit is reduced to 40 minutes. Overtime hours would still be paid at time-and-a-quarter, and the minimum guaranteed wage would rise to £162 per week for each man.

The sales price per unit is £10 and the direct material cost per unit is £4.

Required

Calculate the profit of the company and the wages of the direct labour team if the current wage scheme is maintained, and also if the new scheme is introduced, if sales demand in one week is:

(a)   800 units;
(b)   1,000 units;
(c)   1,200 units.

Ignore overhead costs. Draw conclusions from your figures.

Answer

If *the current wages scheme* is maintained, labour costs would be:

(a)   for 800 units. Time required at 45 minutes per unit = 600 hours. The minimum guaranteed wage is for 20 × 36 = 720 hours, therefore the labour cost would be £2,880;

(b)   for 1,000 units. Time required at 45 minutes per unit = 750 hours.

		£
Cost:	720 hours × £4 per hour	2,880
	30 hours × £5 per hour	150
		3,030

(c)   for 1,200 units. Time required = 900 hours. This is the maximum time available in one week, with 180 hours of overtime.

		£
Cost:	720 hours × £4 per hour	2,880
	180 hours × £5 per hour	900
		3,780

Profitability, ignoring overhead costs:

	800 units	1,000 units	1,200 units
	£	£	£
Labour cost	2,880	3,030	3,780
Materials cost	3,200	4,000	4,800
	6,080	7,030	8,580
Sales	8,000	10,000	12,000
Profit	1,920	2,970	3,420
Profit per unit	£2.40	£2.97	£2.85

With *the new incentive scheme* labour costs would be:

(a)   800 units. Time required 533.3 hours. The minimum guaranteed wage is for 720 hours at £4.50 per hour, and the total labour cost would be £3,240.

(b)   1,000 units. Time required at 40 minutes per unit = 666.7 hours. Once again, the labour cost would be the minimum guaranteed wage of £3,240.

(c)   1,200 units. Time required 800 hours.

		£
Cost:	720 hours × £4.50	3,240
	80 hours × £5.625	450
		3,690

Profitability, ignoring overhead costs:

	800 units £	1,000 units £	1,200 units £
Labour cost	3,240	3,240	3,690
Materials cost	3,200	4,000	4,800
	6,440	7,240	8,490
Sales	8,000	10,000	12,000
Profit	1,560	2,760	3,510
Profit per unit	£1.95	£2.76	2.925

Conclusion

Comparing the current and the proposed wages schemes, from the point of view of both the company and the employees, we find that the company will reduce its profitability at lower volumes of sales and will improve profit, but only slightly, at higher volumes of sales.

Output sales	Gain/(loss) of profit £	Gain in wages £	Increase/(decrease) in hours paid for Hours
800 units	(360)	360	-
1,000 units	(210)	210	(30)
1,200 units	90	(90)	(100)

Since the company loses profit at the expense of wages, or employees lose some wages, albeit for working fewer hours of overtime, it is unlikely that the incentive scheme has much merit, unless it is expected that sales demand and output can be increased to the new maximum level of output. In other words, the incentive scheme has no real value unless the company can benefit from the improved productivity.

If, for example, sales demand were 1,350 units per week, the time required to make the output would be 1,350 units × 40 minutes = 900 hours. The labour cost would be £4.50 × 720 hours plus £5.625 × 180 hours = £4,252.5

	£
Labour cost	4,252.50
Materials cost (1,350 units)	5,400.00
	9,652.50
Sales	13,500.00
Profit	3,847.50

The company would increase its maximum potential profit by (£3,847.50 − 3,420) = £427.50 per week and maximum potential wages would rise by £(4,252.20 − 3,780) = £472.20 per week, or £23.61 per man, per week.

3 RECORDING LABOUR COSTS

Organisation for controlling and measuring labour costs

3.1 Several departments and management groups are involved in the collection, recording and costing of labour. These include the following.

- Personnel
- Production planning
- Timekeeping
- Wages
- Cost accounting

Personnel department

3.2 The **personnel department** is responsible for the following.

- Engagement, transfer and discharge of employees.
- Classification and method of remuneration.

The department is headed by a **professional personnel officer** trained in personnel management, labour laws, company personnel policy and industry conditions who should have an understanding of the needs and problems of the employees.

3.3 Additional labour maybe found as follows.

- Contacting recruitment agencies
- Placing advertisements in newspapers and journals (trade)
- Contacting local schools and technical colleges
- Review any CVs held on file of persons known to be available for work

All potential employees/interviewees should complete an application form.

3.4 When a person is engaged a **personnel record card** should be prepared showing full personal particulars, previous employment, medical category and wage rate. Other details to be included are National Insurance number, address, telephone number, transfers, promotions, changes in wage rates, sickness and accidents and, when an employee leaves, the reason for leaving.

3.5 Personnel departments sometimes **maintain records of overtime and shift working**. Overtime has to be sanctioned by the works manager or personnel office who advise the time-keepers who control the time booked.

3.6 The personnel department is responsible for issuing **reports to management** on normal and overtime hours worked, absenteeism and sickness, lateness, labour turnover and disciplinary action.

Production planning department

3.7 This department is responsible for the following.

- Scheduling work
- Issuing job orders to production departments
- Chasing up jobs when they run late

Timekeeping department

3.8 The **timekeeping department** is responsible for recording the attendance time and job time of the following.

- The time spent in the factory by each worker
- The time spent by each worker on each job

Such timekeeping provides basic data for statutory records, payroll preparation, labour costs of an operation or overhead distribution (where based on wages or labour hours) and statistical analysis of labour records for determining productivity and control of labour costs.

Attendance time

3.9 The bare minimum record of employees' time is a simple **attendance record** showing days absent because of holiday, sickness or other reason. A typical record of attendance is shown as follows.

	1	2	3	4	5	6	7	8	9	10	11	12	13	14	15	16	17	18	19	20	21	22	23	24	25	26	27	28	29	30	31
JAN																															
FEB																															
MAR																															
APR																															
MAY																															
JUNE																															
JULY																															
AUG																															
SEPT																															
OCT																															
NOV																															
DEC																															

NAME: A.N. OTHER   DEPT: 072   NI REF: WD 4847 41C   LEAVE ENTITLEMENT: 20

			Note overleaf: (1) The reasons for special leave (eg bereavement).
Illness: I	Leave: L	Training: T	
Industrial Accident: IA	Unpaid Leave: UL	Jury Service: J	(2) Ensure training is noted on personnel card.
Maternity: M	Special Leave: SL		

RECORD OF ATTENDANCE

3.10 It is also necessary to have a record of the following.

- Time of arrival
- Time of breaks
- Time of departure

These may be recorded as follows.

- In a signing-in book
- By using a time recording clock which stamps the time on a clock card
- By using swipe cards (which made a computer record)

An example of a clock card is shown as follows.

No				Ending	
Name					
HOURS	RATE	AMOUNT	DEDUCTIONS		
Basic				Income Tax	
O/T				NI	
Others				Other	
				Total deduction	
Total					
Less deductions					
Net due					

Time	Day	Basic time	Overtime
1230	T		
0803	T		
1700	M		
1305	M		
1234	M		
0750	M		

Signature _ _ _ _ _ _ _ _ _ _ _

Job time

3.11 **Continuous production**. Where **routine, repetitive** work is carried out it might not be practical to record the precise details. For example if a worker stands at a conveyor belt for seven hours his work can be measured by keeping a note of the number of units that pass through his part of the process during that time.

3.12 **Job costing**. When the work is not of a repetitive nature the records required might be one or several of the following.

(a) **Daily time sheets**. A time sheet is filled in by the employee as a record of how their time has been spent. The total time on the time sheet should correspond with time shown on the attendance record.

(b) **Weekly time sheets**. These are similar to daily time sheets but are passed to the cost office at the end of the week. An example of a weekly timesheet is shown below.

			Time Sheet No. _ _ _ _ _ _ _ _ _ _ _ _ _ _ _ _				
Employee Name _ _ _ _ _ _ _ _ _			Clock Code _ _ _ _ _ _ _ _ _		Dept _ _ _ _ _ _ _		
Date _ _ _ _ _ _ _ _ _ _ _ _ _ _ _ _ _ _			Week No. _ _ _ _ _ _ _ _ _ _ _ _ _				
Job No.	Start Time	Finish Time	Qty	Checker	Hrs	Rate	Extension

(c) **Job cards**. Cards are prepared for each job or batch. When an employee works on a job he or she records on the job card the time spent on that job. Job cards are therefore likely to contain entries relating to numerous employees. On completion of the job it will contain a full record of the times and quantities involved in the job or batch. A typical job card is shown as follows.

JOB CARD			
Department _ _ _ _ _ _ _ _ _ _ _ _ _ _ _ _ _ _ _ Job no _ _ _ _ _ _ _ _ _ _ _ _ _ _ _ _ _ _ _ .			
Date _ . Operation no _ _ _ _ _ _ _ _ _ _ _ _ _ _ _ _ _ _			
Time allowance _ _ _ _ _ _ _ _ _ _ _ _ _ _ _ Time started _ _ _ _ _ _ _ _ _ _ _ _ _ _ _ _ _ _			
	Time finished _ _ _ _ _ _ _ _ _ _ _ _ _ _ _ _ _ _		
	Hours on the job _ _ _ _ _ _ _ _ _ _ _ _ _ _ _ _ .		
Description of job	Hours	Rate	Cost
Employee no _ _ _ _ _ _ _ _ _ _ _ _ _ _ _ _ _ Certified by _ _ _ _ _ _ _ _ _ _ _ _ _ _ _ _ _ _			
Signature _ _ _ _ _ _ _ _ _ _ _ _ _ _ _ _ _ _			

A job card will be given to the employee, showing the work to be done and the expected time it should take. The employee will record the time started and time finished for each job. Breaks for tea and lunch may be noted on the card, as standard times, by the production planning department. The hours actually taken and the cost of those hours will be calculated by the accounting department.

3.13 **Piecework**. The wages of pieceworkers and the labour cost of work done by them is determined from what is known as a **piecework ticket** or an **operation card**. The card records the total number of items (or 'pieces') produced and the number of rejects. Payment is only made for 'good' production.

OPERATION CARD				
Operator's Name _ _ _ _ _ _ _ _ _ _ _ _ _ _ _ _ _ _		Total Batch Quantity _ _ _ _ _ _ _ _ _ _ _ _		
Clock No _		Start Time _ _ _ _ _ _ _ _ _ _ _ _ _ _ _ _ _		
Pay week No _ _ _ _ _ _ _ _ _ Date _ _ _ _ _ _ _		Stop Time _ _ _ _ _ _ _ _ _ _ _ _ _ _ _ _ _		
Part No _		Works Order No _ _ _ _ _ _ _ _ _ _ _ _ _ _		
Operation _		Special Instructions _ _ _ _ _ _ _ _ _ _ _		
Quantity Produced	No Rejected	Good Production	Rate	£
Inspector _		Operative _ _ _ _ _ _ _ _ _ _ _ _ _ _ _ _ _		
Foreman -		Date -		
PRODUCTION CANNOT BE CLAIMED WITHOUT A PROPERLY SIGNED CARD				

Note that the attendance record of a pieceworker is required for calculations of holidays, sick pay and so on.

3.14 **Other types of work**. Casual workers are paid from job cards or time sheets. Time sheets are also used where outworkers are concerned.

3.15 Office work can be measured in a similar way, provided that the work can be divided into distinct jobs. Firms of accountants and advertising agencies, for example, book their staff time to individual clients and so make use of time sheets for salaried staff.

Salaried labour

3.16 Even though salaried staff are paid a flat rate monthly, they may be required to prepare timesheets. The reasons are as follows.

(a) Timesheets provide management with information (eg product costs).

(b) Timesheet information may provide a basis for billing for services provided (eg service firms where clients are billed based on the number of hours work done).

(c) Timesheets are used to record hours spent and so support claims for overtime payments by salaried staff.

3.17 An example of a timesheet (as used in the service sector) is shown as follows.

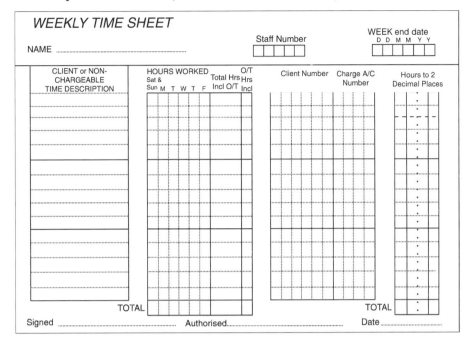

Idle time

3.18 **Idle time** occurs when employees cannot get on with their work, through no fault of their own. Examples are as follows.

- Machine breakdowns
- Shortage of work

3.19 **Idle time** has a cost because employees will still be paid their basic wage or salary for these unproductive hours and so there should be a record of idle time. This may simply comprise an entry on time sheets coded to 'idle time' generally, or separate idle time cards may be prepared. A supervisor might enter the time of a stoppage, its cause, its duration and the employees made idle on an idle time record card. Each stoppage should have a reference number which can be entered on time sheets or job cards.

Wages department

3.20 Responsibilities of the payroll department include the following.

- Preparation of the payroll and payment of wages.
- Maintenance of employee records.
- Summarising wages cost for each cost centre.
- Summarising the hours worked for each cost centre.
- Summarising other payroll information eg bonus payment, pensions etc.
- Providing an internal check for the preparation and payout of wages.

3.21 **Attendance cards** are the basis for payroll preparation. For **time workers**, the gross wage is the product of time attended and rate of pay. To this is added any overtime premium or bonus. For **piece workers**, gross wages are normally obtained by the product of the number of good units produced and the unit rate, with any premiums, bonuses and allowances for incomplete jobs added.

3.22 After calculation of net pay, a pay slip is prepared showing all details of earnings and deductions. The wage envelope or the attendance card may be used for this purpose.

3.23 When the payroll is complete, a coin and note analysis is made and a cheque drawn to cover the total amount. On receipt of the cash, the pay envelopes are made up and sealed. A receipt is usually obtained on payout (the attendance card can be used). Wages of absentees are retained until claimed by an authorised person.

3.24 **Internal checks** are necessary to prevent fraud. One method is to distribute the payroll work so that no person deals completely with any transaction. All calculations should be checked on an adding machine where possible. Makeup of envelopes should not be done by persons who prepare the payroll. The cashier should reconcile his analysis with the payroll summary.

Cost accounting department

3.25 The cost accounting department has the following responsibilities.

- The accumulation and classification of all cost data (which includes labour costs).
- Preparation of cost data reports for management.
- Analysing labour information on time cards and payroll.

3.26 In order to establish the labour cost involved in products, operations, jobs and cost centres, the following documents are used.

- Clock cards
- Job cards
- Idle time cards
- Payroll

3.27 Analyses of labour costs are used for the following.

(a) Charging wages directly attributable to production to the appropriate job or operation.

(b) Charging wages which are not directly attributable to production as follows.

    (i) Idle time of production workers is charged to indirect costs as part of the overheads.

    (ii) Wages costs of supervisors, or store assistants are charged to the overhead costs of the relevant department.

(c) Producing idle time reports which show a summary of the hours lost through idle time, and the cause of the idletime. Idle time may be analysed as follows.

    (i) Controllable eg lack of materials.
    (ii) Uncontrollable eg power failure.

FORMULA TO LEARN

$$\text{Idle time ratio} = \frac{\text{Idle hours}}{\text{Total hours}} \times 100\%$$

3.28 The idle time ratio is useful because it shows the proportion of available hours which were lost as a result of idle time.

4 LABOUR TURNOVER

Exam focus point

Part of an examination question asked candidates to identify the costs associated with labour turnover. There were 5 marks to be gained.

The reasons for labour turnover

4.1 Some employees will leave their job and go to work for another company or organisation. Sometimes the reasons are unavoidable.

- Illness or accidents
- A family move away from the locality
- Marriage, pregnancy or difficulties with child care provision
- Retirement or death

4.2 Other causes of labour turnover are to some extent controllable.

- Paying a lower wage rate than is available elsewhere.
- Requiring employees to work in unsafe or highly stressful conditions.
- Requiring employees to work uncongenial hours.
- Poor relationships between management and staff.
- Lack of opportunity for career enhancement.
- Requiring employees to work in inaccessible places (eg no public transport).
- Discharging employees for misconduct, bad timekeeping or unsuitability.

Measuring labour turnover

KEY TERM

Labour turnover is a measure of the number of employees leaving/being recruited in a period of time expressed as a percentage of the total labour force.

FORMULA TO LEARN

$$\text{Labour turnover rate} = \frac{\text{Replacements}}{\text{Average number of employees in period}} \times 100\%$$

4.3 EXAMPLE : LABOUR TURNOVER RATE

Revolving Doors plc had a staff of 2,000 at the beginning of 20X1 and, owing to a series of redundancies caused by the recession, 1,000 at the end of the year. Voluntary redundancy was taken by 1,500 staff at the end of June, 500 more than the company had anticipated, and these excess redundancies were immediately replaced by new joiners.

The labour turnover rate is calculated as follows.

$$\text{Rate} = \frac{500}{(2,000 + 1,000) \div 2} \times 100\% = 33\%$$

The costs of labour turnover

4.4 The costs of labour turnover can be large and management should attempt to keep labour turnover as low as possible so as to minimise these costs. The **cost of labour turnover** may be divided into the following.

- Preventative costs
- Replacement costs

4.5 **Replacement costs.** These are the costs incurred as a result of hiring new employees. and they include the following.

- Cost of selection and placement
- Inefficiency of new labour; productivity will be lower
- Costs of training
- Loss of output due to delay in new labour becoming available
- Increased wastage and spoilage due to lack of expertise among new staff
- The possibility of more frequent accidents at work
- Cost of tool and machine breakages

4.6 **Preventative costs** are costs incurred in order to prevent employees leaving and they include the following.
- Cost of personnel administration incurred in maintaining good relationships
- Cost of medical services including check-ups, nursing staff and so on
- Cost of welfare services, including sports facilities and canteen meals
- Pension schemes providing security to employees

The prevention of high labour turnover

4.7 Labour turnover will be reduced by the following actions.
- Paying satisfactory wages
- Offering satisfactory hours and conditions of work
- Creating a good informal relationship between members of the workforce
- Offering good training schemes and a well-understood career or promotion ladder
- Improving the content of jobs to create job satisfaction
- Proper planning so as to avoid redundancies
- Investigating the cause of an apparently high labour turnover

5 ACCOUNTING FOR LABOUR COSTS   6/94, 12/95, 12/97, 6/99

Exam focus point

Do not underestimate the importance of accounting for labour costs. In 12/95 a 10 mark question was set on this topic.

5.1 We will use an example to briefly review the principal bookkeeping entries for wages.

5.2 EXAMPLE: THE WAGES CONTROL ACCOUNT

The following details were extracted from a weekly payroll for 750 employees at a factory.

Analysis of gross pay

	Direct workers £	Indirect workers £	Total £
Ordinary time	36,000	22,000	58,000
Overtime: basic wage	8,700	5,430	14,130
premium	4,350	2,715	7,065
Shift allowance	3,465	1,830	5,295
Sick pay	950	500	1,450
Idle time	3,200	-	3,200
	56,665	32,475	89,140
Net wages paid to employees	£45,605	£24,220	£69,825

Required

Prepare the wages control account for the week.

5.3 SOLUTION

(a) **The wages control account** acts as a sort of 'collecting place' for net wages paid and deductions made from gross pay. The gross pay is then analysed between direct and indirect wages.

(b) The first step is to determine which wage costs are **direct** and which are **indirect**. The direct wages will be debited to the work in progress account and the indirect wages will be debited to the production overhead account.

(c) There are in fact only two items of direct wages cost in this example, the ordinary time (£36,000) and the basic overtime wage (£8,700) paid to direct workers. All other payments (including the overtime premium) are indirect wages.

(d) The net wages paid are debited to the control account, and the balance then represents the deductions which have been made for income tax, national insurance, and so on.

WAGES CONTROL ACCOUNT

	£		£
Bank: net wages paid	69,825	Work in progress - direct labour	44,700
Deductions control accounts*		Production overhead control:	
(£89,140 – £69,825)	19,315	Indirect labour	27,430
		Overtime premium	7,065
		Shift allowance	5,295
		Sick pay	1,450
		Idle time	3,200
	89,140		89,140

* In practice there would be a separate deductions control account for each type of deduction made (for example, PAYE and National Insurance).

Chapter roundup

* **Labour** is a major cost in many businesses and it is therefore vital that you have understood this chapter's topics, a summary of them being set out below.

* **Production** is the quantity or volume of output produced. **Productivity** is a measure of the efficiency with which output has been produced. An increase in production without an increase in productivity will not reduce unit costs.

* There are three basic groups of **remuneration** method, **time work**, **piecework** schemes and **bonus/incentive** schemes.

* Labour attendance time is recorded on, for example, an attendance record or clock card. Job time may be recorded on daily time sheets, weekly time sheets or job cards depending on the circumstances. The manual recording of times on time sheets or job cards, is however, liable to error or even deliberate deception and may be unreliable.

* The labour cost of pieceworkers is recorded on a piecework ticket/operation card.

* **Idle time** has a cost and must, therefore, be recorded.

* **Labour turnover** is the rate at which employees leave a company and this rate should be kept as low as possible. The cost of labour turnover can be divided into **preventative** and **replacement** costs.

* The **wages control account** acts as a collecting place for wages before they are analysed to work in progress and production overhead control accounts.

Quick quiz

1   Distinguish between the terms production and productivity. (see key terms)

2   List five types of incentive scheme. (2.16)

3   What are the requirements for a successful individual bonus scheme? (2.21)

4   What is a value added incentive scheme? (2.27)

5   What are the responsibilities of a typical personnel department? (3.2)

6   List four types of document used in time recording. (3.9 - 3.17))

7   What are the responsibilities of a typical wages department? (3.20)

8   Define the idle time ratio. (formulae to learn)

9   List six methods of reducing labour turnover. (4.7)

Question to try	Level	Marks	Time
7	Introductory	n/a	25 mins

Chapter 8

OVERHEAD APPORTIONMENT AND ABSORPTION

Chapter topic list	Syllabus reference
1 Overheads	CA 2(c)(i)
2 Absorption costing: an introduction	CA 2(c)(i), (ii)
3 Product cost build-up using absorption costing	CA 2(c)(i), (ii)
4 Overhead allocation	CA 2(c)(i), (ii)
5 Overhead apportionment	CA 2(c)(i), (ii)
6 Overhead absorption	CA 2(c)(i), (ii)
7 Blanket absorption rates and departmental absorption rates	CA 2(c)(i), (ii)
8 Normal costing	CA 2(c)(iii)
9 Over and under absorption of overheads	CA 2(c)(iii)
10 Non-manufacturing overheads	CA 2(c)(ii)
11 Activity based costing	CA 2(c)(i)

Introduction

Absorption costing is a method of accounting for overheads. It basically a method of sharing out overheads incurred amongst units produced.

This chapter begins by explaining why absorption costing might be necessary and then provides an overview of how the cost of a unit of product is built up under a system of absorption costing. A detailed analysis of this costing method is then provided, covering the three stages of absorption costing: **allocation**, **apportionment** and **absorption**. You will also see how to account for using absorption costing when it comes to preparing the profit and loss account.

The chapter ends with a brief look at a costing method that might be more appropriate than absorption costing in the current industrial environment, **activity based costing**.

1 OVERHEADS

KEY TERM

Overhead is the cost incurred in the course of making a product, providing a service or running a department, but which cannot be traced directly and in full to the product, service or department.

1.1 Overhead is actually the total of the following.

- Indirect materials

- Indirect labour
- Indirect expenses

1.2   The total of these indirect costs is usually split into the following.

- **Production** overhead
- **Administration** overhead
- **Selling and distribution** overhead

1.3   In cost accounting there are two schools of thought as to the correct method of dealing with overheads.

- Absorption costing
- Marginal costing

2   ABSORPTION COSTING: AN INTRODUCTION 6/98

2.1   **The objective of absorption costing is to include in the total cost of a product** (unit, job, process and so on) **an appropriate share of the organisation's total overhead.** An appropriate share is generally taken to mean an amount which reflects the amount of time and effort that has gone into producing a unit or completing a job.

2.2   An organisation with one production department that produces identical units will divide the total overheads among the total units produced. **Absorption costing is a method for sharing overheads between different products on a fair basis.**

Is absorption costing necessary?

2.3   Suppose that a company makes and sells 100 units of a product each week. The prime cost per unit is £6 and the unit sales price is £10. Production overhead costs £200 per week and administration, selling and distribution overhead costs £150 per week. The weekly profit could be calculated as follows.

	£	£
Sales (100 units × £10)		1,000
Prime costs (100 × £6)	600	
Production overheads	200	
Administration, selling and distribution costs	150	
		950
Profit		50

2.4   In absorption costing, overhead costs will be added to each unit of product manufactured and sold.

	£ per unit
Prime cost per unit	6
Production overhead (£200 per week for 100 units)	2
Full factory cost	8

The weekly profit would be calculated as follows.

	£
Sales	1,000
Less factory cost of sales	800
Gross profit	200
Less administration, selling and distribution costs	150
Net profit	50

2.5   Sometimes, but not always, the overhead costs of administration, selling and distribution are also added to unit costs, to obtain a full cost of sales.

	£ per unit
Prime cost per unit	6.00
Factory overhead cost per unit	2.00
Administration etc costs per unit	1.50
Full cost of sales	9.50

The weekly profit would be calculated as follows.

	£
Sales	1,000
Less full cost of sales	950
Profit	50

2.6   It may already be apparent that the weekly profit is £50 no matter how the figures have been presented. So, how does absorption costing serve any useful purpose in accounting?

2.7   The **theoretical justification** for using absorption costing is that all production overheads are incurred in the production of the organisation's output and so each unit of the product receives some benefit from these costs. Each unit of output should therefore be charged with some of the overhead costs.

2.8   The **practical reasons** for using absorption costing are as follows.

(a)   **Stock valuations**. Stock in hand must be valued for two reasons.

(i)   For the closing stock figure in the balance sheet

(ii)   For the cost of sales figure in the profit and loss account

The valuation of stocks will affect profitability during a period because of the way in which the cost of sales is calculated.

    The cost of goods produced
+   the value of opening stocks
−   the value of closing stocks
=   the cost of goods sold.

In our example, closing stocks might be valued at prime cost (£6), but in absorption costing, they would be valued at a fully absorbed factory cost, £8 per unit. (They would not be valued at £9.50, the full cost of sales, because the only costs incurred in producing goods for finished stock are factory costs.)

(b)   **Pricing decisions**. Many companies attempt to fix selling prices by calculating the full cost of production or sales of each product, and then adding a margin for profit. In our example, the company might have fixed a gross profit margin at 25% on factory cost, or 20% of the sales price, in order to establish the unit sales price of £10. 'Full cost plus pricing' can be particularly useful for companies which do jobbing or contract work, where each job or contract is different, so that a standard unit sales price cannot be fixed. Without using absorption costing, a full cost is difficult to ascertain.

(c)   **Establishing the profitability of different products**. This argument in favour of absorption costing is more contentious, but is worthy of mention here. If a company sells more than one product, it will be difficult to judge how profitable each individual product is, unless overhead costs are shared on a fair basis and charged to the cost of sales of each product.

Statement of standard accounting practice 9 (SSAP 9)

2.9 Of these three arguments, the problem of valuing stocks is perhaps the most significant. **Absorption costing is recommended in financial accounting** by the *Statement of standard accounting practice* on stocks and long-term contracts (SSAP 9). SSAP 9 deals with **financial accounting systems**. The cost accountant is (in theory) free to value stocks by whatever method seems best, but where companies integrate their financial accounting and cost accounting systems into a single system of accounting records, the valuation of closing stocks will be determined by SSAP 9.

2.10 SSAP 9 states that costs of all stocks should comprise those costs which have been incurred in the normal course of business in **bringing the product to its 'present location and condition'**. These costs incurred will include all related production overheads, even though these overheads may accrue on a time basis. In other words, in financial accounting, closing stocks should be valued at full factory cost, and it may therefore be convenient and appropriate to value stocks by the same method in the cost accounting system.

3 PRODUCT COST BUILD-UP USING ABSORPTION COSTING

3.1 The procedure of building up the cost of a unit of production (cost unit) under a system of absorption costing is as follows.

(a) **Direct costs** are **allocated** directly to cost units.

(b) **Indirect costs** which are clearly identifiable with particular administration cost centres, production cost centres, service/backup departments or selling and distribution cost centres are **allocated** to those cost centres. Frequently it is not possible to identify a discrete item of cost with one particular cost centre and so the cost is allocated to an overhead cost centre for the overhead.

(c) The **overheads** within the general overhead cost centre have to be split over several cost centres on an agreed basis. Let us consider rates for example. The cost of rates would first be allocated to the rent and rates cost centre. Although rates are levied upon the premises as a whole, for internal costing purposes they need to be **apportioned** between various cost centres. The basis used for apportioning rates is usually the floor area occupied by the various cost centres. The basis upon which the apportionment is made varies from cost to cost but the basis chosen should produce as fair and equitable a division as possible.

(d) The general overheads apportioned to service/backup departments and the overheads directly allocated to those departments then have to be **apportioned** to production departments.

(e) Costs apportioned to administration cost centres, marketing cost centres, distribution cost centres and so on are not usually included as part of the product cost and are deducted from the full cost of production to arrive at the cost of sales.

(f) The overheads both allocated to the production cost centres and apportioned directly and via the service departments cannot be related directly to cost units but do form part of the total product cost. These overheads must therefore be shared out in some equitable fashion among all the cost units produced. The process by which this is done is known as **overhead absorption**.

(g) Product costs (and non-production and non-service department overheads) are then charged to cost of sales.

The above procedures are set out in the following diagram. Don't worry if the process is not totally clear to you, we will be covering it in greater detail as we work through this chapter.

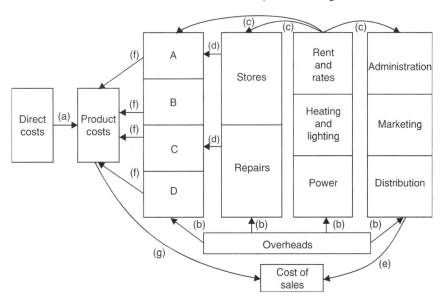

Product cost build-up using absorption costing

4 OVERHEAD ALLOCATION

12/94

KEY TERM

Allocation is the process by which whole cost items are charged direct to a cost unit or cost centre.

4.1 Cost centres may be one of the following types.

(a) A **production department**, to which production overheads are charged

(b) A **production area service department**, to which production overheads are charged

(c) An **administrative department**, to which administration overheads are charged

(d) A **selling** or a **distribution department**, to which sales and distribution overheads are charged

(e) An **overhead cost centre**, to which items of expense which are shared by a number of departments, such as rent and rates, heat and light and the canteen, are charged

4.2 The following costs would therefore be charged to the following cost centres via the process of allocation.

(a) Direct labour will be charged to a production cost centre.
(b) The cost of a warehouse security guard will be charged to the warehouse cost centre.
(c) Paper (recording computer output) will be charged to the computer department.
(d) Costs such as the canteen are charged direct to various overhead cost centres.

BPP
PUBLISHING

4.3 As an example of overhead allocation, consider the following costs of a company.

Wages of the foreman of department A	£200
Wages of the foreman of department B	£150
Indirect materials consumed in department A	£50
Rent of the premises shared by departments A and B	£300

The cost accounting system might include three overhead cost centres.

Cost centre:	101	Department A
	102	Department B
	201	Rent

Overhead costs would be allocated directly to each cost centre, ie £200 + £50 to cost centre 101, £150 to cost centre 102 and £300 to cost centre 201. The rent of the factory will be subsequently shared between the two production departments, but for the purpose of day to day cost recording, the rent will first of all be charged in full to a separate cost centre.

5 OVERHEAD APPORTIONMENT   12/94, 6/98, 6/99, 12/99

Exam focus point

In the majority of cases, the basis of apportionment of overhead is obvious. If you come across an examination question for which two or more bases may appear equally acceptable, use the method you prefer and explain why you have used the chosen method.

First stage: apportioning general overheads

5.1 **Overhead apportionment** follows on from overhead allocation. The first stage of overhead apportionment is to identify all overhead costs as production department, production service department, administration or selling and distribution overhead. The costs for heat and light, rent and rates, the canteen and so on (ie costs allocated to general overhead cost centres) must therefore be shared out between the other cost centres.

Bases of apportionment

5.2 It is considered important that overhead costs should be shared out on a **fair basis**. You will appreciate that because of the complexity of items of cost it is rarely possible to use only one method of apportioning costs to the various departments of an organisation. The bases of apportionment for the most usual cases are given below.

Overhead to which the basis applies	Basis
Rent, rates, heating and light, repairs and depreciation of buildings	Floor area occupied by each department
	Cost or book value of equipment
Depreciation, insurance of equipment	Number of employees, or labour hours worked in each department
Personnel office, canteen, welfare, wages and cost offices, first aid	
Heating, lighting (see above)	Volume of space occupied by each department
Carriage inwards (costs paid for the delivery of material supplies)	Value of material issues to each cost centre/department

5.3 EXAMPLE: OVERHEAD APPORTIONMENT

Fire Bases Ltd has incurred the following overhead costs.

	£
Depreciation of factory	1,000
Factory repairs and maintenance	600
Factory office costs (treat as production overhead)	1,500
Depreciation of equipment	800
Insurance of equipment	200
Heating	390
Lighting	100
Canteen	900
	5,490

Information relating to the production and service departments in the factory is as follows.

	Department			
	Production A	Production B	Service X	Service Y
Floor space (square metres)	1,200	1,600	800	400
Volume (cubic metres)	3,000	6,000	2,400	1,600
Number of employees	30	30	15	15
Book value of equipment	£30,000	£20,000	£10,000	£20,000

(handwritten margin notes: 4000, 13000, 90, 80000)

Required

Determine how the overhead costs should be apportioned between the four departments.

5.4 SOLUTION

		Total	To Department			
Item of cost	*Basis of apportionment*	*cost*	*A*	*B*	*X*	*Y*
		£	£	£	£	£
Factory depreciation	(floor area)	1,000	300	400	200	100
Factory repairs	(floor area)	600	180	240	120	60
Factory office costs	(number of employees)	1,500	500	500	250	250
Equipment depreciation	(book value)	800	300	200	100	200
Equipment insurance	(book value)	200	75	50	25	50
Heating	(volume)	390	90	180	72	48
Lighting	(floor area)	100	30	40	20	10
Canteen	(number of employees)	900	300	300	150	150
Total		5,490	1,775	1,910	937	868

Second stage: service department cost apportionment

5.5 The second stage of overhead apportionment concerns the **treatment of service departments**. A factory is divided into a number of production and service departments, but only the production departments are directly involved in the manufacture of the units. In order to be able to add production overheads to unit costs, it is necessary to have all the overheads charged to the production departments. The next stage in absorption costing is, therefore, to **apportion the costs of service departments to the production departments**. One method by which service department costs can be apportioned is known as the **repeated distribution method**.

The repeated distribution method of service department cost apportionment

> ### KEY TERM
>
> **Apportionment** is a procedure whereby indirect costs are spread fairly between departments.

5.6 It could therefore be argued that a fair sharing of service department costs is not possible unless recognition is given to the work done by each service department for other service departments. A stores department may, for example, use a maintenance department and the maintenance department may in turn use the stores department. The repeated distribution method of apportionment, is best explained by means of an example.

5.7 EXAMPLE: REPEATED DISTRIBUTION METHOD OF APPORTIONMENT

A company has two production and two service departments (stores and maintenance). The following information about activity in the recent costing period is available.

	Production departments		Stores	Maintenance
	A	*B*	*department*	*department*
Overhead costs	£10,030	£8,970	£10,000	£8,000
Cost of material acquisitions	£30,000	£50,000	-	£20,000
Maintenance hours needed	8,000	1,000	1,000	-

Required

Apportion the overheads of the service departments to the two production departments.

5.8 SOLUTION

If we give consideration to the work done by the stores and maintenance departments for each other, service department costs should be apportioned as follows.

	Dept A	*Dept B*	*Stores*	*Maintenance*
Stores (100%)	30%	50%	-	20%
Maintenance (100%)	80%	10%	10%	-

5.9

	Production Dept A	*Production Dept B*	*Stores*	*Maintenance*
	£	*£*	*£*	*£*
Overhead costs	10,030	8,970	10,000	8,000
Apportion stores costs (note (a))	3,000	5,000	(10,000)	2,000
			0	10,000
Apportion maintenance costs	8,000	1,000	1,000	(10,000)
			1,000	0
Repeat: Apportion stores	300	500	(1,000)	200
Repeat: Apportion maintenance	160	20	20	(200)
Repeat: Apportion stores	6	10	(20)	4
Repeat: Apportion maintenance (note (b))	4	-	-	(4)
	21,500	15,500	0	0

Notes

(a) The first apportionment could have been the costs of maintenance, rather than stores; there is no difference to the final results.

(b) When the repeated distributions bring service department costs down to small numbers (here £4) the final apportionment to production departments is an approximate rounding.

Using algebra

5.10 A quicker way, perhaps, of arriving at your conclusions in the example above is to use **algebra** and **simultaneous equations**.

5.11 Let us use the same data as the example above.

(a) Let S be the total stores department overhead for apportionment, after it has been apportioned overhead from Maintenance.

(b) Let M be the total of maintenance department overhead after it has been apportioned overhead from Stores.

5.12 We can set up our equations as follows.

$$S = 0.1M + £10,000 \quad (1)$$
$$M = 0.2S + £8,000 \quad (2)$$

5.13 Multiplying (2) by 5 gives us

$$5M = S + £40,000 \quad \text{(3), which can be rearranged so that}$$
$$S = 5M - £40,000 \quad (4)$$

Subtracting (1) from (4)

$$S = 5M - £40,000 \quad (4)$$
$$S = 0.1M + £10,000 \quad (1)$$

$$0 = 4.9M - £50,000$$

$$M = \frac{£50,000}{4.9} = £10,204$$

Substituting in (1)

$$S = 0.1 \times (£10,204) + £10,000$$
$$S = £11,020$$

5.14 These overheads can be apportioned as follows, using the percentages in Paragraph 5.8. Note that the result is the same as that obtained when using the repeated distribution method.

	Production dept A £	Production dept B £	Stores £	Maintenance £
Overhead costs	10,030	8,970	10,000	8,000
Apportion stores total	3,306	5,510	(11,020)	2,204
Apportion maintenance total	8,164	1,020	1,020	(10,204)
	21,500	15,500	-	-

Question 1

Sandstorm Ltd is a jobbing engineering concern which has three production departments (forming, machines and assembly) and two service departments (maintenance and general).

The following analysis of overhead costs has been made from the year just ended.

	£	£
Rent and rates		8,000
Power		750
Light, heat		5,000
Repairs, maintenance:		
Forming	800	
Machines	1,800	
Assembly	300	
Maintenance	200	
General	100	
		3,200
Departmental expenses:		
Forming	1,500	
Machines	2,300	
Assembly	1,100	
Maintenance	900	
General	1,500	
		7,300
Depreciation:		
Plant		10,000
Fixtures and fittings		250
Insurance:		
Plant		2,000
Buildings		500
Indirect labour:		
Forming	3,000	
Machines	5,000	
Assembly	1,500	
Maintenance	4,000	
General	2,000	
		15,500
		52,500

Other available data are as follows.

	Floor area sq. ft	Plant value £	Fixtures & fittings £	Effective horse-power	Direct cost for year £	Labour hours worked	Machine hours worked
Forming	2,000	25,000	1,000	40	20,500	14,400	12,000
Machines	4,000	60,000	500	90	30,300	20,500	21,600
Assembly	3,000	7,500	2,000	15	24,200	20,200	2,000
Maintenance	500	7,500	1,000	5	-	-	-
General	500	-	500	-	-	-	-
	10,000	100,000	5,000	150	75,000	55,100	35,600

Service department costs are apportioned as follows.

	Maintenance %	General %
Forming	20	20
Machines	50	60
Assembly	20	10
General	10	–
Maintenance	–	10
	100	100

Required

Using the data provided prepare an analysis showing the distribution of overhead costs to departments.

Answer

Analysis of distribution of actual overhead costs

	Basis	Forming £	Machines £	Assembly £	Machining £	General £	Total £
Directly allocated overheads:							
Repairs, maintenance		800	1,800	300	200	100	3,200
Departmental expenses		1,500	2,300	1,100	900	1,500	7,300
Indirect labour		3,000	5,000	1,500	4,000	2,000	15,500
Apportionment of other overheads:							
Rent, rates	1	1,600	3,200	2,400	400	400	8,000
Power	2	200	450	75	25	0	750
Light, heat	1	1,000	2,000	1,500	250	250	5,000
Dep'n of plant	3	2,500	6,000	750	750	0	10,000
Dep'n of F and F	4	50	25	100	50	25	250
Insurance of plant	3	500	1,200	150	150	0	2,000
Insurance of buildings	1	100	200	150	25	25	500
		11,250	22,175	8,025	6,750	4,300	52,500

Basis of apportionment:

1   floor area
2   effective horsepower
3   plant value
4   fixtures and fittings value

Apportionment of service department overheads to production departments, using the repeated distribution method.

	Forming £	Machines £	Assembly £	Maintenance £	General £	Total £
Overheads	11,250	22,175	8,025	6,750	4,300	52,500
	1,350	3,375	1,350	(6,750)	675	
					4,975	
	995	2,985	498	497	(4,975)	
	99	249	99	(497)	50	
	10	30	5	5	(50)	
	1	3	1	(5)		
	13,705	28,817	9,978	0	0	52,500

---

6   OVERHEAD ABSORPTION   6/94, 12/94, 12/95, 6/96, 12/97, 6/98, 12/98

Exam focus point

Absorption costing in one form or another has appeared in most of the new syllabus exams. It is therefore a key syllabus topic. Apart from being able to perform all the relevant techniques and calculations, be prepared to comment on absorption methods used.

6.1   Having allocated and/or apportioned all overheads, the next stage in absorption costing is to add them to, or **absorb them into,** the cost of production or sales.

(a) **Production costs** are added to the **prime cost** (direct materials, labour and expenses) to give the **factory cost,** (full cost of production). Production overheads are therefore included in the value of stocks of finished goods.

(b) **Administration and selling and distribution overheads** are then added, the sum of the factory cost and these overheads being the total cost of sales. These overheads are therefore not included in the value of closing stock.

Use of a predetermined absorption rate

6.2 Overheads are not absorbed on the basis of actual costs but on the basis of **estimated** or **budgeted** figures (calculated prior to the beginning of the period) using what is known as an **absorption rate**. There are a number of reasons for this.

(a) Goods are produced and sold throughout the year, but many actual overheads are not known until the end of the year. It would be inconvenient to wait until the year end in order to decide what overhead costs should be.

(b) An attempt to calculate overhead costs more regularly (such as each month) is possible, although estimated costs must be added for occasional expenditures such as rent and rates (incurred once or twice a year). The difficulty with this approach would be that actual overheads from month to month would fluctuate randomly; therefore, overhead costs charged to production would depend to a certain extent on random events and changes.

6.3 EXAMPLE : USE OF A PREDETERMINED ABSORPTION RATE

Suppose that a company budgets to make 1,200 units of a product in the first half of 20X5. Budgeted production overhead costs, all fixed costs, are £12,000. Due to seasonal demand for the company's product, the volume of production varies from month to month. Actual overhead costs are £2,000 per month. Actual monthly production in the first half of 20X5 is listed below, and total actual production in the period is 1,080 units.

The table below shows the production overhead cost per unit using the following.

(a) A predetermined absorption rate of $\dfrac{£12,000}{1,200} = £10$ per unit

(b) An actual overhead cost per unit each month

(c) An actual overhead cost per unit based on actual six-monthly expenditure of £12,000 and actual six-monthly output of 1,080 units = £11.11 per unit

			Overhead cost per unit		
			(a)	*(b)*	*(c)*
			Predetermined	*Actual cost*	*Average actual cost*
Month	*Expenditure*	*Output*	*unit rate*	*each month*	*in the six months*
	(A)	*(B)*		*(A) ÷ (B)*	
	£	Units	£	£	£
Jan	2,000	100	10	20.00	11.11
Feb	2,000	120	10	16.67	11.11
Mar	2,000	140	10	14.29	11.11
April	2,000	160	10	12.50	11.11
May	2,000	320	10	6.25	11.11
June	2,000	240	10	8.33	11.11
	12,000	1,080			

6.4   *Points to note*

(a)   Methods (a) and (c) give a **constant overhead cost per unit** each month, regardless of seasonal variations in output. Method (b) gives **variable unit overhead costs**, depending on the season of the year. For this reason, it is argued that method (a) or (c) would provide more useful (long-term) costing information.

In addition, if prices are based on full cost with a percentage mark-up for profit, method (b) would give seasonal variations in selling prices, with high prices in low-season and low prices in high-season. Methods (a) and (c) would give a constant price based on 'cost plus'.

(b)   With method (a), overhead costs per unit are known throughout the period, and cost statements can be prepared at any time. This is because **predetermined overhead rates are known in advance**. With method (c), overhead costs cannot be established until after the end of an accounting period. For example, overhead costs of output in January 20X5 cannot be established until actual costs and output for the period are known, which will be not until after the end of June 20X5.

(c)   For the reasons given above, predetermined overhead rates are preferable to rates based on actual overhead costs, in spite of being based on estimates of costs.

6.5   **Overhead absorption rates** are therefore calculated as follows.

(a)   The overhead likely to be incurred during the coming year is estimated.

(b)   The total hours, units, or direct costs on which the overhead absorption rates are to be based (activity level) are estimated.

(c)   The estimated overhead is divided by the budgeted activity level to arrive at an absorption rate.

6.6   The activity level can be based on a number of measures.

Full capacity	Output (expressed in standard hours) that could be achieved if sales orders, supplies and workforce were available for all installed workplaces.
Practical capacity	Full capacity less an allowance for known unavoidable volume losses.
Budgeted capacity	Standard hours planned for the period, taking into account budgeted sales, supplies, workforce availability and efficiency expected.

The examiner might try to confuse you by referring to '**full practical capacity**'. This simply means **100% of practical capacity**.

Choosing the appropriate absorption base

6.7   The different **bases of absorption** (or 'overhead recovery rates') are as follows.

- A percentage of direct materials cost
- A percentage of direct labour cost
- A percentage of prime cost
- A rate per machine hour
- A rate per direct labour hour
- A rate per unit
- A percentage of factory cost (for administration overhead)
- A percentage of sales or factory cost (for selling and distribution overhead)

6.8 The choice of an absorption basis is a matter of judgement and common sense, what is required is an **absorption basis** which realistically reflects the characteristics of a given cost centre and which avoids undue anomalies.

6.9 Many factories use a **direct labour hour rate** or **machine hour rate** in preference to a rate based on a percentage of direct materials cost, wages or prime cost.

(a) A **direct labour** hour basis is most appropriate in a **labour intensive** environment.

(b) A **machine hour** rate would be used in departments where production is controlled or dictated by machines.

(c) A **rate per unit** would be effective only if all units were identical.

6.10 EXAMPLE: OVERHEAD ABSORPTION

The budgeted production overheads and other budget data of Hairy Mammoth Ltd are as follows.

	Production dept A	*Production dept B*
Budget		
Overhead cost	£36,000	£5,000
Direct materials cost	£32,000	
Direct labour cost	£40,000	
Machine hours	10,000	
Direct labour hours	18,000	
Units of production		1,000

Required

Calculate the absorption rate using the various bases of apportionment.

6.11 SOLUTION

(a) Department A

(i) Percentage of direct materials cost $\dfrac{£36,000}{£32,000} \times 100\% = 112.5\%$

(ii) Percentage of direct labour cost $\dfrac{£36,000}{£40,000} \times 100\% = 90\%$

(iii) Percentage of prime cost $\dfrac{£36,000}{£72,000} \times 100\% = 50\%$

(iv) Rate per machine hour $\dfrac{£36,000}{10,000\text{hrs}} = £3.60$ per machine hour

(v) Rate per direct labour hour $\dfrac{£36,000}{18,000\text{hrs}} = £2$ per direct labour hour

(b) The department B absorption rate will be based on units of output.

$\dfrac{£5,000}{1,000\text{units}} = £5$ per unit produced

6.12 The choice of the basis of absorption is significant in determining the cost of individual units, or jobs, produced. Using the previous example, suppose that an individual product has a material cost of £80, a labour cost of £85, and requires 36 labour hours and 23 machine hours to complete. The overhead cost of the product would vary, depending on the basis of absorption used by the company for overhead recovery.

(a) As a percentage of direct material cost, the overhead cost would be
112.5% × £80 = £90.00

(b) As a percentage of direct labour cost, the overhead cost would be
90% × £85 = £76.50

(c) As a percentage of prime cost, the overhead cost would be 50% × £165 = £82.50

(d) Using a machine hour basis of absorption, the overhead cost would be
23 hrs × £3.60 = £82.80

(e) Using a labour hour basis, the overhead cost would be 36 hrs × £2 = £72.00

6.13 In theory, each basis of absorption would be possible, but the company should choose a basis for its own costs which seems to be '**fairest**'. In our example, this choice will be significant in determining the cost of individual products, as the following summary shows, but the total cost of production overheads is the budgeted overhead expenditure, no matter what basis of absorption is selected. It is the relative share of overhead costs borne by individual products and jobs which is affected by the choice of overhead absorption basis. A summary of the product costs in the previous example is shown as follows.

| | *Basis of overhead recovery* | | | | |
	Percentage of materials cost	*Percentage of labour cost*	*Percentage of prime cost*	*Machine hours*	*Direct labour hours*
	£	£	£	£	£
Direct material	80	80.00	80.00	80.00	80
Direct labour	85	85.00	85.00	85.00	85
Production overhead	90	76.50	82.50	82.80	72
Full factory cost	255	241.50	247.50	247.80	237

7 BLANKET ABSORPTION RATES AND DEPARTMENTAL ABSORPTION RATES

> **KEY TERM**
>
> A **blanket overhead absorption rate** is an absorption rate used throughout a factory and for all jobs and units of output irrespective of the department in which they were produced.

7.1 For example, if total overheads were £500,000 and there were 250,000 direct machine hours during the period, the **blanket overhead rate** would be £2 per direct machine hour and all jobs passing through the factory would be charged at that rate. Such a rate is not appropriate, however, if there are a number of departments, and jobs do not spend an equal amount of time in each department.

7.2 It is argued that if a single factory overhead absorption rate is used, some products will receive a higher overhead charge than they ought 'fairly' to bear, whereas other products will be under-charged. By using **a separate absorption rate** for each department, charging of overheads will be equitable and the full cost of production of items will be representative of the cost of the efforts and resources put into making them.

7.3 EXAMPLE: SEPARATE ABSORPTION RATES

Fire Dragon Ltd has two production departments, for which the following budgeted information is available.

	Department A	Department B	Total
Budgeted overheads	£360,000	£200,000	£560,000
Budgeted direct labour hours	200,000 hrs	40,000 hrs	240,000 hrs

If a single factory overhead absorption rate is applied, the rate of overhead recovery would be:

$$\frac{£560,000}{240,000 \text{hours}} = £2.33 \text{ per direct labour hour}$$

If separate departmental rates are applied, these would be:

$$Department\ A = \frac{£360,000}{200,000 \text{hours}} \qquad Department\ B = \frac{£200,000}{40,000 \text{hours}}$$

$$= £1.80 \text{ per direct labour hour} \qquad = £5 \text{ per direct labour hour}$$

Department B has a higher overhead rate of cost per hour worked than department A.

Now let us consider two separate jobs.

Job X has a prime cost of £100, takes 30 hours in department B and does not involve any work in department A.

Job Y has a prime cost of £100, takes 28 hours in department A and 2 hours in department B.

What would be the factory cost of each job, using the following rates of overhead recovery?

(a) A single factory rate of overhead recovery
(b) Separate departmental rates of overhead recovery

7.4 SOLUTION

				Job X		Job Y
(a)	**Single factory rate**			£		£
	Prime cost			100		100
	Factory overhead (30 × £2.33)			70		70
	Factory cost			170		170

				Job X		Job Y
(b)	**Separate departmental rates**			£		£
	Prime cost			100		100.00
	Factory overhead:	department A		0	(28 × £1.80)	50.40
		department B	(30 × £5)	150	(2 × £5)	10.00
	Factory cost			250		160.40

7.5 Using a single factory overhead absorption rate, both jobs would cost the same. However, since job X is done entirely within department B where overhead costs are relatively higher, whereas job Y is done mostly within department A, where overhead costs are relatively lower, it is arguable that job X should cost more than job Y. This will occur if separate departmental overhead recovery rates are used to reflect the work done on each job in each department separately.

7.6 If all jobs do not spend approximately the same time in each department then, to ensure that all jobs are charged with their fair share of overheads, it is necessary to establish **separate overhead rates for each department**.

8 NORMAL COSTING

8.1 We know that the **overhead absorption rate is predetermined** using figures from the **annual budget**. If overheads are to be absorbed on the basis of direct labour hours, the overhead absorption rate will be calculated using the total overheads and the number of direct labour hours included in the annual budget.

8.2 Using the predetermined absorption rate, the *actual* cost of production can be established as follows.

	Direct materials
plus:	direct labour
plus:	direct expenses
plus:	overheads (based on the predetermined recovery rate)
equals:	actual cost of production

This is known as **normal costing**.

8.3 Many students become seriously confused about what can appear a very unusual method of costing. The following example should help clarify this costing method.

8.4 EXAMPLE: NORMAL COSTING

Normal Ltd budgeted to make 100 units of product Z at a cost of £3 per unit in direct materials and £4 per unit in direct labour. The sales price would be £12 per unit, and production overheads were budgeted to amount to £200. A unit basis of overhead recovery is in operation. During the period 120 units were actually produced and sold (for £12 each) and the actual cost of direct materials was £380 and of direct labour, £450. Overheads incurred came to £210.

Required

Determine the cost of sales of product Z, and the profit. Ignore administration, selling and distribution overheads.

8.5 SOLUTION

In normal costing, the cost of production and sales is the actual direct cost plus the cost of overheads, absorbed at a predetermined rate as established in the budget. In our example, the overhead recovery rate would be £2 per unit produced (£200 ÷100 units).

The actual cost of sales is calculated as follows.

	£
Direct materials (actual)	380
Direct labour (actual)	450
Overheads absorbed (120 units × £2)	240
Full cost of sales, product Z	1,070
Sales of product Z (120 units × £12)	1,440
Profit, product Z	370

Notice that the actual overheads **incurred**, £210, are not the same as the overheads **absorbed** into the cost of production, £240. In normal absorption costing £240 is the 'correct' cost. This discrepancy between actual overheads incurred and the overheads absorbed, which is an inevitable feature of normal costing, is only reconciled at the end of an accounting period, as the '**under-absorption**' or '**over-absorption**' of **overhead**.

9 OVER AND UNDER ABSORPTION OF OVERHEADS 12/97, 12/98, 6/99

9.1 **The rate of overhead absorption is based on estimates** (of both numerator and denominator) and it is quite likely that either one or both of the estimates will not agree with what actually occurs.

(a) **Over-absorption** means that the overheads charged to the cost of sales are greater then the overheads actually incurred.

(b) **Under-absorption** means that insufficient overheads have been included in the cost of sales.

It is almost inevitable that at the end of the accounting year there will have been an over absorption or under absorption of the overhead actually incurred.

9.2 Suppose that the budgeted overhead in a production department is £80,000 and the budgeted activity is 40,000 direct labour hours. The overhead recovery rate (using a direct labour hour basis) would be £2 per direct labour hour.

Actual overheads in the period are, say £84,000 and 45,000 direct labour hours are worked.

	£
Overhead incurred (actual)	84,000
Overhead absorbed (45,000 × £2)	90,000
Over-absorption of overhead	6,000

In this example, the cost of produced units or jobs has been charged with £6,000 more than was actually spent. An adjustment to reconcile the overheads charged to the actual overhead is necessary and the over-absorbed overhead will be written as an adjustment to the profit and loss account at the end of the accounting period.

The reasons for under-/over-absorbed overhead

9.3 **The overhead absorption rate is predetermined from budget estimates of overhead cost and the expected volume of activity.** Under- or over-recovery of overhead will occur in the following circumstances.

- Actual overhead costs are different from budgeted overheads
- The actual activity level is different from the budgeted activity level
- Actual overhead costs *and* actual activity level differ from the budgeted costs and level

9.4 EXAMPLE: REASONS FOR UNDER-/OVER-ABSORBED OVERHEAD

Big Lizards Ltd has a budgeted production overhead of £50,000 and a budgeted activity of 25,000 direct labour hours and therefore a recovery rate of £2 per direct labour hour.

Required

Calculate the under-/over-absorbed overhead, and the reasons for the under-/over-absorption, in the following circumstances.

(a) Actual overheads cost £47,000 and 25,000 direct labour hours are worked.
(b) Actual overheads cost £50,000 and 21,500 direct labour hours are worked.
(c) Actual overheads cost £47,000 and 21,500 direct labour hours are worked.

9.5 SOLUTION

(a)

	£
Actual overhead	47,000
Absorbed overhead (25,000 × £2)	50,000
Over-absorbed overhead	3,000

The reason for the over-absorption is that although the actual and budgeted direct labour hours are the same, actual overheads cost less than expected.

(b)

	£
Actual overhead	50,000
Absorbed overhead (21,500 × £2)	43,000
Under-absorbed overhead	7,000

The reason for the under-absorption is that although budgeted and actual overhead costs were the same, fewer direct labour hours were worked than expected.

(c)

	£
Actual overhead	47,000
Absorbed overhead (21,500 × £2)	43,000
Under-absorbed overhead	4,000

The reason for the under absorption is a combination of the reasons in (a) and (b).

9.6 EXAMPLE: UNDER AND OVER ABSORPTION OF OVERHEADS

Rioch Havery Ltd is a small company which manufactures two products, A and B, in two production departments, machining and assembly. A canteen is operated as a separate production service department.

The budgeted production, sales and overheads in the year to 31 March 20X3 are as follows.

	Product A	*Product B*
Sales price per unit	£50	£70
Sales (units)	2,200	1,400
Production (units)	2,000	1,500
Material cost per unit	£14	£12

Direct labour:

	Product A *Hours per unit*	*Product B* *Hours per unit*
Machining department (£4 per hour)	2	3
Assembly department (£3 per hour)	1	2

Machine hours per unit:

Machining department	$3\frac{1}{2}$	4
Assembly department		

Budgeted production overheads:

	Machining department £	*Assembly department* £	*Canteen* £	*Total* £
Allocated costs	10,000	25,000	12,000	47,000
Apportionment of other general production overheads	26,000	12,000	8,000	46,000
	36,000	37,000	20,000	93,000
Number of employees	30	20	1	51
Floor area (square metres)	5,000	2,000	500	5,500

Required

(a) Calculate an absorption rate for overheads in each production department for the year to 31 March 20X3 and the budgeted cost per unit of products A and B.

BPP PUBLISHING

(b) Suppose that actual results in the year to 31 March 20X3 are as follows.

	Product A	Product B	
Sales (units)	2,400	1,400	
Production (units)	2,200	1,500	
Sales price per unit	£50	£70	
Direct materials cost per unit	£14	£12	
Direct labour hours per unit:			
Machining department	2 hrs	3 hrs	(actual cost £4 per hour)
Assembly department	1 hr	2 hrs	(actual cost £3 per hour)
Machining hours:			
Machining department	3 hrs	4 hrs	
Assembly department	½ hr		

	Machining department £	Assembly department £	Canteen £	Total £
Actual production overheads:				
Allocated costs	30,700	27,600	10,000	68,300
Apportioned share of general production overheads	17,000	8,000	5,000	30,000
	47,700	35,600	15,000	98,300

Calculate the 'actual' cost of product A and product B.

9.7 SOLUTION

Step 1. Choose absorption rates

Since machine time appears to be more significant than labour time in the machining department, a machine hour rate of absorption will be used for overhead recovery in this department. In the assembly department, machining is insignificant and a direct labour hour rate of absorption would seem to be the basis which will give the fairest method of overhead recovery.

Step 2. Apportion budgeted overheads

Next we need to apportion **budgeted** overheads to the two production departments. Canteen costs will be apportioned on the basis of the number of employees in each department. (Direct labour hours in each department are an alternative basis of apportionment, but the number of employees seems to be more directly relevant to canteen costs).

	Machining department £	Assembly department £	Total £
Budgeted allocated costs	10,000	25,000	35,000
Share of general overheads	26,000	12,000	38,000
Apportioned canteen costs (30:20)	12,000	8,000	20,000
	48,000	45,000	93,000

Step 3. Calculate overhead absorption rates

The overhead absorption rates are predetermined, using budgeted estimates. Since the overheads are production overheads, the budgeted activity relates to the volume of production, in units (the production hours required for volume of sales being irrelevant).

	Product A	Product B	Total
Budgeted production (units)	2,000	1,500	
Machining department: machine hours	6,000 hrs	6,000 hrs	12,000 hrs
Assembly department: direct labour hours	2,000 hrs	3,000 hrs	5,000 hrs

The overhead absorption rates will be as follows.

	Machining department	Assembly department
Budgeted overheads	£48,000	£45,000
Budgeted activity	12,000 hrs	5,000 hrs
Absorption rate	£4 per machine hour	£9 per direct labour hour

Step 4. Determine a budgeted cost per unit

The budgeted cost per unit would be as follows.

	Product A		Product B	
	£	£	£	£
Direct materials		14		12
Direct labour:				
Machining department	8		12	
Assembly department	3		6	
		11		18
Prime cost		25		30
Production overhead:				
Machining department	12		16	
Assembly department	9		18	
		21		34
Full cost		46		64

Step 5. **Apportion actual service department overhead to production departments**

When the actual costs are analysed, the 'actual' overhead of the canteen department (£15,000) would be split between the machining and assembly departments.

	Machining department	Assembly department	Total
	£	£	£
Allocated cost	30,700	27,600	58,300
Apportioned general overhead	17,000	8,000	25,000
Canteen (30:20)	9,000	6,000	15,000
	56,700	41,600	98,300

Step 6. **Determine an actual cost per unit**

The overhead absorption rate remains as budgeted, £4 per machine hour in the machining department and £9 per direct labour hour in the assembly department.

	Product A	Product B
	£	£
Prime cost per unit (same as budgeted)	25	30
Overhead cost per unit (same as budgeted)	21	34
'Actual' cost per unit	46	64

The actual cost per unit is the same as the budgeted unit cost for the following reasons.

(a) Actual unit costs for direct materials and direct labour were the same as in the budget.

(b) The actual machine hours (machining department) and direct labour hours (assembly department) per unit were the same as in the budget.

Step 7. **Establish the over- or under-absorption of overheads**

There would be an over- or under-absorption of overheads as follows.

		Machining department £		Assembly department £	Total £
Overheads absorbed					
Product A (2,200 units)	(× 12)	26,400	(× 9)	19,800	46,200
Product B (1,500 units)	(× 16)	24,000	(× 18)	27,000	51,000
		50,400		46,800	97,200
Overheads incurred		56,700		41,600	98,300
(Under)/over-absorbed overhead		(6,300)		5,200	(1,100)

The total under-absorbed overhead of £1,100 will be written off to the profit and loss account at the end of the year, to compensate for the fact that overheads charged to production (£97,200) were less than the overheads actually incurred (£98,300).

9.8 The distinction between **overheads incurred** (actual overheads) and **overheads absorbed** is an important one which you must learn and understand. The difference between them is known as under- or over-absorbed overheads.

Question 2

The budgeted and actual data for Tecpointer Ltd for the year to 31 March 20X5 are as follows.

	Budgeted	Actual
Direct labour hours	9,000	9,900
Direct wages	£34,000	£35,500
Machine hours	10,100	9,750
Direct materials	£55,000	£53,900
Units produced	120,000	122,970
Overheads	£63,000	£61,500

The cost accountant of Tecpointer Ltd has decided that overheads should be absorbed on the basis of labour hours.

Required

Calculate the amount of under- or over-absorbed overheads for Tecpointer Ltd for the year to 31 March 20X5.

Answer

Overhead absorption rate = $\dfrac{£63,000}{9,000}$ = £7 per hour

Overheads absorbed by production = 9,900 × £7 = £69,300

	£
Actual overheads	61,500
Overheads absorbed	69,300
Over-absorbed overheads	7,800

10 NON-MANUFACTURING OVERHEADS

10.1 For **external reporting** (eg statutory accounts) it is not necessary to allocate non-manufacturing overheads to products. This is because many for the overheads are non-manufacturing, and are regarded as **period costs**.

10.2 For **internal reporting** purposes and for a number of industries which base the selling price of their product on estimates of **total** cost or even actual cost, a total cost per unit of output may be required. Builders, law firms and garages often charge for their services by adding a percentage profit margin to actual cost. For product pricing purposes and for internal management reports it may therefore be appropriate to allocate non-manufacturing overheads to units of output.

Bases for apportioning non-manufacturing overheads

10.3 A number of non-manufacturing overheads such as delivery costs or salespersons' salaries are clearly identified with particular products and can therefore be classified as direct costs. The majority of non-manufacturing overheads, however cannot be directly allocated to particular units of output. Two possible methods of allocating such non-manufacturing overheads are as follows.

10.4 **Method 1: Choose a basis for the overhead absorption rate** which most closely matches the non-manufacturing overhead such as direct labour hours, direct machine hours and so on. The problem with such a method is that most non-manufacturing overheads are unaffected in the short term by changes in the level of output and tend to be fixed costs.

10.5 **Method 2 : Allocate non-manufacturing overheads on the ability of the products to bear such costs**. One possible approach is to use the manufacturing cost as the basis for allocating non-manufacturing costs to products.

> **FORMULA TO LEARN**
>
> The **overhead absorption rate** is calculated as follows.
>
> $$\text{Overhead absorption rate} = \frac{\text{Estimated non-manufacturing overheads}}{\text{Estimated manufacturing costs}}$$

10.6 If, for example, budgeted distribution overheads are £200,000 and budgeted manufacturing costs are £800,000, the predetermined distribution overhead absorption rate will be 25% of manufacturing cost. Other bases for absorbing overheads are as follows.

Types of overhead	Possible absorption base
Selling and marketing	Sales value
Research and development	Consumer cost (= production cost minus cost of direct materials) or added value (= sales value of product minus cost of bought in materials and services)
Distribution	Sales values
Administration	Consumer cost or added value

Administration overheads

10.7 The administration overhead usually consists of the following.

- Executive salaries
- Office rent and rates
- Lighting
- Heating and cleaning the offices

In cost accounting, administration overheads are regarded as periodic charges which are charged against the gross costing profit for the year (as in financial accounting).

Selling and distribution overheads

10.8 **Selling and distribution overheads** are often considered collectively as one type of overhead but they are actually quite different forms of expense.

(a) **Selling costs** are incurred in order to obtain sales

(b) **Distribution costs** begin as soon as the finished goods are put into the warehouse and continue until the goods are despatched or delivered to the customer

10.9 **Selling overhead** is therefore often absorbed on the basis of sales value so that the more profitable product lines take a large proportion of overhead. The normal cost accounting entry for selling overhead is as follows.

DR Cost of goods sold
CR Selling overhead control account

10.10 **Distribution overhead** is more closely linked to production than sales and from one point of view could be regarded as an extra cost of production. It is, however, more usual to regard production cost as ending on the factory floor and to deal with distribution overhead separately. It is generally absorbed on a percentage of production cost but special circumstances, such as size and weight of products affecting the delivery charges, may cause a different basis of absorption to be used. The cost accounting entry is as follows.

DR Cost of goods sold
CR Distribution overhead control account

11 ACTIVITY BASED COSTING

11.1 **Absorption costing** appears to be a relatively straightforward way of adding overhead costs to units of production using, more often than not, a **volume related absorption basis** (such as direct labour hours or direct machine hours). **Absorption costing assumes that all overheads are related primarily to production volume**. In reality, however, direct labour or direct machine hours may account for only 5% of a product's cost. However, a product may cause the overheads of service support functions (data processing, production scheduling and first item inspection) to increase. Are such overheads affected by the production volume? No – these overheads tend to be affected by the **range** and **complexity** of the products manufactured.

11.2 Because absorption costing tends to allocate too great a proportion of overheads to high volume products (which cause relatively little diversity), and too small a proportion of overheads to low volume products (which cause greater diversity and therefore use more support services), alternative methods of costing have been developed. **Activity based costing (ABC)** is one such development.

11.3 The major ideas behind **activity based costing** are as follows.

(a) **Activities cause costs**. Activities include ordering, materials handling, machining, assembly, production scheduling and despatching.

(b) Products create demand for the activities.

(c) Costs are assigned to products on the basis of a product's consumption of the activities.

Outline of an ABC system

11.4   An ABC costing system operates as follows.

Step 1.   Identify an organisation's major activities.

Step 2.   Identify the factors which determine the size of the costs of an activity/cause the costs of an activity. These are known as **cost drivers**.

Activity	Cost driver
Ordering	Number of orders
Materials handling	Number of production runs
Production scheduling	Number of production runs
Despatching	Number of despatches

For those costs that vary with production levels in the short term, ABC uses **volume-related cost drivers** such as labour or machine hours. The cost of oil used as a lubricant on the machines would therefore be added to products on the basis of the number of machine hours since oil would have to be used for each hour **the machine** ran.

Step 3.   Collect the costs of each activity into what are known as **cost pools** (equivalent to cost centres under more traditional costing methods).

Step 4.   Charge support overheads to products on the basis of their usage of the activity. A product's usage of an activity is measured by the number of the activity's cost driver it generates.

Suppose, for example, that the cost pool for the ordering activity totalled £100,000 and that there were 10,000 orders (the cost driver). Each product would therefore be charged with £10 for each order it required. A batch requiring five orders would therefore be charged with £50.

11.5   **Absorption costing** and **ABC** have many similarities. In both systems, **direct costs go straight to the product and overheads are allocated to production cost centres/cost pools.** The main difference is as follows.

(a)   **Absorption costing** uses usually two **absorption bases** (labour hours and/or machine hours) to charge overheads to products.

(b)   **ABC** uses many **cost drivers** as absorption bases (number of orders, number of dispatches and so on) to charge overheads to products.

11.6   In summary, ABC has absorption rates which are more closely linked to the cause of the overheads.

11.7   A **cost driver** is an activity which generates costs. Examples of cost drivers include the following.

- Sales levels as these **drive** the costs of sales commission
- Miles travelled as these **drive** the fuel costs
- Hours worked as these **drive** the costs of labour

The principal idea of ABC is to identify cost drivers.

11.8   Consider the following.

(a)   **Overheads which vary with output** should be traced to products using volume-related cost drivers eg direct labour hours or direct machine hours.

(b) **Overheads which do not vary with output** should be traced to products using transaction based cost drivers eg number of production runs, or number of orders received and so on.

Chapter roundup

- Product costs are built up using absorption costing by a process of **allocation**, **apportionment** and **absorption**.

- In absorption costing, it is usual to add overheads into product costs by applying a **predetermined overhead absorption rate**. (This is set annually, in the budget).

- To work out the **absorption rate**, budgeted overheads are allocated to production cost centres, service department cost centres or general overhead cost centres. General overheads are then apportioned to production and service department cost centres using an appropriate basis. The service department cost centre overheads are then apportioned to production cost centres. All production overhead is thus identified with cost centres engaged directly in production.

- The **absorption rate** is calculated by dividing the budgeted overhead by the budgeted level of activity (budgeted direct labour hours or budgeted machine hours).

- Management should try to establish an absorption rate that provides a reasonably 'accurate' estimate of overhead costs for jobs, products or services. This means that when a predetermined overhead rate is used the bases for apportioning overhead costs between departments should be 'fair' and separate departmental absorption rates should be used.

- The **overhead absorption rate** is predetermined using figures from the budget. Actual costs of production include overheads based on this predetermined recovery rate. This is known as **normal costing**.

- **If overheads absorbed exceed overheads incurred**, the cost of production (or sales) will have been too high. The amount of **overabsorption** will be written as a 'favourable' adjustment to the profit and loss account. **If overheads absorbed are lower than the amount of overheads incurred**, the cost of production (or sales) will have been too low. The amount of **under-absorption** will be written as an 'adverse' adjustment to the profit and loss account.

- Under- or over-absorbed overhead is inevitable in normal absorption costing because the predetermined overhead absorption rates are based on forecasts (guesses) about overhead expenditure and the level, or volume, of activity.

- **Activity based costing (ABC)** is an alternative to the more traditional absorption costing. ABC involves the identification of the factors **(cost drivers)** which cause the costs of an organisation's major activities. **Support overheads** are charged to products on the basis of their usage of an activity.

Quick quiz

1 What are the reasons for using absorption costing? (see paras 2.7, 2.8)

2 Name the three stages in charging overheads to units of output. (3.1)

3 Why is it common to use *predetermined* overhead absorption rates? (6.2, 6.4)

4 What is the problem with using a single factory overhead absorption rate? (7.3, 7.6)

5 What is normal costing? (8.2)

6 How is under-/over-absorbed overhead accounted for? (9.2)

7 Why does under- or over-absorbed overhead occur? (9.3)

8 What are the major ideas of activity based costing? (11.3)

9 What is the advantage of using cost drivers instead of traditional absorption bases? (11.6)

Question to try	Level	Marks	Time
8	Examination	14	25 mins

BPP
PUBLISHING

Chapter 9

MARGINAL COSTING AND ABSORPTION COSTING

Chapter topic list	Syllabus reference
1 Marginal cost and marginal costing	CA 4(a)
2 Contribution	CA 4(a)(i)
3 The principles of marginal costing	CA 4(a), (b)
4 Marginal costing and absorption costing and the calculation of profit	CA 1(c)(iv), 4(a)(ii)
5 Reconciling the profit figures given by the two methods	CA 1(c)(iv), 4(a)(ii)
6 Marginal costing versus absorption costing - which is better?	CA 1(c)(iv), 4(a)(ii)
7 Introduction to decision making	CA 4(a)

Introduction

This chapter defines **marginal costing** and compares it with absorption costing. Whereas absorption costing recognises fixed costs (usually fixed production costs) as part of the cost of a unit of output and hence as product costs, marginal costing treats all fixed costs as period costs. Two such different costing methods obviously each have their supporters and we will be looking at the arguments both in favour of and against each method, as well as their comparative usefulness for reporting to management, for reporting profits and stock values in externally published accounts and for providing decision-making information. Each costing method, because of the different stock valuation used, produces a different profit figure and we will be looking at this particular point in detail.

1 MARGINAL COST AND MARGINAL COSTING

KEY TERMS

- **Marginal costing** is an alternative method of costing to absorption costing. In marginal costing, only variable costs are charged as a cost of sale and a contribution is calculated (sales revenue minus variable cost of sales). Closing stocks of work in progress or finished goods are valued at marginal (variable) production cost. Fixed costs are treated as a period cost, and are charged in full to the profit and loss account of the accounting period in which they are incurred.

- **Marginal cost** is the cost of a unit of a product or service which would be avoided if that unit were not produced or provided.

1.1 The marginal production cost per unit of an item usually consists of the following.

- Direct materials
- Direct labour
- Variable production overheads

1.2 Direct labour costs might be excluded from marginal costs when the work force is a given number of employees on a fixed wage or salary. Even so, it is not uncommon for direct labour to be treated as a variable cost, even when employees are paid a basic wage for a fixed working week. If in doubt, you should treat direct labour as a variable cost unless given clear indications to the contrary. Direct labour is often a step cost, with sufficiently short steps to make labour costs act in a variable fashion.

1.3 The **marginal cost of sales** usually consists of the marginal cost of production adjusted for stock movements plus the variable selling costs, which would include items such as sales commission, and possibly some variable distribution costs.

2 CONTRIBUTION

> **KEY TERM**
>
> **Contribution** is the difference between sales value and the marginal cost of sales.

2.1 **Contribution** is of fundamental importance in marginal costing, and the term 'contribution' is really short for 'contribution towards covering fixed overheads and making a profit'.

3 THE PRINCIPLES OF MARGINAL COSTING   12/95, 6/96, 12/96, 12/97, 6/99

3.1 The principles of marginal costing are as follows.

(a) Period fixed costs are the same, for any volume of sales and production (provided that the level of activity is within the 'relevant range'). Therefore, by selling an extra item of product or service the following will happen.

- Revenue will increase by the sales value of the item sold.
- Costs will increase by the variable cost per unit.
- Profit will increase by the amount of contribution earned from the extra item.

(b) Similarly, if the volume of sales falls by one item, the profit will fall by the amount of contribution earned from the item.

(c) **Profit measurement should therefore be based on an analysis of total contribution.** Since fixed costs relate to a period of time, and do not change with increases or decreases in sales volume, it is misleading to charge units of sale with a share of fixed costs. Absorption costing is therefore misleading, and it is more appropriate to deduct fixed costs from total contribution for the period to derive a profit figure.

(d) When a unit of product is made, the extra costs incurred in its manufacture are the **variable production costs**. Fixed costs are unaffected, and no extra fixed costs are incurred when output is increased. It is therefore argued that the valuation of closing stocks should be at variable production cost (direct materials, direct labour, direct expenses (if any) and variable production overhead) because these are the only costs properly attributable to the product.

3.2 EXAMPLE: MARGINAL COSTING PRINCIPLES

Rain Until September Ltd makes a product, the Splash, which has a variable production cost of £6 per unit and a sales price of £10 per unit. At the beginning of September 20X0, there were no opening stocks and production during the month was 20,000 units. Fixed costs for the month were £45,000 (production, administration, sales and distribution). There were no variable marketing costs.

Required

Calculate the contribution and profit for September 20X0, using marginal costing principles, if sales were as follows.

(a) 10,000 Splashes
(b) 15,000 Splashes
(c) 20,000 Splashes

3.3 SOLUTION

The first stage in the profit calculation must be to identify the variable cost of sales, and then the contribution. Fixed costs are deducted from the total contribution to derive the profit. All closing stocks are valued at marginal production cost (£6 per unit).

	10,000 Splashes		15,000 Splashes		20,000 Splashes	
	£	£	£	£	£	£
Sales (at £10)		100,000		150,000		200,000
Opening stock	0		0		0	
Variable production cost	120,000		120,000		120,000	
	120,000		120,000		120,000	
Less value of closing stock (at marginal cost)	60,000		30,000		-	
Variable cost of sales		60,000		90,000		120,000
Contribution		40,000		60,000		80,000
Less fixed costs		45,000		45,000		45,000
Profit/(loss)		(5,000)		15,000		35,000
Profit (loss) per unit		£(0.50)		£1		£1.75
Contribution per unit		£4		£4		£4

3.4 The conclusions which may be drawn from this example are as follows.

(a) The **profit per unit varies** at differing levels of sales, because the average fixed overhead cost per unit changes with the volume of output and sales.

(b) The **contribution per unit is constant** at all levels of output and sales. Total contribution, which is the contribution per unit multiplied by the number of units sold, increases in direct proportion to the volume of sales.

(c) Since the **contribution per unit does not change,** the most effective way of calculating the expected profit at any level of output and sales would be as follows.

(i) First calculate the total contribution.
(ii) Then deduct fixed costs as a period charge in order to find the profit.

(d) In our example the expected profit from the sale of 17,000 Splashes would be as follows.

	£
Total contribution (17,000 × £4)	68,000
Less fixed costs	45,000
Profit	23,000

3.5 (a) If total contribution **exceeds fixed costs,** a profit is made

    (b) If total contribution **exactly equals fixed costs,** no profit or loss is made (**breakeven point**)

    (c) If total contribution is **less than fixed costs,** there will be a loss

Exam focus point

In the 6/98 exam, candidates were required to calculate the contribution earned given the **contribution margin**. For example, if the contribution margin is 45% and the sales revenue is £150,000, then the contribution earned will be 45% × £150,000 = £67,500.

Question 1

Argot Slang Ltd makes two products, the Drawl and the Twang. Information relating to each of these products for April 20X1 is as follows.

	Drawl	*Twang*
Opening stock	nil	nil
Production (units)	15,000	6,000
Sales (units)	10,000	5,000
Sales price per unit	₤£20	£30
Unit costs	£	£
Direct materials	8	14
Direct labour	4	2
Variable production overhead	2	1
Variable sales overhead	2	3

Fixed costs for the month	£
Production costs	40,000
Administration costs	15,000
Sales and distribution costs	25,000

Required

(a) Using marginal costing principles and the method in 3.4(d) above, calculate the profit in April 20X1.

(b) Calculate the profit if sales had been 15,000 units of Drawl and 6,000 units of Twang.

Answer

(a)

	£
Contribution from Drawls (unit contribution = £20 − £16 = £4 × 10,000)	40,000
Contribution from Twangs (unit contribution = £30 − £20 = £10 × 5,000)	50,000
Total contribution	90,000
Fixed costs for the period	80,000
Profit	10,000

(b) At a higher volume of sales, profit would be as follows.

	£
Contribution from sales of 15,000 Drawls (× £4)	60,000
Contribution from sales of 6,000 Twangs (× £10)	60,000
Total contribution	120,000
Less fixed costs	80,000
Profit	40,000

Profit or contribution information

3.6 The main advantage of **contribution information** (rather than profit information) is that it allows an easy calculation of profit if sales increase or decrease from a certain level. By comparing total contribution with fixed overheads, it is possible to determine whether profits or losses will be made at certain sales levels. **Profit information**, on the other hand, does not lend itself to easy manipulation but note how easy it was to calculate profits using contribution information in Question 1. **Contribution information** is more useful for **decision making** than profit information, as we shall see in Section 7 of this chapter.

4 MARGINAL COSTING AND ABSORPTION COSTING AND THE CALCULATION OF PROFIT 6/94, 6/97, 12/97, 6/99

Exam focus point

There were four marks available in the 12/97 examination for being able to explain and demonstrate why marginal costing and absorption costing produce different net profit figures.

4.1 **Marginal costing** as a cost accounting system is significantly different from absorption costing. It is an **alternative method** of accounting for costs and profit, which rejects the principles of absorbing fixed overheads into unit costs.

(a) **In marginal costing**

(i) Closing stocks are valued at marginal production cost.

(ii) Fixed costs are charged in full against the profit of the period in which they are incurred.

(b) **In absorption costing** (sometimes referred to as **full costing**)

(i) Closing stocks are valued at full production cost, and include a share of fixed production costs.

(ii) This means that the cost of sales in a period will include some fixed overhead incurred in a previous period (in opening stock values) and will exclude some fixed overhead incurred in the current period but carried forward in closing stock values as a charge to a subsequent accounting period.

4.2 In **marginal costing**, it is necessary to identify the following.

- Variable costs
- Contribution
- Fixed costs

In **absorption costing** it is not necessary to distinguish variable costs from fixed costs.

4.3 EXAMPLE: MARGINAL AND ABSORPTION COSTING COMPARED

Look back at the information contained in Question 1. Suppose that the budgeted production for April 20X1 was 15,000 units of Drawl and 6,000 units of Twang, and production overhead is absorbed on the basis of budgeted direct labour costs.

Required

Calculate the profit if production was as budgeted, and sales were as follows.

(a) 10,000 units of Drawl and 5,000 units of Twang
(b) 15,000 units of Drawl and 6,000 units of Twang

Administration, sales and distribution costs should be charged as a period cost.

4.4 SOLUTION

Budgeted production overhead is calculated as follows.

		£
Fixed		40,000
Variable:	Drawls (15,000 × £2)	30,000
	Twangs (6,000 × £1)	6,000
Total		76,000

The **production overhead absorption rate** would be calculated as follows.

$$\frac{\text{Budgeted production overhead}}{\text{Budgeted direct labour cost}} = \frac{£76,000}{(15,000 \times £4) + (6,000 \times £2)} \times 100\%$$

$$= 105.56\% \text{ of direct labour cost}$$

(a) If sales are 10,000 units of Drawl and 5,000 units of Twang, profit would be as follows.

	Absorption costing		
	Drawls	*Twangs*	*Total*
	£	£	£
Costs of production			
Direct materials	120,000	84,000	204,000
Direct labour	60,000	12,000	72,000
Overhead (105.56% of labour)	63,333	12,667	76,000
	243,333	108,667	352,000
Less closing stocks	(1/3) 81,111	(1/6) 18,111	99,222
Production cost of sales	162,222	90,556	252,778
Administration costs			15,000
Sales and distribution costs			
Variable			35,000
Fixed			25,000
Total cost of sales			327,778
Sales	200,000	150,000	350,000
Profit			22,222

Note. There is no under-/over-absorption of overhead, since actual production is the same as budgeted production.

The profit derived using absorption costing techniques is different from the profit (£10,000) using marginal costing techniques at this volume of sales (see earlier question).

(b) If production and sales are exactly the same, (15,000 units of Drawl and 6,000 units of Twang) profit would be £40,000.

	£
Sales (300,000 + 180,000)	480,000
Cost of sales (352,000★ + 15,000 + 48,000 + 25,000)	440,000
Profit	40,000

★ No closing stock if sales and production are equal.

This is the same as the profit calculated by marginal costing techniques in the earlier question.

4.5   We can draw a number of conclusions from this example.

(a) Marginal costing and absorption costing are different techniques for assessing profit in a period.

(b) If there are **changes in stocks during a period**, so that opening stock or closing stock values are different, **marginal costing and absorption costing give different results** for profit obtained.

(c) **If the opening and closing stock volumes and values are the same, marginal costing and absorption costing will give the same profit figure.** This is because the total cost of sales during the period would be the same, no matter how calculated.

The long-run effect on profit

4.6   **In the long run, total profit for a company will be the same whether marginal costing or absorption costing is used.** Different accounting conventions merely affect the profit of individual accounting periods.

4.7   EXAMPLE: COMPARISON OF TOTAL PROFITS

To illustrate this point, let us suppose that a company makes and sells a single product. At the beginning of period 1, there are no opening stocks of the product, for which the variable production cost is £4 and the sales price £6 per unit. Fixed costs are £2,000 per period, of which £1,500 are fixed production costs.

	Period 1	Period 2
Sales	1,200 units	1,800 units
Production	1,500 units	1,500 units

Required

Determine the profit in each period using the following methods of costing.

(a) Absorption costing. Assume normal output is 1,500 units per period.
(b) Marginal costing.

4.8   SOLUTION

(a) **Absorption costing**: the absorption rate for fixed production overhead is

$$\frac{£1,500}{1,500 \text{ units}} = £1 \text{ per unit}$$

	Period 1		Period 2		Total	
	£	£	£	£	£	£
Sales		7,200		10,800		18,000
Production costs						
Variable	6,000		6,000		12,000	
Fixed	1,500		1,500		3,000	
	7,500		7,500		15,000	
Add opening stock b/f	-		1,500			
	7,500		9,000			
Less closing stock c/f	1,500		-		-	
Production cost of sales	6,000		9,000		15,000	
Other costs	500		500		1,000	
Total cost of sales		6,500		9,500		16,000
Unadjusted profit		700		1,300		2,000
(Under-)/over-absorbed overhead		-		-		-
Profit		700		1,300		2,000

(b) **Marginal costing**

	Period 1		Period 2		Total	
	£	£	£	£	£	£
Sales		7,200		10,800		18,000
Variable production cost	6,000		6,000		12,000	
Add opening stock b/f	-		1,200			
	6,000		7,200			
Less closing stock c/f	1,200		-		-	
Variable production cost						
of sales		4,800		7,200		12,000
Contribution		2,400		3,600		6,000
Fixed costs		2,000		2,000		4,000
Profit		400		1,600		2,000

Notes

(a) **The total profit over the two periods is the same for each method of costing, but the profit in each period is different.**

(b) In absorption costing, fixed production overhead of £300 is carried forward from period 1 into period 2 in stock values, and becomes a charge to profit in period 2. In marginal costing all fixed costs are charged in the period they are incurred, therefore the profit in period 1 is £300 lower and in period 2 is £300 higher than the absorption costing profit.

5 RECONCILING THE PROFIT FIGURES GIVEN BY THE TWO METHODS

5.1 **The difference in profits reported under the two costing systems is due to the different stock valuation methods used.**

5.2 **If stock levels increase between the beginning and end of a period, absorption costing will report the higher profit.** This is because some of the fixed production overhead incurred during the period will be carried forward in closing stock (which reduces cost of sales) to be set against sales revenue in the following period instead of being written off in full against profit in the period concerned.

5.3 **If stock levels decrease, absorption costing will report the lower profit** because as well as the fixed overhead incurred, fixed production overhead which had been carried forward in opening stock is released and is also included in cost of sales.

5.4 EXAMPLE: RECONCILING PROFITS

The profits reported under absorption costing and marginal costing for period 1 in the example in Paragraph 4.7 would be reconciled as follows.

	£
Marginal costing profit	400
Adjust for fixed overhead in stock:	
Stock increase of 300 units × £1 per unit	300
Absorption costing profit	700

Question 2

Reconcile the profits reported under the two systems for period 2 of the example in Paragraph 4.7.

Answer

	£
Marginal costing profit	1,600
Adjust for fixed overhead in stock:	
Stock decrease of 300 units × £1 per unit	(300)
Absorption costing profit	1,300

---

6 MARGINAL COSTING VERSUS ABSORPTION COSTING - WHICH IS BETTER?

6.1 There are accountants who favour each costing method.

(a) **Arguments in favour of absorption costing are as follows**.

    (i) Fixed production costs are incurred in order to make output; it is therefore 'fair' to charge all output with a share of these costs.

    (ii) Closing stock values, by including a share of fixed production overhead, will be valued on the principle required for the financial accounting valuation of stocks by SSAP 9.

    (iii) A problem with calculating the contribution of various products made by a company is that it may not be clear whether the contribution earned by each product is enough to cover fixed costs, whereas by charging fixed overhead to a product we can decide whether it is profitable or not.

    (iv) Where stock building is necessary, such as in fireworks manufacture, fixed costs should be included in stock valuations otherwise a series of losses will be shown in earlier periods, to be offset eventually by excessive profits when the goods are sold.

(b) **Arguments in favour of marginal costing are as follows**.

    (i) It is simple to operate.

    (ii) There are no apportionments, which are frequently done on an arbitrary basis, of fixed costs. Many costs, such as the managing director's salary, are indivisible by nature.

    (iii) Fixed costs will be the same regardless of the volume of output, because they are period costs. It makes sense, therefore, to charge them in full as a cost to the period.

    (iv) The cost to produce an extra unit is the variable production cost. It is realistic to value closing stock items at this directly attributable cost.

    (v) As we have seen, the size of total contribution varies directly with sales volume at a constant rate per unit. For management purposes, better information about expected profit is obtained from the use of variable costs and contribution in the accounting system.

    (vi) It is also argued that absorption costing gives managers the wrong signals. Goods are produced, not to meet market demand, but to absorb allocated overheads. Production in excess of demand in fact increases the overheads (for example warehousing) the organisation must bear.

    (vii) Under- or over-absorption of overheads is avoided.

    (viii) **It is a great aid to decision making, especially when a particular resource is limited**, as we shall see in Section 7. **Absorption costing information is not really appropriate for decision making**.

7   INTRODUCTION TO DECISION MAKING   *6/96, 6/97, 12/98*

7.1   There is one particular situation where marginal costing principles are used as opposed to absorption costing principles. This is when we are dealing with a **scarce resource**.

7.2   What is a scarce resource? We are all affected by scarce resources in our lives. Everyday examples include the following: time; money; and sleep.

We are more likely to say that we don't have enough money, rather than say 'for me, money is a scarce resource'.

7.3   The scarce resource is known as a **limiting factor** or a **key factor** since it limits how we pass our time, or how we spend our money. We all have to make decisions regarding how best to use any scarce resource.

7.4   A manufacturing company, may have a number of possible limiting factors.

- Sales, if there is a limit to sales demand.
- Labour hours, if these are insufficient to meet the level of production demanded.
- Materials, if these are insufficient to meet the level of production demanded.

7.5   If there are insufficient resources to make everything, management is faced with the problem of deciding which products to produce by considering the limiting factors.

7.6   **In limiting factor analysis, it is assumed that management wishes to maximise profit. Profit will be maximised when contribution is maximised** (given that fixed cost do not change). This is where marginal costing principles are applied.

7.7   If materials are the limiting factor, contribution will be maximised by earning the biggest contribution from each kg of material. Similarly, if labour hours are the limiting factor, contribution will be maximised by earning the biggest contribution from each labour hour worked.

7.8   Therefore the **limiting factor decision** involves calculating the contribution earned from each unit of the limiting factor, for each different product.

7.9   EXAMPLE: LIMITING FACTOR

ER Ltd makes two products, the Greene and the Ross. Unit variable costs are as follows.

	Greene	*Ross*
	£	£
Direct materials	1	3
Direct labour (£3 per hour)	6	3
Variable overhead	1	1
	8	7

The sales price per unit is £14 per Greene and £11 per Ross. During July 20X6 the available direct labour is limited to 8,000 hours. Sales demand in July is expected to be 3,000 units for Greenes and 5,000 units for Rosses.

Required

Determine the profit-maximising production mix, assuming that monthly fixed costs are £20,000, and that opening stocks of finished goods and work in progress are nil.

7.10 SOLUTION

(a) The first step in the solution is to confirm that the limiting factor is something other than sales demand.

	Greene	Ross	Total
Labour hours per unit	2 hrs	1 hr	
Sales demand	3,000 units	5,000 units	
Labour hours needed	6,000 hrs	5,000 hrs	11,000 hrs
Labour hours available			8,000 hrs
Shortfall			3,000 hrs

Labour is the limiting factor on production.

(b) The second step is to identify the contribution earned by each product per unit of limiting factor, that is per labour hour worked.

	Greene £	Ross £
Sales price	14	11
Variable cost	8	7
Unit contribution	6	4
Labour hours per unit	2 hrs	1 hr
Contribution per labour hour (= unit of limiting factor)	£3	£4

Although Greenes have a higher unit contribution than Rosses, two Rosses can be made in the time it takes to make one Greene. Because labour is in short supply it is more profitable to make Rosses than Greenes.

(c) The final stage in the solution is to work out the budgeted production and sales mix. Sufficient Rosses will be made to meet the full sales demand, and the remaining labour hours available will then be used to make Greenes.

Product	Demand	Hours required	Hours available	Priority of manufacture
Ross	5,000	5,000	5,000	1st
Greene	3,000	6,000	3,000 (bal)	2nd
		11,000	8,000	

Product	Units	Hours needed	Contribution per unit £	Total £
Ross	5,000	5,000	4	20,000
Greene	1,500	3,000	6	9,000
		8,000		29,000
Less fixed costs				20,000
Profit				9,000

7.11 In conclusion.

(a) Unit contribution is *not* the correct way to decide priorities.

(b) Labour hours are the scarce resource, and therefore **contribution per labour hour** is the correct way to decide priorities.

(c) The Ross earns £4 contribution per labour hour, and the Greene earns £3 contribution per labour hour. Rosses therefore make more profitable use of the scarce resource, and should be manufactured first.

Other considerations regarding limiting factors

7.12 The following points should also be borne in mind when making a decision which involves limiting factors.

(a) In the long run management should seek to remove the limiting factor.

(b) In the short term management may be able to find ways around the limiting factor (such as overtime working and sub-contracting).

(c) It may not be easy to identify the limiting factor.

Chapter roundup

- In your examination you may be asked to calculate the profit for an accounting period using either of the two methods of accounting. **Absorption costing** is most often used for routine profit reporting and must be used for financial accounting purposes. **Marginal costing** provides better management information for planning and decision making.

- **Marginal cost** is the variable cost of one unit of product or service.

- **Contribution** is an important measure in marginal costing, and it is calculated as the difference between sales value and marginal or variable cost.

- **In marginal costing, fixed production costs are treated as period costs** and are written off as they are incurred. **In absorption costing, fixed production costs are absorbed into the cost of units** and are carried forward in stock to be charged against sales for the next period. Stock values using absorption costing are therefore greater than those calculated using marginal costing.

- **Reported profit figures** using marginal costing or absorption costing will differ if there is any change in the level of stocks in the period. If production is equal to sales, there will be no difference in calculated profits using these costing methods.

- **SSAP 9** recommends the use of absorption costing for the valuation of stocks in financial accounts.

- There are a number of arguments both for and against each of the costing systems.

- The distinction between marginal costing and absorption costing is very important and it is vital that you now understand the contrast between the two systems. We have seen how marginal costing principles inform basic decision making. This is a topic which will be expanded greatly in the Professional Stage of your studies.

Quick quiz

1 What is marginal costing? (see key terms)

2 What is a period cost in marginal costing? (key terms)

3 Define contribution. (key terms)

4 What is a breakeven point? (3.5)

5 What is the main difference between marginal costing and absorption costing? (4.1)

6 If opening and closing stock volumes and values are the same, does absorption costing or marginal costing give the higher profit? (4.5)

7 What are the arguments for and against the use of marginal costing? (6.1)

8 What is a limiting factor? (7.3)

Question to try	Level	Marks	Time
9	Examination	14	25 mins

Part C
Costing methods

Chapter 10

COST BOOKKEEPING

Chapter topic list	Syllabus reference
1 Accounting for costs	CA 1(b)(i)
2 Interlocking systems	CA 1(b)(i),(ii)
3 Interlocking systems: the cost ledger and financial	
ledger compared	CA 1(b)(i),(ii)
4 Integrated systems	CA 1(b)(i),(ii)

Introduction

You now know how to determine the major elements of the cost of a unit of product - **material**, **labour**, **overhead** - and how to build these elements up into a cost unit. What you don't know is how to account for these costs within the parameters of the costing method used by an organisation. This chapter will teach you the first step, which is **cost bookkeeping**.

The overall bookkeeping routine will vary from organisation to organisation but either an **integrated** or an **interlocking** system will be used. We will be looking at each of these systems in detail, seeing how to record costs in them and how the two systems differ.

1   ACCOUNTING FOR COSTS

1.1   There are **no statutory requirements** to keep detailed cost records. Some small firms only keep traditional financial accounts and prepare cost information in an ad-hoc fashion. This approach is, however, unsatisfactory for all but the smallest organisations: most firms therefore maintain some form of cost accounting system.

1.2   **Cost accounting systems** range from simple analysis systems to computer based accounting systems. Often systems are tailored to the users' requirements and therefore incorporate unique features. All systems will incorporate a number of common aspects and all records will be maintained using the principles of double entry.

Control accounts

1.3   Cost accounting systems keep the following types of information.

- Value of individual stock items
- Cost of individual products or jobs
- Total costs, which are recorded in control accounts

> **KEY TERM**
>
> A **control account** is an account which records total cost, whereas individual debits and credits are posted to individual ledger accounts.

1.4 Examples of control account include the following.

(a) **Stores control account** (recording total cost of materials in stock and material issues)

(b) **Wages control account** (recording how total wage costs are charged to work in progress, or to production overheads)

(c) **Work in progress control account** (recording the total cost of production, and transfers to finished goods stock control account)

Interlocking and integrated systems

1.5 Recording cost transactions using the self-balancing double entry method of a debit and credit entry for each transaction may be achieved in either of the following ways.

> **KEY TERMS**
>
> • **Interlocking systems.** Separate ledger accounts are kept for both the cost accounting function and the financial accounting function, which necessitates the reconciliation of the profits produced by the separate profit and loss accounts.
>
> • **Integrated systems.** The cost accounting function and the financial accounting function are combined in one system of ledger accounts.

1.6 In interlocking systems, the cost accounts use the same basic data (purchases, wages and so on) as the financial accounts, but frequently adopt different bases for items such as depreciation and stock valuation.

1.7 In integrated systems, the same basis for items such as stock valuation and depreciation will be used and there is no need for a reconciliation between cost profit and financial profit. Financial profit will simply be the cost profit adjusted by non-cost items such as income from investments and charitable donations.

1.8 The principles of double entry bookkeeping are not described in this chapter, but if you have not yet begun your studies of basic financial accounting, you may not be familiar with the concept of 'debits and credits'. Nevertheless you may still be able to follow the explanations below, provided that you remember the **'golden rule' of double entry bookkeeping, that for every entry made in one account, there must be a corresponding balancing entry in another account.**

2   INTERLOCKING SYSTEMS   *6/96, 6/99, 12/99*

> **Exam focus point**
> Parts of questions in the 6/96, 6/99 and 12/99 exams required candidates to complete the cost accounts for a period.

2.1 **The principal accounts in a system of interlocking accounts**

(a) The resources accounts

- Materials control account or stores control account
- Wages (and salaries) control account
- Production overhead control account
- Administration overhead control account
- Selling and distribution overhead control account

(b) Accounts which record the cost of production items from the start of production work through to cost of sales

- Work in progress control account
- Finished goods control account
- Cost of sales control account

(c) Sales account

(d) The costing profit and loss account

(e) The under-/ over-absorbed overhead account

(f) Cost ledger control account (in the cost ledger)

(g) Financial ledger control account (in the financial ledger)

How an interlocking system works

2.2 An **interlocking system** features two ledgers.

(a) The **financial ledger** contains asset, liability, revenue, expense and appropriation (eg dividend) accounts. It is from this ledger that the trial balances is prepared.

(b) The **cost ledger,** is where cost information such as the build-up of work in progress is analysed in more detail.

The cost ledger control account

2.3 There are certain items of cost or revenue which are of no interest to the cost accountant because they are **financial accounting items**. These include the following.

- Interest or dividends received
- Dividends paid
- Discounts allowed or received for prompt payment of invoices

2.4 Some financial accounting items are related to costs and profits, and are of interest to the cost accountant. These items include the following.

- Cash
- Creditors
- Debtors
- Profit and loss reserves

The items listed are *not* included in the separate cost accounting books, but are held in a **cost ledger control account.**

2.5 The **financial ledger control account** is a sort of 'dustbin' account which is used to keep the double entry system working.

BPP PUBLISHING

Accounting entries in a system of cost ledger accounts

2.6   The accounting entries in a system of cost ledger accounts can be confusing and it is important to keep in mind some general principles.

(a)   When **expenditure** is incurred on materials, wages or overheads, the actual amounts paid or payable are debited to the appropriate resources accounts. The credit entries (which in a financial accounting ledger would be in the cash or creditors accounts) are in the cost ledger control account.

(b)   When production begins, **resources are allocated to work in progress**. This is recorded by crediting the resources accounts and debiting the work in progress account. In the case of production overheads, the amount credited to the overhead account and debited to work in progress should be the amount of overhead absorbed. If this differs from the amount of overhead incurred, there will be a difference on the overhead control account; this should be written off to an 'under-/over-absorbed overhead' account. (One other point to remember is that when indirect materials and labour are allocated to production, the entries are to credit the materials and wages accounts and debit production overhead account.)

(c)   As **finished goods** are produced, work in progress is reduced. This is recorded by debiting the finished goods control account and crediting the work in progress control account.

(d)   To establish the **cost of goods sold**, the balances on finished goods control account, administration overhead control account and selling and distribution overhead control account are transferred to cost of sales control account. For a company with a full absorption costing system, the transfers from administration overhead and selling and distribution overhead accounts would be the amounts absorbed, rather than the amounts incurred. Any difference would again be written off to an 'under-/over-absorbed overhead' account.

(e)   **Sales** are debited to the cost ledger control account and credited to sales account.

(f)   **Profit** is established by transferring to the cost profit and loss account the balances on sales account, cost of sales account and under-/over-absorbed overhead accounts.

Accounting entries in absorption costing and marginal costing systems

2.7   The principles outlined above are illustrated for absorption costing and marginal costing systems in the diagrams on the following pages.

Points to note

2.8   (a)   In both diagrams the direct and indirect materials figures, and the direct and indirect labour figures, are extracted from the materials and wages analyses respectively.

(b)   In the diagram of an absorption costing system, the debit in respect of overheads to the WIP account is the absorbed overheads and is found by multiplying the total units of the basis for absorption (labour hours, machines hours and so on) for the period by the overhead absorption rate. For example, if 10,000 direct labour hours were booked to cost units and the overhead absorption rate was £2 per direct labour hour, then £20,000 would be debited to the WIP account for overheads.

(c)   In the diagram of the marginal costing system, only the variable overheads are debited to the WIP account. Fixed overheads are debited direct to the costing profit and loss account.

(d) In the absorption costing diagram, selling and distribution overheads are *not* included in the charges to the WIP account. As these overheads are incurred at the time of sale and delivery, they are charged to the profit and loss account in the same period as the sales to which they relate are credited. In the marginal costing diagram, selling and distribution overheads, both variable and fixed, are deducted after contribution.

(e) The final balance on the overhead account of the absorption costing system is the under- or over-absorbed overhead. There will be no such balance under a marginal costing system.

(f) The closing balances on the WIP and finished goods accounts under absorption costing will be at absorbed cost, but will be at marginal cost under marginal costing.

(g) Our diagrams are highly simplified versions of the full set of cost accounts used in practice.

2.9 EXAMPLE: INTERLOCKING ACCOUNTS

Write up the cost ledger accounts of a manufacturing company for the latest accounting period. The following data is relevant.

(a) There is no stock on hand at the beginning of the period.

(b) Details of the transactions for the period received from the financial accounts department include the following.

	£
Sales	420,000
Indirect wages:	
production	25,000
administration	15,000
sales and distribution	20,000
Materials purchased	101,000
Direct factory wages	153,200
Production overheads	46,500
Selling and distribution expenses	39,500
Administration expenses	32,000

(c) Other cost data for the period includes the following.

Stores issued to production as indirect materials	£15,000
Stores issued to production as direct materials	£77,000
Cost of finished production	£270,200
Cost of goods sold at finished goods stock valuation	£267,700
Standard rate of production overhead absorption	50p per operating hour
Rate of administration overhead absorption	20% of production cost of sales
Rate of sales and distribution overhead absorption	10% of sales revenue
Actual operating hours worked	160,000

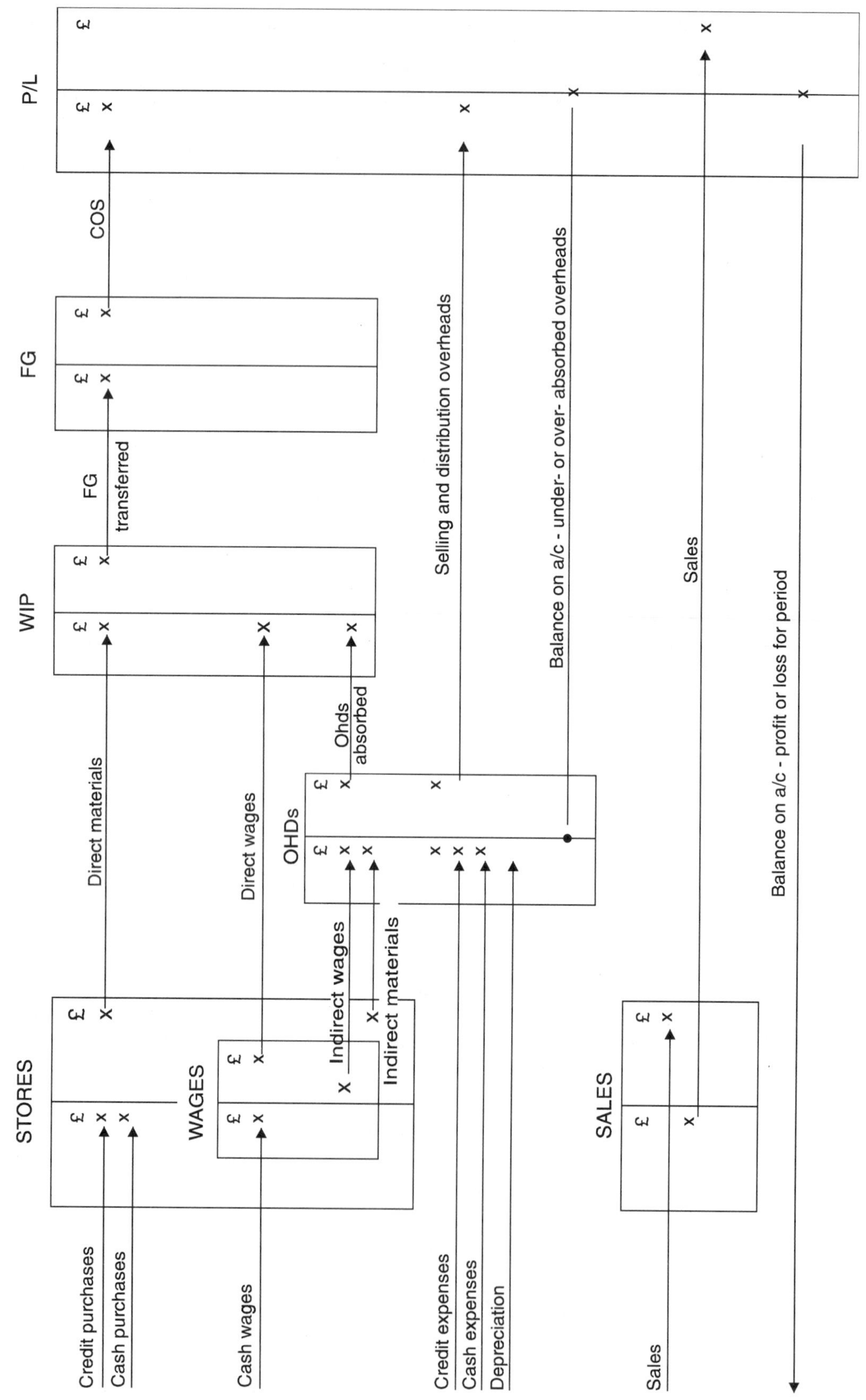

Cost accounting using absorption costing

Cost accounting using marginal costing

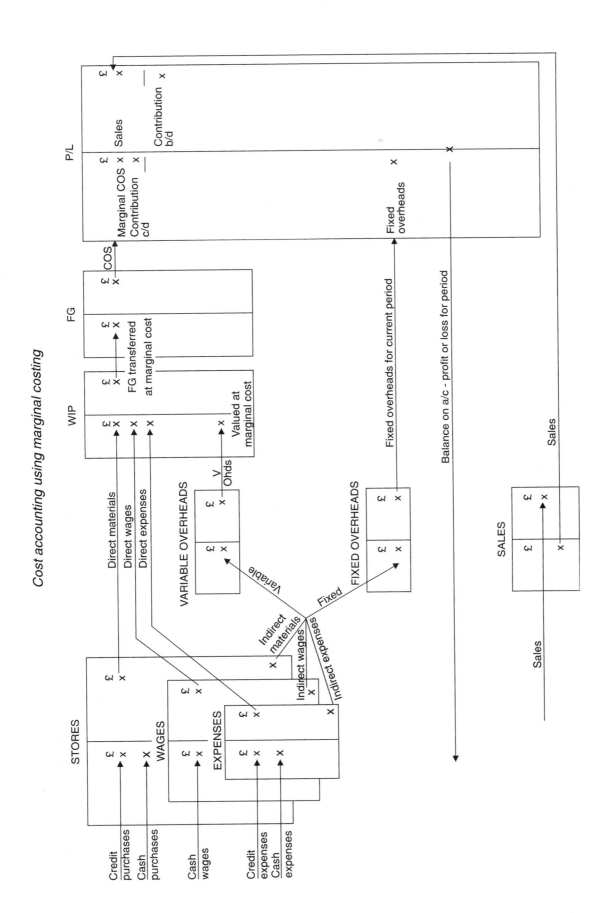

2.10 SOLUTION

The problem should be tackled methodically, in the order suggested by paragraph 2.6 above. The letters in brackets show the sequence in which the various entries are made. Any entries without a letter are merely transfers of closing balances.

COST LEDGER CONTROL (CLC)

	£		£
Sales (a)	420,000	Wages control (b)	213,200
Balance c/d	51,500	Materials control (c)	101,000
		Prod'n o'hd control (d)	46,500
		S & D o'hd control (e)	39,500
		Admin o'hd control (f)	32,000
		Cost profit and loss a/c	39,300
	471,500		471,500
		Balance b/d	51,500

MATERIALS CONTROL

	£		£
CLC (c) - purchases	101,000	Prod'n o'hd control (k)(indirect materials)	15,000
		WIP control (l)(issues to production)	77,000
		∴Closing stock c/d (balancing item)	9,000
	101,000		101,000
Closing stock b/d	9,000		

WAGES CONTROL

	£		£
CLC (b)	213,200	Prod'n o'hd control (g)	25,000
		Admin o'hd control (h)	15,000
		S & D o'hd control (j)	20,000
		WIP control (m)(direct labour)	153,200
	213,200		213,200

PRODUCTION OVERHEAD CONTROL

	£		£
CLC (d)	46,500	WIP control (p)(160,000 × 50p)	
Wages control (g)	25,000	(overheads absorbed)	80,000
Materials control (k)	15,000	∴ O'hds under-absorbed	6,500
	86,500		86,500

ADMINISTRATION OVERHEAD CONTROL

	£		£
CLC (f)	32,000	Cost of sales control (q)	
Wages control (h)	15,000	(20% × £267,700)	53,540
∴ O'hds over-absorbed	6,540		
	53,540		53,540

SELLING AND DISTRIBUTION OVERHEAD CONTROL

	£		£
CLC (e)	39,500	Cost of sales control (r)(o/hds	
Wages control (j)	20,000	absorbed) (10% × £420,000)	42,000
		∴ O'hds under-absorbed	17,500
	59,500		59,500

WORK IN PROGRESS CONTROL

	£		£
Materials control (l)	77,000	Finished goods control (n)	270,200
Wages control (m)	153,200	(transfer of finished production)	
Prod'n o'hd control (p)	80,000	∴ Closing stock of WIP c/d	40,000
	310,200		310,200
Balance b/d	40,000		

FINISHED GOODS CONTROL

	£		£
WIP control (n)	270,200	Cost of sales control (o)	267,700
		∴ Stock of finished goods c/d	2,500
	270,200		270,200
Balance b/d	2,500		

COST OF SALES CONTROL

	£		£
Finished goods control (o)	267,700	Cost profit and loss a/c	363,240
Admin o'hd control (q)	53,540		
S & D o'hd control (r)	42,000		
	363,240		363,240

SALES

	£		£
Cost profit and loss a/c	420,000	CLC (a)	420,000

UNDER-/OVER-ABSORBED OVERHEAD

	£		£
Prod'n o'hd control	6,500	Admin o'hd control	6,540
S & D o'hd control	17,500	∴ Cost profit and loss a/c	17,460
	24,000		24,000

COST PROFIT AND LOSS

	£		£
Cost of sales control	363,240	Sales	420,000
Under-/over-absorbed o'hd	17,460		
CLC (profit for period)	39,300		
	420,000		420,000

Note how the trial balance can be extracted from the accounts.

TRIAL BALANCE

	Debit £	Credit £
Cost ledger control		51,500
Materials stock	9,000	
Work in progress	40,000	
Finished goods stocks	2,500	
	51,500	51,500

Question 1

Ten Days Early Ltd is a company which operates an interlocking cost accounting system, which is not integrated with the financial accounts. At the beginning of February 20X1, the opening balances in the cost ledger were as follows.

	£
Stores ledger control account	36,400
Work in progress control account	23,000
Finished goods control account	15,700
Cost ledger control account	75,100

During February 20X1 the following transactions took place.

	£
Materials purchased	28,700
Materials issued to:	
Production	21,300
Service departments	4,200
Gross factory wages paid	58,900

Of these gross wages, £19,500 were indirect wages.

	£
Production overheads incurred (excluding the items shown above)	1,970
Raw material stocks written off, damaged	1,200
Selling overheads incurred and charged to cost of sales	10,500
Sales	88,000
Material and labour cost of goods sold	52,800

At the end of February 20X1 stocks of work in progress were £7,640 higher than at the beginning of the month. The company operates a marginal costing system.

Required

Prepare the control accounts and costing profit and loss account which would record these transactions in February 20X1.

Answer

The company operates a marginal costing system and hence production overhead is not included in the value of WIP or finished goods but it treated as a period cost and written off directly to the profit and loss account.

(a)
COST LEDGER CONTROL ACCOUNT (CLC)

	£		£
Sales account (h)	88,000	Opening balance b/f	75,100
Profit and loss account (j)	2,170	Stores ledger control (b)	28,700
Closing balance c/f	85,000	Factory wages control (c)	58,900
		Production overhead control (d)	1,970
		Selling overheads control (g)	10,500
	175,170		175,170
		Opening balance b/f	85,000

(b)
STORES LEDGER CONTROL ACCOUNT

	£		£
Opening balance b/f	36,400	WIP control (e)	21,300
Purchases - CLC (a)	28,700	Production overhead control (d)	4,200
		Profit and loss account (stock written off) (j)	1,200
		Closing balance c/f	38,400
	65,100		65,100
Balance b/f	38,400		

(c)
FACTORY WAGES CONTROL ACCOUNT

	£		£
Gross wages - CLC (a)	58,900	WIP control (balancing figure(e)	39,400
		Production overhead control (d)	19,500
	58,900		58,900

(d)
PRODUCTION OVERHEAD CONTROL ACCOUNT

	£		£
Stores ledger control (b)	4,200	Profit and loss account	
Factory wages control (c)	19,500	(balancing figure)(j)	25,670
Other costs - CLC (a)	1,970		
	25,670		25,670

(e)

WORK IN PROGRESS (WIP) CONTROL ACCOUNT

	£		£
Opening balance b/f	23,000	Finished goods control (f)	53,060
Stores ledger control (b)	21,300	(balancing figure)	
Factory wages control (c)	39,400	Closing balance c/f	
		(23,000 + 7,640)	30,640
	83,700		83,700
Balance b/f	30,640		

(f)

FINISHED GOODS CONTROL ACCOUNT

	£		£
Opening balance b/f	15,700	Cost of sales (i)	52,800
WIP control (e)	53,060	Closing balance c/f	15,960
	68,760		68,760
Balance b/f	15,960		

(g)

SELLING OVERHEAD CONTROL ACCOUNT

	£		£
CLC (a)	10,500	Cost of sales a/c (i)	10,500

(h)

SALES ACCOUNT

	£		£
Profit and loss a/c (j)	88,000	CLC - sales (a)	88,000

(i)

COST OF SALES ACCOUNT

	£		£
Finished goods control (f)	52,800	Profit and loss a/c (j)	63,300
Selling overhead control (g)	10,500		
	63,300		63,300

(j)

COSTING PROFIT AND LOSS ACCOUNT

	£		£
Cost of sales account (i)	63,300	Sales account (h)	88,000
Production overhead (d)	25,670	Loss (balance) CLC (a)	2,170
Stores ledger control -			
stock written off (b)	1,200		
	90,170		90,170

TRIAL BALANCE AS AT 28 FEBRUARY 20X1
(not required by the question)

	£	£
Cost ledger control account		85,000
Stores ledger control account	38,400	
Work in progress control account	30,640	
Finished goods control account	15,960	
	85,000	85,000

3 INTERLOCKING SYSTEMS: THE COST LEDGER AND FINANCIAL LEDGER COMPARED

3.1 **If separate cost accounts and financial accounts are maintained, the cost profit will not be the same as the financial profit** (because different profit and loss accounts are prepared). Cost profit and financial profit will therefore need to be reconciled.

3.2 Some examples of items creating differences between the cost accounting and financial accounting profits are listed as follows.

(a) **Items appearing in the financial accounts, but not in the cost accounts.**

(i) Items of income which boost the financial accounts profit, but are excluded from the cost accounts.

- Interest or dividends received
- Discounts received (for early settlement of debts)
- Profits on disposal of fixed assets

(ii) Items of expenditure which reduce the financial accounts profit, but which are excluded from the cost accounts.

- Interest paid
- Discounts allowed (for early settlement of debt)
- Losses on disposal of fixed assets
- Losses on investments
- Fines and penalties

(iii) Items of expenditure which are capitalised as assets in the financial accounts, for example development costs.

(iv) Appropriations of profit in the financial profit and loss account.
- Donations
- Income tax
- Dividends paid and proposed
- Transfers to reserves
- Write-offs of goodwill, investments and other assets

(b) **Differences may arise between the financial and cost accounts in the calculation of actual overhead costs incurred.** For example if the cost accounting books contain a provision for depreciation account, differences may arise in the choice of depreciation method (for example straight line method, reducing balance method, and so on) or in the expected life of the equipment.

(c) **Valuation of stock on hand is likely to be made according to different bases for the respective accounts.** For the financial accounts the basis of stock valuation will be the lower of FIFO cost and net realisable value. For the cost accounts, the basis of stock valuation might be any one of the following.

- LIFO cost
- FIFO cost
- Weighted average cost
- Standard cost
- Replacement cost

Differences in stock valuations

3.3 Differences in stock valuations should be studied carefully. Suppose the financial accounting profit of a company is £10,000, and that the only differences between the financial books and the cost books are the following stock valuations.

	Financial accounts £	Cost accounts £
Opening stock of WIP	4,000	5,000
Closing stock of WIP	6,000	7,500
Opening stock of finished goods	12,000	10,000
Closing stock of finished goods	9,000	8,500

3.4 Opening and closing stock value differences will affect profit, and it may be helpful to use the format of a trading account to work out what the effect of a difference is. Consider the following trading account.

TRADING ACCOUNT

	£		£
Opening stock	10	Sales	100
Purchases	80	Closing stock	20
	90		
Gross profit (balancing figure)	30		
	120		120

This account shows the following.

(a) A higher figure for opening stock reduces profit.
(b) A higher figure for closing stock increases profit.

3.5 If this point is not clear, re-calculate the profit in the following circumstances.

(a) Opening stock is higher, say £15.
(b) Closing stock is higher, say £30.
(c) Opening stock is lower, say £8.
(d) Closing stock is lower, say £16.

The resulting profits, all other items on the account being unchanged, would be £25 (lower), £40 (higher), £32 (higher) and £26 (lower) for (a), (b), (c) and (d) respectively.

3.6 Let us go back to our example in Paragraph 3.3.

(a) Opening stock of WIP: the cost accounts profit will be £1,000 lower.
(b) Closing stock of WIP: the cost accounts profit will be £1,500 higher.
(c) Opening stock of finished goods: the cost accounts profit will be £2,000 higher.
(d) Closing stock of finished goods: the cost accounts profit will be £500 lower.

Question 2

Inspection of Elsewhere Ltd's financial and cost accounts has revealed the following.

Stock type	Financial accounts £	Cost accounts £
Raw materials - opening stock	5,191	4,862
Raw materials - closing stock	5,478	5,397
WIP - opening stock	8,898	8,910
WIP - closing stock	7,990	8,113
Finished goods - opening stock	12,566	12,723
Finished goods - closing stock	12,714	12,730

Required

Calculate the overall difference in financial ledger profit and cost ledger profit due to differences in stock valuations.

Answer

	£
Raw materials - opening stock (5,191 – 4,862)	329
Raw materials - closing stock (5,478 – 5,397)	(81)
WIP - opening stock (8,898 – 8,910)	(12)
WIP - closing stock (7,990 – 8,113)	123
Finished goods - opening stock (12,566 – 12,723)	(157)
Finished goods - closing stock (12,714 – 12,730)	16
	218

Stock valuation differences mean that the financial accounting profit is £218 lower than the cost accounting profit. (There may, of course, be other differences.)

---

4 INTEGRATED SYSTEMS 12/98

4.1 A system of **integrated accounts may be summarised as follows.**

(a) The financial and cost accounts are combined in one set of self-balancing ledger accounts.

(b) There is no need to operate cost ledger control accounts.

(c) There is no need to reconcile the respective cost and financial profits.

(d) The classifications used in the cost ledger are used in the integrated ledger.

(e) In addition to the classifications used in the cost ledger, the following ledger accounts would be required.

- Debtors' and creditors' control accounts.
- Bank account.
- Fixed asset accounts, subdivided into categories of assets (eg motor vehicles).
- Other assets and liabilities accounts.
- Share capital account, retained profit account and other reserve accounts.

4.2 You should be able to refer back to the earlier example of interlocking accounts entries and identify the differences which would appear in a set of integrated accounts.

The advantage and disadvantage of integrated systems

4.3 The **advantage** of integrated systems is the **saving in administrative effort**. Only one set of accounts needs to be maintained instead of two and the possible confusion arising from having two sets of accounts with different figures (eg for stock values and profits) does not exist.

4.4 The **disadvantage** of integrated accounts is that **one set of accounts is expected to fulfil two different purposes.**

- Stewardship of the business, and external reporting
- Provision of internal management information

4.5 At times, these different purposes may conflict; for example, the valuation of stocks will conform to the requirements of SSAP 9, whereas the cost accountants might have preferred, given their own choice, to value closing stocks at, say, marginal cost or replacement cost. In addition, the cost-coding of expenditures, to serve both financial accounting and cost accounting purposes, will be more complex and a double-purpose coding system (with longer numerical cost codes) will probably have to be used.

4.6 In practice however, computers have swept away these objections and most modern cost accounting systems are integrated systems.

4.7 EXAMPLE: INTEGRATED ACCOUNTS

Crediton Debbit Ltd manufactures a range of products which are sold through a network of wholesalers and dealers. A set of integrated accounts is kept, and for the year 20X0 the following information is relevant.

(a) Production overhead is absorbed into the cost of products on the basis of a budgeted rate of 80% of direct labour cost.

(b) Finished stocks are valued at factory cost.

(c)   The selling price to wholesalers and dealers includes a profit margin of 25% on actual production cost.

(d)

	31 March 20X0 £	30 April 20X0 £
Raw materials stock	17,200	15,160
Work in progress	5,600	4,750
Finished goods stock	10,500	12,090
Debtors for goods sold	9,200	11,140
Creditors for raw materials	7,600	9,420
Fixed assets at net book value	6,000	5,800

(e)   Bank transactions for the month of April 20X0 were as follows.

	£
Bank balance at 31 March	1,500
Receipts from debtors	27,560
Payments made	
Direct labour	6,400
Creditors for raw materials	8,960
Production overhead	5,200
Administration overhead	700
Selling and distribution overhead	2,300

Production overhead includes a monthly charge of £200 for depreciation and the opening balance on the production overhead control account each month is nil. Administration, selling and distribution overheads consist entirely of cash items.

Required

(a)   Use the information above to write up the following control accounts.

(i)   Raw materials stock
(ii)   Work in progress
(iii)   Finished goods
(iv)   Production overhead

(b)   Prepare the following statements.

(i)   A profit and loss account for the month of April 20X0
(ii)   A balance sheet as at 30 April 20X0

4.8   SOLUTION

(a)   (i)

RAW MATERIALS STOCK

	£		£
Opening balance	17,200	Work in progress	
Creditors (W3)	10,780	(balancing figure)	12,820
		Balance c/d	15,160
	27,980		27,980
Balance b/d	15,160		

(ii)

WORK IN PROGRESS

	£		£
Opening balance	5,600	Finished goods	
Raw materials stock	12,820	(balancing figure)	25,190
Direct wages	6,400		
Production overhead (W1)	5,120	Balance c/d	4,750
	29,940		29,940
Balance b/d	4,750		

(iii)   FINISHED GOODS

	£		£
Opening balance	10,500	Profit and loss account	
Work in progress	25,190	(Cost of sales)	23,600
		Balance c/d	12,090
	35,690		35,690
Balance b/d	12,090		

Check	£
Production cost of sales	23,600
Profit margin (add 25%)	5,900
Sales	29,500

(iv)   PRODUCTION OVERHEAD

	£		£
Cash	5,200	Work in progress	5,120
Depreciation	200	Profit and loss account	
		(under-absorbed)	280
	5,400		5,400

(b) (i)   PROFIT AND LOSS ACCOUNT
FOR THE MONTH OF APRIL 20X0

	£	£
Sales (W2)		29,500
Production cost of sales		23,600
Gross profit		5,900
Less: administration overhead	700	
sales and distribution overhead	2,300	
under-absorbed production overhead	280	
		3,280
Profit		2,620

(ii)   BALANCE SHEET AS AT 30 APRIL 20X0

	£	£
Fixed assets (net book value)		5,800
Current assets		
Raw materials	15,160	
Work in progress	4,750	
Finished goods	12,090	
Debtors	11,140	
Cash (W4)	5,500	
	48,640	
Less current liabilities		
Creditors	9,420	
		39,220
		45,020
Long-term capital £(42,400 (balancing figure)+ 2,620)		45,020

Workings

1 Direct labour	£6,400
Production overhead absorbed (80%)	£5,120

2   DEBTORS

	£		£
Opening balance	9,200	Cash	27,560
Sales (balancing figure)	29,500	Balance c/f	11,140
	38,700		38,700

3   CREDITORS FOR RAW MATERIALS

	£		£
Cash	8,960	Opening balance	7,600
Balance c/f	9,420	Raw materials purchases	
		(balancing figure)	10,780
	18,380		18,380

4   CASH

	£		£
Opening balance	1,500	Creditors for raw materials	8,960
Debtors	27,560	Direct labour	6,400
		Production overhead	5,200
		Administration overhead	700
		Sales and distribution o'hd	2,300
		Balance c/f	5,500
	29,060		29,060

Exam focus point

These were five marks available in the 12/98 exam for preparing the **materials control account** for a given month in a company's integrated accounting system.

Question 3

Liverpool Ltd operates a costing system which is fully integrated with the financial accounts. The cost clerk has provided you with the following information.

(a) Balances at beginning of month

	£
Stores ledger control account	24,175
Work in progress control account	19,210
Finished goods control account	34,164
Creditors control account	15,187
Prepayments of production overheads	
brought forward from previous month	2,100

(b) Information relating to events during the month

	£
Materials purchased	76,150
Materials issued from stores	29,630
Gross wages paid: direct workers	15,236
indirect workers	4,232
Recorded non-productive time of direct workers	5,230
Payments to creditors	58,320
Selling and distribution overheads incurred	5,240
Other production overheads incurred but not yet paid for	14,200
Sales	75,400
Cost of finished goods sold	59,830
Cost of goods completed and transferred into finished	
goods store during the month	62,130

(c) Balances at end of month

	£
Physical stock value of work in progress at month end	24,800

(d) The production overhead absorption rate is 150% of direct wages.

Required

Prepare the following accounts for the month.

(a)   Stores ledger control account
(b)   Work in progress control account
(c)   Finished goods control account
(d)   Production overhead control account
(e)   Creditors control account
(f)   Profit and loss account

Answer

(a)   STORES LEDGER CONTROL ACCOUNT

	£		£
Opening balance b/f	24,175	Work in progress control	
Creditors control		(materials issued)	29,630
(materials purchased)	76,150	Closing stock c/f	70,695
	100,325		100,325

(b)   WORK IN PROGRESS CONTROL ACCOUNT

	£		£
Opening balance b/f	19,210	Finished goods control	
Stores ledger account		(cost of goods transferred)	62,130
(materials issued)	29,630	Closing stock c/f	24,800
Wages control			
(direct wages)	15,236		
Production overhead control			
(overhead absorbed			
15,236 × 150%)	22,854		
	86,930		86,930

(c)   FINISHED GOODS CONTROL ACCOUNT

	£		£
Opening balance b/f	34,164	Profit and loss account	
Work in progress control		(cost of sales)	59,830
(cost of goods completed)	62,130	Closing stock c/f	36,464
	96,294		96,294

(d)   PRODUCTION OVERHEAD CONTROL ACCOUNT

	£		£
Prepayments b/f	2,100	Work in progress control	
Wages control (idle time		(overheads absorbed)	22,854
of direct workers)	5,230	Profit and loss account (under-	
Wages control (indirect		absorbed overhead) (bal.)	2,908
workers wages)	4,232		
Creditors control (other			
overheads incurred)	14,200		
	25,762		25,762

(e)   CREDITORS CONTROL ACCOUNT

	£		£
Cash account (payments)	58,320	Opening balance b/f	15,187
Creditors c/f	47,217	Stores ledger control	
		(materials purchased)	76,150
		Production overhead control	
		(other overheads)	14,200
	105,537		105,537

(f)

PROFIT AND LOSS ACCOUNT			
	£		£
Finished goods control (cost of goods sold)	59,830	Sales	75,400
Gross profit c/f	15,570		
	75,400		75,400
Selling and distribution overheads	5,240	Gross profit b/f	15,570
Production overhead control (under-absorbed overhead)	2,908		
Net profit c/f	7,422		
	15,570		15,570

Exam focus point

In the previous edition of this Study Text, it was noted that the Paper 3 examiner had stated that an entire question on cost bookkeeping may form part of the examination. Following on from a cost bookkeeping article published in the May 1999 edition of *Students' Newsletter* (written by the Paper 3 examiner himself) there was an entire cost bookkeeping question in the June 1999 examination. Make sure that you take the time to read *Students' Newsletter* and in particular, take note of any articles written by the examiner – they might provide you with some very useful tips!

Chapter roundup

- There are two types of cost accounting system - **interlocking** and **integrated**.

- **Interlocking** accounts contain **separate ledgers** for **cost accounts** and for **financial accounts**. A memorandum financial ledger control account is set up in the financial ledger. It does not form part of the double entry but merely details the data which will be analysed in further detail in the cost ledger. A **cost ledger control account** is maintained in the cost ledger to complete the costing double entry. It represents the financial ledger accounts which are not maintained in the cost ledger (such as cash, debtors and creditors).

- When an organisation operates an **interlocking accounts system**, it is necessary to reconcile the cost accounting profit with the financial accounting profit. Items which create differences between the cost accounting and financial accounting profits include stock valuations, profits and losses on disposal of fixed assets, interest paid and received and appropriations of profit.

- **Integrated systems** combine both financial and cost accounts in one system of ledger accounts. A reconciliation between cost and financial profits is not necessary with an integrated system.

Quick quiz

1   List the principal accounts in a system of interlocking accounts. (see para 2.1)

2   What is the double entry for the following?

(a)   Production overhead absorbed in the cost of production (2.6(b))
(b)   Completed work transferred to finished goods store (2.6(c))

3   List ten items which might appear in a reconciliation of cost accounting profit and financial accounting profit. (3.2)

4   What are the advantages and disadvantages of integrated accounts? (4.3, 4.4)

Question to try	Level	Marks	Time
10	Introductory	n/a	15 mins

Chapter 11

JOB, BATCH AND CONTRACT COSTING

Chapter topic list	Syllabus reference
1 Job costing	CA 3(a)(i),(ii)
2 Job costing for internal services	CA 3(a)(i)
3 Job costing example	CA 3(a)(ii)
4 Batch costing	CA 3(a)(i),(ii)
5 Introduction to contract costing	CA 3(a)(i)
6 Recording contract costs	CA 3(a)(ii)
7 Contract accounts	CA 3(a)(ii)
8 Progress payments	CA 3(a)(i), (ii)
9 Profits on contracts	CA 3(a)(iii)
10 Losses on incomplete contracts	CA 3(a)(iii)
11 Disclosure of long-term contracts in financial accounts	CA 3(a)(iii)

Introduction

Having learnt the basics of bookkeeping in the previous chapter, we will now apply these basics to particular costing methods.

A **costing method** is designed to suit the way goods are processed or manufactured or the way services are provided. Each organisation's costing method will therefore have unique features but costing methods of firms in the same line of business will more than likely have common aspects. On the other hand, organisations involved in completely different activities, such as hospitals and car part manufacturers, will use very different methods.

This chapter begins by covering **job costing**. We will see the circumstances in which job costing should be used and how the costs of jobs are calculated. We will look at how the **costing of individual jobs** fits in with the recording of total costs in control accounts. The chapter then moves on to **batch costing**, the procedure for which is similar to job costing.

The final costing method considered in this chapter is **contract costing**. Contract costing is similar to job costing but the job is of such importance that a formal contract is made between the supplier and the customer. We will see how to record contract costs, how to account for any profits and losses arising on contracts at the end of an accounting period and we will look briefly at how contract balances are disclosed in financial accounts.

BPP PUBLISHING

1   JOB COSTING

KEY TERMS

- A **job** is a cost unit which consists of a single order or contract.

- **Job costing** is a costing method applied where work is undertaken to customers' special requirements and each order is of comparatively short duration

1.1   The work relating to a job is usually carried out within a factory or workshop and moves through processes and operations as a **continuously identifiable unit**.

Procedure for the performance of jobs

1.2   The normal procedure which is adopted in jobbing concerns involves the following.

(a)   The prospective customer approaches the supplier and indicates the requirements of the job.

(b)   A responsible official sees the prospective customer and agrees with him the precise details of the items to be supplied, for example the quantity, quality, size and colour of the goods, the date of delivery and any special requirements.

(c)   The estimating department of the organisation then prepares an estimate for the job. This will include the cost of the materials to be used, the wages expected to be paid, the appropriate amount for factory, administration, selling and distribution overhead, the cost where appropriate of additional equipment needed specially for the job, and finally the supplier's profit margin. The total of these items will represent the quoted selling price.

(d)   At the appropriate time, the job will be 'loaded' on to the factory floor. This means that as soon as all materials, labour and equipment are available and subject to the scheduling of other orders, the job will be started. In an efficient organisation, the start of the job will be timed to ensure that while it will be ready for the customer by the promised date of delivery it will not be loaded too early, otherwise storage space will have to be found for the product until the date it is required by (and was promised to) the customer.

Collection of job costs

1.3   A separate record must be maintained to show the details of individual jobs. The process of collecting job costs may be outlined as follows.

(a)   **Materials requisitions are sent to stores.** Where a perpetual inventory system is maintained, an advance copy of the requisition is used to appropriate from free stock the relevant quantities of materials. The second copy of the requisition is sent as and when the materials are needed.

(b)   **The material requisition note will be used to cost the materials issued to the job** concerned, and this cost may then be recorded on a **job cost sheet**. The cost may include items already in stock and/or items specially purchased.

(c)   **The job ticket is passed to the worker who is to perform the first operation.** The times of his starting and finishing the operation are recorded on the ticket, which is then passed to the person who is to carry out the second operation, where a similar record of the times of starting and finishing is made.

(d) When the job is completed, the **job ticket is sent to the cost office,** where the time spent will be costed and recorded on the job cost sheet.

(e) The **relevant costs** of materials issued, direct labour performed and direct expenses incurred as recorded on the job cost sheet **are charged to the job account** in the work in progress ledger.

(f) **The job account is debited with the job's share of the factory overhead,** based on the absorption rate(s) in operation. If the job is incomplete at the end of an accounting period, it is valued at factory cost in the closing balance sheet (where a system of absorption costing is in operation).

(g) **On completion of the job,** the job account is charged with the appropriate administration, selling and distribution overhead, after which **the total cost of the job can be ascertained.**

(h) The difference between the agreed selling price and the total actual cost will be the supplier's profit (or loss).

Job cost sheet (or card)

1.4 An example of a job cost sheet is shown on page 196. Job cost sheets show the following.

- Detail of relatively small jobs.
- A summary of direct materials, direct labour and so on for larger jobs.

1.5 When jobs are completed, **job cost sheets** are transferred from the **work in progress** category to **finished goods**. When delivery is made to the customer, the costs become a **cost of sale**. If the completed job was carried out in order to build up finished goods stocks (rather than to meet a specific order) the quantity of items produced and their value are recorded on finished goods stores ledger cards.

Rectification costs

> **KEY TERM**
>
> **Rectification cost** is the cost incurred in rectifying sub-standard output.

1.6 If the finished output is found to be sub-standard, it may be possible to rectify the fault. The sub-standard output will then be returned to the department or cost centre where the fault arose. You should know how to deal with such costs in a job costing system.

1.7 **Rectification costs** can be treated in two ways.

(a) If rectification work is not a frequent occurrence, but arises on occasions with specific jobs to which it can be traced directly, then the rectification costs should be **charged as a direct cost to the jobs concerned.**

(b) If rectification is regarded as a normal part of the work carried out generally in the department, then the rectification costs should be **treated as production overheads.** This means that they would be included in the total of production overheads for the department and absorbed into the cost of all jobs for the period, using the overhead absorption rate.

JOB COST CARD

	Job No. B641

Customer	Mr J White	Customer's Order No.	Vehicle make	Peugot 205 GTE
Job Description	Repair damage to offside front door		Vehicle reg. no.	G 614 SOX
Estimate Ref. 2599		Invoice No.	Date to collect	14.6.X1
Quoted price £338.68		**Invoice price** £355.05		

Material / Labour / Overheads

Date	Req. No.	Qty.	Price	Cost £	Cost p	Date	Emp-loyee	Cost Ctre	Hrs.	Rate	Bonus	Cost £	Cost p	Hrs	OAR	Cost £	Cost p
12.6	36815	1	75.49	75	49	12.6	018	B	1.98	6.50	–	12	87	7.9	2.50	19	75
12.6	36816	1	33.19	33	19	13.6	018	B	5.92	6.50	–	38	48				
12.6	36842	5	6.01	30	05						13.65	13	65				
13.6	36881	5	3.99	19	95												
Total C/F				158	68	**Total C/F**						65	00	**Total C/F**		19	75

Expenses

Date	Ref.	Description	Cost £	Cost p
12.6	–	N. Jolley Panel-beating	50	–
Total C/F			50	–

Job Cost Summary

	Actual £	Actual p	Estimate £	Estimate p
Direct Materials B/F	158	68	158	68
Direct Expenses B/F	50	00		
Direct Labour B/F	65	00	180	00
Direct Cost	273	68		
Overheads B/F	19	75		
	293	43		
Admin overhead (add 10%)	29	34		
= Total Cost	322	77	338	68
Invoice Price	355	05		
Job Profit/Loss	32	28		

Comments

Job Cost Card Completed by -

Job costing and computerisation

1.8 **Job costing cards** exist in **manual** systems, but it is increasingly likely that in large organisations the job costing system will be **computerised**, using accounting software specifically designed to deal with job costing requirements. A computerised job accounting system is likely to contain the following features.

(a) Every job will be given a job code number, which will determine how the data relating to the job is stored.

(b) A separate set of codes will be given for the type of costs that any job is likely to incur. Thus, 'direct wages', say, will have the same code whichever job they are allocated to.

(c) In a sophisticated system, costs can be analysed both by job (for example all costs related to Job 456), but also by type (for example direct wages incurred on all jobs). It is thus easy to perform variance analysis and to make comparisons between jobs.

(d) A job costing system might have facilities built into it which incorporate other factors relating to the performance of the job. In complex jobs, sophisticated planning techniques might be employed to ensure that the job is performed in the minimum time possible. Time management features therefore may be incorporated into job costing software.

Cost plus pricing

1.9 The usual method of fixing selling prices within a jobbing concern is known as **cost plus pricing** where a desired profit margin is added to total costs to arrive at the selling price.

1.10 The **disadvantages** of cost plus pricing are as follows.

(a) There are no incentives to **control costs** as a profit is guaranteed.

(b) There is no motive to tackle **inefficiencies** or **waste**.

(c) It doesn't take into account any significant differences in actual and estimated volumes of activity. Since the overhead absorption rate is based upon estimated volumes, there may be **under-/over-absorbed overheads** not taken into account.

(d) Because overheads are apportioned in an arbitrary way, this may lead to **under and over pricing**.

1.11 The **cost plus system** is often adopted where **one-off jobs** are carried out to **customers' specifications**.

> ### Exam focus point
> An exam question about job costing may ask you to accumulate costs to arrive at a job cost, and then to determine a job price by adding a certain amount of profit. To do this, you need to remember the following crucial formula.
>
> | | % |
> |---|---|
> | Cost of job | 100 |
> | + profit | 25 |
> | = price | 125 |
>
> Profit may be expressed either as a percentage of job cost (such as 25% 25/100 mark up) or as a percentage of price (such as 20% (25/125) margin).

2 JOB COSTING FOR INTERNAL SERVICES

2.1 **Job costing systems** may be used to control the costs of **internal service departments,** eg the maintenance department. A job costing system enables the cost of a specific job to be charged to a user department. Therefore instead of apportioning the total costs of service departments, each job done is charged to the individual user department.

2.2 An **internal job costing system** for service departments will have the following advantages.

(a) **Realistic apportionment.** The identification of expenses with jobs and the subsequent charging of these to the department(s) responsible means that costs are borne by those who incurred them.

(b) **Increased responsibility and awareness.** User departments will be aware that they are charged for the specific services used and may be more careful to use the facility more efficiently. They will also appreciate the true cost of the facilities that they are using and can take decisions accordingly.

(c) **Control of service department costs.** The service department may be restricted to charging a standard cost to user departments for specific jobs carried out. It will then be possible to measure the efficiency or inefficiency of the service department by recording the difference between the standard charges and the actual expenditure.

(d) **Budget information.** This information will ease the budgeting process, as the purpose and cost of service department expenditure can be separately identified.

Question 1

Twist and Tern Ltd is a company that carries out jobbing work. One of the jobs carried out in February was job 1357, to which the following information relates.

Direct material Y:	400 kilos were issued from stores at a cost of £5 per kilo.
Direct material Z:	800 kilos were issued from stores at a cost of £6 per kilo. 60 kilos were returned.
Department P:	300 labour hours were worked, of which 100 hours were done in overtime.
Department Q:	200 labour hours were worked, of which 100 hours were done in overtime.

Overtime work is not normal in Department P, where basic pay is £4 per hour plus an overtime premium of £1 per hour. Overtime work was done in Department Q in February because of a request by the customer of another job to complete his job quickly. Basic pay in Department Q is £5 per hour and overtime premium is £1.50 per hour.

Department P had to carry out rectification work which took 20 hours in normal time. These 20 hours are additional to the 300 hours above. This rectification work is normal for a job such as job 1357, and since it was expected, it is included in the direct cost of the job.

Overhead is absorbed at the rate of £3 per direct labour hour in both departments.

Required

Calculate the following.

(a) The direct materials cost of job 1357
(b) The direct labour cost of job 1357
(c) The full production cost of job 1357

Answer

(a)

		£
Direct material Y (400 kilos × £5)		2,000
Direct material Z (800 – 60 kilos × £6)		4,440
Total direct material cost		6,440

(b)

		£
Department P (320 hours × £4)		1,280
Department Q (200 hours × £5)		1,000
Total direct labour cost		2,280

Rectification work, being normal and expected, is included in the direct labour cost of Department P. In Department P, overtime premium will be charged to overhead. In Department Q, overtime premium will be charged to the job of the customer who asked for overtime to be worked.

(c)

	£
Direct material cost	6,440
Direct labour cost	2,280
Production overhead (520 hours × £3)	1,560
	10,280

---

3 JOB COSTING EXAMPLE 12/98

3.1 An example may help to illustrate the principles of job costing, and the way in which the costing of individual jobs fits in with the recording of total costs in control accounts.

3.2 Fateful Morn Ltd is a jobbing company. On 1 June 20X2, there was one uncompleted job in the factory. The job card for this work is summarised as follows.

Job Card, Job No 6832

Costs to date	£
Direct materials	630
Direct labour (120 hours)	350
Factory overhead (£2 per direct labour hour)	240
Factory cost to date	1,220

During June, three new jobs were started in the factory, and costs of production were as follows.

Direct materials	£
Issued to: job 6832	2,390
job 6833	1,680
job 6834	3,950
job 6835	4,420
Damaged stock written off from stores	2,300

Material transfers	£
Job 6834 to job 6833	250
Job 6832 to 6834	620

Materials returned to store	£
From job 6832	870
From job 6835	170

Direct labour hours recorded

Job 6832	430 hrs
Job 6833	650 hrs
Job 6834	280 hrs
Job 6835	410 hrs

The cost of labour hours during June 20X2 was £3 per hour, and production overhead is absorbed at the rate of £2 per direct labour hour. Production overheads incurred during the month amounted to £3,800. Completed jobs were delivered to customers as soon as they were completed, and the invoiced amounts were as follows.

Job 6832	£5,500
Job 6834	£8,000
Job 6835	£7,500

Administration and marketing overheads are added to the cost of sales at the rate of 20% of factory cost. Actual costs incurred during June 20X2 amounted to £3,200.

Required

(a) Prepare the job accounts for each individual job during June 20X2; (the accounts should only show the cost of production, and not the full cost of sale).

(b) Prepare the summarised job cost cards for each job, and calculate the profit on each completed job.

(c) Show how the costs would be shown in the company's cost control accounts.

3.3 SOLUTION

(a) **Job accounts**

JOB 6832

	£		£
Balance b/f	1,220	Job 6834 a/c	620
Materials (stores a/c)	2,390	(materials transfer)	
Labour (wages a/c)	1,290	Stores a/c (materials returned)	870
Production overhead (o'hd a/c)	860	Cost of sales a/c (balance)	4,270
-	5,760		5,760

JOB 6833

	£		£
Materials (stores a/c)	1,680	Balance c/f	5,180
Labour (wages a/c)	1,950		
Production overhead (o'hd a/c)	1,300		
Job 6834 a/c (materials transfer)	250		
	5,180		5,180

JOB 6834

	£		£
Materials (stores a/c)	3,950	Job 6833 a/c (materials transfer)	250
Labour (wages a/c)	840		
Production overhead (o'hd a/c)	560	Cost of sales a/c (balance)	5,720
Job 6832 a/c (materials transfer)	620		
	5,970		5,970

JOB 6835

	£		£
Materials (stores a/c)	4,420	Stores a/c (materials returned)	170
Labour (wages a/c)	1,230		
Production overhead (o'hd a/c)	820	Cost of sales a/c (balance)	6,300
	6,470		6,470

(b) **Job cards, summarised**

	Job 6832	*Job 6833*	*Job 6834*	*Job 6835*
	£	£	£	
Materials	1,530*	1,930	4,320 **	4,250
Labour	1,640	1,950	840	1,230
Production overhead	1,100	1,300	560	820
Factory cost	4,270	5,180	(c/f) 5,720	6,300
Admin & marketing o'hd (20%)	854		1,144	1,260
Cost of sale	5,124		6,864	7,560
Invoice value	5,500		8,000	7,500
Profit/(loss) on job	376		1,136	(60)

* £(630 + 2,390 − 620 − 870)   ** £(3,950 + 620 − 250)

(c) **Control accounts**

STORES CONTROL (incomplete)

	£		£
WIP a/c (returns)	1,040	WIP a/c	
		(2,390 + 1,680 + 3,950 + 4,420)	12,440
		Profit and loss a/c:	
		stock written off	2,300

WORK IN PROGRESS CONTROL

	£		£
Balance b/f	1,220	Stores control a/c (returns)	1,040
Stores control a/c	12,440	Cost of sales a/c	
Wages control a/c	5,310	*(4,270 + 5,720 + 6,300)	16,290
Production o'hd control a/c	3,540	Balance c/f (Job No 6833)	5,180
	22,510		22,510

* 1,770 hours at £3 per hour

COST OF SALES CONTROL

	£		£
WIP control a/c	16,290	Profit and loss	19,548
Admin & marketing o'hd a/c			
(854 + 1,144 + 1,260)	3,258		
	19,548		19,548

SALES

	£		£
Profit and loss	21,000	CLC	21,000
		(5,500 + 8,000 + 7,500)	
	21,000		21,000

PRODUCTION OVERHEAD CONTROL

	£		£
CLC	3,800	WIP a/c	3,540
(overhead incurred)		Under-absorbed o'hd a/c	260
	3,800		3,800

UNDER-/OVER-ABSORBED OVERHEADS

	£		£
Production o'hd control a/c	260	Admin & marketing o'hd a/c	58
		Profit and loss a/c	202
	260		260

ADMIN & MARKETING OVERHEAD CONTROL

	£		£
CLC (overhead incurred)	3,200	Cost of sales a/c	3,258
Over absorbed o'hd a/c	58		
	3,258		3,258

PROFIT AND LOSS

	£		£
Cost of sales a/c	19,548	Sales a/c	21,000
Stores a/c (stock written off)	2,300		
Under-absorbed overhead a/c	202	Loss (CLC) - balance	1,050
	22,050		22,050

FINANCIAL LEDGER CONTROL (CLC) (incomplete)

	£		£
Sales a/c	21,000	Production overhead a/c	3,800
P & L a/c (loss)	1,050	Admin and marketing o'hd a/c	3,200

The loss of £1,050 is the sum of the profits/losses on each completed job £(376 + 1,136 - 60) = £1,452, minus the total of under-absorbed overhead (£202) and the stock write-off (£2,300).

Question 2

A furniture-making business manufactures quality furniture to customers' orders. It has three production departments (A, B and C) which have overhead absorption rates (per direct labour hour) of £12.86, £12.40 and £14.03 respectively.

Two pieces of furniture are to be manufactured for customers. Direct costs are as follows.

	Job XYZ	Job MNO
Direct material	£154	£108
Direct labour	20 hours dept A	16 hours dept A
	12 hours dept B	10 hours dept B
	10 hours dept C	14 hours dept C

Labour rates are as follows: £3.80(A); £3.50 (B); £3.40 (C)

The firm quotes prices to customers that reflect a required profit of 25% on selling price. Calculate the total cost and selling price of each job.

Answer

			Job XYZ £		Job MNO £
Direct material			154.00		108.00
Direct labour:	dept A	(20 × 3.80)	76.00	(16 × 3.80)	60.80
	dept B	(12 × 3.50)	42.00	(10 × 3.50)	35.00
	dept C	(10 × 3.40)	34.00	(14 × 3.40)	47.60
Total direct cost			306.00		251.40
Overhead:	dept A	(20 × 12.86)	257.20	(16 × 12.86)	205.76
	dept B	(12 × 12.40)	148.80	(10 × 12.40)	124.00
	dept C	(10 × 14.03)	140.30	(14 × 14.03)	196.42
Total cost			852.30		777.58
Profit (note)			284.10		259.19
Quoted selling price			1,136.40		1,036.77

(*Note.* If profit is 25% on selling price, this is the same as $33^{1}/3\%$ (25/75) on cost.)

4 BATCH COSTING 12/97

4.1 The procedures for **costing batches** are very similar to those for costing jobs.

(a) The batch is treated as a **job** during production and the costs are collected in the manner already described in this chapter.

(b) Once the batch has been completed, the **cost per unit** can be calculated as the **total batch cost divided by the number of units in the batch**.

4.2 EXAMPLE: BATCH COSTING

A company manufactures widgets to order and has the following budgeted overheads for the year, based on normal activity levels.

Department	Budgeted overheads £	Budgeted activity
Welding	6,000	1,500 labour hours
Assembly	10,000	1,000 labour hours

Selling and administrative overheads are 20% of factory cost. An order for 250 widgets type X128, made as Batch 5997, incurred the following costs.

Materials	£12,000
Labour	100 hours welding shop at £2.50/hour
	200 hours assembly shop at £1/hour

£500 was paid for the hire of special X-ray equipment for testing the welds.

Required

Calculate the cost per unit for Batch 5997.

4.3 SOLUTION

The first step is to calculate the overhead absorption rate for the production departments.

$$\text{Welding} = \frac{£6,000}{1,500} = £4 \text{ per labour hour}$$

$$\text{Assembly} = \frac{£10,000}{1,000} = £10 \text{ per labour hour}$$

Total cost - Batch no 5997

		£	£
Direct material			12,000
Direct expense			500
Direct labour	$100 \times 2.50 =$	250	
	$200 \times 1.00 =$	200	
			450
Prime cost			12,950
Overheads	$100 \times 4 =$	400	
	$200 \times 10 =$	2,000	
			2,400
Factory cost			15,350
Selling and administrative cost (20% of factory cost)			3,070
Total cost			18,420

$$\text{Cost per unit} = \frac{£18,420}{250} = £73.68$$

5   **INTRODUCTION TO CONTRACT COSTING**   12/97

Exam focus point
There were six marks to be gained in the 12/97 exam for describing the key features of three
examples of **specific order costing systems** ie, job, batch and contract costing.

KEY TERMS

- A **contract** is a cost unit or cost centre which is charged with the direct costs of production and an apportionment of head office overheads.

- **Contract costing** is a method of job costing where the job to be carried out is of such magnitude that a formal contract is made between the customer and supplier. It applies where work is undertaken to customers' special requirements and each order is of long duration (as compared with job costing). The work is usually constructional and in general the method is similar to job costing.

5.1   In industries such as building and construction work, civil engineering and shipbuilding, job costing is not usually appropriate. **Contract costing** is.

Features of contract costing

5.2   (a)   A **formal contract** is made between customer and supplier.
      (b)   Work is undertaken to **customers' special requirements**.
      (c)   The work is for a **relatively long duration**.
      (d)   The work is frequently **constructional in nature**.
      (e)   The method of costing is **similar to job costing**.
      (f)   The work is frequently **based on site**.
      (g)   It is not unusual for a site to have its own cashier and time-keeper.

5.3   The problems which may arise in contract costing are as follows.

      (a)   **Identifying direct costs**: because of the large size of the job, many cost items which are usually thought of as production overhead are charged as direct costs of the contract (for example supervision, hire of plant, depreciation and so on).

      (b)   **Low indirect costs**: because many costs normally classed as overheads are charged as direct costs of a contract, the absorption rate for overheads should only apply a share of the cost of those cost items which are not already direct costs.

      (c)   **Difficulties of cost control**: because of the size of some contracts and some sites, there are often cost control problems (material usage and losses, pilferage, labour supervision, damage to and loss of plant and tools and so on).

      (d)   **Dividing the profit between different accounting periods**: when a contract covers two or more accounting periods, how should the profit (or loss) on the contract be divided between the periods?

6 RECORDING CONTRACT COSTS

Direct materials

6.1 The **direct materials** used on a contract may be obtained as follows.

- From the company's central stores
- From the company's suppliers (direct)

6.2 The following points concern **materials obtained from the company's central stores.**

(a) A material requisition note must be sent to the store keeper from the contract site.

(b) The contract manager or foreman must sign all material requisition notes, authorising the issue of materials.

(c) The requisition note provides a record of the cost of the materials issued to the contract.

(d) Contract foreman prefer to have too much material, rather than run out. This means that they will often requisition more material than actually needed. The surplus material will need to be returned to stores via a **material returns note**.

(e) The material returns note must be signed by the foreman and checked by the storekeeper. The accounting entry when materials are returned is as follows.

CREDIT   Contract account (work in progress or 'job' account)
DEBIT   Stores account

(f) Materials on site which relate to an incomplete contract should be carried forward as **'closing stock of materials on site'**.

6.3 When materials are delivered directly from the company's suppliers:

(a) a copy of the goods received note will be sent from the site to the accounting department, and checked against the invoice received from the supplier;

(b) the entire invoice cost will then be charged directly to the contract.

Direct labour

6.4 It is usual for **direct labour** on a contract site to be paid on an hourly basis.

- On a **small site,** the foreman will log the hours worked by each employee.
- On a **large site** there will probably be a resident timekeeper.

Since all the work done is spent exclusively on a single contract, the direct labour cost of the contract should be easily identified from the wages sheets.

6.5 Employees who work on several contracts at the same time, will have to record the time spent on each contract on **time sheets**. Each contract will then be charged with the cost of these recorded hours. Any revenue earned from other small jobs done whilst working on a contract should be treated as follows.

DEBIT   Cash (cash received)
CREDIT   Contract account

6.6 **Payment of wages** depends on the following.

(a) If the **site is nearby,** the wages will be calculated in the head office accounting department, and wage packets made up by the head office cashier. The wages may then be transported from head office to the site by security van, and distributed by the site foreman. Unclaimed wages will be returned to the head office cashier.

(b) If the **site is a long way** from head office, the wages may still be calculated by the accounting department at head office, but the job of distributing wage packets might be given to a site cashier. A local bank will be authorised by head office to issue the appropriate amount of wages to the site cashier.

6.7 The **cost of supervision**, which is usually a production overhead in unit costing, job costing and so on, will be a direct cost of a contract.

Subcontractors

6.8 On large contracts, much work may be done by **subcontractors**. The invoices of subcontractors will be treated as a **direct expense to the contract.**

The cost of plant

6.9 A feature of most contract work is the amount of plant used. Plant used on a contract may be **owned** by the company, or **hired** from a plant hire firm.

(a) If the plant is **hired**, the cost will be a direct expense of the contract.
(b) If the plant is **owned**, a variety of accounting methods may be employed.

Method one: charging depreciation

6.10 **The contract may be charged depreciation on the plant, on a straight line or reducing balance basis.** For example if a company has some plant which cost £10,000 and is depreciated at 10% per annum straight line (to a residual value of nil) and a contract makes use of the plant for six months, a depreciation charge of £500 would be made against the contract. The disadvantage of this method of costing for plant is that the contract site foreman is not made directly responsible and accountable for the actual plant in his charge. The foreman must be responsible for receipt of the plant, returning the plant after it has been used and proper care of the plant whilst it is being used.

Method two: charging the contract with current book value

6.11 **A more common method of costing for plant is to charge the contract with the current book value of the plant.**

CREDIT   Plant account (fixed asset account) - with the value of the plant net of depreciation

DEBIT   Contract account

At the end of an accounting period, the contract account is credited with the written down value of the equipment.

CREDIT   Contract account (plant written down value) carried forward as an opening balance at the start of the next period.

When plant is returned from the site to head office (or transferred to another contract site), the contract account is credited with the written down value of the plant.

CREDIT   Contract account (written down value)
DEBIT   Plant account (or another contract account)

6.12 EXAMPLE : CHARGING THE CONTRACT WITH CURRENT BOOK VALUE

Contract number 123 obtained some plant and loose tools from central store on 1 January 20X2. The book value of the plant was £100,000 and the book value of the loose tools was £8,000. On 1 October 20X2, some plant was removed from the site: this plant had a written down value on 1 October of £20,000. At 31 December 20X2, the plant remaining on site had a written down value of £60,000 and the loose tools had a written down value of £5,000.

CONTRACT 123 ACCOUNT

	£		£
1 January 20X2		*1 October 20X2*	
Plant issued to site	100,000	Plant transferred	20,000
Loose tools issued to site	8,000	*31 December 20X2*	
		Plant value c/f	60,000
		Loose tools value c/f	5,000
		Depreciation (bal fig)	23,000
	108,000		108,000

The difference between the values on the debit and the credit sides of the account (£20,000 for plant and £3,000 for loose tools) is the depreciation cost of the equipment for the year.

Method three: using a plant account

6.13 A third method of accounting for plant costs is to **open a plant account, which is debited with the depreciation costs and the running costs** (repairs, fuel and so on) **of the equipment**. A notional hire charge is then made to contracts using the plant. For example suppose that a company owns some equipment which is depreciated at the rate of £100 per month. Running costs in May 20X3 are £300. The plant is used on 20 days in the month, 12 days on Contract X and 8 days on Contract Y. The accounting entries would be as follows.

PLANT ACCOUNT

	£		£
Depreciation (cost ledger control account)	100	Contract X (hire for 12 days)	240
		Contract Y (hire for 8 days)	160
Running costs (cost ledger control a/c, wages a/c and stores a/c)	300		
	400		400

CONTRACT X

	£		£
Plant account (notional hire)	240		

CONTRACT Y

	£		£
Plant account (notional hire)	160		

Overhead costs

6.14 **Overhead costs** are added periodically (for example at the end of an accounting period) and are based on predetermined overhead absorption rates for the period. You may come across examples where a share of head office general costs is absorbed as an overhead cost to the contract, but this should not happen if the contract is unfinished at the end of the period, because only production overheads should be included in the value of any closing work in progress.

7 CONTRACT ACCOUNTS

7.1 The account for a contract is a **job account,** or **work in progress account,** and is a record of the direct materials, direct labour, direct expenses and overhead charges on the contract. If we ignore, for the moment, profits on a part-finished contract, a typical contract account might appear as shown below. Check the items in the account carefully, and notice how the cost (or value) of the work done emerges as work in progress. On an unfinished contract, where no profits are taken mid-way through the contract, this cost of work in progress is carried forward as a closing stock balance.

7.2 EXAMPLE: A CONTRACT ACCOUNT

CONTRACT 794 - LUTTERBINS HOLIDAY CAMP

	£		£
Materials requisition from stores	15,247	Materials returned to stores or	
Materials and equipment purchased	36,300	transferred to other sites	2,100
Maintenance and operating costs		Proceeds from sale of materials	
of plant and vehicles	14,444	on site and jobbing work for	
Hire charges for plant and		other customers	600
vehicles not owned	6,500	Book value of plant transferred	4,800
Tools and consumables	8,570	Materials on site c/d	7,194
Book value of plant on site b/d	14,300	Book value of plant on site c/d	6,640
Direct wages	23,890		21,334
Supervisors' and engineers' salaries			
(proportion relating to time spent		Cost of work done c/d	
on the contract)	13,000	(balancing item)	139,917
Other site expenses	12,000		
Overheads (apportioned perhaps on			
the basis of direct labour hours)	17,000		
	161,251		161,251
Materials on site b/d	7,194		
Book value of plant on site b/d	6,640		
Cost of work done b/d	139,917		

8 PROGRESS PAYMENTS

8.1 A customer is likely to be required under the terms of the contract to make **progress payments** to the contractor throughout the course of the work. The amount of the payments will be based on the **value of work done** (as a proportion of the contract price) as assessed by the architect or surveyor (for a building contract) or qualified engineer in his certificate. A **certificate** provides confirmation that work to a certain value has been completed, and that some payment to the contractor is now due. The amount of the payment will be calculated as follows.

> **The value of work done and certified by the architect or engineer**

minus   **a retention (commonly 10%)**

minus   **the payments made to date**

equals   **payment due.**

8.2 Thus, if an architect's certificate assesses the value of work done on a contract to be £125,000 and if the retention is 10%, and if £92,000 has already been paid in progress payments the current payment = £125,000 – £12,500 – £92,000 = £20,500

8.3   When **progress payments** are received from the customer, the accounting entry is as follows.

      DEBIT   Bank (or financial ledger control account)
      CREDIT   Cash received on account, or contractee account.

8.4   **Retention monies** are released when the contract is completed and accepted by the customer.

9   PROFITS ON CONTRACTS

      6/96, 6/99

> **Exam focus point**
>
> In the 6/99 exam, there were 7 marks available for determining the expected profit/loss on a contract for a six-month period and for recommending the profit/loss to be included in the company accounts for the period.

9.1   You may have noticed that the progress payments do not necessarily give rise to profit immediately because of **retentions. So how are profits calculated on contracts?**

9.2   EXAMPLE: PROFITS ON CONTRACTS COMPLETED IN ONE ACCOUNTING PERIOD

If a contract is started and completed in the same accounting period, the calculation of the profit is straightforward, sales minus the cost of the contract. Suppose that a contract, No 6548, has the following costs.

	£
Direct materials (less returns)	40,000
Direct labour	35,000
Direct expenses	8,000
Plant costs	6,000
Overhead	11,000
	100,000

The work began on 1 February 20X3 and was completed on 15 November 20X3 in the contractor's same accounting year.

The contract price was £120,000 and on 20 November the inspecting engineer issued the final certificate of work done. At that date the customer had already paid £90,000 and the remaining £30,000 was still outstanding at the end of the contractor's accounting period. The accounts would appear as follows.

CONTRACT 6548 ACCOUNT

	£		£
Materials less returns	40,000	Cost of sales (P&L)	100,000
Labour	35,000		
Expenses	8,000		
Plant cost	6,000		
Overhead	11,000		
	100,000		100,000

WORK CERTIFIED ACCOUNT

	£		£
Turnover (P&L)	120,000	Contractee account	120,000
	120,000		120,000

CONTRACTEE (CUSTOMER) ACCOUNT

	£		£
Work certified a/c - value of work		Cash	90,000
Certified	120,000	Balance c/f	
		(debtor in balance sheet)	30,000
	120,000		120,000

The profit on the contract will be treated in the profit and loss account as follows.

	£
Turnover	120,000
Cost of sales	100,000
	20,000

Taking profits on incomplete contracts

9.3   A more difficult problem emerges when a contract is **incomplete** at the end of an accounting period. The contractor may have spent considerable sums of money on the work, and received substantial progress payments, and even if the work is not finished, the contractor will want to claim some profit on the work done so far.

9.4   Suppose that a company starts four new contracts in its accounting year to 31 December 20X1, but at the end of the year, none of them has been completed. All of the contracts are eventually completed in the first few months of 20X2 and they make profits of £40,000, £50,000, £60,000 and £70,000 respectively, £220,000 in total. If profits are not taken until the contracts are finished, the company would make no profits at all in 20X1, when most of the work was done, and £220,000 in 20X2. Such violent fluctuations in profitability would be confusing not only to the company's management, but also to shareholders and the investing public at large.

9.5   The problem arises because **contracts are for long-term work**, and it is a well-established practice that some profits should be taken in an accounting period, even if the contract is incomplete.

9.6   EXAMPLE: PROFITS ON INCOMPLETE CONTRACTS

Suppose that contract 246 is started on 1 July 20X2. Costs to 31 December 20X2, when the company's accounting year ends, are derived from the following information.

	£
Direct materials issued from store	18,000
Materials returned to store	400
Direct labour	15,500
Plant issued, at book value 1 July 20X2	32,000
Written-down value of plant 31 December 20X2	24,000
Materials on site, 31 December 20X2	1,600
Overhead costs	2,000

As at 31 December, certificates had been issued for work valued at £50,000 and the contractee had made progress payments of £45,000. The company has calculated that more work has been done since the last certificates were issued, and that the cost of work done but not yet certified is £8,000.

9.7 SOLUTION

The contract account would be prepared as follows.

CONTRACT 246 ACCOUNT

	£	£		£
Materials	18,000		Value of plant c/d	24,000
Less returns	400		Materials on site c/d	1,600
		17,600	Cost of work done not	
Labour		15,500	certified c/d	8,000
Plant issued at book value		32,000	Cost of sales (P&L)	33,500
Overheads		2,000		
		67,100		67,100

WORK CERTIFIED ACCOUNT

	£		£
Turnover (P&L)	50,000	Contractee account	50,000
	50,000		50,000

CONTRACTEE ACCOUNT

	£		£
Work certified account	50,000	Cash (progress payment)	45,000
		Balance c/f	5,000
	50,000		50,000

Points to note

(a) **The work done, but not yet certified, must be valued at cost,** and not at the value of the unissued certificates. It would be imprudent to suppose that the work has been done to the complete satisfaction of the architect or engineer, who may not issue certificates until further work is done.

(b) It would appear that £50,000 should be recognised as turnover and £33,500 as cost of sales leaving £16,500 as net profit. However it is often considered imprudent to claim this full amount of profit, and it is commonly argued that the profit taken should be a more conservative figure (in our example, less than £16,500, so that amounts taken to turnover and cost of sales relating to the contract should be less than £50,000 and £33,500 respectively).

(c) We have ignored retentions here.

Estimating the size of the profit

> **Exam focus point**
> The method of calculating profit on an incomplete contract may vary, and you should check any examination question carefully to find out whether a specific method is stated in the text of the question.

9.8 The **concept of prudence** should be applied when estimating the size of the profit on an incomplete contract and the following guidelines should be noted.

(a) **If the contract is in its early stages, no profit should be taken.** Profit should only be taken when the outcome of the contract can be assessed with reasonable accuracy.

(b) **For a contract on which substantial costs have been incurred, but which is not yet near completion** (that is, it is in the region of 35% to 85% complete) a formula which has often been used in the past is as follows.

$$\text{Profit taken} = \tfrac{2}{3} \ (\text{or} \ \tfrac{3}{4} \ ) \ \text{of the notional profit}$$

where notional profit = (the value of work certified to date) − (the cost of the work certified).

In the example above, the notional profit for contract 246 is £16,500 (£(50,000 − 33,500)) and the profit taken for the period using the above formula would be calculated as follows.

$$^2/_3 \text{ of } £16,500 = £11,000 \text{ (or } ^3/_4 \text{ of } £16,500 = £12,375)$$

(c) **Where the contractee withholds a retention, or where progress payments are not made as soon as work certificates are issued**, it would be more prudent to reduce the profit taken by the proportion of retentions to the value of work certified.

$$\textbf{Profit taken} = \, ^2/_3 \, \textbf{(or } ^3/_4\textbf{)} \times \textbf{notional profit} \times \frac{\text{cash received on account}}{\text{value of work certified}}$$

In our example of contract 246, this would be:

$$^2/_3 \times £16,500 \times \frac{£45,000}{£50,000} = £9,900$$

(d) **If the contract is nearing completion, the size of the eventual profit should be foreseeable with reasonable certainty and there is no need to be excessively prudent.** The profit taken may be calculated by one of three methods.

(i) **Work certified to date minus the cost of work certified.** In our example, this would be the full £16,500.

(ii) $$\frac{\textbf{Cost of work done}}{\textbf{Estimated total cost of contract}} \times \textbf{estimated total profit on contract}$$

In our example, if the estimated total cost of the contract 246 is £64,000 and the estimated total profit on the contract is £18,000, the profit taken would be:

$$\frac{£(33,500 + 8,000)}{£64,000} \times £18,000 = £11,672$$

(iii) $$\textbf{Profit taken} = \frac{\textbf{Value of work certified}}{\textbf{contract price}} \times \textbf{estimated total profit}$$

This is perhaps the most-favoured of the three methods. In our example of contract 246, if the final contract price is £82,000 and the estimated total profit is £18,000 the profit taken would be:

$$\frac{£50,000}{£82,000} \times £18,000 = £10,976$$

Some companies may feel that it is prudent to reduce the profit attributed to the current accounting period still further, to allow for retentions of cash by the contractee. In our example, the profit taken would now be:

$$\frac{£50,000}{£82,000} \times £18,000 \times \frac{£45,000}{£50,000} = £9,878$$

This formula simplifies to:

$$\frac{\text{cash received to date}}{\text{contract price}} \times \text{estimated total profit from the contract}$$

(e) **A loss on the contract may be foreseen.** The method of dealing with losses is covered in the next section.

9.9 It should be apparent from these different formulae that the profit taken on an incomplete contract will depend on two things.

- The degree of completion
- The choice of formula

Question 3

Landy Stroyers plc is a construction company. Data relating to one of its contracts, XYZ, for the year to 31 December 20X2, are as follows.

	£'000
Value of work certified to 31 December 20X1	500
Cost of work certified to 31 December 20X1	360
Plant on site b/f at 1 January 20X2	30
Materials on site b/f at 1 January 20X2	10
Cost of contract to 1 January 20X2 b/f	370
Materials issued from store	190
Sub-contractors' costs	200
Wages and salaries	200
Overheads absorbed by contract in 20X2	100
Plant on site c/f at 31 December 20X2	15
Materials on site c/f at 31 December 20X2	5
Value of work certified to 31 December 20X2	1,200
Cost of work certified to 31 December 20X2	950

No profit has been taken on the contract prior to 20X2. There are no retentions.

Required

(a) Calculate the total cumulative cost of contract XYZ to the end of December 20X2.

(b) Turnover on the contract is taken as the value of work certified. Calculate the gross profit for the contract for the year to 31 December 20X2.

Answer

(a)

CONTRACT ACCOUNT

	£'000		£'000
Cost of contract b/f	370	Plant on site c/f	15
Plant on site b/f	30	Materials on site c/f	5
Materials on site b/f	10	Cost of contract c/f (balance)	1,080
Materials from stores	190		
Sub-contractors' costs	200		
Wages and salaries	200		
Overheads	100		
	1,100		1,100

(b) No profit had been taken on the contract prior to 20X2, and so profit is quite simply calculated as follows.

	£'000
Value of work certified to 31.12.X2	1,200
Cost of work certified to 31.12.X2	950
Gross profit to 31.12.X2	250

10 LOSSES ON INCOMPLETE CONTRACTS

10.1 At the end of an accounting period, it may be that instead of finding that the contract is profitable, a loss is expected. When this occurs, the **total expected loss should be taken into account as soon as it is recognised, even though the contract is not yet complete.** The contract account should be debited with the **anticipated future loss** (final cost of contract – full contract price – (cost of work at present – value of work certified at present)) and the profit and loss account debited with the total expected loss (final cost of contract – full contract price).

The same accounting procedure would be followed on completed contracts, as well as incomplete contracts, but it is essential that the full amount of the loss on the total contract, if foreseeable, should be charged against company profits at the earliest opportunity, even if a contract is incomplete. This means that in the next accounting period, the contract should break even, making neither a profit nor a loss, because the full loss has already been charged to the profit and loss account.

10.2 EXAMPLE: LOSS ON CONTRACT

Contract 257 was begun on 22 March 20X3. By 31 December 20X3, the end of the contractor's accounting year, costs incurred were as follows.

	£
Materials issued	24,000
Materials on site, 31 December	2,000
Labour	36,000
Plant issued to site 22 March	40,000
Written-down value of plant, 31 December	28,000
Overheads	6,000

The contract is expected to end in February 20X4 and at 31 December 20X3, the cost accountant estimated that the final cost of the contract would be £95,000. The full contract price is £90,000. Work certified at 31 December was valued at £72,000. The contractee has made progress payments up to 31 December of £63,000.

Required

Prepare the contract account.

10.3 SOLUTION

CONTRACT 257 ACCOUNT

	£		£
Materials issued	24,000	Materials on site c/f	2,000
Labour	36,000	Plant at written-down value, c/f	28,000
Plant issued, written-down value	40,000	Cost of work c/d (balancing figure)	76,000
Overheads	6,000		
	106,000		106,000
Cost of work done, b/d	76,000	Cost of sales (P&L)	77,000
Anticipated future loss*	1,000		
	77,000		77,000

* The total estimated loss on the contract is £5,000 (£90,000 – £95,000). Of this amount £4,000 has been lost in the current period (£76,000 – £72,000) and so £1,000 is anticipated as arising in the future: the company will invoice £18,000 (£90,000 – £72,000) and will incur costs of £19,000 (£95,000 – £76,000). This is taken as a loss in the current period.

The loss is posted £72,000 to turnover and £77,000 to cost of sales (£5,000 net).

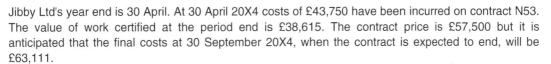

Question 4

Jibby Ltd's year end is 30 April. At 30 April 20X4 costs of £43,750 have been incurred on contract N53. The value of work certified at the period end is £38,615. The contract price is £57,500 but it is anticipated that the final costs at 30 September 20X4, when the contract is expected to end, will be £63,111.

Required

(a) Prepare the contract account.
(b) Calculate the figures for turnover and cost of sales for the period to 30 April 20X4.

Answer

(a) CONTRACT N53

	£		£
Cost of work done b/d	43,750	Cost of sales (P&L)	44,226
Anticipated future loss*	476		
	44,226		44,226

*£[(63,111 – 57,500) – (43,750 – 38,615)] = £476.

(b) Turnover = £38,615

Cost of sales = £44,226

---

11 DISCLOSURE OF LONG-TERM CONTRACTS IN FINANCIAL ACCOUNTS

11.1 **SSAP 9** defines how **stocks** and **work in progress** should be valued in the financial accounts, and makes particular reference to long-term contract work in progress and profits. Although there is no requirement that cost accounting procedures should be the same as financial accounting procedures and standards, it is generally thought that conformity between the financial and cost accounts is desirable in contract costing.

11.2 SSAP 9 makes the following requirements with relation to the profit and loss account.

(a) The profit and loss account will contain turnover and related costs deemed to accrue to the contract over the period, so that the profit and loss account reflects the net profit on the contract taken in the period.

(b) The profit taken needs to reflect the proportion of the work carried out at the accounting date, and to take account of any known inequalities of profitability at the various stages of a contract.

(c) Where the outcome of a contract cannot be reasonably assessed before its completion, no profits should be taken on the incomplete contract.

(d) The amount of profit taken to the profit and loss account for an incomplete contract should be judged with prudence.

(e) If it is expected that there will be a loss on the contract as a whole, provision needs to be made for the whole of the loss as soon as it is recognised (in accordance with the prudence concept). The amount of the loss should be deducted from the amounts for long-term contracts included under stocks, and where a credit balance results, it should be disclosed separately under creditors or provisions for liabilities and charges.

11.3 **SSAP 9** requires the following **disclosures** in the balance sheet.

Balances relating to long-term contracts are split into two elements.

(a) Work done on long-term contracts not yet recognised in the profit and loss account is disclosed under 'stocks' as 'long-term contract balances'.

(b) The difference between

(i)	amounts recognised as turnover	X
(ii)	progress payments received	(X)
		X

will be recognised in debtors as 'amounts recoverable on long-term contracts' if (i) is greater than (ii), or will be offset against the balances in (a) above if (ii) is greater than (i).

Chapter roundup

- **Job costing** is the costing method used where each cost unit is separately identifiable.

- Each job is given a **number** to distinguish it from other jobs.

- Costs for each job are collected on a **job cost sheet** or **job card.**

- Material costs for each job are determined from **material requisition notes**.

- Labour times on each job are recorded on a **job ticket**, which is then costed and recorded on the job cost sheet. Some labour costs, such as overtime premium or the cost of rectifying sub-standard output, might be charged either directly to a job or else as an overhead cost, depending on the circumstances in which the costs have arisen.

- **Overhead** is absorbed into the cost of jobs using the predetermined overhead absorption rates.

- The usual method of fixing prices within a jobbing concern is **cost plus pricing**.

- An **internal job costing system** can be used for costing the work of service departments.

- **Batch costing** is similar to job costing in that each batch of similar articles is separately identifiable. The **cost per unit** manufactured in a batch is the total batch cost divided by the number of units in the batch.

- **Contract costing** is a form of job costing which applies where the job is on a large scale and for a long duration. The majority of costs relating to a contact are direct costs.

- Contract costs are collected in a **contract account**.

- A customer is likely to be required to make **progress payments** which are calculated as the value of work done and certified by the architect or engineer minus a retention minus the payments made to date.

- The long duration of a contract usually means that an estimate must be made of the profit earned on each incomplete contract at the end of the accounting period. There are several different ways of calculating contract profits (which you should learn), but the overriding consideration must be the application of the prudence concept. **If a loss is expected on a contract, the total expected loss should be taken into account as soon as it is recognised, even if the contract is not complete.**

- The loss should be deducted from the amounts for long-term contracts included under stocks in the balance sheet. If the resulting balance is a credit, it should be disclosed separately under creditors or provisions for liabilities and charges.

- **SSAP 9** requires the following disclosures in the balance sheet.

  ○ Work done on long-term contracts which has yet to be recognised in the profit and loss account in disclosed under 'stocks' as 'long-term contract balances'.

  ○ The difference between (a) 'amounts recognised as turnover' and (b) 'progress payments received' will be recognised in debtors as 'amounts recoverable on long-term contracts' if (a) > (b), but will be offset against the stock balance mentioned above if (b) > (a).

Quick quiz

1   Describe the procedures by which job costs are collected. (see paras 1.2, 1.3)

2   How is a job valued at the end of an accounting period if it is incomplete? (1.3)

3   Describe two ways of accounting for rectification costs. (1.7)

4   What is cost plus pricing? (1.9)

5   What are the advantages of an internal job costing system for service departments. (2.2)

6   How is the cost per unit in batch costing calculated? (4.1)

7   List the features of contract costing. (5.2)

8   How would you account for plant depreciation in contract accounts? (6.10 - 6.13)

9   How is the amount of a progress payment calculated? (8.1)

10 What are the three methods of calculating profit on a contract which is nearing completion? (9.8)

11 How would you account for a loss on an incomplete contract? (10.1)

12 What four requirements does SSAP 9 make with relation to the profit and loss account? (11.2)

13 If progress payments received are greater than amounts recognised as turnover, is the difference recognised in debtors or offset against 'long-term contracts balance' in stock? (11.3)

Questions to try	Level	Marks	Time
11	Examination	14	25 mins
12	Examination	14	25 mins

Chapter 12

PROCESS COSTING

Chapter topic list	Syllabus reference
1 Introduction to process costing	CA 3(b)(i), (ii)
2 The basics of process costing	CA 3(b)(i), (ii)
3 Dealing with losses in process	CA 3(b)(iv)
4 Accounting for scrap	CA 3(b)(iv)
5 Losses with a disposal cost	CA 3(b)(iv)
6 Valuing closing work in progress	CA 3(b)(iii)
7 Valuing opening work in progress: FIFO method	CA 3(b)(iii)
8 Valuing opening work in progress: weighted average cost method	CA 3(b)(iii)

Introduction

We have already looked at three costing methods, **job costing**, **batch costing** and **contract costing**. In this chapter we will consider a fourth, **process costing**. The chapter will consider the topic from basics, looking at how to account for the most simple of processes. We then move on to how to account for any **losses** which might occur, as well as what to do with any **scrapped units** which are sold. We also consider how to deal with any **closing work in progress** and then look at two methods of valuing **opening work in progress**. Valuation of both opening and closing work in progress hinges on the concept of **equivalent units**, which will be explained in detail.

1   INTRODUCTION TO PROCESS COSTING

KEY TERM

Process costing is a costing method used where it is not possible to identify separate units of production, or jobs, usually because of the continuous nature of the production processes involved.

1.1   It is common to identify process costing with **continuous production** such as the following.

- Oil refining
- Paper
- Foods and drinks
- Chemicals

Process costing may also be associated with the continuous production of large volumes of low-cost items, such as **cans** or **tins**.

1.2 The following are features of process costing which make it different from job or batch costing.

    (a) The **output** of one process becomes the **input** to the next until the finished product is made in the final process.

    (b) The continuous nature of production in many processes means that there will usually be **closing work in progress which must be valued**. In process costing it is not possible to build up cost records of the cost per unit of output or the cost per unit of closing stock because production in progress is an **indistinguishable homogeneous mass**.

    (c) There is often a **loss in process** due to spoilage, wastage, evaporation and so on.

    (d) Output from production may be a single product, but there may also be a **by-product** (or by-products) and/or **joint products.**

1.3 The aim of this chapter is to describe how cost accountants keep a set of accounts to record the costs of production in a processing industry. The aim of the set of accounts is to derive a cost, or valuation, for output and closing stock.

2 THE BASICS OF PROCESS COSTING

2.1 Where a series of separate processes is required to manufacture the finished product, the output of one process becomes the input to the next until the final output is made in the final process. If two processes are required the accounts would look like this.

PROCESS 1 ACCOUNT

	Units	£		Units	£
Direct materials	1,000	50,000	Output to process 2	1,000	90,000
Direct labour		20,000			
Production overhead		20,000			
	1,000	90,000		1,000	90,000

PROCESS 2 ACCOUNT

	Units	£		Units	£
Materials from process 1	1,000	90,000	Output to finished goods	1,000	150,000
Added materials		30,000			
Direct labour		15,000			
Production overhead		15,000			
	1,000	150,000		1,000	150,000

2.2 Note that direct labour and production overhead may be treated together in an examination question as **conversion cost**.

2.3 **Added** materials, labour and overhead in process 2 are added gradually throughout the process. Materials from process 1, in contrast, will often be introduced in full at the start of process 2.

2.4 The 'units' columns in the process accounts are for **memorandum purposes** only and help you to ensure that you do not miss out any entries.

Framework for dealing with process costing

2.5 Process costing is centred around **four key steps**. The exact work done at each step will depend on whether there are normal losses, scrap, opening and closing stock and so on.

Step 1. **Determine output and losses.** This step involves the following.

- Determining expected output
- Calculating normal loss and abnormal loss and gain
- Calculating equivalent units if there is closing or opening work in progress

Step 2. **Calculate cost per unit of output, losses and WIP.** This step involves calculating cost per unit or cost per equivalent unit.

Step 3. **Calculate total cost of output, losses and WIP.** In some examples this will be straightforward; however in cases where there is closing and/or opening work-in-progress a **statement of evaluation** will have to be prepared.

Step 4. **Complete accounts.** This step involves the following.

- Completing the process account
- Writing up the other accounts required by the question

3 DEALING WITH LOSSES IN PROCESS 6/98

Exam focus point

Examination questions in the past have tested candidates' ability to prepare process accounts where losses and gains are included.

3.1 Losses during processing can happen when liquids evaporate, when there is wastage and if completed units are rejected.

A **loss** therefore occurs when the quantity of materials output from a process is less than the quantities input. How would any losses be costed?

Three different ways of costing losses

3.2 Suppose that input to a process consists of 100 litres of material. Total process costs are £85,652. What is the cost per litre if output is as follows?

(a) 92 litres
(b) 98 litres

Base cost per unit on output

3.3 One way of costing the output is to say that **the cost per unit should be based on actual units produced (output), so that any lost units have no cost at all.**

		Cost per unit		
(a)	If output is 92 litres	$\dfrac{£85,652}{92}$	=	£931 per litre
(b)	If output is 98 litres	$\dfrac{£85,652}{98}$	=	£874 per litre

You should see that the **cost per litre varies** according to the actual loss in the period. Therefore, if some loss in process is unavoidable, and if the amount of loss varies from period to period, this approach to costing will result in **fluctuations** in unit costs.

3.4   It might be more satisfactory to take a **longer-term view of loss**, and calculate **average unit costs** on the basis of **average loss** over a longer period of time. This would give **greater stability** and **consistency** to unit costs of production between one period (such as one month) and the next.

Base cost per unit on input

3.5   A second way of costing the output is to say that **lost units have a cost, which should be charged to the P & L account** whenever they occur. The cost per unit would then be based on units of **input** rather than units of output.

		Cost per unit £	Cost of output £	Cost of loss £
(a)	If output is 92 litres	$\dfrac{£85,652}{100}$ 856.52	(× 92) 78,799.84	(× 8) 6,852.16
(b)	If output is 98 litres	$\dfrac{£85,652}{100}$ 856.52	(× 98) 83,938.96	(× 2) 1,713.04

The cost of the loss would be written off directly to the P & L account.

The main drawback to this method of costing is that if some loss in processing is unavoidable and to be expected, there would be some cost of production unavoidably written off to the P & L account in every period, and this is an unsatisfactory method of costing.

Differentiate between expected and unexpected losses

3.6   The third method of costing loss (described below) is a **compromise system**, which is based on the following view.

   •   If some loss is to be expected, it should not be given a cost.

   •   If there is some loss that 'shouldn't happen', it ought to be given a cost.

Normal loss and abnormal loss/gain

> **KEY TERMS**
>
> •   **Normal loss** is the loss expected during a process. It is not given a cost.
>
> •   **Abnormal loss** is the loss resulting when actual loss is greater than normal or expected loss, and it is given a cost.
>
> •   **Abnormal gain** is the gain resulting when actual loss is less than the normal or expected loss, and it is given a 'negative cost'.

3.7   Normal loss, abnormal loss and abnormal gain can be illustrated using the information in Paragraph 3.2. The cost per unit should be based on **expected output**, which is **input minus normal loss**. Let's suppose that normal loss is 5% of input.

3.8   If actual output is 92 litres, the steps are as follows.

   Step 1.   **Determine output and losses**
           Normal output is 95 litres, and so there is an abnormal loss of 3 litres.

Step 2. **Calculate cost per unit of output, losses and WIP**

$$\text{Cost per unit} = \frac{£85,652}{(100-5)\text{litres}} = \frac{£85,652}{95} = £901.60 \text{ per litre}$$

Step 3. **Calculate total cost of output and losses**

	£
Cost of output (92 × £901.60)	82,947.20
Normal loss	0.00
Abnormal loss (3 litres × £901.60)	2,704.80
	85,652.00

Step 4. **Complete accounts**

The process account and abnormal loss account would be:

PROCESS ACCOUNT

	Units	£		Units	£
Cost of materials,			Finished goods	92	82,947.20
labour and overhead	100	85,652	Normal loss	5	0.00
			Abnormal loss	3	2,704.80
	100	85,652		100	85,652.00

ABNORMAL LOSS A/C

	£		£
Process a/c	2704.80	P & L account	2704.80

3.9 If actual output is 98 litres, the steps are as follows.

Step 1. **Determine output and losses**

Normal output is 95 litres, and normal loss is 5 litres, therefore there is an abnormal gain of (98 – 95) = 3 litres.

Step 2. **Calculate cost per unit of output and losses**

This will be £901.60 as above.

Step 3. **Calculate total cost of output and losses**

	£
Cost of output (98 × £901.60)	88,356.80
Normal loss	0.00
	88,356.80
Abnormal gain (3 litres × £901.60)	(2,704.80)
	85,652.00

Step 4. **Complete accounts**

The process account and abnormal gain account would be as follows.

PROCESS ACCOUNT

	Units	£		Units	£
Cost of materials, labour			Finished goods	98	88,356.80
and overhead	100	85,652.00	Normal loss	5	0.00
Abnormal gain	3	2,704.80			
	103	88,356.80		103	88,356.80

ABNORMAL GAIN A/C

	£		£
P & L account	2704.80	Process a/c	2704.80

3.10 EXAMPLE: NORMAL AND ABNORMAL LOSS

Gunner Ltd operates a manufacturing process, and during March 20X3 the following processing took place.

Opening stock	nil	Closing stock	nil
Units introduced	1,000 units	Output	900 units
Costs incurred	£4,500	Loss	100 units

Required

Determine the cost of output in the following circumstances.

(a) Expected or normal loss is 10% of input.

(b) There is no expected loss, so that the entire loss of 100 units was unexpected.

3.11 SOLUTION

(a) If loss is expected, and is an unavoidable feature of processing, it is argued by cost accountants that there is no point in charging a cost to the loss. It is more sensible to accept that the loss will occur, and spread the costs of production over the expected units of output.

Step 1. **Determine output and losses**

Normal output is 90% of 1,000 units which is 900 units. Normal loss is therefore 100 units (1,000 – 900).

Step 2. **Calculate cost per unit of output, losses and WIP**

$$\text{Cost per unit of output} = \frac{\text{Costs}}{\text{Expected output}} = \frac{£4,500}{900} = £5$$

Step 3. **Calculate total cost of output and losses**

	£
Cost of output (900 × £5)	4,500
Normal loss (100 × £0)	-
	4,500

Step 4. **Complete accounts**

Normal loss is not given any cost, so that the process account would appear as follows.

PROCESS ACCOUNT

	Units	£		Units	£
Costs incurred	1,000	4,500	Normal loss	100	0
			Output units	900	4,500
	1,000	4,500		1,000	4,500

It helps to enter normal loss into the process 'T' account, just to make sure that your memorandum columns for units are the same on the debit and the credit sides of the account.

(b) If loss is unexpected and occurred perhaps as a result of poor workmanship, poor quality materials and so on, it is argued that it would be reasonable to charge a cost to the units of loss. The cost would then be transferred to an 'abnormal loss' account, and eventually written off to the profit and loss account as an item of loss in the period. Units of 'good output' would not be burdened with the cost of the loss, so that the cost per unit remains unaltered.

Step 1. **Determine output and losses**

Normal output is 1,000 units as stated in the question. Therefore abnormal loss is 100 units.

Step 2. **Calculate cost per unit of output, losses and WIP**

$$\text{Cost per unit of output} = \frac{£4,500}{1,000\,\text{units}} = £4.50$$

Step 3. **Calculate total cost of output and losses**

	£
Cost of output (900 × £4.50)	4,050
Abnormal loss (100 × £4.50)	450
	4,500

Step 4. **Complete accounts**

The process account and abnormal loss account would look like this.

PROCESS ACCOUNT

	Units	£		Units	£
Costs incurred	1,000	4,500	Abnormal loss	100	450
			Output units	900	4,050
	1,000	4,500		1,000	4,500

ABNORMAL LOSS ACCOUNT

	Units	£		Units	£
Process account	100	450	Profit and loss account	100	450

3.12 EXAMPLE: ABNORMAL LOSSES AND GAINS

Suppose that input to a process is 1,000 units at a cost of £4,500. Normal loss is 10% and there are no opening or closing stocks. What would be the accounting entries for the cost of output and the cost of the loss if actual output were as follows.

(a)   860 units (so that actual loss is 140 units).

(b)   920 units (so that actual loss is 80 units).

3.13 SOLUTION

The same principles described earlier for evaluating normal and abnormal loss may be applied to situations where normal loss and abnormal loss/gain occur together.

(a)   Normal loss is given no share of cost.

(b)   The cost of output is based on the **expected units of output**, which in our example amount to 90% of 1,000 = 900 units.

(c)   Abnormal loss is given a cost, which is written off to the profit and loss account via an abnormal loss/gain account.

(d)   Abnormal gain is treated in the same way, except that being a gain rather than a loss, it appears as a **debit** entry in the process account (whereas a loss appears as a **credit** entry in this account).

(a)   *Step 1.*   **Determine output and losses**

If actual output is 860 units, the actual loss is 140 units.

	Units
Actual loss	140
Normal loss (10% of 1,000)	100
Abnormal loss	40

Step 2. **Calculate cost per unit of output, losses and WIP**

The cost per unit of output and the cost per unit of abnormal loss are based on expected output.

$$\frac{\text{Costs incurred}}{\text{Expected output}} = \frac{£4,500}{900\text{units}}$$

Cost per unit   £5

Normal loss is not assigned any cost.

Step 3. **Calculate total cost of output and losses**

	£
Cost of output (860 × £5)	4,300
Normal loss (100 × £0)	-
Abnormal loss (40 × £5)	200
	4,500

Step 4. **Complete accounts**

PROCESS ACCOUNT

	Units	£		Units		£
Cost incurred	1,000	4,500	Normal loss	100		0
			Output (finished			
			goods a/c)	860	(× £5)	4,300
			Abnormal loss	40	(× £5)	200
	1,000	4,500		1,000		4,500

ABNORMAL LOSS ACCOUNT

	Units	£		Units	£
Process a/c	40	200	Profit and loss a/c	40	200

(b) *Step 1.* **Determine output and losses**

If actual output is 920 units, the actual loss is 80 units.

	Units
Actual loss	80
Normal loss (10% of 1,000)	100
Abnormal gain	20

Step 2. **Calculate cost per unit of output, losses and WIP**

The cost per unit of output and the cost per unit of abnormal gain are based on expected output.

$$\frac{\text{Costs incurred}}{\text{Expected output}} = \frac{£4,500}{900\text{units}} = £5 \text{ per unit}$$

Step 3. **Calculate total cost of output and losses**

	£
Cost of output (920 × £5)	4,600
Normal loss (100 × £0)	-
Abnormal gain (20 × £5)	(100)
	4,500

(Whether there is abnormal loss or gain does not affect the valuation of units of output. The figure of £5 per unit is exactly the same as when there were 40 units of abnormal loss.)

Step 4. **Complete accounts**

PROCESS ACCOUNT

	Units	£		Units	£
Cost incurred	1,000	4,500	Normal loss	100	0
Abnormal gain a/c	20(× £5)	100	Output	920	(× £5) 4,600
			(finished goods a/c)		
	1,020	4,600		1,020	4,600

ABNORMAL GAIN

	Units	£		Units	£
Profit and loss a/c	20	100	Process a/c	20	100

3.14 EXAMPLE: ABNORMAL LOSSES AND GAINS AGAIN

During a four week period, period 3, costs of input to a process were £29,070. Input was 1,000 units, output was 850 units and normal loss is 10%.

During the next period, period 4, costs of input were again £29,070. Input was again 1,000 units, but output was 950 units.

There were no units of opening or closing stock.

Required

Prepare the process account and abnormal loss or gain account for each period.

3.15 SOLUTION

Step 1. **Determine output and losses**

If normal output is 900 units (90% × 1,000 units), and actual output in period 3 is 850 units, then there is an abnormal loss of 50 units (900 – 850). If actual output is 950 units in period 4, there is an abnormal gain of 50 units (900 – 950).

Step 2. **Calculate cost per unit of output, losses and WIP**

For each period the cost per unit is based on expected output.

$$\frac{\text{Cost of input}}{\text{Expected units of output}} = \frac{£29,070}{900} = £32.30 \text{ per unit}$$

Step 3. **Calculate total cost of output and losses**

Period 3	£
Output (850 × £32.30)	27,455
Normal loss (100 × £0)	-
Abnormal loss (50 × £32.30)	1,615
	29,070

Period 4	£
Output (950 × £32.30)	30,685
Normal loss (100 × £0)	-
Abnormal gain (50 × £32.30)	(1,615)
	29,070

Step 4. **Complete accounts**

PROCESS ACCOUNT

	Units	£		Units	£
Period 3					
Cost of input	1,000	29,070	Normal loss	100	0
			Finished goods a/c	850	27,455
			(× £32.30)		
			Abnormal loss a/c	50	1,615
			(× £32.30)		
	1,000	29,070		1,000	29,070
Period 4					
Cost of input	1,000	29,070	Normal loss	100	0
Abnormal gain a/c	50	1,615	Finished goods a/c	950	30,685
(× £32.30)			(× £32.30)		
	1,050	30,685		1,050	30,685

ABNORMAL LOSS OR GAIN ACCOUNT

	£		£
Period 3		*Period 4*	
Abnormal loss in process a/c	1,615	Abnormal gain in process a/c	1,615

A nil balance on this account will be carried forward into period 5.

(*Note.* It is considered more appropriate to value all units of output at a value based on expected loss (£32.30 per unit) rather than to have random fluctuations in the cost per unit each period due to variations in the loss.

3.16 If there is a closing balance in the abnormal loss or gain account when the profit for the period is calculated, this balance is taken to the profit and loss account: an abnormal gain will adjust profit upwards and an abnormal loss will adjust profit downwards.

Question 1

3,000 units of material are input to a process. Process costs are as follows.

Material £11,700
Conversion costs £6,300

Output is 2,000 units. Normal loss is 20% of input.

Required

Prepare a process account and the appropriate abnormal loss/gain account.

Answer

Step 1. **Determine output and losses**

We are told that output is 2,000 units.

Normal loss = 20% × 3,000 = 600 units

Abnormal loss = (3,000 − 600) − 2,000 = 400 units

Step 2. **Calculate cost per unit of output and losses**

$$\text{Cost per unit} = \frac{£(11,700 + 6,300)}{2,400} = £7.50$$

Step 3. **Calculate total cost of output and losses**

		£
Output	(2,000 × £7.50)	15,000
Normal loss		0
Abnormal loss	(400 × £7.50)	3,000
		18,000

Step 4. **Complete accounts**

PROCESS ACCOUNT

	Units	£		Units	£
Material	3,000	11,700	Output	2,000	15,000
Conversion costs		6,300	Normal loss	600	
			Abnormal loss	400	3,000
	3,000	18,000		3,000	18,000

ABNORMAL LOSS ACCOUNT

	£		£
Process a/c	3,000	P&L account	3,000

4 ACCOUNTING FOR SCRAP   6/94, 6/98

4.1 **Loss or spoilage may have a scrap value.** When loss or spoilage is sold as scrap, there are two ways of accounting for the income.

(a) **Add** the revenue from the scrap sales to total sales revenue in the period.

(b) **Subtract** the sales revenue from the scrap from the costs of production and the cost of abnormal loss in the period. This is the more usual method to adopt.

4.2 If a distinction is made between normal loss and abnormal loss/gain the accounting treatment of scrap in process costing is as follows.

(a) The scrap value of normal loss will probably be deducted from the cost of materials in the process. This is done in the cost accounts themselves by crediting the scrap value of normal loss to the process account.

(b) The scrap value of **abnormal loss (or abnormal gain)** will probably be set off against its cost, in an abnormal loss (abnormal gain) account, and only the balance on the account will be written to the P & L account at the end of the period.

4.3 Accounting for scrap fits into our process costing framework as follows.

Step 1. **Determine output and losses**

This stage is important, as the scrap value of normal losses will be accounted for differently.

Steps 2 **Calculate costs of output and losses**
and 3. To do this we must first **separate** the scrap value of normal loss from abnormal loss. Then we will subtract the scrap value of normal loss from the cost of the process and divide by the expected output to determine cost per unit, and subsequently total costs.

Step 4. **Complete accounts**

In the process account the units of **normal loss** will be costed at their **scrap value**. The units of **abnormal loss/gain** will be costed at the cost per unit calculated in Steps 2 and 3.

The other relevant accounting entries are as follows.

• For **normal losses**

DEBIT   Scrap account
CREDIT   Process account

with the scrap value of normal loss.

- For **abnormal losses**

  DEBIT   Scrap account
  CREDIT   Abnormal loss account

  with the scrap value of abnormal loss.

- For **abnormal gains**

  DEBIT   Abnormal gain account
  CREDIT   Scrap account

  with the scrap value of abnormal gain.

- **Complete scrap account**

  DEBIT   Cash received
  CREDIT   Scrap account

  with cash received from sale of actual scrap.

4.4 EXAMPLE: SCRAP AND NORMAL LOSS

Suppose that input to a process costs £1,370, normal loss is 10% and units scrapped sell for £2 each. 100 units are input and 90 units output.

Required

Show the process account and the scrap account.

4.5 SOLUTION

Step 1. **Determine output and losses**

Normal loss is 10% of 100 units, ie 10 units. Normal output is therefore 90 units (100 – 10). There is therefore no abnormal loss or gain.

Step 2. **Calculate costs of output and losses**

The total value of scrap is $10 \times £2 = £20$. The scrap value of normal loss is deducted from the materials cost, in order to calculate the output cost per unit, before it is credited to the process account as a value for normal loss.

The cost per unit of output would be calculated as follows.

	£	
Cost of input	1,370	
Less scrap value of normal loss		
(10 units × £2)	(20)	
	1,350	
Expected units of output	90	units
Cost per unit (£1,350 ÷ 90)	£15	per unit

Step 3. **Calculate total costs of output and losses**

	£
Output (90 × £15)	1,350
Normal loss (100 × £0)	-
	1,350

Step 4. **Complete accounts**

The accounting entries would be as follows.

PROCESS ACCOUNT

	Units	£		Units	£
Input costs	100	1,370	Normal loss ** (scrap a/c) 10		20
			Output (finished goods a/c)90		1,350
	100	1,370		100	1,370

SCRAP ACCOUNT

	£		£
Scrap value of normal loss in process **	20	Cash a/c or financial ledger control = actual cash received for scrap	20
	20		20

4.6 If there is abnormal loss or abnormal gain, the scrap value of actual loss will differ from the normal loss scrap value. This discrepancy is ignored in the process account and is dealt with instead in the abnormal loss or gain account and the scrap account.

Question 2

Nan Ltd has a factory which operates two production processes. Normal spoilage in each process is 10%, and scrapped units out of process 1 sell for 50p per unit whereas scrapped units out of process 2 sell for £3. Output from process 1 is transferred to process 2: output from process 2 is finished output ready for sale.

Relevant information about costs for period 5 are as follows.

	Process 1		Process 2	
	Units	£	Units	£
Input materials	2,000	£8,100		
Transferred to process 2	1,750			
Materials from process 1			1,750	
Added materials			1,250	£1,900
Labour and overheads		£10,000		£22,000
Output to finished goods			2,800	

Required

Prepare the following cost accounts.

(a) Process 1
(b) Process 2
(c) Abnormal loss
(d) Abnormal gain
(e) Scrap

Answer

(a) *Process 1*

Step 1. Determine output and losses

The normal loss is 10% of 2000 units = 200 units, and the actual loss is (2000 - 1750) = 250 units. This means that there is abnormal loss of 50 units.

Actual output	1,750 units
Abnormal loss	50 units
Expected output (90% of 2,000)	1,800 units

Step 2. Calculate cost per unit of output and losses

(i) The total value of scrap is 250 units at 50p per unit = £125. We must split this between the scrap value of normal loss and the scrap value of abnormal loss.

	£
Normal loss	100
Abnormal loss	25
Total scrap (250 units × 50p)	125

(ii) The scrap value of normal loss is first deducted from the materials cost in the process, in order to calculate the output cost per unit and then credited to the process account as a 'value' for normal loss. The cost per unit in process 1 is calculated as follows.

	Total cost		Cost per expected unit of output
	£		£
Materials	8,100		
Less normal loss scrap value *	100		
	8,000	(÷ 1,800)	4.44
Labour and overhead	10,000	(÷ 1,800)	5.56
Total	18,000	(÷ 1,800)	10.00

* It is usual to set this scrap value of normal loss against the cost of materials.

Step 3. Calculate total cost of output and losses

		£
Output	(1,750 units × £10.00)	17,500
Normal loss	(200 units × £0.50)	100
Abnormal loss	(50 units × £10.00)	500
		18,100

Step 4. Complete accounts

Now we can put the process 1 account together.

PROCESS 1 ACCOUNT

	Units	£		Units	£
Materials	2,000	8,100	Output to process 2*	1,750	17,500
Labour and			Normal loss		
overhead		10,000	(scrap a/c)	200	100
			Abnormal loss a/c*	50	500
	2,000	18,100		2,000	18,100

* At £10 per unit.

(b) *Process 2*

Step 1. Determine output and losses

The normal loss is 10% of the units processed = 10% of (1,750 (from process 1) + 1,250) = 300 units. The actual loss is (3,000 - 2,800) = 200 units, so that there is abnormal gain of 100 units. These are *deducted* from actual output in arriving at the number of expected units (normal output) in the period.

Expected units of output

	Units
Actual output	2,800
Abnormal gain	(100)
Expected output (90% of 3,000)	2,700

Step 2. Calculate cost per unit of output and losses

(i) The total value of scrap is 200 units at £3 per unit = £600. We must split this between the scrap value of normal loss and the scrap value of abnormal gain. Abnormal gain's scrap value is 'negative'.

		£
Normal loss scrap value	300 units × £3	900
Abnormal gain scrap value	100 units × £3	(300)
Scrap value of actual loss	200 units × £3	600

(ii) The scrap value of normal loss is first deducted from the cost of materials in the process, in order to calculate a cost per unit of output, and then credited to the process account as a 'value' for normal loss. The cost per unit in process 2 is calculated as follows.

	Total cost		Cost per expected unit of output
	£		£
Materials:			
Transferred from process 1	17,500		
Added in process 2	1,900		
	19,400		
Less scrap value of normal loss	900		
	18,500	(÷ 2,700)	6.85
Labour and overhead	22,000	(÷ 2,700)	8.15
	40,500	(÷ 2,700)	15.00

Step 3. Calculate total cost of output and losses

		£
Output	(2,800 × £15.00)	42,000
Normal loss	(300 units × £3.00)	900
		42,900
Abnormal gain	(100 units × £15.00)	(1,500)
		41,400

Step 4. Complete accounts

PROCESS 2 ACCOUNT

	Units	£		Units	£
From process 1	1,750	17,500	Finished output	2,800	42,000
Added materials	1,250	1,900			
Labour and overhead		22,000	Normal loss (scrap a/c)	300	900
	3,000	41,400			
Abnormal gain a/c	100	1,500			
	3,100	42,900		3,100	42,900

(c) and (d)

Abnormal loss and abnormal gain accounts

For each process, one or the other of these accounts will record three items.

(i) The cost/value of the abnormal loss/gain. This is the corresponding entry to the entry in the process account.

(ii) The scrap value of the abnormal loss or gain, to set off against it.

(iii) A balancing figure, which is written to the P&L account as an adjustment to the profit figure.

ABNORMAL LOSS ACCOUNT

	£		£
Process 1	500	Scrap a/c (scrap value of abnormal loss)	25
		Profit and Loss a/c (balance)	475
	500		500

ABNORMAL GAIN ACCOUNT

	£		£
Scrap a/c (scrap value of abnormal gain units)	300	Process 2	1,500
Profit & Loss a/c (balance)	1,200		
	1,500		1,500

(e) *Scrap account*

This is credited with the cash value of actual units scrapped. The other entries in the account should all be identifiable as corresponding entries to those in the process accounts, and abnormal loss and abnormal gain accounts.

SCRAP ACCOUNT

	£		£
Normal loss:		Cash: sale of	
Process 1 (200 × 50p)	100	process 1 scrap (250 × 50p)	125
Process 2 (300 × £3)	900	Cash: sale of	
Abnormal loss a/c	25	process 2 scrap (200 × £3)	600
		Abnormal gain a/c	300
	1,025		1,025

Question 3

Look back at Question 1. Suppose the units of loss could be sold for £1 each. Prepare appropriate accounts.

Answer

Step 1. **Determine output and losses**

Actual output	2,000 units
Abnormal loss	400 units
Expected output	2,400 units

Step 2. **Calculate cost per unit of output and losses**

	£
Scrap value of normal loss	600
Scrap value of abnormal loss	400
Total scrap (1,000 units × £1)	1,000

Step 3. **Calculate total cost of output and losses**

		£
Output	(2,000 × £7.25)	14,500
Normal loss	(600 × £1.00)	600
Abnormal loss	(400 × £7.25)	2,900
		18,000

$$\text{Cost per expected unit} = \frac{£\big((11,700 - 600) + 6,300\big)}{2,400} = £7.25$$

Step 4. **Complete accounts**

PROCESS ACCOUNT

	Units	£		Units	£
Material	3,000	11,700	Output	2,000	14,500
Conversion costs		6,300	Normal loss	600	600
			Abnormal loss	400	2,900
	3,000	18,000		3,000	18,000

ABNORMAL LOSS ACCOUNT

	£		£
Process a/c	2,900	Scrap a/c	400
		P&L a/c	2,500
	2,900		2,900

SCRAP ACCOUNT

	£		£
Normal loss	600	Cash	1,000
Abnormal loss	400		
	1,000		1,000

Question 4

'No Friction' is an industrial lubricant which is formed by subjecting certain crude chemicals to two successive processes. The output of process 1 is passed to process 2 where it is blended with other chemicals. The process costs for period 3 were as follows.

Process 1

Material	3,000 kg at £0.25 per kg
Labour	£120
Process plant time	12 hours at £20 per hour

Process 2

Material	2,000 kg at £0.40 per kg
Labour	£84
Process plant time	20 hours at £13.50 per hour

General overhead for period 3 amounted to £357 and is absorbed into process costs on a budgeted labour cost basis. Actual labour costs were identical to budgeted labour costs.

The normal output of process 1 is 80% of input and of process 2, 90% of input. Waste matter from process 1 is sold for £0.20 per kg and that from process 2 for £0.30 per kg.

The output for period 3 was as follows.

Process 1	2,300 kgs
Process 2	4,000 kgs

There was no stock of work in progress at either the beginning or the end of the period and it may be assumed that all available waste matter had been sold at the prices indicated.

Required

Show how the foregoing data would be recorded in a system of cost accounts.

Answer

Process 1

Step 1.   Determine output and losses

	kg
Normal output (80% × 3,000 kg)	2,400
Actual output	2,300
Abnormal loss	100

Therefore normal loss = 20% × 3,000 kg = 600kg.

Step 2.   Calculate cost per unit of output and losses

(a)   The total value of scrap is 700 kg at £0.20 per kg = £140.

We must split this between the scrap value of normal loss and the scrap value of abnormal loss.

	£
Normal loss scrap value (600 kg × £0.20)	120
Abnormal loss scrap value (100 kg × £0.20)	20
Scrap value of actual loss	140

(b)   The scrap value of normal loss is first deducted from the cost of materials in the process, in order to calculate a cost per unit of output and is then credited to the process account as a 'value' for normal loss. The cost per unit in process 1 is therefore calculated as follows.

	£
Materials (3,000 × £0.25)	750
Labour	120
Process plant time (12 × £20)	240
General overhead (W1)	210
	1,320
Less scrap value of normal loss	120
	1,200

$$\text{Cost per unit} = \frac{\text{Total cost}}{\text{Expected units of output}} = \frac{£1,200}{2,400} = £0.50$$

Step 3. **Calculate total cost of output and losses**

	£
Output (2,300 × £0.50)	1,150
Normal loss (600 × £0.20)	120
Abnormal loss (100 × £0.50)	50
	1,320

Step 4. **Complete accounts**

At this stage, we only need to be concerned with completing the process 1 account. The finished stock account, scrap account and abnormal loss and gain account can be prepared once the process 2 account has been completed.

PROCESS 1 ACCOUNT

	kg	£		kg	£
Material	3,000	750	Normal loss to scrap a/c		
Labour		120	(20%)	600	120
Process plant time		240	Production transferred to		
General overhead (W1)		210	process 2	2,300	1,150
			Abnormal loss a/c	100	50
	3,000	1,320		3,000	1,320

PROCESS 2

Step 1. **Determine output and losses**

Input to process 2	kg
Transfer from process 1	2,300
Materials added	2,000
	4,300

Normal loss (10% × 4,300 kg) = 430 kg.

Normal output is therefore 90% of input, ie 90% × 4,300 = 3,870 kg.

Actual output was 4,000 kg.

Therefore, abnormal gain = (4,000 kg – 3,870 kg) = 130 kg

Step 2. **Calculate cost per unit of output and losses**

The retail value of scrap is 300kg at £0.30 per kg = £90. However, we must split this between the scrap value of normal loss and the scrap value of abnormal gain.

	£
Normal loss scrap value (430kg × £0.30)	129
Abnormal gain scrap value (130kg × £0.30)	(39)
	90

The cost per unit in process 2 is calculated as follows.

	£
Transfer from process 1 (as calculated earlier)	1,150
Materials (200 kg × £0.40)	800
Labour	84
Process plant time (20 hours × £13.50)	270
General overhead (W1)	147
	2,451

$$\text{Cost per unit} = \frac{\text{Total cost - scrap value of normal loss}}{\text{Expected units of ouptut}}$$

$$= \frac{£2,45 - £129}{3,870} = £0.60$$

Step 3. **Calculate total cost of output and losses**

	£
Output (4,000 kg × £0.60)	2,400
Scrap value of normal loss (430 kg × £0.3)	129
	2,529
Abnormal gain (130 × £0.60)	(78)
	2,451

Step 4. Complete accounts

PROCESS 2 ACCOUNT

	kg	£		kg	£
Transferred from process 1	2,300	1,150	Normal loss to scrap a/c		
Material added	2,000	800	(10%)	430	129
Labour		84	Production transferred to		
Process plant time		270	finished stock	4,000	2,400
General overhead		147			
	4,300	2,451			
Abnormal gain	130	78			
	4,430	2,529		4,430	2,529

FINISHED STOCK ACCOUNT

	kg	£
Process 2	4,000	2,400

SCRAP ACCOUNT

	kg	£		kg	£
Process 1	600	120	Scrap value of abnormal		
Process 2	430	129	gains (see workings)	130	39
Abnormal loss (process 1)	100	20	Cash	1,000	230
	1,130	269		1,130	269

ABNORMAL LOSS AND GAIN ACCOUNT

	kg	£		kg	£
Process 1 (loss)	100	50	Scrap value of process 1's		
Scrap value of abnormal			abnormal loss	100	20
gain (see workings)	130	39	Process 2 (gain)	130	78
Profit and loss		9			
	230	98		230	98

(*Note.* In this answer, a single account has been prepared for abnormal loss/gain. Your answer will probably have separated this single account into two separate accounts, one for abnormal gain and one for abnormal loss.)

Workings

1 Allocation of general overhead

Total labour cost = £120 + £84 = £204

∴ Overheads allocated to process 1 $= \dfrac{120}{204} \times £357 = £210$

and overheads allocated to process 2 $= \dfrac{84}{204} \times £357 = £147$

2 The scrap value of the normal loss from process 2 of 430 kg is overstated because of the abnormal gain.

The actual scrap from process 2 is only 300 kg therefore 130 kg is written off from the scrap account and charged to abnormal gain at 30p per kg.

5 LOSSES WITH A DISPOSAL COST

5.1 As well as being able to deal with questions in which scrap or loss units are **worthless** or have a **scrap value**, you must also be able to deal with losses which have a **disposal cost**.

5.2 The basic calculations required in such circumstances are as follows.

(a) Increase the process costs by the cost of disposing of the units of normal loss and use the resulting cost per unit to value good output and abnormal loss/gain.

(b) The normal loss is given no value in the process account.

(c) Include the disposal costs of normal loss on the debit side of the process account.

(d) Include the disposal costs of abnormal loss in the abnormal loss account and hence in the transfer of the cost of abnormal loss to the profit and loss account.

5.3   Suppose that input to a process was 1,000 units at a cost of £4,500. Normal loss is 10% and there are no opening and closing stocks. Actual output was 860 units and loss units had to be disposed of at a cost of £0.90 per unit.

Normal loss = 10% × 1,000 = 100 units. ∴ Abnormal loss = 900 – 860 = 40 units

$$\text{Cost per unit} = \frac{£4,500 + (100 \times £0.90)}{900} = £5.10$$

5.4   The relevant accounts would be as follows.

PROCESS ACCOUNT

	Units	£		Units	£
Cost of input	1,000	4,500	Output	860	4,386
Disposal cost of			Normal loss	100	-
normal loss		90	Abnormal loss	40	204
	1,000	4,590		1,000	4,590

ABNORMAL LOSS ACCOUNT

	£		£
Process a/c	204	Profit and loss a/c	240
Disposal cost (40 × £0.90)	36		
	240		240

6   VALUING CLOSING WORK IN PROGRESS   12/96, 6/97, 12/99

> **Exam focus point**
> In 6/97 candidates were required to prepare process accounts in which opening and closing work in process were not 100% complete.

6.1   In the examples we have looked at so far we have assumed that opening and closing stocks of work in process have been nil. We must now look at more realistic examples and consider how to allocate the costs incurred in a period between completed output (that is, finished units) and partly completed closing stock.

6.2   Some examples will help to illustrate the problem, and the techniques used to share out (apportion) costs between finished output and closing stocks.

6.3   Suppose that we have the following account for Process 2 for period 9.

PROCESS ACCOUNT

	Units	£		Units	£
Materials	1,000	6,200	Finished goods	800	?
Labour and overhead		2,850	Closing WIP	200	?
	1,000	9,050		1,000	9,050

How do we value the finished goods and closing work in process?

6.4   With any form of process costing involving closing WIP, we have to apportion costs between output and closing WIP. To apportion costs 'fairly' we make use of the concept of **equivalent units of production**.

Equivalent units

KEY TERM

Equivalent units are notional whole units which represent incomplete work, and which are used to apportion costs between work in process and completed output.

6.5 We will assume that in the example above the degree of completion is as follows.

(a) **Direct materials**. These are added in full at the start of processing, and so any closing WIP will have 100% of their direct material content. (This is not always the case in practice. Materials might be added gradually throughout the process, in which case closing stock will only be a certain percentage complete as to material content. We will look at this later in the chapter.)

(b) **Direct labour and production overhead.** These are usually assumed to be incurred at an even rate through the production process, so that when we refer to a unit that is 50% complete, we mean that it is half complete for labour and overhead, although it might be 100% complete for materials.

6.6 Let us also assume that the closing WIP is 100% complete for materials and 25% complete for labour and overhead.

6.7 How would we now put a value to the finished output and the closing WIP?

In **Step 1** of our framework, we have been told what output and losses are. However we also need to calculate **equivalent units**.

STATEMENT OF EQUIVALENT UNITS

| | | Materials | | Labour and overhead | |
	Total units	Degree of completion	Equivalent units	Degree of completion	Equivalent units
Finished output	800	100%	800	100%	800
Closing WIP	200	100%	200	25%	50
	1,000		1,000		850

Exam focus point
In the 12/99 exam, part of a question required candidates to explain the concept of equivalent units and to explain its relevance in a process costing system.

6.8 In **Step 2** the important figure is **average cost per equivalent unit**. This can be calculated as follows.

STATEMENT OF COSTS PER EQUIVALENT UNIT

	Materials	Labour and overhead
Costs incurred in the period	£6,200	£2,850
Equivalent units of work done	1,000	850
Cost per equivalent unit (approx)	£6.20	£3.3529

6.9 To calculate total costs for **Step 3**, we prepare a statement of evaluation to show how the costs should be apportioned between finished output and closing WIP.

 238

STATEMENT OF EVALUATION

| | | Materials | | | Labour and overheads | | |
Item	Equivalent units	Cost per equivalent units £	Cost £	Equivalent units	Cost per equivalent units £	Cost £	Total cost £
Finished output	800	6.20	4,960	800	3.3529	2,682	7,642
Closing WIP	200	6.20	1,240	50	3.3529	168	1,408
	1,000		6,200	850		2,850	9,050

6.10 The process account (work in progress, or work in process account) would be shown as follows.

PROCESS ACCOUNT

	Units	£		Units	£
Materials	1,000	6,200	Finished goods	800	7,642
Labour overhead		2,850	Closing WIP	200	1,408
	1,000	9,050		1,000	9,050

Different rates of input

6.11 In many industries, materials, labour and overhead may be **added at different rates** during the course of production.

(a) Output from a previous process (for example the output from process 1 to process 2) may be introduced into the subsequent process all at once, so that closing stock is 100% complete in respect of these materials.

(b) Further materials may be added gradually during the process, so that closing stock is only partially complete in respect of these added materials.

(c) Labour and overhead may be 'added' at yet another different rate. When production overhead is absorbed on a labour hour basis, however, we should expect the degree of completion on overhead to be the same as the degree of completion on labour.

When this situation occurs, **equivalent units**, and a **cost per equivalent unit**, should be calculated separately for each type of material, and also for conversion costs.

6.12 EXAMPLE: EQUIVALENT UNITS AND DIFFERENT DEGREES OF COMPLETION

Suppose that Columbine Ltd is a manufacturer of processed goods, and that results in process 2 for April 20X3 were as follows.

Opening stock	nil
Material input from process 1	4,000 units
Costs of input:	£
material from process 1	6,000
added materials in process 2	1,080
conversion costs	1,720

Output is transferred into the next process, process 3.

Closing work in process amounted to 800 units, complete as to:

process 1 material	100%
added materials	50%
conversion costs	30%

Required

Prepare the account for process 2 for April 20X3.

6.13 SOLUTION

(a) STATEMENT OF EQUIVALENT UNITS (OF PRODUCTION IN THE PERIOD)

							Equivalent units of production			
			Process 1 material		Added materials		Labour and overhead	
Input	Output	Total						
Units		Units	Units	%	Units	%	Units	%
4,000	Completed production	3,200	3,200	100	3,200	100	3,200	100
	Closing stock	800	800	100	400	50	240	30
4,000		4,000	4,000		3,600		3,440	

(b) STATEMENT OF COST (PER EQUIVALENT UNIT)

Input	Cost	Equivalent production in units	Cost per unit
	£		£
Process 1 material	6,000	4,000	1.50
Added materials	1,080	3,600	0.30
Labour and overhead	1,720	3,440	0.50
	8,800		2.30

(c) STATEMENT OF EVALUATION (OF FINISHED WORK AND CLOSING STOCKS)

Production	Cost element	Number of equivalent units	Cost per equivalent unit	Total	Cost
			£	£	£
Completed production		3,200	2.30		7,360
Closing stock:	process 1 material	800	1.50	1,200	
	added material	400	0.30	120	
	labour and overhead	240	0.50	120	
					1,440
					8,800

(d)

PROCESS ACCOUNT

	Units	£		Units	£
(ex process 1 a/c)					
Process 1 material (Stores a/c)	4,000	6,000	Process 3 a/c (finished output)	3,200	7,360
Added material (Wages a/c and o'h a/c)		1,080			
Conversion costs		1,720	Closing stock c/f	800	1,440
	4,000	8,800		4,000	8,800

7 VALUING OPENING WORK IN PROGRESS: FIFO METHOD 6/94, 6/97, 6/98

7.1 Opening work in progress is partly complete at the beginning of a period and is valued at the cost incurred to date. In the example in Paragraph 6.12, closing work in progress of 800 units at the end of April 20X3 would be carried forward as opening stock, value £1,440, at the beginning of May 20X3.

7.2 It therefore follows that the work required to complete units of opening stock is 100% minus the work in progress done in the previous period. For example, if 100 units of opening stock are 70% complete at the beginning of June 20X2, the equivalent units of production would be as follows.

Equivalent units in previous period	(May 20X2) (70%)	=	70
Equivalent units to complete work in current period	(June 20X2) (30%)	=	30
Total work done			100

7.3 **The FIFO method of valuation** deals with production on a first in, first out basis. The assumption is that the first units completed in any period are the units of opening stock that were held at the beginning of the period.

7.4 EXAMPLE: WIP AND FIFO

Suppose that information relating to process 1 of a two-stage production process is as follows, for August 20X2.

Opening stock 500 units: degree of completion	60%
cost to date	£2,800

	£
Costs incurred in August 20X2	
Direct materials (2,500 units introduced)	13,200
Direct labour	6,600
Production overhead	6,600
	26,400

Closing stock 300 units: degree of completion	80%

There was no loss in the process.

Required

Prepare the process 1 account for August 20X2.

7.5 SOLUTION

As the term implies, first in, first out means that in August 20X2 the first units completed were the units of opening stock.

Opening stocks:	work done to date =	60%
	plus work done in August 20X2 =	40%

The cost of the work done up to 1 August 20X2 is known to be £2,800, so that the cost of the units completed will be £2,800 plus the cost of completing the final 40% of the work on the units in August 20X2.

Once the opening stock has been completed, all other finished output in August 20X2 will be work started as well as finished in the month.

	Units
Total output in August 20X2 ★	2,700
Less opening stock, completed first	500
Work started and finished in August 20X2	2,200

(★ Opening stock plus units introduced minus closing stock = 500 + 2,500 – 300)

What we are doing here is taking the total output of 2,700 units, and saying that we must divide it into two parts as follows.

(a)   The opening stock, which was first in and so must be first out.

(b)   The rest of the units, which were 100% worked in the period.

Dividing finished output into two parts in this way is a necessary feature of the FIFO valuation method.

Continuing the example, closing stock of 300 units will be started in August 20X2, but not yet completed.

The total cost of output to process 2 during 20X2 will be as follows.

		£
Opening stock	cost brought forward	2,800 (60%)
	plus cost incurred during August 20X2,	
	to complete	x (40%)
		2,800 + x
Fully worked 2,200 units		y
Total cost of output to process 2, FIFO basis		2,800 + x + y

Equivalent units will again be used as the basis for apportioning **costs incurred during August 20X2**. Be sure that you understand the treatment of 'opening stock units completed', and can relate the calculations to the principles of FIFO valuation.

Step 1.   **Determine output and losses**

STATEMENT OF EQUIVALENT UNITS

	Total units		Equivalent units of production in August 20X2
Opening stock units completed	500	(40%)	200
Fully worked units	2,200	(100%)	2,200
Output to process 2	2,700		2,400
Closing stock	300	(80%)	240
	3,000		2,640

Step 2.   **Calculate cost per unit of output and losses**

The cost per equivalent unit in August 20X2 can now be calculated.

STATEMENT OF COST PER EQUIVALENT UNIT

$$\frac{\text{Cost incurred}}{\text{Equivalent units}} \quad = \quad \frac{£26,400}{2,640}$$

Cost per equivalent unit =   £10

Step 3.   **Calculate total costs of output, losses and WIP**

STATEMENT OF EVALUATION

	Equivalent units	Valuation £
Opening stock, work done in August 20X2	200	2,000
Fully worked units	2,200	22,000
Closing stock	240	2,400
	2,640	26,400

The total value of the completed opening stock will be £2,800 (brought forward) plus £2,000 added in August before completion = £4,800.

Step 4. **Complete accounts**

PROCESS 1 ACCOUNT

	Units	£		Units	£
Opening stock	500	2,800	Output to process 2:		
Direct materials	2,500	13,200	Opening stock completed	500	4,800
Direct labour		6,600	Fully worked units	2,200	22,000
Production o'hd		6,600		2,700	26,800
			Closing stock	300	2,400
	3,000	29,200		3,000	29,200

We now know that the value of x is £(4,800 – 2,800) = £2,000 and the value of y is £22,000.

Question 5

The following information relates to process 3 of a three-stage production process for the month of January 20X4.

Opening stock

		£
300 units complete as to:		
materials from process 2	100%	4,400
added materials	90%	1,150
labour	80%	540
production overhead	80%	810
		6,900

In January 20X4, a further 1,800 units were transferred from process 2 at a valuation of £27,000. Added materials amounted to £6,600 and direct labour to £3,270. Production overhead is absorbed at the rate of 150% of direct labour cost. Closing stock at 31 January 20X4 amounted to 450 units, complete as to:

process 2 materials	100%
added materials	60%
labour and overhead	50%

Required

Prepare the process 3 account for January 20X4 using FIFO valuation principles.

Answer

Step 1. **STATEMENT OF EQUIVALENT UNITS**

	Total units	Process 2 materials	Added materials		Conversion costs	
Opening stock	300	0	(10%)	30	(20%)	60
Fully worked units *	1,350	1,350		1,350		1,350
Output to finished goods	1,650	1,350		1,380		1,410
Closing stock	450	450	(60%)	270	(50%)	225
	2,100	1,800		1,650		1,635

* Transfers from process 2, minus closing stock.

Step 2. **STATEMENT OF COSTS PER EQUIVALENT UNIT**

	Total cost	Equivalent units	Cost per equivalent unit
	£		£
Process 2 materials	27,000	1,800	15.00
Added materials	6,600	1,650	4.00
Direct labour	3,270	1,635	2.00
Production overhead (150% of £3,270)	4,905	1,635	3.00
			24.00

Step 3. STATEMENT OF EVALUATION

	Process 2 materials £		Additional materials £		Labour £		Overhead £	Total £
Opening stock cost b/f	4,400		1,150		540		810	6,900
Added in Jan 20X4	-	(30x£4)	120	(60x£2)	120	(60x£3)	180	420
	4,400		1,270		660		990	7,320
Fully worked units	20,250		5,400		2,700		4,050	32,400
Output to finished Goods	24,650		6,670		3,360		5,040	39,720
Closing stock (450x£15)	6,750	(270x£4)	1,080	(225x£2)	450	(225x£3)	675	8,955
	31,400		7,750		3,810		5,715	48,675

Step 4. COMPLETE ACCOUNTS

PROCESS 3 ACCOUNT

	Units	£		Units	£
Opening stock b/f	300	6,900	Finished goods a/c	1,650	39,720
Process 2 a/c	1,800	27,000			
Stores a/c		6,600			
Wages a/c		3,270			
Production o'hd a/c		4,905	Closing stock c/f	450	8,955
	2,100	48,675		2,100	48,675

8 VALUING OPENING WORK IN PROGRESS: WEIGHTED AVERAGE COST METHOD

8.1 An alternative to FIFO is the **weighted average cost method of stock valuation** which calculates a weighted average cost of units produced from both opening stock and units introduced in the current period.

By this method **no distinction is made between units of opening stock and new units introduced** to the process during the accounting period. The cost of opening stock is added to costs incurred during the period, and completed units of opening stock are each given a value of one full equivalent unit of production.

8.2 EXAMPLE: WEIGHTED AVERAGE COST METHOD

Magpie Ltd produces an item which is manufactured in two consecutive processes. Information relating to process 2 during September 20X3 is as follows.

Opening stock 800 units
Degree of completion:

		£
process 1 materials	100%	4,700
added materials	40%	600
conversion costs	30%	1,000
		6,300

During September 20X3, 3,000 units were transferred from process 1 at a valuation of £18,100. Added materials cost £9,600 and conversion costs were £11,800.

Closing stock at 30 September 20X3 amounted to 1,000 units which were 100% complete with respect to process 1 materials and 60% complete with respect to added materials. Conversion cost work was 40% complete.

Magpie Ltd uses a weighted average cost system for the valuation of output and closing stock.

Required

Prepare the process 2 account for September 20X3.

8.3 SOLUTION

Step 1. Opening stock units count as a full equivalent unit of production when the weighted average cost system is applied. Closing stock equivalent units are assessed in the usual way.

STATEMENT OF EQUIVALENT UNITS

	Total units		Process 1 material	Added material	Conversion costs
				Equivalent units	
Opening stock	800	(100%)	800	800	800
Fully worked units *	2,000	(100%)	2,000	2,000	2,000
Output to finished goods	2,800		2,800	2,800	2,800
Closing stock	1,000	(100%)	1,000	(60%) 600	(40%) 400
	3,800		3,800	3,400	3,200

(* 3,000 units from process 1 minus closing stock of 1,000 units)

Step 2. The cost of opening stock is added to costs incurred in September 20X3, and a cost per equivalent unit is then calculated.

STATEMENT OF COSTS PER EQUIVALENT UNIT

	Process 1 material £	Added materials £	Conversion costs £
Opening stock	4,700	600	1,000
Added in September 20X3	18,100	9,600	11,800
Total cost	22,800	10,200	12,800
Equivalent units	3,800 units	3,400 units	3,200 units
Cost per equivalent unit	£6	£3	£4

Step 3. STATEMENT OF EVALUATION

	Process 1 material £	Added materials £	Conversion costs £	Total cost £
Output to finished goods (2,800 units)	16,800	8,400	11,200	36,400
Closing stock	6,000	1,800	1,600	9,400
				45,800

Step 4. PROCESS 2 ACCOUNT

	Units	£		Units	£
Opening stock b/f	800	6,300	Finished goods a/c	2,800	36,400
Process 1 a/c	3,000	18,100			
Added materials		9,600			
Conversion costs		11,800	Closing stock c/f	1,000	9,400
	3,800	45,800		3,800	45,800

Which method should be used?

8.4 **FIFO stock valuation is more common than the weighted average method, and should be used unless an indication is given to the contrary.** You may find that you are presented with limited information about the opening stock, which forces you to use either the FIFO or the weighted average method. The rules are as follows.

(a) If you are told the degree of completion of each element in opening stock, but not the value of each cost element, then you must use the **FIFO method.**

(b) If you are not given the degree of completion of each cost element in opening stock, but you are given the value of each cost element, then you must use the **weighted average method.**

Chapter roundup

- Many students find process costing daunting. It shouldn't be. Use our suggested four-step approach to dealing with questions and you should find the topic quite straightforward.

    Step 1. Determine output and losses

    Step 2. Calculate cost per unit of output, losses and WIP

    Step 3. Calculate total cost of output, losses and WIP

    Step 4. Complete accounts

- **Process costing** is used where there is a continuous flow of identical units.

- Losses may occur in process. If a certain level of loss is expected, this is known as **normal loss**. If losses are greater than expected, the extra loss is **abnormal loss**. If losses are less than expected, the difference is known as **abnormal gain**.

- It is conventional for the **scrap value** of normal loss to be deducted from the cost of materials before a cost per equivalent unit is calculated.

- Abnormal losses and gains never affect the cost of good units of production. The scrap value of abnormal losses is not credited to the process account, and abnormal loss and gain units carry the same full cost as a good unit of production.

- When units are partly completed at the end of a period (and hence there is closing work in progress), it is necessary to calculate the **equivalent units of production** in order to determine the cost of a completed unit.

- Account can be taken of opening work in progress using either the **FIFO** method or the **weighted average cost method.**

Quick quiz

1   What are the distinguishing features of process costing? (see para 1.2)

2   Distinguish between normal loss and abnormal loss. (key terms)

3   Why are normal and abnormal losses accounted for in different ways? (3.11)

4   Is an abnormal gain a debit or credit entry in the process account? (3.13)

5   What are the different accounting treatments for the scrap value of normal loss and the scrap value of abnormal loss? (4.2)

6   What is an equivalent unit? (key terms)

7   What three 'statements' are usually prepared when answering a process costing question? (6.7 - 6.9)

8   Distinguish between the FIFO and weighted average cost methods of valuing opening WIP. (7.3, 8.1)

9   Unless given an indication to the contrary, which method of valuing opening WIP should be used? (8.4)

Question to try	Level	Marks	Time
13	Examination	14	25 mins

Chapter 13

PROCESS COSTING, JOINT PRODUCTS AND BY-PRODUCTS

Chapter topic list	Syllabus reference
1 Contrasting joint products and by-products	CA 3(b)(iv)
2 Problems in accounting for joint products	CA 3(b)(iv)
3 Dealing with common costs	CA 3(b)(iv)
4 Joint products in process accounts	CA 3(b)(iv)
5 Accounting for by-products	CA 3(b)(iv)

Introduction

You should now be aware of the most simple and the more complex areas of process costing. In this chapter we are going to turn our attention to the methods of accounting for **joint products** and **by-products** which arise as a result of a **continuous process**.

1   CONTRASTING JOINT PRODUCTS AND BY-PRODUCTS

KEY TERMS

- **Joint products** are two or more products which are output from the same processing operation, but which are indistinguishable from each other up to their point of separation.

- A **by-product** is a supplementary or secondary product (arising as the result of a process) whose value is small relative to that of the principal product.

1.1 (a) Joint products have a **substantial sales value**. Often they require further processing before they are ready for sale. Joint products arise, for example, in the oil refining industry where diesel fuel, petrol, paraffin and lubricants are all produced from the same process.

(b) The distinguishing feature of a by-product is its **relatively low sales value** in comparison to the main product. In the timber industry, for example, by-products include sawdust, small offcuts and bark.

1.2 **What exactly separates a joint product from a by-product?**

(a) A **joint product** is regarded as an important saleable item, and so it should be **separately costed**. The profitability of each joint product should be assessed in the cost accounts.

(b) A **by-product** is not important as a saleable item, and whatever revenue it earns is a 'bonus' for the organisation. Because of their relative insignificance, by-products are **not separately costed**.

2 PROBLEMS IN ACCOUNTING FOR JOINT PRODUCTS 6/95

> **Exam focus point**
> In 6/95, there were 3 marks to be gained by distinguishing between the accounting treatment of joint products and of by-products.

2.1 Joint products are not separately identifiable until a certain stage is reached in the processing operations. This stage is the '**split-off point**', sometimes referred to as the **separation point**. Costs incurred prior to this point of separation are **common** or **joint costs,** and these need to be allocated (apportioned) in some manner to each of the joint products. In the following sketched example, there are two different split-off points.

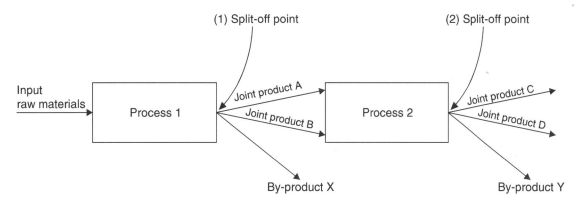

2.2 The **problems in accounting for joint products** are basically of two different sorts.

(a) How common costs should be apportioned between products, in order to put a value to closing stocks and to the cost of sale (and profit) for each product.

(b) Whether it is more profitable to sell a joint product at one stage of processing, or to process the product further and sell it at a later stage.

3 DEALING WITH COMMON COSTS 12/98

3.1 The problem of costing for joint products concerns **common costs,** that is those common processing costs shared between the units of eventual output up to their 'split-off point'. Some method needs to be devised for sharing the common costs between the individual joint products for the following reasons.

(a) To put a value to closing stocks of each joint product.
(b) To record the costs and therefore the profit from each joint product.
(c) Perhaps to assist in pricing decisions.

3.2 Here are some examples of the common costs problem.

(a) How to spread the common costs of oil refining between the joint products made (petrol, naphtha, kerosene and so on).

(b) How to spread the common costs of running the telephone network between telephone calls in peak and cheap rate times, or between local and long distance calls.

3.3   Various methods that might be used to establish a basis for apportioning or allocating common costs to each product are as follows.

- Physical measurement
- Relative sales value apportionment method; sales value at split-off point

Dealing with common costs: physical measurement

3.4   With physical measurement, **the common cost is apportioned to the joint products on the basis of the proportion that the output of each product bears by weight or volume to the total output.** An example of this would be the case where two products, product 1 and product 2, incur common costs to the point of separation of £3,000 and the output of each product is 600 tons and 1,200 tons respectively.

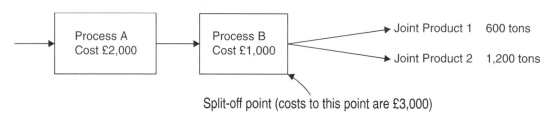

Split-off point (costs to this point are £3,000)

Product 1 sells for £4 per ton and product 2 for £2 per ton.

The division of the common costs (£3,000) between product 1 and product 2 could be based on the tonnage of output.

	Product 1		Product 2	Total
Output	600 tons	+	1,200 tons	1,800 tons
Proportion of common cost	$\dfrac{600}{1,800}$	+	$\dfrac{1,200}{1,800}$	
	£		£	£
Apportioned cost	1,000		2,000	3,000
Sales	2,400		2,400	4,800
Profit	1,400		400	1,800
Profit/sales ratio	58.3%		16.7%	37.5%

3.5   Physical measurement has the following limitations.

(a)   Where the products separate during the processes into different states, for example where one product is a gas and another is a liquid, this method is unsuitable.

(b)   This method does not take into account the relative income-earning potentials of the individual products, with the result that one product might appear very profitable and another appear to be incurring losses.

Dealing with common costs: sales value at split-off point

3.6   With relative sales value apportionment of common cost, **the cost is allocated according to the product's ability to produce income.** This method is most widely used because the assumption that some profit margin should be attained for all products under normal marketing conditions is satisfied. The common cost is apportioned to each product in the proportion that the sales (market) value of that product bears to the sales value of the total output from the particular processes concerned. Using the previous example where the sales price per unit is £4 for product 1 and £2 for product 2.

(a)	Common costs of processes to split-off point	£3,000
(b)	Sales value of product 1 at £4 per ton	£2,400
(c)	Sales value of product 2 at £2 per ton	£2,400

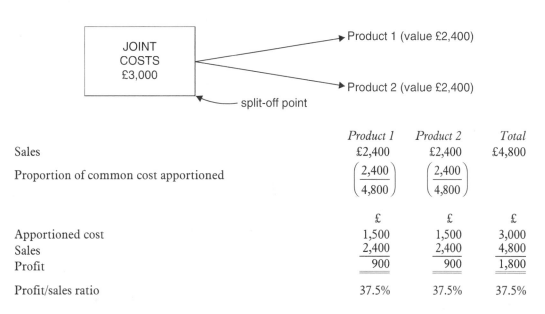

	Product 1	*Product 2*	*Total*
Sales	£2,400	£2,400	£4,800
Proportion of common cost apportioned	$\left(\dfrac{2,400}{4,800}\right)$	$\left(\dfrac{2,400}{4,800}\right)$	
	£	£	£
Apportioned cost	1,500	1,500	3,000
Sales	2,400	2,400	4,800
Profit	900	900	1,800
Profit/sales ratio	37.5%	37.5%	37.5%

3.7 A comparison of the gross profit margin resulting from the application of the above methods for allocating common costs will illustrate the greater acceptability of the relative sales value apportionment method. Physical measurement gives a higher profit margin to product 1, not necessarily because product 1 is highly profitable, but because it has been given a smaller share of common costs.

4 JOINT PRODUCTS IN PROCESS ACCOUNTS

4.1 This example illustrates how joint products are incorporated into process accounts.

EXAMPLE: JOINT PRODUCTS AND PROCESS ACCOUNTS

Three joint products are manufactured in a common process, which consists of two consecutive stages. Output from process 1 is transferred to process 2, and output from process 2 consists of the three joint products, Hans, Nils and Bumpsydaisies. All joint products are sold as soon as they are produced.

Data for period 2 of 20X6 are as follows.

	Process 1	*Process 2*
Opening and closing stock	None	None
Direct material		
(30,000 units at £2 per unit)	£60,000	-
Conversion costs	£76,500	£226,200
Normal loss	10% of input	10% of input
Scrap value of normal loss	£0.50 per unit	£2 per unit
Output	26,000 units	10,000 units of Han
		7,000 units of Nil
		6,000 units of Bumpsydaisy

Selling prices are £18 per unit of Han, £20 per unit of Nil and £30 per unit of Bumpsydaisy.

Required

(a) Prepare the Process 1 account.
(b) Prepare the Process 2 account using the sales value method of apportionment.
(c) Prepare a profit statement for the joint products.

4.2 SOLUTION

(a) **Process 1 equivalent units**

	Total units	*Equivalent units*
Output to process 2	26,000	26,000
Normal loss	3,000	0
Abnormal loss (balance)	1,000	1,000
	30,000	27,000

Costs of process 1

	£
Direct materials	60,000
Conversion costs	76,500
	136,500
Less scrap value of normal loss (3,000 × £0.50)	1,500
	135,000

Cost per equivalent unit $\dfrac{£135,000}{27,000} = £5$

PROCESS 1 ACCOUNT

	£		£
Direct materials	60,000	Output to process 2	
Conversion costs	76,500	(26,000 × £5)	130,000
		Normal loss (scrap value)	1,500
		Abnormal loss a/c	
		(1,000 × £5)	5,000
	136,500		136,500

(b) **Process 2 equivalent units**

	Total units	*Equivalent units*
Units of Hans produced	10,000	10,000
Units of Nils produced	7,000	7,000
Units of Bumpsydaisies produced	6,000	6,000
Normal loss (10% of 26,000)	2,600	0
Abnormal loss (balance)	400	400
	26,000	23,400

Costs of process 2

	£
Material costs - from process 1	130,000
Conversion costs	226,200
	356,200
Less scrap value of normal loss (2,600 × £2)	5,200
	351,000

Cost per equivalent unit $\dfrac{£351,000}{23,400} = £15$

Cost of good output (10,000 + 7,000 + 6,000) = 23,000 units × £15 = £345,000

The sales value of joint products, and the apportionment of the output costs of £345,000, is as follows.

	Sales value		*Costs (process 2)*
	£	%	£
Hans (10,000 × £18)	180,000	36	124,200
Nils (7,000 × £20)	140,000	28	96,600
Bumpsydaisy (6,000 × £30)	180,000	36	124,200
	500,000	100	345,000

PROCESS 2 ACCOUNT

	£		£
Process 1 materials	130,000	Finished goods accounts	
Conversion costs	226,200	- Hans	124,200
		- Nils	96,600
		- Bumpsydaisies	124,200
		Normal loss (scrap value)	5,200
		Abnormal loss a/c	6,000
	356,200		356,200

(c) PROFIT STATEMENT

	Hans	*Nils*	*Bumpsydaisies*
	£'000	£'000	£'000
Sales	180.0	140.0	180.0
Costs	124.2	96.6	124.2
Profit	55.8	43.4	55.8
Profit/ sales ratio	31%	31%	31%

Question 1

Prepare the Process 2 account and a profit statement for the joint products in the above example using the units basis of apportionment.

Answer

PROCESS 2 ACCOUNT

	£		£
Process 1 materials	130,000	Finished goods accounts	
Conversion costs	226,200	- Hans (10,000 × £15)	150,000
		- Nils (7,000 × £15)	105,000
		- Bumpsydaisies (6,000 × £15)	90,000
		Normal loss (scrap value)	5,200
		Abnormal loss a/c (400 × £15)	6,000
	356,200		356,200

PROFIT STATEMENT

	Hans	*Nils*	*Bumpsydaisies*
	£'000	£'000	£'000
Sales	180	140	180
Costs	150	105	90
Profit	30	35	90
Profit/ sales ratio	16.7%	25%	50%

5   ACCOUNTING FOR BY-PRODUCTS   6/95

5.1 The by-product has some commercial value and its accounting treatment of income may be as follows.

(a) Income (minus any post-separation further processing or selling costs) from the sale of the by-product may be **added to sales of the main product,** thereby increasing sales turnover for the period.

(b) The sales of the by-product may be **treated as a separate, incidental source of income** against which are set only post-separation costs (if any) of the by-product. The revenue would be recorded in the profit and loss account as 'other income'.

(c) The sales income of the by-product may be **deducted from the cost of production** or cost of sales of the main product.

(d) The **net realisable value of the by-product may be deducted from the cost of production of the main product**. The net realisable value is the final saleable value of the by-product minus any post-separation costs. Any closing stock valuation of the main product or joint products would therefore be reduced.

The choice of method (a), (b), (c) or (d) will be influenced by the circumstances of production and ease of calculation, as much as by conceptual correctness. The method you are most likely to come across in examinations is method (d). An example will help to clarify the distinction between the different methods.

5.2 EXAMPLE: METHODS OF ACCOUNTING FOR BY-PRODUCTS

During November 20X3, Splatter Ltd recorded the following results.

Opening stock	main product P, nil
	by-product Z, nil
Cost of production	£120,000

Sales of the main product amounted to 90% of output during the period, and 10% of production was held as closing stock at 30 November.

Sales revenue from the main product during November 20X2 was £150,000.

A by-product Z is produced, and output had a net sales value of £1,000. Of this output, £700 was sold during the month, and £300 was still in stock at 30 November.

Required

Calculate the profit for November using the four methods of accounting for by-products.

5.3 SOLUTION

The four methods of accounting for by-products are shown below.

(a) Income from by-product added to sales of the main product

	£	£
Sales of main product (£150,000 + £700)		150,700
Opening stock	0	
Cost of production	120,000	
	120,000	
Less closing stock (10%)	12,000	
Cost of sales		108,000
Profit, main product		42,700

The closing stock of the by-product has no recorded value in the cost accounts.

(b) **By-product income treated as a separate source of income**

	£	£
Sales, main product		150,000
Opening stock	0	
Cost of production	120,000	
	120,000	
Closing stock (10%)	12,000	
Cost of sales, main product		108,000
Profit, main product		42,000
Other income		700
Total profit		42,700

The closing stock of the by-product again has no value in the cost accounts.

(c) **Sales income of the by-product deducted from the cost of production in the period**

	£	£
Sales, main product		150,000
Opening stock	0	
Cost of production (120,000 – 700)	119,300	
	119,300	
Less closing stock (10%)	11,930	
Cost of sales		107,370
Profit, main product		42,630

Although the profit is different from the figure in (a) and (b), the by-product closing stock again has no value.

(d) **Net realisable value of the by-product deducted from the cost of production in the period**

	£	£
Sales, main product		150,000
Opening stock	0	
Cost of production (120,000 – 1,000)	119,000	
	119,000	
Less closing stock (10%)	11,900	
Cost of sales		107,100
Profit, main product		42,900

As with the other three methods, closing stock of the by-product has no value in the books of accounting, but the value of the closing stock (£300) has been used to reduce the cost of production, and in this respect it has been allowed for in deriving the cost of sales and the profit for the period.

Question 2

Randolph Ltd manufactures two joint products, J and K, in a common process. A by-product X is also produced. Data for the month of December 20X2 were as follows.

Opening stocks		nil	
Costs of processing	direct materials	£25,500	
	direct labour	£10,000	

Production overheads are absorbed at the rate of 300% of direct labour costs.

		Production	Sales
		Units	Units
Output and sales consisted of:	product J	8,000	7,000
	product K	8,000	6,000
	by-product X	1,000	1,000

The sales value per unit of J, K and X is £4, £6 and £0.50 respectively. The saleable value of the by-product is deducted from process costs before apportioning costs to each joint product. Costs of the common processing are apportioned between product J and product K on the basis of sales value of production.

Required

Calculate the profit for December 20X2. Analyse this profit by individual products.

Answer

The sales value of production was £80,000.

	£	
Product J (8,000 × £4)	32,000	(40%)
Product K (8,000 × £6)	48,000	(60%)
	80,000	

The costs of production were as follows.

	£
Direct materials	25,500
Direct labour	10,000
Overhead (300% of £10,000)	30,000
	65,500
Less sales value of by-product (1,000 × 50p)	500
Net production costs	65,000

The profit statement would appear as follows (nil opening stocks).

	Product J			Product K		Total
		£			£	£
Production costs	(40%)	26,000	(60%)		39,000	65,000
Less closing stock	(1,000 units)	3,250	(2,000 units)		9,750	13,000
Cost of sales		22,750			29,250	52,000
Sales	(7,000 units)	28,000	(6,000 units)		36,000	64,000
Profit		5,250			6,750	12,000

Chapter roundup

- Joint products are two or more products separated in a process, each of which has a significant value compared to the other. A by-product is an incidental product from a process which has an insignificant value compared to the main product.

- The point at which joint and by-products become separately identifiable is known as the split-off point or separation point. Costs incurred up to this point are called common costs or joint costs.

- There are four methods of apportioning joint costs, each of which can produce significantly different results. These methods are as follows.

  - Physical measurement

  - Relative sales value apportionment method; sales value at split-off point

  - Relative sales value apportionment method; sales value of end product less further processing costs after split-off point

  - Weighted average method

- The relative sales value method is most widely used because (ignoring the effect of further processing costs) it assumes that all products achieve the same profit margin.

- The most common method of accounting for by-products is to deduct the net realisable value of the by-product from the cost of the main products.

Quick quiz

1   What is the difference between a joint product and a by-product? (see key terms)

2   What is meant by the term 'split-off' point? (2.1)

3   Name two methods of apportioning common costs to joint products. (3.3)

4   Describe the four methods of accounting for by-products. (5.1)

Question to try	Level	Marks	Time
14	Examination	14	25 mins

Chapter 14

SERVICE COSTING

Chapter topic list	Syllabus reference
1 What is service costing?	CA 3(c)(i)
2 Unit cost measures	CA 3(c)(ii)
3 Service cost analysis	CA 3(c)(iii)
4 Service cost analysis in internal service situations	CA 3(c)(iii)
5 The usefulness of costing services that do not earn revenue	CA 3(c)(iii)
6 Service cost analysis in service industry situations	CA 3(c)(iii)

Introduction

Having covered job, batch, contract and process costing, we will now turn our attention to **service costing**, the service being a **specialist service** provided to third parties or an **internal service** provided within an organisation. The chapter looks at the calculation of a cost per unit of service and at methods of cost accounting in both types of situation.

1   WHAT IS SERVICE COSTING?   6/99

> **KEY TERM**
>
> **Service costing** (or **function costing**) is a costing method concerned with establishing the costs, not of items of production, but of services rendered.

1.1 Service costing is used in the following circumstances.

(a) A company operating in a service industry will cost its services, for which sales revenue will be earned; examples are electricians, car hire services, road, rail or air transport services and hotels.

(b) A company may wish to establish the cost of services carried out by some of its departments; for example the costs of the vans or lorries used in distribution, the costs of the computer department, or the staff canteen.

1.2 Service costing differs from product costing (such as job or process costing) in the following ways.

(a) With many services, the cost of direct materials consumed will be relatively small compared to the labour, direct expenses and overheads cost. In product costing the direct materials are often a greater proportion of the total cost.

(b) Although many services are revenue-earning, others are not (such as the distribution facility or the staff canteen). This means that the purpose of service costing may not be to establish a profit or loss (nor to value closing stocks for the balance sheet) but may rather be to provide management information about the comparative costs or efficiency of the services, with a view to helping managers to budget for their costs using historical data as a basis for estimating costs in the future and to control the costs in the service departments.

(c) The procedures for recording material costs, labour hours and other expenses will vary according to the nature of the service.

2 UNIT COST MEASURES

2.1 One particular problem with service costing is the **difficulty in defining a realistic cost unit** that represents a suitable measure of the service provided. Frequently, a composite cost unit may be deemed more appropriate. Hotels, for example, may use the 'occupied bed-night' as an appropriate unit for cost ascertainment and control.

2.2 Typical cost units used by companies operating in a service industry are shown below.

Service	Cost unit
Road, rail and air transport services	Passenger/mile or kilometre, ton/mile, tonne/kilometre
Hotels	Occupied bed-night
Education	Full-time student
Hospitals	Patient
Catering establishment	Meal served

Question 1

Can you think of examples of cost units for internal services such as canteens, distribution and maintenance?

Answer

Service	Cost unit
Canteen	Meal served
Vans and lorries used in distribution	Mile or kilometre, ton/mile, tonne/kilometre
Maintenance	Man hour

2.3 Each organisation will need to ascertain the **cost unit** most appropriate to its activities. If a number of organisations within an industry use a common cost unit, then valuable comparisons can be made between similar establishments. This is particularly applicable to hospitals, educational establishments and local authorities. Whatever cost unit is decided upon, the calculation of a cost per unit is as follows.

FORMULA TO LEARN

$$\text{Cost per service unit} = \frac{\text{Total costs for period}}{\text{Number of service units in the period}}$$

3 SERVICE COST ANALYSIS   12/95, 6/99

Exam focus point

In 12/95, part of a question tested candidates' ability to calculate the profitability of services provided by a public transport business. There were 10 marks to be gained.

3.1   **Service cost analysis** should be performed in a manner which ensures that the following objectives are attained.

   (a)   Planned costs should be compared with actual costs.

         Differences should be investigated and corrective action taken as necessary.

   (b)   A cost per unit of service should be calculated.

         If each service has a number of variations (such as maintenance services provided by plumbers, electricians and carpenters) then the calculation of a cost per unit of each service may be necessary.

   (c)   The cost per unit of service should be used as part of the control function.

         For example, costs per unit of service can be compared, month by month, period by period, year by year and so on and any unusual trends can be investigated.

   (d)   Prices should be calculated for services being sold to third parties.

         The procedure is similar to job costing. A mark-up is added to the cost per unit of service to arrive at a selling price.

   (e)   Costs should be analysed into fixed, variable and semi-variable costs to help assist management with planning, control and decision making.

4 SERVICE COST ANALYSIS IN INTERNAL SERVICE SITUATIONS   12/98

Transport costs

4.1   **'Transport costs'** is a term used here to refer to the costs of the transport services used by a company, rather than the costs of a transport organisation, such as British Rail.

4.2   If a company has a fleet of lorries or vans which it uses to distribute its goods, it is useful to know how much the department is costing for a number of reasons.

   (a)   Management should be able to budget for expected costs, and to control actual expenditure on transport by comparing actual costs with budgeted costs.

   (b)   The company may charge customers for delivery or 'carriage outwards' costs, and a charge based on the cost of the transport service might be appropriate.

   (c)   If management knows how much its own transport is costing, a comparison can be made with alternative forms of transport (independent transport companies, British Rail) to decide whether a cheaper or better method of delivery can be found.

   (d)   Similarly, if a company uses, say, a fleet of lorries, knowledge of how much transport by lorry costs should help management to decide whether another type of vehicle, say vans, would be cheaper to use.

4.3   Transport costs may be analysed to provide the cost of operating one van or lorry each year, but it is more informative to analyse costs as follows.

(a) The cost per mile or kilometre travelled.

(b) The cost per ton/mile or tonne/kilometre (the cost of carrying one tonne of goods for one kilometre distance) or the cost per kilogram/metre.

4.4 For example, suppose that a company lorry makes five deliveries in a week.

Delivery	Tonnes carried	Distance (one way) Kilometres	Tonne/kilometres carried
1	0.4	180	72
2	0.3	360	108
3	1.2	100	120
4	0.8	250	200
5	1.0	60	60
			560

If the costs of operating the lorry during the week are known to be £840, the cost per tonne/kilometre would be:

$$\frac{£840}{560 \text{ tonne/kilometre}} = £1.50 \text{ per tonne/kilometre}$$

4.5 Transport costs might be collected under five broad headings.

(a) **Running costs** such as petrol, oil, drivers' wages
(b) **Loading costs** (the labour costs of loading the lorries with goods for delivery)
(c) **Servicing, repairs,** spare parts and tyre usage
(d) **Annual direct expenses** such as road tax, insurance and depreciation
(e) **Indirect costs of the distribution department** such as the wages of managers

4.6 The role of the cost accountant is to provide a system for **recording and analysing costs**. Just as production costs are recorded by means of material requisition notes, labour time sheets and so on, so too must transport costs be recorded by means of log sheets or time sheets, and material supply notes.

The purpose of a lorry driver's log sheet is to record distance travelled, or the number of tonne/kilometres and the drivers' time.

Canteen costs

4.7 Another example of service costing is the cost of a company's **canteen services**. A feature of canteen costing is that some revenue is earned when employees pay for their meals, but the prices paid will be insufficient to cover the costs of the canteen service. The company will subsidise the canteen and a major purpose of canteen costing is to establish the size of the subsidy.

4.8 If the costs of the canteen service are recorded by a system of service cost accounting, the likely headings of expense would be as follows.

(a) **Food and drink**: separate canteen stores records may be kept, and the consumption of food and drink recorded by means of 'materials issues' notes.

(b) **Labour costs of the canteen staff**: hourly paid staff will record their time at work on a time card or time sheet. Salaried staff will be 'fixed' cost each month.

(c) **Consumable stores** such as crockery, cutlery, glassware, table linen and cleaning materials will also be recorded in some form of stock control system.

(d) **The cost of gas and electricity** may be separately metered; otherwise an apportionment of the total cost of such utilities for the building as a whole will be made to the canteen department.

(e) Asset records will be kept and **depreciation charges** made for major items of equipment like ovens and furniture.

(f) An apportionment of other **overhead costs** of the building (rent and rates, building insurance and maintenance and so on) may be charged against the canteen.

Cash income from canteen sales will also be recorded.

4.9 Suppose that a canteen recorded the following costs and revenue during the month.

	£
Food and drink	11,250
Labour	11,250
Heating and lighting	1,875
Repairs and consumable stores	1,125
Financing costs	1,000
Depreciation	750
Other apportioned costs	875
Revenue	22,500

The canteen served 37,500 meals in the month.

The size of the subsidy could be easily identified as follows:

	£
The total costs of the canteen	28,125
Revenue	22,500
Loss, to be covered by the company	5,625

The cost per meal averages 75p and the revenue per meal 60p. If the company decided that the canteen should pay its own way, without a subsidy, the average price of a meal would have to be raised by 15 pence.

5 THE USEFULNESS OF COSTING SERVICES THAT DO NOT EARN REVENUE

5.1 The techniques for costing services are similar to the techniques for costing products, but why should we want to establish a cost for 'internal' services, services that are provided by one department for another, rather than sold externally to customers? In other words, what is the purpose of service costing for non-revenue-earning services?

5.2 Service costing has two basic purposes.

(a) **To control the costs in the service department.** If we establish a distribution cost per tonne kilometre, a canteen cost per employee, or job costs of repairs, we can establish control measures in the following ways.

  (i) Comparing actual costs against a target or standard
  (ii) Comparing current actual costs against actual costs in previous periods

(b) **To control the costs of the user departments**, and prevent the unnecessary use of services. If the costs of services are charged to the user departments in such a way that the charges reflect the use actually made by each department of the service department's services then the following will occur.

  (i) The overhead costs of user departments will be established more accurately; indeed some service department variable costs might be identified as directly attributable costs of the user department.

(ii)   If the service department's charges for a user department are high, the user department might be encouraged to consider whether it is making an excessively costly and wasteful use of the service department's service.

(iii)   The user department might decide that it can obtain a similar service at a lower cost from an external service company.

5.3   EXAMPLE: COSTING INTERNAL SERVICES

(a) If maintenance costs in a factory are costed as jobs (that is, if each bit of repair work is given a job number and costed accordingly) repair costs can be charged to the departments on the basis of repair jobs actually undertaken, instead of on a more generalised basis, such as apportionment according to machine hour capacity in each department. Departments with high repair costs could then consider their high incidence of repairs, the age and reliability of their machines, or the skills of the machine operatives.

(b) If mainframe computer costs are charged to a user department on the basis of a cost per hour, the user department would assess whether it was getting good value from its use of the mainframe computer and whether it might be better to hire the service of a computer bureau, or perhaps install a stand-alone microcomputer system in the department.

6   SERVICE COST ANALYSIS IN SERVICE INDUSTRY SITUATIONS

Distribution costs

6.1   EXAMPLE: SERVICE COST ANALYSIS IN THE SERVICE INDUSTRY

This example shows how a rate per tonne/kilometre can be calculated for a distribution service.

Rick Shaw Ltd operates a small fleet of delivery vehicles. Standard costs have been established as follows.

Loading	1 hour per tonne loaded
Loading costs:	
Labour (casual)	£2 per hour
Equipment depreciation	£80 per week
Supervision	£80 per week
Drivers' wages (fixed)	£100 per man per week
Petrol	10p per kilometre
Repairs	5p per kilometre
Depreciation	£80 per week per vehicle
Supervision	£120 per week
Other general expenses (fixed)	£200 per week

There are two drivers and two vehicles in the fleet.

During a slack week, only six journeys were made.

Journey	Tonnes carried (one way)	One-way distance of journey Kilometres
1	5	100
2	8	20
3	2	60
4	4	50
5	6	200
6	5	300

Required

Calculate the expected average full cost per tonne/kilometre for the week.

6.2 SOLUTION

Variable costs	Journey	1	2	3	4	5	6
		£	£	£	£	£	£
Loading labour		10	16	4	8	12	10
Petrol (both ways)		20	4	12	10	40	60
Repairs (both ways)		10	2	6	5	20	30
		40	22	22	23	72	100

Total costs

	£
Variable costs (total for journeys 1 to 6)	279
Loading equipment depreciation	80
Loading supervision	80
Drivers' wages	200
Vehicles depreciation	160
Drivers' supervision	120
Other costs	200
	1,119

Journey		One way distance	
	Tonnes	Kilometres	Tonne/kilometres
1	5	100	500
2	8	20	160
3	2	60	120
4	4	50	200
5	6	200	1,200
6	5	300	1,500
			3,680

Cost per tonne/kilometre $\dfrac{£1,119}{3,680} = £0.304$

Note that the large element of fixed costs may distort this measure but that a variable cost per tonne/kilometre of £279/3,680 = £0.076 may be useful for budgetary control.

Education

6.3 The techniques described in the preceding paragraphs can be applied, in general, to any service industry situation. Attempt the following question about education.

Question 2

A university with annual running costs of £3 million has the following students.

Classification	Number	Attendance weeks per annum	Hours per week
3 year	2,700	30	28
4 year	1,500	30	25
Sandwich	1,900	35	20

Required

Calculate a cost per suitable cost unit for the university to the nearest penny.

Answer

We need to begin by establishing a cost unit for the university. Since there are three different categories of students we cannot use 'a student' as the cost unit. Attendance hours would seem to be the most appropriate cost unit. The next step is to calculate the number of units.

Number of students		Weeks		Hours		Total hours per annum
2,700	×	30	×	28	=	2,268,000
1,500	×	30	×	25	=	1,125,000
1,900	×	35	×	20	=	1,330,000
						4,723,000

The cost per unit is calculated as follows.

$$\text{Cost per unit} = \frac{\text{Total cost}}{\text{Number of units}} = £(\frac{3,000,000}{4,723,000}) = \underline{£0.64}$$

Exam focus point

Candidates in the 6/99 exam were asked to outline the key factors to consider when introducing a service costing system to a stores operations department. There were 7 marks available.

Chapter roundup

* **Service costing** can be used by companies operating in a service industry or by companies wishing to establish the cost of services carried out by some of their departments.

* Service costing for **internal services** adds to the administrative burdens of an organisation because it costs time and money. The benefits of the system should therefore exceed the costs of its operation.

* Not all service departments can be costed using the approach laid out in this chapter. For example, it would be difficult to work out a job cost or service unit cost for the accounting department, personnel department or general administration work at head office. These service costs would be charged as general overheads and then apportioned between user departments on a suitable basis.

* A problem faced in both service costing situations is the **selection of an appropriate cost unit**. The unit will often be a two part one, such as the tonne/kilometre. Whatever cost unit is decided upon, the calculation of a cost per unit will be the total costs for the period divided by the number of service units in the period.

Quick quiz

1 Describe three differences between service costing and product costing. (see para 1.2)

2 Suggest five headings under which the costs of a transport department might be collected. (4.5)

3 Why is it useful to cost non-revenue-earning services? (5.2)

Question to try	Level	Marks	Time
15	Examination	14	25 mins

Part D
Business statistics

Chapter 15

THE COLLECTION OF DATA

Chapter topic list	Syllabus reference
1　Data	QT 5(a), (b)
2　Conducting a statistical enquiry	QT 5(b)
3　Random sampling	QT 5(b)
4　Quasi-random sampling	QT 5(b)
5　Non-random sampling	QT 5(b)
6　Data collection methods	QT 5(b)
7　Sampling and auditing	QT 5(b)

Introduction

The words 'quantitative techniques' often strike terror into the hearts of students. They conjure up images of complicated mathematical formulae, scientific analysis of reams of computer output and the drawing of strange graphs and diagrams. Such images are wrong. Quantitative techniques simply involves the following.

- **Collecting** data
- **Presenting** the data in a useful form
- **Inspecting** the data

A study of the subject will demonstrate that quantitative techniques is nothing to be afraid of and that a knowledge of it is extremely advantageous in your working environment. The main advantage of quantitative techniques are that they offer methods which can be used to **make sense of numbers**. In a business environment, for example, a manager may collect all sorts of data on production levels, costs and sales, but on their own the numbers are unlikely to mean very much. By using quantitative techniques, a manager can try to make sense out of the numbers, which in turn should help in making sensible business decisions.

We will start our study of quantitative techniques by looking at **data collection**. In the next chapter we will consider how to present data once they have been collected.

1　DATA

1.1　Here are some examples of data.

- The number of people who pass their driving test each year with red hair
- The number of goals scored by each football team in the second division
- The profit after tax for the past ten years of the four biggest supermarket chains

Types of data

1.2 Data may be of several types.

(a) **Quantitative and qualitative data**

- **Quantitative data** are data that can be **measured**, and include the following.

  ○ The temperature on each day of August (which can be measured in degrees fahrenheit or celsius).

  ○ The time it takes you to travel to work each day this week (which can be measured in hours and minutes).

- **Qualitative data** are **data that cannot be measured** but reflect some quality of what is being observed. For example, whether somebody is male or female: there is no measure of how male or how female somebody is.

(b) **Discrete and continuous data**. Quantitative data can be further classified as **discrete** or **continuous**.

- Data are **discrete** if they can take on only certain **definite** and **separate values** eg British shoe sizes.

- Data which can take on **absolutely any value** (perhaps restricted to a certain limited range and as long as they can be measured accurately enough) are **continuous** eg height (1.62m, 1.59m, 1.85m and so on).

(c) **Primary and secondary data**

Data can also be either **primary** or **secondary**.

- **Primary data** are data collected specifically for the current purpose.

- **Secondary data** are data which have already been collected elsewhere, for some other purpose, but which can be used or adapted for the current purpose.

Primary data have to be gathered from a source. The advantage of using primary data is that the **source** of the data, the **circumstances under which they are collected** and any **limitations** or **inadequacies** in the data are known to you. The data are **tailor-made** to your requirements and likely to be more **up-to-date** than anything from a published source.

Any limitations in secondary data, on the other hand, **might not be known** by the current user of the data because he or she did not collect them. Nor may the data be entirely suitable for the purpose they are being used for. Secondary data can sometimes be used despite their inadequacies because they are available cheaply (the extra cost of collecting primary data outweighing their extra value) and because you, as a private individual or representative of your firm, are unlikely to have direct access to the primary data sources.

Examples of secondary data include the following.

- **Published statistics**. The government, for example, publishes statistics through the Office for National Statistics (ONS) (following the merger of the Central Statistical Office and the Office of Population, Censuses and Surveys in April 1996). The European Community (EC) and the United Nations also publish statistics, as do various newspapers and accountancy bodies.

- **Historical records**. The type of historical record used depends on why it is required. An accountant producing an estimate of future company sales might use historical records of past sales.

(d) **Raw and aggregated data**

The result of any census or sample enquiry is a mass of data which is usually called raw data. Aggregated data, on the other hand, is the mass of data after they have been reduced to manageable proportions by classifying and summarising them.

(e) **Sample and population data**

> **KEY TERM**
>
> A **population** is the group of people or objects of interest to the data collector.

If you were concerned with the level of service a bank provides for its customers, the relevant population is all of the bank's customers. Data arising as a result of investigating the population is known as **population data.**

Where the relevant identified population is too large for a cost effective enquiry into the entire population to be conducted, a sample of that population must be selected, and individual responses generalised to represent the facts about, or views of, the entire population. Data arising as a result of investigating the sample are known as **sample data**.

Descriptive and inferential statistics

> **KEY TERMS**
>
> • **Descriptive statistics** are statistics which describe the actual state of a situation as it exists now or as it existed in the past.
>
> • **Inferential statistics** describe the future by inferring the future from records of the past and present.

1.3   For example, every car has a display of the total mileage it has travelled since it was new. This display of total mileage is a statistic that describes the present state of how much the car has been used. Suppose that the population of Ruritania at the end of 1982 was 10 million. This total population is a statistic that describes the past state of Ruritania's population. Descriptive statistics do not describe the future.

1.4   Marketing analysts may be able to infer future sales of a new product from results of a market research survey being carried out and/or from records of sales of similar products in the past.

2   CONDUCTING A STATISTICAL ENQUIRY

Stages in a statistical enquiry

2.1

Step 1.   **State the problem**. The problem must be stated explicitly so as to provide terms of reference from which those conducting the enquiry can start to collect relevant data for analysis.

Step 2.   **Decide on how to tackle the problem**. In the light of the terms of reference set in Step 1, a decision as to how to tackle the problem must be made. The same problem may have already been faced and suitable secondary data may already exist in-house. Alternatively, new data (primary data) may need to be collected.

Step 3. **Determine the depth of enquiry needed.** Is a complete enquiry to be made of all members of the population or will it be sufficient to take a sample?

Step 4. **Decide how the data is to be collected.**

Step 5. **Collect the data.**

Step 6. **Edit and classify the data.** A mass of raw data may need editing and organising before it can be analysed.

Step 7. **Analyse and interpret the data.** The data should be analysed and interpreted by those who are knowledgeable about the subject matter and skilled in the statistical methods used, so that appropriate conclusions can be drawn.

Step 8. **Present conclusions of statistical enquiry.** The conclusions drawn in Step 7 above may need presenting in a certain format, such as graphs or charts. A report, including recommendations, may be required by senior management.

Obtaining data

2.2 There are basically three ways of obtaining data.

- Find the data yourself. (Primary data)
- Use somebody else's data. (Secondary data)
- Use published data. (Secondary data)

2.3 The question of whether to use primary or secondary data is often a matter of compromise. Are we prepared to settle for secondary data which may not be exactly what we are looking for but which are readily and fairly cheaply available, or is the accuracy of the data so important that we are prepared to pay for it in terms of time, money and effort?

Finding data yourself

2.4 We need to define the population we are interested in. This is not as obvious as it sounds. We have to be extremely specific in our definition, especially if part-time market research interviewers are to do some of the data collection. If you tell your interviewers to question 'accountants', does this mean qualified accountants or students still training to be accountants? Does the term include certified, management and chartered accountants? Do the 'accountants' have to be working full time? If you intended the term to be interpreted in one particular way and your interviewers interpret it differently your results may be invalid and even misleading.

2.5 It is unlikely that we will be able to collect information from *every* member of our defined population. If all members of a population are examined we are conducting a **census**. The advantage of a census is that it should give a completely accurate view of the population but it is usually impractical and too costly. If therefore makes sense to study only a **portion** or **sample** of the population and hope that the results we get from our sample will not be too far from those which would apply to the population as a whole.

2.6 **Disadvantages of a census**

In practice, a 100% survey (census) never achieves the completeness required.

- The higher cost of a census may exceed the value of results.

- Things are always changing: it could well be out of date by the time you complete it.

Advantages of a sample

- It can be shown mathematically that once a certain sample size has been reached, very little extra accuracy is gained by examining more items.

- It is possible to ask more questions with a sample.

2.7 One of the most important requirements of data is that they should be **complete**. That is, the data should cover all areas of the population to be examined. If this requirement is not met, then the sample will be **biased**.

2.8 For example, suppose you wanted to survey the productivity of workers in a factory, and you went along every Monday and Tuesday for a few months to measure their output. Would these data be complete? The answer is no. You might have gathered very thorough data on what happens on Mondays and Tuesdays, but you would have missed out the rest of the week. It could be that the workers, keen and fresh after the weekend, work better at the start of the week than at the end. If this is the case, then your data will give you a misleadingly high productivity figure. Careful attention must therefore be given to the sampling method employed to produce a sample.

2.9 Sampling methods fall into three main groups.

- Random sampling
- Quasi-random sampling
- Non-random sampling

3 RANDOM SAMPLING

6/95, 12/98

> **Exam focus point**
> There were 4 marks available in the 6/95 exam for outlining the advantages and disadvantages of simple random sampling.

3.1 To ensure that the sample selected is free from bias, **random sampling** must be used. Inferences about the population being sampled can then be made validly.

3.2 A simple random sample is a sample **selected** in such a way that **every item** in the population has an **equal chance** of being included.

3.3 For example, if you wanted to take a random sample of library books, it would not be good enough to pick them off the shelves, even if you picked them at random. This is because the books which were out on loan would stand no chance of being chosen. You would either have to make sure that all the books were on the shelves before taking your sample, or find some other way of sampling (for example, using the library index cards).

3.4 A random sample is not necessarily a perfect sample. For example, you might pick what you believe to be a completely random selection of library books, and find that every one of them is a detective thriller. It is a remote possibility, but it could happen. The only way to eliminate the possibility altogether is to take a 100% survey (a census) of the books, which, unless it is a tiny library, is impractical.

BPP PUBLISHING

Sampling frames

> ### KEY TERM
>
> A **sampling frame** is simply a numbered list of all the items in the population.

3.5 If random sampling is used then it is necessary to construct a sampling frame. Once such a list has been made, it is easy to select a random sample, simply by generating a list of random numbers.

3.6 For instance, if you wanted to select a random sample of children from a school, it would be useful to have a list of names:

0   J Absolam
1   R Brown
2   S Brown
...

Now the numbers 0, 1, 2 and so on can be used to select the random sample. It is normal to start the numbering at 0, so that when 0 appears in a list of random numbers it can be used.

3.7 Sometimes it is not possible to draw up a sampling frame. For example, if you wanted to take a random sample of Americans, it would take too long to list all Americans.

3.8 A sampling frame should have the following characteristics.

- **Completeness**. Are all members of the population included on the list?
- **Accuracy**. Is the information correct?
- **Adequacy**. Does it cover the entire population?
- **Up to dateness**. Is the list up to date?
- **Convenience**. Is the sampling frame readily accessible?
- **Non-duplication**. Does each member of the population appear on the list only once?

3.9 Two readily available sampling frames for the human population of Great Britain are the **council tax register** (list of dwellings) and the **electoral register** (list of individuals).

Random number tables

3.10 Assuming that a sampling frame can be drawn up, then a random sample can be picked from it by one of the following methods.

- The **lottery method** (picking numbered pieces of paper out of a box)
- The use of **random number tables**

3.11 Set out below is part of a typical random number table.

93716	16894	98953	73231
32886	59780	09958	18065
92052	06831	19640	99413
39510	35905	85244	35159
27699	06494	03152	19121
92962	61773	22109	78508
10274	12202	94205	50380
75867	20717	82037	10268
85783	47619	87481	37220

(a)   The sample is found by selecting groups of random numbers with the number of digits depending on the total population size, as follows.

Total population size	Number of random digits
1 - 10	1
1 - 100	2
1 - 1,000	3

The items selected for the sample are those corresponding to the random numbers selected.

(b)   The starting point on the table should be selected at random. After that, however, numbers must be selected in a consistent manner. In other words, you should use the table row by row or column by column. By jumping around the table from place to place, personal bias may be introduced.

(c)   In many practical situations it is more convenient to use a computer to generate a list of random numbers, especially when a large sample is required.

3.12   EXAMPLE: RANDOM NUMBER TABLES

An investigator wishes to select a random sample from a population of 800 people, who have been numbered 000, 001, ...799. As there are three digits in 799 the random numbers will be selected in groups of three. Working along the first line of the table given earlier, the first few groups are as follows.

$$937 \quad 161 \quad 689 \quad 498 \quad 953 \quad 732$$

Numbers over 799 are discarded. The first four people in the sample will therefore be those numbered 161, 689, 498 and 732.

Drawbacks of random sampling

3.13   (a)   The selected items are subject to the full range of variation inherent in the population.

(b)   An unrepresentative sample may result.

(c)   The members of the population selected may be scattered over a wide area, adding to the cost and difficulty of obtaining the data.

(d)   An adequate sampling frame might not exist.

(e)   The numbering of the population might be laborious.

Quasi- and non-random sampling

3.14   In many situations it might be too expensive to obtain a random sample, in which case quasi-random sampling is necessary, or else it may not be possible to draw up a sampling frame. In such cases, non-random sampling has to be used.

4   QUASI-RANDOM SAMPLING   6/96, 6/97, 12/98

Exam focus point

In the 6/97 exam there were 9 marks available for describing systematic sampling and multistage sampling and listing the advantages and potential limitations of each.

4.1 Quasi-random sampling, which provides a **good approximation to random sampling**, necessitates the existence of a sampling frame.

The main methods of quasi-random sampling are as follows.

- Systematic sampling
- Stratified sampling
- Multistage sampling

Systematic sampling

4.2 Systematic sampling may provide a good approximation to random sampling. It works by selecting every nth item after a random start. For example, if it was decided to select a sample of 20 from a population of 800, then every 40th (800 ÷ 20) item after a random start in the first 40 should be selected. The starting point could be found using the lottery method or random number tables. If (say) 23 was chosen, then the sample would include the 23rd, 63rd, 103rd, 143rd ... 783rd items. The gap of 40 is known as the **sampling interval**.

4.3 Systematic sampling has the following **advantages**.

- It is easy to select the sample items given a sampling frame.
- It is reasonably random, providing that there is no pattern to the distribution of items.

Systematic sampling has the following **limitations**.

- It requires a sampling frame.
- It requires access to the whole population.
- If there is a regular pattern to the distribution of items, the sample may be biased.
- It may be expensive to select the required sample (every nth item).

Stratified sampling

Exam focus point
In the 6/96 exam there were 7 marks available for explaining the term stratified sampling and listing its merits and potential drawbacks as a sampling technique.

4.4 In many situations **stratified sampling** is the best method of choosing a sample. The population must be divided into **strata** or **categories**.

If we took a random sample of all cost and management accountants in the country, it is conceivable that the entire sample might consist of members of the ACCA working in public companies. Stratified sampling removes this possibility as random samples could be taken from each type of employment, the number in each sample being proportional to the total number of cost and management accountants in each type of organisation.

4.5 EXAMPLE: STRATIFIED SAMPLING

The number of cost and management accountants in each type of work in a particular country are as follows.

Partnerships	500
Public companies	500
Private companies	700
Public practice	800
	2,500

If a sample of 20 was required the sample would be made up as follows.

		Sample
Partnerships	$\dfrac{500}{2,500} \times 20$	4
Public companies	$\dfrac{500}{2,500} \times 20$	4
Private companies	$\dfrac{700}{2,500} \times 20$	6
Public practice	$\dfrac{800}{2,500} \times 20$	6
		$\overline{\underline{20}}$

4.6 The strata frequently involve multiple classifications. In social surveys, for example, there is usually stratification by age, sex and social class. This implies that the sampling frame must contain information on these three variables before the threefold stratification of the population can be made.

4.7 Advantages of stratification are as follows.

(a) It ensures a representative sample since it guarantees that every important category will have elements in the final sample.

(b) The structure of the sample will reflect that of the population if the same proportion of individuals is chosen from each stratum.

(c) Each stratum is represented by a randomly chosen sample and therefore inferences can be made about each stratum.

(d) Precision is increased. Sampling takes place within strata and, because the range of variation is less in each stratum than in the population as a whole and variation between strata does not enter as a chance effect, higher precision is obtainable. (For this to occur, the items in each stratum must be as similar as possible and the difference between the individual strata must be as great as possible.)

4.8 Note, however, that **stratification requires prior knowledge of each item in the population**. Sampling frames do not always contain this information. Stratification from the electoral register as to age structure would not be possible because the electoral register does not contain information about age.

Multistage sampling

4.9 Multistage sampling is normally used to cut down the number of investigators and the costs of obtaining a sample. An example will show how the method works.

4.10 EXAMPLE: MULTISTAGE SAMPLING

A survey of spending habits is being planned to cover the whole of Britain. It is obviously impractical to draw up a sampling frame, so random sampling is not possible. Multi-stage sampling is to be used instead.

The country is divided into a number of areas and a small sample of these is selected at random. Each of the areas selected is subdivided into smaller units and again, a smaller number of these is selected at random. This process is repeated as many times as necessary and finally, a random sample of the relevant people living in each of the smallest units is taken. A fair approximation to a random sample can be obtained.

Thus, we might choose a random sample of eight areas, and from each of these areas, select a random sample of five towns. From each town, a random sample of 200 people might be selected so that the total sample size is $8 \times 5 \times 200 = 8,000$ people.

4.11 The main advantages of this method are as follows.

- It does not require a sampling frame
- It is relatively cheap, because samples may be collected quickly

4.12 The main disadvantages are as follows.

(a) It is **not truly random,** as once the final sampling areas have been selected, the rest of the population cannot be in the sample.

(b) The sample **may be biased** if only a small number of regions are selected.

4.13 The sampling methods looked at so far have necessitated the existence of a sampling frame (or in multistage sampling, sampling frames of areas, sub-areas and items within selected sub-areas). It is often impossible to identify a satisfactory sampling frame and, in such instances, other sampling methods have to be employed.

5   NON-RANDOM SAMPLING   12/98

5.1 There are two main methods of non-random sampling. They are used when a sampling frame cannot be established.

- Quota sampling
- Cluster sampling

Quota sampling

> **KEY TERM**
>
> **Quota sampling** is a sampling method commonly used by market researchers, and which involves stratifying the population and restricting the sample to a fixed number in each strata.

5.2 Investigators are told to interview all of the people that they meet up to a certain quota. The quota may be further divided to ensure that the sample mirrors the structure or stratification of the population. The actual choice of the individuals to be interviewed is left to the investigator.

Advantages of quota sampling

5.3 (a) It is **cheap** and **administratively easy**.

(b) A much **larger sample can be studied,** and hence more information can be gained at a faster speed for a given outlay than when compared with a fully randomised sampling method.

(c) Although a fairly detailed knowledge of the characteristics of a population is required, **no sampling frame is necessary** because the interviewer questions every person he meets up to the quota.

(d) Quota sampling may be the only possible approach in certain situations, such as television audience research.

(e) Given suitable, trained and properly briefed field workers, quota sampling yields enough **accurate information** for many forms of commercial market research.

Disadvantages of quota sampling

5.4 (a) The method can result in certain biases (although these can often be allowed for and/or may be unimportant for the purpose of the research).

(b) The non-random nature of the method rules out any valid estimate of the sampling error (you will meet this later on) in estimates derived from the sample.

5.5 Quota sampling cannot be regarded as ultimately satisfactory in research where it is important that theoretically valid results should be obtained. It can be argued, however, that when other large sources of error, such as non response, exist, it is pointless to worry too much about sampling error.

5.6 EXAMPLE: QUOTA SAMPLING

Consider the figures in Paragraph 4.5 above, but with the following additional information relating to the sex of the cost and management accountants.

	Male	Female
Partnerships	300	200
Public companies	400	100
Private companies	300	400
Public practice	300	500

An investigator's quotas might be as follows.

	Male	Female	Total
Partnerships	30	20	50
Public companies	40	10	50
Private companies	30	40	70
Public practice	30	50	80
			250

Using quota sampling, the investigator would interview the first 30 male cost and management accountants in partnerships that he met, the first 20 female cost and management accountants in partnerships that he met and so on.

Cluster sampling

5.7 **Cluster sampling** involves selecting one definable subsection of the population as the sample, that subsection taken to be representative of the population in question. The pupils of one school might be taken as a cluster sample of all children at school in one county. Cluster sampling benefits from **low costs** in the same way as multistage sampling.

5.8 **Advantages of cluster sampling**

- It is a good alternative to multistage sampling if a satisfactory sampling frame does not exist.

- It is inexpensive to operate because little organisation or structure is involved.

Disadvantage of cluster sampling

- The potential for considerable bias.

Question 1

Describe four methods a brewery could employ to test the market for a new canned beer. Discuss the relative advantages and disadvantages of each method chosen.

Answer

(a) The brewery could try to supply the beer to a random sample of beer drinkers, and then ask for their views. Such samples are taken in such a way that every member of the population (in this case, all beer drinkers and perhaps all potential beer drinkers) has an equal chance of being selected for the sample. The main advantage of random sampling is that it allows mathematical analysis of the data to be carried out. The main disadvantage is that a random sample can be difficult and expensive to collect. The brewery may well find that it is impossible to compile a list of all beer drinkers from which to select a sample.

(b) Stratified sampling may well be appropriate. The population would first be divided into groups, perhaps by age or by weekly beer consumption, and then samples would be selected from each group (reflecting the proportion of the population in the group). The main advantage of stratified sampling is that it ensures that each group is represented in the sample. The main disadvantage is that preliminary work is needed to determine which groupings are likely to be useful and the proportion of the population in each group.

(c) Cluster sampling may well be a practical alternative, giving some of the benefits of both random sampling and stratified sampling. The population could be divided geographically into beer drinkers at public houses in different regions of the country and beer purchasers at off licences within these regions. A sample of regions could be selected, and a sample of public houses and off licences in each selected region could be chosen. All consumers at the chosen public houses and off licences would then form the sample. The main advantage of cluster sampling is its relative cheapness. The main disadvantage is that the sample obtained will not be truly random, so some forms of statistical analysis will not be possible.

(d) Quota sampling has the advantage of being even cheaper than cluster sampling, but the disadvantage of producing a sample which is even further from being random. Researchers would simply visit a selection of public houses and off licences and interview the first beer drinkers they met until they had fulfilled some quota (say ten men and ten women).

Question 2

A company owning a chain of newsagents wishes to undertake a customer service survey. Interviewers will be despatched to a sample of 100 branches to question customers in the shops.

The number of newsagents owned in each area is as follows.

Central	360
North West	240
North	200
North East	100
Greater London	700
Scotland	200
Wales	140
South	60

Required

Explain how the 100 newsagents might be chosen, given the relative advantages and disadvantages of each method, if the survey is to be performed using the following sampling methods.

(a) Stratified random sampling
(b) Systematic sampling
(c) Cluster sampling

Answer

(a) *Stratified sampling*

Each area could be taken as a stratum. There are 2,000 newsagents altogether, so 100/2,000 = 5% of the newsagents in each area must be included in the sample.

In the Central area, for example, $360 \times 5\% = 18$ newsagents would be included. These should be selected randomly from the 360 newsagents. The newsagents should be numbered from 000 to 359, and three-digit random numbers used to select the sample.

Stratified sampling has the advantage that the same proportion of newsagents from each area will be included in the sample. It gives a closer approximation to random sampling than cluster sampling, and may give a closer approximation to random sampling than systematic sampling. Statistical calculations generally require that the samples on which they are based be random or nearly so.

The disadvantage of stratified sampling is that it is likely to be more expensive than the other two methods.

(b) *Systematic sampling*

In order to take a systematic sample, the 2,000 newsagents must first be arranged in some order. Any order will do, but orders which might produce some cyclical patterns (such as by size within one area, they by size with the next area, and so on) should be avoided if possible. The sample then comprises every $2,000/100 = 20$th newsagent in the order, with the first newsagent chosen at random from among the first 20 in the order.

The advantage of systematic sampling is that, provided a complete list of newsagents is available, it is cheap and easy to obtain the sample. The disadvantage is that if there is any cyclical pattern in the ordering, an unrepresentative sample may be obtained.

(c) *Cluster sampling*

Each area could be regarded as a cluster. Each area could be divided into sub-clusters (perhaps towns and their surrounding areas, or London boroughs), and a random sample of sub-clusters from each cluster would then be taken. The sample would comprise all the newsagents within the selected sub-clusters.

This method is fairly cheap to use, but the sub-clusters must first be identified. It is possible that a sample smaller or larger than 100 newsagents will be obtained. The sample will also not be random, invalidating certain statistical calculations.

---

6 DATA COLLECTION METHODS

6.1 Once a sample has been determined, primary data can actually be collected using either of the following methods.

- Surveys
- Observation

Surveys

6.2 Although surveys offer a quick, efficient and cost-effective way of obtaining the required data, they are not straightforward. Without skill, tact and expertise the results may easily become contaminated with bias and error and the conclusions subsequently drawn will be useless. There are two main types of survey.

- Interviews
- Postal questionnaires

Interviews

6.3 There are basically two types of interview that can be used to collect data.

- The personal (face to face) interview
- The telephone interview

(a) In a **personal interview**, an interviewer asks a number of questions from a questionnaire. **Advantages** of personal interviews are as follows.

- Interviewers are able to reduce anxiety and embarrassment of respondents
- Increased response rate
- Increased accuracy of responses
- Interviewers can ask for clarification of answer given
- Questions can be asked in a fixed order
- Answers can be recorded in a standard manner
- Survey costs are reduced because less skilled interviewers can be used
- Pictures, signs and objects can be used
- Routing of questions is easier

Disadvantages of personal interviews are as follows.

- Time consuming
- Cost per completed interview can be higher than with other survey methods
- Questionnaires can be difficult to design

(b) **Telephone interviews** are most useful when only a small amount of information is required. **Advantages** are as follows.

- The response is rapid.
- It is relatively cheap.
- A wide geographical area can be covered from a central location.
- It may be easier to ask sensitive or embarrassing questions.
- The interview does not take up much of the respondent's time.

Disadvantages include the following.

- A biased sample may result as it won't include people who do not have telephones and people who are ex-directory.
- It is not possible to use 'showcards' or pictures.
- The refusal rate is much higher than with face-to-face interviews.
- It is not possible to see the interviewee's expression or to develop the rapport that is possible with personal interviews.
- The interview must be short.
- Respondents may be unwilling to participate for fear of being sold something.

Postal questionnaires

6.4   Postal questionnaires have the following advantages over personal interviews.

(a)   The cost per person is likely to be less, so more people can be sampled.

(b)   It is usually possible to ask more questions because the people completing the forms (the respondents) can do so in their own time.

(c)   All respondents are presented with questions in the same way. There is no opportunity for an interviewer to influence responses (interviewer bias) or to misrecord them.

(d)   It may be easier to ask personal or embarrassing questions in a postal questionnaire than in a personal interview.

(e) Respondents may need to look up information for the questionnaire. This will be easier if the questionnaire is sent to their home or place of work.

6.5 On the other hand, the use of personal interviews does have certain advantages over the use of postal questionnaires.

(a) Large numbers of postal questionnaires may not be returned or may be returned only partly completed. This may lead to biased results if those replying are not representative of all people in the survey. Response rates are likely to be higher with personal interviews, and the interviewer can encourage people to answer all questions. Low response rates are a major problem with postal questionnaires.

(b) Misunderstanding is less likely with personal interviews because the interviewer can explain questions which the interviewee does not understand.

(c) Personal interviews are more suitable when deep or detailed questions are to be asked, since the interviewer can take the time required with each interviewee to explain the implications of the question. Also, the interviewer can probe for further information and encourage the respondent to think deeper.

Observation

6.6 **Observation** as a method of data collection is suitable if data needs either counting (such as the number of shoppers entering a store between 9 and 10 am) or measuring (such as the length of time taken to perform a task).

7 SAMPLING AND AUDITING

7.1 An external auditor's main role is to ensure that a company's financial statements show a true and fair view. In the early days of auditing it was quite common for the auditor to check all of the company's transactions during the accounting period. It is now much more usual for only a small portion of transactions to be checked and then a generalised statement concerning the entire population of transactions to be made using the information gained from the small portion checked. This, of course, is sampling. In theory, the auditor can plan to select a sample **judgementally**, or **statistically**.

Judgement sampling

7.2 **Judgement sampling** means deciding **how large** a sample should be, and **what items** to include in the sample, using judgement and 'common sense'. Although judgement sampling is simple to understand and easy to use, the auditor's personal bias may affect the choice of items (for example, by selecting the purchase orders which are easy to find). As a result, the auditor will not know how representative the sample has been and consequently it will be difficult to draw any useful conclusions relating to the population as a whole. Judgement sampling is not commonly used.

Statistical sampling

KEY TERM

Statistical sampling means taking a random sample (rather than a judgmental sample), and then following it up with a statistical evaluation.

7.3 It gives the best possible chance of selecting a representative sample, and then goes on to measure the risk that the sample is, after all, not representative.

7.4 **Selecting a representative sample**

   (a) The selection method should be **free from bias** (which explains why a judgement sample cannot lead to statistical conclusions)

   (b) Each transaction in the population under review should have a known and **equal chance** of selection

   (c) The sample size should be looking **large enough** so that the risk of it not being a typical sample is insignificant

7.5 Some form of random selection gives the best chance of selecting a representative sample, because by definition it guarantees conditions (a) and (b) above. However, there is still a risk that the sample is non-representative because it is not large enough (condition (c) above). The only way to prevent this risk is to choose a 100% sample, which does not happen in practice. The auditor therefore determines the risk that he is prepared to take, and uses statistical tables to look up the corresponding sample size.

7.6 **Advantages of using statistical sampling**

   (a) It provides an estimate of the degree of probability that the sample is representative of the whole population. This cannot be provided by means of judgement sampling.

   (b) The size of the sample required can be estimated accurately on a scientific basis which enables the auditor to justify the number of items selected.

   (c) The sample may be smaller than one selected by traditional means.

   (d) The use of statistical methods of sampling enables the auditor to predict the total number of errors in a population from errors found in a sample, and also to estimate the maximum possible error rate.

Sampling plans

7.7 **Estimation sampling of variables**. A randomly selected sample of items which can take any value within a continuous range of possible values is used to provide conclusions as to the monetary value of a population. The values of assets and liabilities are frequently determined using this method, which estimates the value of a population by extrapolating statistically the value of a representative sample of items drawn from the population.

7.8 **Estimation sampling of attributes** plan enables the auditor to estimate the maximum possible error rate in the population. This can then be compared with the auditor's **maximum acceptable error rate**, which in turn will depend on the characteristic being tested. If for example an error is taken as being the lack of authorisation then the auditor would be less concerned with errors in the approval of overtime working than with those in the authorisation of major capital expenditure.

7.9 **Discovery sampling**. This type of plan is designed so that if the actual error rate in the population exceeds the auditor's maximum acceptable error rate, he will be certain to find at least one error in the sample he tests. If no errors are found, the auditor infers that with a known confidence the error rate in the population is within acceptable limits. The maximum acceptable error rates are often set so that the discovery of one or more errors in the sample indicates a major breakdown in internal control. The discovery of an error will involve the auditor in further tests, possibly starting with the use of estimation sampling to find the maximum possible error rate.

7.10 **Acceptance sampling.** More widely used in quality control than in auditing, the plan is structured to enable the auditor to 'accept' or 'reject' the population on the basis of the number of errors found. For example, the auditor might use the following plan. If, from a population of 1,000, a sample of 150 items is drawn and three or fewer errors are found, then he would have the desired assurance that the population error rate did not exceed (say) 4%, where the figure of 4% represents the maximum acceptable error rate.

7.11 **Monetary unit sampling** method of sampling is useful for estimating the value of error in the population from a sample of items. MUS has two main characteristics. Items are selected for testing by weighting the items in proportion to their value (an item valued at £5 is five times more likely to be included than an item valued at £1) and inferences are drawn based on attribute sampling concepts.

7.12 Once a sampling plan has been established, the actual sample can be selected using any one of the methods considered earlier in this Chapter.

Criticisms of statistical sampling

7.13 Statistical sampling still has a number of criticisms.

- It is time consuming

- It is not convenient to produce sample data at random

- An experienced auditor can often produce a more suitable judgemental sample than one produced by random sampling

---

Chapter roundup

- There are a number of different types of data: **quantitative** and **qualitative** data, **discrete** and **continuous** data, **primary** and **secondary** data, **raw** and **aggregated** data and **sample** and **population** data. Statistics can be **descriptive** or **inferential**.

- There are three ways of obtaining data: you can find the data yourself, use somebody else's data or use published data.

- Data are often collected from a **sample** rather than the population. A sample can be selected using **random** sampling, **quasi-random** sampling (systematic, stratified and multistage sampling) or **non-random** sampling (quota and cluster sampling). We will be looking at how to draw conclusions from sample data in Chapter 22 which covers sampling theory.

- Once a sample has been determined, data can actually be collected using **surveys** (interviews or postal questionnaires) or **observation**.

- Most accountancy firms tend to use statistical sampling. **Statistical sampling** methods appropriate for auditing purposes include estimation sampling of variables, estimation sampling of attributes, discovery sampling, acceptance sampling and MUS.

- Once data have been collected they need to be presented and analysed. It is important to remember that if the data have not been collected properly, no amount of careful presentation or interpretation can remedy the defect.

Quick quiz

1   Distinguish between quantitative and qualitative data. (see para 1.2)

2   Distinguish between discrete and continuous data. (1.2)

3   Distinguish between primary and secondary data. (1.2)

4   Distinguish between descriptive and inferential statistics. (key terms)

5   List the arguments in favour of using a sample. (2.6)

6   What is a random sample? (3.2)

7   What are the three methods of quasi-random sampling? (4.1)

8   What are the two methods of non-random sampling? (5.1)

9   What are the advantages of personal interviews as a method of data collection? (6.3)

10 What statistical sampling methods are appropriate to auditing? (7.2-7.6)

Question to try	Level	Marks	Time
16	Introductory	n/a	15 mins

Chapter 16

DATA PRESENTATION

Chapter topic list	Syllabus reference
1 Tables	QT 1(c), 5(e)
2 Charts	QT 1(c), 5(d), 5(e)
3 Frequency distributions	QT 1(c), 5(e)
4 Histograms	QT 1(c), 5(d), 5(e)
5 Graphs	QT 1(c), 5(d), 5(e)

Introduction

You now know how to collect data. So what do we do now? We have to **present** the data we have collected so that it can be of use. This chapter begins by looking at how data can be presented in **tables** and **charts**. Such methods are helpful in presenting key data in a **concise** and **easy to understand** way. They are, however, purely **descriptive** and offer little opportunity for further detailed numerical analysis of a situation.

Data that are a mass of numbers can usefully be summarised into a **frequency distribution** (effectively a table which details the frequency with which a particular value occurs). **Histograms** and ogives are the pictorial representation of grouped and **cumulative frequency distributions** and provide the link between the purely descriptive approach to data analysis and the numerical approach which we will be covering in Chapters 17 and 18.

1   TABLES

12/95

> **KEY TERMS**
>
> • **Raw data** are primary data which have not been processed.
>
> • **Tabulation** means putting data into tables. A table is a matrix of data in rows and columns, with the rows and the columns having titles.

1.1   Raw data need to be summarised and analysed, to give them meaning. One of the most basic ways of presenting data is **tabulation**.

1.2   Since a table is **two-dimensional**, it can only show **two variables**. For example, the resources required to produce items in a factory could be tabulated, with one dimension (rows or columns) representing the items produced and the other dimension representing the resources.

BPP
PUBLISHING

Resources for production: all figures in pounds

	Product items				
Resources	*A*	*B*	*C*	*D*	*Total*
Direct material A	X	X	X	X	X
Direct material B	X	X	X	X	X
Direct labour grade 1	X	X	X	X	X
Direct labour grade 2	X	X	X	X	X
Supervision	X	X	X	X	X
Machine time	X	X	X	X	X
Total	X	X	X	X	X

Guidelines for tabulation

1.3 Having established what the two dimensions represent, the following guidelines should be applied when presenting data in tabular form.

- The table should be given a clear title.
- All columns should be clearly labelled.
- The data should be inserted into the appropriate places in the table.
- Where appropriate, there should be clear sub-totals.
- A total column may be presented; this would usually be the right-hand column.
- A total figure is often advisable at the bottom of each column of figures.
- Tables should not contain too much data (and thus be difficult to read).

1.4 EXAMPLE: TABLES

The total number of employees in a certain trading company is 1,000. They are employed in three departments: production, administration and sales. 600 people are employed in the production department and 300 in administration. There are 110 male juveniles in employment, 110 female juveniles, and 290 adult females. The remaining employees are adult males.

In the production department there are 350 adult males, 150 adult females and 50 male juveniles, whilst in the administration department there are 100 adult males, 110 adult females and 50 juvenile males.

Required

Draw up a table to show all the details of employment in the company and its departments and provide suitable secondary statistics to describe the distribution of people in departments.

1.5 SOLUTION

The basic table required has the following two dimensions.

- Departments
- Age/sex analysis

Secondary statistics (not the same thing as secondary data) are supporting figures that are **supplementary** to the main items of data, and which clarify or amplify the main data. A major example of secondary statistics is percentages. In this example, we could show one of the following.

(a) The percentage of the total work force in each department belonging to each age/sex group

(b)   The percentage of the total of each age/sex group employed in each department

In this example, (a) has been selected but you might consider that (b) would be more suitable. Either could be suitable, depending of course on what purposes the data are being collected and presented for.

Analysis of employees

	Production		Administration		Sales		Total	
	No	%	No	%	No	%	No	%
Adult males	350	58.4	100	33.3	40**	40	490*	49
Adult females	150	25.0	110	36.7	30**	30	290	29
Male juveniles	50	8.3	50	16.7	10**	10	110	11
Female juveniles	50*	8.3	40*	13.3	20**	20	110	11
Total	600	100.0	300	100.0	100	100	1,000	100

*   Balancing figure to make up the column total

**   Balancing figure then needed to make up the row total

Rounding errors

1.6   Rounding errors may become apparent when, for example, a percentages column does not add up to 100%. Any rounding should therefore be to the nearest unit and the potential size of errors should be kept to a tolerable level by rounding to a small enough unit (for example to the nearest £10, rather than to the nearest £1,000).

2   CHARTS

2.1   Instead of presenting data in a table, it might be preferable to give a visual display in the form of a **chart**.

2.2   The purpose of a chart is to convey the data in a way that will demonstrate its meaning more clearly than a table of data would. Charts are not always more appropriate than tables, and the most suitable way of presenting data will depend on the following.

(a)   What the data are intended to show. Visual displays usually make one or two points quite forcefully, whereas tables usually give more detailed information.

(b)   Who is going to use the data. Some individuals might understand visual displays more readily than tabulated data.

Pictograms

> **KEY TERM**
>
> A **pictogram** is a statistical diagram in which quantities are represented by pictures or symbols.

2.3   EXAMPLE: PICTOGRAMS

A pictogram showing the number of employees at a factory would represent the quantities of employees using pictures of people.

287

Number of employees

In this example, each picture represents ten employees, and to represent a smaller quantity, a part-picture can be drawn. Here, there were 45 men employed in 20X6.

2.4 Guidelines for drawing a pictogram

- The symbols should be clear and simple.
- The quantity that each symbol represents should be clearly shown in a key .
- Bigger quantities ought to be shown by more symbols, not by bigger symbols.

For example, if sales of boxes of dishwasher powder double between 20X5 and 20X6, a pictogram should show:

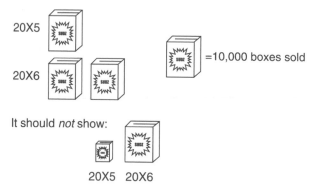

In this pictogram, the bigger symbol does not give a true impression of sales growth.

2.5 Advantages of pictograms

- They present data in a simple, readily understood way
- They convey their message to the reader at a glance

2.6 Disadvantages of pictograms

- They can only convey a limited amount of information
- They lack precision

Each symbol must represent quite a large number of items, otherwise a pictogram would contain too many symbols. Using portions of a symbol to represent smaller quantities gives some extra precision, but not much.

 represents 1,000 men then

 represents less than 1,000 men, but how many exactly? 400? 500? 600?

Pie charts

2.7 A **pie chart** shows pictorially the **relative sizes of component elements** of a total. It is called a pie chart because it is circular, and so has the shape of a pie in a round pie dish and because the 'pie' is cut into slices. Each slice represents a part of the total.

2.8 Pie charts have sectors of varying sizes, and you need to be able to draw sectors fairly accurately. To do this, you need a protractor. Working out sector sizes involves converting parts of the total into equivalent degrees of a circle.

2.9 EXAMPLE: PIE CHARTS

The costs of production at Factory A and Factory B during March 20X2 were as follows.

	Factory A		Factory B	
	£'000	%	£'000	%
Direct materials	70	35	50	20
Direct labour	30	15	125	50
Production overhead	90	45	50	20
Office costs	10	5	25	10
	200	100	250	100

Required

Show the costs for the factories in pie charts.

2.10 SOLUTION

To convert the components into degrees of a circle, we can use either the percentage figures or the actual cost figures.

(a) Using the percentage figures, the total percentage is 100%, and the total number of degrees in a circle is 360°. To convert from one to the other, we multiply each percentage value by 360°/100% = 3.6.

	Factory A		Factory B	
	%	Degrees	%	Degrees
Direct materials	35	126	20	72
Direct labour	15	54	50	180
Production overhead	45	162	20	72
Office costs	5	18	10	36
	100	360	100	360

(b) Using the actual cost figures, we would multiply each cost by

	Factory A	Factory B
$\dfrac{\text{Number of degrees}}{\text{Total cost}}$	$\dfrac{360}{200} = 1.8$	$\dfrac{360}{250} = 1.44$

	Factory A		Factory B	
	£'000	Degrees	£'000	Degrees
Direct materials	70	126	50	72
Direct labour	30	54	125	180
Production overhead	90	162	50	72
Office costs	10	18	25	36
	200	360	250	360

A pie chart could be drawn for each factory (using a protractor), as follows.

289

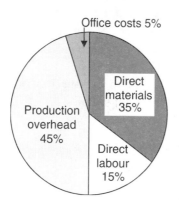

Factory A

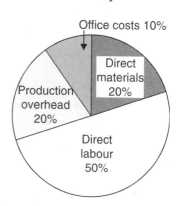

Factory B

2.11 The **advantages of pie charts** are as follows.

- They give a simple pictorial display of the relative sizes of elements of a total.
- They show clearly when one element is much bigger than others.
- They can sometimes clearly show differences in the elements of two different totals.

In the example above, the pie charts for factories A and B show how factory A's costs mostly consist of production overhead and direct materials, whereas at factory B, direct labour is the largest cost element.

2.12 The **disadvantages of pie charts** are as follows.

- They show only the relative sizes of elements.

In the example of the two factories, for instance, the pie charts do not show that costs at Factory B were £50,000 higher in total than at Factory A.

- It can be time consuming calculating degrees of a circle and drawing sectors accurately.
- It is sometimes difficult to compare sector sizes accurately by eye.

Bar charts

6/96, 12/98

KEY TERM

A **bar chart** is a method of presenting data in which quantities are shown in the form of bars on a chart, the length of the bars being proportional to the quantities.

2.13 The bar chart is one of the most common methods of presenting data in a visual form. There are three main types of bar chart.

- Simple bar charts
- Component bar charts, including percentage component bar charts
- Multiple (or compound) bar charts

Simple bar charts

2.14 A **simple bar chart** is a chart consisting of one or more bars, in which the length of each bar indicates the magnitude of the corresponding data item.

2.15 EXAMPLE: A SIMPLE BAR CHART

A company's total sales for the years from 20X1 to 20X6 are as follows.

Year	Sales
	£'000
20X1	800
20X2	1,200
20X3	1,100
20X4	1,400
20X5	1,600
20X6	1,700

The data could be shown on a simple bar chart as follows

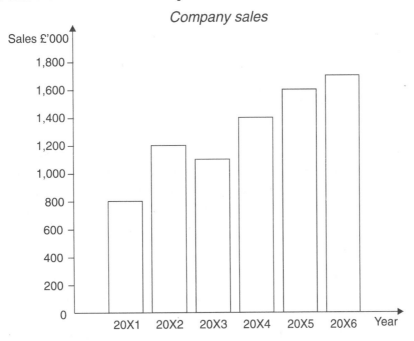

Each axis of the chart must be clearly labelled, and there must be a scale to indicate the magnitude of the data. Here, the y axis includes a scale for the amount of sales, and so readers of the bar chart can see not only that sales have been rising year by year (with 20X3 being an exception) but also what the actual sales have been each year.

2.16 Simple bar charts serve two purposes.

(a) They show the actual magnitude of each item.
(b) By comparing the lengths of bars on the chart, magnitudes may be compared.

Component bar charts   **12/95**

2.17 A **component bar chart** is a chart that gives a breakdown of each total into its components.

2.18 EXAMPLE: A COMPONENT BAR CHART

Charbart plc's sales for the years from 20X7 to 20X9 are as follows.

	20X7	20X8	20X9
	£'000	£'000	£'000
Product A	1,000	1,200	1,700
Product B	900	1,000	1,000
Product C	500	600	700
Total	2,400	2,800	3,400

A component bar chart would show the following.

- How total sales have changed from year to year
- The components of each year's total

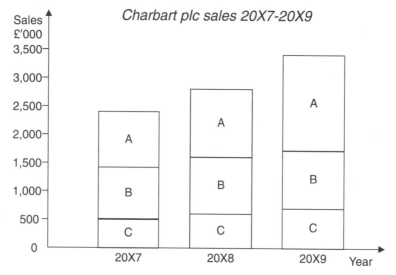

In this diagram the growth in sales is illustrated and the significance of growth in product A sales as the reason for the total sales growth is also fairly clear. The growth in product A sales would have been even clearer if product A had been drawn as the bottom element in each bar instead of the top one.

Percentage component bar charts

2.19 The **difference** between a **component bar chart** and a **percentage component bar chart** is that with a **component bar chart**, the total length of **each bar** (and the length of each component in it) **indicates magnitude**. A bigger amount is shown by a longer bar. With a **percentage component bar chart, total magnitudes are not shown**. If two or more bars are drawn on the chart, the total length of each bar is the same. The only varying lengths in a percentage component bar chart are the lengths of the sections of a bar, which vary according to the relative sizes of the components.

2.20 EXAMPLE: A PERCENTAGE COMPONENT BAR CHART

The information in the previous example of sales of Charbart plc could have been shown in a percentage component bar chart as follows.

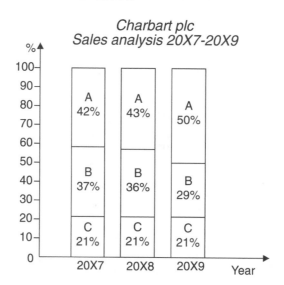

Working

	20X7		20X8		20X9	
	£'000	%	£'000	%	£'000	%
Product A	1,000	42	1,200	43	1,700	50
Product B	900	37	1,000	36	1,000	29
Product C	500	21	600	21	700	21
Total	2,400	100	2,800	100	3,400	100

This chart shows that sales of C have remained a steady proportion of total sales, but the proportion of A in total sales has gone up quite considerably, while the proportion of B has fallen correspondingly.

Multiple bar charts (compound bar charts)

2.21 A **multiple bar chart** (or compound bar chart) is a bar chart in which two or more separate bars are used to present sub-divisions of data.

2.22 EXAMPLE: A MULTIPLE BAR CHART

The data on Charbart plc's sales could be shown in a multiple bar chart as follows.

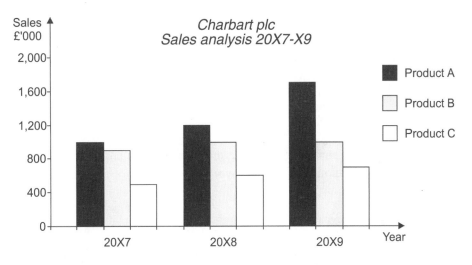

2.23 A multiple bar chart uses several bars for each total. In the above example, the sales in each year are shown as three separate bars, one for each product, X, Y and Z.

Multiple bar charts are sometimes drawn with the bars horizontal instead of vertical.

2.24 Multiple bar charts present similar information to component bar charts, except for the following.

(a) Multiple bar charts do not show the grand total (in the above example, the total output each year) whereas component bar charts do.

(b) Multiple bar charts illustrate the comparative magnitudes of the components more clearly than component bar charts.

3   FREQUENCY DISTRIBUTIONS   6/99

3.1 Frequently the data collected from a statistical survey or investigation is simply a mass of numbers. The output in units of 20 employees during one week is as follows.

65	69	70	71	70	68	69	67	70	68
72	71	69	74	70	73	71	67	69	70

3.2 The raw data shown yields little information as it stands. The data could, be arranged in order size (an array) and the lowest and highest data items, as well as a typical items, could be identified.

> ### KEY TERM
>
> A **frequency distribution** is the distribution of the number of times the value of a particular variable occurs.

3.3 Many sets of data, however, contain a limited number of data values, even though there may be many occurrences of each value. It can therefore be useful to organise the data into what is known as a **frequency distribution (or frequency table)**. A frequency distribution for the data in Paragraph 3.1 is as follows.

Output Units	*Number of employees (frequency)*
65	1
66	0
67	2
68	2
69	4
70	5
71	3
72	1
73	1
74	1
	20

3.4 When the data are arranged in this way it is immediately obvious that 69 and 70 units are the most common volumes of output per employee per week.

Grouped frequency distributions 6/97

> ### KEY TERM
>
> A **grouped frequency distribution** is the distribution of the number of times values within ranges of particular values occur.

3.5 If there is a large set of data or if most data items are different, it is often convenient to **group** frequencies together into **bands** or **classes**. Suppose that the output produced by another group of 20 employees during one week was as follows, in units.

1,087	850	1,084	792
924	1,226	1,012	1,205
1,265	1,028	1,230	1,182
1,086	1,130	989	1,155
1,134	1,166	1,129	1,160

3.6 The range of output from the lowest to the highest producer is 792 to 1,265, a range of 473 units. This range could be divided into classes of say, 100 units (the class width or class interval), and the number of employees producing output within each class could then be grouped into a single frequency, as follows.

Output	Number of employees (frequency)
Units	
700 - 799	1
800 - 899	1
900 - 999	2
1,000 - 1,099	5
1,100 - 1,199	7
1,200 - 1,299	4
	20

3.7 Once items have been 'grouped' in this way their individual values are lost.

Grouped frequency distributions of continuous variables

3.8 As well as being used for discrete variables (as above), grouped frequency distributions (or grouped frequency tables) can be used to present data for continuous variables.

3.9 EXAMPLE: A GROUPED FREQUENCY DISTRIBUTION FOR A CONTINUOUS VARIABLE

Suppose we wish to record the heights of 50 different individuals. The information might be presented as a grouped frequency distribution, as follows.

Height	Number of individuals (frequency)
cm	
Up to and including 154	1
Over 154, up to and including 163	3
Over 163, up to and including 172	8
Over 172, up to and including 181	16
Over 181, up to and including 190	18
Over 190	4
	50

Note the following points.

(a) It would be wrong to show the ranges as 0 - 154, 154 - 163, 163 - 172 and so on, because 154 cm and 163 cm would then be values in two classes, which is not permissible. Although each value should only be in one class, we have to make sure that each possible value can be included. Classes such as 154-162, 163-172 would not be suitable since a height of 162.5 cm would not belong in either class. Such classes could be used for discrete variables, however.

(b) There is an **open ended** class at each end of the range. This is because heights up to 154 cm and over 190 cm are thought to be uncommon, so that a single 'open ended' class is used to group all the frequencies together.

Preparing grouped frequency distributions

3.10 To prepare a grouped frequency distribution, a decision must be made about **how wide each class should be**. In an examination, you might be told how many classes to use, or what the class interval should be. Consider the following guidelines.

(a) The size of each class should be appropriate to the nature of the data being recorded, and the most appropriate class interval varies according to circumstances.

(b) The upper and lower limits of each class interval should be suitable 'round' numbers for class intervals which are in multiples of 5, 10, 100, 1,000 and so on. For example, if the class interval is 10, and data items range in value from 23 to 62 (discrete values), the class intervals should be 20-29, 30-39, 40-49, 50-59 and 60-69, rather than 23-32, 33-42, 43-52 and 53-62.

(c)   With **continuous variables**, either:

(i)   the upper limit of a class should be 'up to and including ...' and the lower limit of the next class should be 'over ...'; or

(ii)   the upper limit of a class should be 'less than...', and the lower limit of the next class should be 'at least ...'.

Question 1

The commission earnings for May 20X3 of the assistants in a department store were as follows (in £).

60	35	53	47	25	44	55	58	47	71
63	67	57	44	61	48	50	56	61	42
43	38	41	39	61	51	27	56	57	50
55	68	55	50	25	48	44	43	49	73
53	35	36	41	45	71	56	40	69	52
36	47	66	52	32	46	44	32	52	58
49	41	45	45	48	36	46	42	52	33
31	36	40	66	53	58	60	52	66	51
51	44	59	53	51	57	35	45	46	54
46	54	51	39	64	43	54	47	60	45

Required

Prepare a grouped frequency distribution classifying the commission earnings into categories of £5 commencing with '£25 and under £30'.

Answer

We are told what classes to use, so the first step is to identify the lowest and highest values in the data. The lowest value is £25 (in the first row) and the highest value is £73 (in the fourth row). This means that the class intervals must go up to '£70 and under £75'.

We can now set out the classes in a column, and then count the number of items in each class using tally marks.

Class interval	Tally marks	Total
£25 and less than £30	///	3
£30 and less than £35	////	4
£35 and less than £40	‖‖ ‖‖	10
£40 and less than £45	‖‖ ‖‖ ‖‖	15
£45 and less than £50	‖‖ ‖‖ ‖‖ ///	18
£50 and less than £55	‖‖ ‖‖ ‖‖ ‖‖	20
£55 and less than £60	‖‖ ‖‖ ///	13
£60 and less than £65	‖‖ ///	8
£65 and less than £70	‖‖ /	6
£70 and less than £75	///	3
	Total	100

3.11   You should be able to interpret a grouped frequency distribution and express an interpretation in writing. In the example in Paragraph 3.9, an interpretation of the data is fairly straightforward.

*   Most heights fell between 154 cm and 190 cm.

*   Most heights were in the middle of this range, with few people having heights in the lower and upper ends of the range.

Cumulative frequency distributions

> **KEY TERM**
>
> A **cumulative frequency distribution** (or **cumulative frequency table**) is a table which can be used to show the total number of times that a value above or below a certain amount occurs.

3.12   There are two possible cumulative frequency distributions for the grouped frequency distribution in Paragraph 3.6.

	Cumulative frequency		*Cumulative frequency*
≥ 700	20	< 800	1
≥ 800	19	< 900	2
≥ 900	18	<1,000	4
≥ 1,000	16	<1,100	9
≥ 1,100	11	<1,200	16
≥ 1,200	4	<1,300	20

Notes

(a)   The first cumulative frequency distribution shows that of the total of 20 employees, 19 produced 800 units or more, 18 produced 900 units or more, 16 produced 1,000 units or more and so on.

(b)   The second cumulative frequency distribution shows that, of the total of 20 employees, one produced under 800 units, two produced under 900 units, four produced under 1,000 units and so on.

> **Exam focus point**
>
> Part of a question in the 6/99 exam required candidates to draw up a frequency distribution of reject rates.

Tabular presentation

3.13   Instead of the style of presentation we have looked at so far, you may come across a more formal **tabular presentation** style. Consider the following example.

3.14   EXAMPLE: GROUPED FREQUENCY AND CUMULATIVE FREQUENCY TABLES

Suppose that 20 people threw three dice each and obtained the following totals.

Total of three dice thrown

7	15	17	5	9
11	13	18	3	10
6	12	12	7	9
13	15	14	10	4

Required

Prepare a grouped frequency table and a cumulative frequency table.

3.15 SOLUTION

	Frequency of scores			
	Score interval			
	3-5	6-10	11-15	16 - 18
Frequency	3	7	8	2

	Cumulative frequency of scores			
	Score interval			
	3-5	0-10	0-15	0-18
Cumulative frequency	3	10	18	20

4 HISTOGRAMS

6/94, 12/99

> **Exam focus point**
>
> Remember that you can pick up easy marks in an examination for drawing a graph neatly. Always use a ruler, label your axes and use an appropriate scale.

> **KEY TERM**
>
> A **histogram** is a data presentation method for (usually) grouped data of a continuous variable. It is visually similar to a bar chart but frequencies are represented by areas covered by the bar rather than by their height.

Histograms of frequency distributions with equal class intervals

4.1 If all the class intervals are the same, as in the frequency distribution in Paragraph 3.6

- The bars of the histogram will all have the same width.
- The heights will be proportional to the frequencies.

The histogram looks almost identical to a bar chart except that the bars are joined together. Because the bars are joined together, when presenting discrete data the data must be treated as continuous so that there are no gaps between class intervals. For example, for a cricketer's scores in various games the classes would have to be ≥ 0 but < 10, ≥ 10 but < 20 and so on, instead of 0-9, 10-19 and so on.

4.2 A histogram of the distribution in Paragraph 3.6 would be drawn as follows.

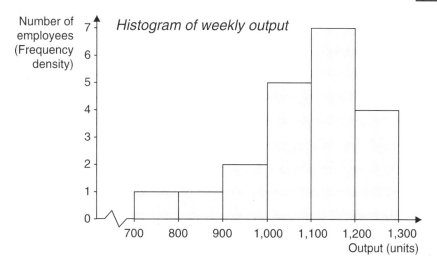

4.3   Note that the discrete data have been treated as continuous, the intervals being changed to >700 but ≤ 800, >800 but ≤ 900 and so on.

Histograms of frequency distributions with unequal class intervals

4.4   If a distribution has **unequal** class intervals, the heights of the bars have to be adjusted for the fact that the bars do not have the same width.

4.5   EXAMPLE: A HISTOGRAM WITH UNEQUAL CLASS INTERVALS

The weekly wages of employees of Salt Lake Ltd are as follows.

Wages per employee	*Number of employees*
Up to and including £60	4
> £60 ≤ £80	6
> £80 ≤ £90	6
> £90 ≤£120	6
More than £120	3

The class intervals for wages per employee range from £10 to £30.

A histogram is drawn as follows.

(a)   The width of each bar on the chart must be proportionate to the corresponding class interval. In other words, the bar representing wages of > £60 ≤ £80, a range of £20, will be oncewide as the bar representing wages of > £80 ≤ £90, a range of only £10.

(b)   A standard width of bar must be selected. This should be the size of class interval which occurs most frequently. In our example, class intervals £10, £20 and £30 each occur once. An interval of £20 will be selected as the standard width.

(c)   Open-ended classes must be closed off. It is usual for the width of such classes to be the same as that of the adjoining class. In this example, the class 'up to and including £60' will become >£40 ≤ £60 and the class 'more than £120' will become >£120 ≤ £150.

(d)   Each frequency is then multiplied by (standard class width ÷ actual class width) to obtain the height of the bar in the histogram.

(e)   The height of bars no longer corresponds to **frequency** but rather to **frequency density** and hence the vertical axis should be labelled frequency density.

(f)   Note that the data is considered to be continuous since the gap between, for example, £79.99 and £80.00 is very, very small.

Class interval	Size of interval	Frequency	Adjustment	Height of bar
> £40 ≤ £60	20	4	× 20/20	4
> £60 ≤ £80	20	6	× 20/20	6
> £80 ≤ £90	10	6	× 20/10	12
> £90 ≤ £120	30	6	× 20/30	4
> £120 ≤ £150	30	3	× 20/30	2

The first two bars will be of normal height.

The third bar will be twice as high as the class frequency (6) would suggest, to compensate for the fact that the class interval, £10, is only half the standard size.

The fourth and fifth bars will be two thirds as high as the class frequencies (6 and 3) would suggest, to compensate for the fact that the class interval, £30, is 150% of the standard size.

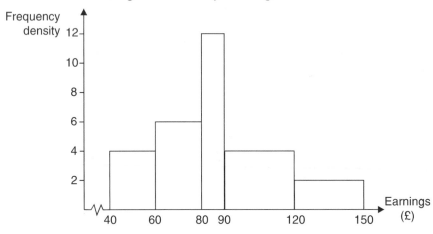

Histogram of weekly earnings: Salt Lake Ltd

Question 2

The sales force of a company have just completed a successful sales campaign. The performances of individual sales staff have been analysed as follows, into a grouped frequency distribution.

Sales	Number of sales staff
Up to £10,000	1
> £10,000 ≤ £12,000	10
> £12,000 ≤ £14,000	12
> £14,000 ≤ £18,000	8
> £18,000 ≤ £22,000	4
> £22,000	1

Required

Draw a histogram from this information.

Answer

Before drawing the histogram, we must decide on the following.

(a) A standard class width: £2,000 will be chosen.

(b) An open-ended class width. It is usual for the width to be the same as that of the adjoining class. In this example, the open-ended class width will therefore be £2,000 for class 'up to £10,000' and £4,000 for the class '> £22,000'.

Class interval	Size of width £	Frequency	Adjustment	Height of block
Up to £10,000	2,000	1	× 2/2	1
> £10,000 ≤ £12,000	2,000	10	× 2/2	10
> £12,000 ≤ £14,000	2,000	12	× 2/2	12
> £14,000 ≤ £18,000	4,000	8	× 2/4	4
> £18,000 ≤ £22,000	4,000	4	× 2/4	2
> £22,000	4,000	1	× 2/4	¹/₂

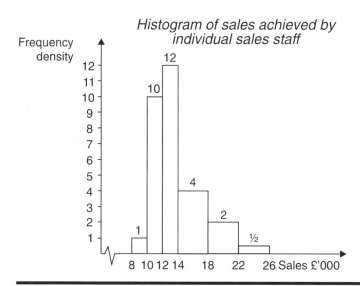

Histogram of sales achieved by individual sales staff

The advantages and disadvantages of histograms

4.6 **Advantages** of histograms include the following.

- They clearly display grouped frequency distributions graphically.
- They indicate the range of the values, and whether it is narrow or wide.
- They indicate where the most frequently occurring value is.

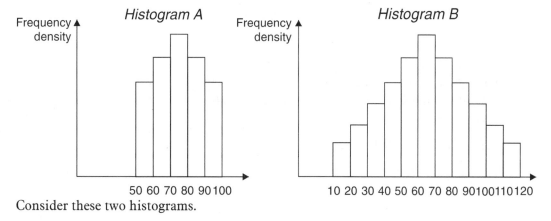

Consider these two histograms.

- In (A) there is a narrower range of values than in (B).
- Both have the most frequently occurring value somewhere in the middle of the range.

Now compare these two histograms.

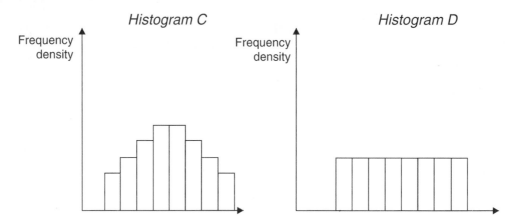

Histogram C   *Histogram D*

- The most frequently occurring values in histogram C are in the middle of the range.
- In histogram D, values occur with equal frequency across the entire range.

4.7 The main **disadvantages** of histograms are as follows.

- They may give a false sense of accuracy if representing sample data.
- If class widths vary, they may be more difficult for the lay person to understand.
- They are not particularly accurate because they **assume** that **frequencies occur evenly** throughout the class interval.

Frequency polygons

> **KEY TERM**
>
> A **frequency polygon** is a chart derived from a histogram which makes the assumption that the frequency of occurrence of data items is *not* evenly spread.

4.8 A **frequency polygon** is drawn from a histogram, in the following way.

- Mark the mid-point of the top of each bar in the histogram.
- Join up all these points with straight lines.

4.9 The ends of the diagram (the mid-points of the two end bars) should be joined to the base line at the mid-points of the next class intervals outside the range of observed data. These intervals should be taken to be of the same size as the last class intervals for observed data.

4.10 **EXAMPLE: A FREQUENCY POLYGON**

The following grouped frequency distribution relates to the number of occasions during the past 40 weeks that a particular cost has been a given amount.

Cost	Number of occasions
£	
> 800 ≤ 1,000	4
> 1,000 ≤ 1,200	10
> 1,200 ≤ 1,400	12
> 1,400 ≤ 1,600	10
> 1,600 ≤ 1,800	4
	40

Required

Prepare a frequency polygon.

4.11 SOLUTION

A histogram is first drawn, in the way described earlier. All classes are of the same width.

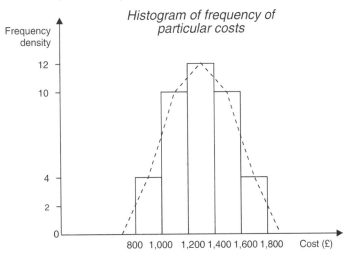

The mid-points of the class intervals outside the range of observed data are 700 and 1,900.

Frequency curves

4.12 Because a frequency polygon has straight lines between points, it too can be seen as an inaccurate way of presenting data. One method of obtaining greater accuracy would be to make the class intervals smaller. If the class intervals of a distribution were made small enough the frequency polygon would become very smooth. It would become a curve.

> **Exam focus point**
> There were 3 marks available in the 12/99 exam for explaining how to convert a histogram into a frequency polygon.

5   GRAPHS   6/96, 6/99

Ogives

5.1   Just as a grouped frequency distribution can be graphed as a histogram, a cumulative frequency distribution can be graphed as an **ogive**.

> **KEY TERM**
>
> An **ogive** is a graph which shows the cumulative number of items with a value less than or equal to, or alternatively greater than or equal to, a certain amount.

5.2   EXAMPLE: OGIVES

Consider the following frequency distribution.

Number of faulty units rejected on inspection	Frequency	Cumulative frequency
1	5	5
2	5	10
3	3	13
4	1	14
	14	

An ogive would be drawn as follows.

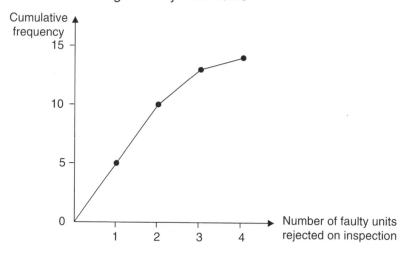

Ogive of rejected items

5.3   When we have a **grouped** frequency distribution, we plot the **upper limits of the class** eg for the class internal of $> 2 \le 3$, we would plot the cumulative frequency against 3.

5.4   Drawing ogives involves plotting the cumulative frequencies on a graph.

- A cumulative frequency polygon (or diagram) is an ogive drawn with straight lines.
- A cumulative frequency curve is an ogive drawn as a curve.

Question 3

A grouped frequency distribution for the volume of output produced at a factory over a period of 40 weeks is as follows.

Output (units)	Number of times output achieved
> 0 ≤ 200	4
>200 ≤ 400	8
>400 ≤ 600	12
>600 ≤ 800	10
>800 ≤1,000	6
	40

Required

Draw an appropriate ogive, and estimate the number of weeks in which output was 550 units or less.

Answer

Upper limit of interval	Frequency	Cumulative frequency
200	4	4
400	8	12
600	12	24
800	10	34
1,000	6	40

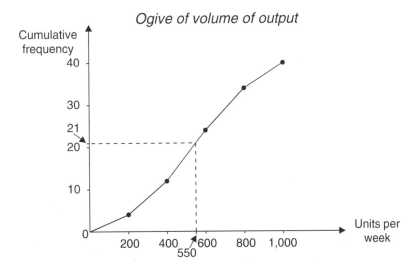

Ogive of volume of output

The dotted lines indicate that output of up to 550 units was achieved in 21 out of the 40 weeks.

5.5 We can also draw ogives to show the cumulative number of items with values greater than or equal to some given value.

5.6 EXAMPLE: DOWNWARD SLOPING OGIVES

Output at a factory over a period of 80 weeks is shown as follows.

Output per week	Number of times output achieved
Units	
> 0 ≤ 100	10
> 100 ≤ 200	20
> 200 ≤ 300	25
> 300 ≤ 400	15
> 400 ≤ 500	10
	80

If we wished to draw an ogive to show the number of weeks in which output exceeded a certain value, the cumulative total would begin at 80 and drop to 0. In drawing an ogive when we work down through values of the variable, the descending cumulative frequency should be plotted against the lower limit of each class interval.

Lower limit of interval	Frequency	Cumulative ('more than') frequency
0	10	80
100	20	70
200	25	50
300	15	25
400	10	10
500	0	0

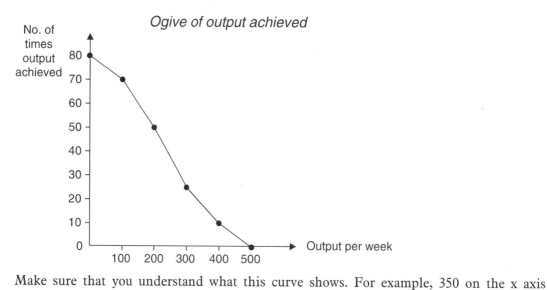

Ogive of output achieved

Make sure that you understand what this curve shows. For example, 350 on the x axis corresponds with about 18 on the y axis. This means that output of 350 units or more was achieved 18 times out of the 80 weeks.

Lorenz curves   6/94

5.7   A **Lorenz curve** makes use of cumulative frequencies to show the extent to which a variable is distributed throughout the population.

> **KEY TERM**
>
> A **Lorenz curve** is a graphical means of data presentation which measures one cumulative amount against another.

5.8   A common application of the Lorenz curve is to show the distribution of wealth.

5.9   EXAMPLE: LORENZ CURVES

The national wealth of Ruritania is spread as follows.

Wealth in roubles per person	*No of people*	*Wealth* '000 roubles
< 500	13,000	5,200
≥ 500 < 1,000	16,000	12,800
≥ 1,000 < 5,000	16,000	48,000
≥ 5,000 < 40,000	2,000	50,000
≥ 40,000	500	25,000
	47,500	141,000

The cumulative number of people and the cumulative wealth can be calculated as follows.

No of people	*Cumulative* no of people	%	*Wealth* '000 roubles	*Cumulative wealth* '000 roubles	%
13,000	13,000	27	5,200	5,200	4
16,000	29,000	61	12,800	18,000	13
16,000	45,000	95	48,000	66,000	47
2,000	47,000	99	50,000	116,000	82
500	47,500	100	25,000	141,000	100

The graph is plotted from the percentage columns.

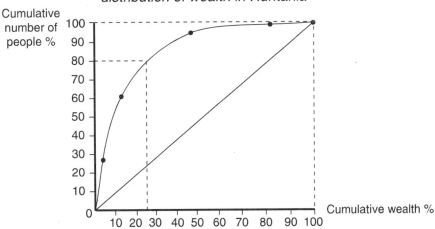

Lorenz curve showing the
distribution of wealth in Ruritania

A straight line is also drawn through the origin to point (100%, 100%). This diagonal line is called the **line of uniform distribution**, and represents zero concentration of wealth. Note the following points.

- 80% of the population own 25% of the wealth.

- Therefore, 20% of the population own 75% of the wealth.

- The more the Lorenz curve deviates from the line of uniform distribution, the greater the concentration of wealth.

- The main application of the Lorenz curve is to make comparisons, by comparing where the curve is in relation to the line of uniform distribution.

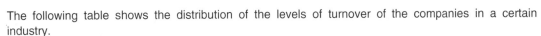

Question 4

The following table shows the distribution of the levels of turnover of the companies in a certain industry.

Turnover £'000	Number of companies
over 500 - 1,000	32
over 1,000 - 1,500	58
over 1,500 - 2,000	41
over 2,000 - 2,500	33
over 2,500 - 3,000	28
over 3,000 - 3,500	16

Required

(a) Construct a Lorenz curve from these data. Use the mid-point of each class as the turnover of each company in the class.

(b) State what this chart shows.

Answer

(a)

Calculation of figures for Lorenz curve

Turnover £'000	Class midpoint, x £'000	No of cos, f	Total turnover, fx	Cumulative turnover	%	Cumulative companies	%
over 500 - 1,000	750	32	24,000	24,000	6.46	32	15.38
over 1,000 - 1,500	1,250	58	72,500	96,500	25.97	90	43.26
over 1,500 - 2,000	1,750	41	71,750	168,250	45.29	131	62.98
over 2,000 - 2,500	2,250	33	74,250	242,500	65.28	164	78.85
over 2,500 - 3,000	2,750	28	77,000	319,500	86.00	192	92.30
over 3,000 - 3,500	3,250	16	52,000	371,500	100.00	208	100.00

The Lorenz curve is now drawn. The number of companies has been recorded on the y axis and turnover on the x axis, but it would be equally suitable to have turnover on the y axis and the number of companies on the x axis.

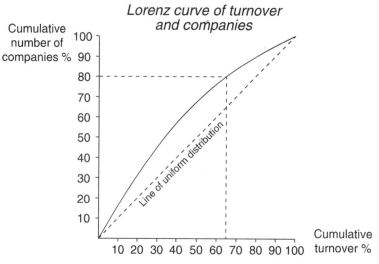

Lorenz curve of turnover and companies

(b) The Lorenz curve in this example shows the degree of concentration of total revenue within the population of companies. The further the curve is away from the diagonal the greater is the degree of concentration of revenue.

In this case it appears that there is a moderate degree of concentration of turnover. Approximately 80% of companies share only about 65% of the total turnover, so the top 20% of companies have 35% of total turnover.

Chapter roundup

- **Tables** are a simple way of presenting information about two variables.

- Charts often convey the meaning or significance of data more clearly than would a table. Make sure that you are able to construct **pictograms**, **pie charts** and **bar charts**.

- There are three main types of bar chart: **simple**, **component** (including percentage component) and **multiple** (or compound).

- **Frequency distributions** are used if values of particular variables occur more than once. Make sure that you know the difference between grouped frequency and cumulative frequency distributions.

- A frequency distribution can be represented pictorially by means of a histogram. The number of observations in a class is represented by the area covered by the bar, rather than by its height. **Frequency polygons** and **frequency curves** are perhaps more accurate methods of data presentation than the standard histogram.

- An **ogive** shows the cumulative number of items with a value less than or equal to, or alternatively greater than or equal to, a certain amount.

- A **Lorenz curve** is a form of cumulative frequency curve which measures one cumulative amount against another. Both the x and y axes are often shown in terms of percentages. This type of graph is used to show degrees of concentration.

Quick quiz

1   What are the main guidelines for tabulation? (see para 1.3)

2   What are the advantages of pictograms? (2.5)

3   What are the disadvantages of pie charts? (2.12)

4   Name the three main types of bar chart. (2.13)

5   How would you prepare a grouped frequency distribution? (3.10)

6   What is a cumulative frequency distribution? (key terms)

7   What are the computations needed to draw a histogram? (4.5)

8   How would you draw a frequency polygon from a histogram? (4.8)

9   How would you draw an ogive? (5.2 - 5.4)

10   What is the purpose of a Lorenz curve? (5.7)

Question to try	Level	Marks	Time
17	Examination	14	25 mins

BPP PUBLISHING

Chapter 17

AVERAGES

Chapter topic list	Syllabus reference
1 The arithmetic mean	QT 6(a)
2 The mode	QT 6(a)
3 The median	QT 6(a)

Introduction

Sometimes you might need more information than that provided by the diagrammatic representations of data that we looked at in Chapter 16. In such circumstances you may need to apply some sort of **numerical analysis**.

There are two initial measures that we can take from a set of data: a **measure of centrality** (average) and a **measure of spread**.

An average is a **representative** figure that is used to give some impression of the size of all the items in the population. You may have thought that an average is simply 'an average' but there are in fact three main types of average.

* Arithmetic mean
* Mode
* Median

In this chapter, we will be looking at each of these averages in turn, their calculation and their advantages and disadvantages.

1   THE ARITHMETIC MEAN

6/95, 12/97, 6/98, 12/99

1.1   This is the best known type of average.

FORMULA TO LEARN

Arithmetic mean for ungrouped data $\bar{x} = \dfrac{\text{Sum of values of items}}{\text{Number of items}}$

1.2   EXAMPLE: THE ARITHMETIC MEAN

The demand for a product on each of 20 days was as follows (in units).

3   12   7   17   3   14   9   6   11   10   1   4   19   7   15   6   9   12   12   8

The arithmetic mean of daily demand is

$$\frac{\text{Sum of demand}}{\text{Number of days}} = \frac{185}{20} = 9.25 \text{ units}$$

1.3   The **arithmetic mean** of a variable x is shown as $\overline{x}$ ('x bar'). Thus in the above example $\overline{x}$ = 9.25 units. Demand on any one day is never actually 9.25 units. The arithmetic mean is merely an **average representation of demand** on each of the 20 days.

Finding the arithmetic mean of data in a frequency distribution

1.4   It is more likely that an arithmetic mean of a frequency distribution will be required. In our previous example, the frequency distribution would be shown as follows.

Daily demand x	Frequency f	Demand ×frequency fx
1	1	1
3	2	6
4	1	4
6	2	12
7	2	14
8	1	8
9	2	18
10	1	10
11	1	11
12	3	36
14	1	14
15	1	15
17	1	17
19	1	19
	20	185

$$\overline{x} = \frac{185}{20} = 9.25$$

Sigma, Σ

> **KEY TERM**
>
> Σ means 'the sum of' and is used as shorthand to mean the sum of a set of values.

1.5   Therefore, in the previous example:

- Σf would mean the sum of all the frequencies, which is 20;

- Σfx would mean the sum of all the values of 'frequency multiplied by daily demand', that is, all 14 values of fx, so Σ fx = 185;

- Σx^2 would mean the sum of all the values of 'x multiplied by x';

- (Σx)^2 would mean the square of the sum of all the values of x (sum all the values of x and then square the total).

The symbolic formula for the arithmetic mean of a frequency distribution

> **FORMULA TO LEARN**
>
> The **arithmetic mean of a frequency distribution** $\overline{x} = \dfrac{\Sigma fx}{n}$ or $\dfrac{\Sigma fx}{\Sigma f}$
>
> where n is the number of values recorded, or the number of items measured.

Finding the arithmetic mean of grouped data in class intervals 6/95

1.6 Another common problem is to calculate (or at least approximate) the arithmetic mean of a frequency distribution, where the frequencies are shown in class intervals.

1.7 EXAMPLE: GROUPED DATA

Using the example in Paragraph 1.4, the frequency distribution might have been shown as follows.

Daily demand	Frequency
$> 0 \leq 5$	4
$> 5 \leq 10$	8
$>10 \leq 15$	6
$>15 \leq 20$	2
	20

There is an extra difficulty with finding the average now; as the data have been collected into classes, a certain amount of detail has been lost and the values of the variables to be used in the calculation of the mean are not clearly specified. To calculate the arithmetic mean of grouped data we therefore need to decide on a value which best represents all of the values in a particular class interval.

The mid-point of each class interval is conventionally taken, on the assumption that the frequencies occur evenly over the class interval range. In the example above, the variable is discrete, so the first class includes 1, 2, 3, 4 and 5, giving a mid-point of 3. With a continuous variable (such as quantities of fuel consumed in litres), the mid-points would have been 2.5, 7.5 and so on. Once the value of x has been decided, the mean is calculated in exactly the same way as shown in the formula to learn.

Daily demand	Mid point	Frequency	
	x	f	fx
$> 0 \leq 5$	3	4	12
$> 5 \leq 10$	8	8	64
$>10 \leq 15$	13	6	78
$>15 \leq 20$	18	2	36
		$\Sigma f = 20$	$\Sigma\Sigma fx = 190$

$$\text{Arithmetic mean } \overline{x} = \frac{\Sigma fx}{\Sigma f} = \frac{190}{20} = 9.5 \text{ units}$$

Because the assumption that frequencies occur evenly within each class interval is not quite correct in this example, our approximate mean of 9.5 is not exactly correct, and is in error by 0.25. As the frequencies become larger, the size of this approximating error decreases.

Finding the arithmetic mean of combined data

1.8 If the mean age of a group of five people is 27 and the mean age of another group of eight people is 32. How would we find the mean age of the whole group of 13 people?

1.9 Remember that the arithmetic mean $= \dfrac{\text{Sum of values of items}}{\text{Number of items}}$

The sum of the ages in the first group is $5 \times 27 \quad = 135$
The sum of the ages in the second group is $8 \times 32 \quad = 256$
The sum of all 13 ages is $135 + 256 \qquad = 391$

The mean age is therefore $\dfrac{391}{13} = 30.07$ years.

Question 1

The mean weight of 10 units at 5 kgs, 10 units at 7 kgs and 20 units at X kgs is 8 kgs. What is the value of X?

Answer

$$\text{Mean} = \frac{\text{Sum of values of items}}{\text{Number of items}}$$

Sum of first 10 units = $5 \times 10 = 50$ kgs

Sum of second 10 units = $7 \times 10 = 70$ kgs

Sum of third 20 units = $20 \times X = 20X$

Sum of all 40 units = $50 + 70 + 20X = 120 + 20X$

$$\therefore \text{ Arithmetic mean} = 8 = \frac{120 + 20X}{40}$$

$$\therefore \quad 8 \times 40 = 120 + 20X$$

$$320 - 120 = 20X$$

$$10 = X$$

The advantages and disadvantages of the arithmetic mean

1.10 Advantages of the arithmetic mean

- It is easy to calculate.

- It is widely understood.

- The value of every item is included in the computation of the mean and so it can be determined with arithmetical precision and is representative of the whole set of data.

- It is supported by mathematical theory and is suited to further statistical analysis.

1.11 Disadvantages of the arithmetic mean

(a) Its value may not correspond to any actual value. For example, the 'average' family might have 2.3 children, but no family has exactly 2.3 children.

(b) An arithmetic mean might be distorted by extremely high or low values. For example, the mean of 3, 4, 4 and 6 is 4.25, but the mean of 3, 4, 4, 6 and 15 is 6.4. The high value, 15, distorts the average and in some circumstances the mean would be a misleading and inappropriate figure.

(c) The arithmetic mean is not always the correct average to use when taking averages of percentages (or averages of averages). For example, if the average mark of one group of students is 70% and that of another group 80%, the average mark is not 75% unless the number of students in each group is the same.

Question 2

For the week ended 29 May, the wages earned by the 69 operators employed in the machine shop of Mechaids Ltd were as follows.

Wages	Number of Operatives
under £ 60	3
£60 and under £70	11
£70 and under £80	16
£80 and under £90	15
£90 and under £100	10
£100 and under £110	8
£110 and under £120	6
	69

Required

Calculate the arithmetic mean wage of the operators of Mechaids Ltd for the week ended 29 May.

Answer

The mid point of the range 'under £60' is assumed to be £55, since all other class intervals are £10. This is obviously an approximation which might result in a loss of accuracy (there is no better alternative assumption to use). Note that the mid points of the classes are half way between their end points, because wages can vary in steps of only 1p so are virtually a continuous variable.

Mid point of class	Frequency	
x	f	fx
£		
55	3	165
65	11	715
75	16	1,200
85	15	1,275
95	10	950
105	8	840
115	6	690
	69	5,835

Arithmetic mean = $\dfrac{£5,835}{69}$ = £84.57

2   THE MODE

KEY TERM

The **mode** is an average which means 'the most frequently occurring value'.

2.1   EXAMPLE: THE MODE

The daily demand for stock in a ten day period is as follows.

Demand	Number of days
Units	
6	3
7	6
8	1
	10

The mode is 7 units, because it is the value which occurs most frequently.

Finding the mode of a grouped frequency distribution

2.2 In a grouped frequency distribution, the mode can be estimated in two ways.

- Using the formula
- Using a histogram

Using the formula

2.3 The method of making this estimate is as follows.

Step 1. Establish which is the class with the highest value of frequency/class width (the modal class).

- Where all classes have the **same width,** this is the class with the **highest frequency**
- Where **class widths differ** this is the class with the **highest frequency class width**

Step 2. Identify the following.

L = the lower limit of the modal class
F_0 = the frequency of the next class below the modal class
F_1 = the frequency of the modal class
F_2 = the frequency of the next class above the modal class
c = the width of the modal class.

Step 3. Calculate the mode using the following equation. $L + \dfrac{(F_1 - F_0) \times c}{2F_1 - F_0 - F_2}$

NB. This method will only work when the modal class width is the same as the classes' widths above and below it.

2.4 EXAMPLE: THE FORMULA FOR THE MODE

Calculate the mode of the following frequency distribution.

Value		*Frequency*
At least	*Less than*	
10	25	6
25	40	19
40	55	12
55	70	7
70	85	3

2.5 SOLUTION

Step 1. All classes have the same width, so the modal class is the class interval with the highest frequency, that is, the class ≥ 25 and < 40.

Step 2.
L = 25
F_0 = 6
F_1 = 19
F_2 = 12
C = 15

Step 3. The estimated mode is

$$25 + \frac{(19-6) \times 15}{(2 \times 19) - 6 - 12} = 25 + \frac{(13 \times 15)}{(38 - 18)} = 25 + 9.75 = 34.75$$

BPP
PUBLISHING

Using a histogram

2.6 The mode of a grouped frequency distribution can also be calculated from a histogram. Using this method, it does not matter if the class intervals vary, because the modal class is **always** the class with the **tallest bar**.

2.7 EXAMPLE: FINDING THE MODE FROM A HISTOGRAM

Consider the following grouped frequency distribution

Value		Frequency
At least	Less than	
0	10	0
10	20	50
20	30	150
30	40	100

The modal class (the one with the highest frequency) is 'at least 20, less than 30'. But how can we find a single value to represent the mode?

Step 1. Draw a histogram of the frequency distribution.

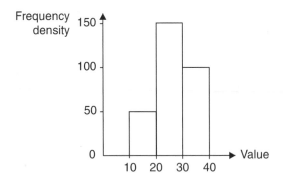

Step 2. Identify the modal class with the tallest bar.

Step 3. Estimate the mode graphically as follows.

- Join with a straight line the top left hand corner of the bar for the modal class and the top left hand corner of the next bar to the right.

- Join with a straight line the top right hand corner of the bar for the modal class and the top right hand corner of the next bar to the left.

- Identify where these two lines intersect.

Histogram showing mode

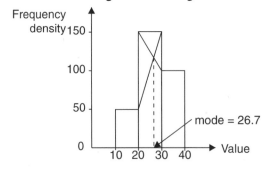

Using the formula for the mode, we would arrive at the same answer.

$$\text{Mode} = 20 + \frac{(150-50)\times10}{(2\times150)-50-100} = 20 + \frac{1,000}{150} = 26.7$$

Again, using both the formula and the graphical approach, we are assuming that the frequencies occur evenly within each class interval but this may not always be correct. It is unlikely that the 150 values in the modal class occur evenly. Hence the mode in a grouped frequency distribution is only an estimate.

The advantages and disadvantages of the mode

2.8 The mode will be a more appropriate average to use than the mean in situations where it is useful to know the **most common value**. For example, if a manufacturer wishes to start production in a new industry, it might be helpful to know what sort of product made by the industry is most in demand with customers.

2.9 **Advantages of the mode**

- It is easy to find.
- It is not influenced by a few extreme values.
- It can be used for data which are not even numerical (unlike the mean and median).
- It can be the value of an actual item in the distribution.

2.10 **Disadvantages of the mode**

- It may be unrepresentative; it only represents the most common value.

- It does not take every value into account

- There can be two or more modes within a set of data.

- If the modal class is only very slightly bigger than another class, just a few more items in this other class could mean a substantially different result, suggesting some instability in the measure.

3 THE MEDIAN   12/95, 12/97

> **Exam focus point**
> In the 12/95 exam, there were easy marks to be gained by explaining and calculating the median of given data.

> **KEY TERM**
>
> The **median** (Q_2) is the value of the middle member of a distribution once all of the items have been arranged in order of magnitude.

3.1 The median of a set of ungrouped data is found by arranging the items in ascending or descending order of value, and selecting the item in the middle of the range. A list of items in order of value is called an **array**.

3.2 EXAMPLE : THE MEDIAN

The median of the following nine values:

8   6   9   12   15   6   3   20   11

is found by taking the middle item (the fifth one) in the array:

3	6	6	8	9	11	12	15	20

The median is 9. The middle item of an odd number of items is calculated as the $\frac{(n+1)}{2}^{th}$ item.

3.3 Consider the following array.

8	6	7	2	1	11	3	2	5	2

1	2	2	2	3	5	6	7	8	11

The median is 4 because, with an even number of items, we have to take the arithmetic mean of the two middle ones (in this example, $(3 + 5)/2 = 4$). When there are many items, however, it is not worth doing this.

Finding the median of an ungrouped frequency distribution

3.4 The median of an ungrouped frequency distribution is found in a similar way.

Value x	Frequency f	Cumulative frequency
8	3	3
12	7	10
16	12	22
17	8	30
19	5	35
	35	

The median would be the $(35 + 1)/2 = 18$th item. The 18th item has a value of 16, as we can see from the cumulative frequencies in the right hand column of the above table.

Finding the median of a grouped frequency distribution

3.5 The median of a grouped frequency distribution, like the arithmetic mean and the mode, can only be estimated approximately using one of two methods.

- Using the formula
- Using an ogive

Using the formula

Step 1. Find the class interval to which the middle item belongs.

Step 2. c the size of the class interval
f the frequency of the class
R is the difference between the middle member ($(n + 1)/2$ for odd n, n/2 for even n) and the cumulative total of frequencies up to the end of the preceding class.

Step 3. Calculate the median using the following formula.

$$\text{Median} = \text{value of lower limit to the class} + \left(\frac{R}{F} \times c\right)$$

3.6 EXAMPLE: THE MEDIAN OF A GROUPED FREQUENCY DISTRIBUTION

The average monthly earnings of 135 employees of Comedian Ltd have been analysed as a grouped frequency distribution as follows.

Average monthly earnings			
More than	Not more than	No of employees	Cumulative frequency
£	£		
120	140	12	12
140	160	49	61
160	180	25	86
180	200	18	104
200	220	17	121
220	240	14	135

Required

Calculate the median monthly earnings of employees of Comedian Ltd.

3.7 SOLUTION

Step 1.   The middle member is the $(135 + 1)/2 = 68$th item. This occurs in the class £160 – £180.

Step 2. $c = 20$
$f = 25$
$R = 68 - 61$

Step 3.   Median $= £160 + \left(\dfrac{68 - 61}{25} \times £20 \right) = £165.60$

Note that, because we are assuming that the values are spread out evenly within each class, the median calculated is only approximate.

Using an ogive

3.8   Instead of using the formula to estimate the median of a grouped frequency distribution, we could establish the median from an **ogive**.

3.9 EXAMPLE: THE MEDIAN FROM AN OGIVE

Construct an ogive of the following frequency distribution and establish the median.

Class	Frequency	Cumulative frequency
£		
≥ 340, < 370	17	17
≥ 370, < 400	9	26
≥ 400, < 430	9	35
≥ 430, < 460	3	38
≥ 460, < 490	2	40
	40	

3.10 SOLUTION

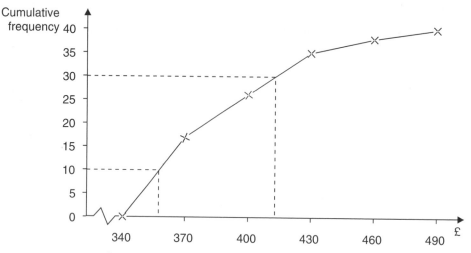

The median is at the $^{1}/_{2} \times 40 = 20$th item. Reading off from the horizontal axis on the ogive, the value of the median is approximately £380.

3.11 Note that, because we are assuming that the values are spread evenly within each class, the median calculated is only approximate.

The advantages and disadvantages of the median

3.12 The median is only of interest where there is a **range of values** and the middle item is of some significance. Perhaps the most suitable application of the median is in comparing changes in a 'middle of the road' value over time.

3.13 **Advantages of the median**

- It is easy to understand.
- It is unaffected by extremely high or low values.
- It can be the value of an actual item in the distribution.

3.14 **Disadvantages of the median**

- It fails to reflect the full range of values.
- It is unsuitable for further statistical analysis.
- It can be time-consuming when arranging the data in size order.

Question 3

The following grouped frequency distribution gives the annual wages of 200 employees in an engineering firm.

Wages £	Number of employees
5,000 and less than 5,500	4
5,500 and less than 6,000	26
6,000 and less than 6,500	133
6,500 and less than 7,000	35
7,000 and less than 7,500	2

Required

Calculate the mean, the median and the mode of annual wages (using formulae rather than a histogram and/or ogive).

Answer

(a) The mean

Mid point x £	Frequency f	fx	Cumulative frequency
5,250	4	21,000	4
5,750	26	149,500	30
6,250	133	831,250	163
6,750	35	236,250	198
7,250	2	14,500	200
	200	1,252,500	

$$\text{Mean} = \frac{1,252,500}{200} = £6,262.50$$

(b) The median value is the value of the 100th item. This is estimated as

$$£6,000 + \frac{100-30}{133} \times £500 = £6,000 + £263.16 = £6,263.16$$

(c) The modal value is in the range £6,000 and less than £6,500. It is estimated as

$$£6,000 + \frac{(133-26) \times £500}{(2 \times 133) - 26 - 35} = £6,000 + \frac{£53,500}{205} = £6,260.98$$

Question 4

Give a specific business, commercial or industrial example of when:

(a) the median would be used in preference to the arithmetic mean;
(b) the mode would be used in preference to the median;
(c) the arithmetic mean would be used in preference to any other average.

Answer

(a) Whenever a distribution is significantly skewed or expensive to measure, the median will be the most appropriate measure: salaries of employees, turnover of a large set of companies, time to destruction in tests of components.

(b) The mode is the most useful measure of location when the most common/popular item is required: number of customers in a queue, number of defects in a sample, sales of shirts by neck sizes.

(c) The mean should always be chosen in symmetric distributions or where further statistical calculations or analysis might be required: number of items produced per day on a large assembly line, number of orders received per month by a firm.

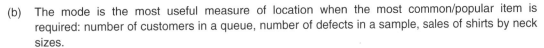

Chapter roundup

- The **arithmetic mean** is the best known type of average and is widely understood. The mean is used for further statistical analysis.

- The **mode** is the most frequently occurring value.

- The **median** is the value of the middle member of an array.

- The arithmetic mean, mode and median of a grouped frequency distribution can only be estimated approximately.

- You should now be able to calculate any of the three averages for a basic set of values, an ungrouped frequency distribution and a grouped frequency distribution.

Quick quiz

1   State a formula for the arithmetic mean of a frequency distribution. (see formulae to learn)

2   Define the mode. (key terms)

3   Explain how to estimate the mode from a histogram of a distribution. (2.7)

4   Define the median. (key terms)

5   State the formula for estimating the median of a grouped frequency distribution. (3.5)

Question to try	Level	Marks	Time
18	Examination	14	25 mins

Chapter 18

MEASURES OF SPREAD

Chapter topic list	Syllabus reference
1 The range	QT 6(b)
2 The quartile deviation and the inter-quartile range	QT 6(b)
3 The mean deviation	QT 6(b)
4 The standard deviation	QT 6(b)
5 The coefficient of variation	QT 6(b)
6 Skewness	QT 6(b)

Introduction

In Chapter 17 we introduced the first type of statistic that can be used to describe certain aspects of a set of data - **averages**. Averages are a method of determining the '**location**' or **central point** of a distribution, but they give no information about the **spread of values** in the distribution.

Measures of spread give some idea of the **dispersion** of a variable about its average. The main measures are discussed in sections 1 to 5 of the chapter. Section 6 looks at a concept which affects the topics covered both in this chapter and Chapter 17, **skewness**.

1 THE RANGE

KEY TERM

The **range** is the difference between the highest observation and the lowest observation.

1.1 The main properties of the range as a measure of spread are as follows.

- It is easy to find and to understand.
- It is easily affected by one or two extreme values.
- It gives no indication of spread between the extremes.
- It is not suitable for further statistical analysis.

Question 1

Calculate the mean and the range of each of the following sets of data.

(a) x_1 =   4   8   7   3   5   16   24   5

(b) x_2 =   10   7   9   11   11   8   9   7

Answer

(a) $\bar{x}_1 = \dfrac{72}{8} = 9$

The figures have a mean of 9 and a range of 24 - 3 = 21.

(b) $\bar{x}_2 = \dfrac{72}{8} = 9$

The figures have a mean of 9 and a range of 11 - 7 = 4.

The set of data x_1 is more widely dispersed than the set of data x_2.

---

2   THE QUARTILE DEVIATION AND THE INTER-QUARTILE RANGE

12/95

Exam focus point

In the 12/95 exam, you had to explain and calculate two measures of spread. Many candidates failed to spot that the frequencies given by the examiner were cumulative. You **must** read the information given in an examination **very** carefully.

Quartiles

KEY TERMS

Quartiles are one means of identifying the range within which most of the values in the population occur.

- The **lower quartile** (Q_1) is the value below which 25% of the population fall
- The **upper quartile** (Q_3) is the value above which 25% of the population fall

2.1   If we had 11 data items,

- $Q_1 = 11 \times \frac{1}{4} = 2.75 = 3^{rd}$ item
- $Q_3 = 11 \times \frac{3}{4} = 8.25 = 9^{th}$ item
- $Q_2 = 11 \times \frac{1}{2} = 5.5 = 6^{th}$ item

The quartile deviation

2.2   The lower and upper quartiles can be used to calculate a measure of spread called the **quartile deviation**.

KEY TERM

The **quartile deviation** is half the difference between the lower and upper quartiles and is sometimes called the **semi inter-quartile range**, $\dfrac{(Q_3 - Q_1)}{2}$

2.3   For example, if the lower and upper quartiles of a frequency distribution were 6 and 11, the quartile deviation of the distribution would be $(11 - 6)/2 = 2.5$ units. This shows that the average distance of a quartile from the median is 2.5. The smaller the quartile deviation, the less dispersed is the distribution.

2.4 As with the range, the quartile deviation may be misleading as a measure of spread. If the majority of the data are towards the lower end of the range then the third quartile will be considerably further above the median than the first quartile is below it, and when the two distances from the median are averaged the difference is disguised. Therefore it is often better to quote the actual values of the two quartiles, rather than the quartile deviation.

The inter-quartile range

> ### KEY TERM
>
> The **inter-quartile range** is the upper quartile minus the lower quartile ($Q_3 - Q_1$).

Question 2

Can you think of some advantages and disadvantages of the semi inter-quartile range?

Answer

Advantages

(a) It is easy to understand.
(b) It is unaffected by extreme values.
(c) It can be calculated even if the values of extreme items are not known.

Disadvantages

(a) It does not take all values into account.
(b) Data has to be arranged in order of size.
(c) It is unsuitable for use in further statistical analysis.

2.5 EXAMPLE: QUARTILES

Calculate the following of the grouped frequency distribution below.

(a) The lower and upper quartiles and the median
(b) The quartile deviation

Value x		Frequency f	Cumulative frequency
more than £	not more than £		
0	10	3	3
10	20	6	9
20	30	11	20
30	40	15	35
40	50	12	47
50	60	7	54
60	70	6	60
		60	

2.6 SOLUTION

(a) Establish which items are Q_1, Q_2, and Q_3

$Q_1 = 60 \times \frac{1}{4} = 15^{th}$ item

$Q_3 = 60 \times \frac{3}{4} = 45^{th}$ item

Q_2 (median) $= 60 \times \frac{1}{2} = 30^{th}$ item

Calculate the values of Q_1, Q_2, and Q_3 in the same way as the median of a grouped frequency distribution is calculated.

$$\text{Median} = \text{value of lower limit of the class} + \left(\frac{R}{f} \times c\right)$$

where c = the size of the class interval

f = the frequency of the class

R = the quartile member minus the cumulative frequency up to the end of the preceding class

	Class £	c	f	R	Quartile value
$Q_1 = $ 15th item	20 – 30	10	11	(15 – 9)	$20 + \left(\dfrac{15-9}{11} \times 10\right) = 25.45$
$Q_2 = 30^{th}$ item	30 – 40	10	15	(30 – 20)	$30 + \left(\dfrac{30-20}{15} \times 10\right) = 36.67$
$Q_3 = 45^{th}$ item	40 – 50	10	12	(45 – 35)	$40 + \left(\dfrac{45-35}{12} \times 10\right) = 48.33$

(b)   The quartile deviation is $\dfrac{Q_3 - Q_1}{2} = \dfrac{48 - 25}{2} = 11.5$ units

2.7   Alternatively, the quartiles can be found from an ogive.

Question 3

Using an ogive, find the values of the upper and lower quartiles of the frequency distribution detailed in Paragraph 3.9 of Chapter 17.

Answer

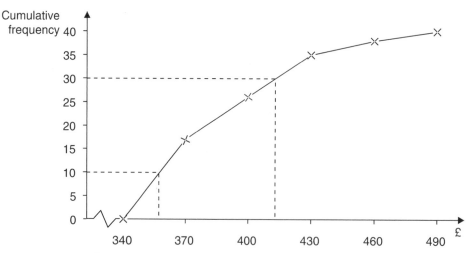

The upper quartile is the $\frac{3}{4} \times 40 = $ 30th value.

The lower quartile is the $\frac{1}{4} \times 40 = $ 10th value.

Reading off from the ogive these values are at approximately £358 and £412 respectively.

3 THE MEAN DEVIATION

3.1 Because it only uses the middle 50% of the population, the inter-quartile range is a useful measure of dispersion if there are **extreme values** in the distribution. If there are no extreme values which could potentially distort a measure of dispersion, however, it seems unreasonable to exclude 50% of the data. The mean deviation (the topic of this section), and the standard deviation (the topic of Section 4) are often more useful measures.

KEY TERM

The **mean deviation** is a measure of the average amount by which the values in a distribution differ from the arithmetic mean.

FORMULA TO LEARN

$$\text{Mean deviation} = \frac{\Sigma f |x - \bar{x}|}{n}$$

3.2 (a) $|x - \bar{x}|$ is the difference between each value (x) in the distribution and the arithmetic mean $\bar{x}$ of the distribution. When calculating the mean deviation for grouped data the deviations should be measured to the midpoint of each class: that is, x is the midpoint of the class interval. The vertical bars mean that all differences are taken as positive since the total of all of the differences, if this is not done, will always equal zero. Thus if x = 3 and $\bar{x}$ = 5, then $x - \bar{x}$ = –2 but $|x - \bar{x}|$ = 2.

(b) $f |x - \bar{x}|$ is the value in (a) above, multiplied by the frequency for the class.

(c) $\Sigma f |x - \bar{x}|$ is the sum of the results of all the calculations in (b) above.

(d) n (which equals Σf) is the number of items in the distribution.

3.3 EXAMPLE: THE MEAN DEVIATION

Calculate the mean deviation of the frequency distribution in Paragraph 2.5.

3.4 SOLUTION

Midpoint x	f	fx	$\|x - \bar{x}\|$	$f\|x - \bar{x}\|$
5	3	15	32	96
15	6	90	22	132
25	11	275	12	132
35	15	525	2	30
45	12	540	8	96
55	7	385	18	126
65	6	390	28	168
	$\Sigma f = 60$	$\Sigma fx = 2,220$		780

$$\text{Arithmetic mean } \bar{x} = \frac{\Sigma fx}{\Sigma f} = \frac{2,220}{60} = 37$$

$$\text{Mean deviation} = \frac{780}{60} = 13 \text{ hours}$$

Question 4

Calculate the mean deviation of the following frequency distribution.

Value	Frequency of occurrence
5	4
15	6
25	8
35	20
45	6
55	6
	50

Answer

x	f	fx	$|x - \bar{x}|$	$f|x - \bar{x}|$
5	4	20	27.2	108.8
15	6	90	17.2	103.2
25	8	200	7.2	57.6
35	20	700	2.8	56.0
45	6	270	12.8	76.8
55	6	330	22.8	136.8
	50	1,610		539.2

Arithmetic mean $\bar{x} = \dfrac{1,610}{50} = 32.2$

Mean deviation $= \dfrac{539.2}{50} = 10.784$, say 10.8.

3.5 Summary of the **mean deviation**.

(a) It is a measure of dispersion which shows by how much, on average, each item in the distribution differs in value from the arithmetic mean of the distribution.

(b) Unlike quartiles, it uses all values in the distribution to measure the dispersion, but it is not greatly affected by a few extreme values because an average is taken.

(c) It is not, however, suitable for further statistical analysis.

4   THE STANDARD DEVIATION   6/95, 6/97, 6/98, 12/97, 6/98, 12/98, 12/99

Exam focus point

In the 12/97 exam, there were six marks available for calculating the standard deviation of a cumulative frequency distribution, and a further 6 marks to be gained for describing what the standard deviation measures and how it may be used in statistical analysis. In the 6/98 exam candidates were required to **explain clearly** how to calculate the arithmetic mean and standard deviation of a grouped frequency distribution. Make sure that you are able to explain these statistics clearly in addition to being able to calculate them.

KEY TERM

The **variance**, σ^2, is the average of the squared mean deviation for each value in a distribution.

4.1　σ is the Greek letter sigma (in lower case). The variance is therefore called 'sigma squared'.

4.2　Calculation of the variance for ungrouped data

Step 1.	Difference between value and mean	$x - \bar{x}$
Step 2.	Square of the difference	$(x - \bar{x})^2$
Step 3.	Sum of the squares of the difference	$\Sigma(x - \bar{x})^2$
Step 4.	Average of the sum (= variance = σ^2)	$\dfrac{\Sigma(x-\bar{x})^2}{n}$

The units of the variance are the square of those in the original data because we squared the differences. We therefore need to take the square root to get back to the units of the original data. **The standard deviation = square root of the variance.**

4.3　The standard deviation measures the spread of data around the mean. In general, the larger the standard deviation value in relation to the mean, the more dispersed the data.

4.4　Calculation of the variance for grouped data

Step 1.	Difference between value and mean	$(x - \bar{x})$
Step 2.	Square of the difference	$(x - \bar{x})^2$
Step 3.	Sum of the squares of the difference	$\Sigma f(x - \bar{x})^2$
Step 4.	Average of the sum (= variance = σ^2)	$\dfrac{\Sigma f(x-\bar{x})^2}{\Sigma f}$

4.5　There are a number of formulae which you may use to calculate the standard deviation; use whichever one you feel comfortable with. The standard deviation formulae provided in your examination are shown as follows.

EXAM FORMULAE

Standard deviation (for **ungrouped data**) $= \sqrt{\dfrac{\Sigma(x-\bar{x})^2}{n}} = \sqrt{\dfrac{\Sigma x^2}{n} - \bar{x}^2}$

Standard deviation (for **grouped data**) $= \sqrt{\dfrac{\Sigma f(x-\bar{x})^2}{\Sigma f}} = \sqrt{\dfrac{\Sigma fx^2}{\Sigma f} - \left(\dfrac{\Sigma fx}{\Sigma f}\right)}$

4.6　EXAMPLE: THE VARIANCE AND THE STANDARD DEVIATION

Calculate the variance and the standard deviation of the frequency distribution in Paragraph 2.5

Exam focus point

Note that you do not have to learn the standard deviation formulae: they are provided in your examination.

4.7   SOLUTION

Using the formula provided in the examination, the calculation is as follows.

Midpoint x	f	x^2	fx^2
5	3	25	75
15	6	225	1,350
25	11	625	6,875
35	15	1,225	18,375
45	12	2,025	24,300
55	7	3,025	21,175
65	6	4,225	25,350
	60		97,500

$$\text{Mean} = \frac{\Sigma fx}{\Sigma f} = \text{(from Paragraph 3.4)} = 37$$

$$\text{Variance} = \frac{\Sigma fx^2}{\Sigma f} - \left(\frac{\Sigma fx}{\Sigma f}\right)^2 = \frac{97,500}{60} - (37)^2 = 256 \text{ hours}$$

$$\text{Standard deviation} = \sqrt{256} = 16 \text{ hours}$$

Question 5

Calculate the variance and the standard deviation of the frequency distribution in Question 4.

Answer

x	f	x^2	fx^2
5	4	25	100
15	6	225	1,350
25	8	625	5,000
35	20	1,225	24,500
45	6	2,025	12,150
55	6	3,025	18,150
	50		61,250

Mean = 32.2 (from Question 4)

$$\text{Variance} = \frac{61,250}{50} - (32.2)^2 = 188.16$$

$$\text{Standard deviation} = \sqrt{188.16} = 13.72$$

The main properties of the standard deviation

4.8   The standard deviation's main properties are as follows.

- It is based on **all the values in the distribution** and so is more comprehensive than dispersion measures based on quantiles, such as the quartile deviation.

- It is suitable for **further statistical analysis**.

- It is **more difficult to understand** than some other measures of dispersion.

The importance of the standard deviation lies in its suitability for further statistical analysis (we shall consider this further in Chapter 22).

The variance and the standard deviation of several items together

4.9 You may need to calculate the variance and standard deviation for n items together, given the variance and standard deviation for one item alone.

4.10 EXAMPLE: SEVERAL ITEMS TOGETHER

The daily demand for an item of stock has a mean of 6 units, with a variance of 4 and a standard deviation of 2 units. Demand on any one day is unaffected by demand on previous days or subsequent days.

Required

Calculate the arithmetic mean, the variance and the standard deviation of demand for a five day week.

4.11 SOLUTION

If we let

- Arithmetic mean = $\bar{x}$ = 6
- Variance = σ^2 = 4
- Standard deviation = σ = 2
- Number of days in week = n = 5

The following rules apply to $\bar{x}$, σ^2 and σ when we have several items together.

- **Arithmetic mean** = $n\bar{x}$ = 5 × 6 = 30 units
- **Variance** = $n\sigma^2$ = 5 × 4 = 20 units
- **Standard deviation** = $\sqrt{n\sigma^2}$ = $\sqrt{20}$ = 4.47 units

---

Question 6

The weights of three items X, Y and Z vary independently and have the following means and standard deviations.

	Mean weight kg	Standard deviation kg
X	10	2
Y	14	2
Z	6	1

The three items are sold together in a single packet.

Required

Calculate the mean weight of a packet of one unit each of X, Y and Z, and the standard deviation of the weights of packets.

Answer

Mean of X + Y + Z = (10 + 14 + 6) kg = 30 kg

Variance of X + Y + Z = $(2^2 + 2^2 + 1^2)$ = 9 kg

Standard deviation of X + Y + Z = $\sqrt{9}$ = 3 kg.

Packets of one of each of X, Y and Z have a mean weight of 30 kg and a standard deviation of weights of 3 kg.

---

5   THE COEFFICIENT OF VARIATION

5.1   It is sometimes useful to be able to compare the spreads of two distributions. This comparison can be done using the **coefficient of variation**.

> **ORMULA TO LEARN**
>
> Coefficient of variation (coefficient of relative spread) = $\dfrac{\text{Standard deviation}}{\text{mean}}$

5.2   The bigger the coefficient of variation, the wider the spread. For example, suppose that two sets of data, A and B, have the following means and standard deviations.

	A	*B*
Mean	120	125
Standard deviation	50	51
Coefficient of variation	0.417	0.408

Although B has a higher standard deviation in absolute terms (51 compared to 50) its relative spread is a bit less than A's since the coefficient of variation is a bit smaller.

Question 7

Calculate the coefficient of variation of the distribution in Questions 4 and 5.

Answer

Coefficient of variation = $\dfrac{\text{standard deviation}}{\text{mean}} = \dfrac{13.72}{32.2} = 0.426$

6   SKEWNESS   12/95, 6/97

> **Exam focus point**
> 2 Marks were available in 12/95 for explaining the coefficient of skewness.

6.1   As well as being able to calculate the average and spread of a frequency distribution, you should be aware of the **skewness** of a distribution.

6.2   A symmetrical frequency distribution (a normal distribution) can be drawn as follows.

Symmetrical frequency distribution

- Its mean, mode and median all have the same value, μ
- Its two halves are mirror images of each other

6.3   A **positively skewed** distribution's graph will lean towards the left hand side, with a tail stretching out to the right, and can be drawn as follows.

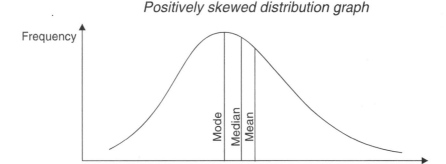

Positively skewed distribution graph

- Its mean, mode and median all have different values
- The mode will have a lower value than the median
- Its mean will have a higher value than the median (and than most of the distribution)
- It does not have two halves which are mirror images of each other

6.4   A **negatively skewed distribution's** graph will lean towards the right hand side, with a tail stretching out to the left, and can be drawn as follows.

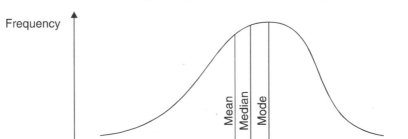

Negatively skewed distribution graph

- Its mean, median and mode all have different values
- The mode will be higher than the median
- The mean will have a lower value than the median (and than most of the distribution)

6.5   Since the mean is affected by extreme values, it may not be representative of the items in a very skewed distribution.

Coefficient of skewness

6.6   The **skewness of frequency distribution curves** can be compared using **Pearson's coefficient of skewness**.

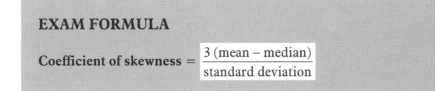

EXAM FORMULA

$$\text{Coefficient of skewness} = \frac{3\,(\text{mean} - \text{median})}{\text{standard deviation}}$$

BPP PUBLISHING

Question 8

What do you think is indicated by the following coefficient values?

(a) 0
(b) +3
(c) −3

Answer

(a) A symmetrical distribution
(b) Maximum positive skewness
(c) Maximum negative skewness

6.7 EXAMPLE: SKEWNESS

In a quality control test, the weights of standard packages were measured to give the following grouped frequency table.

Weights in grams	Number of packages
198 and less than 199	3
199 and less than 200	8
200 and less than 201	93
201 and less than 202	148
202 and less than 203	48

Required

(a) Calculate the mean, standard deviation, mode and median of the weights of the packages.
(b) Explain whether or not you think that the distribution is symmetrical.
(c) Calculate the coefficient of skewness and comment on the result.

6.8 SOLUTION

Weight g	Mid point x	f	fx	$x - \bar{x}$	$f(x - \bar{x})^2$
198 and less than 199	198.5	3	595.5	−2.77	23.0187
199 and less than 200	199.5	8	1,596.0	−1.77	25.0632
200 and less than 201	200.5	93	18,646.5	−0.77	55.1397
201 and less than 202	201.5	148	29,822.0	0.23	7.8292
202 and less than 203	202.5	48	9,720.0	1.23	72.6192
		300	60,380.0		183.6700

$$\text{Mean} = \frac{\Sigma fx}{\Sigma f} = \frac{60,380}{300} = 201.27g$$

$$\text{Standard deviation} = \sqrt{\frac{183.67}{300}} = 0.78g$$

The distribution appears not to be symmetrical, but negatively skewed.

(a) The mean is in the higher end of the range of values at 201.27 g.
(b) The mode could be estimated as

$$201 + \frac{(148-93)\times1}{(2\times148)-93-48} = 201.35g$$

(c) The median (the 150th item) could be estimated as

$$201 + \frac{(150 - 93 - 8 - 3)}{148} = 201.31\text{g}$$

The median has a higher value than the mean, and the mode has a higher value than the median. This suggests that the frequency distribution is negatively skewed.

$$\text{Coefficient of skewness} = \frac{3\,(\text{mean} - \text{median})}{\text{standard deviation}}$$

$$= \frac{3(201.27 - 201.31)}{0.78}$$

$$= -0.15$$

The distribution is negatively skewed but the skewness is relatively small.

Chapter roundup

- **Measures of spread** give some idea of the spread of variables about the average.

- The **range** is the difference between the highest and lowest observations.

- The **quartiles** and the **median** divide the population into four groups of equal size.

- The **quartile deviation** is half the difference between the two quartiles.

- The **interquartile range** is the difference between the upper and lower quartiles.

- The **mean deviation** is a measure of the average amount by which the values in a distribution differ from the arithmetic mean.

- The **standard deviation**, which is the square root of the variance, is the most important measure of spread used in statistics. Make sure you understand how to calculate the standard deviation of a set of data.

- The spreads of two distributions can be compared using the **coefficient of variation**.

- **Skewness** is the asymmetry of a frequency distribution curve.

- Measures of spread are valuable in giving a full picture of a frequency distribution. We would nearly always want to be told an average for a distribution, but just one more number, a measure of spread, can be very informative.

Quick quiz

1 Why may the quartile deviation be misleading? (see para 2.4)

2 When calculating the mean deviation for grouped data, to where should the deviations be measured? (3.2)

3 Give a formula for the variance for data in a frequency distribution. (exam formulae)

4 Define the coefficient of variation of a distribution. (formulae to learn)

5 Distinguish between positive skewness and negative skewness. (6.3, 6.4)

Now try illustrative question 19 at the end of the Study Text

Question to try	Level	Marks	Time
19	Introductory	n/a	15 mins

Chapter 19

INDEX NUMBERS

Chapter topic list	Syllabus reference
1 Basic terminology	QT 6(c)
2 Simple indices	QT 6(c)
3 Index relatives	QT 6(c)
4 Composite index numbers	QT 6(c)
5 Laspeyre and Paasche indices	QT 6(c)
6 Practical issues	QT 6(c)
7 The Retail Prices Index for the United Kingdom	QT 6(c)

Introduction

A number of the methods of data presentation looked at in Chapter 16 can be used to identify visually the **trends** in data over a period of time but it may also be useful to identify trends using statistical rather than visual means. This is frequently achieved by constructing a set of **index numbers.**

Index numbers provide a **standardised way of comparing the values, over time**, of prices, wages, volume of output and so on. They are used extensively in business, government and commerce.

No doubt you will be aware of some index numbers - the **RPI**, the **Financial Times All Share Index** and so on. This chapter will explain to you how to construct indices and will look at associated issues such as their limitations.

1   BASIC TERMINOLOGY

KEY TERM

An **index** is a measure, over time, of the average changes in the values (prices or quantities) of a group of items.

1.1   An index comprises a series of **index numbers**. It is possible to prepare an index for a single item, although such an index would probably be unnecessary. When there is a group of items, a simple list of changes in their values over time might become rather hard to interpret. An index, however, would be able to provide a useful single **measure of comparison.**

Price indices and quantity indices

1.2   An index may be a **price index** or a **quantity index**.

(a) A **price index** measures the **change in the money value** of a group of items over time. The best known price index in the UK is the Retail Prices Index (RPI) which measures changes in the costs of items of expenditure of the average household.

(b) A **quantity index** (also called a **volume index**) measures the **change in the non-monetary values** of a group of items over time. An example is a productivity index, which measures changes in the productivity of various departments.

Index points

1.3 The term 'points' refers to the difference between the index values in two years. For example, suppose that the index of food prices in 20X1 – 20X6 was as follows.

20X1	180
20X2	200
20X3	230
20X4	250
20X5	300
20X6	336

The index has risen 156 points between 20X1 and 20X6. This is an increase of $(156/180) \times 100 = 86.7\%$. Similarly, the index rose 36 points between 20X5 and 20X6, a rise of 12%.

The base period, or base year

1.4 Index numbers normally take the value for a **base date**, usually the starting point of the series though it could be part way through the series, as 100.

2 SIMPLE INDICES

FORMULAE TO LEARN

- **Price index** (where one commodity in under consideration)$= \dfrac{p_n}{p_o} \times 100$

  where p_n is the price for the period under consideration and p_o is the price for the base period.

- **Quantity index** (where one commodity in under consideration)$= \dfrac{q_n}{q_o} \times 100$

  where q_n is the quantity for the period under consideration and q_o is the quantity for the base period.

2.1 EXAMPLE: SINGLE-ITEM INDICES

If the price of a cup of coffee was 40p in 20X0, 50p in 20X1 and 76p in 20X2, then using 20X0 as a base year the price index numbers (price relatives) for 20X1 and 20X2 would be as follows.

$$20X1 \text{ price index} = \frac{50}{40} \times 100 = 125$$

$$20X2 \text{ price index} = \frac{76}{40} \times 100 = 190$$

If the number of cups of coffee sold in 20X0 was 500,000, in 20X1 700,000 and in 20X2 600,000, then using 20X0 as a base year, the quantity index numbers (quantity relatives) for 20X1 and 20X2 would be as follows.

$$20X1 \text{ quantity index} = \frac{700,000}{500,000} \times 100 = 140$$

$$20X2 \text{ quantity index} = \frac{600,000}{500,000} \times 100 = 120$$

3   INDEX RELATIVES   6/98, 12/98

3.1   An **index relative** (sometimes just called a relative) is the name given to an index number which measures the **change in a single distinct commodity**.

Time series of relatives

3.2   Given the values of some commodity over time (a time series), there are two ways in which index relatives can be calculated.

3.3   In the **fixed base method,** a base year is selected (index 100), and all subsequent changes are measured against this base. Such an approach should only be used if **the basic nature of the commodity is unchanged over time**.

3.4   In the **chain base method,** changes are calculated with respect to the value of the commodity in the period immediately before. This approach can be used for any set of commodity values but must be used if **the basic nature of the commodity is changing over time**.

3.5   EXAMPLE: FIXED BASE AND CHAIN BASE METHODS

The price of commodity was £2.70 in 20X0, £3.11 in 20X1, £3.42 in 20X2 and £3.83 in 20X3. Construct both a chain base index and a fixed base index for the years 20X0 to 20X3 using 20X0 as the base year.

3.6   SOLUTION

Chain base index	20X0	100	
	20X1	115	$(3.11/2.70 \times 100)$
	20X2	110	$(3.42/3.11 \times 100)$
	20X3	112	$(3.83/3.42 \times 100)$
Fixed base index	20X0	100	
	20X1	115	
	20X2	127	$(3.42/2.70 \times 100)$
	20X3	142	$(3.83/2.70 \times 100)$

The chain base relatives show the rate of change in prices from year to year, whereas the fixed base relatives show changes relative to prices in the base year.

Changing the base of fixed base relatives

3.7   It is sometimes necessary to change the base of a time series of fixed base relatives, perhaps because the base time point is too far in the past. The following time series has a base date of 1970 which would probably be considered too out of date.

	1990	*1991*	*1992*	*1993*	*1994*	*1995*
Index (1970 = 100)	451	463	472	490	499	505

To change the base date (to **rebase**), divide each relative by the relative corresponding to the new base time point and multiply the result by 100.

Question 1

Rebase the index in Paragraph 3.7 to 1993.

Answer

	1990	*1991*	*1992*	*1993*	*1994*	*1995*
Index (1993 = 100)	92*	94	96	100**	102***	103

    *   451/490 × 100
    **   490/490 × 100
    *** 499/490 × 100

Comparing sets of fixed base relatives

3.8   You may be required to compare two sets of time series relatives. For example, an index of the annual number of advertisements placed by an organisation in the press and the index of the number of the organisation's product sold per annum might be compared. If the base years of the two indices differ, however, comparison is extremely difficult.

	20W8	*20W9*	*20X0*	*20X1*	*20X2*	*20X3*	*20X4*
Number of advertisements Placed (20X0 = 100)	90	96	100	115	128	140	160
Volumes of sales (20W0 = 100)	340	347	355	420	472	515	572

3.9   From the figures above it is impossible to determine whether sales are increasing at a greater rate than the number of advertisements placed, or vice versa. This difficulty can be overcome by **rebasing** one set of relatives so that the base dates are the same. For example, we could rebase the index of volume of sales to 20X0.

	20W8	*20W9*	*20X0*	*20X1*	*20X2*	*20X3*	*20X4*
Number of advertisements Placed (20X0 = 100)	90	96	100	115	128	140	160
Volumes of sales (20X0 = 100)	96	98*	100	118	133**	145	161

    ★ 347/355 × 100
    ★★ 472/355 × 100

3.10   The two sets of relatives are now much easier to compare. They show that volume of sales is increasing at a faster rate, in general, than the number of advertisements placed.

Time series deflation   6/95, 12/95

3.11   The **real value** of a commodity can only be measured in terms of some '**indicator**' such as the **rate of inflation** (normally represented by the Retail Prices Index) or the Index of Output of Production Industries. For example the cost of a commodity may have been £10 in 20X0 and £11 in 20X1, representing an increase of 10%. However, if we are told the prices in general (as measured by the RPI) increased by 12% between 20X0 and 20X1, we can argue that the **real** cost of the commodity has decreased.

3.12 EXAMPLE: DEFLATION

Mack Johnson works for Pound of Flesh Ltd. Over the last five years he has received an annual salary increase of £500. Despite his employer assuring him that £500 is a reasonable annual salary increase, Mack is unhappy because, although he agrees £500 is a lot of money, he finds it difficult to maintain the standard of living he had when he first joined the company. Consider the figures below.

Year	(a) Wages £	(b) RPI	(c) Real wages £	(d) Real wages index
1	12,000	250	12,000	100.0
2	12,500	260	12,019	100.2
3	13,000	275	11,818	98.5
4	13,500	295	11,441	95.3
5	14,000	315	11,111	92.6

(a) This column shows Mack's wages over the five-year period.

(b) This column shows the current RPI.

(c) This column shows what Mack's wages are worth taking prices, as represented by the RPI, into account. The wages have been deflated relative to the new base period (year 1). Economists call these deflated wage figures **real wages**. The real wages in real terms, for years 2 and 4, for example, are calculated as follows.

Year 2: £12,500 × 250/260 = £12,019
Year 4: £13,500 × 250/295 = £11,441

(d) This column is calculated by dividing the entries in column (c) by £12,000:

$$\text{Real index} = \frac{\text{current value}}{\text{base value}} \times \frac{\text{base indicator}}{\text{current indicator}}$$

So, for example, the real wage index in year 4 $= \dfrac{13,500}{12,000} \times \dfrac{250}{295} \times 100 = 95.3$

The real wages index shows that the real value of Mack's wages has fallen by 7.4% over the five-year period. In real terms he is now earning £11,111 compared to £12,000 in year 1. He is probably justified, therefore, in being unhappy.

Exam focus point

In both the 6/95 and 12/95 exams, the examiner has said that many candidates demonstrated poor understanding of both inflation and the use of index numbers. Make sure that you are happy with the basic principles of index numbers.

Question 2

The mean weekly take-home pay of the employees of Staples Ltd and a price index for the 11 years from 20X0 to 20Y0 are as follows.

Year	Weekly wage £	Price index (20X0 = 100)
20X0	150	100
20X1	161	103
20X2	168	106
20X3	179	108
20X4	185	109
20X5	191	112
20X6	197	114
20X7	203	116
20X8	207	118
20X9	213	121
20Y0	231	123

Required

Construct a time series of real wages for 20X0 to 20Y0 using a price index with 20X6 as the base year.

Answer

The index number for each year with 20X6 as the base year will be the original index number divided by 1.14, and the real wages for each year will be (money wages × 100)/index number for the year.

Year	Index	Real wage £
20X0	88	170
20X1	90	179
20X2	93	181
20X3	95	188
20X4	96	193
20X5	98	195
20X6	100	197
20X7	102	199
20X8	104	199
20X9	106	201
20Y0	108	214

Question 3

Given a cash flow of £X in n year's time (year n) and an inflation index of a in the current year and b in year n, how would you calculate the value of £X today?

Answer

Deflated value = $£X \times \dfrac{a}{b}$

4   **COMPOSITE INDEX NUMBERS**   6/94

> ### Exam focus point
> In 6/94, 5 marks were to be gained by explaining the term 'weighted index'.

> ### KEY TERM
> A **composite index number** is an index which covers more than one item.

4.1   The RPI, considers components such as food, alcoholic drink, tobacco and housing and is an example of a composite index number.

4.2 Suppose that the cost of living index is calculated from only three commodities: bread, tea and caviar, and that the prices for 20X1 and 20X2 were as follows.

	20X1	*20X2*
Bread	20p a loaf	40p a loaf
Tea	25p a packet	30p a packet
Caviar	450p a jar	405p a jar

FORMULA TO LEARN

The **simple aggregate price index** is $\dfrac{\Sigma p_n}{\Sigma p_0} \times 100$.

It is a simple index which is calculated by adding the prices for single items in a given year, and dividing by the corresponding sum in the base year.

4.3 We can calculate the **simple aggregate price index** for 20X1 and 20X2 as follows.

	p_0 20X1 £	p_n 20X2 £
Bread	0.20	0.40
Tea	0.25	0.30
Caviar	4.50	4.05
	$\Sigma p_0 = 4.95$	$\Sigma p_n = 4.75$

Year	$\Sigma p_n / \Sigma p_0$	*Simple aggregate price index*
20X1	4.95/4.95 = 1.00	100
20X2	4.75/4.95 = 0.96	96

4.4 **Disadvantages** of the simple aggregate price index

- It ignores quantities of each item consumed
- It ignores the units to which the price refers

Average relatives indices

4.5 To overcome the problem of different units we consider the changes in prices as **ratios** rather than **absolutes** so that all price movements, whatever their absolute values, are treated as equally important.

FORMULA TO LEARN

The **average price relatives index** is calculated as

$\dfrac{1}{K} \Sigma (p_n / p_0) \times 100$ where K is the number of goods

4.6 Price changes are considered as ratios by calculating the average price relatives index.

4.7 Using the information in Paragraph 4.2, we can construct the **average price relatives index** as follows.

Commodity	p_0 £	p_n £	p_n/p_0
Bread	0.20	0.40	2.00
Tea	0.25	0.30	1.20
Caviar	4.50	4.05	0.90
			4.10

Year	$\dfrac{1}{K}\,\Sigma(p_n/p_0)\times 100$	*Average price relatives index*
20X1	$^1/_3 \times 3.00 = 1.00$	100
20X2	$^1/_3 \times 4.10 = 1.37$	137

There has therefore been an average price increase of 37% between 20X1 and 20X2. We could, of course, construct an **average quantity relatives index** if we had been given information on quantities purchased per time period.

4.8 No account has been taken of the **relative importance** of each item, however, in this index. Bread is probably more important than caviar. To overcome both the problem of quantities in different units and the need to attach importance to each item, we can use **weightings** which reflects the importance of each item. To decide the weightings of different items in an index, it is necessary to obtain information, perhaps by market research, about the relative importance of each item. Thus, in our example of a simple cost of living index, it would be necessary to find out how much the average person or household spends each week on each item to determine weightings.

4.9 There are two types of index which give different weights to different items.

- Weighted means of relatives indices
- Weighted aggregate indices

Weighted means of relatives indices

4.10 This method of weighting involves:

- Calculating index relatives for each of the components;
- Using the weights given to obtain a weighted average of the relatives.

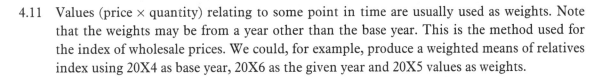

FORMULA TO LEARN

The general form of a **weighted means of relatives index number** is $\dfrac{\Sigma wI}{\Sigma w}$

where   w is the weighting factor
and   I is the index relative

4.11 Values (price × quantity) relating to some point in time are usually used as weights. Note that the weights may be from a year other than the base year. This is the method used for the index of wholesale prices. We could, for example, produce a weighted means of relatives index using 20X4 as base year, 20X6 as the given year and 20X5 values as weights.

4.12 Weighted means of relatives are very important in practice, the great majority of indices published in the UK being of this type.

4.13 EXAMPLE: WEIGHTED MEANS OF RELATIVES INDICES

Use both the information in Paragraph 4.2 and the following details about quantities purchased by each household in a week in 20X1 to determine a weighted means of price relatives index number for 20X2 using 20X1 as the base year.

	Quantity
Bread	6
Tea	2
Caviar	0.067

4.14 SOLUTION

Price relatives (I)	Bread	$40/20 =$	2.00
	Tea	$30/25 =$	1.20
	Caviar	$405/450 =$	0.90
Weightings (w)	Bread	$6 \times 0.20 =$	1.20
	Tea	$2 \times 0.25 =$	0.50
	Caviar	$0.067 \times 4.50 =$	0.30
	$\Sigma w =$		$\overline{2.00}$
Index	Bread	$2 \times 1.2 =$	2.40
	Tea	$1.2 \times 0.5 =$	0.60
	Caviar	$0.9 \times 0.3 =$	0.27
	$\Sigma wI =$		$\overline{3.27}$

Index number $= \dfrac{3.27}{2} \times 100 = 163.5$

Weighted aggregate indices   6/94, 12/96

4.15   This method of weighting involves multiplying each component value by its corresponding weight and adding these products to form an **aggregate**. This is done for both the base period and the period in question. The aggregate for the period under consideration is then divided by the base period aggregate. Laspeyre and Paasche indices are special cases of weighted aggregate indices and are the topic of the next section.

5   LASPEYRE AND PAASCHE INDICES   6/94, 12/98

Exam focus point

If you get confused between Laspeyre and Paasche indices, remember that 'L' for (Laspeyre) comes before 'P' (for Paasche) in the alphabet and that Laspeyre indices use weights from the base year, which comes *before* the current year, the provider of weights for Paasche indices.

5.1   Laspeyre indices use weights from the **base period** and are therefore sometimes called **base weighted indices**.

5.2   Paasche indices use **current time period weights**. In other words the weights are changed every time period.

FORMULAE TO LEARN

- A **Laspeyre price index** uses quantities consumed in the base period as weights and can be expressed as follows.

$$\text{Laspeyre price index} = \frac{\Sigma p_n q_o}{\Sigma p_o q_o} \times 100$$

- A **Laspeyre quantity index** uses prices from the base period as weights and can be expressed as follows.

$$\text{Laspeyre quantity index} = \frac{\Sigma q_n p_o}{\Sigma q_o p_o} \times 100$$

- **Paasche price index** uses quantities consumed in the current period as weights and can be expressed as follows.

$$\text{Paasche price index} = \frac{\Sigma p_n q_n}{\Sigma p_o q_n} \times 100$$

- A **Paasche quantity index** uses prices from the current period as weights and can be expressed as follows.

$$\text{Paasche quantity index} = \frac{\Sigma q_n p_n}{\Sigma q_o p_n} \times 100$$

5.3 EXAMPLE: LASPEYRE AND PAASCHE PRICE INDICES

The wholesale price index in Ruritania is made up from the prices of five items. The price of each item, and the average quantities purchased by manufacturing and other companies each week were as follows, in 20X0 and 20X2.

Item	Quantity 20X0 '000 units	Price per unit 20X0 Roubles	Quantity 20X2 '000 units	Price per unit 20X2 Roubles
P	60	3	80	4
Q	30	6	40	5
R	40	5	20	8
S	100	2	150	2
T	20	7	10	10

Required

Calculate the price index in 20X2, if 20X0 is taken as the base year, using the following.

(a) A Laspeyre index
(b) A Paasche index

5.4 SOLUTION

Workings

Item	p_o	q_o	p_n	q_n	*Laspeyre* $p_o q_o$	$p_n q_o$	*Paasche* $p_n q_n$	$p_o q_n$
P	3	60	4	80	180	240	320	240
Q	6	30	5	40	180	150	200	240
R	5	40	8	20	200	320	160	100
S	2	100	2	150	200	200	300	300
T	7	20	10	10	140	200	100	70
					900	1,110	1,080	950

20X2 index numbers are as follows.

(a) Laspeyre index $= \dfrac{1,110}{900} \times 100 = 123.3$

(b) Paasche index $= \dfrac{1,080}{950} \times 100 = 113.7$

The Paasche index reflects the decline in consumption of the relatively expensive items R and T since 20X0. The Laspeyre index fails to reflect this change.

Question 4

A baker has listed the ingredients he used and their prices, in 20X3 and 20X4, as follows.

	Kgs used 20X3 '000s	Price per kg 20X3 £	Kgs used 20X4 '000s	Price per kg 20X4 £
Milk	3	1.20	4	1.50
Eggs	6	0.95	5	0.98
Flour	1	1.40	2	1.30
Sugar	4	1.10	3	1.14

Required

Calculate the following quantity indices for 20X4 (with 20X3 as the base year).

(a) A Laspeyre index
(b) A Paasche index

Answer

Workings

	p_0	q_0	p_n	q_n	*Laspeyre* $p_0 q_0$	$q_n p_0$	*Paasche* $p_n q_n$	$q_0 p_n$
Milk	1.20	3	1.50	4	3.60	4.80	6.00	4.50
Eggs	0.95	6	0.98	5	5.70	4.75	4.90	5.88
Flour	1.40	1	1.30	2	1.40	2.80	2.60	1.30
Sugar	1.10	4	1.14	3	4.40	3.30	3.42	4.56
					15.10	15.65	16.92	16.24

Quantity index numbers for 20X4 are as follows.

(a) Laspeyre method $= \dfrac{15.65}{15.10} \times 100 = 103.64$

(b) Paasche method $= \dfrac{16.92}{16.24} \times 100 = 104.19$

Which to use - Paasche or Laspeyre ?

5.5 Both patterns of consumption and prices change and a decision therefore has to be made as to whether a Paasche or a Laspeyre index should be used. The following points should be considered when deciding which type of index to use.

PAASCHE INDICES	LASPEYRE INDICES
(use weights from the current time period)	**(use weights from the base period)**
(a) Requires quantities to be ascertained each year which may be costly.	Requires quantities to be ascertained for base year only.
(b) The denominator has to be recalculated each year. The index cannot be calculated until the end of a period when the current prices/quantities are known.	The donominator is fixed. The index may therefore be calculated as soon as current prices/quantities are known.
(c) Because the denominator has to be recalculated each year, comparisons can only be drawn directly between the current year and the base year.	Because the denominator is fixed, the Laspeyre index numbers for several years can be directly compared.
(d) Paasche indices are updated each year.	The weights for a Laspeyre index become out of date.
(e) The effect of current year weighting means that greater importance is placed on goods that are relatively cheaper now than they were in the base year. Inflation could therefore be understated.	Assumes that whatever the price changes, the quantities purchased will remain the same. It therefore assumes that as goods become relatively more expensive, the same quantities will be purchased. Inflation could therefore be overstated.

In practice, it is common to use a Laspeyre index and revise the weights every few years. (Where appropriate, a new base year may be created when the weights are changed.)

6 PRACTICAL ISSUES

What items to include

6.1 The purpose to which the index is to be put must be carefully considered. Once this has been done, the items selected must be as **representative** as possible, taking into account this purpose. Care must be taken to ensure that the items are unambiguously defined and that their values are readily ascertainable.

6.2 For some indices, the choice of items might be relatively straightforward. For example, the FT Actuaries All-Share Index, compiled jointly by the Financial Times, the Institute of Actuaries and the Faculty of Actuaries, is made up of the share prices of approximately 800 companies quoted on The Stock Exchange. The weights are based on the market capitalisations of the companies (the number of shares in issue multiplied by their market value).

6.3 For other indices, the choice of items will be more difficult. The **Retail Prices Index** is an excellent example of the problem. It would be impossible to include all items of domestic spending and a selective, representative basket of goods and services must be found, ranging from spending on mortgages and rents, to cars, public transport, food and drink, electricity, gas, telephone, clothing, leisure activities and so on.

Collecting the data

6.4 Data are required to determine the following.

- The values for each item
- The weight that will be attached to each item

Consider as an example a **cost of living index**. The prices of a particular commodity will vary from place to place, from shop to shop and from type to type. Also the price will vary during the period under consideration. The actual prices used must obviously be some sort of average. The way in which the average is to be obtained should be clearly defined at the outset.

6.5 When constructing a **price index,** it is common practice to use the quantities consumed as weights; similarly, when constructing a **quantity index**, the prices may be used as weights. Care must be taken in selecting the basis for the weighting. For example, in a cost of living index, it may be decided to use the consumption of a typical family as the weights, but some difficulty may be encountered in defining a typical family.

The choice of a base year

6.6 There is no special procedure involved in choosing a base period except that it should have the following properties.

- It should be representative
- It should not be a period in which prices or quantities were extreme

The information conveyed by an index is independent of which base period is chosen. It is, however, necessary to change the base period from time to time and to 'put the clock back' to 100. There are two basic reasons for this.

(a) The actual index numbers may become too large for calculation purposes.

(b) An index should reflect patterns at some particular time. Such patterns need to be regularly updated so that the index does not become irrelevant to what it is trying to measure. For example, expenditure on leisure services is now much more significant than it was 40 years ago.

The limitations and misinterpretation of index numbers

Limitations

6.7 Index numbers are usually only **approximations** of changes in price or quantity over time, and must be interpreted with care.

(a) As we have seen, **weightings become out of date over time**. Unless a Paasche index is used, the weightings will gradually cease to reflect current reality.

(b) **New products or items may appear, and old ones may cease to be significant.** For example, spending has changed in recent years, to include new items such as personal computers and video recorders, whereas the demand for twin tub washing machines has declined. These changes would make the weightings of a price index for such goods out of date.

(c) **The data used to calculate index numbers might be incomplete, out of date, or inaccurate.** For example, the quantity indices of imports and exports are based on records supplied by traders which may be prone to error.

(d) The base year of an index should be a normal year, but there is **probably no such thing as a perfectly normal year**. Some error in the index will be caused by atypical values in the base period.

(e) **The 'basket of items' in an index is often selective**. For example, the Retail Prices Index (RPI) is constructed from a sample of households and from a basket of less than 400 items.

(f) **A national index may not be very relevant to an individual town or region**. For example, if the national index of wages and salaries rises from 100 to 115, we cannot conclude that the wages and salaries of people in, say, Hull, have gone up by 15%.

(g) **An index may exclude important items**: for example, the RPI excludes payments of income tax out of gross wages.

Misinterpretation

6.8 **You must be careful not to misinterpret index numbers**. Several possible mistakes will be explained using the following example of a retail prices index.

20X0		*20X1*		*20X2*	
January	340.0	January	360.6	January	436.3
		February	362.5	February	437.1
		March	366.2	March	439.5
		April	370.0	April	442.1

(a) It would be wrong to say that prices rose by 2.6% between March and April 20X2. It is correct to say that prices rose 2.6 points, or 0.6% (2.6 ÷ 439.5).

(b) It would be correct to say that the annual rate of price increases (the rate of inflation) fell between March and April 20X2. It would be a mistake, however, to suppose that a fall in the rate of inflation means that prices are falling, therefore the price index is falling.

The rate of price increases has slowed down, but the trend of prices is still upwards.

(i) The annual rate of inflation from March 20X1 to March 20X2 is

$$\left(\frac{439.5 - 366.2}{366.2} \right) = 20\%$$

(ii) The annual rate of inflation from April 20X1 to April 20X2 is

$$\left(\frac{442.1 - 370.0}{370.0} \right) = 19.5\%$$

Thus the annual rate of inflation has dropped from 20% to 19.5% between March and April 20X2, even though prices went up in the month between March and April 20X2 by 0.6%. (The price increase between March and April 20X1 was over 1%. This is included in the calculation of the rate of inflation between March 20X1 and March 20X2, but is excluded in the comparison between April 20X1 and April 20X2 where it has been replaced by the lower price increase, 0.6%, between March and April 20X2.)

7 THE RETAIL PRICES INDEX FOR THE UNITED KINGDOM

7.1 The **Retail Prices Index** measures the **change in the cost of living**. It is published monthly (on a Tuesday) near the middle of the month by the Department of Employment and is displayed (to different levels of complexity) in the *Monthly Digest of Statistics*, the *Annual Abstract of Statistics*, the *Department of Employment Gazette* and *Economic Trends*. Since it measures the monthly change in the cost of living its principle use is as a **measure of inflation**.

7.2   The index measures the **percentage changes**, month by month, in the average level of prices of 'a representative basket of goods' purchased by the great majority of households in the United Kingdom. It takes account of practically all wage earners and most small and medium salary earners.

7.3   Each month the 350 items in the basket and the quantities bought of those items are listed in the Family Expenditure Survey. The Family Expenditure Survey is a continuing enquiry conducted by the Department of Employment into the general characteristics of households, their income and their expenditures. From this information the representative basket of goods is divided into main groups. Each group is divided into sections and these sections may be further split into separate items. Each group, section and specific item is weighted according to information from the Family Expenditure Survey to account for its relative importance in the basket.

7.4   Prices are collected from all over the United Kingdom by Department of Employment staff from different types of retail outlet each month. To ensure uniformity, the same ones are used each month. **Price relatives** are calculated for each item covered by the RPI for each retail outlet and averaged for a local area. The averages of local areas are averaged to obtain a national average (for each of the 350 items covered by the RPI).

7.5   The weights are then used to calculate **composite indices** using the average of relatives method for items in the sections, sections within groups and finally groups. The RPI is therefore a **weighted average of relatives** of each group with base date January 1987.

7.6   Each month, an **overall index** is published, as well as **indices for each group**, section and specific item.

7.7   The representative basket of goods is divided into the following main groups. In a recent year, the weights were as follows.

(a)	Food and catering	189
(b)	Alcohol and tobacco	113
(c)	Housing and household expenditure	336
(d)	Personal expenditure	97
(e)	Travel and leisure	265
		1,000

The weights are always calculated to add to 1000.

7.8   Certain items of expenditure are not included in the RPI. These include the following.

- Income tax and National Insurance payments
- Insurance and pension payments
- Mortgage payments (except for interest payments which are included)
- Gambling, gifts, charity

The items and their weights in the basket of goods are continually revised to ensure that they remain as representative as possible.

Chapter roundup

- An **index** is a measure, over time, of the average changes in the value (price or quantity) of a group of items relative to the situation at some period in the past.

- An **index relative** is an index number which measures the change in a single distinct commodity.

- Index relatives can be calculated using the **fixed base method** or the **chain base method**.

- In order to compare two time series of relatives, each series should have the same base period and hence one (or both) may need rebasing.

- The real value of a commodity can only be measured in terms of some 'indicator' (such as the **RPI**).

- **Time series deflation** is a technique used to obtain a set of index relatives that measure the changes in the real value of some commodity with respect to some given indicator.

- **Composite indices** cover more than one item.

- **Weighting** is used to reflect the importance of each item in the index.

- **Weighted means of relatives indices** are found by calculating indices and then applying weights.

- There are two types of **weighted aggregate index**, the **Laspeyre** (which uses quantities/prices from the base period as the weights) and the **Paasche** (which uses quantities/prices from the current period as weights).

Quick quiz

1 How are index relatives calculated using the chain base method? (see para 3.4)

2 How is a time series of relatives rebased? (3.9)

3 Why must the real value of a commodity be measured in terms of some indicator? (3.11)

4 What is the general form of a weighted means of relatives index? (formulae to learn)

5 What do Laspeyre indices use as weights? (5.1)

6 What are the limitations of index numbers? (6.7)

7 Give some examples of how index numbers might be misinterpreted. (6.8)

Question to try	Level	Marks	Time
20	Introductory	n/a	15 mins

Chapter 20

INTRODUCTION TO PROBABILITY

Chapter topic list	Syllabus reference
1 The concept of probability	QT 1(c), 4(a)
2 The laws of probability	QT 1(c), 4(a)
3 Prior and posterior probabilities	QT 1(c), 4(a)
4 Venn diagrams	QT 1(c), 4(a)

Introduction

We are now going to move away from the summary and analysis of data and look at a new topic area, **sampling** and **probability**.

'The likelihood of rain this afternoon is fifty percent' warns the weather report from your radio alarm clock. 'There's no chance of you catching that bus' grunts the helpful soul as you puff up the hill. The headline on your newspaper screams 'Odds of Rainbow Party winning the election rise to one in four'.

'Likelihood' and 'chance' are expressions used in our everyday lives to denote a level of uncertainty. Probability, a word which often strikes fear into the hearts of students, is simply the mathematical term used when we need to imply a degree of uncertainty.

There are a number of ways of analysing. Underlying all of these methods is, however, one concept: **probability**. This chapter will therefore explain various techniques for assessing probability and look at how it can be applied in business decision making.

1   THE CONCEPT OF PROBABILITY

KEY TERM

Probability is a measure of likelihood and can be stated as a percentage, a ratio, or more usually as a number from 0 to 1.

1.1   Consider the following.

- Probability = 0 = impossibility
- Probability = 1 = certainty
- Probability = ½ = a 50% chance of something happening
- Probability = ¼ = a 1 in 4 chance of something happening

1.2   In statistics, probabilities are more commonly expressed as proportions than as percentages. Consider the following possible outcomes.

Possible outcome	*Probability as a percentage*	*Probability as a proportion*
A	15.0%	0.150
B	20.0%	0.200
C	32.5%	0.325
D	7.5%	0.075
E	12.5%	0.125
F	12.5%	0.125
	100.0%	1.000

1.3 Suppose a businessman estimates that if the selling price of a product is raised by 20p, there would be a 90% probability that demand would fall by 30%. How do you think he would have reached his estimate of 90% probability?

1.4 There are several ways of assessing probabilities.

- They may be measurable with mathematical certainty.

  o If a coin is tossed, there is a 0.5 probability that it will come down heads, and a 0.5 probability that it will come down tails.

  o If a die is thrown, there is a one-sixth probability that a 6 will turn up.

- They may be measurable from an analysis of past experience.

- Probabilities can be estimated from research or surveys.

1.5 It is important to note that **probability is a measure of the likelihood of an event happening in the long run**, or **over a large number of times**.

2 THE LAWS OF PROBABILITY 6/95, 6/98, 12/99

2.1 It is the year 2020 and examiners are extinct. A mighty but completely fair computer churns out examinations that are equally likely to be easy or difficult. There is no link between the number of questions on each paper, which is arrived at on a fair basis by the computer, and the standard of the paper. You are about to take five examinations.

Simple probability

2.2 It is vital that the first examination is easy as it covers a subject which you have tried, but failed to understand. What is the probability that it will be an easy examination?

2.3 Obviously (let us hope), the probability of an easy paper is $^1/_2$ (or 50% or 0.5). This reveals a very important principle (which holds if each result is equally likely).

FORMULA TO LEARN

Probability of achieving the desired result

$$= \frac{\text{Number of ways of achieving desired result (heads)}}{\text{Total number of possible outcomes (heads or tails)}}$$

Let us apply the principle to our example.

Total number of possible outcomes = 'easy' or 'difficult'	= 2
Total number of ways of achieving the desired result (which is 'easy')	= 1
The probability of an easy examination, or P(easy examination)	= $^1/_2$

2.4 EXAMPLE: SIMPLE PROBABILITY

If a coin is tossed in the air, what is the probability that it will come down heads?

2.5 SOLUTION

$$P(\text{heads}) = \frac{\text{Number of ways of achieving desired result (heads)}}{\text{Total number of possible outcomes (heads or tails)}}$$

$$= \quad ^1/_2 \text{ or } 50\% \text{ or } 0.5.$$

Complementary outcomes

2.6 You are keen to pass more examinations than your sworn enemy but, unlike you, he is more likely to pass the first examination if it is difficult. (He is very strange!!) What is the probability of the first examination being more suited to your enemy's requirements?

2.7 We know that the probability of certainty is one. The certainty in this scenario is that the examination will be easy or difficult.

P(easy or difficult examination)	=	1
From Paragraph 2.3, P(easy examination)	=	$^1/_2$
P(not easy examination)	=	P(difficult examination)
	=	1 − P(easy examination)
	=	$1 - ^1/_2$
	=	$^1/_2$

> **FORMULA TO LEARN**
>
> $P(\overline{X}) = 1 - P(X)$, where $\overline{X}$ is 'not X'.

2.8 EXAMPLE: COMPLEMENTARY OUTCOMES

If there is a 25 per cent chance of the Rainbow Party winning the next general election, use the law of complementary events to calculate the probability of the Rainbow Party *not* winning the next election.

2.9 SOLUTION

P(winning)	=	$25\% = ^1/_4$
P(not winning)	=	$1 - P(\text{winning}) = 1 - ^1/_4 = ^3/_4$

The simple addition or OR law

2.10 The time pressure in the second examination is enormous. The computer will produce a paper which will have between five and nine questions. You know that, easy or difficult, the examination must have six questions at the most for you to have any hope of passing it.

What is the probability of the computer producing an examination with six or fewer questions? In other words, what is the probability of an examination with five *or* six questions?

2.11 Don't panic. Let us start by using the basic principle.

$$P(5 \text{ questions}) = \frac{\text{Total number of ways of achieving a five question examination}}{\text{Total number of possible outcomes } (= 5,6,7,8 \text{ or } 9 \text{ questions})}$$

$$= \quad {}^1\!/_5$$

Likewise $P(6 \text{ questions}) = {}^1\!/_5$

Either five questions or six questions would be acceptable, so the probability of you passing the examination must be greater than if just five questions or just six questions (but not both) were acceptable. We therefore add the two probabilities together so that the probability of passing the examination has increased.

2.12 So $P(5 \text{ or } 6 \text{ questions}) = P(5 \text{ questions}) + P(6 \text{ questions})$

$$= \quad {}^1\!/_5 + {}^1\!/_5 = {}^2\!/_5 .$$

> **FORMULA TO LEARN**
>
> The **simple addition law** or **OR law** is:
>
> $P(X \text{ or } Y \text{ or } Z) = P(X) + P(Y) + P(Z)$
>
> where X, Y and Z are **mutually exclusive outcomes**, which means that the occurrence of one of the outcomes excludes the possibility of any of the others happening.

In the example the outcomes are **mutually exclusive** because it is impossible to have five questions *and* six questions in the same examination.

2.13 EXAMPLE: MUTUALLY EXCLUSIVE OUTCOMES

The delivery of an item of raw material from a supplier may take up to six weeks from the time the order is placed. The probabilities of various delivery times are as follows.

Delivery time	Probability
≤ 1 week	0.10
$> 1, \leq 2$ weeks	0.25
$> 2, \leq 3$ weeks	0.20
$> 3, \leq 4$ weeks	0.20
$> 4, \leq 5$ weeks	0.15
$> 5, \leq 6$ weeks	0.10
	1.00

Required

Calculate the probability that a delivery will take the following times.

(a) Two weeks or less

(b) More than three weeks

2.14 SOLUTION

(a) $P(\leq 1 \text{ or } > 1, \leq 2 \text{ weeks}) = P(\leq 1 \text{ week}) + P(>1, \leq 2 \text{ weeks}) = 0.10 + 0.25 = 0.35$

(b) $P(> 3, \leq 6 \text{ weeks}) = P(> 3, \leq 4 \text{ weeks}) + P(> 4, \leq 5 \text{ weeks}) + P(> 5, \leq 6 \text{ weeks}) = 0.20 + 0.15 + 0.10 = 0.45$

The simple multiplication or AND law

2.15 You still have three examinations to sit: astrophysics, geography of the moon and computer art. Stupidly, you forgot to revise for the astrophysics examination, which will have between

15 and 20 questions. You think that you may scrape through this paper if it is easy *and* if there are only 15 questions.

What is the probability that the paper the computer produces will exactly match your needs? Do not forget that there is no link between the standard of the examination and the number of questions.

2.16   The best way to approach this question is diagrammatically, showing all the possible outcomes.

		Number of questions				
	15	*16*	*17*	*18*	*19*	*20*
Type of paper						
Easy (E)	E and 15★	E and 16	E and 17	E and 18	E and 19	E and 20
Difficult (D)	D and 15	D and 16	D and 17	D and 18	D and 19	D and 20

The diagram shows us that, of the twelve possible outcomes, there is only one 'desired result' (which is asterisked). We can therefore calculate the probability as follows.

P(easy paper *and* 15 questions) = $^1/_{12}$.

2.17   The answer can be found more easily as follows.

P(easy paper *and* 15 questions) = P(easy paper) × P(15 questions) = $^1/_2 × ^1/_6 = ^1/_{12}$.

FORMULA TO LEARN

The **simple multiplication law** or **AND law** is: $P(X \text{ and } Y) = P(X) P(Y)$

where X and Y are **independent** events, which means that the occurrence of one event in no way affects the outcome of the other events.

2.18   The number of questions has no effect on, nor is it affected by whether it is an easy or difficult paper.

2.19   EXAMPLE: INDEPENDENT EVENTS

A die is thrown and a coin is tossed simultaneously. What is the probability of throwing a 5 and getting heads on the coin?

2.20   SOLUTION

The probability of throwing a 5 on a die is $^1/_6$
The probability of a tossed coin coming up heads is $^1/_2$
The probability of throwing a 5 and getting heads on a coin is $^1/_2 × ^1/_6 = ^1/_{12}$

The general rule of addition

2.21   The three examinations you still have to sit are placed face down in a line in front of you at the final examination sitting. There is an easy astrophysics paper, a difficult geography of the moon paper and a difficult computer art paper. Without turning over any of the papers you are told to choose one of them. What is the probability that the first paper that you select is difficult or is the geography of the moon paper?

2.22 Let us think about this carefully. There are two difficult papers, so P(difficult) = $^2/_3$. There is one geography of the moon paper, so P(geography of the moon) = $^1/_3$

2.23 If we use the OR law and add the two probabilities then we will have double counted the difficult geography of the moon paper. It is included in the set of difficult papers and in the set of geography of the moon papers. In other words, we are *not* faced with mutually exclusive outcomes because the occurrence of a geography of the moon paper does not exclude the possibility of the occurrence of a difficult paper. We therefore need to take account of this double counting.

P(difficult paper or geography of the moon paper) = P(difficult paper) + P(geography of the moon paper) – P(difficult paper and geography of the moon paper).

Using the AND law, P(difficult paper or geography of the moon paper) = $^2/_3$ + $^1/_3$ – ($^1/_3$) = $^2/_3$.

FORMULA TO LEARN

The **general rule of addition** is:

P(X or Y) = P(X) + P(Y) – P(X and Y)

where the word 'or' is used in an inclusive sense: either X or Y or both. X and Y are therefore *not* mutually exclusive.

2.24 Since it is *not* impossible to have an examination which is difficult *and* about the geography of the moon, these two events are not mutually exclusive.

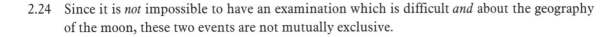

Question 1

If one card is drawn from a normal pack of 52 playing cards, what is the probability of getting an ace or a spade?

Answer

P(ace) = 4/52

P (spade) = 13/52

P(ace of spades) = 1/52

∴ P(ace or spades) = $\dfrac{4}{52} + \dfrac{13}{52} - \dfrac{1}{52} = \dfrac{16}{52} = \dfrac{4}{13}$

The general rule of multiplication

2.25 Computer art is your last examination. Understandably you are very tired and you are uncertain whether you will be able to stay awake. You believe that there is a 70% chance of your falling asleep if it becomes too hot and stuffy in the examination hall. It is well known that the air conditioning system serving the examination hall was installed in the 1990s and is therefore extremely unreliable. There is a 1 in 4 chance of it breaking down during the examination, thereby causing the temperature in the hall to rise. What is the likelihood that you will drop off?

2.26 The scenario in Paragraph 2.25 has led us to face what is known as **conditional probability**. We can rephrase the information provided as 'the probability that you will fall asleep, given that it is too hot and stuffy, is equal to 70%' and we can write this as P(fall asleep/too hot and stuffy) = 70%.

2.27 Whether you fall asleep is **conditional** upon whether the hall becomes too hot and stuffy. The events are not, therefore, independent and so we cannot use the simple multiplication law. So: P(it becomes too hot and stuffy and you fall asleep)

= P(too hot and stuffy) × P(fall asleep/too hot and stuffy)
= 25% × 70% = 0.25 × 0.7 = 0.175 = 17$\frac{1}{2}$%

> **FORMULA TO LEARN**
>
> The **general rule of multiplication** is: P(X and Y) $=$ P(X) × P(Y/X)
>
> $=$ P(Y) × P(X/Y)
>
> where X and Y are **dependent events**, the occurrence of the second event being dependent upon the occurrence of the first.

2.28 When X and Y are independent events, then P(Y/X) = P(Y) since, by definition, the occurrence of Y (and therefore P(Y)) does not depend upon the occurrence of X. Similarly P(X/Y) = P(X).

2.29 EXAMPLE: CONDITIONAL PROBABILITY

The board of directors of Shuttem Ltd has warned that there is a 60% probability that a factory will be closed down unless its workforce improves its productivity. The factory's manager has estimated that the probability of success in agreeing a productivity deal with the workforce is only 30%.

Required

Determine the likelihood that the factory will be closed.

2.30 SOLUTION

If outcome A is the shutdown of the factory and outcome B is the failure to improve productivity:

P (A and B)   =   P(B) × P(A/B) = 0.7 × 0.6 = 0.42

Another method of dealing with conditional probabilities is by using contingency tables.

2.31 EXAMPLE: CONTINGENCY TABLES

A cosmetics company has developed a new anti-dandruff shampoo which is being tested on volunteers. Seventy percent of the volunteers have used the shampoo whereas others have used a normal shampoo, believing it to be the new anti-dandruff shampoo. Two sevenths of those using the new shampoo showed no improvement whereas one third of those using the normal shampoo had less dandruff.

Required

A volunteer shows no improvement. What is the probability that he used the normal shampoo?

2.32 SOLUTION

The problem is solved by drawing a contingency table, showing 'improvement' and 'no improvement', volunteers using normal shampoo and volunteers using the new shampoo.

Let us suppose that there were 1,000 volunteers (we could use any number). We could depict the results of the test on the 1,000 volunteers as follows.

	New shampoo	*Normal shampoo*	*Total*
Improvement	***500	****100	600
No improvement	**200	200	400
	*700	***300	1,000

* $70\% \times 1,000$ ** $^2/_7 \times 700$

*** Balancing figure   **** $^1/_3 \times 300$

We can now calculate P(used normal shampoo/showed no improvement)

P(shows no improvement) = 400/1,000

P(used normal shampoo/shows no improvement) = 200/400 = $^1/_2$

Other probabilities are just as easy to calculate.

P(shows improvement/used new shampoo) = 500/700 = $^5/_7$

P(used new shampoo/shows improvement) = 500/600 = $^5/_6$

Addition and multiplication rules combined

2.33 Question 2 shows how addition and multiplication rules may be combined in one question.

Question 2

The independent probabilities that the three sections of a management accounting department will encounter one computer error in a week are respectively 0.1, 0.2 and 0.3. There is never more than one computer error encountered by any one section in a week. Calculate the probability that there will be the following number of errors encountered by the management accounting department next week.

(a) At least one computer error
(b) One and only one computer error
(c) One or two computer errors

Answer

(a) The probability of at least one computer error is 1 minus the probability of no error. The probability of no error is $0.9 \times 0.8 \times 0.7 = 0.504$.

(Since the probability of an error is 0.1, 0.2 and 0.3 in each section, the probability of no error in each section must be 0.9, 0.8 and 0.7 respectively.)

The probability of at least one error is $1 - 0.504 = 0.496$.

(b) Y = yes, N = no

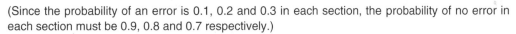

		Section 1	Section 2	Section 3
(i)	Error?	Y	N	N
(ii)	Error?	N	Y	N
(iii)	Error?	N	N	Y
		Probabilities		
(i)	$0.1 \times 0.8 \times 0.7 =$	0.056		
(ii)	$0.9 \times 0.2 \times 0.7 =$	0.126		
(iii)	$0.9 \times 0.8 \times 0.3 =$	0.216		
	Total	0.398		

The probability of only one error only is 0.398.

(c)   We begin by calculating P (two errors).

		Section 1	Section 2	Section 3
(i)	Error?	Y	Y	N
(ii)	Error?	Y	N	Y
(iii)	Error?	N	Y	Y

		Probabilities
(i)	$0.1 \times 0.2 \times 0.7$	= 0.014
(ii)	$0.1 \times 0.8 \times 0.3$	= 0.024
(iii)	$0.9 \times 0.2 \times 0.3$	= 0.054
		Total 0.092

The probability of one or two computer errors = P (1 error) + P (2 errors) = 0.398 + 0.092 = 0.49

Question 3

A glass bottle manufacturer has three inspection points: one for size, the second for colour and the third for flaws such as cracks and bubbles in the glass. The probability that each inspection point will incorrectly accept or reject a bottle is 0.02.

Required

Calculate the following probabilities.

(a)   A perfect bottle will be passed through all inspection points.
(b)   A bottle faulty in colour and with a crack will be passed through all inspection points.
(c)   A bottle faulty in size only will be passed through all inspection points.

Answer

The probability of incorrect testing is 0.02 at each stage, and so the probability of correct testing is 0.98.

(a)   A perfect bottle has a 98% probability of passing each stage, and so the probability of its passing all three stages is $0.98 \times 0.98 \times 0.98 = 0.941192$.

(b)   A bottle faulty in colour and with a crack must pass three stages.

Size:	probability	0.98
Colour:	probability	0.02
Flaws:	probability	0.02

Probability of passing = $0.98 \times 0.02 \times 0.02 = 0.000392$

(c)   A bottle faulty in size only must pass three stages.

Size:	probability	0.02
Colour:	probability	0.98
Flaws:	probability	0.98

Probability of passing = $0.02 \times 0.98 \times 0.98 = 0.019208$

3   PRIOR AND POSTERIOR PROBABILITIES

3.1   Consider a situation in which we are considering the sex and hair colour of people in a given group or population consisting of 70% men and 30% women. We have established the probabilities of hair colourings as follows.

	Men	*Women*
Brown	0.60	0.35
Blonde	0.35	0.55
Red	0.05	0.10

These probabilities of sex and hair colouring might be referred to as prior probabilities, to distinguish them from posterior probabilities.

Posterior probabilities consider the situation in reverse or retrospect, so that we can ask, for example: 'Given that a person taken at random from the population is brown-haired what is the probability that the person is male?'

3.2   Posterior probabilities can be established by drawing a probability tree as follows.

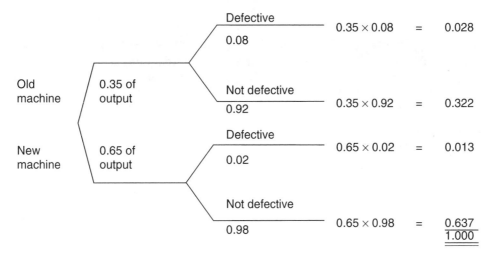

Joint probabilities

Brown	0.60	$0.7 \times 0.60 =$	0.420
Blonde	0.35	$0.7 \times 0.35 =$	0.245
Red	0.05	$0.7 \times 0.05 =$	0.035
Brown	0.35	$0.3 \times 0.35 =$	0.105
Blonde	0.55	$0.3 \times 0.55 =$	0.165
Red	0.10	$0.3 \times 0.10 =$	0.030
			1.000

The probability of being a man, given that a person is brown haired, is

$$\frac{\text{Probability of being a man and brown haired}}{\text{Probability of being a man or woman and brown haired}} = \frac{0.42}{0.42 + 0.105}$$

$$= \frac{0.42}{0.525} = 0.80$$

3.3   EXAMPLE: POSTERIOR PROBABILITIES

Two machines produce the same product. The older machine produces 35% of the total output but eight units in every 100 are defective. The newer machine produces 65% of the total output but two units in every 100 are defective.

Required

Determine the probability that a defective unit picked at random was produced by the older machine.

3.4   SOLUTION

We want to establish the posterior probability that, given a defective unit, it was produced by the older machine.

		Defective		
		0.08	0.35×0.08	= 0.028
Old machine	0.35 of output	Not defective		
		0.92	0.35×0.92	= 0.322
		Defective		
New machine	0.65 of output	0.02	0.65×0.02	= 0.013
		Not defective		
		0.98	0.65×0.98	= 0.637
				1.000

The probability of a defective unit being from the older machine is $\dfrac{0.028}{0.028 + 0.013} = 0.683$.

4   VENN DIAGRAMS

> **KEY TERM**
>
> A **Venn diagram** is a pictorial representation of divisions and subdivisions of a universal set.

4.1

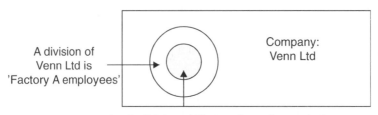

Venn diagram showing divisions and sub-divisions of a category

4.2   If we use the following symbols:

U   (Universal) = the set of all the company's employees
A   = the set of Factory A employees
B   = the set of direct production workers in Factory A

the Venn diagram can be shown as follows.

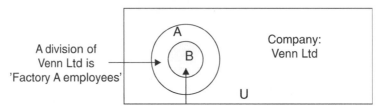

Venn diagram showing divisions and sub-divisions of a category

4.3   If we used B to represent the set of all direct production workers, whether inside Factory A or in other factories of Venn Ltd, we could draw Venn diagrams as follows.

Venn diagrams of sets of Factory A employees and direct production workers

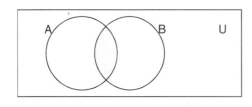

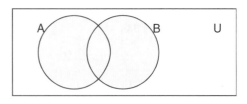

(a)   (b)

(a)   The shading on this diagram picks out the company's production workers within Factory A, that is those who are both employed in Factory A and employed as production workers. This area is called the **intersection of A and B** and is written $A \cap B$.

(b) The shading on this diagram picks out those employees who are either direct production workers or who work in Factory A (or who come into both categories). This area is called the **union of A and B** and is written $A \cup B$.

Venn diagrams and probability

4.4 It is possible to use **Venn diagrams** to **solve probability problems**. For example, if there are two outcomes they can be depicted by two overlapping circles, one for each outcome. The known probabilities can be filled in, then the unknown probabilities can be derived from the fact that all the probabilities on the diagram must add up to 1.

4.5 EXAMPLE: VENN DIAGRAMS

Two outcomes are denoted by M and N. $\overline{M}$ denotes 'not M' and $\overline{N}$ denotes 'not N'. The following probabilities are given.

$$P(M) = 0.50 \qquad P(M \text{ and } N) = 0.15 \qquad P(\overline{M} \text{ and } \overline{N}) = 0.10$$

What is $P(N)$ and $P(M \text{ or } N)$?

4.6 SOLUTION

We can draw a Venn diagram with a circle for each outcome, M and N.

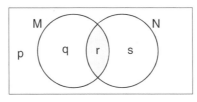

The given probabilities are as follows.

$P(M) \qquad = q + r = 0.50$
$P(M \text{ and } N) \quad = r = M \cap N = 0.15$
$P(\overline{M} \text{ and } \overline{N}) \quad = p = 0.10$

We want to know $P(N)$ and $P(M \text{ or } N)$.

$P(N)$ is equal to $r + s$ and therefore we need to deduce s.

$p + (q + r) + s \quad = 1.00$
$0.10 + 0.50 + s \quad = 1.00$
$\qquad\qquad\quad s \quad = 1.00 - 0.10 - 0.50 = 0.40$
$P(N) = \quad r + s \quad = 0.15 + 0.40$
$\qquad\qquad\qquad = 0.55$

$P(M \text{ or } N) = q + r + s = P(M \cup N) = 0.5 + 0.4 = 0.9$

Did you notice how we threw the $\cup$ and $\cap$ symbols into the solution above?

$P(M \text{ or } N) \qquad = P(M) \text{ or } P(N) \text{ or } P(M \text{ and } N)$

$\qquad\qquad\qquad = \quad q \quad + \quad r \quad + \quad s = P(M \cup N)$

and $P(M \text{ and } N) \quad = P(M) \text{ and } P(N) = r = P(M \cap N)$

BPP
PUBLISHING

Exam focus point

Use Venn diagrams to solve probability problems by using circles to depict different outcomes. Known probabilities can be filled in, and unknown probabilities can be derived, because the total probabilities must add up to 1.

Question 4

A cosmetics company runs a campaign in a department store in Britain, stopping 100 customers at random and asking their opinions about three new perfumes, A, B and C. It discovers the following.

Number who like A	= 35
Number who like B	= 43
Number who like C	= 57
Number who like A and B	= 21
Number who like A and C	= 20
Number who like B and C	= 31
Number who like all three	= 15

Required

Determine the following probabilities.

(a) A customer likes exactly one perfume only.
(b) A customer likes none of the perfumes.

Answer

Venn diagram of people liking perfumes

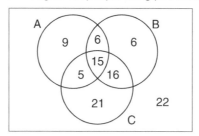

The figures are found by entering the 15 who like all three perfumes first, then finding the numbers who like only two as balancing figures (for example A, B, not C = 21 – 15 = 6), then finding the numbers who like only one, and finally the number who like none.

(a) The probability that a customer likes exactly one perfume is (9 + 6 + 21)/100 = 0.36.
(b) The probability that a customer likes none of the perfumes is 22/100 = 0.22.

Chapter roundup

- **Mutually exclusive outcomes** are outcomes where the occurrence of one of the outcomes excludes the possibility of any of the others happening.

- **Independent events** are events where the occurrence of one event in no way affects the outcome of the other events.

- **Dependent or conditional events** are events where the occurrence of one event depends on the occurrence of the others.

- The **addition laws** for two events, X and Y, are as follows.

  $P(X \text{ or } Y) = P(X) + P(Y)$ when X and Y are mutually exclusive outcomes.
  $P(X \text{ or } Y) = P(X) + P(Y) - P(X \text{ and } Y)$ when X and Y are independent events.

- The **multiplication laws** for two events, X and Y, are as follows.

  $P(X \text{ and } Y) = 0$ when X and Y are mutually exclusive outcomes.
  $P(X \text{ and } Y) = P(X) P(Y)$ when X and Y are independent events.
  $P(X \text{ and } Y) = P(X) P(Y/X) = P(Y) P(X/Y)$ when X and Y are dependent/conditional events.

- **Venn diagrams** can be used to help solve probability problems.

Quick quiz

1   What is the probability of certainty? (see para 1.1)

2   What is the probability of $\overline{x}$? (formulae to learn)

3   Define mutually exclusive outcomes. (formulae to learn)

4   Define independent events. (formulae to learn)

5   Define conditional events. (2.26, 2.27)

6   What is the general rule of multiplication of probabilities? (formulae to learn)

7   How can the intersection of two sets X and Y be written using Venn diagram terminology? (4.3)

Question to try	Level	Marks	Time
21	Examination	14	25 mins

BPP PUBLISHING

Chapter 21

DECISION MAKING

Chapter topic list	Syllabus reference
1 Expected values	QT 1(c), 4(c)
2 Decision making with expected values	QT 1(c), 4(c)
3 Decision trees	QT 1(c), 4(a), (c)

Introduction

The previous chapter provided an introduction to probability. We begin this chapter by examining the related topic of **expected values** and we will see how the concept can be used to assist decision making.

Although simple decisions can be made using expected values, more complex problems, although solvable using the basic principles, require a clear logical approach to ensure that all possible choices and outcomes of a decision are taken into consideration. **Decision trees**, the topic of the third section of this chapter, are a useful way of interpreting such problems.

1 EXPECTED VALUES

12/94, 12/97, 6/98, 12/98

> **KEY TERM**
>
> An **expected value** (or EV) is a weighted average value, based on probabilities.

1.1 If the probability of an outcome of an event is p, then the expected number of times that this outcome will occur in n events (the expected value) is equal to n × p. For example, suppose that the probability that a transistor is defective is 0.02. How many defectives would we expect to find in a batch of 4,000 transistors?

$$EV = 4,000 \times 0.02$$
$$= 80 \text{ defectives would be expected.}$$

1.2 EXAMPLE: EXPECTED VALUES

The daily sales of Product T may be as follows.

Units	Probability
1,000	0.2
2,000	0.3
3,000	0.4
4,000	0.1
	1.0

Required

Calculate the expected daily sales.

1.3 SOLUTION

The EV of daily sales may be calculated by multiplying each possible outcome (volume of daily sales) by the probability that this outcome will occur.

Units	*Probability*	*Expected value* Units
1,000	0.2	200
2,000	0.3	600
3,000	0.4	1,200
4,000	0.1	400
	EV of daily sales	2,400

In the long run the expected value should be approximately the actual average, if the event occurs many times over. In the example above, we do not expect sales on any one day to equal 2,400 units, but in the long run, over a large number of days, average sales should equal 2,400 units a day.

Expected values and single events

1.4 The point made in the preceding paragraph is an important one. An **expected value** can be calculated when the **event will only occur once or twice**, but it will not be a true long-run average of what will actually happen, because there is no long run.

1.5 Suppose, for example, that a businessman is trying to decide whether to invest in a project. He estimates that there are three possible outcomes.

Outcome	*Profit/(loss)* £	*Probability*
Success	10,000	0.2
Moderate success	2,000	0.7
Failure	(4,000)	0.1

The expected value of profit may be calculated as follows.

Profit/(loss) £	*Probability*	*Expected value* £
10,000	0.2	2,000
2,000	0.7	1,400
(4,000)	0.1	(400)
	Expected value of profit	3,000

1.6 In this example, the project is a one-off event, and as far as we are aware, it will not be repeated. The actual profit or loss will be £10,000, £2,000 or £(4,000), and the average value of £3,000 will not actually happen. There is no long-run average of a single event.

1.7 Nevertheless, the expected value can be used to help the manager decide whether or not to invest in the project. Generally the following rules apply.

- A project with a **positive EV** (EV is a profit) should be **accepted**
- A project with a **negative EV** (EV is a loss) should be **rejected**

1.8 Provided that we understand the limitations of using expected values for single events, they can offer a helpful guide for management decisions, and suggest to managers whether any particular decision is worth the risk of taking (subject, of course, to reasonable accuracy in the estimates of the probabilities themselves).

Question 1

A company manufactures and sells product D. The selling price of the product is £6 per unit, and estimates of demand and variable costs of sales are as follows.

Probability	Demand	Probability	Variable cost per unit
	Units		£
0.3	5,000	0.1	3.00
0.6	6,000	0.3	3.50
0.1	8,000	0.5	4.00
		0.1	4.50

The unit variable costs do not depend on the volume of sales.

Fixed costs will be £10,000.

Required

Calculate the expected profit.

Answer

The EV of demand is as follows.

Demand	Probability	Expected value
Units		Units
5,000	0.3	1,500
6,000	0.6	3,600
8,000	0.1	800
	EV of demand	5,900

The EV of the variable cost per unit is as follows.

Variable costs	Probability	Expected value
£		£
3.00	0.1	0.30
3.50	0.3	1.05
4.00	0.5	2.00
4.50	0.1	0.45
	EV of unit variable costs	3.80

		£
Sales	5,900 units × £6.00	35,400
Less variable costs	5,900 units × £3.80	22,420
Contribution		12,980
Less fixed costs		10,000
Expected profit		2,980

The expected value of a probability

1.9 You might be required to calculate a **weighted average probability** of an event occurring: an EV of a probability. Consider the following example.

1.10 EXAMPLE: THE EXPECTED VALUE OF A PROBABILITY

A salesman has three small areas to cover, areas A, B and C. He never sells more than one item per day, and the probabilities of making a sale when he visits each area are as follows.

Area	Probability
A	30%
B	25%
C	10%

He visits only one area each day. He visits Area A as often as he visits Area B, but he only visits Area C half as often as he visits Area A.

Required

(a) Calculate the probability that on any one day he will visit Area C.
(b) Calculate the probability that he will make a sale on any one day.
(c) Calculate the probability that if he does make a sale, it will be in Area A.

1.11 SOLUTION

(a) The probabilities of visiting each area are obtained from the ratios in which he visits them.

Area	Ratio	Probability
A	2	0.4
B	2	0.4
C	1	0.2
	5	1.0

The probability that he will visit Area C is 0.2.

(b) The probability of making a sale on any one day is found as follows.

Area	Probability of a sale x	Probability of visiting area p	EV of probability of a sale px
A	0.30	0.4	0.12
B	0.25	0.4	0.10
C	0.10	0.2	0.02
			0.24

The probability of making a sale is 0.24 or 24%.

(c) The probability of making a sale is 0.24 and the probability that the sale will be in Area A rather than B or C can be established as follows.

$$\frac{\text{EV of probability of sale in A}}{\text{EV of probability of sale in A, B or C}} = \frac{0.12}{0.24} = 0.5.$$

One half of all sales will be made in Area A.

FORMULA TO LEARN

$E(x) = \Sigma x P(x)$

This is read as '**the expected value of "x"** is equal to the sum of the products of each value of x and the corresponding probability of that value of x occurring'.

2 DECISION MAKING WITH EXPECTED VALUES 12/97

2.1 The **expected values** for single events can offer a helpful guide for management decisions: a project with a positive EV should be accepted; a project with a negative EV should be rejected.

2.2 Another decision rule involving expected values that you are likely to come across is the choice of an option which has the **highest EV of profit** (or the lowest EV of cost).

2.3 Choosing the option with the highest EV of profit is a decision rule that has both merits and drawbacks, as the following example will show.

2.4 EXAMPLE: THE EXPECTED VALUE CRITERION

Suppose that there are two mutually exclusive projects with the following possible profits.

Project A		Project B	
Probability	*Profit*	*Probability*	*Profit/(loss)*
	£		£
0.8	5,000	0.1	(2,000)
0.2	6,000	0.2	5,000
		0.6	7,000
		0.1	8,000

Required

Determine which project should be chosen.

Solution

2.5 The EV of profit for each project is as follows. £

(a) Project A $(0.8 \times 5,000) + (0.2 \times 6,000) =$ 5,200

(b) Project B $(0.1 \times (2,000)) + (0.2 \times 5,000) + (0.6 \times 7,000) + (0.1 \times 8,000) =$ 5,800

Project B has a higher EV of profit. This means that on the balance of probabilities, it could offer a better return than A, and so is arguably a better choice.

On the other hand, the minimum return from project A would be £5,000 whereas with B there is a 0.1 chance of a loss of £2,000. So project A might be a safer choice.

3 DECISION TREES 12/97

3.1 **Expected values** are generally used for making **simple decisions**. More **complex problems** are best solved with the use of **decision trees**.

3.2 Exactly how does the use of a decision tree permit a clear and logical approach?

- All possible choices that can be made are shown as **branches** on the tree.
- All possible outcomes of each choice are shown as **subsidiary branches** on the tree.

3.3 There are two stages to preparing a decision tree.

- Drawing the tree itself, to show all the choices and outcomes
- Putting in the numbers (the probabilities, outcome values and EVs)

Drawing a decision tree: the basic rules

3.4 Every decision tree starts from a **decision point** with the **decision options** that are being considered.

(a) There should be a line, or branch, for each option or alternative.

(b) It helps to identify the decision point, and any subsequent decision point in the tree, with a symbol. Here, we shall use a square shape.

(c) There is no accepted convention on the shapes used at the points of a decision tree. If you have to investigate a ready-drawn tree, remember that the very first (leftmost) point will always be a decision point.

3.5 It is conventional to draw decision trees from left to right, and so a decision tree will start as follows.

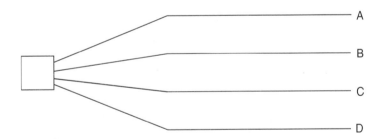

The square is the decision point, and A, B, C and D represent four alternatives from which a choice must now be made.

3.6 If the outcome from any choice or alternative is **100% certain**, the branch of the decision tree for that alternative is **complete**.

3.7 If the outcome of a particular alternative is **uncertain**, the various possible outcomes must be shown. We show this on a decision tree by inserting an **outcome or event point** on the branch of the tree. Each possible outcome is then shown as a subsidiary branch, coming out from the outcome point. The probability of each outcome occurring should be written on to the branch of the tree which represents that outcome.

3.8 To distinguish decision points from outcome points, a circle will be used as a symbol for an outcome or event point.

In the example above, there are two choices facing the decision maker, A and B. The outcome if A is chosen is known with certainty, but if B is chosen, there are two possible outcomes, high sales (0.6 probability) or low sales (0.4 probability).

3.9 Clarity becomes an issue when the options are more complex. For example a company might be considering three options.

- Launch a new product, and advertise nationally.
- Launch a new product, and do not advertise.
- Don't launch the product.

This could be shown in either of two ways, as shown below. Usually, the first method will be clearer than the second method.

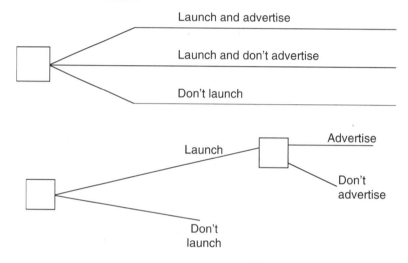

3.10 When several outcomes are uncertain, it is usually simpler to show two or more stages of outcome points on the decision tree.

3.11 For example suppose that a company can choose to launch a new product XYZ or not. If the product is launched, expected sales and expected unit costs might be as follows.

Sales		Unit costs	
Units	Probability	£	Probability
10,000	0.8	6	0.7
15,000	0.2	8	0.3

(a)   The decision tree could be drawn as follows.

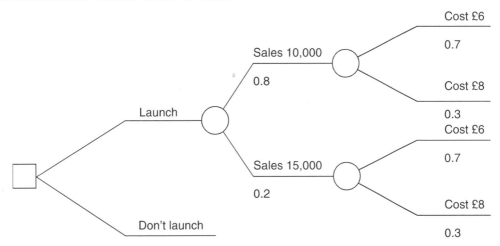

(b)   The layout shown above will usually be less complex than working out the alternative way of drawing the tree, which is shown below.

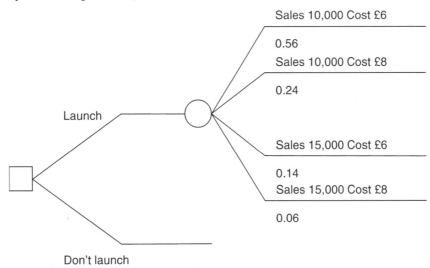

3.12   Occasionally, a decision taken now will influence another decision which might then have to be taken at some time in the future, depending on how results turn out. When this situation arises, the decision tree can be drawn as a **two-stage tree**, as follows.

In this tree, either decision A or B or else decision C or D is dependent on the outcome which occurs as a consequence of choosing decision X.

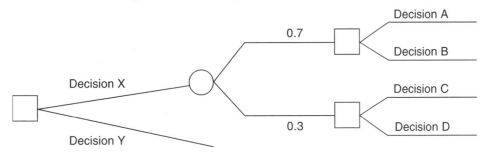

Evaluating the decision with a decision tree: rollback analysis

3.13   The EV of each decision option can be evaluated, using the decision tree to help keep the logic properly sorted out. The basic rules are as follows.

(a) We start on the right hand side of the tree and work back towards the left hand side and the current decision under consideration.

(b) It helps if we label each decision point and outcome point on the tree, to give it an identification.

(c) Working from right to left, we calculate the EV of revenue, cost, contribution or profit at each outcome point on the tree.

3.14 Suppose that the following decision tree represents a decision under consideration.

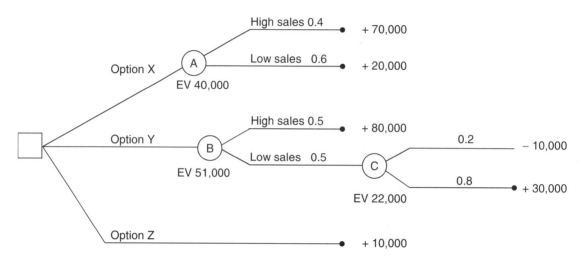

3.15 At outcome point C (the right-most outcome point) the EV is calculated as follows.

Profit	*Probability*	
x	*p*	*px*
(10,000)	0.2	(2,000)
30,000	0.8	24,000
	EV =	22,000

At outcome point B therefore, the EV is as follows.

Profit	*Probability*	
x	*p*	*px*
80,000	0.5	40,000
22,000	0.5	11,000
	EV =	51,000

It remains to calculate the EV at outcome point A.

Profit	*Probability*	
x	*p*	*px*
70,000	0.4	28,000
20,000	0.6	12,000
	EV =	40,000

The calculation of EVs, first at outcome points A and C and then at outcome point B, brings us back to the initial decision, where the choices can now be compared, as follows.

Option

X:	EV = EV at A = £40,000
Y:	EV = EV at B = £51,000
Z:	Certain value £10,000.

If the decision is to select the option with the highest EV of profit, the evaluation of the decision tree would then point to option Y.

3.16 The decision tree should be drawn in '**chronological order**' from **left to right**. When there are two-stage decision trees, the first decision in time should be drawn on the left. This is the decision of immediate concern to management.

3.17 When there are two decision stages in the decision tree, the second stage decision must be evaluated first so that we can evaluate the part of the decision tree to the left of it.

3.18 EXAMPLE: DRAWING AND EVALUATING A DECISION TREE

These rules for drawing decision trees might seem quite simple when you look at an example.

Beethoven Ltd has a new wonder product, the vylin, of which it expects great things. At the moment the company has two courses of action open to it, to test market the product or abandon it. If they test it, it will cost £100,000 and the market response could be positive or negative with probabilities of 0.60 and 0.40. If the response is positive the company could either abandon the product or market it full scale. If it markets the vylin full scale, the outcome might be low, medium or high demand, and the respective net pay offs would be (200), 200 or 1,000 in units of £1,000 (ie the result could range from a net loss of £200,000 to a gain of £1,000,000). These outcomes have probabilities of 0.20, 0.50 and 0.30 respectively.

If the result of the test marketing is negative and the company goes ahead and markets the product, estimated losses would be £600,000. If, at any point, the company abandons the product, there would be a net gain of £50,000 from the sale of scrap. All the financial values have been discounted to the present.

Required

(a) Draw a decision tree.
(b) Include figures for cost, loss or profit on the appropriate branches of the tree.
(c) Evaluate the options and state what option you think should be chosen.

3.19 SOLUTION

(a) The starting point for the tree is to establish what decision has to be made now. What are the alternative options? In this case, they are to test market or to abandon.

(b) The outcome of the 'abandon' option is known with certainty. There are two possible outcomes of the option to test market, positive response and negative response.

(c) Depending on the outcome of the test market, another decision will then be made, to abandon the product or to go ahead with the market launch.

(d) This is the logical structure on which the decision tree should be drawn, as follows.

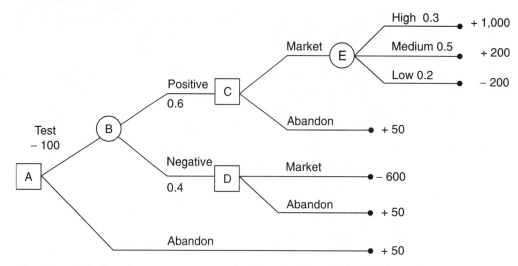

(e) The right-hand-most outcome point is point E, and the EV is as follows.

	Profit (£'000)	Probability	
	x	*p*	*px*
High	1,000	0.3	300
Medium	200	0.5	100
Low	(200)	0.2	(40)
			EV 360

This is the EV of the decision to market the product if the test market shows a positive response.

(f) (i) At decision point C, the choices are as follows.

- Market, EV + 360 (the EV at point E)
- Abandon, value + 50

The choice would be to market the product, and so the EV at decision point C is +360.

(ii) At decision point D, the choices are as follows.

- Market, value − 600
- Abandon, value +50

The choice would be to abandon, and so the EV at decision point D is +50.

The second stage decisions have therefore been made. If the original decision is to test market, the company will market the product if the test shows positive customer response, and will abandon the product if the test results are negative.

(g) The evaluation of the decision tree is completed as follows.

(i) Calculate the EV at outcome point B.

0.6×360 (EV at C) $+ 0.4 \times 50$ (EV at D) $= 216 + 20 = 236$

(ii) Compare the options at point A.

- Test: EV = EV at B minus test marketing cost = 236 − 100 = 136
- Abandon: value 50

The choice would be to test market the product, because it has a higher EV of profit.

Question 2

A software company has just won a contract worth £80,000 if it delivers a successful product on time, but only £40,000 if it is late. It faces the problem now of whether to produce the work in-house or to sub-contract it. To sub-contract the work would cost £30,000, but the local sub-contractor is so fast and reliable as to make it certain that successful software is produced on time.

If the work is produced in-house the cost would be only £20,000 but, based on past experience, would have only a 90% chance of being successful. In the event of the software *not* being successful, there would be insufficient time to rewrite the whole package internally, but there would still be the options of either a 'late rejection' of the contract (at a further cost of £10,000) or of 'late sub-contracting' the work on the same terms as before. With this late start the local sub-contractor is estimated to have only a 50/50 chance of producing the work on time or of producing it late. In this case the sub-contractor still has to be paid £30,000, regardless of whether he meets the deadline or not.

Required

(a) Draw a decision tree for the software company, using squares for decision points and circles for outcome (chance) points, including all relevant data on the diagram.

(b) Calculate expected values as appropriate and recommend a course of action to the software company with reasons.

Answer

(a) *All values in £'000*

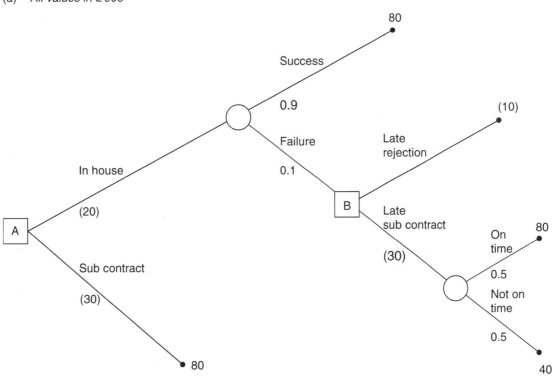

(b) *At decision point B*

EV of late rejection = −10
EV of late sub-contract = (80 × 0.5) + (40 × 0.5) − 30 = 30
The optimum strategy at B is therefore to subcontract with EV = 30.

At decision point A

EV of sub-contract = 80 − 30 = 50
EV of in-house = (80 × 0.9) + (30* × 0.1) − 20 = 55
The optimum strategy at A is therefore to produce in-house with EV = 55.
*This is the optimum EV at decision point B.

Conclusions

The decisions which will maximise expected profits are to attempt initially to produce in-house and if this fails to sub-contract. The expected profit is £55,000.

Assuming that the probabilities have been correctly estimated, the company has a 90% chance of making a profit of £60,000, a 5% chance of making £30,000 and a 5% chance of making a

£10,000 loss. If the company is not willing to risk making a loss, the initial option of subcontracting should be taken since this offers a guaranteed profit of £50,000.

Chapter roundup

- An **expected value** is a weighted average value based on probabilities. The expected value of a probability is equal to the sum of the products of each value of x and the corresponding probability of that value of x occurring

- **Decision trees** ensure that all possible choices and outcomes of a decision are taken into account by the adoption of a clear and logical approach.

- The steps in **rollback analysis**, which evaluates the EV of each decision option, are as follows.

    o   Work from right to left, to the particular decision under consideration.
    o   Label each decision point and outcome point.
    o   Work from left to right and calculate EVs at each outcome point.

Quick quiz

1   How do you calculate an expected value? (see para 1.1)

2   What is the drawback of the decision rule to choose the alternative with the highest EV of profit? (2.5)

3   How does a decision tree aid the answering of complex probability questions? (key terms, 3.1, 3.2)

4   What are the rules for drawing decision trees? (3.4 - 3.12)

Question to try	Level	Marks	Time
22	Examination	14	25 mins

Chapter 22

THE NORMAL DISTRIBUTION, ESTIMATION AND TESTING

Chapter topic list	Syllabus reference
1 Probability distributions	QT 4(b)
2 The normal distribution	QT 4(b)
3 Statistical inference	QT 6(d)
4 Sampling distribution of the mean	QT 4(b), 6(d)
5 The size of a sample	QT 6(d)
6 Hypothesis testing	QT 6(d)

Introduction

In Chapter 20 we looked at the calculation and interpretation of probability and uncertainty. This chapter begins by examining **probability distributions**. The importance of probability distributions is that they extend the areas to which probability can be applied and they provide a method of arriving at the probability of an event without having to go through all the probability rules examined in Chapter 20. We will then turn our attention to a particular probability distribution: the **normal distribution**.

Having examined the normal distribution we will use it to study **sampling theory**. Sampling theory allows us to make estimates of population values using information from samples.

Finally we will study **hypothesis testing**, which looks at whether or not a belief about a population is supported by sample values.

1 PROBABILITY DISTRIBUTIONS

1.1 On converting the frequencies into proportions, we get a **probability distribution**.

Marks out of 10 (statistics test)	Number of students (frequency distribution)	Proportion or probability (probability distribution)
0	0	0.00
1	0	0.00
2	1	0.02
3	2	0.04
4	4	0.08
5	10	0.20
6	15	0.30
7	10	0.20
8	6	0.12
9	2	0.04
10	0	0.00
	50	1.00

BPP PUBLISHING

> ### KEY TERM
>
> A **probability distribution** is an analysis of the proportion of times each particular value occurs in a set of items.

1.2 A graph of the probability distribution would be the same as the graph of the frequency distribution, but with the vertical axis marked in proportions rather than in numbers.

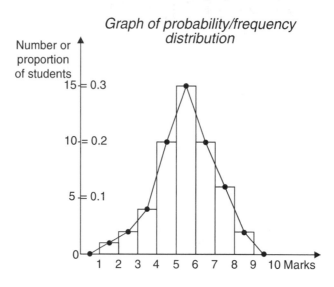

Graph of probability/frequency distribution

1.3 The area under the curve in the frequency distribution represents the total number of students whose marks have been recorded, 50 people. The area under the curve in a probability distribution is 100%, or 1 (the total of all the probabilities).

1.4 There are a number of different probability distributions but we shall confine our attention to just one: the **normal distribution**.

2 THE NORMAL DISTRIBUTION 12/96, 6/98

> ### Exam focus point
> Make sure that you are confident with reading normal distribution tables. Marks are allocated in the examination for correctly reading values from the tables.

2.1 The normal distribution is an important probability distribution which is often applied to **continuous variables**. In other words, in calculating P(x), x can be any value, and does not have to be a whole number.

2.2 Examples of continuous variables include the following.

   (a) The **heights of people**. The height of a person need not be an exact number of centimetres, but can be anything within a range of possible figures.

   (b) The **temperature of a room**. It need not be an exact number or degrees, but can fall anywhere within a range of possible values.

2.3 The normal distribution can also apply to **discrete variables** which can take **many possible values**. For example, the volume of sales, in units, of a product might be any whole number in the range 100 – 5,000 units. There are so many possibilities within this range that the variable is for all practical purposes continuous.

2.4   The normal distribution can be drawn as a graph, and it would be a **bell-shaped curve**.

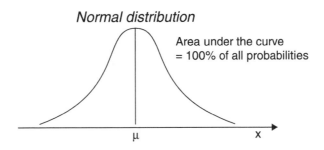

Normal distribution

Area under the curve
= 100% of all probabilities

2.5   Properties of the normal distribution are as follows.

- It is symmetrical.
- μ is the mean of the distribution (μ is pronounced 'mu').
- The area to the left of μ is the mirror image of the area to the right of μ.
- The area under the curve totals exactly 1.

2.6   The normal distribution is important because in the practical application of statistics, it has been found that **many probability distributions** are **close** enough **to a normal distribution** to be treated as one without any significant loss of accuracy.

The standard deviation and the normal distribution

2.7   For any normal distribution, the **dispersion** around the mean of the frequency of occurrences can be measured exactly in terms of the **standard deviation** (a concept we covered in Chapter 18).

2.8   The entire frequency curve represents all the possible outcomes and their frequencies of occurrence and the normal curve is **symmetrical**; therefore 50% of occurrences have a value greater than the mean value, and 50% of occurrences have a value less than the mean value.

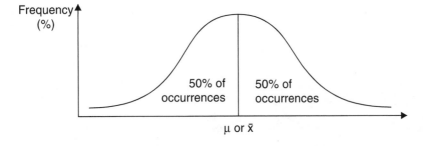

Frequency (%)

50% of occurrences

50% of occurrences

μ or $\bar{x}$

2.9   **About 68% of frequencies have a value within one standard deviation either side of the mean.** Thus if a normal distribution has a mean of 80 and a standard deviation of 3, 68% of the total frequencies would occur within the range ± one standard deviation from the mean, that is, within the range 77 – 83. Since the curve is symmetrical, 34% of the values must fall in the range 77 – 80 and 34% in the range 80 – 83.

BPP
PUBLISHING

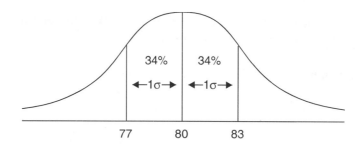

2.10 **95% of the frequencies in a normal distribution occur in the range ± 1.96 standard deviations from the mean.**

In our example, when μ = 80, and σ = 3, 95% of the frequencies in the distribution would occur in the range

80 ± 1.96 (3) = 80 ± 5.88 (the range 74.12 to 85.88)

47½% would be in the range 74.12 to 80 and 47½% would be in the range 80 to 85.88.

2.11 **99% of the frequencies occur in the range ± 2.58 standard deviations from the mean.**

In our example, 99% of frequencies in a normal distribution with μ = 80 and σ = 3 would lie in the range

80 ± 2.58 (3) = 80 ± 7.74 = 72.26 to 87.74.

Normal distribution tables

2.12 Although there is an infinite number of normal distributions, depending on values of the mean μ and the standard deviation σ, **the relative dispersion of frequencies around the mean, measured as proportions of the total population, is exactly the same for all normal distributions.** In other words, whatever the normal distribution, 47½% of outcomes will always be in the range between the mean and 1.96 standard deviations below the mean, 49.5% of outcomes will always be in the range between the mean and 2.58 standard deviations below the mean and so on.

2.13 A normal distribution table, shown in the Appendix at the end of this Study Text, gives the proportion of the total which lies above (or below) any point lying any number of standard deviation units above (or below) the mean. You will be given a copy of this table in your examination.

FORMULA TO LEARN

Distances above or below the mean are expressed in numbers of **standard deviations, z.**

$$z = \frac{x - \mu}{\sigma}$$

where z = the number of standard deviations above or below the mean
      x = the value of the variable under consideration
      μ = the mean
      σ = the standard deviation.

2.14 EXAMPLE: THE NORMAL DISTRIBUTION

A frequency distribution is normal, with a mean of 100 and a standard deviation of 10.

Required

Calculate the proportion of the total frequencies which will be:

(a)   above 80;
(b)   above 90;
(c)   above 100;
(d)   above 115;
(e)   below 85;
(f)   below 95;
(g)   below 108;
(h)   in the range 80 - 110;
(i)   in the range 90 - 95.

2.15 SOLUTION

Calculate the proportion of frequencies above a certain value as follows.

- If the value is below the mean, the total proportion is:

  0.5 plus proportion between the value and the mean.

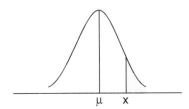

- If the value is above the mean, the proportion can be read straight from the table.

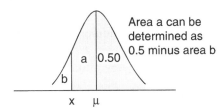

Calculate the proportion of frequencies below a certain value as follows.

- If the value is below the mean, the proportion required can be read straight from the table.

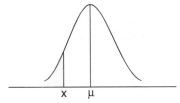

- If the value is above the mean, the proportion required is 0.5 plus the proportion between the value and the mean.

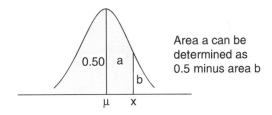

(a)   80 is $\frac{80-100}{10}$ = 2 standard deviations below the mean. From the tables, where

z = 2 the proportion is 0.02275.

The proportion of frequencies above 80 is 0.5 + (0.5 – 0.02275) = 0.5 + 0.47725 = 0.97725.

(b)   90 is $\frac{90-100}{10}$ = 1 standard deviation below the mean. From the tables, when

z = 1, the proportion is 0.1587.

The proportion of frequencies above 90 is 0.5 + (0.5 – 0.1587) = 0.5 + 0.3413 = 0.8413.

(c)   100 is the mean. The proportion above this is 0.5.

(d)   115 is $\frac{115-100}{10}$ = 1.5 standard deviations above the mean. From the tables, where z

= 1.5, the proportion is 0.0668.

The proportion of frequencies above 115 is therefore 0.0668.

(e)   85 is 1.5 standard deviations below the mean. The proportion of frequencies   below 85
is therefore the same as the proportion above 115, 0.0668.

(f)   95 is $\frac{95-100}{10}$ = 0.5 standard deviations below the mean. When z = 0.5, the proportion

from the tables is 0.3085. The proportion of frequencies below 95 is therefore 0.3085.

(g)   108 is $\frac{108-100}{10}$ = 0.8 standard deviations above the mean. From the tables for

z = 0.8 the proportion is 0.2119.

The proportion of frequencies below 108 is 0.5 + (0.5 – 0.2119) = 0.5 + 0.2881 = 0.7881.

(h)   The range 80 to 110 may be divided into two parts:

(i)   80 to 100 (the mean);
(ii)   100 to 110.

The proportion in the range 80 to 100 is (2 standard deviations) 0.47725

The proportion in the range 100 to 110 is (1 standard deviation) 0.3413

The proportion in the total range 80 to 110 is 0.47725 + 0.3413 = 0.81855

(i)   The range 90 to 95 may be analysed as:

(i)   the proportion below 95;
(ii)   minus the proportion below 90.

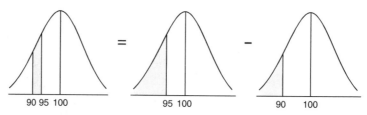

above 95 (and below the mean).

Proportion below 95 (0.5 standard deviations)	0.3085
Proportion above below 90 (1 standard deviation)	0.1587
Proportion between 90 and 95	0.1498

Question 1

The salaries of employees in an industry are normally distributed, with a mean of £14,000 and a standard deviation of £2,700.

Required

(a) Calculate the proportion of employees who earn less than £12,000.

(b) Calculate the proportion of employees who earn between £11,000 and £19,000.

Answer

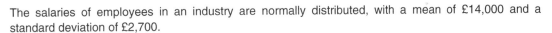

(a) (12,000 – 14,000)/2,700 = –0.74

From tables, the proportion of the normal distribution more than 0.74 standard deviations below the mean is 0.2296.

(b) (11,000 – 14,000)/2,700 = –1.11

(19,000 – 14,000)/2,700 = 1.85

The proportion with earnings between £11,000 and £14,000 is 0.5 – 0.1335 = 0.3665.

The proportion with earnings between £14,000 and £19,000 is 0.5 – 0.0322 = 0.4678.

The required proportion is 0.3665 + 0.4678 = 0.8343.

2.16 Note that **the normal distribution is, in fact, a way of calculating probabilities**. In the previous question, for example, the **probability** that an employee earns less than £12,000 (part (a)) is 0.2296 and the probability that an employee earns between £11,000 and £19,000 is 0.8343.

3   STATISTICAL INFERENCE

3.1 During the run up to a general election we are bombarded with the results of countless opinion polls predicting who will be forming the next government, but have you ever wondered about the basis for these predictions? It would be almost physically impossible and financially undesirable to question the entire population of the country so small samples are taken and opinions gleaned from the samples. From these results the pollsters can then infer the opinions of the entire population.

> **KEY TERM**
>
> **Statistical inference** is a process by which conclusions are drawn about some measure or attribute of a population based upon analysis of sample data.

3.2 Samples are taken and analysed in order to draw conclusions about the whole population. A sample is ideally **representative of the population** from which it is taken.

3.3 Sampling is **quicker** and **cheaper** than testing the entire population and is often the only feasible method of obtaining information about the population.

4 SAMPLING DISTRIBUTION OF THE MEAN 12/94, 6/99, 12/99

> **KEY TERM**
>
> A **sampling distribution of the mean** is a frequency distribution of the mean of a large number of samples.

4.1 Suppose that we wish to estimate the mean of a population, say the average weight of a product made in a factory. A sample of, say, 100 units of the product might be taken, and the mean weight per unit of the sample might be, say, 5.8 kg.

Another sample of 100 units might then be taken and the mean weight might be, say, 6.3 kg.

A large number of samples might be taken and the mean of each sample calculated. These means will not all be the same and they can be plotted as a frequency distribution. This distribution is called a **sampling distribution of the mean**.

4.2 In our example, a frequency distribution of the mean weight per unit in each of 250 samples (of 100 units per sample) might be as follows.

Mean weight per unit kg	Mid-point of class interval	Frequency (No of samples)
5.45 and < 5.55	5.5	3
5.55 and < 5.65	5.6	7
5.65 and < 5.75	5.7	16
5.75 and < 5.85	5.8	30
5.85 and < 5.95	5.9	44
5.95 and < 6.05	6.0	50
6.05 and < 6.15	6.1	44
6.15 and < 6.25	6.2	30
6.25 and < 6.35	6.3	16
6.35 and < 6.45	6.4	7
6.45 and < 6.55	6.5	3
		250 samples

The mean weight per unit of 100 units in a sample might thus range from 5.45 to 6.55 kg. The true mean of the population, that is, the true mean weight of all units produced, presumably lies somewhere within this range.

4.3 A sampling distribution of the mean has the following important properties.

(a) It is very close to being normally distributed.

(b) The mean of the sampling distribution is the same as the population mean, μ. Thus by using sample data, we are able to make estimates about the mean of the population.

(c) The sampling distribution has a standard deviation which is called the **standard error of the mean**.

4.4 (a) In our example, the 250 samples give an estimate of the population mean. This distribution of sample means would be (approximately) normally distributed, with a mean of about 6 kg (weight per unit of product).

(b) This mean of 6 kg would be the same as the population mean, μ, so that we would be able to state that the true population mean is about 6 kg.

(c) The standard deviation of the sampling distribution (which could be calculated as 0.2 kg: workings not shown) is the standard error (se).

The standard error

4.5   Since, σ is not normally known, we take **the standard deviation of the sample (s) to be the best estimate of the standard deviation of the whole population (σ).**

4.6   For reasons which will become apparent in later studies, we will use a formula for s which is slightly different from that used to find the standard deviation of a population when we have data on every member.

The central limit theorem

4.7   **The greater the sample size, the more closely will the sampling distribution approximate to a normal distribution.**

Confidence levels, limits and intervals

4.8   From our knowledge of the properties of a normal distribution, together with the rule that sample means are normally distributed around the true population mean, with a standard deviation equal to the standard error, we can predict (using normal distribution tables) the following.

- 68% of all sample means will be within one standard error of the population mean.
- 95% of all sample means will be within 1.96 standard errors of the population mean.
- 99% of all sample means will be within 2.58 standard errors of the population mean.

4.9   Let us look at it another way.

- With 68% probability, the population mean lies within the range: sample mean ± one standard error.

- With 95% probability, the population mean lies within the range: sample mean ± 1.96 standard errors.

- With 99% probability, the population mean lies within the range: sample mean ± 2.58 standard errors.

These degrees of certainty (such as 95%) are known as **confidence levels**, and the ends of the ranges (such as sample mean + 2.58 standard errors) around the sample mean are called **confidence limits**. The ranges (such as sample mean ± one standard error) are called **confidence intervals**.

EXAM FORMULA

Confidence intervals can be calculated using the following formula

$$\bar{x} \pm z\, \sigma/\sqrt{n}$$

where z is the number of standard errors

4.10 EXAMPLE: CONFIDENCE INTERVALS

From a random sample of 576 of a company's 20,000 employees, it was found that the average number of days each person was absent from work due to illness was eight days a year, with a standard deviation (found using the formula with n–1 as the denominator) of 3.6 days.

Required

Calculate the confidence limits for the average number of days absence a year through sickness per employee for the company as a whole at the following confidence levels.

(a) 95%
(b) 99%

4.11 SOLUTION

We must first calculate the standard error, which is estimated as $s/\sqrt{n}$ (because we do not know the standard deviation of the entire population).

se = $3.6/\sqrt{576}$ = 0.15.

(a) At the 95% level of confidence z = 1.96 and therefore the true average number of days absence a year is in the range $8 \pm (1.96 \times 0.15)$

   = 8 ± 0.294 = 7.706 days to 8.294 days, say 7.7 days to 8.3 days.

(b) At the 99% level of confidence z = 2.58 and therefore the true average number of days absence a year is in the range 8 ± (2.58 × 0.15)

= 8 ± 0.387 = 7.613 days to 8.387 days, say 7.6 days to 8.4 days.

4.12 Why is it necessary to calculate confidence limits? If the sample mean were eight days would it not be sufficient to use eight days as a point estimate of the population mean?

4.13 In practice, a sample mean might indeed be used as a 'point estimate' of the population mean. However, we could not be sure how reliable the estimate might be, without first considering the size of the standard error. The sample mean might be above or below the true population mean, but we can say with 95% confidence that the sample mean is no more than 1.96 standard errors above or below the true population mean. We are therefore 95% confident that the average number of days absence a year through sickness per employee is in the range 7.7 days to 8.3 days.

4.14 If the confidence limits cover a wide range of values, a point estimate of the population mean from the sample would not be reliable. On the other hand, if the confidence limits cover a narrow range of values, a point estimate of the population mean, using the sample mean, would be reliable.

Question 2

The cost of assembling an item of equipment has been estimated by obtaining a sample of 144 jobs. The average cost of assembly derived from the sample was £4,000 with a standard deviation of £1,500.

Required

Estimate confidence limits for the true average cost of assembly. Use the 95% level of confidence.

Answer

The standard error is estimated as 1,500/√144 = £125.

At the 95% level of confidence, the population mean is in the range £(4,000 ± (1.96 × 125)) = £(4,000 ± 245), that is, £3,755 to £4,245.

Sampling distribution of a proportion

4.15 The **arithmetic mean** is a very important statistic, and sampling is often concerned with **estimating the mean of a population**. Many surveys, however, especially those concerned with attitudes or opinions about an issue or the percentage of times an event occurs (for example, the proportion of faulty items out of the total number of items produced in a manufacturing department) attempt to estimate a proportion rather than an arithmetic mean.

Suppose for example, that we wished to know what proportion of an electorate intends to vote for the Jacobin party at the forthcoming general election. Several samples might be obtained, and the proportion of pro-Jacobin voters in a sample might vary, say from 37% to 45%. The central limit theorem would apply, and the proportion of pro-Jacobin voters in each sample could be arranged into a **sampling distribution** (the sampling distribution of a proportion) with the following features.

- It is normally distributed.
- It has a mean equal to the proportion of pro-Jacobin voters in the population.
- It has a standard deviation equal to the standard error of a proportion.

EXAM FORMULAE

- The **standard error of a proportion** is $\sqrt{\dfrac{p(1-p)}{n}}$

  where   p is the proportion in the population
  n is the size of the sample

  We use the sample proportion p as an estimate of the population proportion.

- **Confidence intervals** can therefore be calculated using the formula:

  $$\hat{p} \pm z\sqrt{\frac{p(1-p)}{n}}$$

  where $\hat{p}$ is the sample proportion and z the number of standard errors.

4.16 EXAMPLE: A CONFIDENCE INTERVAL FOR A PROPORTION

In a random sample of 500 out of 100,000 employees, 320 were members of a trade union. Estimate the proportion of trade union members in the entire organisation at the 95% confidence level.

4.17 SOLUTION

The sample proportion is 320/500 = 0.64.

$$\text{Standard error} = \sqrt{\frac{0.64 \times (1-0.64)}{500}} = \sqrt{\frac{0.64 \times 0.36}{500}} = 0.0215$$

An estimate of the population proportion at the 95% confidence level (z = 1.96) is the sample proportion ± 1.96 standard errors.

The population proportion is 0.64 ± (1.96 × 0.0215) = 0.64 ± 0.04. The percentage of employees who are trade union members is between 60% and 68% at the 95% level of confidence.

Question 3

A researcher wishes to know the proportion of people who regularly travel by train. Of a sample of 400 people, 285 said they did so.

Required

Estimate the population proportion with 99% confidence.

Answer

The sample proportion is 285/400 = 0.7125.

The standard error is $\sqrt{\dfrac{0.7125 \times (1-0.7125)}{400}} = 0.0226$

The 99% confidence interval for the population proportion is

  0.7125 ± (2.58 × 0.0226)

= 0.7125 ± 0.0583

= 0.6542 to 0.7708

5 THE SIZE OF A SAMPLE

12/94, 6/96, 6/99, 12/99

Selecting a sample size in order to estimate the arithmetic mean

5.1 Suppose that a trade association wants to find out the average salary to within £10 of all those working in the trade in question. A previous investigation estimated it to be £18,000, with a standard deviation of £50. How could the trade association decide on the size of the sample required to be able to estimate the true average salary to within £10?

5.2 We know that, at the 95% level of confidence, the population mean = $\bar{x} \pm 1.96$ se (where $\bar{x}$ is a sample mean). If we require the estimate to be within $\pm £10$ then 1.96 se $= 10$

$$\therefore 1.96\,\sigma/\sqrt{n} = 10$$

$$\therefore \frac{1.96 \times £50}{\sqrt{n}} = 10$$

$$\therefore \left(\frac{1.96 \times £50}{10}\right)^2 = n = 96.04, \text{ say } 97 \text{ (we have to round up)}$$

A sample size of 97 is therefore required to be able to estimate the true mean salary to within $\pm £10$.

5.3 In general terms the size of sample required to estimate a population mean with a sufficient degree of accuracy ® at a given level of confidence $= n = (1.96\sigma/r)^2$. An estimate must be provided for σ even before the sample is collected. At the 99% confidence level, 1.96 is replaced by 2.58.

EXAM FORMULA

The **sample size required in order to calculate the arithmetic mean with sufficient accuracy** is

$$n \geq \left(\frac{zs}{I}\right)^2$$

where   z   = the number of standard errors
        s   = standard deviation of the population
        I   = degree of accuracy required in terms of units from the true mean
        n   = sample size required

5.4 EXAMPLE: SAMPLE SIZES

The management of a company making a certain type of car component wish to ascertain the average number of components per hour produced by the workers. Based on a previous sample, it is estimated that the average number produced by each employee every hour is

100, with a standard deviation of 25. The management now wish to know the true average to within two units. Calculate the sample size at the 99% confidence level.

5.5 SOLUTION

At a 99% level of confidence, $n = [2.58 \times 25/2]^2 = 32.25^2$

$= 1,040.06$ workers, say 1,041.

To have 99% confidence about the accuracy of the sample mean as an estimate of the population mean to within two units, the sample size would need to be 1,041 workers.

Selecting a sample size in order to estimate a proportion

5.6 Let r be the degree of accuracy required, expressed as units of the population proportion. Thus if we require an estimate of the proportion which is accurate to within 3%, r would be 0.03. We know that, at the 95% level of confidence:

$$r = 1.96 \text{ se} = 1.96 \sqrt{[pq/n]}$$

$$r^2 = \frac{1.96^2 \times pq}{n}$$

$$n = \frac{1.96^2 \times pq}{r^2}$$

At the 99% confidence level, 1.96 is replaced by 2.58.

EXAM FORMULA

The sample size required in order to calculate the proportion of a population with sufficient accuracy is

$$n \geq \frac{z^2 p(1 - p)}{I^2}$$

where z = the number of standard errors
         p = the population proportion
         I = degree of accuracy required in terms of units from the true mean
         n = sample size required

5.7 EXAMPLE: SAMPLE SIZES FOR ESTIMATING PROPORTIONS

A manufacturer wishes to estimate the proportion of defective components. He would be satisfied if he obtained an estimate within 0.5% of the true proportion, and was 99% confident of his result. An initial (large) sample indicated that p = 0.02. Determine the size of sample that he should examine.

5.8 SOLUTION

p =   0.02, therefore q = 1 – p = 0.98
r =   0.5% = 0.005

At a 99% level of confidence

$$n = \frac{2.58^2 \times 0.02 \times 0.98}{0.005^2}$$

$$= 5{,}218.6 \text{ units, say } 5{,}219 \text{ units}$$

The sample would need to consist of 5,219 units.

5.9 If we have no initial idea of the population proportion, we work out a required sample size using $p = 0.5$, as this gives the largest possible value for $p(1 - p)$, and hence the largest possible value for n. We will thus at least achieve the required accuracy.

Sample sizes and the standard error

> **Exam focus point**
> In 12/94 there were 3 marks to be gained for describing how and why the standard error changes with the sample size.

5.10 The standard error is given as $\sigma / \sqrt{n}$. As the **sample size increases, the standard error therefore decreases** (since σ remains the same whatever the sample size). In other words, the variability of the data around the mean decreases the larger the sample size taken.

Sample sizes from an administrative viewpoint

5.11 Remember that as well as calculating a sample size from a statistical point of view other, administrative-type, factors may have to be taken into account. These factors are summarised below.

(a) Two basic statistical facts

(i) The larger the sample size, the more precise will be the information given about the population.

(ii) Above a certain size, little extra information is given by increasing the size.

A sample therefore only need be large enough to be reasonably representative of the population.

(b) The amount of money and time available

(c) Aims of the survey

(d) Degree of precision required

(e) Number of sub-samples required

6 HYPOTHESIS TESTING

What is hypothesis testing?

> **KEY TERM**
>
> **Hypothesis testing** is the process of setting up a theory or hypothesis about some characteristics of the population and then sampling in order to ascertain whether the hypothesis is supported or not.

6.1 Hypothesis testing, (or **significance testing** as it is sometimes called) is the process of testing a belief or opinion by statistical means. For example, if we choose to test the belief that all BBP employees drive to work, we would need to establish the following **hypotheses**.

(a) The **null hypothesis**. This is the first hypothesis which we need to state, and in our example it would be our claim '**All BPP employees drive to work**'.

(b) The **alternative hypothesis**. This hypothesis describes the alternative situation to the null hypothesis, ie what the situation will be if the null hypothesis were in fact not true. In our example, this second hypothesis would be stated as '**Not all BPP employees drive to work**'.

6.2 Once we have started our hypotheses, we might wish to ask a sample of BPP's employees whether they drive to work, and each employee questioned should answer '**yes**' or '**no**'. The emphasis here is therefore, on testing whether a set of sample results support or are consistent with the **null hypothesis** 'All BPP employees drive to work'. Look carefully at the step-by-step guide to hypothesis testing in the next paragraph.

6.3 The procedure for hypothesis testing is as follows.

Step 1. State the following hypotheses:
H_0 **null hypothesis** eg the mean value of a company's invoices is £200
H_1 **alternative hypothesis** eg the mean value of a company's invoices is **not** £200

Step 2. Select a **significance level**. This is the chance we take of wrongly rejecting the null hypothesis

Step 3. **Test** the null hypothesis. Are the sample results near enough what we would expect to get if the H_0 were true?

Step 4. Draw a **conclusion**

6.4 Bear in mind that with hypothesis testing we are dealing with **samples** and can never be 100% sure of our results. We therefore conduct our tests at a **particular level**, for example 5% or 1%. These percentages represent the chance of drawing the wrong conclusion.

6.5 EXAMPLE: HYPOTHESIS TESTING (1) (A TWO-TAIL TEST)

A company's management accountant has estimated that the average direct cost of providing a certain service to a customer is £40.

A sample has been taken, consisting of 150 service provisions, and the mean direct cost for the sample was £45 with a standard deviation (adjusted by Bessel's correction factor) of £10.

Required

Assess whether the sample is consistent with the estimate of an average cost of £40.

6.6 SOLUTION

Step 1. Let H_0 be that the average direct cost per unit of service is £40
Let H_1 be that the average direct cost per unit of service is **not** £40

Step 2. **Select a significance level**. Here, we will use 5%. 5% is a common choice. The lower the significance level, the lower the probability of wrongly rejecting the null hypothesis, but the higher the probability of wrongly accepting it. However, the probability of wrongly accepting the null hypothesis is *not* (100 - significance level) %. You do not need to know how to compute this probability.

Our choice of 5% means that we shall assume that the sample mean (£45) is consistent with our estimated population mean (£40) provided that the sample mean is within what would be a 100% – 5% = 95% confidence interval around a sample mean equal to the mean given by H_0.

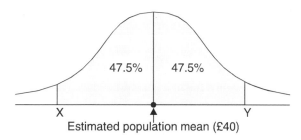

Estimated population mean (£40)

You may prefer to think of this in terms of the diagram above. If the sample mean of £45 is within the range from X to Y, we will conclude that our null hypothesis is acceptable.

X and Y are each 1.96 standard errors from the mean. From our sample, we can calculate the standard error as $s/\sqrt{n} = 10/\sqrt{150} = 0.816$.

Step 3. **Test the null hypothesis**. The sample mean is £5 higher than our hypothesised population mean, and this is 5/0.816 = 6.1 standard errors above the mean.

At the 5% level of significance we would expect the sample mean to be within 1.96 standard errors of the hypothesised mean. It is not, and so at this level of significance, we reject the null hypothesis.

Step 4. **Conclusion**. The average direct cost per unit of service is not £40, and the management accountant is wrong.

6.7 EXAMPLE: HYPOTHESIS TESTING (2) (A ONE-TAIL TEST)

In a manufacturing operation, the standard level of scrapped units is 8% of input. During one week, 18,400 units were input to the operation of which 1,580 were scrapped.

Required

Assess whether the level of rejects appears to exceed the expected level. Test at the 5% level of significance.

6.8 SOLUTION

Step 1. Let H_0 be that the true level of rejects is 8% or 0.08.
Let H_1 be that the level of rejects is greater than 8%.

The actual level of rejects is $\dfrac{1,580}{18,400} = 0.08587$

Step 2. **Select a significance level**. This has already be stated in the question. We must therefore establish a limit for the number of units scrapped, so as to ensure that there is only a 5% probability of the number of rejects in the sample exceeding the limit, if the average rejection rate for the population is in fact 8%. This may be shown in a diagram as follows.

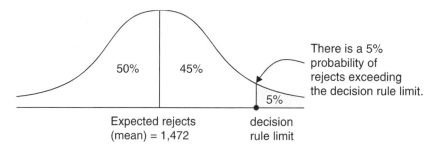

Expected rejects   decision
(mean) = 1,472   rule limit

The decision rule limit (as shown in the diagram) must be such that there is only a 5% probability of the actual scrapped units in the sample being a greater amount. This means that 95% of the frequency distribution must lie to the left hand side of the limit. From normal distribution tables, 0.05 of the distribution lies more than 1.65 standard errors above the mean.

The standard error of the proportion, calculated from the proportion in the null hypothesis, is $\sqrt{[pq/n]} = \sqrt{[0.08 \times 0.92/18,400]} = 0.002$.

Step 3. **Test the null hypothesis**. The actual level of rejects is 0.00587 above the expected level. This represents $0.00587/0.002 = 2.935$ standard errors.

At the 5% level of significance, we would expect the sample proportion to be not more than 1.65 standard errors above the hypothesised mean. It is not since it is 2.935 standard errors above the hypothesised mean. We therefore reject the null hypothesis and conclude that the level of rejects is higher than 8% (at the 5% level of significance).

Step 4. **Conclusion**. The level of rejects is higher than 8% at the 5% level of significance.

One-tail tests and two-tail tests

6.9   There are two different types of hypothesis test.

- One-tail (one sided)
- Two-tail (two sided)

6.10   **One-tail tests** are used to determine at a given level of significance whether the results from a sample differ from expected results in **one direction** only and the alternative hypothesis is of the form

- 'is less than' or
- 'is greater than'

6.11   **Two-tail tests** are used to determine whether the sample results differ from expected results in **two directions**. The alternative hypothesis is generally of the form '**does not equal**'.

Question 4

It is thought that the mean net weight of bags of sugar produced by a machine is at least 1.03 kg. A sample of 230 bags had a mean net weight of 1.02 kg, with a standard deviation of weights of 0.02 kg.

Required

Test the hypothesis that the population mean is at least 1.03 kg at the 1% significance level.

Answer

$H_0 : \mu \geq 1.03$ kg

$H_1 : \mu < 1.03$ kg

This is a one-tail test, so the critical value for 1% significance is -2.33. (The minus sign is put in because we will reject H_0 if the sample mean is more than 2.33 standard errors *below* the hypothesised mean.)

Standard error = $0.02/\sqrt{230}$ = 0.00132

$(1.02 - 1.03)/0.00132$ = -7.58.

H_0 should be rejected. There is clear evidence that the population mean weight is below 1.03 kg.

Chapter roundup

- The **normal distribution** is a probability distribution which usually applies to variables with a **continuous range of possible values** (continuous variables), such as distance and time. The distribution can be drawn as a bell-shaped curve, the area under the curve being exactly equal to one. The distance of a point above or below the mean is expressed in numbers of standard deviations, z, and 68%/95%/99% of frequencies are $\pm 1/\pm 1.96/\pm 2.58$ standard deviations from the mean.

- If a large number of samples are taken from the population, their means calculated and the means plotted as a frequency distribution, this distribution (the sampling distribution of the mean) will be very close to being normally distributed (**central limit theorem**).

- The mean of this sampling distribution is the same as the population mean, μ. The standard deviation of the distribution is called the **standard error of the mean (se)** and is estimated using the **standard deviation, s, of a sample**.

- Armed with knowledge of the central limit theorem and properties of the sampling distribution of the mean, we can say, with a certain **level of confidence** and using sample data, the range within which the true population mean falls.

- As well as being able to do this, you should also be able to calculate the **size of the sample** required to obtain a sufficient degree of accuracy at a given level of confidence in the estimation of the population mean.

- The **sampling distribution of a proportion** is normally distributed, has a mean equal to the **population proportion** and has a standard deviation called the **standard error of a proportion**.

- **Hypothesis testing** looks at whether or not a belief about a population is supported by sample values.

Quick quiz

1   What is the area under a curve in a probability distribution? (see para 1.3)

2   What is the formula for the number of standard deviations z? (formulae to learn)

3   What is the sampling distribution of the mean? (key terms)

4   What is the statistical rule covered by the central limit theorem? (key terms)

5   What is the standard error of the mean? (4.3)

6   What is the formula for the standard error of the mean? (exam formulae)

7   What is used as the best estimate of the standard deviation of the whole population when calculating the standard error? (4.5)

8   Define confidence intervals, confidence levels and confidence limits. (4.9)

9   What are the features of a sampling distribution of a proportion? (4.15)

10 What is the formula for the standard error of a proportion? (exam formulae)

11 What administrative-type factors need to be taken into account when deriving a sample size? (5.11)

12 What is the procedure for hypothesis testing? (6.1)

13 What is a one-tail test? (6.10)

Question to try	Level	Marks	Time
23	Examination	14	25 mins

Part E
Business mathematics

Chapter 23

EQUATIONS

Chapter topic list	Syllabus reference
1 Linear equations	QT 3(b)
2 Linear equations and graphs	QT 3(a), (b)
3 Simultaneous linear equations	QT 3(a), (b); CA 2(c) (ii)
4 Non-linear equations	QT 3(a)
5 Quadratic equations	QT 3(a), (b)

Introduction

You are over the moon. You have just been awarded a £1,000 pay rise. If the man on the Clapham omnibus asks you to explain your new salary in terms of your old salary, what would you say? You might say something like 'my new salary equals my old salary plus £1,000'. Easy. What would you say, on the other hand, to the mathematics professor who asks you to give a mathematical equation which describes your new salary in terms of your old salary? Like many students, you may be perfectly capable of answering the man on the omnibus, but not the professor. Your reply to the professor should be something like 'y = x + 1,000' but many students get completely confused when they have to deal with mathematical symbols and letters instead of simple words. There is, however, no need to worry about equations: they are simply a shorthand method of expressing words. Work through this chapter and it should help to make things clearer.

1   LINEAR EQUATIONS

Structure

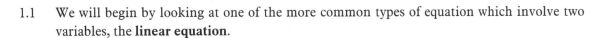

KEY TERM

An **equation** is an expression of the relationship between variables.

1.1   We will begin by looking at one of the more common types of equation which involve two variables, the **linear equation**.

1.2   Let us establish some basic linear equations. Suppose that it takes Joe Bloggs 15 minutes to walk one mile. How long does it take Joe to walk two miles? Obviously it takes him 30 minutes. How did you calculate the time? You probably thought that if the distance is doubled then the time must be doubled. How do you explain (in words) the relationships between the distance walked and the time taken? One explanation would be that every mile walked takes 15 minutes.

1.3   That is an explanation in words. Can you explain the relationship with an equation?

1.4 First you must decide which is the **dependent variable** and which is the **independent variable**. In other words, does the time taken depend on the number of miles walked or does the number of miles walked depend on the time it takes to walk a mile? Obviously the time depends on the distance. We can therefore let **y be the dependent variable** (time taken in minutes) and **x be the independent variable** (distance walked in miles).

1.5 We now need to **determine** the **constants a and b**. There is no fixed amount so a = 0. To ascertain b, we need to establish the number of times by which the value of x should be multiplied to derive the value of y. Obviously y = 15x where y is in minutes. If y were in hours then y = $^x/_4$.

FORMULA TO LEARN

A **linear equation** has the general form $y = a + bx$

where   y   is the dependent variable, depending for its value on the value of x;

        x   is the independent variable whose value helps to determine the corresponding value of y;

        a   is a constant, that is, a fixed amount;

        b   is also a constant, being the coefficient of x (that is, the number by which the value of x should be multiplied to derive the value of y).

1.6 EXAMPLE: DERIVING A LINEAR EQUATION

A salesman's weekly wage is made up of a basic weekly wage of £100 and commission of £5 for every item he sells.

Required

Derive an equation which describes this scenario.

1.7 SOLUTION

    x   = number of items sold
    y   = weekly wage
    a   = £100
    b   = £5
∴ y   = 5x + 100

1.8 Note that the letters used in an equation do not have to be x and y. It may be sensible to use other letters, for example we could use p and q if we are describing the relationship between the price of an item and the quantity demanded.

Exam focus point

It is vital that you are able to construct, rearrange and solve equations confidently. Many exam questions will require that you are able to do so.

2   LINEAR EQUATIONS AND GRAPHS

2.1   One of the clearest ways of presenting the relationship between two variables is by plotting a **linear equation** as a **straight line** on a graph.

The rules for drawing graphs

2.2   A **graph** has a **horizontal** axis, the **x axis** and a **vertical** axis, the **y axis**. The **x axis** is used to represent the **independent** variable and the **y axis** is used to represent the **dependent** variable.

2.3   If calender time is one variable, it is always treated as the independent variable. When time is represented on the x axis of a graph, we have a time series.

2.4   (a)   If the data to be plotted are derived from calculations, rather than given in the question, make sure that there is a neat table in your working papers.

   (b)   The scales on each axis should be selected so as to use as much of the graph paper as possible. Do not cramp a graph into one corner.

   (c)   In some cases it is best not to start a scale at zero so as to avoid having a large area of wasted paper. This is acceptable as long as the scale adopted is clearly shown on the axis. One way of avoiding confusion is to break the axis concerned, as follows.

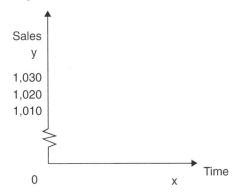

   (d)   The scales on the x axis and the y axis should be marked. For example, if the y axis relates to amounts of money, the axis should be marked at every £1, or £100 or at whatever other interval is appropriate. The axes must be marked with values to give the reader an idea of how big the values on the graph are.

   (e)   A graph should not be overcrowded with too many lines. Graphs should always give a clear, neat impression.

   (f)   A graph must always be given a title, and where appropriate, a reference should be made to the source of data.

2.5   EXAMPLE: DRAWING GRAPHS

Plot the graph for the relationship $y = 4x + 5$. Consider the range of values from $x = 0$ to $x = 10$.

2.6   SOLUTION

The first step is to draw up a table. Although the problem mentions $x = 0$ to $x = 10$, it is not necessary to calculate values of y for $x = 1, 2, 3$ etc. A graph of a linear equation can actually be drawn from just two (x, y) values but it is always best to calculate a number of values in case you make an arithmetical error. We have calculated six values.

x	0	2	4	6	8	10
y	5	13	21	29	37	45

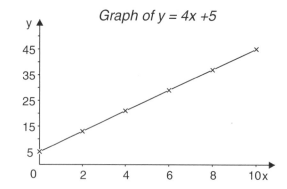

The intercept and the slope

2.7 The graph of a linear equation is determined by two things, the **gradient** (or slope) of the straight line and the point at which the straight line crosses the y axis.

2.8 The point at which the straight line crosses the y axis is known as the **intercept**. Look back at Paragraph 2.6. The intercept of $y = 4x + 5$ is (0, 5). It is no coincidence that the intercept is the same as the constant represented by a in the general form of the equation $y = a + bx$. a is the value y takes when $x = 0$, in other words a constant, and so is represented on a graph by the point (0, a).

2.9 The gradient of the graph of a linear equation is $(y_2 - y_1)/(x_2 - x_1)$ where (x_1, y_1) and (x_2, y_2) are two points on the straight line.

The slope of $y = 4x + 5 = (21 - 13)/(4 - 2) = 8/2 = 4$ where $(x_1, y_1) = (2, 13)$ and $(x_2, y_2) = (4, 21)$

Question 1

Find the gradient of $y = 10 - x$

Answer

Gradient $= -1$

2.10 Note that the gradient of $y = 4x + 5$ is positive whereas the gradient of $y = 10 - x$ is negative. A positive gradient slopes upwards from left to right whereas a negative gradient slopes downwards from left to right. The greater the value of the gradient, the steeper the slope.

2.11 Just as the intercept can be found by inspection of the linear equation, so can the gradient. It is represented by the coefficient of x (b in the general form of the equation). The slope of the graph $y = 7x - 3$ is therefore 7 and the slope of the graph $y = 3,597 - 263x$ is -263.

Question 2

Find the intercept and slope of the graph $4y = 16x - 12$

Answer

$4y = 16x - 12$

Equation must be form $y = a + bx$

$$y = -\frac{12}{4} + \frac{16}{4}x = -3 + 4x$$

Intercept = a = –3 ie (0, –3)

Slope = 4

---

3   SIMULTANEOUS LINEAR EQUATIONS

KEY TERM

Simultaneous equations are two or more equations which are satisfied by the same variable values.

3.1   Examples of linear equations are as follows.

$$y = 3x + 16$$
$$2y = x + 72$$

3.2   There are two unknown values, x and y, and there are two different equations which both involve x and y. There are as many equations as there are unknowns and so we can find the values of x and y.

Exam focus point

In the June 1998 exam, candidates were given the total cost function for a product and asked to explain the cost behaviour assumptions implied by this equation. For example, if a product has total costs equal to 200x + 50,000, this implies that the product has variable costs of £200 per unit and fixed costs of £50,000 which are incurred at any level of production or sales. Be prepared to interpret equations as well as solve them.

Graphical solution

3.3   One way of finding a solution is by a graph. If both equations are satisfied together, the values of x and y are where the straight line graphs of the equations intersect.

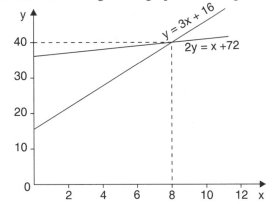

Since both equations are satisfied, the values of x and y must lie on both the lines. Since this happens only once, at the intersection of the lines, the values are x = 8, y = 40.

Algebraic solution

3.4   A more common method of solving simultaneous equations is by algebra.

(a)   Returning to the original equations, we have:

$$y = 3x + 16 \qquad (1)$$
$$2y = x + 72 \qquad (2)$$

(b) Rearranging these, we have:

$$y - 3x = 16 \qquad (3)$$
$$2y - x = 72 \qquad (4)$$

(c) If we now multiply equation (4) by 3, so that the coefficient for x becomes the same as in equation (3) we get:

$$6y - 3x \quad = 216 \qquad (5)$$
$$y - 3x \quad = 16 \qquad (3)$$

(d) Subtracting (3) from (5) we get:

$$5y \quad = 200$$
$$y \quad = 40$$

(e) Substituting 40 for y in any equation, we can derive a value for x. Thus substituting in equation (4) we get:

$$2(40) - x \quad = 72$$
$$80 - 72 \quad = x$$
$$8 \qquad = x$$

(f) The solution is y = 40, x = 8.

Question 3

Solve the following simultaneous equations to derive values for x and y.

$$4x + 3y = 23 \qquad (1)$$
$$5x - 4y = -10 \qquad (2)$$

Answer

If we multiply equation (1) by 4 and equation (2) by 3, we will obtain coefficients of +12 and −12 for y in our two products.

$$16x + 12y = 92 \qquad (3)$$
$$15x - 12y = -30 \qquad (4)$$

Add (3) and (4).

$$31x = 62$$
$$x = 2$$

Substitute x = 2 into (1)

$$4(2) + \quad 3y \quad = \quad 23$$
$$3y \quad = \quad 23 - 8 = 15$$
$$y \quad = \quad 5$$

The solution is x = 2, y = 5.

4 NON-LINEAR EQUATIONS

KEY TERM

A **non-linear equation** is one in which one variable varies with the nth power of another, where n > 1.

4.1 The following are examples of non-linear equations.

$$y = x^2; \; y = 3x^3 + 2; \; 2y = 5x^4 - 6; \; y = -x^{12} + 3$$

4.2 It is common for a non-linear equation to include a number of terms, all to different powers. Here are some examples.

$$y = x^2 + 6x + 10 \qquad\qquad y = -12x^9 + 3x^6 + 6x^3 + 3x^2 - 1$$
$$2y = 3x^3 - 4x^2 - 8x + 10 \qquad 3y = 22x^8 + 7x^7 + 3x^4 - 12$$

4.3 Non-linear equations can be expressed in the form

$$y = ax^n + bx^{n-1} + cx^{n-2} + dx^{n-3} + \ldots + \text{constant.}$$ Consider the following equation.

$$y = -12x^9 + 3x^6 + 6x^3 + 2x^2 - 1$$

In this equation $a = -12$, $b = 0$, $c = 0$, $d = 3$, $e = 0$, $f = 0$, $g = 6$, $h = 2$, $i = 0$, constant $= -1$ and $n = 9$.

Graphing non-linear equations

4.4 The **graph of a linear equation**, as we saw earlier, **is a straight line**. The **graph of a non-linear equation**, on the other hand, **is not a straight line**. Let us consider an example.

4.5 EXAMPLE: GRAPHING NON-LINEAR EQUATIONS

Graph the equation $y = -2x^3 + x^2 - 2x + 10$.

4.6 SOLUTION

The graph of this equation can be plotted in the same way as the graph of a linear equation is plotted. Take a selection of values of x, calculate the corresponding values of y, plot the pairs of values and join the points together. The joining must be done using as smooth a curve as possible.

x	-3	-2	-1	0	1	2	3
$-2x$	6	4	2	0	-2	-4	-6
x^2	9	4	1	0	1	4	9
$-2x^3$	54	16	2	0	-2	-16	-54
10	10	10	10	10	10	10	10
y	79	34	15	10	7	-6	-41

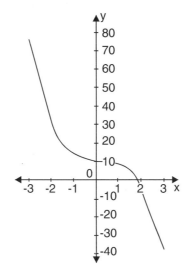

5   **QUADRATIC EQUATIONS**   12/97

> **KEY TERM**
>
> **Quadratic equations** are a type of non-linear equation in which one variable varies with the square (or second power) of the other variable.

5.1   The following equations are all examples of quadratic equations.

$y - x^2$ $y = 5x^2 + 7$ $2y = -2x^2 - 3$ $y = x^2 + 3$

5.2   A quadratic equation may include both a term involving the square and also a term involving the first power of a variable. Here are some examples.

$y = x^2 + 6x + 10$ $2y = 3x^2 - 4x - 8$ $y = 2x^2 + 3x + 6$

5.3   All quadratic equations can be expressed in the **form $y = ax^2 + bx + c$**. For instance, in the equation $y = 3x^2 + 2x - 6$, $a = 3$, $b = 2$, $c = -6$.

Graphing a quadratic equation

5.4   The graph of a quadratic equation can be plotted using the same method as that illustrated in Paragraph 4.6.

5.5   **EXAMPLE: GRAPHING A QUADRATIC EQUATION**

Graph the equation $y = -2x^2 + x - 3$.

5.6   **SOLUTION**

x	-3	-2	-1	0	1	2	3
$-2x^2$	-18	-8	-2	0	-2	-8	-18
-3	-3	-3	-3	-3	-3	-3	-3
y	-24	-13	-6	-3	-4	-9	-18

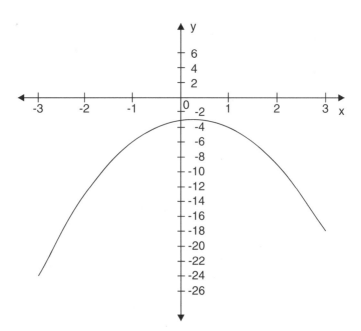

5.7 Graphs shaped like that in Paragraph 5.6 are sometimes referred to as **parabolas** and illustrate a number of points about the graph of the equation $y = ax^2 + bx + c$.

  (a) The constant term 'c' determines the value of y at the point where the curve crosses the y axis (the **intercept**). In the graph above $c = -3$ and the curve crosses the y axis at $y = -3$.

  (b) The sign of 'a' determines the way up the curve appears. If a is positive, the curve is shaped like a **ditch**, but if a is negative, the curve is shaped like a **bell**.

   A **ditch-shaped curve** is said to have a **minimum point** whereas a **bell-shaped curve** is said to have a **maximum point**.

  (c) The graph enables us to find the values of x when $y = 0$ (if there are any). In other words the graph allows us to solve the quadratic equation $0 = ax^2 + bx + c$.

   For the curve in Paragraph 5.6 we see that there are no such values (that is, $0 = -2x^2 + x - 3$ cannot be solved)

Solving quadratic equations

5.8 There are many situations in business mathematics which call for the solution to a quadratic equation and the graphical method is not, in practice, the most efficient way to determine the solution.

5.9 **Many quadratic equations have two values of x** (called '**solutions for x**' or '**roots of the equation**') which satisfy the equation for any particular value of y. These values can be found using the following formula.

> **EXAM FORMULA**
>
> If, $ax^2 + bx + c = 0$ then $x = \dfrac{-b \pm \sqrt{(b^2 - 4ac)}}{2a}$

5.10 EXAMPLE: QUADRATIC EQUATIONS

Solve $x^2 + x - 2 = 0$.

5.11 SOLUTION

$$x = \frac{-1 \pm \sqrt{\left(1^2 - \left(4 \times 1 \times (-2)\right)\right)}}{2 \times 1} = \frac{-1 \pm \sqrt{(1+8)}}{2} = \frac{-1 \pm 3}{2} = \frac{-4}{2} \text{ or } \frac{2}{2}$$
So $x = -2$ or $x = 1$

Quadratic equations with a single value for x

5.12 Sometimes, $b^2 - 4ac = 0$, and so there is only one solution to the quadratic equation. Let us solve $x^2 + 2x + 1 = 0$.

$$x = \frac{-2 \pm \sqrt{\left(2^2 - (4 \times 1 \times 1)\right)}}{2} \qquad x = \frac{-2 \pm 0}{2} = -1$$

This quadratic equation can only be solved by one value of x.

Chapter roundup

- A **linear equation** has the general form $y = a + bx$, where x is the **independent** variable and y the dependent variable, and a and b are fixed amounts.

- The graph of a linear equation is a **straight line**. The **intercept** of the line on the y axis is 'a' in $y = a + bx$ and the slope of the line is 'b'.

- **Simultaneous equations** are two or more equations which are satisfied by the same variable values. They can be solved **graphically** or **algebraically**.

- In **non-linear equations**, one variable varies with the nth power of another, where n > 1. The graph of a non-linear equation is not a straight line.

- **Quadratic equations** are non-linear equations in which one variable varies with the square of the other variable. The graphs of quadratic equations are parabolas, the sign of 'a' in the general form of the quadratic equation ($y = ax^2 + bx + c$) determining the way up the curve appears. Quadratic equations can be solved by the formula $x = \dfrac{-b \pm \sqrt{\left(b^2 - 4ac\right)}}{2a}$

Quick quiz

1   What is the general form of a linear equation? (see formulae to learn)

2   On which axis of a graph is the independent variable represented? (2.2)

3   What are the rules for drawing graphs? (2.2 - 2.4)

4   What is the intercept? (2.8)

5   In which direction does a positive gradient slope? (2.10)

6   What are simultaneous equations? (key terms)

7   If the graph of a quadratic curve has a minimum point, is 'a' positive or negative? (5.7)

8   What is the formula for solving a quadratic equation? (exam formulae)

Question to try	Level	Marks	Time
24	Introductory	n/a	15 mins

Chapter 24

COST BEHAVIOUR

Chapter topic list	Syllabus reference
1 The importance of understanding cost behaviour	CA 1(c)(i), (ii)
2 Cost behaviour and levels of activity	CA 1(c)(ii)
3 Cost behaviour patterns	QT 3(a); CA 1(c)(i), (ii)
4 Determining the fixed and variable elements of semi-variable costs	QT 3(a), (b); CA 1(c)(i),(ii)
5 The linear assumption of cost behaviour	QT 3(a); CA 1(c)(ii)
6 Factors affecting the influence of activity level	CA 1(c)(ii)

Introduction

Chapter 23 provided the foundation for this and the following two chapters, since it covered equations which are the basis of **business models**. A **model** is basically a representation of a **'real-world' situation**.

The **high-low method** is a model representing **cost behaviour**, and it is used to determine the **fixed** and **variable** elements of semi-variable costs. We shall be looking at this model in detail in this chapter, along with other aspects of cost behaviour.

1 THE IMPORTANCE OF UNDERSTANDING COST BEHAVIOUR   12/95

Cost behaviour and decision making

> **KEY TERM**
>
> **Cost behaviour** is the way in which costs are affected by changes in the volume of output.

1.1 Management decisions will often be based on how costs and revenues vary at different activity levels. Examples of such decisions are as follows.

- What should the **planned activity level** be for the next period?
- Should the **selling price** be reduced in order to sell more units?
- Should a particular component be **manufactured internally** or **bought in**?
- Should a **contract** be undertaken?

Cost behaviour and cost control

1.2 If the accountant does not know the level of costs which should have been incurred as a result of an organisation's activities, how can he or she hope to control costs?

Cost behaviour and budgeting

1.3   Knowledge of cost behaviour is obviously essential for the tasks of **budgeting, decision making** and **control accounting**.

1.4   EXAMPLE: COST BEHAVIOUR AND PRODUCTION LEVEL

Fixed and variable cost analysis enables management to decide whether an incentive scheme would be attractive to both employers and employees.

Suppose that Given Hann Hoffa Ltd is a company which manufactures a single product which sells for £20. The costs of production have been estimated to be as follows.

Fixed costs per month	£1,000
Variable costs	£12 per unit

The variable costs have been analysed further.

(a)   Labour costs (2 hours at £2 per hour) = £4
(b)   Material and other costs = £8

Demand for the product varies from 400 units to 800 units per month. The maximum output which can be achieved is currently only 600 units per month, because the available labour hours are restricted to 1,200 hours per month. The nature of the product is such that stocks of work-in-progress or finished goods cannot be stored.

An incentive scheme has been proposed whereby the payment to employees will be increased from £2 to £3 per hour, provided that the time taken to produce each unit is reduced from 2 hours to 1½ hours.

Required

(a)   Ascertain the effect of the incentive scheme on employees' wages and company profits at the following output levels.

(i)   At the minimum level of output per month
(ii)   At the current maximum level of output per month

(b)   Show by how much the company would profit if output and sales were increased to the new maximum level.

(c)   Draw conclusions from these figures about the effects of the incentive scheme.

1.5   SOLUTION

(a)   (i)   **400 units per month**

	With the incentive scheme £	£	Without the incentive scheme £	£
Sales (400 × £20)		8,000		8,000
Materials etc costs (400 × £8)	3,200		3,200	
Labour costs (400 × £3 × 1½ hrs)	1,800		(400 × £2 × 2hrs) 1,600	
Total variable costs		5,000		4,800
Contribution		3,000		3,200
Fixed costs		1,000		1,000
Profit		2,000		2,200

The labour force would work fewer hours (600 instead of 800) but would receive £200 more in pay. Company profits would fall by £200 if the scheme is introduced and demand is 400 units.

(ii) **600 units per month**

	With the incentive scheme £	With the incentive scheme £	Without the incentive scheme £	Without the incentive scheme £
Sales (600 × £20)		12,000		12,000
Materials etc costs (600 × £8)	4,800		4,800	
Labour costs (600 × £3 × 1½ hrs)	2,700		(600 × £2 × 2hrs) 2,400	
Total variable costs		7,500		7,200
		4,500		4,800
Fixed costs		1,000		1,000
Profit		3,500		3,800

The labour force would again work fewer hours (900 instead of 1,200) but would receive £300 more in pay. With the introduction of the scheme, company profits would be £300 lower if demand is only 600 units.

(b) Maximum output = 1,200 hrs ÷ 1½ hrs per unit
= 800 units per month

This is also the maximum demand per month.

	With the incentive scheme	£	£
Sales	(800 × £20)		16,000
Materials etc costs	(800 × £8)	6,400	
Labour costs	(800 × 1½ hrs × £3)	3,600	
Total variable costs			10,000
			6,000
Fixed costs			1,000
Profit			5,000

Employees would receive higher wages, and company profits would be capable of reaching £5,000 per month if maximum demand is achieved.

(c) The particular incentive scheme under review does not benefit the company unless actual output and sales exceed the current maximum levels, that is unless the improved productivity results in improved sales volumes.

1.6 EXAMPLE: COST BEHAVIOUR AND ACTIVITY LEVEL

Hans Bratch Ltd has a fleet of company cars for sales representatives. Running costs have been estimated as follows.

(a) Cars cost £12,000 when new, and have a guaranteed trade-in value of £6,000 at the end of two years. Depreciation is charged on a straight-line basis.

(b) Petrol and oil cost 15 pence per mile.

(c) Tyres cost £300 per set to replace; replacement occurs after 30,000 miles.

(d) Routine maintenance costs £200 per car (on average) in the first year and £450 in the second year.

(e) Repairs average £400 per car over two years and are thought to vary with mileage. The average car travels 25,000 miles per annum.

(f) Tax, insurance, membership of motoring organisations and so on cost £400 per annum per car.

Required

Calculate the average cost per annum of cars which travel 20,000 miles per annum and 30,000 miles per annum.

1.7 SOLUTION

Costs may be analysed into fixed, variable and stepped cost items, a stepped cost being a cost which is fixed in nature but only within certain levels of activity.

(a) **Fixed costs**

	£ per annum
Depreciation £(12,000 – 6,000) ÷ 2	3,000
Routine maintenance £(200 + 450) ÷ 2	325
Tax, insurance etc	400
	3,725

(b) **Variable costs**

	Pence per mile
Petrol and oil	15.0
Repairs (£400 ÷ 50,000 miles)	0.8
	15.8

(c) Step costs are tyre replacement costs, which are £300 at the end of every 30,000 miles.

(i) If the car travels less than or exactly 30,000 miles in two years, the tyres will not be changed. Average cost of tyres per annum = £0.

(ii) If a car travels more than 30,000 miles and up to (and including) 60,000 miles in two years, there will be one change of tyres in the period. Average cost of tyres per annum = £150 (£300 ÷ 2).

(iii) If a car exceeds 60,000 miles in two years (up to 90,000 miles) there will be two tyre changes. Average cost of tyres per annum = £300. (£600 ÷ 2).

The estimated costs per annum of cars travelling 20,000 miles per annum and 30,000 miles per annum would therefore be as follows.

	20,000 miles per annum £	*30,000 miles per annum* £
Fixed costs	3,725	3,725
Variable costs (15.8p per mile)	3,160	4,740
Tyres	150	150
Cost per annum	7,035	8,615

Exam focus point
Remember that the behavioural analysis of costs is important for planning, control and decision-making.

2 COST BEHAVIOUR AND LEVELS OF ACTIVITY 12/95

2.1 There are many factors which may influence costs. The major influence is **volume of output**, or the **level of activity**. The level of activity may refer to one of the following.

- Value of items sold
- Number of items sold
- Number of invoices issued
- Number of units of electricity consumed

Basic principles of cost behaviour

2.2 The basic principle of cost behaviour is that **as the level of activity rises, costs will usually rise**. It will cost more to produce 2,000 units of output than it will cost to produce 1,000 units.

414

2.3 This principle is common sense. The problem for the accountant, however, is to determine, for each item of cost, the way in which costs rise and by how much as the level of activity increases. For our purposes here, the level of activity for measuring cost will generally be taken to be the **volume of production**.

3 COST BEHAVIOUR PATTERNS 12/95

Fixed costs

> **KEY TERM**
>
> A **fixed cost** is a cost which tends to be unaffected by increases or decreases in the volume of output.

3.1 Fixed costs are a **period charge**, in that they relate to a span of time; as the time span increases, so too will the fixed costs (which are sometimes referred to as period costs for this reason). It is important to understand that **fixed costs always have a variable element**, since an increase or decrease in production may also bring about an increase or decrease in fixed costs.

3.2 A sketch graph of a fixed cost would look like this.

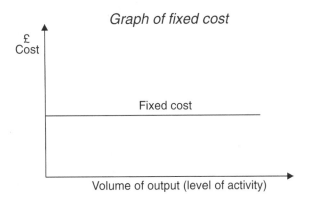

Graph of fixed cost

Examples of a fixed cost would be as follows.

- The salary of the managing director (per month or per annum)
- The rent of a single factory building (per month or per annum)
- Straight line depreciation of a single machine (per month or per annum)

Step costs 12/94

> **KEY TERM**
>
> A **step cost** is a cost which is fixed in nature but only within certain levels of activity.

3.3 Consider the depreciation of a machine which may be fixed if production remains below 1,000 units per month. If production exceeds 1,000 units, a second machine may be required, and the cost of depreciation (on two machines) would go up a step. A sketch graph of a step cost could look like this.

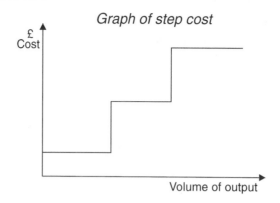

Graph of step cost

£
Cost

Volume of output

Other examples of step costs are as follows.

(a) Rent is a step cost in situations where accommodation requirements increase as output levels get higher.

(b) Basic pay of employees is nowadays usually fixed, but as output rises, more employees (direct workers, supervisors, managers and so on) are required.

(c) Royalties.

Variable costs

> **KEY TERM**
>
> A **variable cost** is a cost which tends to vary directly with the volume of output. The variable cost per unit is the same amount for each unit produced.

3.4

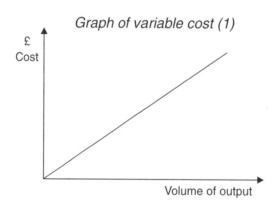

Graph of variable cost (1)

£
Cost

Volume of output

3.5 A constant variable cost per unit implies that the price per unit of say, material purchased is constant, and that the rate of material usage is also constant.

(a) The most important variable cost is the **cost of raw materials** (where there is no discount for bulk purchasing since bulk purchase discounts reduce the cost of purchases).

(b) **Direct labour costs** are, for very important reasons, classed as a variable cost even though basic wages are usually fixed.

(c) **Sales commission** is variable in relation to the volume or value of sales.

(d) **Bonus payments** for productivity to employees might be variable once a certain level of output is achieved, as the following diagram illustrates.

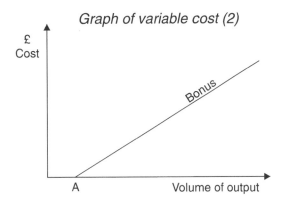

Graph of variable cost (2)

Up to output A, no bonus is earned.

Non-linear or curvilinear variable costs

> **KEY TERM**
>
> If the relationship between total variable cost and volume of output can be shown as a curved line on a graph, the relationship is said to be **curvilinear**.

3.6   Two typical relationships are as follows.

(a)

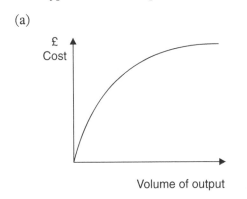

(b)

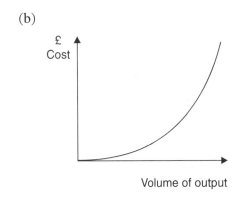

Each extra unit of output in graph (a) causes a **less than proportionate** increase in cost whereas in graph (b), each extra unit of output causes **a more than proportionate** increase in cost.

3.7   The cost of a piecework scheme for individual workers with differential rates could behave in a **curvilinear** fashion if the rates increase by small amounts at progressively higher output levels.

Semi-variable costs (or semi-fixed costs or mixed costs)   12/94

> **KEY TERM**
>
> A **semi-variable/semi-fixed/mixed cost** is a cost which contains both fixed and variable components and so is partly affected by changes in the level of activity.

BPP
PUBLISHING

3.8   Examples of these costs include the following.

(a) **Electricity and gas bills**

- Fixed cost = standing charge
- Variable cost = charge per unit of electricity used

(b) **Salesman's salary**

- Fixed cost = basic salary
- Variable cost = commission on sales made

(c) **Costs of running a car**

- Fixed cost = road tax, insurance
- Variable costs = petrol, oil, repairs (which vary with miles travelled)

Other cost behaviour patterns

3.9   Other cost behaviour patterns may be appropriate to certain cost items. The cost of materials after deduction of a bulk purchase is shown as follows.

(a)

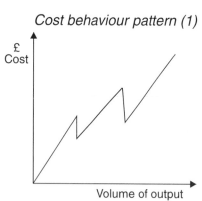

Cost behaviour pattern (1)

(b)

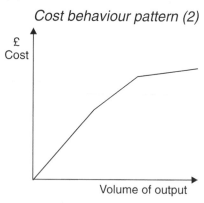

Cost behaviour pattern (2)

(i)   Graph (a) shows a bulk purchase discount which applies retrospectively to all units purchased.

(ii)   Graph (b) shows a discount which applies only to units purchased in excess of a certain quantity.

(c)

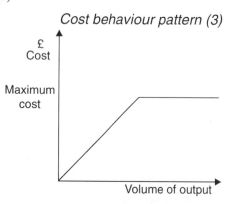

Cost behaviour pattern (3)

(d)

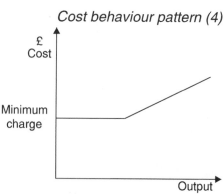

Cost behaviour pattern (4)

(i)   Graph (c) represents an item of cost which is variable with output up to a certain maximum level of cost.

(ii)   Graph (d) represents a cost which is variable with output, subject to a minimum (fixed) charge.

Cost behaviour and total and unit costs

3.10   The following table relates to different levels of production of the zed. The variable cost of producing a zed is £5. Fixed costs are £5,000.

	1 zed £	10 zeds £	50 zeds £
Total variable cost	5	50	250
Variable cost per unit	5	5	5
Total fixed cost	5,000	5,000	5,000
Fixed cost per unit	5,000	500	100
Total cost (fixed and variable)	5,005	5,050	5,250
Total cost per unit	5,005	505	105

What happens when activity levels rise can be summarised as follows.

- The variable cost per unit remains constant
- The fixed cost per unit falls
- The total cost per unit falls

This may be illustrated graphically as follows.

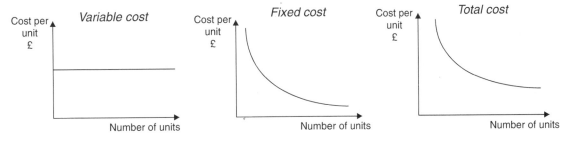

Question 1

Are the following likely to be fixed, variable or mixed costs?

(a)   Telephone bill
(b)   Annual salary of the chief accountant
(c)   The management accountant's annual membership fee to CIMA (paid by the company)
(d)   Cost of materials used to pack 20 units of product X into a box
(e)   Wages of warehousemen

Answer

(a)   Mixed
(b)   Fixed
(c)   Fixed
(d)   Variable
(e)   Variable

4 DETERMINING THE FIXED AND VARIABLE ELEMENTS OF SEMI-VARIABLE COSTS   12/95, 12/99

4.1 It is generally assumed that costs are one of the following.

- Variable
- Fixed
- Semi-variable

Cost accountants tend to separate semi-variable costs into their variable and fixed elements. They therefore generally tend to treat costs as either **fixed** or **variable**.

4.2 There are several methods for identifying the fixed and variable elements of semi-variable costs. Each method is only an estimate, and each will produce different results. One of the principal methods is the **high-low method.**

High-low method

4.3 Follow the steps below to estimate the fixed and variable elements of semi-variable costs.

Step 1. Review records of costs in previous periods.

- Select the period with the **highest** activity level.
- Select the period with the **lowest** activity level.

Step 2. If inflation makes it difficult to compare costs, adjust by indexing up or down.

Step 3. Determine the following.

- Total cost at high activity level
- Total costs at low activity level
- Total units at high activity level
- Total units at low activity level

Step 4. Calculate the following.

$$\frac{\text{Total cost at high activity level} - \text{total cost at low activity level}}{\text{Total units at high activity level} - \text{total units at low activity level}}$$

= variable cost per unit (v)

Step 5. The fixed costs can be determined as follows. (Total cost at high activity level) –(total units at high activity level × variable cost per unit)

4.4 The following graph demonstrates the high-low method.

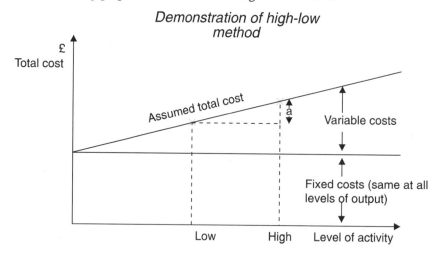

Demonstration of high-low method

4.5 EXAMPLE: THE HIGH-LOW METHOD WITH INFLATION

TS Ltd has recorded the following total costs during the last five years.

Year	Output volume	Total cost	Average price level index
	Units	£	
20X0	65,000	145,000	100
20X1	80,000	179,200	112
20X2	90,000	209,100	123
20X3	60,000	201,600	144
20X4	75,000	248,000	160

Required

Calculate the total cost that should be expected in 20X5 if output is 85,000 units and the average price level index is 180.

4.6 SOLUTION

Step 1.

- Period with highest activity = 20X2
- Period with lowest activity = 20X3

Step 2.

- Adjust costs so that they can be compared.

$$\text{20X2 indexed cost} = £209,100 \times \frac{100}{123} = £170,000$$

$$\text{20X0 indexed cost} = £201,600 \times \frac{100}{144} = £140,000$$

Step 3.

- Total cost at high activity level = 170,000
- Total cost at low activity level = 140,000
- Total units at high activity level = 90,000
- Total units at low activity level =– 60,000

Step 4. Variable cost per unit

$$= \frac{\text{total cost at high activity level} - \text{total cost at low activity level}}{\text{total units at high activity level} - \text{total units at low activity level}}$$

$$= \frac{170,000 - 140,000}{90,000 - 60,000} = \frac{30,000}{30,000} = £1 \text{ per unit}$$

Step 5. Fixed costs = (total cost at high activity level) – (total units at high activity level × variable cost per unit)

= 170,000 – (90,000 × 1) = 170,000 – 90,000 = £80,000

Therefore the costs in 20X5 for output of 85,000 units are as follows.

		£
Variable costs =	85,000 × £1 =	85,000
Fixed costs =		80,000
		165,000

However, we must now index up the 20X5 costs to reflect 20X5 price levels.

$$£165,000 \times \frac{180}{100} = £297,000$$

4.7 The step-by-step guide has been covered in order that you fully understand the process involved. The answer to Question 2 will cover all of these steps, without stating so each time, as this is how you would present your answer in an examination.

> ### Exam focus point
>
> In the December exams of 1995 and 1999 easy marks were available for using the high-how method to analyse the costs of data given in the question into fixed and variable components. Remember to use the highest and lowest points in your calculations when using the high-low method. The examiner has commented that some candidates have failed to do so when answering exam questions.

Question 2

W Ltd has operated a restaurant for the last two years. Revenue and operating costs over the two years have been as follows.

	Year 1	Year 2
	£'000	£'000
Revenue	1,348,312	1,514,224
Operating costs		
Food and beverage	698,341	791,919
Wages	349,170	390,477
Other overheads	202,549	216,930

The number of meals served in year 2 showed an 8% increase on the year 1 level of 151,156. An increase of 10% over the year 2 level is budgeted for year 3.

All staff were given hourly rate increases of 6% last year (in year 2). In year 3 hourly increases of 7% are to be budgeted.

The inflation on 'other overheads' last year was 5%, with an inflationary increase of 6% expected in the year ahead.

Food and beverage costs are budgeted to average £5.14 per meal in year 3. This is expected to represent 53% of sales value.

Required

From the information given above, and using the high-low method of cost estimation, determine the budgeted expenditure on wages and other overhead for year 3. (Round your final answer for each to the nearest £'000.)

Answer

Wages

We need to discover the variable wages cost, by using the high-low method. There are only two years, so one is taken is 'high' and one as 'low'.

	Year 1 Meals		Year 2 Meals	Increase
Number of meals	151,156	(× 108%)	163,248	12,092
	£		£	£
Wages cost	349,170		390,477	41,307

We must account for inflation, however, to 'equalise' the two years by adjusting year 1 to year 2 costs. The figure used is the 6% hourly rate increase.

	£	£	£
£349,170 × 106% =	370,120	390,477	20,357

In year 2, the variable wages cost of a meal is $\dfrac{£20,357}{12,092} = £1.68$

In year 1, adjusting back for inflation

	£
$\left(\dfrac{£20{,}357}{12{,}092}\right) \times 151{,}156$ meals $\div 106\% =$ Variable wages cost (year 1)	240,068
Fixed wages cost (year 1) (balance)	109,102
Total wages cost (year 1)	349,170

So, in year 3

		£
Variable cost	$\left(\dfrac{£20{,}357}{12{,}092}\right) \times 179{,}573$ meals (W1) $\times 107\%$	323,475
Fixed cost	£109,102 $\times$ 106% (year 2) $\times$ 107% (year 3)	123,743
Total wages cost (year 3)		447,218

Overheads

	Year 1 Meals	Year 2 Meals	Increase
Number of meals	151,156	163,248	12,092
	£	£	£
Overhead costs	202,549	216,930	14,381
Adjusting for inflation to year 2 cost			
£202,549 $\times$ 105% =	212,676	216,930	4,254

$\therefore$ Variable overhead cost in year 2 is $\dfrac{£4{,}254}{12{,}092} = £0.352$ per meal

$\therefore$ In year 1

	£
$151{,}156 \times \left(\dfrac{£0.352}{1.05}\right) =$ variable overhead cost	50,673
Fixed overhead cost (balance)	151,876
Total overhead cost (year 1)	202,549

$\therefore$ In year 3

	£
£0.352 $\times$ 179,573 meals (W1) $\times$ 106% (variable)	67,003
£151,876 $\times$ 105% $\times$ 106% (fixed)	169,038
Total overhead costs (year 3)	236,041

---

5 THE LINEAR ASSUMPTION OF COST BEHAVIOUR

5.1 It is usual for the cost accountant to make the following assumptions.

(a) Costs are generally considered to be fixed, variable or mixed (semi-fixed, semi-variable) within a normal range of output.

(b) Departmental costs are assumed to be mixed costs, with a fixed element and a variable element. The fixed costs and variable costs per unit may be estimated, with varying degrees of probable accuracy, by a variety of methods, of which the high-low method is perhaps the simplest to use (but the least accurate in its estimations).

(c) Departmental costs are therefore assumed to rise in a straight line (linear) fashion as the volume of activity increases.

5.2 A worthwhile question to answer at this stage is: are the assumptions in (b) and (c) above correct? In other words, is it true to say that costs may be divided into a fixed element and a variable cost per unit which is the same for every unit produced? There is a good argument that the variable cost per unit, (or the marginal cost per unit in the language of economics), changes with the level of output. Due to growing economies of scale (in other words, cost savings as activity levels increase) up to a certain level, a view put forward in basic economics is that the variable cost per unit could be graphed as follows.

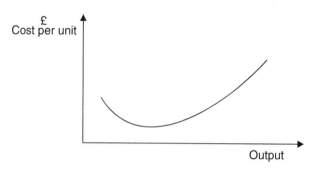

Total costs would therefore appear as a curved line, as follows.

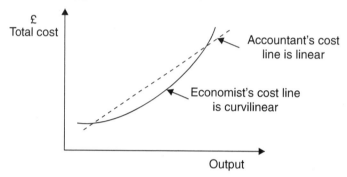

5.3   It is sufficient at this stage to be aware of the difference of views between the 'accountant' and the 'economist', and to understand that the accountant justifies the linear assumption of cost behaviour for the following reasons.

(a)   It is easier to understand than curvilinear cost behaviour.

(b)   Fixed and variable costs are easier to estimate, and easier to use.

(c)   The assumption of linear costs is only used in practice within normal ranges of output, ie within a **relevant range of activity**.

(d)   Within this relevant range of activity, the cost estimates of the economist and the accountant would not differ greatly, if at all; therefore linear costs should be used because sufficient accuracy is achieved with less effort (and for less cost).

6   FACTORS AFFECTING THE INFLUENCE OF ACTIVITY LEVEL

6.1   You are by now aware that it is not possible to say that a certain type of cost is always a fixed cost, or that another type is always variable. There are several factors which affect the extent to which a cost is influenced by a change in activity.

(a)   **The make-up of the labour force.** The company's activities will determine whether there is a large production workforce. Where this is the case, a large increase in activity may necessitate hiring extra workers. In a non-labour intensive industry, increased output may result in a very low increase in costs.

(b)   **The attitude of management to the change in activity.** This will depend on the nature of the cost and the management's objectives in the long and short term. Management may have the power to control the amount by which the cost rises in the case of some indirect costs such as administration and advertising charges.

(c) **The length of time the change in activity is observed**. Changes in cost behaviour may not be noticeable or even occur at all unless a change in activity is sustained.

(d) **The extent to which the company is operating at full capacity**. Where machines were lying idle prior to an increase in activity, the extra demand may be met with a minimal rise in costs.

(e) **The general economic climate**. This may affect the availability of suitable resources and thereby the firm's ability to respond to a change of activity.

(f) **The particular environment of the firm**. This includes the quality of the workforce and industrial relations, and the motivation of the staff.

6.2 It is important to establish the **time span under consideration** in determining cost behaviour patterns. For instance, some fixed costs may become variable in the long run, and, in the very short term, costs which are normally considered to be variable may in fact be fixed.

Chapter roundup

- Costs which are not affected by the level of activity are **fixed** costs or **period** costs.

- Even though fixed costs in total remain constant over a range of activity, the cost per unit will tend to reduce as the level of activity rises because the same fixed cost is being spread over a greater number of units.

- **Step costs** are fixed within a certain range of activity.

- **Variable costs** increase or decrease with the level of activity, and although they can behave in a **curvilinear** fashion, it is usually assumed that there is a linear relationship between cost and activity.

- **Semi-fixed**, **semi-variable** or **mixed costs** are costs which are part fixed and part variable.

- It is often possible to assume that, within the normal range of output, costs are either variable, fixed or semi-variable.

- The fixed and variable elements of semi-variable costs can be determined by the **high-low method**.

Quick quiz

1 For which three tasks is the knowledge of cost behaviour essential? (see para 1.3)

2 Define cost behaviour. (key terms)

3 Give an example of a fixed cost and a step cost. (3.2, 3.3)

4 Describe the steps involved in the high-low method. (4.3)

5 Contrast an accountant's and an economist's views of cost behaviour. (5.2, 5.3)

6 List six factors which affect the extent to which cost is influenced by a change in activity. (6.1)

Question to try	Level	Marks	Time
25	Examination	14	25 mins

BPP PUBLISHING

Chapter 25

COST-VOLUME-PROFIT (BREAKEVEN) ANALYSIS

Chapter topic list	Syllabus reference
1 CVP analysis and breakeven point	QT 3(b); CA 4(c)(i), (ii)
2 The Contribution/Sales (C/S) ratio	QT 3(b); CA 4(c)(i), (ii)
3 The margin of safety	QT 3(b); CA 4(c)(i), (ii)
4 Breakeven arithmetic	QT 3(b); CA 4(c)(i), (ii)
5 Breakeven charts, contribution charts and profit/volume charts	QT 3(a); CA 4(c)(i), (ii)
6 Limitations of CVP analysis	CA 4(c)(i), (ii)

Introduction

You should by now realise that the cost accountant needs estimates of **fixed** and **variable costs**, and **revenues**, at various output levels. The cost accountant, must also be fully aware of **cost behaviour** because, to be able to estimate costs, he must know what a particular cost will do given particular conditions.

An understanding of cost behaviour is not all that you may need to know, however. The application of **cost-volume-profit analysis**, which is based on the cost behaviour principles and marginal costing ideas, is sometimes necessary so that the appropriate decision-making information can be provided. As you may have guessed, this chapter is going to look at that very topic, **cost-volume-profit analysis**.

1   CVP ANALYSIS AND BREAKEVEN POINT   6/94, 6/95, 12/95, 6/99

KEY TERM

Cost-volume-profit (CVP)/breakeven analysis is the study of the interrelationships between costs, volume and profit at various levels of activity.

1.1   The management of an organisation usually wishes to know the profit likely to be made if the aimed-for production and sales for the year are achieved. Management may also be interested to know the following.

(a)   The **breakeven** point which is the activity levels at which there is neither profit nor loss.

(b)   The **amount** by which actual **sales can fall** below anticipated sales, **without** a **loss** being incurred.

1.2   The breakeven point (BEP) can be calculated arithmetically.

426

FORMULA TO LEARN

$$\text{Breakeven point} = \frac{\text{Total fixed costs}}{\text{Contribution per unit}} = \frac{\text{Contribution required to break even}}{\text{Contribution per unit}}$$

$$= \text{Number of units of sale required to break even.}$$

1.3 EXAMPLE: BREAKEVEN POINT

Expected sales	10,000 units at £8 = £80,000
Variable cost	£5 per unit
Fixed costs	£21,000

Required

Compute the breakeven point.

1.4 SOLUTION

The contribution per unit is £(8–5)	=	£3
Contribution required to break even	=	fixed costs = £21,000
Breakeven point (BEP)	=	21,000 ÷ 3
	=	7,000 units
In revenue, BEP	=	(7,000 × £8) = £56,000

Sales above £56,000 will result in profit of £3 per unit of additional sales and sales below £56,000 will mean a loss of £3 per unit for each unit by which sales fall short of 7,000 units. In other words, profit will improve or worsen by the amount of contribution per unit.

	7,000 units		*7,001 units*
	£		£
Revenue	56,000		56,008
Less variable costs	35,000		35,005
Contribution	21,000		21,003
Less fixed costs	21,000		21,000
Profit	0	(= breakeven)	3

2 THE CONTRIBUTION/SALES (C/S) RATIO   6/94, 6/95, 6/98

2.1 An alternative way of calculating the breakeven point to give an answer in terms of sales revenue is as follows.

FORMULA TO LEARN

$$\frac{\text{Required contribution} = \text{Fixed costs}}{\text{C / S ratio}} = \text{Sales revenue at breakeven point}$$

(The **C/S (contribution/sales) ratio** is also sometimes called a profit/volume or P/V ratio).

2.2 In the example in Paragraph 1.3 the C/S ratio is $\dfrac{£3}{£8} = 37.5\%$

Breakeven is where sales revenue equals $\dfrac{\pounds 21{,}000}{37.5\%} = \pounds 56{,}000$

At a price of £8 per unit, this represents 7,000 units of sales.

The C/S ratio is a measure of how much contribution is earned from each £1 of sales. The C/S ratio of 37.5% in the above example means that for every £1 of sales, a contribution of 37.5p is earned. Thus, in order to earn a total contribution of £21,000 and if contribution increases by 37.5p per £1 of sales, sales must be:

$$\frac{\pounds 1}{37.5\text{p}} \times \pounds 21{,}000 = \pounds 56{,}000$$

Question 1

The C/S ratio of product W is 20%. IB Ltd, the manufacturer of product W, wishes to make a contribution of £50,000 towards fixed costs. How may units of product W must be sold if the selling price is £10 per unit?

Answer

$\dfrac{\text{Required contribution}}{\text{C / S ratio}} = \dfrac{\pounds\,50{,}000}{20\%} = \pounds 250{,}000$

∴ Number of units = £250,000 ÷ £10 = 25,000.

Exam focus point

In 6/95 there were 3 marks to be gained for simply **stating** and **explaining** the formula for the calculation of breakeven sales revenue. In 6/94 there were 7 marks to be gained for calculating the breakeven sales revenue figure. This formula is not given in the examination. Make sure that you know it.

3   THE MARGIN OF SAFETY   6/98

KEY TERM

The **margin of safety** is the difference in units between the budgeted sales volume and the breakeven sales volume and it is sometimes expressed as a percentage of the budgeted sales volume.

3.1   The margin of safety may also be expressed as the difference between the budgeted sales revenue and breakeven sales revenue, expressed as a percentage of the budgeted sales revenue.

3.2   EXAMPLE: MARGIN OF SAFETY

Mal de Mer Ltd makes and sells a product which has a variable cost of £30 and which sells for £40. Budgeted fixed costs are £70,000 and budgeted sales are 8,000 units.

Required

Calculate the breakeven point and the margin of safety.

3.3 SOLUTION

(a) Breakeven point $= \dfrac{\text{Total fixed costs}}{\text{Contribution per unit}} = \dfrac{£70,000}{£(40-30)}$

$$= 7,000 \text{ units}$$

(b) Margin of safety $= 8,000 - 7,000 \text{ units} = 1,000 \text{ units}$

which may be expressed as $\dfrac{1,000 \text{ units}}{8,000 \text{ units}} \times 100\% = 12\tfrac{1}{2}\%$ of budget

(c) The margin of safety indicates to management that actual sales can fall short of budget by 1,000 units or 12½% before the breakeven point is reached and no profit at all is made.

4 BREAKEVEN ARITHMETIC

6/97, 6/98, 12/98

> **FORMULA TO LEARN**
>
> At the **breakeven point**, sales revenue equals total costs and there is no profit.
>
> $\quad$ S $\;=$ V + F
>
> where $\quad$ S $\;=$ Sales revenue
> $\qquad\quad$ V $\;=$ Total variable costs
> $\qquad\quad$ F $\;=$ Total fixed costs
>
> Subtracting $\;$ V from each side of the equation, we get:
> $\qquad\quad$ S $-$ V $=$ F, that is, **total contribution = fixed costs**

4.1 EXAMPLE: BREAKEVEN ARITHMETIC

Butterfingers Ltd makes a product which has a variable cost of £7 per unit.

Required

If fixed costs are £63,000 per annum, calculate the selling price per unit if the company wishes to break even with a sales volume of 12,000 units.

4.2 SOLUTION

Contribution required to break even (= Fixed costs)	=	£63,000
Volume of sales	=	12,000 units
		£
Required contribution per unit (S – V)	= £63,000 ÷ 12,000 =	5.25
Variable cost per unit (V)	=	7.00
Required sales price per unit (S)	=	12.25

Target profits

4.3 A similar formula may be applied where a company wishes to achieve a certain profit during a period. To achieve this profit, sales must cover all costs and leave the required profit.

FORMULA TO LEARN

The target profit is achieved when: $S = V + F + P$,
　　where P = required profit
Subtracting V from each side of the equation, we get:

$$S - V = F + P, \text{ so}$$
$$\text{Total contribution required} = F + P$$

4.4 EXAMPLE: TARGET PROFITS (1)

Riding Breeches Ltd makes and sells a single product, for which variable costs are as follows.

	£
Direct materials	10
Direct labour	8
Variable production overhead	6
	24

The sales price is £30 per unit, and fixed costs per annum are £68,000. The company wishes to make a profit of £16,000 per annum.

Required

Determine the sales required to achieve this profit.

4.5 SOLUTION

Required contribution = fixed costs + profit = £68,000 + £16,000 = £84,000

Required sales can be calculated in one of two ways.

(a) $\dfrac{\text{Required contribution}}{\text{Contribution per unit}}$ = $\dfrac{£84,000}{£(30-24)}$ = 14,000 units, or £420,000 in revenue

(b) $\dfrac{\text{Required contribution}}{\text{C/S ratio}}$ = $\dfrac{£84,000}{20\%}$ = £420,000 of revenue, or 14,000 units.

Question 2

Seven League Boots Ltd wishes to sell 14,000 units of its product, which has a variable cost of £15 to make and sell. Fixed costs are £47,000 and the required profit is £23,000.

Required

Calculate the sales price per unit.

Answer

Required contribution	=	fixed costs plus profit
	=	£47,000 + £23,000
	=	£70,000
Required sales		14,000 units

	£
Required contribution per unit sold	5
Variable cost per unit	15
Required sales price per unit	20

4.6   EXAMPLE: TARGET PROFITS (2)

Tripod Ltd makes and sells three products, X, Y and Z. The selling price per unit and costs are as follows.

	X	Y	Z
Selling price per unit	£80	£50	£70
Variable cost per unit	£50	£10	£20

Fixed costs per month = £160,000

The maximum sales demand per month is 2,000 units of each product and the minimum sales demand is 1,000 of each.

Required

(a) Comment on the potential profitability of the company.

(b) Suppose that there is a fixed demand for X and Y of 1,500 units per month, which will not be exceeded, but for which firm orders have been received. Determine how many units of Z would have to be sold to achieve a profit of at least £25,000 per month.

4.7   SOLUTION

(a) When there is no indication about whether marginal or absorption costing is in use, it is simpler to assess profitability with contribution analysis and marginal costing. This is the requirement in part (a) of the problem. The obvious analysis to make is a calculation of the worst possible and best possible results.

	Best possible			*Worst possible*		
	Sales units	*Contrib'n per unit*	*Total cont'n*	*Sales units*	*Contrib'n per unit*	*Total cont'n*
		£	£		£	£
X	2,000	30	60,000	1,000	30	30,000
Y	2,000	40	80,000	1,000	40	40,000
Z	2,000	50	100,000	1,000	50	50,000
Total contribution			240,000			120,000
Fixed costs			160,000			160,000
Profit/(loss)			80,000			(40,000)

The company's potential profitability ranges from a profit of £80,000 to a loss of £40,000 per month.

(b) The second part of the problem is a variation of a 'target profit' calculation.

	£	£
Required (minimum) profit per month		25,000
Fixed costs per month		160,000
Required contribution per month		185,000
Contribution to be earned from:		
product X 1,500 × £30	45,000	
product Y 1,500 × £40	60,000	
		105,000
Contribution required from product Z		80,000
Contribution per unit of Z		£50
Minimum required sales of Z per month in units		1,600

Decisions to change sales price or costs

4.8   You may come across a problem in which you will be expected to offer advice as to the effect of altering the selling price, variable cost per unit or fixed cost. Such problems are slight variations on basic breakeven arithmetic.

4.9 EXAMPLE: CHANGE IN SELLING PRICE

Stomer Cakes Ltd bake and sell a single type of cake. The variable cost of production is 15p and the current sales price is 25p. Fixed costs are £2,600 per month, and the annual profit for the company at current sales volume is £36,000. The volume of sales demand is constant throughout the year.

The sales manager, Ian Digestion, wishes to raise the sales price to 29p per cake, but considers that a price rise will result in some loss of sales.

Required

Ascertain the minimum volume of sales required each month to raise the price to 29p.

4.10 SOLUTION

The minimum volume of demand which would justify a price of 29p is one which would leave total profit at least the same as before, ie £3,000 per month. Required profit should be converted into required contribution, as follows.

	£
Monthly fixed costs	2,600
Monthly profit, minimum required	3,000
Current monthly contribution	5,600
Contribution per unit (25p – 15p)	10p
Current monthly sales	56,000 cakes

The minimum volume of sales required after the price rise will be an amount which earns a contribution of £5,600 per month, no worse than at the moment. The contribution per cake at a sales price of 29p would be 14p.

$$\text{Required sales} = \frac{\text{required contribution}}{\text{contribution per unit}} = \frac{£5,600}{14p} = 40,000 \text{ cakes per month.}$$

4.11 EXAMPLE: CHANGE IN PRODUCTION COSTS

Close Brickett Ltd makes a product which has a variable production cost of £8 and a variable sales cost of £2 per unit. Fixed costs are £40,000 per annum, the sales price per unit is £18, and the current volume of output and sales is 6,000 units.

The company is considering whether to have an improved machine for production. Annual hire costs would be £10,000 and it is expected that the variable cost of production would fall to £6 per unit.

Required

(a) Determine the number of units that must be produced and sold to achieve the same profit as is currently earned, if the machine is hired.

(b) Calculate the annual profit with the machine if output and sales remain at 6,000 units per annum.

4.12 SOLUTION

The current unit contribution is £(18 – (8 + 2)) = £8

		£
(a)	Current contribution (6,000 × £8)	48,000
	Less current fixed costs	40,000
	Current profit	8,000

With the new machine fixed costs will go up by £10,000 to £50,000 per annum. The variable cost per unit will fall to £(6 + 2) = £8, and the contribution per unit will be £10.

	£
Required profit (as currently earned)	8,000
Fixed costs	50,000
Required contribution	58,000
Contribution per unit	£10
Sales required to earn £8,000 profit	5,800 units

(b) **If sales are 6,000 units**

	£	£
Sales (6,000 × £18)		108,000
Variable costs: production (6,000 × £6)	36,000	
sales (6,000 × £2)	12,000	
		48,000
Contribution (6,000 × £10)		60,000
Less fixed costs		50,000
Profit		10,000

	£
Alternative calculation	
Profit at 5,800 units of sale (see (a))	8,000
Contribution from sale of extra 200 units (× £10)	2,000
Profit at 6,000 units of sale	10,000

Sales price and sales volume

4.13 It may be clear by now that, given no change in fixed costs, **total profit is maximised when the total contribution is at its maximum**. Total contribution in turn depends on the unit contribution and on the sales volume.

4.14 An increase in the sales price will increase unit contribution, but sales volume is likely to fall because fewer customers will be prepared to pay the higher price. A decrease in sales price will reduce the unit contribution, but sales volume may increase because the goods on offer are now cheaper. The **optimum combination** of sales price and sales volume is arguably the one which **maximises total contribution**.

4.15 EXAMPLE: PROFIT MAXIMISATION

C Ltd has developed a new product which is about to be launched on to the market. The variable cost of selling the product is £12 per unit. The marketing department has estimated that at a sales price of £20, annual demand would be 10,000 units.

However, if the sales price is set above £20, sales demand would fall by 500 units for each 50p increase above £20. Similarly, if the price is set below £20, demand would increase by 500 units for each 50p stepped reduction in price below £20.

Required

Determine the price which would maximise C Ltd's profit in the next year.

4.16 SOLUTION

At a price of £20 per unit, the unit contribution would be £(20 − 12) = £8. Each 50p increase (or decrease) in price would raise (or lower) the unit contribution by 50p. The total contribution is calculated at each sales price by multiplying the unit contribution by the expected sales volume.

	Unit price £	Unit contribution £	Sales volume Units	Total contribution £
	20.00	8.00	10,000	80,000
(a) **Reduce price**				
	19.50	7.50	10,500	78,750
	19.00	7.00	11,000	77,000
(b) **Increase price**				
	20.50	8.50	9,500	80,750
	21.00	9.00	9,000	81,000
	21.50	9.50	8,500	80,750
	22.00	10.00	8,000	80,000
	22.50	10.50	7,500	78,750

The total contribution would be maximised, and therefore profit maximised, at a sales price of £21 per unit, and sales demand of 9,000 units.

Quadratic equations and breakeven points

4.17 In the problems that we have looked at so far, the relationships have all been linear. We shall now look at relationships which are expressed as quadratic equations.

4.18 EXAMPLE: QUADRATICS AND BREAKEVEN ANALYSIS

A company manufactures a product. Total fixed costs are £75 and the variable cost per unit is £5x, where x is the quantity of the product produced and sold. The total revenue function is given by R = (25 − x)x.

Required

Find the breakeven point.

4.19 SOLUTION

Total costs (C) = fixed costs + variable costs

= £(75 + 5x)

Total revenue (R) = $25x - x^2$

Breakeven point occurs when C = R

ie when $75 + 5x = 25x - x^2$

ie when $0 = x^2 - 20x + 75$

$$x = \frac{20 \pm \sqrt{400 - (4 \times 1 \times 75)}}{2} = \frac{20 \pm 10}{2} = 5 \text{ or } 15$$

Therefore the company will breakeven when it produces either 5 or 15 units.

5 BREAKEVEN CHARTS, CONTRIBUTION CHARTS AND PROFIT/VOLUME CHARTS

6/98, 6/99, 12/99

Breakeven charts

5.1 **The breakeven point can also be determined graphically using a breakeven chart.** This is a chart which shows approximate levels of profit or loss at different sales volume levels within a limited range.

5.2 A breakeven chart has the following axes.

- A **horizontal** axis showing the **sales/output** (in value or units)
- A **vertical axis** showing £ for **sales revenues** and **costs**

The following lines are drawn on the breakeven chart.

(a) The **sales line**
- Starts at the origin
- Ends at the point signifying expected sales

(b) The **fixed costs line**
- Runs parallel to the horizontal axis
- Meets the vertical axis at a point which represents total fixed costs

(c) The **total costs line**
- Starts where the fixed costs line meets the vertical axis
- Ends at the point which represents anticipated sales on the horizontal axis and total costs of anticipated sales on the vertical axis.

5.3 The **breakeven point** is the **intersection** of the **sales line** and the **total costs line**.

5.4 The distance between the **breakeven point** and the **expected (or budgeted) sales**, in units, indicates the **margin of safety**.

5.5 EXAMPLE: A BREAKEVEN CHART

The budgeted annual output of a factory is 120,000 units. The fixed overheads amount to £40,000 and the variable costs are 50p per unit. The sales price is £1 per unit.

Required

Construct a breakeven chart showing the current breakeven point and profit earned up to the present maximum capacity.

5.6 SOLUTION

We begin by calculating the profit at the budgeted annual output.

	£
Sales (120,000 units)	120,000
Variable costs	60,000
Contribution	60,000
Fixed costs	40,000
Profit	20,000

Breakeven chart (1) is shown on the following page.

The chart is drawn as follows.

(a) The **vertical axis** represents **money** (costs and revenue) and the **horizontal axis** represents the **level of activity** (production and sales).

(b) The fixed costs are represented by a **straight line parallel to the horizontal axis** (in our example, at £40,000).

(c) The **variable costs** are added 'on top of' fixed costs, to give **total costs**. It is assumed that fixed costs are the same in total and variable costs are the same per unit at all levels of output.

The line of costs is therefore a straight line and only two points need to be plotted and joined up. Perhaps the two most convenient points to plot are total costs at zero output, and total costs at the budgeted output and sales.

(i) At zero output, costs are equal to the amount of fixed costs only, £40,000, since there are no variable costs.

(ii) At the budgeted output of 120,000 units, costs are £100,000.

	£
Fixed costs	40,000
Variable costs 120,000 × 50p	60,000
Total costs	100,000

(d) The sales line is also drawn by plotting two points and joining them up.

(i) At zero sales, revenue is nil.

(ii) At the budgeted output and sales of 120,000 units, revenue is £120,000.

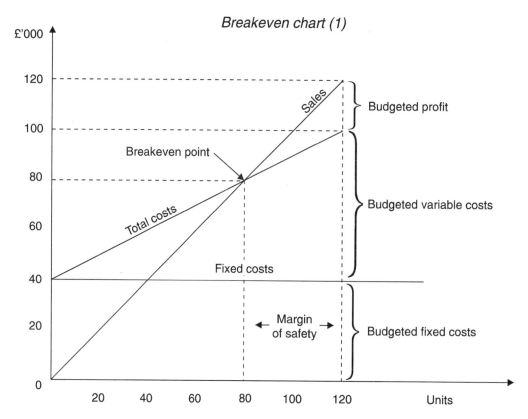

Breakeven chart (1)

5.7 **The breakeven point is where total costs are matched exactly by total revenue.** From the chart, this can be seen to occur at output and sales of 80,000 units, when revenue and costs are both £80,000. This breakeven point can be proved mathematically as:

$$\frac{\text{Required contribution} = \text{fixed costs}}{\text{Contribution per unit}} = \frac{£40,000}{\text{50p per unit}} = 80,000 \text{ units}$$

5.8 The **margin of safety** can be seen on the chart as the **difference** between the **budgeted level of activity** and the **breakeven level**.

The value of breakeven charts

5.9 Breakeven charts are used as follows.

- To **plan** the production of a company's products
- To **market** a company's products
- To given a **visual display** of breakeven arithmetic

5.10 EXAMPLE: VARIATIONS IN THE USE OF BREAKEVEN CHARTS

Breakeven charts can be used to **show variations** in the possible **sales price**, **variable costs** or **fixed costs**. Suppose that a company sells a product which has a variable cost of £2 per unit. Fixed costs are £15,000. It has been estimated that if the sales price is set at £4.40 per unit, the expected sales volume would be 7,500 units; whereas if the sales price is lower, at £4 per unit, the expected sales volume would be 10,000 units.

Required

Draw a breakeven chart to show the budgeted profit, the breakeven point and the margin of safety at each of the possible sales prices.

5.11 SOLUTION

Workings	*Sales price £4.40 per unit*		*Sales price £4 per unit*
	£		£
Fixed costs	15,000		15,000
Variable costs (7,500 × £2.00)	15,000	(10,000 × £2.00)	20,000
Total costs	30,000		35,000
Budgeted revenue (7,500 × £4.40)	33,000	(10,000 × £4.00)	40,000

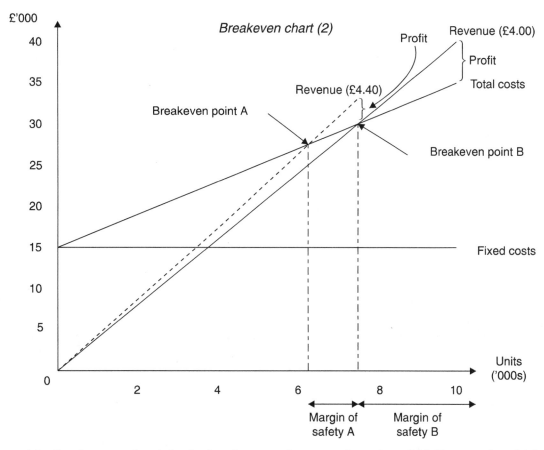

(a) Breakeven point A is the breakeven point at a sales price of £4.40 per unit, which is 6,250 units or £27,500 in costs and revenues.

$$\left(\text{check: } \frac{\text{Required contribution to breakeven}}{\text{Contribution per unit}} \quad \frac{£150,00}{£2.40 \text{ per unit}} = 6,250 \text{ units}\right)$$

The margin of safety (A) is 7,500 units – 6,250 units = 1,250 units or 16.7% of expected sales.

BPP PUBLISHING

(b) Breakeven point B is the breakeven point at a sales price of £4 per unit which is 7,500 units or £30,000 in costs and revenues.

(check: $\dfrac{\text{Required contribution to breakeven}}{\text{Contribution per unit}}$ $\dfrac{£150,00}{£2 \text{ per unit}}$ = 7,5000 units)

The margin of safety (B) = 10,000 units − 7,500 units = 2,500 units or 25% of expected sales.

5.12 Since a price of £4 per unit gives a higher expected profit and a wider margin of safety, this price will probably be preferred even though the breakeven point is higher than at a sales price of £4.40 per unit.

Contribution (or contribution breakeven) charts

5.13 As an alternative to drawing the fixed cost line first, it is possible to start with that for variable costs. This is known as a **contribution chart**. An example is shown below using the example in Paragraphs 5.5 and 5.6.

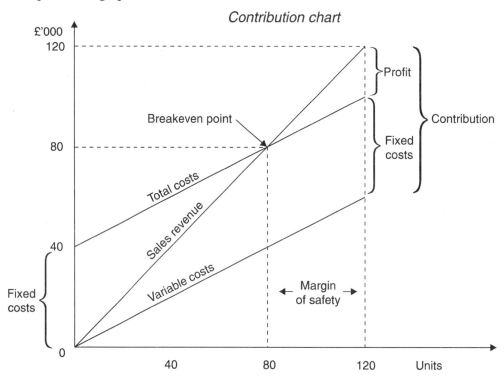

Contribution chart

5.14 One of the **advantages** of the contribution chart is that is shows clearly the **contribution** for **different levels of production** (indicated here at 120,000 units, the budgeted level of output) as the 'wedge' shape between the sales revenue line and the variable costs line. At the **breakeven point**, the **contribution equals fixed costs** exactly. At levels of output **above** the **breakeven** point, the **contribution** is **larger**, and not only covers fixed costs, but also leaves a profit. **Below** the **breakeven** point, the **loss** is the amount by which contribution fails to cover fixed costs.

The Profit/Volume (P/V) chart

> ### KEY TERM
>
> The **profit/volume (P/V) chart** is a variation of the breakeven chart which illustrates the relationship of costs and profit to sales, and the margin of safety.

5.15 A P/V chart is constructed as follows (look at the chart in the example that follows as you read the explanation).

(a) 'P' is on the y axis and actually comprises not only 'profit' but contribution to profit (in monetary value), extending above and below the x axis with a zero point at the intersection of the two axes, and the negative section below the x axis representing fixed costs. This means that at zero production, the firm is incurring a loss equal to the fixed costs.

(b) 'V' is on the x axis and comprises either volume of sales or value of sales (revenue).

(c) The profit-volume line is a straight line drawn with its starting point (at zero production) at the intercept on the y axis representing the level of fixed costs, and with a gradient of contribution/unit (or the C/S ratio if sales value is used rather than units). The P/V line will cut the x axis at the breakeven point of sales volume. Any point on the P/V line above the x axis represents the profit to the firm (as measured on the vertical axis) for that particular level of sales.

5.16 EXAMPLE: P/V CHART

Let us draw a P/V chart for our example. At sales of 120,000 units, total contribution will be $120,000 \times £(1 - 0.5) = £60,000$ and total profit will be £20,000.

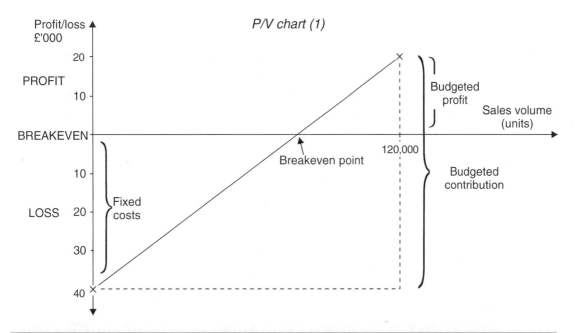

Exam focus point
There were 8 marks available in the 12/99 exam for drawing a P/V chart.

The advantage of the P/V chart

5.17 **The P/V chart shows clearly the effect on profit and breakeven point of any changes in selling price, variable cost, fixed cost and/or sales demand**. If the budgeted selling price of the product in our example is increased to £1.20, with the result that demand drops to 105,000 units despite additional fixed costs of £10,000 being spent on advertising, we could add a line representing this situation to our P/V chart.

5.18 At sales of 105,000 units, contribution will be $105,000 \times £(1.20 - 0.50) = £73,500$ and total profit will be £23,500 (fixed costs being £50,000).

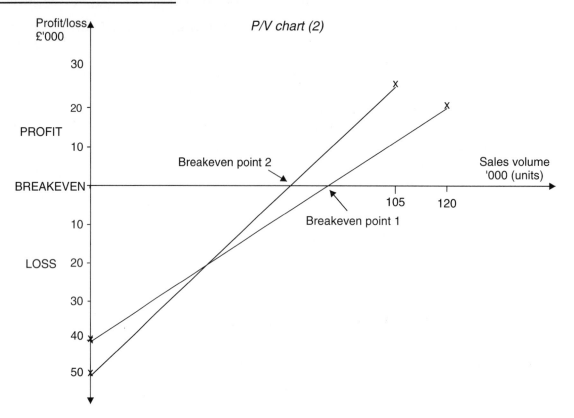

5.19 The diagram shows that if the selling price is increased, the breakeven point occurs at a lower level of sales revenue (71,429 units instead of 80,000 units), although this is not a particularly large increase when viewed in the context of the projected sales volume. It is also possible to see that for sales above 50,000 units, the profit achieved will be higher (and the loss achieved lower) if the price is £1.20. For sales volumes below 50,000 units the first option will yield lower losses.

5.20 The P/V chart is the clearest way of presenting such information; two conventional breakeven charts on one set of axes would be very confusing.

5.21 Changes in the variable cost per unit or in fixed costs at certain activity levels can also be easily incorporated into a P/V chart. The profit or loss at each point where the cost structure changes should be calculated and plotted on the graph so that the profit/volume line becomes a series of straight lines.

5.22 For example, suppose that in our example, at sales levels in excess of 120,000 units the variable cost per unit increases to £0.60 (perhaps because of overtime premiums that are incurred when production exceeds a certain level). At sales of 130,000 units, contribution would therefore be $130,000 \times £(1 - 0.60) = £52,000$ and total profit would be £12,000.

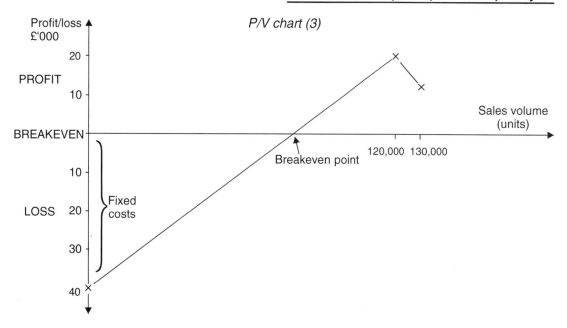

P/V chart (3)

The multi-product breakeven and P/V chart   6/94

5.23   Since most companies sell more than one product, a multi-product chart of some type might be required.

5.24   **A very serious limitation of breakeven charts is that they can show the costs, revenues, profits and margins of safety for a single product only,** or for a single 'sales mix' of products.

5.25   For example suppose that Farmyard Ltd sells three products, X, Y and Z, which have variable unit costs of £3, £4 and £5 respectively. The sales price of X is £8, the price of Y is £6 and the price of Z is £6. Fixed costs per annum are £10,000.

5.26   A breakeven chart cannot be drawn, because we do not know the proportions of X, Y and Z in the sales mix. (If you are not sure about this point, you should try to draw a breakeven chart with the information given. It should not be possible.)

5.27   If, however, we now assume that budgeted sales are as follows:

    X   2,000 units
    Y   4,000 units
    Z   3,000 units

a breakeven chart can be drawn. The chart would make the assumption that output and sales of X, Y and Z are in the proportions 2,000 : 4,000 : 3,000 at all levels of activity, in other words that the sales mix is 'fixed' in these proportions.

(a)   *Workings*

Budgeted costs		*Costs* £	*Budgeted revenue*	*Revenue* £
Variable costs of X	(2,000 × £3)	6,000	X (2,000 × £8)	16,000
Variable costs of Y	(4,000 × £4)	16,000	Y (4,000 × £6)	24,000
Variable costs of Z	(3,000 × £5)	15,000	Z (3,000 × £6)	18,000
Total variable costs		37,000		58,000
Fixed costs		10,000		
Total budgeted costs		47,000		

(b)   The breakeven chart can now be drawn.

441

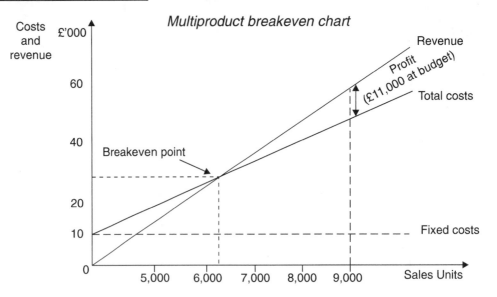

Multiproduct breakeven chart

5.28 The same information could be shown on a P/V chart, as follows.

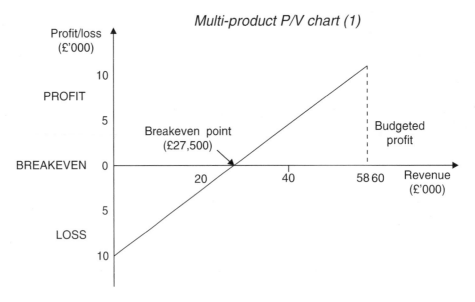

Multi-product P/V chart (1)

5.29 The breakeven point is approximately £27,500. This may either be read from the breakeven chart or computed mathematically. The budgeted C/S ratio for all three products together is

$$\frac{\text{contribution}}{\text{sales}} = \frac{£(58,000 - 37,000)}{£58,000} = 36.21\%$$

The required contribution to break even is £10,000, the amount of fixed costs. The breakeven point is

$$\frac{£10,000}{36.21\%} = £27,500 \text{ (approx) in sales revenue}$$

5.30 An addition to the P/V chart would now be made to show further information about the contribution earned by each product individually, so that their performance and profitability can be compared.

	Contribution £	Sales £	C/S ratio %
Product X	10,000	16,000	62.50
Product Y	8,000	24,000	33.33
Product Z	3,000	18,000	16.67
Total	21,000	58,000	36.21

5.31 By convention, the products are shown individually on a P/V chart from left to right, in order of the size of their C/S ratio. In this example, product X will be plotted first, then product Y and finally product Z. A dotted line is used to show the cumulative profit/loss and the cumulative sales as each product's sales and contribution in turn are added to the sales mix.

Product	Cumulative sales £		Cumulative profit £
X	16,000	(£10,000 – £10,000)	-
X and Y	40,000		8,000
X, Y and Z	58,000		11,000

You will see on the graph which follows that these three pairs of data are used to plot the dotted line, to indicate the contribution from each product. The solid line which joins the two ends of this dotted line indicates the average profit which will be earned from sales of the three products in this mix.

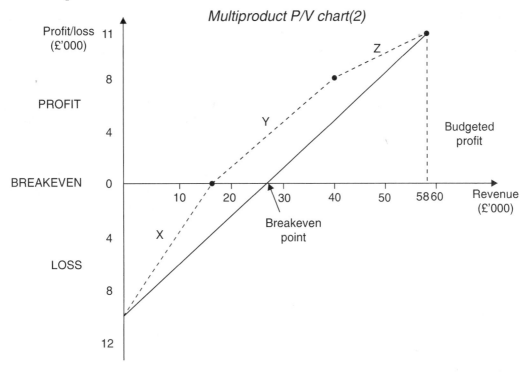

Multiproduct P/V chart(2)

5.32 From this diagram, it may be apparent that since X is the most profitable in terms of C/S ratio, it might be worth considering an increase in the sales of X, even if there is a consequent fall in the sales of Z. Alternatively, the pricing structure of the products should be reviewed and a decision made as to whether the price of product Z should be raised so as to increase its C/S ratio (although an increase is likely to result in some fall in sales volume).

5.33 The **multi-product P/V chart** is therefore **helpful** in identifying the following.

(a) The overall company breakeven point.

(b) Which products should be expanded in output and which should be discontinued.

(c) How changes in selling price/sales volume will effect the company's breakeven point/profit.

6 LIMITATIONS OF CVP ANALYSIS

6.1 Breakeven analysis is a useful technique for managers. Breakeven arithmetic can provide **simple** and **quick** estimates. **Breakeven charts** provide a **graphical representation** of breakeven arithmetic. Breakeven analysis has a number of limitations.

- It **can only apply to a single product** or a single mix of a group of products.
- A breakeven chart may be **time-consuming** to prepare.
- It **assumes** fixed costs are constant at all levels of output.
- It **assumes** that **variable costs** are the **same** per unit at all levels of output.
- It **assumes** that **sales prices** are **constant** at all levels of output.
- It assumes **production** and **sales** are the **same** (stock levels are ignored).
- It **ignores** the **uncertainty** in the estimates of fixed costs and variable cost per unit.

Chapter roundup

- CVP analysis has a number of purposes: to provide information to management about cost behaviour for routine planning and 'one-off' decision making; to determine what volume of sales is needed at any given budgeted sales price in order to break even; to identify the 'risk' in the budget by measuring the margin of safety; to calculate the effects on profit of changes in variable costs, C/S ratios, sales price and volume, product mix, and so on.

- Make sure that you understand how to calculate the breakeven point, the C/S ratio, the margin of safety and target profits, and can apply the principles of CVP analysis both to decisions about whether to change sales prices or costs and to problems of profit maximisation. You should also be able to construct breakeven, contribution and profit/volume charts.

- CVP analysis does have limitations: it is only valid within a 'relevant range' of output volumes; it measures profitability, but does not consider the volume of capital employed to achieve such profits, and so ignores return on capital employed; and it is subject to certain other limitations described earlier in this chapter.

Quick quiz

1 What is the formula for calculating the breakeven point in terms of the number of units required to break even? (see formulae to learn)

2 Give the formula which uses the C/S ratio to calculate the breakeven point. (formulae to learn)

3 What is the margin of safety? (key terms)

4 Give three uses of breakeven charts? (5.9)

5 Sketch a breakeven chart which shows the contribution at different levels of production. (5.13)

6 What is a profit/volume chart? (key terms)

7 What are the limitations of breakeven charts and CVP analysis? (6.1)

Question to try	Level	Marks	Time
26	Introductory	n/a	15 mins

Chapter 26

LINEAR PROGRAMMING

Chapter topic list	Syllabus reference
1 Formulating the problem	QT 3(c)
2 Graphing the model	QT 3(a), (c)
3 Finding the best solution	QT 1(c), 3(b), (c)

Introduction

As with the other models we have looked at, Chapter 23 on equations and Chapter 24 on cost behaviour provide the foundations for this chapter on **linear programming models**. But what is linear programming?

Linear programming is a technique for solving problems of

- **profit maximisation**
- **cost minimisation**
- **resource allocation**

We are all faced with **resource allocation decisions** on a daily basis. For example, we may consider that we don't have enough money. Money is therefore a **scarce resource**, and we have to decide as to how best to spend it. This chapter looks at the way in which maximisation, minimisation and resource allocation problems are best solved.

1   FORMULATING THE PROBLEM   12/94

1.1   In common with many quantitative methods, we need a rather simple example to illustrate the basic linear programming techniques. Let us imagine that Barkers Ltd makes just two models of kennel, the Super and the Deluxe, and that the only constraint faced by the company is that monthly machine capacity is restricted to 400 hours. The Super requires 5 hours of machine time per unit and the Deluxe 1.5 hours. Government restrictions mean that the maximum number of kennels that can be sold each month is 150, that number being made up of any combination of the Super and the Deluxe.

1.2   Let us now work through the steps involved in setting up a linear programming model.

Step 1. Define variables

1.3   What are the quantities that the company can vary? Obviously not the number of machine hours or the maximum sales, which are fixed by external circumstances beyond the company's control. The only things which it can determine are the number of each type of kennel to manufacture. It is these numbers which Jack Russell has to determine in such a way as to get the maximum possible profit. Our variables will therefore be as follows.

Let x = the number of units of the Super kennel manufactured.
Let y = the number of units of the Deluxe kennel manufactured.

Step 2. **Establish constraints**

1.4   Having defined these two variables we can now translate the two constraints into inequalities involving the variables.

1.5   Let us first consider the machine hours constraint. Each Super requires 5 hours of machine time. Producing five Supers therefore requires $5 \times 5 = 25$ hours of machine time and, more generally producing x Supers will require 5x hours. Likewise producing y Deluxes will require 1.5y hours. The total machine hours needed to make x Supers and y Deluxes is 5x + 1.5y. We know that this cannot be greater than 400 hours so we arrive at the following inequality.

$$5x + 1.5y \le 400$$

1.6   We can obtain the other inequality more easily. The total number of Supers and Deluxes made each month is x + y but this has to be less than 150 due to government restrictions. The sales order constraint is therefore as follows.

$$x + y \le 150$$

1.7   The variables in linear programming models should usually be non-negative in value. In this example, for instance, you cannot make a negative number of kennels and so we need the following constraints.

$$x \ge 0; y \ge 0$$

Do not forget these non-negativity constraints when formulating a linear programming model.

Step 3. **Establish objective function**

1.8   We have yet to introduce the question of profits. Let us assume that the profit on each type of kennel is as follows.

	£
Super	100
Deluxe	200

1.9   The objective of Barkers Ltd is to maximise profit and so the objective function to be maximised is as follows.

Profit (P) = 100x + 200y

1.10   The problem has now been reduced to the following four inequalities and one equation.

$$5x + 1.5y \;\le 400$$
$$x + y \;\le 150$$
$$x \;\ge 0$$
$$y \;\ge 0$$
$$P \;= 100x + 200y$$

1.11   Have you noticed that the inequalities are all **linear expressions**? If plotted on a graph, they would all give straight lines. This explains why the technique is called **linear programming** and also gives a hint as to how we should proceed with trying to find the solution to Jack's problem.

1.12 EXAMPLE: FORMULATING A PROBLEM

Maxim Wise Ltd makes three products, A, B and C. Each product is made by the same grades of labour, and the time required to make one unit of each product is as follows.

	A	B	C
Skilled labour	3 hours	4 hours	1 hour
Unskilled labour	2.5 hours	2 hours	6 hours

The variable costs per unit of A, B and C are £28, £30 and £26 respectively. The products sell for £40, £40 and £34 respectively.

In March 20X3 the company expects to have only 600 hours of skilled labour and 2,000 hours of unskilled labour available. There is a minimum requirement for 40 units of B and 120 units of C in the month.

Monthly fixed costs are £1,500.

Required

Formulate a linear programming problem.

1.13 SOLUTION

The variables are the products A, B and C. We want to decide how many of each to produce in the month.

Let the number of units of product A made be a.
Let the number of units of product B made be b.
Let the number of units of product C made be c.

The objective is to maximise the monthly profit. Since fixed costs are a constant value of £1,500, which will be incurred regardless of which production plan is selected, these are irrelevant to the objective function, which can be stated as 'to maximise profit by maximising contribution'. The contribution per unit is £12 for A, £10 for B and £8 for C.

The objective is therefore to maximise $12a + 10b + 8c$ (contribution).

There are constraints relating to the availability of skilled labour and unskilled labour, and the minimum requirements for B and C. In addition, there are the constraints that A, B and C cannot have negative values, but since B and C must exceed 40 and 120 respectively, the non-negativity constraints are redundant for these two variables.

The programme may therefore be formulated as follows.

Objective: maximise $12a + 10b + 8c$ (contribution)
subject to the constraints:

$3a + 4b + c$	$\leq$	600	(skilled labour)
$2.5a + 2b + 6c$	$\leq$	2,000	(unskilled labour)
b	$\geq$	40	(requirement for B)
c	$\geq$	120	(requirement for C)
a	$\geq$	0	

2   GRAPHING THE MODEL   12/98

2.1   We have looked at how to formulate a problem and in this section we will look at solving a problem using graphs.

2.2   A **graphical solution** is only **possible** when there are **two variables** in the problem. One variable is represented by the x axis and one by the y axis of the graph. Since non-negative values are not usually allowed, the graph shows only zero and positive values of x and y.

2.3   A linear equation with one or two variables is shown as a straight line on a graph.
       Thus y = 6 would be shown as follows.

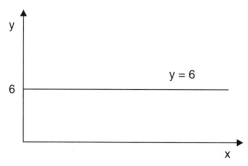

If the problem included a constraint that y could not exceed 6, the inequality $y \leq 6$ would be represented by the shaded area of the graph below.

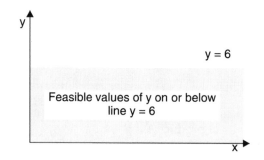

2.4   The equation 4x + 3y = 24 is also a straight line on a graph. To draw any straight line, we need only to plot two points and join them up. The easiest points to plot are the following.

(a)   x = 0 (in this example, if x = 0, 3y = 24, y = 8)
(b)   y = 0 (in this example, if y = 0, 4x = 24, x = 6)

By plotting the points, (0, 8) and (6, 0) on a graph, and joining them up, we have the line for 4x + 3y = 24.

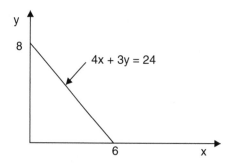

2.5   If we had a constraint $4x + 3y \leq 24$, any combined value of x and y within the shaded area below (on or below the line) would satisfy the constraint.

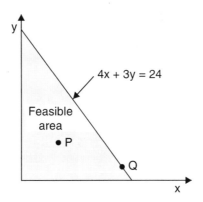

For example, at point P where (x = 2, y = 2) 4x + 3y = 14 which is less than 24; and at point Q where x = 5.5, y = 2/3, 4x + 3y = 24. Both P and Q lie within the feasible area (the area where the inequality is satisfied, also called the **feasible region**). A feasible area enclosed on all sides may also be called a feasible polygon.

2.6   The inequalities y ≥ 6, x ≥ 6 and 4x + 3y ≥ 24, would be shown graphically as follows.

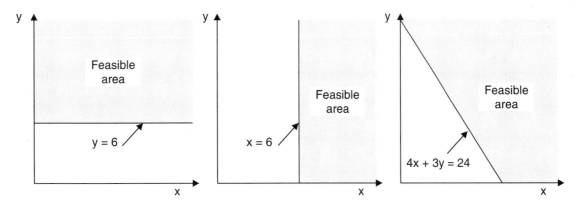

2.7   When there are several constraints, the feasible area of combinations of values of x and y must be an area where all the inequalities are satisfied.

Thus, if y ≤ 6 *and* 4x + 3y ≤ 24 the feasible area would be the shaded area in the following graph.

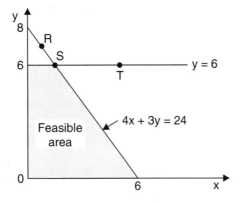

(a)   Point R (x = 0.75, y = 7) is not in the feasible area because although it satisfies the inequality 4x + 3y ≤ 24, it does not satisfy y ≤ 6.

(b)   Point T (x = 5, y = 6) is not in the feasible area, because although it satisfies the inequality y ≤ 6, it does not satisfy 4x + 3y ≤ 24.

(c)   Point S (x = 1.5, y = 6) satisfies both inequalities and lies just on the boundary of the feasible area since y = 6 exactly, and 4x + 3y = 24. Point S is thus at the intersection of the two equation lines.

2.8 Similarly, if y ≥ 6 and 4x + 3y ≥ 24 but x ≤ 6, the feasible area would be the shaded area in the graph below.

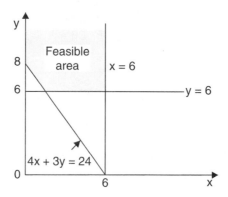

Question 1

Draw the feasible region which arises from the constraints facing Barkers.

Answer

If 5x + 1.5y = 400, then if x = 0, y = 267 and if y = 0, x = 80.
If x + y = 150, then if x = 0, y = 150 and if y = 0, x = 150.

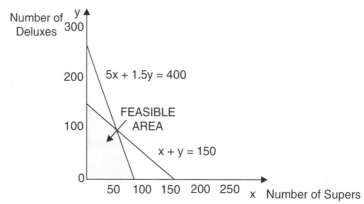

Question 2

Draw the feasible area for the following inequalities.

2x + 3y ≤ 12
y   ≥ 2x
x   ≥ 0, y ≥ 0

Answer

The new problem here is the inequality y ≥ 2x. The equation y = 2x is a straight line, and you need to plot two points to draw it, for example:

(a) when x = 0, y = 0
(b) when x = 2, y = 4

Since y ≥ 2x, feasible combinations of x and y lie above this line (if x = 2, y must be 4 or more).

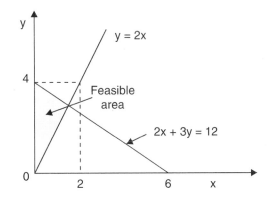

---

3 FINDING THE BEST SOLUTION

3.1 Having found the feasible region (which includes all the possible solutions to the problem) we need to find which of these possible solutions is 'best' in the sense that it yields the maximum possible profit. We could do this by finding out what profit each of the possible solutions would give, and then choosing as our 'best' combination the one for which the profit is greatest.

3.2 Consider, however, the feasible region of the problem faced by Barkers Ltd (see the solution to Question 1). Even in such a simple problem as this, there are a great many possible solution points within the feasible area. Even to write them all down would be a time consuming process and also an unnecessary one, as we shall see.

3.3 Let us look again at the graph of Barker's problem.

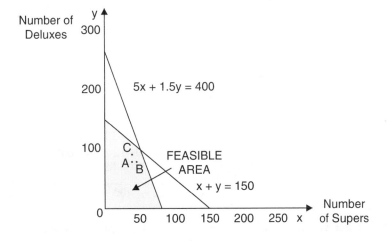

Consider, for example, the point A at which 40 Supers and 80 Deluxes are being manufactured. This will yield a profit of $((40 \times 100) + (80 \times 200)) = £20,000$. We would clearly get more profit at point B, where the same number of Deluxes are being manufactured but where the number of Supers being manufactured has increased by five, or from point C where the same number of Supers but 10 more Deluxes are manufactured. This argument suggests that the 'best' solution is going to be a point on the edge of the feasible area rather than in the middle of it.

3.4 This still leaves us with quite a few points to look at but there is a way we can narrow down the candidates for the best solution still further. Suppose that Barkers wish to make a profit of £10,000. The company could sell the following combinations of Supers and Deluxes.

(a) 100 Super, no Deluxe

    (b) No Super, 50 Deluxe

    (c) A proportionate mix of Super and Deluxe, such as 80 Super and 10 Deluxe or 50 Super and 25 Deluxe

3.5   The possible combinations of Supers and Deluxes required to earn a profit of £10,000 could be shown by the straight line $100x + 200y = 10,000$.

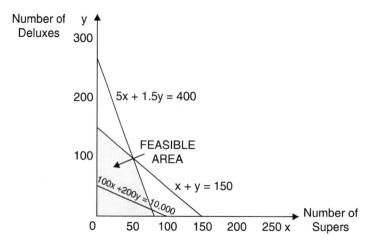

3.6   For a total profit of £15,000, a similar line $100x + 200y = 15,000$ could be drawn to show the various combinations of Supers and Deluxes which would achieve the total of £15,000. Similarly a line $100x + 200y = 8,000$ would show the various combinations of Supers and Deluxes which would earn a total profit of £8,000.

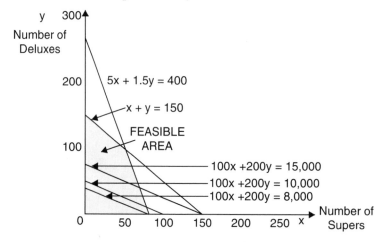

3.7   These profit lines are all parallel. (They are called **iso-profit lines**, 'iso' meaning equal.) A similar line drawn for any other total profit would also be parallel to the three lines shown here. This means that if we wish to know the slope or gradient of the profit line, for any value of total profit, we can simply draw one line for any convenient value of profit, and we will know that all the other lines will be parallel to the one drawn: they will have the same slope.

3.8   **Bigger profits are shown by lines further from the origin** ($100x + 200y = 15,000$), **smaller profits by lines closer to the origin** ($100x + 200y = 8,000$). As Barkers try to increase possible profit we need to slide the profit line outwards from the origin, while always keeping it parallel to the other profit lines.

3.9   As we do this there will come a point at which, if we were to move the profit line out any further, it would cease to lie in the feasible region and therefore larger profits could not be achieved in practice because of the constraints. In our example concerning Barkers this will happen, as you should test for yourself, where the profit line is just passing through the intersection of x + y = 150 with the y axis (at (0, 150)). The point (0, 150) will therefore give us the best production combination of the Super and the Deluxe, that is, to produce 150 Deluxe models and no Super models.

3.10 EXAMPLE: A MAXIMISATION PROBLEM

Brunel Ltd manufactures plastic-covered steel fencing in two qualities, standard and heavy gauge. Both products pass through the same processes, involving steel-forming and plastic bonding.

Standard gauge fencing sells at £18 a roll and heavy gauge fencing at £24 a roll. Variable costs per roll are £16 and £21 respectively. There is an unlimited market for the standard gauge, but demand for the heavy gauge is limited to 1,300 rolls a year. Factory operations are limited to 2,400 hours a year in each of the two production processes.

	Processing hours per roll	
Gauge	*Steel-forming*	*Plastic-bonding*
Standard	0.6	0.4
Heavy	0.8	1.2

Required

Determine the production mix which will maximise total contribution. Calculate the total contribution.

3.11 SOLUTION

Let S be the number of standard gauge rolls per year.
Let H be the number of heavy gauge rolls per year.

The objective is to maximise 2S + 3H (contribution) subject to the following constraints.

$$0.6S + 0.8H \leq 2,400 \quad \text{(steel-forming hours)}$$
$$0.4S + 1.2H \leq 2,400 \quad \text{(plastic-bonding hours)}$$
$$H \leq 1,300 \quad \text{(sales demand)}$$
$$S, H \geq 0$$

Note that the constraints are inequalities, and are not equations. There is no requirement to use up the total hours available in each process, nor to satisfy all the demand for heavy gauge rolls.

If we take the production constraint of 2,400 hours in the steel-forming process

$$0.6S + 0.8H \leq 2,400$$

it means that since there are only 2,400 hours available in the process, output must be limited to a maximum of:

(a) $\dfrac{2,400}{0.6}$ = 4,000 rolls of standard gauge;

(b) $\dfrac{2,400}{0.8}$ = 3,000 rolls of heavy gauge; or

(c) a proportionate combination of each.

This maximum output represents the boundary line of the constraint, where the inequality becomes the equation 0.6S + 0.8H = 2,400.

The line for this equation may be drawn on a graph by joining up two points on the line (such as S = 0, H = 3,000; H = 0, S = 4,000).

The other constraints may be drawn in a similar way with lines for the following equations.

$$0.4S + 1.2H = 2,400 \quad \text{(plastic-bonding)}$$
$$H = 1,300 \quad \text{(sales demand)}$$

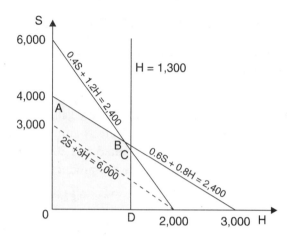

To satisfy all the constraints simultaneously, the values of S and H must lie on or below each constraint line. The outer limits of the feasible polygon are the lines, but all combined values of S and H within the shaded area are feasible solutions.

The next step is to find the **optimal solution**, which **maximises the objective function**. Since the objective is to maximise contribution, the solution to the problem must involve relatively high values (within the feasible polygon) for S, or H or a combination of both.

If, as is likely, there is only one combination of S and H which provides the optimal solution, this combination will be one of the outer corners of the feasible polygon. There are four such corners, A, B, C and D. However, it is possible that any combination of values for S and H on the boundary line between two of these corners might provide solutions with the same total contribution.

To solve the problem we establish the slope of the iso-contribution lines, by drawing a line for any one level of contribution. In our solution, a line 2S + 3H = 6,000 has been drawn. (6,000 was chosen as a convenient multiple of 2 and 3). This line has no significance except to indicate the slope of every iso-contribution line for 2S + 3H.

Using a ruler to judge at which corner of the feasible polygon we can draw an iso-contribution line which is as far to the right as possible, (away from the origin) but which still touches the feasible polygon.

This occurs at corner B where the constraint line 0.4S + 1.2H = 2,400 crosses with the constraint line 0.6S + 0.8H = 2,400. At this point, there are simultaneous equations, from which the exact values of S and H may be calculated.

$$
\begin{array}{llll}
0.4S + & 1.2H & = & 2,400 & \quad (1) \\
0.6S + & 0.8H & = & 2,400 & \quad (2) \\
1.2S + & 3.6H & = & 7,200 & \quad (3)\ ((1) \times 3) \\
1.2S + & 1.6H & = & 4,800 & \quad (4)\ ((2) \times 2) \\
 & 2H & = & 2,400 & \quad (5)\ ((3) - (4)) \\
 & H & = & 1,200 & \quad (6)
\end{array}
$$

Substituting 1,200 for H in either equation, we can calculate that S = 2,400.

The contribution is maximised where H = 1,200, and S = 2,400.

	Units	Contribution per unit £	Total contribution £
Standard gauge	2,400	2	4,800
Heavy gauge	1,200	3	3,600
			8,400

Question 3

The Dervish Chemical Company operates a small plant. Operating the plant requires two raw materials, A and B, which cost £5 and £8 per litre respectively. The maximum available supply per week is 2,700 litres of A and 2,000 litres of B.

The plant can operate using either of two processes, which have differing contributions and raw materials requirements, as follows.

Process	Raw materials consumed (litres per processing hour)		Contribution per hour £
	A	B	
1	20	10	70
2	30	20	60

The plant can run for 120 hours a week in total, but for safety reasons, process 2 cannot be operated for more than 80 hours a week.

Required

Formulate a linear programming model, and then solve it, to determine how many hours process 1 should be operated each week and how many hours process 2 should be operated each week.

Answer

The decision variables are processing hours in each process. If we let the processing hours per week for process 1 be P_1 and the processing hours per week for process 2 be P_2 we can formulate an objective and constraints as follows.

The objective is to maximise $70P_1 + 60P_2$, subject to the following constraints.

$$
\begin{array}{llll}
20P_1 & + \ 30P_2 & \leq & 2,700 \quad \text{(material A supply)} \\
10P_1 & + \ 20P_2 & \leq & 2,000 \quad \text{(material B supply)} \\
P_2 & & \leq & 80 \quad \text{(maximum time for } P_2 \text{)} \\
P_1 + P_2 & & \leq & 120 \quad \text{(total maximum time)} \\
P_1, P_2 & & \geq & 0
\end{array}
$$

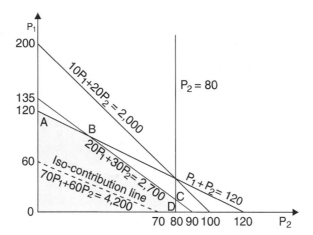

The feasible area is ABCDO.

The optimal solution, found by moving the iso-contribution line outwards, is at point A, where $P_1 = 120$ and $P_2 = 0$.

Total contribution would be $120 \times 70 = £8,400$ a week.

Minimisation problems in linear programming

3.12   Decision problems with limiting factors usually involve the maximisation of contribution. Sometimes there may be a requirement to minimise costs. **We can solve minimisation problems by finding a total cost line which touches the feasible area as near to the origin as possible.**

3.13   EXAMPLE: A MINIMISATION PROBLEM

Stewart Ltd has undertaken a contract to supply a customer with at least 260 units in total of two products, X and Y, during the next month. At least 50% of the total output must be units of X. The products are each made by two grades of labour, as follows.

	X	Y
	Hours	*Hours*
Grade A labour	4	6
Grade B labour	4	2
Total	8	8

Although additional labour can be made available at short notice, the company wishes to make use of 1,200 hours of Grade A labour and 800 hours of Grade B labour which has already been assigned to working on the contract next month. The total variable cost per unit is £120 for X and £100 for Y. Stewart Ltd wishes to minimise expenditure on the contract next month.

Required

Calculate how much of X and Y should be supplied in order to meet the terms of the contract.

3.14   SOLUTION

Let the number of units of X supplied be x, and the number of units of Y supplied be y.

The objective is to minimise $120x + 100y$ (costs), subject to the following constraints.

$x + y$	$\geq$	260	(supply total)
x	$\geq$	$0.5 (x + y)$	(proportion of x in total)
$4x + 6y$	$\geq$	1,200	(Grade A labour)
$4x + 2y$	$\geq$	800	(Grade B labour)
x, y	$\geq$	0	

The constraint $x \geq 0.5 (x + y)$ needs simplifying further.

x	$\geq 0.5 (x + y)$
$2x$	$\geq \quad x + y$
x	$\geq \quad y$

In a graphical solution, the line will be $x = y$.

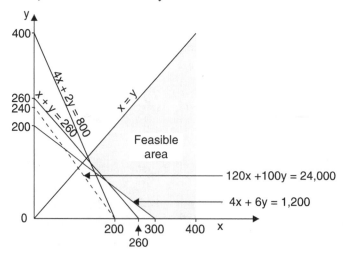

The cost line 120x + 100y = 24,000 has been drawn to show the slope of every cost line 120x + 100y. Costs are minimised where a cost line touches the feasible area as close as possible to the origin of the graph. This occurs where the constraint line 4x + 2y = 800 crosses the constraint line x + y = 260. This point is found as follows.

$$
\begin{array}{lll}
x + y & = \ 260 & (1) \\
4x + 2y & = \ 800 & (2) \\
2x + y & = \ 400 & (3) \ ((2) \times 2) \\
x & = \ 140 & (4) \ ((3) - (1)) \\
y & = \ 120 & (5)
\end{array}
$$

Costs will be minimised by supplying the following.

	Unit cost £	Total cost £
140 units of X	120	16,800
120 units of Y	100	12,000
		28,800

The proportion of units of X in the total would exceed 50%, and demand for Grade A labour would exceed the 1,200 hours minimum.

The use of simultaneous equations   12/94, 6/97

3.15 You might think that a lot of time could be saved if we started by solving the simultaneous equations in a linear programming problem and did not bother to draw the graph. Certainly, this procedure may give the right answer, but in general it is *not* recommended until you have shown graphically which constraints are effective in determining the optimal solution. (In particular, if a question requires 'the graphical method', you *must* draw a graph.) To illustrate this point, consider the following graph.

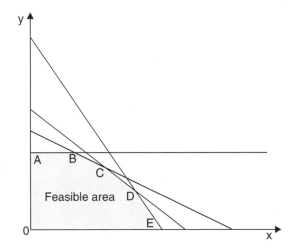

3.16 No figures have been given on the graph but the feasible area is OABCDE. When solving this problem, we would know that the optimum solution would be at one of the corners of the feasible area. We need to work out the profit at each of the corners of the feasible area and pick the one where the profit is greatest. Once the optimum point has been determined graphically, simultaneous equations can be applied to find the exact values of x and y at this point.

Question 4

Given the following constraints and objective function, determine the optimal production level of product X and product Y.

Constraints

$$Y \leq \text{}^{-X}/_2 + 5 \quad (1)$$
$$Y \leq 2X \quad (2)$$
$$X \geq 0 \quad (3)$$
$$Y \geq 0 \quad (4)$$

Objective function

Profit = 3X + 4Y

Answer

Feasible solutions are at the intersection of the constraints:

(1) and (2)	*(1) and (3)*	*(1) and (4)*	*(2) and (3) (2) and (4) (3) and (4)*
X = 2, Y = 4	X = 0, Y = 5	X = 10, Y = 0	X = 0, Y = 0
Profit = 22	Profit = 20	Profit = 30	Profit = 0

Profit is maximised when 10 units of product X and no units of product Y are produced.

Full utilisation of resources
6/96

3.17 If a question states that you are to determine a production plan which will fully utilise *all* available production resources, you can simply construct equations to represent the constraints, treat them as simultaneous equations and solve, without drawing a graph, since there must be only one possible solution if all resources are to be used.

Exam focus point

You must be able to determine the optimal solution graphically and using simultaneous equations. If you have to draw a graph, make sure that it has a title, the axes are labelled and that the constraint lines and the feasible area are clearly identified.

Chapter roundup

- **Linear programming** is a technique that can be carried out in the following stages.

  - Define variables
  - Establish constraints (including non-negativity)
  - Construct objective function
  - Draw a graph of the constraints
  - Establish the feasible region
  - Add an iso-profit/contribution line
  - Determine optimal solution

- Linear programming has a number of practical limitations.

  - In all practical situations there are likely to be substantial problems involved in estimating the total quantities of **scarce resources** available. Furthermore, the final estimates used are likely to be subject to considerable uncertainty.

  - There is an assumption of **linearity**. Each extra unit of a given product is supposed to change the contribution and the consumption of resources by the same amount. In practice, this assumption may be invalid except over small ranges. For example, in a profit maximisation problem, it might be found that there are substantial changes in unit variable costs arising from increasing/decreasing returns to scale.

  - The linear programming model is essentially **static** and is therefore not really suitable for analysing in detail the effects of changes over time.

  - In some circumstances, a solution derived from a linear programming model may be of limited use if, for example, the variables may only take on integer values. A solution can be found by a combination of rounding up or down and trial and error, but this sort of approach is not really suitable for large-scale practical problems.

  - The **graphical method** can only cope with two variables, whereas many companies have more than two products competing for the same resources. You will discover how to deal with this type of situation in later studies.

Quick quiz

1   What is meant by an objective function? (see para 1.9)

2   What would the inequality $4x + 3y \leq 24$ look like when drawn on a graph? (2.5)

3   What is the feasible region? (2.5)

4   What is an iso-profit line? (3.7)

5   How does the graphical solution of minimisation problems differ from that of maximisation problems? (3.12)

Question to try	Level	Marks	Time
27	Examination	14	25 mins

Chapter 27

DIFFERENTIAL CALCULUS

Chapter topic list	Syllabus reference
1 Differential calculus	QT 3(d)
2 Differentiation and quadratic equations	QT 3(d)
3 The use of differentiation in a business context	QT 1(c), 3(d)

Introduction

In this chapter we will be looking at one of the most important branches of mathematics, **calculus**. Calculus is concerned with **measuring change**. It provides the methodology to allow both the calculation of a **rate of change** and determination of whether that rate of change is **increasing** or **decreasing**.

Differential calculus (of differentiation) has many business applications. It can, for example, provide additional information about the graphs of equations. It also enables **profit-maximising**, **revenue-maximising** and **cost-minimising** output levels to be calculated and it can be used to derive a **cost-minimising stock order quantity formula**. In this chapter we will look at differentiation and its application to graphs of equations and profit and revenue maximisation/cost minimisation.

1   DIFFERENTIAL CALCULUS

6/95, 12/97

KEY TERM

Differentiation measures the **rate of change** in one variable (usually denoted y) resulting from a change in another variable (usually denoted x) at a particular point.

1.1   To understand what we mean by 'rate of change' let us consider a simple example.

1.2   Suppose that the annual cost to Sid (in £s) of running his car is described by the function y $= {}^x/_5 + 200$ where y is the total annual cost and x is the number of miles travelled by the car per annum.

1.3   How do we interpret this equation? Let us start by considering the situation in which Sid does not drive his car at all during the year. If the car travels no miles then x = 0. Total cost is therefore £200 ($^0/_5 + 200$). This £200 represents costs such as road tax and insurance that are incurred even if a car is not driven.

1.4   If Sid drives 1 mile per annum, his costs are now £200.20 (y $= {}^1/_5 + 200$). If he drives two miles his costs are £200.40 (y $= {}^2/_5 + 200$), if he drives three miles his costs are £200.60 (y $= {}^3/_5 + 200$) and so on. For each additional mile, Sid's costs increase by 20p.

1.5 What is the rate of change of the total cost, y? When the number of miles travelled, x, is 1, costs increases by 20p; when x = 2, y increases by 40p; when x = 3, y increases by 60p; and when x = 100, y increases by £20. It is therefore obvious that y is increasing at $^1/_5$ the rate at which x increases. The rate of change is therefore $^1/_5$.

1.6 Suppose, however, that we were trying to determine the rate at which the population of a country increases or decreases as the average monthly household income (in £) increases or decreases. Suppose that the relationships between population and average household income per month is described by $y = 9x^4 + 3x^3 + 2x^2 + 15x + 952$. It is far more difficult to ascertain a rate of change when faced with such a complicated equation but, using differential calculus, we can work out the rate of change in a matter of moments.

How to differentiate

1.7 If we have a function $y = ax^n$ where x is the independent variable and y is the dependent variable, we can find the rate of change of y with respect to changes in x by **differentiating y with respect to x** to get dy/dx (pronounced 'dee-y by dee-x').

When $y = ax^n$, $dy/dx = nax^{n-1}$.

dy/dx, the result of differentiating, is called the first derivative of y with respect to x and gives the rate of change of y for any given value of x.

1.8 Let us go back to our example about Sid. The cost function was $y = {^x/_5} + 200$. Rewrite this (for ease of comprehension as $y = {^1/_5}.x^1 + 200 x^0$ (where $x^0 = 1$)

Differentiating, we have dy/dx
$$\begin{aligned} &= 1.{^1/_5}.x^{1-1} + 0.200.x^{0-1} \\ &= {^1/_5}.x^0 + 0 \\ &= {^1/_5} \text{ (as before)} \end{aligned}$$

1.9 Here are two examples.

(a) If $y = 3x^4$, $dy/dx = 4 \times 3 \times x^{4-1} = 12x^3$

So when x = 1, y rises $12 \times 1^3 = 12$ times as fast as x; when x = 2, y rises $12 \times 2^3 = 96$ times as fast as x, and so on.

(b) If $p = 5q^2$, we can differentiate p with respect to q (in exactly the same way as differentiating y with respect to x) such that $dp/dq = 2 \times 5 \times q^{2-1} = 10q$.

1.10 The following points should be noted.

(a) **On differentiation, any constant disappears.** For example, if $y = 3x^2 + 8$, the constant, 8, disappears on differentiation, and
$dy/dx = 2 \times 3 \times x^{2-1} = 6x$

(b) **If the 'power' of x is one, the corresponding value on differentiation is the coefficient of x in the original function.** Thus, if $y = 7x$
$dy/dx = 1 \times 7 \times x^{1-1} = 7 \times x^0 = 7 \times 1 = 7$

(c) **If there are several expressions in the function, each element in the function may be differentiated separately.** For example, if $y = 3x^4 - 2x^3 + 6x^2 - 8x + 24$
$$\begin{aligned} dy/dx &= (4 \times 3 \times x^3) - (3 \times 2 \times x^2) + (2 \times 6 \times x) - (8) \\ &= 12x^3 - 6x^2 + 12x - 8 \end{aligned}$$

(d) The rule also applies when negative powers are involved. For example, if
$$y = 3/x^2 = 3x^{-2},$$

$$\frac{dy}{dx} = -2 \times 3 \times x^{-3} = -6^{-3} = -6/x^3$$

Question 1

Differentiate the following.

(a) y　　　$= 6x + 9$

(b) p　　　$= q^3 + 2q$

(c) s　　　$= 3t^3 + 4t^2 - 2t + 5$

(d) 2y　　$= 5x^2 - 4x + 7$

(e) y　　　$= \frac{1}{x^2} - \frac{3}{2x^3} + \frac{5}{4x^4}$

Answer

(a) $\frac{dy}{dx}$　$= 6$

(b) $\frac{dp}{dq}$　$= 3q^2 + 2$

(c) $\frac{ds}{dt}$　$= 9t^2 + 8t - 2$

(d) y　　$= \frac{5}{2}x^2 - 2x + \frac{7}{2}$

　　$\frac{dy}{dx}$　$= 5x - 2$

(e) y　　$= x^{-2} \ \frac{3}{2}x^{-3} + \frac{5}{4}x^{-4}$

　　$\frac{dy}{dx}$　$= -2x^{-3} + \frac{9}{2}x^{-4} - 5x^{-5}$

　　　　$= \frac{-2}{x^3} + \frac{9}{2x^4} - \frac{5}{x^5}$

2　DIFFERENTIATION AND QUADRATIC EQUATIONS　　6/95, 6/96, 12/97

2.1　If we draw a graph of the linear equation $y = 3x + 2$, we get a straight line as follows.

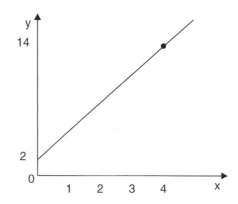

We can differentiate $y = 3x + 2$, such that $\frac{dy}{dx} = 3$. In other words, the **rate of change** in y at any point on the graph is equal to a **constant amount** of 3 per extra unit of x. Another way of expressing this idea is that the gradient or slope of the line at any point on the line shows a constant ratio between increases in y and increases in x of $+3 : 1$.

2.2　Similarly, if we draw a curve of $y = x^2$

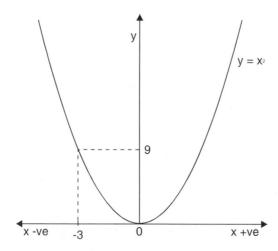

$dy/dx = 2x$. **The rate of change in y at any point on the curve is shown by the gradient or slope of the curve at that point**. This gradient is equal to twice the value of x at that point. Thus at the point (–3,9) the rate of change in y at that point is twice the value of x, $2 \times (-3)$ = –6, and the gradient of the curve is –6.

2.3　You may find it difficult to picture the gradient of a curve at a particular point since gradients are normally associated with straight lines. If, however, you were to draw what is known as a tangent at (–3,9) (a **tangent** being a **straight line** that just **touches** the **curve** at the **point** in question) then the gradient of the curve at that point would be the same as the gradient of the tangent at that point.

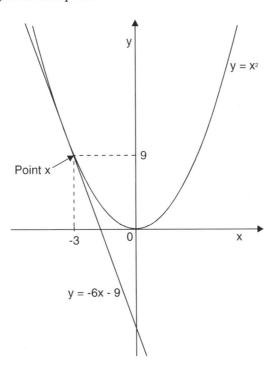

Positive and negative gradients

2.4　The **gradient** of a **straight line** that is **upward sloping** (when travelling from left to right) is **positive** whereas the **gradient** of a **straight line** that is **downward sloping** (when travelling from left to right) is **negative**. For example, if $y = 3x^2 + 4x - 6$, then $dy/dx = 6x + 4$. When x = 1, the gradient of the curve, and hence of a tangent to the curve at x = 1, is 10 ((6×1) + 4). This means that the tangent at x = 1 would be upward sloping since the gradient is positive (+ 10)

Turning points

2.5　Suppose that $y = 5x - 0.001x^2$, then $dy/dx = 5 - 0.002x$.

Now if x = 1,000, $dy/dx = 5 - 2 = 3$ which is **positive**. This means that when x is 1,000, the value of y is still increasing as x increases, and the **gradient** of the curve at that point is **positive**.

However if x = 3,000, $dy/dx = 5 - 6 = -1$, which is **negative**. This means that when x is 3,000, the value of y is decreasing as x increases, and the **gradient** of the curve is **negative**.

Clearly the curve 'flips over' somewhere between x = 1,000 and x = 3,000.

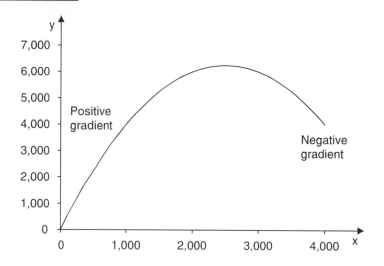

2.6 This **'flip over'** point is known as a **turning point** or **stationary point** and occurs when dy/dx (in other words, the gradient of the curve) is zero.

2.7 To find the turning points of an equation we follow a number of steps.

Step 1. Differentiate the equation.
Step 2. Let $dy/dx = 0$.
Step 3. Solve the resulting equation for x.
Step 4. Substitute the value for x into the original equation to determine the value for y.

2.8 EXAMPLE: TURNING POINTS

Find the turning points of the following equations.

(a) $y = x^2 - 4x + 3$
(b) $4y = 20x^2 - 48x + 32$

2.9 SOLUTION

(a) $\quad\quad y = x^2 - 4x + 3$

Step 1. $dy/dx = 2x - 4$
Step 2. $\quad 0 = 2x - 4$
Step 3. $\quad 4 = 2x$
$\quad\quad 2 = x$
Step 4. $\quad \therefore y = 4 - 8 + 3 = -1$
Turning point at $(2, -1)$

(b) $\quad\quad 4y = 20x^2 - 48x + 32$
$\quad\quad\quad y = 5x^2 - 12x + 8$

Step 1. $dy/dx = 10x - 12$
Step 2. $\quad 0 = 10x - 12$
Step 3. $\quad 12 = 10x$
$\quad\quad {}^6/_5 = x$
Step 4. $\quad \therefore y = (5 \times {}^6/_5 \times {}^6/_5) - (12 \times {}^6/_5) + 8 = {}^{36}/_5 - {}^{72}/_5 + {}^{40}/_5 = {}^4/_5$.

Turning point at $({}^6/_5, {}^4/_5)$

Finding turning points algebraically

2.10   The coordinates of the turning points of a quadratic function can also be found algebraically.

Step 1.   Calculate the roots of the equation using the formula $x = \dfrac{-b \pm \sqrt{b^2 - 4ac}}{2a}$

Step 2.   Calculate the midpoint between the two roots, which will be the turning point.

$$\text{Turning point (x coordinate)} = \frac{\text{Lowest root} + \text{highest root}}{2}$$

Let us use the example in Paragraph 2.8(a).

If $y = x^2 - 4x + 3$, then the roots of the equation are

Step 1. $x = \dfrac{4 \pm \sqrt{16 - (4 \times 1 \times 3)}}{2} = \dfrac{4 \pm 2}{2} = 1 \text{ or } 3$

Step 2. $\therefore$ Turning point (x coordinate) $= \dfrac{1 + 3}{2} = 2$

$\therefore$ Turning point (y coordinate) $= 4 - 8 + 3 = -1$

$\therefore$ Turning point $= (2, -1)$ (the result we arrived at in Paragraph 2.9(a))

Maximum and minimum turning points

2.11   A turning point on the graph of a curve may be one of the following.

- A maximum ('the top of a hill')
- A minimum ('the bottom of a ditch')

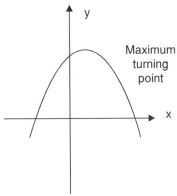
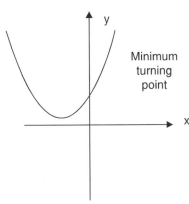

2.12   If we draw a graph, we can determine whether there is a maximum or a minimum point. We can also determine maximum and minimum points **without** drawing a graph. We do this by calculating the **second derivative of the function**.

The second derivative

> **KEY TERM**
>
> The **second derivative of a function** is the derivative of dy/dx, and is written as d^2y/dx^2 (pronounced 'd – two - y - by - d - x- squared').

2.13 **The second derivative may be used to calculate the rate at which the gradient of the curve $y = ax^n$ is increasing or decreasing.**

(a) If $y = 3x^3 - 2x^2 + 4x - 20$

then $dy/dx = 9x^2 - 4x + 4$

and $d^2y/dx^2 = 18x - 4$

(b) If $y = 28/x - 3/x^2 + 5x^4$

then $dy/dx = -28/x^2 + 6/x^3 + 20x^3$

and $d^2y/dx^2 = 56/x^3 - 18/x^4 + 60x^2$

The second derivative is then used to test for maximum or minimum points.

The rule for testing maximum and minimum points

2.14 The rules for testing whether a point is a maximum or a minimum are as follows.

- If $d^2y/dx^2 > 0$ there is a minimum point.

- If $d^2y/dx^2 < 0$ there is a maximum point.

2.15 EXAMPLE: MAXIMUM AND MINIMUM POINTS

Let us look again at the two equations in Paragraph 2.8.

(a) If $y = x^2 - 4x + 3$, the turning point is at $(2, -1)$

$dy/dx = 2x - 4$

$d^2y/dx^2 = 2$

$d^2y/dx^2 > 0$

The turning point is therefore a minimum.

(b) If $4y = 20x^2 - 48x + 32$, the turning point is at $(^6/_5, ^4/_5)$

$y = 5x^2 - 12x + 8$

$dy/dx = 10x - 12$

$d^2y/dx^2 = 10$

$d^2y/dx^2 > 0$

Again the turning point is a minimum.

2.16 POINTS OF INFLEXION

Occasionally, the second derivative of a function is zero when the first derivative is zero.

Where this occurs, the point on the graph is **neither a maximum nor a minimum point**, but is a '**point of inflexion**'. This is a 'point of rest' between two upward or two downward sloping parts of a curve.

2.17 EXAMPLE: A POINT OF INFLEXION

Consider the graph of $y = x^3$

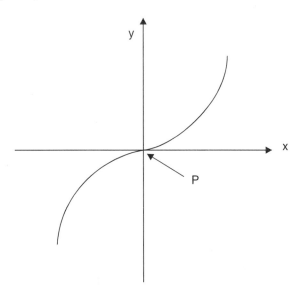

Point P is a point of inflexion for the following reasons.

(a) $^{dy}/dx = 3x^2$: this is zero when x = 0.

(b) $^{d^2y}/dx^2 = 6x$: when x = 0, this also equals 0.

3 THE USE OF DIFFERENTIATION IN A BUSINESS CONTEXT
6/95, 6/96, 6/97, 12/97, 6/98, 6/99

3.1 Business situations and economic relationships can often be described mathematically. The breakeven point of an organisation can be determined using equations and, by expressing total overheads as an equation, the split between fixed and variable overheads can be calculated using the high-low method.

3.2 We are not, however, always interested in what is happening at a certain level of output or at a certain price. We may be interested in the **rate** at which total sales revenue **changes** with the volume of units sold or how demand for a product varies with its price. This is where differential calculus can help.

3.3 We have looked at the basic rules for differentiating functions, so we will now consider these more practical uses of differential calculus in the following examples.

3.4 EXAMPLE: MARGINAL COST

A Ltd's total production costs are fixed costs of £30,000 and variable costs of £5 per unit.

Required

Use differential calculus to find the marginal cost.

3.5 SOLUTION

The first step is to translate the above situation into an equation. The equation obviously has to include costs as the dependent variable but what affects the level of costs (and is therefore the independent variable)? Costs increase and decrease according to the level of output: output is therefore the independent variable.

Let total costs = c and output = x

Total costs = 30,000 + 5x because for every additional unit produced costs increase by £5 but if no units are produced the company still incurs costs of £30,000.

Marginal cost is the additional costs which arise when one extra unit is produced. This being a simple example we have already arrived at the marginal cost of £5. Let us try to get the same answer using differential calculus.

Differential calculus will find the rate at which total costs (c) change as output (x) changes (in other words the marginal cost).

$c = 30,000 + 5x$
$dc/dx = 5$
Marginal cost = £5

3.6 EXAMPLE: MARGINAL REVENUE

Wib Ltd's total revenue (R) from producing the Wibbet can be expressed as

$4x^3 - 9x^2 - 10x - 13$ where x is the number of Wibbets sold.

Required

Use differential calculus to find the marginal revenue when 10 Wibbets are sold.

3.7 SOLUTION

Marginal revenue is simply the additional revenue from selling one extra Wibbet. We can use differential calculus to find the rate at which total revenue (R) changes as the number of Wibbets sold (x) changes.

$R = 4x^3 - 9x^2 - 10x - 13$
$dR/dx = 12x^2 - 18x - 10$

Marginal revenue = $12x^2 - 18x - 10$

We are interested in the marginal revenue when 10 Wibbets are sold (x = 10)

Marginal revenue $(12 \times 10^2) - (18 \times 10) - 10 = 1,200 - 180 - 10 = $ £1,010.

3.8 The marginal revenue function still contains x's. Different values of x substituted into the equation will therefore give different marginal revenues.

3.9 EXAMPLE: PROFIT MAXIMISATION

Cat Ltd believes that demand for its product can be represented by P = 10 − 0.003Q, where P is the unit price in pounds and Q is the quantity of sales. The total cost function is (in £s) $C = 1,000 + 3Q + 0.004Q^2$.

Required

(a) Calculate the level of output and the unit price at which profit will be maximised.

(b)   Calculate the amount of profit at this level.

3.10   SOLUTION

(a)   If P = 10 – 0.003Q, then total revenue R is found by multiplying the number of units sold by the price per unit.

R = PQ = (10 – 0.003Q)Q = 10Q – 0.003Q^2

The marginal revenue function (the rate of change of revenue with quantity) is found by differentiating R with respect to Q.

$^{dR}/_{dQ}$ = MR = 10 – 0.006Q

Since C = 1,000 + 3Q + 0.004Q^2 , the marginal cost function (the rate of change of cost with quantity) is $^{dC}/_{dQ}$ = MC = 3 + 0.008Q

Profit is maximised where MC = MR, as above that point each additional unit will increase total costs by more than total revenue.

$$3 + 0.008\,Q = 10 – 0.006Q$$
$$0.014Q = 7$$
$$Q = 500$$

The unit price is P = 10 – 0.003Q
                      = 10 – 0.003(500)
                      = £8.50

(b)

	£
Revenue (500 × 8.50)	4,250
Less costs (1,000 + 3(500) + 0.004(500)^2)	3,500
Profit	750

3.11   EXAMPLE: MARGINAL COST AND MARGINAL REVENUE

The costs of selling a product are c = x^2 – 2x + 20 where

x   =   output in batches
c   =   costs, in thousands of pounds

The revenue from the product is r = 8.5x^2 – x^3 + 20x where

r   =   value in thousands of pounds
x   =   sales in batches

Required

(a)   Calculate the volume of output at which total costs would be minimised.

(b)   Calculate the volume of sales at which total revenue would be maximised.

(c)   Using the principle that profits are maximised where marginal cost equals marginal revenue (MC = MR), calculate the volume of output and sales which will maximise profits.

(d)   Prove your solution in (c) by formulating the profit function, and calculating where this has a maximum point.

3.12   SOLUTION

(a)   c = x^2 – 2x + 20

$^{dc}/_{dx}$ = 2x – 2

This is a maximum or minimum point when $2x - 2 = 0$

$$2x = 2$$
$$x = 1$$

$d^2c/dx^2 = 2$

This is a positive number, therefore when $x = 1$, there is a minimum point.

(b) $r = 8.5x^2 - x^3 + 20x$

$dr/dx = 17x - 3x^2 + 20$

This is a maximum or minimum point when $-3x^2 + 17x + 20 = 0$

$$x = \frac{-17 \pm \sqrt{[289 - (4 \times (-3) \times 20)]}}{-6}$$

$$= \frac{-17 - 23}{-6} \text{ or } \frac{-17 + 23}{-6}$$

$$= 6^2/_3 \text{ or } -1$$

Since output cannot be negative, we have a maximum or minimum point when $x = 6^2/_3$

$d^2r/dx^2 = -6x + 17$

When $x = 6^2/_3$, this equals $-40 + 17 = -23$. This is a negative number, therefore when $x = 6^2/_3$, there is a maximum point. Total revenue is maximised when $6^2/_3$ batches are sold.

(c) Marginal cost (MC) $= dc/dx = 2x - 2$

Marginal revenue (MR) $= dr/dx = -3x^2 + 17x + 20$

Profits are maximised when MC = MR: $2x - 2 = -3x^2 + 17x + 20$

$$3x^2 - 15x - 22 = 0$$

$$x = \frac{+15 \pm \sqrt{[225 - (4 \times 3 \times (-22))]}}{6}$$

$$= \frac{+15 + 22.1}{6} \text{ or } \frac{+15 - 22.1}{6}$$

$$= 6.2 \text{ or } -1.2$$

Since x cannot be negative, profit is maximised when $x = 6.2$.

(d) Profit equals revenue minus costs.

Revenue $= -x^3 + 8.5x^2 + 20x$

Costs $= x^2 - 2x + 20$

Profit (p) $= -x^3 + 7.5x^2 + 22x - 20$

$dp/dx = -3x^2 + 15x + 22$

There is a maximum or minimum point when $-3x^2 + 15x + 22 = 0$.

As in (c) above, $-3x^2 + 15x + 22 = 0$ when $x = 6.2$ (or -1.2)

$d^2p/dx^2 = -6x + 15$

When $x = 6.2$, $d^2p/dx^2 = -22.2$. This is a maximum point. Profits must therefore be at a maximum when $x = 6.2$.

Question 2

A building firm has won a contract to build a new sports centre. The contract profit will be determined by the size of the work force involved; if the workforce is too small, it is unlikely that the work will be finished on time and the firm will incur penalty payments; if the workforce is too large there are likely to be high rectification costs due to using unskilled labour.

The profit function has been determined as

Profit (£'000) = $x^2 - 80x + 1,431$

where x is the number of workers.

Required

(a) Calculate the limits on the size of the workforce which will ensure that the firm makes a profit.
(b) Calculate the number of workers which will result in maximum profit.

Answer

(a) Profit (p) = $-x^2 + 80x - 1,431$

$$x = \frac{-80 \pm \sqrt{80^2 - (4 \times -1 \times -1,431)}}{-2} = \frac{-80 \pm \sqrt{676}}{-2} = 27 \text{ or } 53$$

∴ Provided that the number of workers is more than 27 and less than 53, the firm will make a profit. (When there are 27 or 53 workers the firm breaks even).

(b) Profit is maximised when $dp/dx = 0$ and $d^2p/dx^2 < 0$.

$dp/dx = -2x + 80$ and so profit is minimised when $0 = -2x + 80$ and $d^2p/dx^2 < 0$.

$d^2p/dx^2 = -2 < 0$

∴ Profit is maximised when $0 = -2x + 80$, ie if there are 40 workers.

The graphical approach to finding the profit-maximising output

Exam focus point

6 marks were available in 6/95 for drawing a graph showing marginal revenue and marginal cost. A sharp pencil and a ruler are essential when drawing graphs in examinations, especially if the question asks for information which you need to read off the graph.

3.13 **Instead of equating the equations for MC and MR and solving algebraically we could plot the two equations on a graph and find the point where the two lines intersect.**

3.14 EXAMPLE: GRAPHICAL APPROACH

Draw a graph showing marginal cost and marginal revenue as calculated in paragraph 3.13(c) above, for output between 0 and 9 batches, clearly indicating the profit-maximising output.

BPP PUBLISHING

3.15 SOLUTION

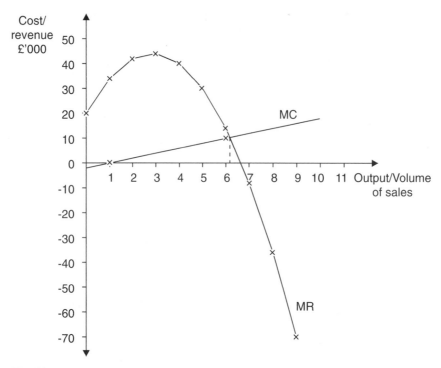

Workings

x	MC	MR
0	–2	20
1	0	34
2	2	42
3	4	44
4	6	40
5	8	30
6	10	14
7	12	–8
8	14	–36
9	16	–70

We need to find the turning point of the MR curve.

MR $= -3x^2 + 17x + 20$

$dMR/dx = -6x + 17$

$0 = -6x + 17$
$17 = 6x$
$17/6 = x$
$\therefore MR = 44.08$

The profit-maximising output is at an output level of 6.2 batches.

Question 3

(a) A company manufactures a product. For the accounting period, the total costs are £1,050 when the output is 20 units and £1,850 when the output is 40 units. Assuming linearity, find an expression for total costs in terms of q, the quantity of output.

(b) When the price is £20, the demand in the accounting period is 40 units. If the price is reduced to £10, the demand increases to 45 units. Assuming linearity, obtain the relationship between price and demand (q).

(c) Obtain an expression for the revenue function and hence show that the profit function is

$P = -2q^2 + 60q - 250$

By a graphical method or otherwise find the output which maximises profits.

Answer

(a) When q rises by 20 units (from 20 units to 40 units) total costs rise by £800 (from £1,050 to £1,850). This is a rise of £800/20 = £40 a unit, so variable costs are £40 a unit. At 20 units, we have:

Fixed costs + 20 × £40 = £1,050

Fixed costs = £1,050 − £800 = £250

The required expression for total costs is therefore T = 250 + 40q.

(b) Let p = price, and assume that p = a + bq

Then 20	=	a + 40b	(1)
10	=	a + 45b	(2)
10	=	−5b	(3) (subtract (2) from (1))
b	=	−2	(4)
20	=	a −80	(5) (from (1))
a	=	100	(6)

The required relationship is p = 100 − 2q.

(c) Revenue = pq = q(100 −2q) = $100q − 2q^2$
Profit = P= revenue − costs
= $100q − 2q^2 − (250 + 40q)$
= $-2q^2 + 60q - 250$

A graph may be plotted using the following values.

q	$-2q^2 + 60q - 250$
5	0
10	150
15	200
20	150
25	0

We can see from the graph that profit is maximised at q = 15. At this point, profit = £200.

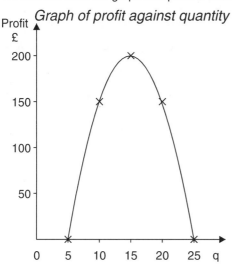

Graph of profit against quantity

Question 4

A firm has analysed their operating conditions, prices and costs and has developed the following functions, where Q is the number of units sold.

Revenue (£): R = $200Q - 3Q^2$

Cost (£): C = $2Q^2 + 50Q + 10$

The firm's objective is to maximise profit.

Required

(a) Calculate the quantity that should be sold.
(b) Calculate the price at which the product should be sold.
(c) Calculate the profit that the company will earn.

Answer

(a) R = $200Q - 3Q^2$

$dR/dQ = 200 - 6Q$ = marginal revenue

C = $2Q^2 + 50Q + 10$

$dC/dQ = 4Q + 50$ = marginal cost

Profit is maximised when MR = MC

ie when 200 − 6Q = 4Q + 50
200 − 50 = 10Q
150 = 10Q
15 = Q

(b) R = $200Q - 3Q^2$
R = Q(200 − 3Q) = quantity × price
Price = 200 − 3Q = 200 − (3 × 15) = £155

		£
(c) Revenue	= ((200 × 15) − (3 × 225))	2,325
Cost	= ((2 × 15^2) + (50 × 15) + 10))	1,210
Profit		1,115

Cost minimisation and revenue maximisation

3.16 We know that by **differentiating a function** we can **find turning points** and then by determining the **second differential** we can ascertain whether the turning point is a **maximum** or **minimum** point. This being the case we can:

(a) differentiate a function representing an organisation's costs, determine the second differential and ascertain the production level at which costs are minimised; or

(b) differentiate a function representing an organisation's revenue, determine the second differential and ascertain the sales level at which revenue is maximised.

3.17 We could also find the point at which costs are maximised or the point at which revenue is minimised. Sounds complicated? Let us have a look at an example.

3.18 EXAMPLE: COST MINIMISATION

A company's costs are given by the function

$$C = 2,000q + \frac{27,000}{q^2} \quad \text{where q is the quantity produced.}$$

Required

Use differential calculus to determine the production level at which costs are minimised and hence calculate the minimum costs.

3.19 SOLUTION

$$C = 2{,}000q + \frac{27{,}000}{q^2} = 2{,}000q + 27{,}000q^{-2}$$

$$\frac{dC}{dq} = 2{,}000 - 54{,}000q^{-3}$$

To find a maximum or minimum point we let dC/dq = 0

$$0 = 2{,}000 - 54{,}000q^{-3} = 2{,}000 - \frac{54{,}000}{q^3}$$

$$\therefore \frac{54{,}000}{q^3} = 2{,}000$$

$$\therefore \frac{54{,}000}{2{,}000} = q^3 = 27$$

$$\therefore q = 3$$

We now need to see whether a production level of 3 leads to minimum costs.

$$\frac{d^2C}{dq^2} = 162q^{-4}$$

If q = 3, $\dfrac{d^2C}{dq^2} = 2 > 0$

When $\dfrac{d^2C}{dq^2} > 0$ we have a minimum point.

Let us calculate the minimum costs.

$$C = 2{,}000q + \frac{27{,}000}{q^2}$$

When q = 3, C = £9,000

At a production level of 30, minimum costs of £9,000 are incurred. The approaches to finding maximum revenue, maximum cost and minimum revenue are exactly the same. Try this question which requires you to determine maximum revenue.

Question 5

The demand for AB Ltd's product X is dependent on price, the price function for product X being

$P = \dfrac{q^2}{3} - \dfrac{45q}{2} + 450$, where q is the quantity sold.

Use differential calculus to find both the sales volume at which revenue is maximised and the maximum revenue available from the sales of product X.

Answer

Revenue (R) = price × quantity sold = Pq

$$R = \left(\frac{q^2}{3} - \frac{45q}{2} + 450 \right) \times q = \frac{q^3}{3} - \frac{45}{2}q^2 + 450q$$

BPP PUBLISHING

$$\frac{dR}{dq} = \frac{3q^2}{3} - \frac{90}{2}q + 450 = q^2 - 45q + 450$$

For a maximum or minimum $0 = q^2 - 45q + 450$. We therefore need to use the formula for solving a quadratic equation to determine values for q.

$$q = \frac{+45 \pm \sqrt{45^2 - (4 \times 1 \times 450)}}{2} = \frac{+45 \pm \sqrt{225}}{2} = \frac{45 \pm 15}{2}$$

$\therefore$ q = 30 or 15

To find the revenue-maximising sales volume we calculate $\frac{d^2R}{dq^2}$.

$$\frac{d^2R}{dq^2} = 2q - 45$$

When q = 15, $\frac{d^2R}{dq^2} = -15 < 0$ and so revenue is maximised when q = 15 (because if q = 30, $\frac{d^2R}{dq^2} > 0$)

If q = 15, R = £2,812.50

$\therefore$ When 15 units are sold maximum revenue of £2,812.50 can be earned.

Chapter roundup

*   **Differential calculus** has very practical applications in business. The basic rule of differentiation is that if $y = ax^n$, then $dy/dx = nax^{n-1}$.

*   The **gradient** of a curve at a particular point can be determined since gradient = dy/dx. You should be able to identify whether a curve is **upward** sloping at a particular point ($dy/dx > 0$) or **downward** sloping ($dy/dx < 0$) at a particular point.

*   The distinction between **maximum** and **minimum** turning points should now be clear to you. We find a turning point by letting $dy/dx = 0$ and then we identify the type of turning point by letting d^2y/dx^2 (the **second derivative**) = 0. If $d^2y/dx^2 > 0$ there is a minimum point and if $d^2y/dx^2 < 0$ there is a maximum point. A **point of inflexion** occurs if $d^2y/dx^2 = 0$.

*   As far as using calculus in a business context is concerned, you should be able to calculate marginal costs, marginal revenues, the point at which profits are maximised (when MC = MR), maximum/minimum revenues and maximum/minimum costs.

Quick quiz

1   If $y = ax^n$, what is the formula for the first derivative of y with respect to x? (see para 1.7)

2   Does a positive first derivative at a particular point indicate that a graph is upwards sloping (from left to right) or downward sloping (from left to right) at that point? (2.4)

3   What is a turning point? (2.6)

4   If the second derivative is greater than 0, does this indicate a maximum or minimum point? (2.14)

5   What is a point of inflexion? (2.16)

6   At what point are profits maximised? (3.10)

Question to try	Level	Marks	Time
28	Examination	14	25 mins

Chapter 28

STOCK CONTROL

Chapter topic list	Syllabus reference
1 The costs of stock	CA 2(a)(ii)
2 The economic order quantity	QT 3(d), CA 2(a)(ii)
3 Refinements of the basic formula	QT 3(d), CA 2(a)(ii)
4 Limitations of the EOQ model	CA 2(a)(ii)

Introduction

The previous chapters have introduced a variety of mathematical techniques. In this chapter we will look at the basic model (the **EOQ model**) used in stock control decisions. The EOQ formula is derived using the mathematical technique of differentiation covered in this part of the Study Text. You do *not* need to be able to derive the EOQ formula.

1   THE COSTS OF STOCK

1.1   We need to begin this chapter by reminding ourselves of the main types of stock cost.

Question 1

Provide examples of the four groups of stock costs which we looked at in Chapter 5.

Answer

(a)   **Holding costs** are comprised of the following.

    (i)   The cost of capital tied up
    (ii)   Warehousing and handling costs
    (iii) Deterioration
    (iv) Obsolescence
    (v)   Insurance
    (vi) Pilferage

(b)   **Procurement costs** (costs of obtaining stock) depend on how the stock is obtained.

    (i)   If goods are obtained from outside suppliers then a business incurs *ordering costs* which include clerical costs, telephone charges, documentation, payment of invoices, receiving goods into stores and so on.

    (ii)   If goods are manufactured internally then a business will incur *production set upcosts* which include the following.

        (1)   The costs of lost production while a production run is being set up.

        (2)   Any variable costs associated with both production planning and preparing the labour force and machinery for a production run to make the batch of items required.

(c)   **Stockout (or shortage) costs** arise because a company that runs out of stock will normally suffer some loss as a result. Any of the following may be the cost of a stock-out (running out of stock).

BPP PUBLISHING

     (i)   The loss of a sale and the contribution from the sale

     (ii)   The extra cost of having to buy an emergency supply of stocks at a higher price

     (iii)   The cost of lost production and sales, where the stock-out brings an entire process to a halt

(d)   The **cost of the stock itself**, the supplier's price or the direct cost per unit of production, will also need to be considered, especially in the following circumstances.

     (i)   The supplier offers a discount on orders for purchases in bulk.
     (ii)   There are savings in the direct cost of production on longer runs.

Cost behaviour and order quantity

1.2   If orders are placed only occasionally then, to cover annual requirements, the quantity ordered will be relatively high and thus stock holding costs will be incurred unnecessarily.

   (a) **Larger stocks** require **more storage space** and possibly **extra staff** and **equipment** to control and handle them.

   (b) **Holding stocks** involves the **tying up** of **capital** on which interest must be paid.

   (c) The **larger** the **value of stocks** held, the **greater insurance** premiums.

   (d) When **materials** or **components** become **out-of-date** and are no longer required, existing stocks must be thrown away and their **cost written off** to the profit and loss account.

   (e) When **materials** in store **deteriorate** to the extent that they are unusable, they must be thrown away (with the likelihood that disposal costs are incurred) and again, the **value written off plus the disposal costs** will be a **charge** to the profit and loss account.

   (f) **Theft** is a **greater risk** with larger stockholdings.

1.3   These costs tend to increase with the level of stocks and so could be reduced by ordering the annual requirement in smaller amounts more frequently during a year.

1.4   There is the danger if stocks are too low, of production stoppages and consequent customer dissatisfaction, loss of revenue and increased cost of emergency action.

1.5   On the other hand, costs associated with ordering from suppliers tend to increase if small orders are placed, because a larger number of orders would then be needed for a given annual demand.

1.6   This can be shown graphically.

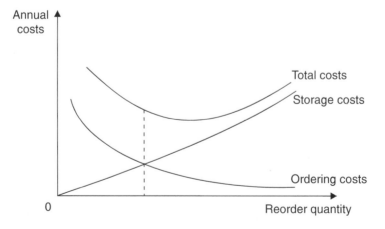

The **larger** the **reorder quantity**, the more **costly stockholding** will become; however, since the number of orders each year will reduce, the **ordering costs will fall**. The **minimum cost** occurs where **holding costs** per annum and **ordering costs** per annum are **equal**.

1.7 It is possible to establish this cost-minimising reorder level using the economic order quantity (EOQ) model.

2 THE ECONOMIC ORDER QUANTITY   6/94, 6/98, 12/98, 6/99, 12/99

Exam focus point
Remember that information about buffer stock is not needed to determine the EOQ or frequency of ordering and that holding costs are based on the average stock level (half the quantity ordered) and *not* quantities purchased.

KEY TERM

The **economic order quantity** is the order quantity which minimises the total costs associated with holding and reordering stock.

2.1 The benefits of buying a large quantity of stock on a small number of occasions must be weighed against the consequent costs of ordering or holding stock.

2.2 The assumptions used in the EOQ model are as follows.

- Demand is certain, constant and continuous over time.
- Supply lead time (the time from placing an order to receiving supplies) is constant.
- Customers' orders cannot be held while fresh stocks are awaited.
- No stock-outs (having orders from customers but no stocks) are permitted.
- All prices are constant and certain. There are no bulk purchase discounts.
- The cost of holding stock is proportional to the quantity of stock held.

2.3 At this stage, some symbols must be introduced.

Let D = usage in units for one year (demand)

         C_0/C_2 = cost of making one order

         C_H/C_1 = holding cost per unit of stock for one year $\Big\}$ relevant costs only

         Q = order quantity

2.4 If the lead time is zero or is known with certainty, and we have constant, certain demand, then fresh stocks can be obtained when stocks have been completely run down. Just before each delivery, therefore, stocks will be zero and when the order quantity (Q) arrives, stocks will be at their maximum level which is Q. As demand is constant, average stock will be $Q \div 2$. This is illustrated in the diagram below. As C_H is the holding cost per unit of stock, the cost of holding the average stock for one year is $(Q \div 2)C_H$.

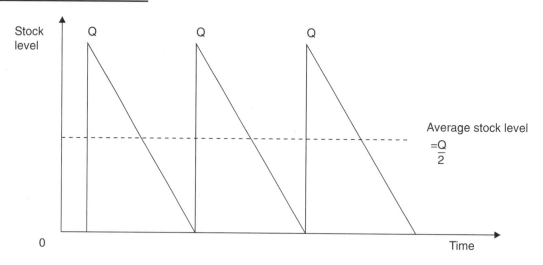

2.5   The **number of orders** for stock made in a year **depends** upon the **annual usage** (D) and the **order quantity** (Q).

- The number of orders made in a year will equal D/Q
- The total ordering costs for the year will equal C_oD/Q

> **Exam focus point**
>
> In the 6/99 exam, candidates were required to calculate a retailer's average stockholding level. In organisations where a safety stock level (or minimum level) draws management's attention to the fact that stocks are approaching a dangerously low level, the average stock is calculated as follows. **Average stock = safety stock (or minimum level) + (EOQ ÷ 2).** In the 12/99 exam, candidates were required to calculate the **average stock investment**. This is simply the average stock × cost per kg of stock.

EOQ - tabulation method

2.6   Jones Ltd purchases raw material from Beswetherick Ltd at a cost of £16 per unit. Jones Ltd's annual demand for the raw material is 25,000 units. The holding cost per unit is £6.40 and the cost of placing an order is £32.

2.7   We can tabulate the annual relevant costs for various order quantities as follows.

Order quantity (units)		100	200	300	400	500	600	800	1,000
Average stock (units)	(a)	50	100	150	200	250	300	400	500
Number of orders	(b)	250	125	83	63	50	42	31	25
		£	£	£	£	£	£	£	£
Annual holding cost	(c)	320	640	960	1,280	1,600	1,920	2,560	3,200
Annual order cost	(d)	8,000	4,000	2,656	2,016	1,600	1,344	992	800
Total relevant cost		8,320	4,640	3,616	3,296	3,200	3,264	3,552	4,000

(a)   Average stock = Order quantity ÷ 2 = Q ÷ 2

(b)   Number of orders = annual demand ÷ order quantity = D/Q

(c)   Annual holding cost = Average stock × £6.40 = $(Q ÷ 2)C_H$

(d)   Annual order cost = Number of orders × £32 = C_oD/Q

2.8   You will see that the order quantity which minimises total annual relevant costs (the economic order quantity) is 500 units.

EOQ - graphical method

2.9 As we saw briefly in Chapter 5, we can present the information tabulated in Paragraph 2.7 in graphical form. The vertical axis represents the relevant annual costs for the investment in stocks, and the horizontal axis can be used to represent either the various order quantities or the average stock levels; two scales are actually shown on the horizontal axis so that both items can be incorporated. The graph shows that, as the average stock level and order quantity increase, the holding cost increases. On the other hand, the ordering costs decline as stock levels and order quantities increase. The total cost line represents the sum of both the holding and the ordering costs.

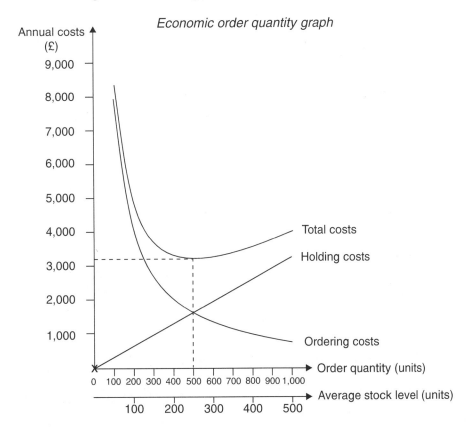

2.10 Note that the total cost line is at a minimum for an order quantity of 500 units and occurs at the point where the ordering cost curve and holding cost curve intersect. The EOQ is therefore found at the point where holding costs equal ordering costs.

Question 2

A fast-food restaurant places orders for various items of disposable catering equipment (such as serviettes and straws) at quarterly intervals.

In respect of an item of stock coded MS 1, data are as follows.

Annual usage quantity	5,000	boxes
Minimum order quantity	500	boxes
Cost per box	£2	

Usage of MS 1 is on a regular basis and, on average, half of the amount purchased is held in stock. The cost of storing the stock is considered to be 25% of its value. The average cost of placing an order is estimated to be £12.50.

Required

(a)   Tabulate the costs of storage and ordering item MS 1 for each level of orders from four to 10 each year.

(b)   Ascertain from the tabulation the number of orders which should be placed in a year to minimise costs.

Answer

(a)

No of orders pa	4	5	6	7	8	9	10
Order quantity (boxes)	1,250	1,000	833	714	625	556	500
Cost of average stock (£)*	1,250	1,000	833	714	625	556	500
Annual holding cost (£)	312.50	250.00	208.25	178.50	156.25	139.00	125.00
Annual ordering cost (£)	50.00	62.50	75.00	87.50	100.00	112.50	125.00
Total relevant cost (£)	362.50	312.50	283.25	266.00	256.25	251.50	250.00

Average stock in boxes = order quantity/2

*Average stock cost = average stock in boxes × £2 = $\dfrac{\text{order quantity}}{2} \times £2$

(b)   The economic order quantity is therefore 500 boxes (the minimum order quantity).

EOQ - formula method

2.11   The EOQ can also be calculated by using a formula.

EXAM FORMULA

$$EOQ = \sqrt{\frac{2C_oD}{C_H}} \qquad EOQ = \sqrt{\frac{2C_2D}{C_1}}$$

See the terminology used earlier in this chapter.

2.12   EXAMPLE: THE ECONOMIC ORDER QUANTITY

The demand for a commodity is 40,000 units a year, at a steady rate. It costs £20 to place an order, and 40p to hold a unit for a year.

Required

Find the order size to minimise inventory costs, the number of orders placed per year, and the frequency of orders.

2.13   SOLUTION

$$Q = \sqrt{\frac{2C_oD}{C_H}} = \sqrt{\frac{2 \times 20 \times 40,000}{0.4}} = 2,000 \text{ units}$$

This means that there will be $\dfrac{40,000}{2,000} = 20$ orders placed each year.

The frequency of orders is therefore every $\dfrac{52\,\text{weeks}}{20\,\text{orders}}$ = 2.6 weeks.

2.14 Many questions on stock control contain irrelevant cost figures. You must remember that the **costs we want are marginal figures**. In other words, the figure you use for **stockholding costs** should be equal to the **additional cost** that would be incurred if **one more unit of stock** were held for one time period and, similarly, the figure you use for **ordering costs** should be equal to the **extra costs** that would be incurred if **one more order** were placed.

Question 3

A company requires 25,000 units of a commodity each year, at a steady rate. It costs £40 to place an order, and storage costs £2 per unit per year.

Required

Calculate the period of time between deliveries.

Answer

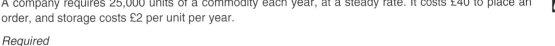

$$Q = \sqrt{\dfrac{2C_0 D}{C_H}} = \sqrt{\dfrac{2 \times 40 \times 25{,}000}{2}} = 1{,}000$$

The company needs $\dfrac{25{,}000}{1{,}000}$ = 25 deliveries per year.

The time between deliveries is therefore $\dfrac{52\text{ weeks}}{25}$ = 2.08 weeks.

---

3 REFINEMENTS OF THE BASIC FORMULA

Economic batch quantity

3.1 You may come across a problem in which the **basic EOQ formula requires modification because re-supply is gradual, instead of instantaneous**. Typically, a manufacturing company might hold stocks of a finished item, which is produced in batches. Once the order for a new batch has been placed, and the production run has started, finished output might be used before the batch run has been completed.

3.2 If the daily demand for an item of stock is ten units, and the storekeeper orders 100 units in a batch. The rate of production is 50 units a day.

   (a) On the first day of the batch production run, the stores will run out of its previous stocks, and re-supply will begin. 50 units will be produced during the day, and ten units will be consumed. The closing stock at the end of day 1 will be 50 – 10 = 40 units.

   (b) On day 2, the final 50 units will be produced and a further ten units will be consumed. Closing stock at the end of day 2 will be (40 + 50 –10) = 80 units.

   (c) In eight more days, stocks will fall to zero.

3.3 The minimum stock in this example is zero, and the maximum stock is 80 units. The maximum stock is the quantity ordered (Q = 100) minus demand during the period of the batch production run which is $Q \times D/R$, where

D   is the rate of demand

R   is the rate of production

Q   is the quantity ordered.

In our example, the maximum stock is $(100 - \dfrac{10}{50} \times 100) = 100 - 20 = 80$ units.

The maximum stock level, given gradual re-supply, is thus $Q - \dfrac{QD}{R} = Q(1 - D/R)$.

3.4   The position can be represented graphically as follows.

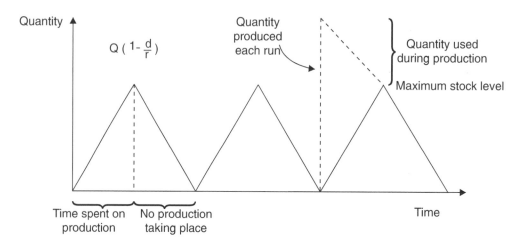

3.5   An amended EOQ (economic batch quantity, or EBQ) formula is required because average stocks are not Q/2 but Q(1 – D/R)/2.

FORMULA TO LEARN

The **EBQ** is $\sqrt{\dfrac{2C_oD}{C_H(1-D/R)}}$

where R = the production rate per time period (which must exceed the stock usage)

Q = the amount produced in each batch

D = the usage per time period

C_o = the set up cost per batch

C_H = the holding cost per unit of stock per time period

Question 4

A company is able to manufacture its own components for stock at the rate of 4,000 units a week. Demand for the component is at the rate of 2,000 units a week. Set up costs for each production run are £50. The cost of holding one unit of stock is £0.001 a week.

Required

Calculate the economic production run.

Answer

$$Q = \sqrt{\dfrac{2 \times 50 \times 2{,}000}{0.001\left(1 - 2{,}000 / 4{,}000\right)}} = 20{,}000 \text{ units (giving a stock cycle of 10 weeks)}$$

Bulk discounts

3.6 The solution obtained from using the simple EOQ formula may need to be modified if bulk discounts (also called quantity discounts) are available. The following graph shows the effect that discounts granted for orders of certain sizes may have on total costs.

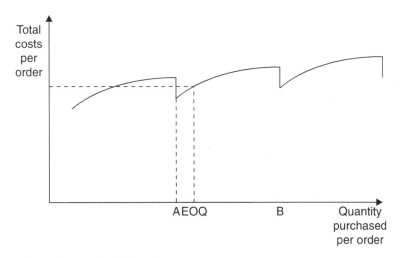

The graph above shows the following.

- Differing bulk discounts are given when the order quantity exceeds A, B and C
- The minimum total cost (ie when quantity B is ordered rather than the EOQ)

3.7 To decide mathematically whether it would be worthwhile taking a discount and ordering larger quantities, it is necessary to **minimise** the total of the following.

- Total material costs
- Ordering costs
- Stock holding costs

3.8 The **total cost** will be **minimised** at one of the following.

- At the **pre-discount EOQ level**, so that a discount is not worthwhile
- At the **minimum order size** necessary to earn the discount

3.9 EXAMPLE: BULK DISCOUNTS

The annual demand for an item of stock is 45 units. The item costs £200 a unit to purchase, the holding cost for one unit for one year is 15% of the unit cost and ordering costs are £300 an order.

The supplier offers a 3% discount for orders of 60 units or more, and a discount of 5% for orders of 90 units or more.

Required

Calculate the cost-minimising order size.

3.10 SOLUTION

(a) The EOQ ignoring discounts is $\sqrt{\dfrac{2 \times 300 \times 45}{15\% \text{ of } 200}} = 30$

	£
Purchases (no discount) 45 × £200	9,000
Holding costs 15 (30 ÷ 2) units × £30	450
Ordering costs 1.5 orders × £300	450
Total annual costs	9,900

(b) With a discount of 3% and an order quantity of 60 units costs are as follows.

	£
Purchases £9,000 × 97%	8,730
Holding costs 30 units × 15% of 97% of £200	873
Ordering costs 0.75 orders × £300	225
Total annual costs	9,828

(c) With a discount of 5% and an order quantity of 90 units costs are as follows.

	£
Purchases £9,000 × 95%	8,550.0
Holding costs 45 units × 15% of 95% of £200	1,282.5
Ordering costs 0.5 orders × £300	150.0
Total annual costs	9,982.5

The cheapest option is to order 60 units at a time.

3.11 Note that the value of C_H varied according to the size of the discount, because C_H was a percentage of the purchase cost. This means that **total holding costs are reduced because of a discount**. This could easily happen if, for example, most of C_H was the cost of insurance, based on the cost of stock held.

Question 5

A company uses an item of stock as follows.
Purchase price: £96 per unit
Annual demand: 4,000 units
Ordering cost: £300
Annual holding cost: 10% of purchase price
Economic order quantity: 500 units

Required

Ascertain whether the company should order 1,000 units at a time in order to secure an 8% discount.

Answer

The total annual cost at the economic order quantity of 500 units is as follows.

	£
Purchases 4,000 × £96	384,000
Ordering costs £300 × (4,000/500)	2,400
Holding costs £96 × 10% × (500/2)	2,400
	388,800

The total annual cost at an order quantity of 1,000 units would be as follows.

	£
Purchases £384,000 × 92%	353,280
Ordering costs £300 × (4,000/1,000)	1,200
Holding costs £96 × 92% × 10% × (1,000/2)	4,416
	358,896

The company should order the item 1,000 units at a time, saving £(388,800 − 358,896) = £29,904 a year.

4 LIMITATIONS OF THE EOQ MODEL

4.1 The EOQ has the following limitations.

- It assumes that holding cost per unit is constant.
- It assumes that demand is certain, constant and continuous over time.

It is unlikely that these assumptions will be correct for all items, at all times.

Chapter roundup

- The components of total stock costs are holding costs, procurement costs, storage costs and the costs of the stock itself.

- **Storage costs** tend to increase as the reorder quantity increases.

- **Ordering costs** tend to decrease as the reorder quantity increases.

- Total costs are at a minimum when **holding costs and ordering costs are equal**.

- The **EOQ model** determines an order quantity which minimises stock holding and ordering costs. Make sure that you know the assumptions upon which the model is based.

- The EOQ can be determined using **tabulation** or **graphical** methods or the formula.

- The EOQ model needs modifying if there is **gradual replenishment** of stocks or if bulk discounts are available.

Quick quiz

1 What are the four groups into which stock costs can be divided? (see Question 1)

2 Sketch on a graph the behaviour of ordering costs, storage costs and total costs as the order quantity increases. (1.6)

3 What are the assumptions used in the simple EOQ model? (2.2)

4 When using the graphical method, the EOQ is found at the intersection of which lines? (2.10)

5 Write down the formula for the EOQ. (exam formulae)

6 At what two points could total costs (when bulk discounts are available) be minimised? (3.8)

Question to try	Level	Marks	Time
29	Introductory	n/a	15 mins

Chapter 29

INTEREST AND DISCOUNTING

Chapter topic list	Syllabus reference
1 Simple interest	QT 2(c)
2 Compound interest	QT 2(c)
3 Effective and nominal rates of interest	QT 2(c)
4 The concept of discounting	QT 2(c)
5 The net present value (NPV) method	QT 2(c)
6 The internal rate of return (IRR) method	QT 2(c)

Introduction

In general, financial mathematics deals with problems of investing money, or capital. If a company (or an individual investor) puts some capital into an investment, a financial return will be expected.

The two major techniques of financial mathematics are **compounding** and **discounting**. These techniques are very closely related to each other. The major application of discounting in business is in the **evaluation of capital expenditure projects**, to decide whether they offer a satisfactory return to the investor. We will be looking at two methods of using discounting to appraise capital expenditure projects, the **net present value (NPV)** method and the **internal rate of return (IRR)** method.

1   SIMPLE INTEREST

KEY TERMS

- **Interest** is the amount of money which an investment earns over time.

- **Simple interest** is interest which is earned in equal amounts every period and which is a given proportion of the original investment (the principal).

1.1   If a sum of money is invested for a period of time, then the amount of simple interest which accrues is equal to the number of periods × the interest rate × the amount invested.

FORMULA TO LEARN
$S_n = P + nrP$

where   P   =   the original sum invested

       r   =   the interest rate (expressed as a proportion, so 10% = 0.1)

       n   =   the number of periods (normally years)

       S_n =   the sum invested after n periods, consisting of the original capital (P) plus interest earned (the terminal value).

1.2 EXAMPLE: SIMPLE INTEREST

What is the terminal value after five years if an investor invests £1,000 at 10% simple interest per annum?

1.3 SOLUTION

$$S_n = £1,000 + (5 \times 0.1 \times £1,000)$$
$$= £1,500$$

1.4 If, for example, the sum of money is invested for 3 months and the interest rate is a rate per annum, then $n = {}^3/_{12} = {}^1/_4$. If the investment period is 197 days and the rate is an annual rate, then $n = {}^{197}/_{365}$.

2 COMPOUND INTEREST   6/99

2.1 Interest is normally calculated by means of compounding. If a sum of money, the principal, is invested at a fixed rate of interest such that the interest is added to the principal and no withdrawals are made, then the amount invested will grow by an increasing number of pounds in each successive time period, because interest earned in earlier periods will itself earn interest in later periods.

2.2 Suppose, for example, that £2,000 is invested to earn 10% interest. After one year, the original principal plus interest will amount to £2,200.

	£
Original investment	2,000
Interest in the first year (10%)	200
Total investment at the end of one year	2,200

(a) After two years the total investment will be £2,420.

	£
Investment at end of one year	2,200
Interest in the second year (10%)	220
Total investment at the end of two years	2,420

The second year interest of £220 represents 10% of the original investment, and 10% of the interest earned in the first year.

(b) Similarly, after three years, the total investment will be £2,662.

	£
Investment at the end of two years	2,420
Interest in the third year (10%)	242
Total investment at the end of three years	2,662

FORMULA TO LEARN

The basic formula for **compound interest** is $S_n = P(1 + r)^n$

where P = the original sum invested
       r = the interest rate, expressed as a proportion (so 5% = 0.05)
       n = the number of periods
       S_n = the sum invested after n periods.

2.3 In the previous example, £2,000 invested at 10% per annum for three years would increase in value to

$$£2,000 \times 1.10^3 = £2,000 \times 1.331 = £2,662.$$

The interest earned over three years is £662.

Question 1

(a) What would be the total value of £5,000 invested now:

(i) after three years, if the interest rate is 20% per annum;
(ii) after four years, if the interest rate is 15% per annum;
(iii) after three years, if the interest rate is 6% per annum?

(b) At what annual rate of compound interest will £2,000 grow to £2,721 after four years?

Answer

(a) (i) $£5,000 \times 1.20^3 = £8,640.00$
(ii) $£5,000 \times 1.15^4 = £8,745.03$
(iii) $£5,000 \times 1.06^3 = £5,955.08$

(b)
$$2,721 = 2,000 \times (1 + r)^4$$
$$(1 + r)^4 = 2,721/2,000 = 1.3605$$
$$1 + r = \sqrt[4]{1.3605} = 1.08$$
$$r = 0.08 = 8\%.$$

Inflation

2.4 The same **compounding formula** can be used to **predict future prices** after allowing for inflation. For example, if we wish to predict the salary of an employee in five years time, given that he earns £8,000 now and wage inflation is expected to be 10% per annum, the formula would be applied as follows.

$$S_n = P(1 + r)^n = £8,000 \times 1.10^5 = £12,884.08\text{, say }£12,900.$$

Withdrawals of capital or interest

2.5 If an investor takes money out of an investment, it will cease to earn interest. Thus, if an investor puts £3,000 into a bank deposit account which pays interest at 8% per annum, and makes no withdrawals except at the end of year 2, when he takes out £1,000, what would be the balance in his account after four years?

	£
Original investment	3,000.00
Interest in year 1 (8%)	240.00
Investment at end of year 1	3,240.00
Interest in year 2 (8%)	259.20
Investment at end of year 2	3,499.20
Less withdrawal	1,000.00
Net investment at start of year 3	2,499.20
Interest in year 3 (8%)	199.94
Investment at end of year 3	2,699.14
Interest in year 4 (8%)	215.93
Investment at end of year 4	2,915.07

2.6 A quicker approach would be as follows.

£

£3,000 invested for 2 years at 8% would increase in value to
£3,000 × 1.08² =   3,499.20
Less withdrawal   1,000.00
                                                                              2,499.20

£2,499.20 invested for a further two years at 8% would increase in value to £2,499.20 × 1.08²
= £2,915.07

Changes in the rate of interest

2.7   If the **rate of interest changes** during the period of an investment, the **compounding formula must be amended** slightly, as follows.

> ### FORMULA TO LEARN
>
> The **sum invested after n periods $S_n = P(1 + r_1)^x (1 + r_2)^{n-x}$**
>
> where r_1 = the initial rate of interest
> x = the number of years in which the interest rate r_1 applies
> r_2 = the next rate of interest
> $n - x$ = the (balancing) number of years in which the interest rate r_2 applies
> S_n = the sum invested after n periods.

Question 2

(a)   If £8,000 is invested now, to earn 10% interest for three years and 8% thereafter, what would be the size of the total investment at the end of five years?

(b)   An investor puts £10,000 into an investment for ten years. The annual rate of interest earned is 15% for the first four years, 12% for the next four years and 9% for the final two years. How much will the investment be worth at the end of ten years?

(c)   An item of equipment costs £6,000 now. The annual rates of inflation over the next four years are expected to be 16%, 20%, 15% and 10%. How much would the equipment cost after four years?

Answer

(a) $£8,000 × 1.10^3 × 1.08^2$ = £12,419.83
(b) $£10,000 × 1.15^4 × 1.12^4 × 1.09^2$ = £32,697.64
(c)   £6,000 × 1.16 × 1.20 × 1.15 × 1.10   = £10,565.28

3   EFFECTIVE AND NOMINAL RATES OF INTEREST   6/96

Effective annual rate of interest

3.1   In the previous examples, interest has been calculated annually, but this need not be the case. **Interest** may be compounded **daily, weekly, monthly** or **quarterly**. The **effective annual rate of interest**, when interest is compounded at shorter intervals, may be calculated as follows.

3.2 EXAMPLE: THE EFFECTIVE ANNUAL RATE OF INTEREST

Calculate the effective annual rate of interest of:

(a)   1.5% per month, compound;
(b)   4.5% per quarter, compound;
(c)   9% per half year, compound.

3.3 SOLUTION

(a) $(1.015)^{12} - 1$ $= 0.1956 = 19.56\%$
(b) $(1.045)^{4} - 1$ $= 0.1925 = 19.25\%$
(c) $(1.09)^{2} - 1$ $= 0.1881 = 18.81\%$

Nominal rates of interest and the annual percentage rate

3.4   Most **interest rates** are **expressed as per annum figures** even when the interest is compounded over periods of less than one year. In such cases, the given interest rate is called a **nominal rate**. We can, however, work out the **effective rate**. It is this effective rate (shortened to one decimal place) which is quoted in advertisements as the **annual percentage rate (APR),** sometimes called the **compound annual rate CAR**).

Depending on whether the compounding is done daily, weekly, monthly, quarterly or six monthly, the APR will vary by differing amounts from the nominal rate.

3.5 EXAMPLE: NOMINAL AND EFFECTIVE RATES OF INTEREST

A building society may offer investors 10% per annum interest payable half-yearly. If the 10% is a nominal rate of interest, the building society would in fact pay 5% every six months, compounded so that the effective annual rate of interest would be

$$[(1.05)^{2} - 1] = 0.1025 = 10.25\% \text{ per annum.}$$

3.6   Similarly, if a bank offers depositors a nominal 12% per annum, with interest payable quarterly, the effective rate of interest would be 3% compound every three months, which is $[(1.03)^{4} - 1] = 0.1255 = 12.55\%$ per annum.

Question 3

Calculate the effective annual rate of interest of:

(a)   15% nominal per annum compounded quarterly;
(b)   24% nominal per annum compounded monthly.

Answer

(a) 15% per annum (nominal rate) is 3.75% per quarter. The effective annual rate of interest is

$$[1.0375^4 - 1] = 0.1587 = 15.87\%$$

(b) 24% per annum (nominal rate) is 2% per month. The effective annual rate of interest is

$$[1.02^{12} - 1] = 0.2682 = 26.82\%$$

---

4 THE CONCEPT OF DISCOUNTING 6/99

The basic principles of discounting

> **KEY TERM**
>
> The basic principle of **compounding** is that if we invest £P now for n years at r% interest per annum, we should obtain $£P (1 + r)^n$ in n years time.

4.1 Thus if we invest £10,000 now for four years at 10% interest per annum, we will have a total investment worth $£10,000 \times 1.10^4 = £14,641$ at the end of four years (that is, at year 4 if it is now year 0).

> **KEY TERM**
>
> The basic principle of **discounting** is that if we wish to have £S in n years' time, we need to invest a certain sum *now* (year 0) at an interest rate of r% in order to obtain the required sum of money in the future.

4.2 For example, if we wish to have £14,641 in four years time, how much money would we need to invest now at 10% interest per annum? This is the reverse of the situation described in Paragraph 4.1.

Let P be the amount of money invested now.

$$£14,641 = P \times 1.10^4$$
$$P = £14,641 \times \frac{1}{1.10^4} = £10,000$$

4.3 £10,000 now, with the capacity to earn a return of 10% per annum, is the equivalent in value of £14,641 after four years. We can therefore say that £10,000 is the present value of £14,641 at year 4, at an interest rate of 10%.

Present value

> **KEY TERM**
>
> **Present value** means the amount of money which must be invested now for n years at an interest rate of r%, to earn a given future sum of money at the time it will be due.

The formula for discounting

FORMULA TO LEARN

The **discounting formula** is $P = S_n \times \dfrac{1}{(1+r)^n}$

where
- S_n is the sum to be received after n time periods
- P is the present value of that sum
- r is the rate of return, expressed as a proportion
- n is the number of time periods (usually years).

The rate r is sometimes called a cost of capital.

4.4 EXAMPLE: DISCOUNTING

(a) Calculate the present value of £60,000 at year 6, if a return of 15% per annum is obtainable.

(b) Calculate the present value of £100,000 at year 5, if a return of 6% per annum is obtainable.

(c) Calculate the amount a person needs to invest now at 12% to earn £4,000 at year 2 and £4,000 at year 3.

4.5 SOLUTION

(a) $PV = 60{,}000 \times \dfrac{1}{1.15^6} = 60{,}000 \times 0.432 = £25{,}920$

(b) $PV = 100{,}000 \times \dfrac{1}{1.06^5} = 100{,}000 \times 0.747 = £74{,}700$

(c) $PV = (4{,}000 \times \dfrac{1}{1.12^2}) + (4{,}000 \times \dfrac{1}{1.12^3}) = 4{,}000 \times (0.797 + 0.712) = £6{,}036$

This calculation can be checked as follows.

	£
Year 0	6,036.00
Interest for the first year (12%)	724.32
	6,760.32
Interest for the second year (12%)	811.24
	7,571.56
Less withdrawal	(4,000.00)
	3,571.56
Interest for the third year (12%)	428.59
	4,000.15
Less withdrawal	(4,000.00)
Rounding error	0.15

Question 4

What is the present value of £16,000 received in year 12 when r = 7%?

Answer

$$PV = £16,000 \times \frac{1}{1.07^{12}} = £7,104$$

Capital expenditure appraisal

4.6 **Discounted cash flow techniques** can be used to **evaluate capital expenditure proposals** (investments).

4.7 **Discounted cash flow (DCF)** involves the **application of discounting arithmetic** to the **estimated future cash flows** (receipts and expenditures) from a project in order to decide whether the project is expected to earn a satisfactory rate of return.

There are two methods of using DCF techniques.

- The net present value (NPV) method
- The internal rate of return (IRR) method

5 THE NET PRESENT VALUE (NPV) METHOD 12/94, 12/95, 12/96, 12/97, 6/98, 6/99

> **Exam focus point**
> Discounting in general, and the determination of a project's NPV in particular, are popular exam topics. The examiner expects you to be able to integrate discounting and decision making: you could be asked to calculate the **expected NPV** of a project (as in 12/94, 12/97 and 6/98).

> **KEY TERM**
>
> The **net present value (NPV)** is a capital expenditure appraisal method which works out the present values of all items of income and expenditure related to an investment at a given rate of return, and then works out a net total. If it is **positive**, the investment is considered to be **acceptable**. If it is **negative**, the investment is considered to be **unacceptable**.

5.1 EXAMPLE: THE NET PRESENT VALUE OF A PROJECT

Spender Fortune Ltd is considering whether to spend £5,000 on an item of equipment. The 'cash profits', the excess of income over cash expenditure, from the project would be £3,000 in the first year and £4,000 in the second year.

The company will not invest in any project unless it offers a return in excess of 15% per annum.

Required

Assess whether the investment is worthwhile, or 'viable'.

5.2 SOLUTION

In this example, an outlay of £5,000 now promises a return of £3,000 *during* the first year and £4,000 *during* the second year. It is a convention in DCF, however, that cash flows spread over a year are assumed to occur *at the end of the year*, so that the cash flows of the project are as follows.

	£
Year 0 (now)	(5,000)
Year 1 (at the end of the year)	3,000
Year 2 (at the end of the year)	4,000

The NPV method takes the following approach.

(a) The project offers £3,000 at year 1 and £4,000 at year 2, for an outlay of £5,000 now.

(b) The company might invest elsewhere to earn a return of 15% per annum.

(c) If the company did invest at exactly 15% per annum, how much would it need to invest now, at 15%, to earn £3,000 at the end of year 1 plus £4,000 at the end of year 2?

(d) Is it cheaper to invest £5,000 in the project, or to invest elsewhere at 15%, in order to obtain these future cash flows?

If the company did invest elsewhere at 15% per annum, the amount required to earn £3,000 in year 1 and £4,000 in year 2 would be as follows.

Year	Cash flow £	Discount factor 15%	Present value £
1	3,000	$\dfrac{1}{1.15} = 0.870$	2,610
2	4,000	$\dfrac{1}{(1.15)^2} = 0.756$	3,024
			5,634

The choice is to invest £5,000 in the project, or £5,634 elsewhere at 15%, in order to obtain these future cash flows. We can therefore reach the following conclusion.

- It is cheaper to invest in the project, by £634.
- The project offers a return of over 15% per annum.

The net present value is the difference between the present value of cash inflows from the project (£5,634) and the present value of future cash outflows (in this example, £5,000 × $1/1.15^0$ = £5,000).

An NPV statement could be drawn up as follows.

Year	Cash flow £	Discount factor 15%	Present value £
0	(5,000)	1.000	(5,000)
1	3,000	$\dfrac{1}{1.15} = 0.870$	2,610
2	4,000	$\dfrac{1}{(1.15)^2} = 0.756$	3,024
		Net present value	+634

The project has a positive net present value, so it is acceptable.

Question 5

A company is wondering whether to spend £18,000 on an item of equipment, in order to obtain cash profits as follows.

Year	£
1	6,000
2	8,000
3	5,000

| | 4 | | 1,000 |

The company requires a return of 10% per annum.

Required

Use the NPV method to assess whether the project is viable.

Answer

	Cash flow £	Discount factor 10%	Present value £
0	(18,000)	1.000	(18,000)
1	6,000	$\dfrac{1}{1.10} = 0.909$	5,454
2	8,000	$\dfrac{1}{1.10^2} = 0.826$	6,608
3	5,000	$\dfrac{1}{1.10^3} = 0.751$	3,755
4	1,000	$\dfrac{1}{1.10^4} = 0.683$	683
		Net present value	(1,500)

The NPV is negative. We can therefore draw the following conclusions.

(a) It is cheaper to invest elsewhere at 10% than to invest in the project.
(b) The project would earn a return of less than 10%.
(c) The project is not viable.

Discount tables

5.3 Assuming that money earns, say, 10% per annum:

(a) the PV (present value) of £1 at year 1 is $£1 \times \dfrac{1}{1.10}$ = £1 × 0.909;

(b) similarly, the PV of £1 at year 2 is $£1 \times \dfrac{1}{(1.10)^2}$ = £1 × 0.826;

(c) the PV of £1 at year 3 is $£1 \times \dfrac{1}{(1.10)^3}$ = £1 × 0.751.

Discount tables show the value of $1/(1 + r)^n$ for different values of r and n. The 10% discount factors of 0.909, 0.826 and 0.751 are shown in the discount tables at the end of this Study Text in the column for 10%. (You will be given discount tables in your examination.)

Question 6

Flower Potts Ltd is considering whether to make an investment costing £28,000 which would earn £8,000 cash per annum for five years. The company expects to make a return of at least 11% per annum.

Required

Assess whether the project is viable.

Answer

Year	Cash flow £	Discount factor 11%	Present value £
0	(28,000)	1.000	(28,000)
1	8,000	0.901	7,208
2	8,000	0.812	6,496
3	8,000	0.731	5,848
4	8,000	0.659	5,272
5	8,000	0.593	4,744
		NPV	1,568

The NPV is positive, therefore the project is viable because it earns more than 11% per annum.

Project comparison

5.4 **The NPV method can also be used to compare two or more investment options**. For example, suppose that Daisy Ltd can choose between the investment outlined in Question 5 above *or* a second investment, which also costs £28,000 but which would earn £6,500 in the first year, £7,500 in the second, £8,500 in the third, £9,500 in the fourth and £10,500 in the fifth. Which one should Daisy Ltd choose?

5.5 **The decision rule is to choose the option with the highest NPV**. We therefore need to calculate the NPV of the second option.

Year	Cash flow £	Discount factor 11%	Present value £
0	(28,000)	1.000	(28,000)
1	6,500	0.901	5,857
2	7,500	0.812	6,090
3	8,500	0.731	6,214
4	9,500	0.659	6,261
5	10,500	0.593	6,227
		NPV =	2,649

Daisy Ltd should therefore invest in the second option since it has the higher NPV.

Expected values and discounting

5.6 Future cash flows cannot be predicted with complete accuracy. To take account of this uncertainty an **expected net present value** can be calculated

> **KEY TERM**
>
> An **expected net present value** is a weighted average net present value based on the probabilities of different sets of circumstances occurring.

5.7 EXAMPLE: EXPECTED NET PRESENT VALUE

An organisation with a cost of capital of 5% is contemplating investing £340,000 in a project which has a 25% chance of being a big success and producing cash inflows of £210,000 after one and two years. There is, however, a 75% change of the project not being quite so successful, in which case the cash inflows will be £162,000 after one year and £174,000 after two years.

Required

Calculate an ENPV and hence advise the organisation.

5.8 SOLUTION

Year	Discount factor 5%	Success Cash flow £'000	PV £'000	Failure Cash flow £'000	PV £'000
0	1.000	(340)	(340.00)	(340)	(340.000)
1	0.952	210	199.92	162	154.224
2	0.907	210	190.47	174	157.818
			50.39		(27.958)

ENPV = (25% × 50.39) + (75% × –27.958) = –8.371

The ENPV is – £8,371 and hence the organisation should not invest in the project.

> **Exam focus point**
>
> The 6/99 exam required candidates to calculate the NPV of a project, taking the effects of inflation into account. This simply requires that cash flows are increased by the annual rate of inflation before they are discounted. Many candidates encountered problems with dealing with inflation and discounting together.

6 THE INTERNAL RATE OF RETURN (IRR) METHOD 12/95, 12/96, 6/98, 6/99

6.1 The **internal rate of return (IRR) method** of evaluating investments is an **alternative** to the **NPV method**.

6.2 The **NPV method** of discounted cash flow **determines** whether an investment earns a **positive** or a **negative NPV** when discounted at a given rate of interest. If the NPV is zero (that is, the present values of costs and benefits are equal) the return from the project would be exactly the rate used for discounting.

> **KEY TERM**
>
> The **internal rate of return** is the rate of return at which the net present value of an investment is zero.

6.3 EXAMPLE: THE IRR METHOD OVER ONE YEAR

If £500 is invested today and generates £600 in one year's time, the internal rate of return (r) can be calculated as follows.

PV of cost   =   PV of benefits

$$500 \quad = \quad \frac{600}{(1+r)}$$

$$500(1+r) \quad = \quad 600$$

$$1+r \quad = \quad \frac{600}{500} = 1.2$$

$$r \quad = 0.2 = 20\%$$

BPP PUBLISHING

6.4 EXAMPLE: THE IRR METHOD OVER TWO YEARS

If £1,000 is invested today and generates £700 in the first year and £600 in the second year the internal rate of return can be calculated as follows.

PV of cost $\qquad$ = $\qquad$ PV of benefits

$$1,000 \qquad = \frac{700}{(1+r)} + \frac{600}{(1+r)^2}$$

Multiply both sides by $(1 + r)^2$

$$1,000 (1 + r)^2 \qquad = \quad 700(1 + r) + 600$$

$$1,000 + 2,000r + 1,000r^2 \quad = \quad 700 + 700r + 600$$

$$1,000r^2 + 1,300r - 300 \quad = \quad 0$$

$$10r^2 + 13r - 3 \qquad = \quad 0$$

$$r \quad = \frac{-13 \pm \sqrt{[169 - (4 \times 10 \times (-3))]}}{20}$$

$$= \frac{-13 - 17}{20} \text{ or } \frac{-13 + 17}{20}$$

$$= -1.5 \qquad \text{or } +0.2$$

$$= -150\% \quad \text{or } 20\%$$

Since high negative returns are not a practical proposition, r = 20%.

6.5 **The IRR method will indicate that a project is viable if the IRR exceeds the minimum acceptable rate of return.** Thus if the company expects a minimum return of, say, 15%, a project would be viable if its IRR is more than 15%.

6.6 The examples so far used to illustrate the IRR method have been for one or two year projects. The arithmetic is more complicated for investments and cash flows extending over a longer period of time. **A technique known as the interpolation method can be used to calculate an approximate IRR.**

6.7 EXAMPLE: INTERPOLATION

A project costing £800 in year 0 is expected to earn £400 in year 1, £300 in year 2 and £200 in year 3.

Required

Calculate the internal rate of return.

6.8 SOLUTION

The IRR is calculated by first of all finding the NPV at each of two interest rates. Ideally, one interest rate should give a small positive NPV and the other a small negative NPV. The IRR would then be somewhere between these two interest rates: above the rate where the NPV is positive, but below the rate where the NPV is negative.

A very rough guideline for estimating at what interest rate the NPV might be close to zero, is to take

$$\frac{2}{3} \times \left(\frac{\text{profit}}{\text{cost of the project}} \right)$$

In our example, the total profit over three years is £(400 + 300 + 200 − 800) = £100

$\frac{2}{3} \times \frac{100}{800} = 0.08$ approx. A starting point is to try 8%.

(a) Try 8%

Year	Cash flow	Discount factor	Present value
	£	8%	£
0	(800)	1.000	(800.0)
1	400	0.926	370.4
2	300	0.857	257.1
3	200	0.794	158.8
		NPV	(13.7)

The NPV is negative, therefore the project fails to earn 8% and the IRR must be less than 8%.

(b) Try 6%

Year	Cash flow	Discount factor	Present value
	£	6%	£
0	(800)	1.000	(800.0)
1	400	0.943	377.2
2	300	0.890	267.0
3	200	0.840	168.0
		NPV	12.2

The NPV is positive, therefore the project earns more than 6% and less than 8%.

The IRR is now calculated by interpolation. The result will not be exact, but it will be a close approximation. Interpolation assumes that the NPV falls in a straight line from +12.2 at 6% to −13.7 at 8%.

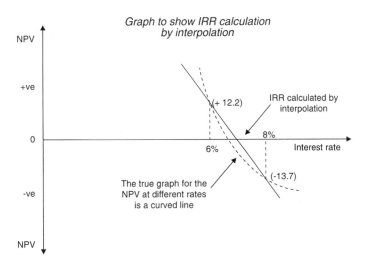

Graph to show IRR calculation by interpolation

Exam focus point

You may be asked to draw a graph in order to estimate the internal rate of return of a project (as in the 12/96 exam where there were 4½ marks to be gained). Do make sure you earn all of the easy marks that you can, and don't forget that ruler and sharp pencil!

FORMULA TO LEARN

The IRR, where the NPV is zero, can be calculated as:

$$a\% + [\frac{A}{A - B} \times (b - a)]\% \text{ where}$$

a is one interest rate

b is the other interest rate

A is the NPV at rate a

B is the NPV at rate b

$$\text{IRR} = 6\% + [\frac{12.2}{(12.2 + 13.7)} \times (8 - 6)]\% = (6 + 0.94)\% = 6.94\% \text{ (approx)}$$

The answer is only an approximation because the NPV falls in a slightly curved line and not a straight line between +12.2 and –13.7. Provided that NPVs close to zero are used, the linear assumption used in the interpolation method is nevertheless fairly accurate.

Note that the formula will still work if A and B are both positive, or both negative, and even if a and b are a long way from the true IRR, but the results will be less accurate.

Chapter roundup

- **Simple interest** is interest which is earned in equal amounts every year (or month) and which is a given proportion of the principal. The simple interest formula is $S_n = P + nrP$.

- **Compounding** means that, as interest is earned, it is added to the original investment and starts to earn interest itself. The basic formula for compound interest is $S_n = P(1+r)^n$.

- If the rate of interest changes during the period of an investment, the compounding formula must be amended slightly to $S_n = P(1+r_1)^x (1 +r_2)^{n-x}$.

- An **effective annual rate of interest** is the corresponding annual rate when interest is compounded at intervals shorter than a year.

- A **nominal rate** of interest is a rate expressed as a per annum figure although the interest is compounded over a period of less than one year. The corresponding effective rate of interest shortened to one decimal place is the **annual percentage rate (APR).**

- **Discounting** is the reverse of compounding. The discounting formula is $P = S_n \times 1/(1+r)^n$.

- The concept of **present value** can be thought of in two ways. It is the value today of an amount to be received some time in the future and it is the amount which would have to be invested today to produce a given amount at some future date.

- **Discounted cash flow techniques** can be used to evaluate capital expenditure projects. There are two methods: the **NPV** method and the **IRR** method.

- The **NPV** method works out the present values of all items of income and expenditure related to an investment at a given rate of return, and then works out a **net total**. If it is positive, the investment is considered to be acceptable. If it is negative, the investment is considered to be unacceptable.

- The **IRR** method is to determine the rate of interest (the IRR) at which the NPV is 0. **Interpolation**, using the following **formula**, is often necessary. The project is viable if the IRR **exceeds** the minimum acceptable return.

$$\text{IRR} = a\% + \left[\frac{A}{A - B} \times (b - a)\right]\%$$

Quick quiz

1   If a sum P is invested earning a simple annual interest rate of r, how much will the investor have after n years? (see formulae to learn)

2   If a sum P is invested earning a compound annual interest rate of r, how much will the investor have after n years? (formulae to learn)

3   How should withdrawals of money be dealt with in compound interest calculations? (2.5, 2.6)

4   How should changes in the rate of interest be dealt with in compound interest calculations? (2.7, formulae to learn)

5   What is meant by an effective annual rate of interest? (3.1)

6   What is the meaning of the term 'present value'? (key terms)

7   What is the present value of a sum of money S_n in n years time, given an interest rate of r? (formulae to learn)

8   What are the two usual methods of capital expenditure appraisal using DCF techniques? (4.7)

9   What is the internal rate of return of an investment? (key terms)

10 How would you determine the internal rate of return of a series of cash flows using interpolation? (6.8)

Question to try	Level	Marks	Time
30	Introductory	n/a	15 mins

Appendix: Mathematical tables

FORMULAE

Standard deviation:

ungrouped data $\sqrt{\dfrac{\Sigma(x-\bar{x})^2}{n}} = \sqrt{\dfrac{\Sigma x^2}{n} - \bar{x}^2}$

grouped data $\sqrt{\dfrac{\Sigma f(x-\bar{x})^2}{\Sigma f}} = \sqrt{\dfrac{\Sigma fx^2}{\Sigma f} - \left(\dfrac{\Sigma fx}{\Sigma f}\right)^2}$

Standard error:

mean $\dfrac{\sigma}{\sqrt{n}}$

proportion $\sqrt{\dfrac{p(1-p)}{n}}$

Confidence interval:

mean $\bar{x} \pm z\dfrac{\sigma}{\sqrt{n}}$

proportion $\hat{p} \pm z\sqrt{\dfrac{p(1-p)}{n}}$

Sample size:

mean $n \geq \left(\dfrac{Zs}{l}\right)^2$

proportion $n \geq \dfrac{Z^2 p(1-p)}{l^2}$

Roots of a quadratic equation: $\dfrac{-b \pm \sqrt{b^2 - 4ac}}{2a}$

Economic order quantity: $\sqrt{\dfrac{2C_2 D}{C_1}}$ or $\sqrt{\dfrac{2C_o D}{C_H}}$

AREA UNDER THE NORMAL CURVE

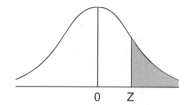

$Z=\dfrac{(X-\mu)}{\sigma}$	0.00	0.01	0.02	0.03	0.04	0.05	0.06	0.07	0.08	0.09
0.0	.5000	.4960	.4920	.4880	.4840	.4801	.4761	.4721	.4681	.4641
0.1	.4602	.4562	.4522	.4483	.4443	.4404	.4364	.4325	.4286	.4247
0.2	.4207	.4168	.4129	.4090	.4052	.4013	.3974	.3936	.3897	.3859
0.3	.3821	.3783	.3745	.3707	.3669	.3632	.3594	.3557	.3520	.3483
0.4	.3446	.3409	.3372	.3336	.3300	.3264	.3228	.3192	.3156	.3121
0.5	.3085	.3050	.3015	.2981	.2946	.2912	.2877	.2843	.2810	.2776
0.6	.2743	.2709	.2676	.2643	.2611	.2578	.2546	.2514	.2483	.2451
0.7	.2420	.2389	.2358	.2327	.2296	.2266	.2236	.2206	.2177	.2148
0.8	.2119	.2090	.2061	.2033	.2005	.1977	.1949	.1922	.1894	.1867
0.9	.1841	.1814	.1788	.1762	.1736	.1711	.1685	.1660	.1635	.1611
1.0	.1587	.1562	.1539	.1515	.1492	.1469	.1446	.1423	.1401	.1379
1.1	.1357	.1335	.1314	.1292	.1271	.1251	.1230	.1210	.1190	.1170
1.2	.1151	.1131	.1112	.1093	.1075	.1056	.1038	.1020	.1003	.0985
1.3	.0968	.0951	.0934	.0918	.0901	.0885	.0869	.0853	.0838	.0823
1.4	.0808	.0793	.0778	.0764	.0749	.0735	.0721	.0708	.0694	.0681
1.5	.0668	.0655	.0643	.0630	.0618	.0606	.0594	.0582	.0571	.0559
1.6	.0548	.0537	.0526	.0516	.0505	.0495	.0485	.0475	.0465	.0455
1.7	.0446	.0436	.0427	.0418	.0409	.0401	.0392	.0384	.0375	.0367
1.8	.0359	.0351	.0344	.0336	.0329	.0322	.0314	.0307	.0301	.0294
1.9	.0287	.0281	.0274	.0268	.0262	.0256	.0250	.0244	.0239	.0233
2.0	.02275	.02222	.02169	.02118	.02068	.02018	.01970	.01923	.01876	.01831
2.1	.01786	.01743	.01700	.01659	.01618	.01578	.01539	.01500	.01463	.01426
2.2	.01390	.01355	.01321	.01287	.01255	.01222	.01191	.01160	.01130	.01101
2.3	.01072	.01044	.01017	.00990	.00964	.00939	.00914	.00889	.00866	.00842
2.4	.00820	.00798	.00776	.00755	.00734	.00714	.00695	.00676	.00657	.00639
2.5	.00621	.00604	.00587	.00570	.00554	.00539	.00523	.00508	.00494	.00480
2.6	.00466	.00453	.00440	.00427	.00415	.00402	.00391	.00379	.00368	.00357
2.7	.00347	.00336	.00326	.00317	.00307	.00298	.00289	.00280	.00272	.00264
2.8	.00256	.00248	.00240	.00233	.00226	.00219	.00212	.00205	.00199	.00193
2.9	.00187	.00181	.00175	.00169	.00164	.00159	.00154	.00149	.00144	.00139

PRESENT VALUE TABLE

Present value of 1 ie $(1+r)^{-n}$

where r = discount rate

n = number of periods until payment

Periods					Discount rates (r)					
(n)	1%	2%	3%	4%	5%	6%	7%	8%	9%	10%
1	0.990	0.980	0.971	0.962	0.952	0.943	0.935	0.926	0.917	0.909
2	0.980	0.961	0.943	0.925	0.907	0.890	0.873	0.857	0.842	0.826
3	0.971	0.942	0.915	0.889	0.864	0.840	0.816	0.794	0.772	0.751
4	0.961	0.924	0.888	0.855	0.823	0.792	0.763	0.735	0.708	0.683
5	0.951	0.906	0.863	0.822	0.784	0.747	0.713	0.681	0.650	0.621
6	0.942	0.888	0.837	0.790	0.746	0.705	0.666	0.630	0.596	0.564
7	0.933	0.871	0.813	0.760	0.711	0.665	0.623	0.583	0.547	0.513
8	0.923	0.853	0.789	0.731	0.677	0.627	0.582	0.540	0.502	0.467
9	0.914	0.837	0.766	0.703	0.645	0.592	0.544	0.500	0.460	0.424
10	0.905	0.820	0.744	0.676	0.614	0.558	0.508	0.463	0.422	0.386
11	0.896	0.804	0.722	0.650	0.585	0.527	0.475	0.429	0.388	0.350
12	0.887	0.788	0.701	0.625	0.557	0.497	0.444	0.397	0.356	0.319
13	0.879	0.773	0.681	0.601	0.530	0.469	0.415	0.368	0.326	0.290
14	0.870	0.758	0.661	0.577	0.505	0.442	0.388	0.340	0.299	0.263
15	0.861	0.743	0.642	0.555	0.481	0.417	0.362	0.315	0.275	0.239

	11%	12%	13%	14%	15%	16%	17%	18%	19%	20%
1	0.901	0.893	0.885	0.877	0.870	0.862	0.855	0.847	0.840	0.833
2	0.812	0.797	0.783	0.769	0.756	0.743	0.731	0.718	0.706	0.694
3	0.731	0.712	0.693	0.675	0.658	0.641	0.624	0.609	0.593	0.579
4	0.659	0.636	0.613	0.592	0.572	0.552	0.534	0.516	0.499	0.482
5	0.593	0.567	0.543	0.519	0.497	0.476	0.456	0.437	0.419	0.402
6	0.535	0.507	0.480	0.456	0.432	0.410	0.390	0.370	0.352	0.335
7	0.482	0.452	0.425	0.400	0.376	0.354	0.333	0.314	0.296	0.279
8	0.434	0.404	0.376	0.351	0.327	0.305	0.285	0.266	0.249	0.233
9	0.391	0.361	0.333	0.308	0.284	0.263	0.243	0.225	0.209	0.194
10	0.352	0.322	0.295	0.270	0.247	0.227	0.208	0.191	0.176	0.162
11	0.317	0.287	0.261	0.237	0.215	0.195	0.178	0.162	0.148	0.135
12	0.286	0.257	0.231	0.208	0.187	0.168	0.152	0.137	0.124	0.112
13	0.258	0.229	0.204	0.182	0.163	0.145	0.130	0.116	0.104	0.093
14	0.232	0.205	0.181	0.160	0.141	0.125	0.111	0.099	0.088	0.078
15	0.209	0.183	0.160	0.140	0.123	0.108	0.095	0.084	0.074	0.065

LOGARITHMS

Logarithm and antilogarithm tables are not supplied in the examination.

	0	1	2	3	4	5	6	7	8	9
10	0000	0043	0086	0128	0170	0212	0253	0294	0334	0374
11	0414	0453	0492	0531	0569	0607	0645	0682	0719	0755
12	0792	0828	0864	0899	0934	0969	1004	1038	1072	1106
13	1139	1173	1206	1239	1271	1303	1335	1367	1399	1430
14	1461	1492	1523	1553	1584	1614	1644	1673	1703	1732
15	1761	1790	1818	1847	1875	1903	1931	1959	1987	2014
16	2041	2068	2095	2122	2148	2175	2201	2227	2253	2279
17	2304	2330	2355	2380	2405	2430	2455	2480	2504	2529
18	2553	2577	2601	2625	2648	2672	2695	2718	2742	2765
19	2788	2810	2833	2856	2878	2900	2923	2945	2967	2989
20	3010	3032	3054	3075	3096	3118	3139	3160	3181	3201
21	3222	3243	3263	3284	3304	3324	3345	3365	3385	3404
22	3424	3444	3464	3483	3502	3522	3541	3560	3579	3598
23	3617	3636	3655	3674	3692	3711	3729	3747	3766	3784
24	3802	3820	3838	3856	3874	3892	3909	3927	3945	3962
25	3979	3997	4014	4031	4048	4065	4082	4099	4116	4133
26	4150	4166	4183	4200	4216	4232	4249	4265	4281	4298
27	4314	4330	4346	4362	4378	4393	4409	4425	4440	4456
28	4472	4487	4502	4518	4533	4548	4564	4579	4594	4609
29	4624	4639	4654	4669	4683	4698	4713	4728	4742	4757
30	4771	4786	4800	4814	4829	4843	4857	4871	4886	4900
31	4914	4928	4942	4955	4969	4983	4997	5011	5024	5038
32	5051	5065	5079	5092	5105	5119	5132	5145	5159	5172
33	5185	5198	5211	5224	5237	5250	5263	5276	5289	5302
34	5315	5328	5340	5353	5366	5378	5391	5403	5416	5428
35	5441	5453	5465	5478	5490	5502	5514	5527	5539	5551
36	5563	5575	5587	5599	5611	5623	5635	5647	5658	5670
37	5682	5694	5705	5717	5729	5740	5752	5763	5775	5786
38	5798	5809	5821	5832	5843	5855	5866	5877	5888	5899
39	5911	5922	5933	5944	5955	5966	5977	5988	5999	6010
40	6021	6031	6042	6053	6064	6075	6085	6096	6107	6117
41	6128	6138	6149	6160	6170	6180	6191	6201	6212	6222
42	6232	6243	6253	6263	6274	6284	6294	6304	6314	6325
43	6335	6345	6355	6365	6375	6385	6395	6405	6415	6425
44	6435	6444	6454	6464	6474	6484	6493	6503	6513	6522
45	6532	6542	6551	6561	6571	6580	6590	6599	6609	6618
46	6628	6637	6646	6656	6665	6675	6684	6693	6702	6712
47	6721	6730	6739	6749	6758	6767	6776	6785	6794	6803
48	6812	6821	6830	6839	6848	6857	6866	6875	6884	6893
49	6902	6911	6920	6928	6937	6946	6955	6964	6972	6981
50	6990	6998	7007	7016	7024	7033	7042	7050	7059	7067
51	7076	7084	7093	7101	7110	7118	7126	7135	7143	7152
52	7160	7168	7177	7185	7193	7202	7210	7218	7226	7235
53	7243	7251	7259	7267	7275	7284	7292	7300	7308	7316
54	7324	7332	7340	7348	7356	7364	7372	7380	7388	7396

	0	1	2	3	4	5	6	7	8	9
55	7404	7412	7419	7427	7435	7443	7451	7459	7466	7474
56	7482	7490	7497	7505	7513	7520	7528	7536	7543	7551
57	7559	7566	7574	7582	7589	7597	7604	7612	7619	7627
58	7634	7642	7649	7657	7664	7672	7679	7686	7694	7701
59	7709	7716	7723	7731	7738	7745	7752	7760	7767	7774
60	7782	7789	7796	7803	7810	7818	7825	7832	7839	7846
61	7853	7860	7868	7875	7882	7889	7896	7903	7910	7917
62	7924	7931	7938	7945	7952	7959	7966	7973	7980	7987
63	7993	8000	8007	8014	8021	8028	8035	8041	8048	8055
64	8062	8069	8075	8082	8089	8096	8102	8109	8116	8122
65	8129	8136	8142	8149	8156	8162	8169	8176	8182	8189
66	8195	8202	8209	8215	8222	8228	8235	8241	8248	8254
67	8261	8267	8274	8280	8287	8293	8299	8306	8312	8319
68	8325	8331	8338	8344	8351	8357	8363	8370	8376	8382
69	8388	8395	8401	8407	8414	8420	8426	8432	8439	8445
70	8451	8457	8463	8470	8476	8482	8488	8494	8500	8506
71	8513	8519	8525	8531	8537	8543	8549	8555	8561	8567
72	8573	8579	8585	8591	8597	8603	8609	8615	8621	8627
73	8633	8639	8645	8651	8657	8663	8669	8675	8681	8686
74	8692	8698	8704	8710	8716	8722	8727	8733	8739	8745
75	8751	8756	8762	8768	8774	8779	8785	8791	8797	8802
76	8808	8814	8820	8825	8831	8837	8842	8848	8854	8859
77	8865	8871	8876	8882	8887	8893	8899	8904	8910	8915
78	8921	8927	8932	8938	8943	8949	8954	8960	8965	8971
79	8976	8982	8987	8993	8998	9004	9009	9015	9020	9025
80	9031	9036	9042	9047	9053	9058	9063	9069	9074	9079
81	9085	9090	9096	9101	9106	9112	9117	9122	9128	9133
82	9138	9143	9149	9154	9159	9165	9170	9175	9180	9186
83	9191	9196	9201	9206	9212	9217	9222	9227	9232	9238
84	9243	9248	9253	9258	9263	9269	9274	9279	9284	9289
85	9294	9299	9304	9309	9315	9320	9325	9330	9335	9340
86	9345	9350	9355	9360	9365	9370	9375	9380	9385	9390
87	9395	9400	9405	9410	9415	9420	9425	9430	9435	9440
88	9445	9450	9455	9460	9465	9469	9474	9479	9484	9489
89	9494	9499	9504	9509	9513	9518	9523	9528	9533	9538
90	9542	9547	9552	9557	9562	9566	9571	9576	9581	9586
91	9590	9595	9600	9605	9609	9614	9619	9624	9628	9633
92	9638	9643	9647	9652	9657	9661	9666	9671	9675	9680
93	9685	9689	9694	9699	9703	9708	9713	9717	9722	9727
94	9731	9736	9741	9745	9750	9754	9759	9763	9768	9773
95	9777	9782	9786	9791	9795	9800	9805	9809	9814	9818
96	9823	9827	9832	9836	9841	9845	9850	9854	9859	9863
97	9868	9872	9877	9881	9886	9890	9894	9899	9903	9908
98	9912	9917	9921	9926	9930	9934	9939	9943	9948	9952
99	9956	9961	9965	9969	9974	9978	9983	9987	9991	9996

ANTILOGARITHMS

	0	1	2	3	4	5	6	7	8	9
.00	1000	1002	1005	1007	1009	1012	1014	1016	1019	1021
.01	1023	1026	1028	1030	1033	1035	1038	1040	1042	1045
.02	1047	1050	1052	1054	1057	1059	1062	1064	1067	1069
.03	1072	1074	1076	1079	1081	1084	1086	1089	1091	1094
.04	1096	1099	1102	1104	1107	1109	1112	1114	1117	1119
.05	1122	1125	1127	1130	1132	1135	1138	1140	1143	1146
.06	1148	1151	1153	1156	1159	1161	1164	1167	1169	1172
.07	1175	1178	1180	1183	1186	1189	1191	1194	1197	1199
.08	1202	1205	1208	1211	1213	1216	1219	1222	1225	1227
.09	1230	1233	1236	1239	1242	1245	1247	1250	1253	1256
.10	1259	1262	1265	1268	1271	1274	1276	1279	1282	1285
.11	1288	1291	1294	1297	1300	1303	1306	1309	1312	1315
.12	1318	1321	1324	1327	1330	1334	1337	1340	1343	1346
.13	1349	1352	1355	1358	1361	1365	1368	1371	1374	1377
.14	1380	1384	1387	1390	1393	1396	1400	1403	1406	1409
.15	1413	1416	1419	1422	1426	1429	1432	1435	1439	1442
.16	1445	1449	1452	1455	1459	1462	1466	1469	1472	1476
.17	1479	1483	1486	1489	1493	1496	1500	1503	1507	1510
.18	1514	1517	1521	1524	1528	1531	1535	1538	1542	1545
.19	1549	1552	1556	1560	1563	1567	1570	1574	1578	1581
.20	1585	1589	1592	1596	1600	1603	1607	1611	1614	1618
.21	1622	1626	1629	1633	1637	1641	1644	1648	1652	1656
.22	1660	1663	1667	1671	1675	1679	1683	1687	1690	1694
.23	1698	1702	1706	1710	1714	1718	1722	1726	1730	1734
.24	1738	1742	1746	1750	1754	1758	1762	1766	1770	1774
.25	1778	1782	1786	1791	1795	1799	1803	1807	1811	1816
.26	1820	1824	1828	1832	1837	1841	1845	1849	1854	1858
.27	1862	1866	1871	1875	1879	1884	1888	1892	1897	1901
.28	1905	1910	1914	1919	1923	1928	1932	1936	1941	1945
.29	1950	1954	1959	1963	1968	1972	1977	1982	1986	1991
.30	1995	2000	2004	2009	2014	2018	2023	2028	2032	2037
.31	2042	2046	2051	2056	2061	2065	2070	2075	2080	2084
.32	2089	2094	2099	2104	2109	2113	2118	2123	2128	2133
.33	2138	2143	2148	2153	2158	2163	2168	2173	2178	2183
.34	2188	2193	2198	2203	2208	2213	2218	2223	2228	2234
.35	2239	2244	2249	2254	2259	2265	2270	2275	2280	2286
.36	2291	2296	2301	2307	2312	2317	2323	2328	2333	2339
.37	2344	2350	2355	2360	2366	2371	2377	2382	2388	2393
.38	2399	2404	2410	2415	2421	2427	2432	2438	2443	2449
.39	2455	2460	2466	2472	2477	2483	2489	2495	2500	2506
.40	2512	2518	2523	2529	2535	2541	2547	2553	2559	2564
.41	2570	2576	2582	2588	2594	2600	2606	2612	2618	2624
.42	2630	2636	2642	2649	2655	2661	2667	2673	2679	2685
.43	2692	2698	2704	2710	2716	2723	2729	2735	2742	2748
.44	2754	2761	2767	2773	2780	2786	2793	2799	2805	2812
.45	2818	2825	2831	2838	2844	2851	2858	2864	2871	2877
.46	2884	2891	2897	2904	2911	2917	2924	2931	2938	2944
.47	2951	2958	2965	2972	2979	2985	2992	2999	3006	3013
.48	3020	3027	3034	3041	3048	3055	3062	3069	3076	3083
.49	3090	3097	3105	3112	3119	3126	3133	3141	3148	3155

	0	1	2	3	4	5	6	7	8	9
.50	3162	3170	3177	3184	3192	3199	3206	3214	3221	3228
.51	3236	3243	3251	3258	3266	3273	3281	3289	3296	3304
.52	3311	3319	3327	3334	3342	3350	3357	3365	3373	3381
.53	3388	3396	3404	3412	3420	3428	3436	3443	3451	3459
.54	3467	3475	3483	3491	3499	3508	3516	3524	3532	3540
.55	3548	3556	3565	3573	3581	3589	3597	3606	3614	3622
.56	3631	3639	3648	3656	3664	3673	3681	3690	3698	3707
.57	3715	3724	3733	3741	3750	3758	3767	3776	3784	3793
.58	3802	3811	3819	3828	3837	3846	3855	3864	3873	3882
.59	3890	3899	3908	3917	3926	3936	3945	3954	3963	3972
.60	3981	3990	3999	4009	4018	4027	4036	4046	4055	4064
.61	4074	4083	4093	4102	4111	4121	4130	4140	4150	4159
.62	4169	4178	4188	4198	4207	4217	4227	4236	4246	4256
.63	4266	4276	4285	4295	4305	4315	4325	4335	4345	4355
.64	4365	4375	4385	4395	4406	4416	4426	4436	4446	4457
.65	4467	4477	4487	4498	4508	4519	4529	4539	4550	4560
.66	4571	4581	4592	4603	4613	4624	4634	4645	4656	4667
.67	4677	4688	4699	4710	4721	4732	4742	4753	4764	4775
.68	4786	4797	4808	4819	4831	4842	4853	4864	4875	4887
.69	4898	4909	4920	4932	4943	4955	4966	4977	4989	5000
.70	5012	5023	5035	5047	5058	5070	5082	5093	5105	5117
.71	5129	5140	5152	5164	5176	5188	5200	5212	5224	5236
.72	5248	5260	5272	5284	5297	5309	5321	5333	5346	5358
.73	5370	5383	5395	5408	5420	5433	5445	5458	5470	5483
.74	5495	5508	5521	5534	5546	5559	5572	5585	5598	5610
.75	5623	5636	5649	5662	5675	5689	5702	5715	5728	5741
.76	5754	5768	5781	5794	5808	5821	5834	5848	5861	5875
.77	5888	5902	5916	5929	5943	5957	5970	5984	5998	6012
.78	6026	6039	6053	6067	6081	6095	6109	6124	6138	6152
.79	6166	6180	6194	6209	6223	6237	6252	6266	6281	6295
.80	6310	6324	6339	6353	6368	6383	6397	6412	6427	6442
.81	6457	6471	6486	6501	6516	6531	6546	6561	6577	6592
.82	6607	6622	6637	6653	6668	6683	6699	6714	6730	6745
.83	6761	6776	6792	6808	6823	6839	6855	6871	6887	6902
.84	6918	6934	6950	6966	6982	6998	7015	7031	7047	7063
.85	7079	7096	7112	7129	7145	7161	7178	7194	7211	7228
.86	7244	7261	7278	7295	7311	7328	7345	7362	7379	7396
.87	7413	7430	7447	7464	7482	7499	7516	7534	7551	7568
.88	7586	7603	7621	7638	7656	7674	7691	7709	7727	7745
.89	7762	7780	7798	7816	7834	7852	7870	7889	7907	7925
.90	7943	7962	7980	7998	8017	8035	8054	8072	8091	8110
.91	8128	8147	8166	8185	8204	8222	8241	8260	8279	8299
.92	8318	8337	8356	8375	8395	8414	8433	8453	8472	8492
.93	8511	8531	8551	8570	8590	8610	8630	8650	8670	8690
.94	8710	8730	8750	8770	8790	8810	8831	8851	8872	8892
.95	8913	8933	8954	8974	8995	9016	9036	9057	9078	9099
.96	9120	9141	9162	9183	9204	9226	9247	9268	9290	9311
.97	9333	9354	9376	9397	9419	9441	9462	9484	9506	9528
.98	9550	9572	9594	9616	9638	9661	9683	9705	9727	9750
.99	9772	9795	9817	9840	9863	9886	9908	9931	9954	9977

BPP PUBLISHING

Exam question bank

1 COST ACCOUNTING *15 mins*

Explain what you understand by the term 'cost accounting' and describe the benefits which a cost accounting system produces for an organisation. (You may refer to your own experience relating to costing systems in your answer).

2 CALCULATORS AND RATIOS *15 mins*

The Secretary of the Resident's Association of a block of flats has asked your advice on how to divide the annual buildings insurance premium between the owners of the various flats in the block.

There are nine flats in all: six three-bedroom flats and three two-bedroom flats. Five of the three-bedroom flats and one of the two-bedroom flats have a garage; the remainder have no garage.

The residents have agreed that the annual premium should be split between a three-bedroom flat, a two-bedroomed flat and a garage in the ratio 11:10:1. The total annual premium payable is £1,364.76.

Required

Calculate the premium payable by the owner of each type of flat.

3 SOFTWARE CATEGORIES (14 marks) *25 mins*

The term *software* can be used to refer to *all* the programs that are run on a computer system. Within this overall definition, however, a number of different categories of software can be identified.

Three different categories of software that you would expect to find in a typical small computer system used by a firm of accountants are *application packages, operating systems* and *utility (or service) programs.*

Required

Describe the main functions of each category of software and give examples of the uses to which it would be put.

4 CLASSIFYING COSTS (14 marks) *25 mins*

Your company is considering installing a costing system and is examining ways in which different classifications of cost can assist management.

Required

Prepare a report for your finance director which outlines the following.

(a) How costs can be classified (5 marks)
(b) How the different classifications can assist management (9 marks)

5 COMPONENT BCD *15 mins*

From the information below relating to component BCD you are required to calculate the following.

(a) Reorder level
(b) Reorder quantity
(c) Minimum level
(d) Average stock held

Maximum stock has been set at 5,500 units

Usage per month:	maximum	1,100 units
	minimum	900 units
Estimated delivery period	maximum	4 months
	minimum	2 months

6 **BLACK ASTERIOD LTD** (14 marks)   *25 mins*

Black Asteroid Ltd is a distributor of moon buggies, a new model of a large-wheeled bicycle. At 30 June, stock in hand was 200 units which had a value of £8,400.

Transactions for the six months to 31 December were as follows.

Date	Purchases Units	Cost per unit £
July	200	46.00
August	500	49.40
October	1,000	52.50 (net)

Alice Commette, the purchasing manager, obtained a bulk purchase discount of £7.50 per unit on the October purchases.

Date	Sales Units	Unit sales price £
September	500	66.00
November	700	70.00
December	500	75.00

There were no sales during the first three months of the period.

Required

Use the FIFO and LIFO methods of stock valuation to do the following.

(a) Show the stores ledger records, including the closing stock valuation.   (7 marks)

(b) Prepare trading accounts for the six month period, using each of the valuation methods.
                                                                                    (5 marks)

(c) Indicate which valuation method is the best measure of profit, and why.   (2 marks)

7 **INCENTIVE SCHEME**   *25 mins*

A company previously paid its direct labour workers on a time basis but is now contemplating moving over to an incentive scheme.

Draft a memo to the chief accountant outlining the general characteristics and advantages of employing a successful incentive scheme.

8 **TOWERS OF ILIUM LTD** (14 marks)   *25 mins*

Towers of Ilium Ltd has two production departments (machining and assembly) and two service departments (maintenance and stores).

The budgeted overheads for period 2 were - machining £18,000; assembly £15,000.

The machining department uses a machine hour rate basis for overhead absorption (budget 720 machine hours) and the assembly department a direct labour hour rate (budget 4,800 direct labour hours).

In budgeting production department overheads, service department overheads were dealt with as follows.

Maintenance department:	70% to machining department
	20% to assembly department
	10% to stores department
Stores department:	40% to machining department
	30% to assembly department
	30% to maintenance department

During period 2 the machining department worked for 703 machine hours and the direct labour hours recorded in the assembly department were 5,256.

Overhead incurred was as follows.

	Machining £	Assembly £	Maintenance £	Stores £
Directly allocated:				
Materials	2,400	3,600	4,200	800
Labour	1,400	1,800	6,000	2,300
Other items	1,700	1,500	600	400
	5,500	6,900	10,800	3,500
Apportioned	2,200	3,100	1,700	1,000
	7,700	10,000	12,500	4,500

Required

(a)   Write up the overhead account for each production department.   (9 marks)
(b)   Explain how the under-/over-absorption occurred for each department.   (5 marks)

9   **ABSORPTION VERSUS MARGINAL (14 marks)**   *25 mins*

(a)   What are the most important features which distinguish marginal costing from absorption costing?
          (5 marks)

(b)   To help decision making during budget preparation, Costain Baddley Ltd has prepared the following estimates of sales revenue and cost behaviour for a one-year period, relating to a product item called Allergic.

Activity	60%	100%
Sales and production (thousands of units)	36	60
	£'000	£'000
Sales	432	720
Production costs:		
Variable and fixed	366	510
Sales, distribution and administration costs:		
Variable and fixed	126	150

The normal level of activity for the current year is 60,000 units, and fixed costs are incurred evenly throughout the year.

There were no stocks of Allergic at the start of the quarter, in which 16,500 units were made and 13,500 units were sold. Actual fixed costs were the same as budgeted.

Required

(i)   Using absorption costing, calculate the following.

   (1)   The amount of fixed production costs absorbed by Allergic
   (2)   The over-/under-absorption of fixed product costs
   (3)   The profit for the quarter   (6 marks)

(ii)   Using marginal costing, calculate the net profit or loss for the quarter.   (3 marks)

You may assume that sales revenue and variable costs per unit are as budgeted.

10   **INTEGRATION**   *15 mins*

Draw a diagram or flowchart to show the flow of accounting entries within an integrated system for the following transactions.

(a)   Purchase of raw materials, on credit terms
(b)   Issue to production of part of the consignment received in (a) above
(c)   Cash payment of wages to direct workers and to indirect workers associated with production
(d)   Electricity for production purposes, obtained on credit
(e)   Depreciation of machinery used for production
(f)   Absorption of production overhead, using a predetermined rate

11   **THE PARTY SOFA LTD (14 marks)**   *25 mins*

Collette O'Day, the managing director of The Party Sofa Ltd, has asked you as cost accountant to prepare certain information about the costs of various production orders (for custom-built furniture).

Work on four orders (job numbers 355 - 358) made up the entire production effort in week no. 38.

You are aware of the following balances at the beginning of week 38.

	£
Raw materials	41,600
Work in progress	82,000
Finished goods (awaiting delivery)	12,000
Under-/over-absorbed overhead account	3,400 (debit bal.)

The work in progress account is supported by the following job cost sheets.

Job number	Direct materials £	Direct labour £	Production overhead £	Total cost £
355	11,200	9,500	13,300	34,000
356	16,600	6,000	8,400	31,000
357	5,000	5,000	7,000	17,000
	32,800	20,500	28,700	82,000

During week 38, the following transactions occurred.

		£
Raw material purchases		23,500
Special components for Job No 358		700
Material requisitions from store for		
Job No 355		7,200
356		5,600
357		6,300
358 (excludes special components)		4,100
Transfer of materials from Job no 356 to Job no 358		1,300

			£
Direct labour employees:			
Total time recorded		8,700 hours	18,000
including Job No 355	(1,400 hours)		3,000
356	(2,400 hours)		4,500
357	(1,800 hours)		4,000
358	(2,600 hours)		5,100

	£
Indirect labour employees	4,800
Supervision	2,600
Employer's national insurance contributions	1,800
Depreciation of machinery	2,900
Factory depreciation	1,000
Heating and lighting	500
Power	300
Maintenance	3,600
Indirect materials issued to production from stores	4,700
Other production overhead expenses	2,900

Factory overhead is applied at the rate of £2.50 per direct labour hour.

At the end of week 38 Job No 355 was completed and delivered to the customer. The invoiced value of the job was £55,000.

Required

(a)   Show the raw materials control account for week 38.   (3 marks)

(b)   Calculate the profit on Job no 355.   (3 marks)

(c)   Calculate the closing value of the work in progress for each remaining job at the end of week 38.
                                                                                  (8 marks)

12   PORT FRISBY (14 marks)   *25 mins*

An engineering firm prepares its accounts annually to 31 March. Contract No 282 - Port Frisby - commenced on 1 June 20X6. The costing records contained the following information in respect of the contract for the period to 31 March 20X7.

	£
Materials charged to site	43,000
Wages	100,220
Overheads	12,620

A machine costing £30,000 has been brought unused onto the site at the beginning of the contract and will be kept there until the contract is completed. Its working life is estimated to be five years, at the end of which its scrap value will be £2,000. A supervisor has spent half of his total time on this contract. His salary is £12,000 per annum. Other expenses charged to the contract amounted to £25,220 and materials on site at 31 March 20X7 were valued at a cost of £4,960. The contract price is £400,000.

At 31 March 20X7 two thirds of the contract was completed and architects' certificates had been issued for £240,000. An amount of £200,000 had been received by way of progress payments. Work done but not yet certified at 31 March 20X7 amounted to £1,764.

Required

(a)   Prepare a contract account in respect of contract No 282.   (10 marks)

(b)   Estimate the amount of profit or loss to be taken on that contract for the period to 31 March 20X7.
                                                                                    (4 marks)

Notes

(a)   The formula to calculate profit taken in this example should be:

$$\tfrac{3}{4} \times \text{notional profit} \times \frac{\text{cash received}}{\text{value of work certified}}$$

(b)   Plant is valued at cost less depreciation. Depreciation is charged on a daily basis, so that the charge to the contract in 20X6/X7 (1 June 20X6 - 31 March 20X7) is for 304 days. A year, for the purposes of calculating depreciation, is taken as 365 days.

13   ATM CHEMICALS (14 marks)   *25 mins*

ATM Chemicals produces product XY by putting it through a single process. You are given the following details for November 20X1.

Input costs	
Material costs	25,000 kilos at £2.48 per kilo
Labour costs	8,000 hours at £5.50 per hour
Overhead costs	£61,600

You are also told the following.

(a)   Normal loss is 4% of input.
(b)   Scrap value of normal loss is £2.00 per kilo.
(c)   Finished output amounted to 21,000 units.
(d)   There was no opening or closing work-in-progress.

Required

(a)   Prepare the process account for the month of November 20X1.   (12 marks)
(b)   Prepare an abnormal loss account.   (2 marks)

14   JAKE SPEARS LTD (14 marks)   *25 mins*

Jake Spears Ltd produces four joint products through a single process from which there is also a by-product output.

BPP
PUBLISHING

The process cost for the month of April 20X0 was made up as follows.

	£
Direct materials	465,000
Direct labour	127,500
Production overhead	382,500
	975,000

Production and sales during the month were as follows.

	Amount produced Units	Amount sold Units	Sales price per unit £
Joint products:			
Goneril	7,000	6,300	90.00
Regan	9,000	7,000	30.00
Cordelia	8,000	6,400	22.50
Lear	4,000	3,800	90.00
By-product:			
Macbeth	15,000	15,000	£1.00

There were no stocks on hand at the beginning of April 20X0.

Required

Prepare a statement showing the value of the closing stocks at the end of April 20X0 and a profit statement for the month of April 20X0 for Jake Spears Ltd.

You should assume that the cost accounting treatment of the by-product would be to credit the process account with the net sale proceeds of the by-product.

15 STEER AND WHEEL LTD (14 marks)   *25 mins*

Steer and Wheel Ltd distributes its goods to a regional dealer using a single lorry. The dealer's premises are 40 kilometres away by road. The lorry has a capacity of 10½ tonnes, and makes the journey twice a day fully loaded on the outward journeys and empty on the return journeys. The following information is available for a four-week budget control period, period 8, during 20X4.

Petrol consumption	8 kilometres per 5 litres petrol
Petrol cost	£0.36 per litre
Oil	£8 per week
Driver's wages and national insurance	£140 per week
Repairs	£72 per week
Garaging	£4 per day (based on a seven-day week)
Cost of lorry when new (excluding tyres)	£18,750
Life of the lorry	80,000 kilometres
Insurance	£650 per annum
Cost of a set of tyres	£1,250
Life of a set of tyres	25,000 kilometres
Estimated sales value of lorry at end of its life	£2,750
Vehicle licence cost	£234 per annum
Other overhead costs	£3,900 per annum

The lorry operates on a five-day week.

Required

Prepare a statement to show the total costs of operating the vehicle in period 8, 20X4 analysed into running costs and standing costs.

16 SAMPLING FRAMES   *15 mins*

(a) Suggest a suitable sampling frame for each of the following in which statistical data will be collected.

    (i) An investigation into the reactions of workers in a large factory to new proposals for shift working.

(ii)   A survey of students at a college about the relevance and quality of the teaching for their professional examinations.

(iii)   An enquiry into the use of home computers by school children in a large city.

(b)   Explain briefly, with reasons, the type of sampling method you would recommend in each of the three situations given above.

---

17   INCOMES (14 marks)   *25 mins*

The following data show income before tax and benefits and after tax and benefits of sections of a population.

Population	Income before tax and benefits	Income after tax and benefits
Millions	£m	£m
40	25	37.5
40	25	37.5
40	50	75.0
20	100	75.0
20	200	75.0
160	400	300.0

(a)   Construct two Lorenz curves, before and after tax and benefits. Full tabular workings must be shown.   (10 marks)

(b)   Describe what the curves actually show.   (3 marks)

(c)   Give one other example of the use of the Lorenz curve.   (1 mark)

---

18   HANDLING COSTS (14 marks)   *25 mins*

The cost accountant of Ware Howser Ltd has calculated standard costs for handling items of stock in a warehouse. The costs are based on the labour time required to deal with stock movements, and are as follows.

Time required for job of handling stock	Standard cost
Minutes	£
Less than 10	9
≥ 10 and up to 20	11
≥ 20 and up to 40	13
≥ 40 and up to 60	15
≥ 60 and up to 90	23
≥ 90 and up to 120	29
≥ 120 and up to 180	38

The warehouse operates a working day of seven hours, and a five-day week. There are 12 people employed.

An examination of the time sheets for a typical week showed that the following costs had been incurred.

Standard cost	Frequency
£	
9	240
11	340
13	150
15	120
23	20
29	20
38	10

Required

(a)   Estimate the mean handling time for a stock movement.   (9 marks)

(b)   Estimate the total number of hours in the week spent actively moving items of stock. (3 marks)

(c) Calculate the average number of jobs handled by each employee per week if each job is dealt with by one person. (2 marks)

---

19   SERVICE CHARGE   *15 mins*

The manager of a repairs depot is reviewing the price charged to customers for repairs. An analysis of the time required to carry out repairs over a typical one-month period is as follows.

Repair time			Number of occasions
Hours			
Less than		2	3
2 and	<	4	8
4 and	<	6	21
6 and	<	8	37
8 and	<	10	62
10 and	<	12	38
12 and	<	14	20
14 and	<	16	8
16 and	<	18	3

Required

Calculate the mean and the standard deviation of repair times.

---

20   PRICE AND QUANTITY   *15 mins*

Compute a price index at 1 July 20X6 for the following basket of items (using the Laspeyre method) taking 1 July 20X2 as the base date.

Items	Quantity used per week 1 July 20X2 Units	Quantity used per week 1 July 20X6 Units	Cost of the item 1 July 20X2 £ per unit	Cost of the item 1 July 20X6 £ per unit
Widgets	18	19	8	6
Fidgets	12	11	7	8
Splodgets	24	27	2	4
Tudgets	15	11	6	7
Ringlets	8	12	10	9

---

21   PROBABILITIES (14 marks)   *25 mins*

(a) Probability theory is a branch of statistics which attempts to predict the likelihood of a particular event occurring out of a large population of events. Explain and elaborate on this statement.(4 marks)

(b) Here are some data.

Age in years	Number surviving at each age Male	Number surviving at each age Female
0	100,000	100,000
10	89,023	91,083
25	85,824	88,133
50	74,794	78,958
80	16,199	24,869

Required

Calculate for each sex the following probabilities.

(i) (1) At birth of reaching the age of 80 years   (2 marks)
     (2) That a person aged 25 years will *not* survive to the age of 50   (2 marks)
     (3) That a new born baby will survive the first ten years of life   (2 marks)
     (4) That a person aged 50 will *not* survive to the age of 80   (2 marks)

(ii) Comment on your results.   (2 marks)

22   **GEOLOGICAL TESTS (14 marks)**   *25 mins*

An oil company has recently acquired rights in a certain area to conduct surveys and test drillings, to lead to extracting oil where it is found in commercially exploitable quantities.

The area is already considered to have good potential for finding oil in commercial quantities. At the outset the company has the choice to conduct further geological tests or to carry out a drilling programme immediately. Given the known conditions, the company estimates that there is a 70% chance of further tests showing a 'success'.

Whether the tests show the possibility of ultimate success or not, or even if no tests are undertaken at all, the company could still pursue its drilling programme or alternatively consider selling its rights to drill in the area. Thereafter, however, if it carries out the drilling programme, the likelihood of final success or failure depends on the foregoing stages.

If 'successful' tests have been carried out, the probability of success in drilling is 80%.

If tests have indicated 'failure', then the probability of success in drilling is 20%.

If no tests have been carried out at all, the probability of success in drilling is 55%.

Costs and revenues have been estimated for all possible outcomes and the net cash flow of each is given below.

Outcome	*Net cash flow* £m
Success	
With prior tests	100
Without prior tests	120
Failure	
With prior tests	– 50
Without prior tests	– 40
Sales of exploitation rights	
Prior tests show 'success'	65
Prior tests show 'failure'	15
Without prior tests	45

Required

(a)   Draw up a decision tree to represent the above information.   (9 marks)

(b)   Evaluate the tree in order to advise the company on its best course of action.   (5 marks)

23   **INELASTIC ROPE (14 marks)**   *25 mins*

(a)   Your company requires a special type of inelastic rope which is available from only two suppliers. Supplier A's ropes have a mean breaking strength of 1,000 kg with a standard deviation of 100 kg. Supplier B's ropes have a mean breaking strength of 900 kg with a standard deviation of 75 kg. The distribution of the breaking strengths of each type of rope is normal. Your company requires that the breaking strength of a rope must be not less than 750 kg.

Required

Decide which rope you should buy, and why.   (4 marks)

(b)   The factory manager of Dry Gulch Ltd maintains that the average time required to make one unit of a product, the sloon, is not more than 48 minutes.

In one sample of 49 trials taken in January 20X3, the average time was 50 minutes, with a standard deviation (applying Bessel's correction) of 2.02 minutes.

Required

(i)   Test the manager's claim, at the 1% level of significance.   (6 marks)

(ii)   Place 80% confidence limits on the mean production time per unit of sloon.   (4 marks)

BPP PUBLISHING

24 QUADRATIC EQUATIONS
15 mins

(a) Solve the following quadratic equations.

    (i) $x^2 - 1.28x - 5.16 = 0$
    (ii) $4x^2 + 33x + 68 = 0$
    (iii) $-3x^2 + 6x + 30 = 6$
    (iv) $x^2 - 4.8x + 5.76 = 0$

(b) If q units of a product are sold at a price of p pounds a unit, the $p = 600 - 0.15q$. q cannot exceed 4,000. What value or values of q will give total revenue of £450,000?

25 VARIABLE OR FIXED (14 marks)
25 mins

(a) Evaluate whether the assumption that costs are readily identifiable as either fixed or variable throughout a range of production is realistic.

    Give examples of any alternative classification.   (8 marks)

(b) Production labour has traditionally been regarded as a directly variable cost.

    Required

    Discuss the factors or circumstances which would make this treatment inappropriate. You may draw on your own experience in answering.   (6 marks)

26 BUILDING COMPANY
15 mins

A building company constructs a standard unit which sells for £30,000. The company's costs can be readily identifiable between fixed and variable costs.

Budgeted data for the coming six months includes the following.

	Sales Units	Profit £
January	18	70,000
February	20	100,000
March	30	250,000
April	22	130,000
May	24	160,000
June	16	40,000

You are told that the fixed costs for the six months have been spread evenly over the period under review to arrive at the monthly profit projections.

Required

Prepare a graph for total sales, costs and output for the six months under review that shows the breakeven point in units and revenue, total fixed costs, the variable cost line and the margin of safety for the total budgeted sales.

27 WALLOP LTD (14 marks)
25 mins

Wallop Ltd manufactures two similar products, hakes and panes, using the same labour force and machines for each. Information about the selling price and costs of each product is as follows.

	Hake £	Hake £	Pane £	Pane £
Selling price		116		120
Variable costs				
Direct materials	43		36	
Direct labour	32		24	
Machining	25		40	
		100		100
Contribution		16		20

The cost of direct labour is £4 an hour and the variable cost of machining is £5 an hour.

In any one month, direct labour hours are restricted to 9,600 hours and machine hours are restricted to 8,125 hours.

There is a maximum monthly demand for hakes of 1,000 units.

Required

(a) Formulate the linear programming problem to determine the monthly production levels of each product. (5 marks)

(b) Solve the problem graphically. (9 marks)

---

28 CHALK AND CHEESE (14 marks) *25 mins*

Chalk Ltd is a company which sells all its output to Cheese Ltd for £200 a unit. The cost of sales each week in Chalk Ltd is given by the function $C = 2q^2 + 40q + 80$ where q = the volume of weekly sales.

Cheese Ltd uses the output of Chalk Ltd to manufacture a product whose demand depends on the selling price. The revenue each week of Cheese Ltd is given by the function

$$R = 1,000q - 16q^2$$

and the costs per week of Cheese Ltd *excluding* the cost of the products bought from Chalk Ltd are given by the function

$$C = 2q^2 + 80q + 400$$

Chalk Ltd can restrict its weekly supply of its product to Cheese Ltd, but cannot raise the unit price above £200.

The two companies are considering whether to merge into a single company, Chalk and Cheese Ltd, and their directors have met to discuss whether there might be any mutual advantage in such a proposal.

Required

(a) Decide on the level of weekly sales at which Chalk Ltd would maximise its profits. Calculate the profit or loss of Cheese Ltd if Chalk Ltd were able to supply a profit-maximising quantity of its product each week. (5 marks)

(b) Decide on the level of weekly sales at which Cheese Ltd would maximise its profits. Calculate the weekly profits of Chalk Ltd. (5 marks)

(c) Suppose that the two companies were to merge into one. Calculate the profit-maximising weekly output and the weekly profit. (4 marks)

---

29 REED JUICES LTD *15 mins*

Reed Juices Ltd purchases 25,000 litres of a material each year from a single supplier. At the moment, the company obtains the material in batches of 800 litres. The material costs £16 per litre; the cost of ordering a new batch from the supplier is £32, and the cost of holding one litre in stock is £4 a year plus an interest cost equal to 15% of the purchase price of the material.

Required

Calculate the economic order quantity and the annual savings which would be obtained if this order quantity replaced the current order size.

---

30 DAISY HOOF LTD *15 mins*

Daisy Hoof Ltd is considering a project to purchase some equipment which would have the following cash flows.

Year	Cash flow
	£
0	(50,000)
1	18,000
2	25,000
3	15,000
4	10,000

The estimated trade-in value of the equipment, which is £2,000, has not been included in the cash flows above.

The company has a cost of capital of 16%.

Required

Calculate the following.

(a)   The NPV of the project
(b)   The IRR of the project

Exam
answer bank

1 COST ACCOUNTING

Cost accounting is a part of the management accounting system, which is the accounting system of an organisation that is specifically concerned with producing information for management to help with routine planning and control decisions and also with occasional one-off decisions. To help with planning and control, management must have the following.

(a) A formal plan, which can be based on a budget or standards of performance
(b) A knowledge of what the actual performance has been

Cost accounting is a system of providing much of this information by doing the following.

(a) Establishing a budget in financial terms and standard costs.

(b) Recording actual costs of products and services, operations and processes or departments.

(c) Comparing actual results against the budget or standard and reporting measures of performance such as variances and profitability.

The detailed analysis of costs and profits is far more extensive than the records of income and expenditure required for financial accounting.

The techniques of cost accounting include the following.

(a) Classifying costs as direct costs or overheads.

(b) Allocating direct costs to products or cost centres.

(c) Apportioning overhead costs to products, services or departments, in absorption costing. Otherwise, marginal costing might be used to measure product costs and profits.

(d) Using methods such as job costing and process costing to measure costs.

(e) Applying standard costing techniques where suitable for cost analysis.

The benefits of cost accounting come from the nature and quality of information that it makes available for management. In large organisations, managers who are responsible for the activities of a part of their organisation might be unaware of what costs they are incurring, how much cost they ought to be incurring and whether their activities are efficient and effective or profitable. Cost accounting information is needed to help managers to recognise what they ought to be doing and whether they have been successful. Since most business organisations exist to earn a profit, or if they do not they must at least operate within certain financial constraints (for example government departments), then it follows that information about plans and actual results ought to be measured in terms of expenditures, revenues and profits. In other words, planning and control information ought to be cost, revenue and profit information, which explains the significance of cost accounting.

The more specific benefits of cost accounting are therefore as follows.

(a) To establish budgets in which every manager can be made aware of the targets for his own area of operations and to establish efficiency and expenditure standards.

(b) To monitor actual results and measure performance as a matter of routine, enabling managers to identify when and how actual results are unsatisfactory, so that control measures can be taken.

(c) To help with one-off management decisions, when managers are expected to choose the more profitable course of action out of two or more alternatives.

(d) To help with pricing decisions when prices are set so as to give a profit margin on costs.

(e) To help with recognising the level of capacity needed to bring unit costs down to a level where profits can be made at current market prices.

(f) To establish what products, services, departments, and so on are actually costing to make, provide and operate.

2 CALCULATORS AND RATIOS

Type	Proportion	Number	Shares
3 bed flat and garage	11 + 1 = 12	5	60
3 bed flat, no garage	11 = 11	1	11
2 bed flat and garage	10 + 1 = 11	1	11
2 bed flat, no garage	10 = 10	2	20
			102

BPP PUBLISHING

Total premium of £1,364.76 is divided by 102. Each share is therefore worth £13.38.

The premium per flat is therefore £13.38 × proportion.

		£
3 bed flat and garage	12 × £13.38	= 160.56
3 bed flat, no garage	11 × £13.38	= 147.18
2 bed flat and garage	11 × £13.38	= 147.18
2 bed flat, no garage	10 × £13.38	= 133.80

Check

£		Number	Total £
160.56	×	5	802.80
147.18	×	1	147.18
147.18	×	1	147.18
133.80	×	2	267.60
			1,364.76

3   SOFTWARE CATEGORIES

Application packages are programs to deal with particular user applications. A firm of accountants would probably make use of specially written programs for payroll, sales ledger, purchase ledger, nominal ledger, stock control and partners time allocation. Use would also probably be made of such general purpose packages as word processing and spreadsheets. A small computer system would probably make use of packages "off the peg" produced by a software house, although the accountancy firm could design and produce its own software if desired.

The application package carries out the specific functions required by the user and a well designed package should enable some adaptation through the user choosing options from a range of choices offered by the package.

An operating system is the software which controls the overall operation of a computer. The functions of an operating system are many and include the following.

(a)   Control of the selection and use of input and output devices, including priority allocation where a multi-user system exists

(b)   Error signalling and handling, such as reporting faults or inoperative peripherals

(c)   Scheduling, loading and running programs

(d)   Maintaining security including checking passwords and protecting data files and programs from unauthorised users (also logging the use of computer resources)

(e)   Communications with users and complying with their requests, informing operators when to load tapes and so on.

The operating system is a set of programs whose job it is to manage hardware and software as efficiently as possible, and to act as a buffer between the user and the complex working of the computer itself.

Utility programs are the middlemen between operating systems and applications software, and ensure that the applications programs are written and run efficiently. They are special programs that perform single and common tasks, and examples include the following.

(a)   Compilers which convert programs into code that computers can handle

(b)   Data base management systems (DBMS) to handle enquiries about a large quantity of intricately organised data

(c)   File management programs to find, search, edit and combine files

(d)   Sort/merge routines to restructure files

(e)   Diagnostic and trace routines to locate errors in program logic

Utility programs are usually supplied as part of the operating system.

4 CLASSIFYING COSTS

REPORT

To: Finance Director
From Cost Accountant
Date: 1 January 20X1
Subject: Cost classification

(a) Costs can be classified in the following ways.

   (i) Direct and indirect cost
   (ii) By function (manufacturing, administration, marketing)
   (iii) By element of cost
   (iv) Fixed and variable cost
   (v) Controllable and uncontrollable cost

(b) Cost classification assists management in decision making, planning and control.

   (i) Direct and indirect cost classification is especially useful for decision making and for control purposes. For example, if managers know the direct cost of a unit they can assess its individual profitability and the direct cost of a cost centre can help in judging the efficiency and effectiveness of the centre. This type of classification also allows the identification of overheads and their subsequent apportionment and absorption.

   (ii) Collecting costs by function allows the cost accountant to cost a product or service.

   (iii) Classification by element will improve control because management will be able to allocate responsibilities more effectively and then be able to concentrate on the more important and significant elements of cost.

   (iv) If managers know which costs are fixed and which are variable they can plant to achieve a desired level of profit and can determine the breakeven point. A knowledge of cost behaviour will also help them to understand the effect on cost of any proposed change in activity levels and it will assist in various ad hoc decisions such as dropping a product line and make or buy decisions.

   (v) In a budgetary control system, control reports which provide an analysis of the costs which are within a manager's control (controllable costs) and those over which the manager cannot exercise control (uncontrollable costs) are part of the feedback. Highlighting the controllable costs will concentrate management attention on the areas where their control action is likely to be worthwhile. This analysis will also avoid the motivational problem which can arise when managers are held responsible for a cost over which they have no control.

5 COMPONENT BCD

(a) Reorder level = maximum usage × maximum delivery period
= 1,100 units × 4 months
= 4,400 units

(b) Reorder quantity = maximum stock – (reorder level – minimum usage in minimum delivery period)
= 5,500 units – (4,400 units – (900 × 2 months))
= 2,900 units

(c) Minimum level = reorder level – (average usage × average delivery period)
= 4,400 units – (1,000 units × 3 months)
= 1,400 units

(d) Average stock held = minimum stock + ½ reorder quantity
= 1,400 units + 1,450 units
= 2,850 units

6 BLACK ASTEROID LTD

(a) *FIFO*

	Receipts		Issues		Receipts		Balance of stock value
	Units	£	Units	£	Units	£	£
Opening balance					200	42.0	8,400
July	200	46.0			200	42.0	17,600
					200	46.0	
August	500	49.4			200	42.0	
					200	46.0	
					500	49.4	42,300
September			200	42.0	400	49.4	19,760
			200	46.0			
			100	49.4			
October	1,000	52.5			400	49.4	
					1,000	52.5	72,260
November			400	49.4	700	52.5	36,750
			300	52.5			
December			500	52.5	200	52.5	10,500

LIFO

	Receipts		Issues		Balance		Balance of stock value
	Units	£	Units	£	Units	£	£
Opening balance					200	42.0	8,400
July	200	46.0			200	42.0	
					200	46.0	17,600
August	500	49.4			200	42.0	
					200	46.0	
					500	49.4	42,300
September			500	49.4	200	42.0	
					200	46.0	17,600
October	1,000	52.5			200	42.0	
					200	46.0	
					1,000	52.5	70,100
November			700	52.5	200	42.0	
					200	46.0	
					300	52.5	33,350
December			300	52.5	200	42.0	8,400
			200	46.0			

(b)   TRADING ACCOUNTS FOR THE PERIOD 1 JULY - 31 DECEMBER

		FIFO	LIFO
	£	£	£
Sales			
500 at £66	33,000		
700 at £70	49,000		
500 at £75	37,500		
		119,500	119,500
Closing stock		10,500	8,400
		130,000	127,900
Opening stock		(8,400)	(8,400)
Purchases			
200 at £46.00	9,200		
500 at £49.40	24,700		
1,000 at £52.50	52,500		
		(86,400)	(86,400)
Gross profit		35,200	33,100

(c)   The most appropriate form of stock pricing in a period of inflation is LIFO, because the price of materials charged against sales is the price closest to the current replacement value of the materials sold/consumed. The profit and loss account is therefore charged with a cost which approximates to the cost of replacing the materials used, and the profit is accordingly reduced. It is inappropriate to price materials lower and thereby increase profit when a portion of this 'profit' is required for material replacement.

7   INCENTIVE SCHEME

MEMORANDUM

To: Chief accountant
From: Cost accountant
Date: 31 March 20X1
Subject: Incentive schemes

The general characteristics of a successful incentive scheme are as follows.

(a)   Its objective should be clearly stated and attainable by the employees.

(b)   The rules and conditions of the scheme should be easy to understand and not liable to be misinterpreted.

(c)   It should be seen to be fair to employees and employers. Other groups of employees should not feel unjustly excluded from the scheme, as their work might be affected by their dissatisfaction.

(d)   It must win the full acceptance of everyone concerned, including trade union negotiators and officials.

(e)   The bonus should be paid as soon as possible after the extra effort has been made by the employees, to associate the ideas of effort and reward.

(f)   Allowances should be made for external factors outside the employees' control which reduce their productivity (for example machine breakdowns or raw material shortages).

(g)   Only those employees who actually make the extra effort should be rewarded.

The advantages of such a scheme are as follows.

(a)   Employees will be paid more for their efficiency.

(b)   In spite of the extra labour cost, the unit cost of output is reduced and the profit earned per unit of sale is increased. Thus the profit arising from productivity improvements are shared between employer and employee.

(c)   The morale of employees should be expected to improve, since they are seen to receive extra reward for extra effort.

8   **TOWERS OF ILIUM LTD**

(a)   The actual overhead may be apportioned to the production departments from the service departments by means of the repeated distribution method calculation.

	Machining	Assembly	Maintenance	Stores
	£	£	£	£
Actual overhead	7,700	10,000	12,500	4,500
Apportion maintenance	8,750	2,500	(12,500)	1,250
			0	5,750
Apportion stores	2,300	1,725	1,725	(5,750)
			1,725	0
Apportion maintenance	1,208	345	(1,725)	172
			0	172
Apportion stores	69	52	51	(172)
			51	0
Apportion maintenance	36	10	(51)	5
Apportion stores (say)	3	2		(5)
	20,066	14,634	–	–

The total overheads of £34,700 are therefore apportioned as shown to become 'actual' overheads of the two production departments.

Absorbed overhead	Machining	Assembly
Budgeted overhead	£18,000	£15,000
Budgeted activity	720 machine hours	4,800 direct labour hours
Absorption rate	£25 per machine hour	£3.125 per direct labour hour
Actual activity	703 machine hours	5,256 direct labour hours
Absorbed overhead	£17,575	£16,425

MACHINING DEPARTMENT OVERHEAD ACCOUNT

	£		£
Overhead incurred	20,066	Work in progress (machining department)	17,575
		Under-absorbed overhead account	2,491
	20,066		20,066

ASSEMBLY DEPARTMENT OVERHEAD ACCOUNT

	£		£
Overhead incurred	14,634	Work in progress (assembly department)	16,425
Over-absorbed overhead a/c	1,791		
	16,425		16,425

(b)   In the machining department, the under-absorbed overhead occurred because actual expenditure was in excess of budgeted expenditure, and actual activity was below the budget of 720 machine hours. The excess spending and under-capacity should be investigated to learn their cause.

In the assembly department, the over-absorption of overhead was due to the extra capacity (the number of direct labour hours worked was in excess of budget) and also because actual expenditure was below the budget of £15,000.

9   **ABSORPTION VERSUS MARGINAL**

(a)   The features which distinguish marginal costing from absorption costing are as follows.

(i)   In absorption costing, items of stock are costed to include a 'fair share' of fixed production overhead, whereas in marginal costing, stocks are valued at variable production cost only. Closing stocks will therefore be valued more highly in absorption costing than in marginal costing.

(ii)   As a consequence of carrying forward an element of fixed production overheads in closing stock values, the cost of sales used to determine profit in absorption costing will:

(1)   include some fixed production overhead costs incurred in a previous period but carried forward into opening stock values of the current period;

(2)   exclude some fixed production overhead costs incurred in the current period by including them in closing stock values.

In contrast marginal costing charges the actual fixed costs of a period in full into the profit and loss account of the period. (Marginal costing is therefore sometimes known as period costing.)

(iii)   In absorption costing, 'actual' fully absorbed unit costs are reduced by producing in greater quantities, whereas in marginal costing, unit variable costs are unaffected by the volume of production (that is, provided that variable costs per unit remain unaltered at the changed level of production activity). Profit in any period can be affected by the actual volume of production in absorption costing; this is not the case in marginal costing.

(iv)   In marginal costing, the identification of variable costs and of contribution enables management to use cost information more easily for decision-making purposes (such as in budget decision making). It is easy to decide by how much contribution (and therefore profit) will be affected by changes in sales volume. (Profit would be unaffected by changes in production volume).

In absorption costing, however, the effect on profit in a period of changes in both:

(1)   production volume; and
(2)   sales volume;

is not easily seen, because behaviour is not analysed and incremental costs are not used in the calculation of actual profit.

(b)   *Working*

	Production costs £	Sales etc costs £
Total costs of 60,000 units (fixed plus variable)	510,000	150,000
Total costs of 36,000 units (fixed plus variable)	366,000	126,000
Difference = variable costs of 24,000 units	144,000	24,000
Variable costs per unit	£6	£1

It therefore follows that:

	£	£
Total costs of 60,000 units	510,000	150,000
Variable costs of 60,000 units	360,000	60,000
Fixed costs	150,000	90,000

The rate of absorption of fixed production overheads will therefore be:

$$\frac{£150,000}{60,000} = £2.50 \text{ per unit}$$

(i)   (1)   The fixed production overhead absorbed by Allergic would be 16,500 units produced × £2.50 = £41,250.

	£
(2) Budgeted annual fixed production overhead	150,000
Budgeted = actual quarterly overhead	37,500
Absorbed into production (see (1) above)	41,250
Over-absorption of fixed production costs	3,750

BPP PUBLISHING

(3)   Profit for the quarter, using absorption costing

	£	£
Sales (13,500 × £12)		162,000
Costs of production (no opening stocks)		
Value of stocks produced (16,500 × £8.50)	140,250	
Less value of closing stocks		
(3,000 units × full production cost £8.50)	25,500	
Production cost of sales	114,750	
Sales etc costs	£	
Variable (13,500 × £1)	13,500	
Fixed (¼ of £90,000)	22,500	
		36,000
Total cost of sales		150,750
Less over-absorbed production overhead		3,750
		147,000
Profit		15,000

(_Tutorial note_. Several alternative methods of presenting the profit statement would be acceptable. Students are advised, however, that an absorption costing statement should include the overheads absorbed in production costs and the adjustment for under-/over- absorption of overhead.)

(ii)   Profit statement using marginal costing

	£	£
Sales		162,000
Variable costs of production (16,500 × £6)	99,000	
Less value of closing stocks (3,000 × £6)	18,000	
Variable production cost of sales	81,000	
Variable sales etc costs	13,500	
Total variable cost of sales (13,500 × £7)		94,500
Contribution (13,500 × £5)		67,500
Fixed costs: production	37,500	
sales etc	22,500	
		60,000
Profit		7,500

(_Tutorial note_. The difference between the profit in (i) and (ii) of £7,500 is caused by the difference in closing stock values, which amounts to the fixed overhead absorbed on the 3,000 units at £2.50 per unit. Had there been any opening stocks, the difference in their valuation would also have affected the comparative figures.)

10   INTEGRATION

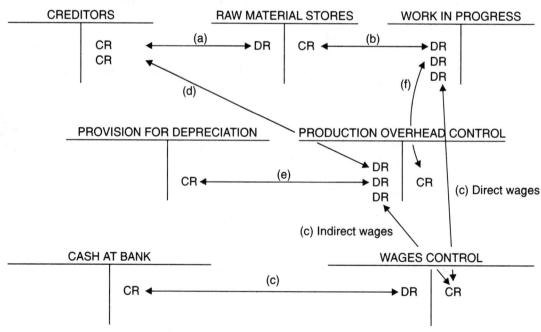

11 THE PARTY SOFA LTD

(a)

RAW MATERIALS CONTROL ACCOUNT

	£			£	£
Opening stock	41,600	Work in progress			
Purchases (CLC)	23,500	Job No 355		7,200	
		356		5,600	
		357		6,300	
		358		4,100	
					23,200
		Production overhead a/c			4,700
		Closing stock			37,200
	65,100				65,100

(b)

JOB NO 355 ACCOUNT

	£		£
Opening work in progress	34,000	Finished goods	
Raw materials account	7,200	(or cost of sales)	47,700
Direct labour account	3,000		
Production overhead a/c	3,500		
(1,400 hrs × £2.50)			
	47,700		47,700

The profit on Job 355 was:	£
Sales	55,000
Less cost of sales	47,700
Profit	7,300

(c)

JOB NO 356 ACCOUNT

	£		£
Opening WIP	31,000	Job No 358 account	1,300
Raw materials account	5,600	Closing work in progress	45,800
Direct labour account	4,500		
Production overhead a/c			
(2,400 × £2.50)	6,000		
	47,100		47,100

JOB NO 357 ACCOUNT

	£		£
Opening work in progress	17,000	Closing work in progress	31,800
Raw materials account	6,300		
Direct labour account	4,000		
Production overhead a/c			
(1,800 × £2.50)	4,500		
	31,800		31,800

JOB NO 358 ACCOUNT

	£		£
Special purchases (CLC)	700	Closing work in progress	17,700
Raw materials account	4,100		
Job No 356 account	1,300		
Direct labour account	5,100		
Production overhead account			
(2,600 × £2.50)	6,500		
	17,700		17,700

PRODUCTION OVERHEAD ACCOUNT

	£		£	£
Indirect labour - wages a/c	4,800	Work in progress:		
Supervision - wages a/c	2,600	Job No: 355	3,500	
Employer's Nat. Ins. - CLC	1,800	356	6,000	
Indirect materials - raw mats a/c	4,700	357	4,500	
		358	6,500	
Depreciation:				20,500
Machinery - CLC	2,900			
Factory - CLC	1,000	Under-absorbed overhead a/c		6,000
Heating and lighting - CLC	500			
Power - CLC	300			
Maintenance - CLC	3,600			
Other expenses - CLC	2,900			
Idle time (note) - Wages a/c	1,400			
	26,500			26,500

(*Note.* Idle time is the difference between the cost of direct labour hours paid for and the cost of the time recorded against each job.)

12   PORT FRISBY

(a)

CONTRACT 282 - PORT FRISBY

	£		£
Materials	43,000	Materials on site c/f	4,960
Wages	100,220	Plant at valuation c/f (W)	25,336
Overhead	12,620	Cost of sales (see (b))	115,000
Plant at cost	30,000	Work certified not allocated	
Supervisor's salary (½ × 10		to cost of sales (see (b))	69,000
months × £12,000 pa)	5,000	Work not certified	1,764
Other expenses	25,220		
	216,060		216,060

WORK CERTIFIED ACCOUNT

	£		£
Turnover (P&L) (see (b))	150,000	Contractee ledger account	240,000
Balance	90,000		
	240,000		240,000

CONTRACTEE ACCOUNT

	£		£
Work certified account	240,000	Bank	200,000
		Balance c/f	40,000
	240,000		240,000

Working

Calculation of plant value carried down

Number of days in current period that plant was used (1.6.X6 - 31.3.X7)	304 days
Total number of days in expected life of the plant (5 × 365 days)	1,825 days
Loss of value of plant over expected working life £(30,000 – 2,000)	£28,000
Loss of value of plant during 10 months to 31.3.X7 = £28,000 × $\frac{304}{1,825}$	£4,664
Value of plant carried down at 31.3.X7 = £30,000 – £4,664	£25,336

(b)   Profit taken comprises the following.

	£
Turnover = £240,000 × ¾ × $\frac{£200,000}{£240,000}$ =	150,000
Cost of sales (£185,764 – £1,764) × ¾ × $\frac{£200,000}{£240,000}$	115,000
Net profit taken on the contract	35,000

Work certified not allocated to cost of sales is thus (£185,764 – £1,764) – £115,000 = £69,000.

13 ATM CHEMICALS

Step 1. Determine output and losses

STATEMENT OF EQUIVALENT UNITS

	Total Units
Output	21,000
Abnormal loss	3,000
Normal loss	1,000
	25,000

Step 2. Calculate cost per unit of output, losses and WIP

$$\text{Cost per equivalent unit } \frac{£(62,000 + 44,000 + 61,600 - 2,000)}{24,000} = £6.90$$

Step 3. Calculate total cost of output, losses and WIP

STATEMENT OF EVALUATION

	£
Output (21,000 × £6.90)	144,900
Abnormal loss (3,000 × £6.90)	20,700
	165,600

Step 4. Complete accounts

(a)

PROCESS ACCOUNT

	Units	£		Units	£
Materials	25,000	62,000	Normal loss	1,000	2,000
Labour		44,000	Abnormal loss	3,000	20,700
Overheads		61,600	Finished output	21,000	144,900
	25,000	167,600		25,000	167,600

(b)

ABNORMAL LOSS ACCOUNT

	£		£
Process account	20,700	P&L account	20,700

Assumption. Abnormal loss has no scrap value.

14 JAKE SPEARS LTD

Although joint processing costs may be apportioned between joint products on the basis of units produced, the basis of apportionment chosen here is the relative sales value of the items produced.

Joint product	*Units produced*	*Sales price per unit* £	*Sales value* £'000	*Proportion of total*
Goneril	7,000	90.00	630	0.4375
Regan	9,000	30.00	270	0.1875
Cordelia	8,000	22.50	180	0.1250
Lear	4,000	90.00	360	0.2500
			1,440	1.0000

The apportionment of joint costs will be as follows.

	£
Joint process costs	975,000
Less sales proceeds of by-product Macbeth	15,000
Net joint process costs	960,000

Apportioned to		£	
Goneril	(0.4375)	420,000	
Regan	(0.1875)	180,000	
Cordelia	(0.1250)	120,000	
Lear	(0.25)	240,000	
		960,000	

JAKE SPEARS LTD
PROFIT STATEMENT FOR THE MONTH OF APRIL 20X0

	Goneril		Regan		Cordelia		Lear		Total
	Units	£'000	Units	£'000	Units	£'000	Units	£'000	£'000
Production costs	7,000	420	9,000	180	8,000	120	4,000	240	960
Less closing stock	700	42	2,000	40	1,600	24	200	12	118
Cost of sales	6,300	378	7,000	140	6,400	96	3,800	228	842
Sales		567		210		144		342	1,263
Profit		189		70		48		114	421

15 STEER AND WHEEL LTD

Tonnes travelled per day	$40 \times 2 \times 2 = 160$ km
Tonnes travelled in the period	160×5 days $\times 4$ weeks = 3,200 km
Tonnes travelled in the period fully loaded (½ of 3,200)	1,600 km
Tonnes carried, per trip	10½ tonnes
Tonnes/kilometres in the period	16,800 tonne/kilometres

STATEMENTS OF COSTS PERIOD 8 20X4

(a) Running costs

	£
Petrol (3,200 miles ÷ 8 km per 5 litres × £0.36 per litre)	720
Oil and grease (£8 × 4 weeks)	32
Repairs (£72 × 4 weeks)	288
Wages (£140 × 4 weeks)	560
Tyres cost (£1,250 ÷ 25,000 km × 3,200 km)	160
Depreciation ((£18,750 − 2,750) ÷ 80,000 km × 3,200 km)	640
Running costs	2,400

Note Depreciation is assumed to be a running cost, charged on distance travelled, rather than a fixed charge per period.

(b) Standing costs

	£
Garaging (£4 per day × 7 days × 4 weeks)	112
Insurance (£650 ÷ 13)	50
Licence cost (£234 ÷ 13)	18
Other overheads (£3,900 ÷ 13)	300
	480

(c) Total costs

	£
Running costs	2,400
Standing costs	480
Total costs, period 8	2,880

16   SAMPLING FRAMES

(a)   (i)   The sampling frame should be a list of all workers who will be affected by the new proposals. The personnel department should be able to provide such a list.

(ii)   The college registration department should be able to provide a list of all students attending courses to prepare them for their professional examinations.

(iii) The Education department of the local authority should be able to provide a list of all schoolchildren in the city, or a list of schools which could supply lists of their pupils. These lists of pupils could then be combined to form the sampling frame.

(b)   In the large factory, the recommended type of sampling method would depend on whether the workers affected by the new proposals were homogeneous and in one department, or whether they logically fitted into separate levels of seniority, different departments and so on. In the former case, simple random sampling would be appropriate. In the latter case, stratified random sampling would be appropriate.

In the college it is likely that the different years of each course would be given separate tuition which was more or less relevant to the professional examinations. Stratified random sampling should therefore be performed, taking as the strata each year of each course.

In the large city, each of simple random sampling and stratified random sampling would be prohibitively expensive to carry out. A system such as multi-stage sampling would be more appropriate. A random sample would be taken from each school in a random selection of schools from throughout the city.

17   INCOMES

(a)

Population			Income before tax and benefits			Income after tax and benefits		
Millions	%	Cum %	£m	%	Cum %	£m	%	Cum %
40	25.0	25.0	25	6.25	6.25	37.5	12.5	12.50
40	25.0	50.0	25	6.25	12.50	37.5	12.5	25.00
40	25.0	75.0	50	12.50	25.00	75.0	25.0	50.00
20	12.5	87.5	100	25.00	50.00	75.0	25.0	75.00
20	12.5	100.0	200	50.00	100.00	75.0	25.0	100.00
160	100.0		400	100.00		300.0	100.0	

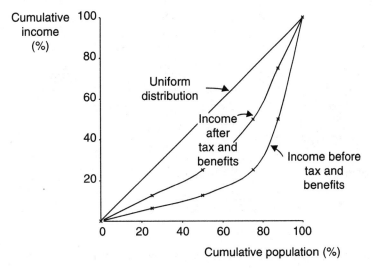

(b)   The two Lorenz curves show the degrees of concentration of pre-tax and post-tax incomes between the population. The further away from the diagonal line a curve is, the more concentrated is the distribution. We see from the graph that pre-tax income is spread less evenly than post-tax income, as might be expected in an equitable tax system.

(c)   A Lorenz curve could also be used to show whether the turnovers of all companies in an industry are fairly similar, or whether a large proportion of the turnover is concentrated in the hands of a few large companies.

18 HANDLING COSTS

(a) The frequency distribution of stock movements per week is given below.

Handling time		Mid point		
At least	Less than	x	f	fx
0	10	5	240	1,200
10	20	15	340	5,100
20	40	30	150	4,500
40	60	50	120	6,000
60	90	75	20	1,500
90	120	105	20	2,100
120	180	150	10	1,500
			900	21,900

Mean $\bar{x}$ $= \dfrac{21,900}{900}$

$= 24.33$ minutes

(b) Using the mid-points of the class intervals, the estimated total number of minutes spent each week in moving items of stock is 21,900 (Σ fx).

In hours, this is $\dfrac{21,900}{60} = 365$ person hours per week.

(c) The average number of jobs handled by each employee per week is

$$\dfrac{\text{Expected number of jobs}}{\text{Number of people}} = \dfrac{900}{12} = 75$$

19 SERVICE CHARGE

Mid point			
x	f	fx	fx^2
1	3	3	3
3	8	24	72
5	21	105	525
7	37	259	1,813
9	62	558	5,022
11	38	418	4,598
13	20	260	3,380
15	8	120	1,800
17	3	51	867
	200	1,798	18,080

$\bar{x}$ $= \dfrac{1,798}{200}$

$= 8.99$, say 9

The standard deviation is $\sqrt{\dfrac{18,080}{200} - (8.99)^2}$

$= \sqrt{90.4 - 80.8201}$

$= 3.10$

The repair times have a mean of 9 hours and a standard deviation of 3.1 hours.

20 PRICE AND QUANTITY

Item	Quantity	Price 1.7.X2	Price 1.7.X6		
	q_0	p_0 £	p_n £	$p_0 q_0$	$p_n q_0$
Widgets	18	8	6	144	108
Fidgets	12	7	8	84	96
Splodgets	24	2	4	48	96
Tudgets	15	6	7	90	105
Ringlets	8	10	9	80	72
				446	477

Index at 1.7.X6 $= \dfrac{477}{446} \times 100 = 107$

21 PROBABILITIES

(a) The *probability* of an outcome is the likelihood or chance of it happening. It is usually expressed as a proportion: for example, the probability of a tossed coin coming up heads is ½. The sum of the probabilities of all the (mutually exclusive) outcomes which could happen is always 1: for example, P(heads) + P(tails) = ½ + ½ = 1. If the probability of something is 1, then it *must* happen. On the other hand, if the probability of something is 0, then it *cannot* happen.

Probability theory uses formulae to compute the probabilities of various combinations of outcomes occurring. The appropriate formula depends on the relationships between events and between their outcomes. Here are some examples.

(i) Two outcomes are *mutually exclusive* when one of them cannot occur if the other occurs. Several outcomes are mutually exclusive if the occurrence of any one of them excludes the possibility of any of the others occurring.

(ii) Events are said to be *independent* if the outcome of one of them in no way affects the probabilities of the various outcomes of the others.

If several outcomes, X, Y and Z are mutually exclusive, then the probability that one of X, Y and Z will occur is given by the simple addition or OR law.

P (X, Y or Z) = P(X) + P(Y) + P(Z)

A more general rule of addition must be applied when outcomes are not mutually exclusive. If A and B are two possible outcomes then we apply the general rule of addition.

P(A or B) = P(A) + P(B) – P(A and B)

The probability of outcomes A and B of two independent events both occurring is given by the simple multiplication or AND law.

P(A and B) = P(A) × P(B)

If the probability of one outcome occurring is affected by whether another outcome occurs, then the probability that both outcomes will occur is given by the general rule of multiplication.

P(A and B) = P(A) × P(B|A) = P(B) × P(A|B)

where P(B|A) means the probability of B occurring given that A occurs.

(b) (i) (1) P(male reaching age of 80) $= \dfrac{16{,}199}{100{,}000} = 0.16199$

P(female reaching age of 80) $= \dfrac{24{,}869}{100{,}000} = 0.24869$

(2) P(male of 25 not reaching age of 50)

$= \dfrac{85{,}824 - 74{,}794}{85{,}824} = \dfrac{11{,}030}{85{,}824} = 0.1285$

P(female of 25 not reaching age of 50)

$= \dfrac{88{,}133 - 78{,}958}{88{,}133} = \dfrac{9{,}175}{88{,}133} = 0.1041$

(3) P(new born male survives until 10)

$$= \frac{89,023}{100,000} \qquad = 0.89023$$

P(new born female survives until 10)

$$= \frac{91,083}{100,000} \qquad = 0.91083$$

(4) P(male of 50 not reaching age of 80)

$$= \frac{74,794 - 16,199}{74,794} \qquad = \frac{58,595}{74,794} \ = 0.7834$$

P(female of 50 not reaching age of 80)

$$= \frac{78,958 - 24,869}{78,958} \qquad = \frac{54,089}{78,958} \ = 0.6850$$

(ii) A glance at the table of figures shows that females are likely to live longer than males. The probability calculations confirm that conclusion. Such data are used by life assurance companies, which use the statistics on the large numbers of people taking out life assurance policies to determine premiums. Note that reliable statistics can only be compiled on the basis of large samples, and that life assurance companies can only use them appropriately if they write many policies. If only one person has a policy, and he or she dies early, the assurer would suffer a loss even if that person had been 'likely' to live to a great age.

22 GEOLOGICAL TESTS

(a)

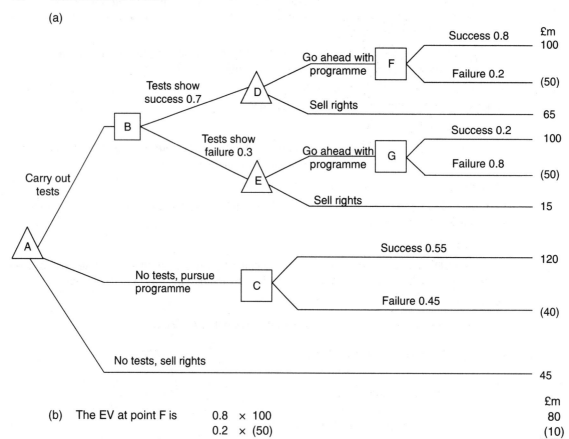

£m

(b) The EV at point F is

0.8 × 100	80
0.2 × (50)	(10)
	70

The decision at point D will be to pursue the programme rather than sell the rights for £65,000,000, and the EV at point D is therefore £70,000,000.

£m

The EV at point G is

0.2 × 100	20
0.8 × (50)	(40)
	(20)

The decision at point E will be to sell the rights rather than pursue the programme, and the EV at point E is £15,000,000.

		£m
The EV at point C is	0.55 × 120	66
	0.45 × (40)	(18)
		48

		£m
The EV at point B is	0.7 × 70	49.0
	0.3 × 15	4.5
		53.5

The decision at point A is between

(i)	conducting tests	EV	£53,500,000
(ii)	not conducting tests and pursuing the programme	EV	£48,000,000
(iii)	not conducting tests and selling the rights	EV	£45,000,000

The EV at point A, choosing option (i) with the highest EV, is £53,500,000.

23   INELASTIC ROPE

Supplier A

(a)   750 kg lies 250 kg below the mean which is 250/100 = 2.5 standard deviations below the mean.

From tables, the probability of the breaking strength being at least 750 kg is 1 − 0.00621 = 0.99379.

Supplier B

750 kg lies 150 kg below the mean, which is 150/75 = 2 standard deviations below the mean.

From tables, the probability of the breaking strength being at least 750 kg is 1 − 0.02275 = 0.97725.

If the company is most concerned about the breaking strength not being less than 750 kg (rather than with the mean breaking strength of each supplier's rope) it would be better to purchase supplier A's rope.

(b)   (i)   The standard error of the sample mean is $2.02/\sqrt{49}$ = 0.2886 minutes.

The null hypothesis is that the population mean is 48 minutes. The alternative hypothesis is that it is more than 48 minutes. This is a one-tail test at 1% significance, so the cut-off level is 2.33 standard errors.

50 − 48 = 2 minutes = 2/0.2886 = 6.9 standard errors.

We therefore reject the null hypothesis and conclude that the average time per unit in January 20X3 was longer than 48 minutes. The claim of the factory manager is rejected.

(ii)   80% confidence limits would be 1.28 standard errors either side of the sample mean of 50 minutes.

Confidence limits = 50 ± (1.28 × 0.2886) minutes
  = 50 ± 0.3694 minutes
  = 49.63 and 50.37 minutes.

24   QUADRATIC EQUATIONS

(a)   (i) x = $[+1.28 \pm \sqrt{((-1.28^2) + 4 \times 1 \times 5.16)}]/(2 \times 1)$
  = $[+1.28 \pm \sqrt{22.2784}]/2$
  = $[+1.28 \pm 4.72]/2$
  = 3 or −1.72.

(ii) x = $[-33 \pm \sqrt{(33^2 - 4 \times 4 \times 68)}]/(2 \times 4)$
  = $[-33 \pm \sqrt{1}]/8$
  = $[-33 \pm 1]/8$
  = −4 or −4.25.

BPP PUBLISHING

(iii) $x = [-6 \pm \sqrt{(6^2 + 4 \times 3 \times 24)}]/(2 \times -3)$

$= [-6 \pm \sqrt{324}]/(-6)$

$= [-6 \pm 18]/(-6)$

$= -2$ or $+4$.

(iv) $x = [+4.8 \pm \sqrt{((-4.8)^2 - 4 \times 1 \times 5.76)}]/(2 \times 1)$

$= (+4.8 \pm \sqrt{0})/2$

$= 2.4$.

(b) Total revenue = $pq = 600q - 0.15q^2 = 450,000$

$-0.15q^2 + 600q - 450,000 = 0$

$q = [-600 \pm \sqrt{(600^2 - 4 \times 0.15 \times 450,000)}]/(2 \times -0.15)$

$= [-600 \pm \sqrt{90,000}]/(-0.3)$

$= [-600 \pm 300]/(-0.3)$

$= 1,000$ or $3,000$ units.

25 VARIABLE OR FIXED

(a) It is an over-simplification to say that costs are readily identifiable as either fixed or variable throughout a range of production.

While many variable costs approximate to a linear behaviour pattern (rise in a straight line fashion as the volume of activity increases), some variable costs are in fact curvilinear, becoming either more expensive or cheaper per unit as activity levels change. A unit variable cost which might increase as activity increases is direct labour. Bonus payments might be paid progressively as certain levels of production are reached. An example of a variable cost becoming progressively cheaper per unit as activity increases is direct materials. Discounts are sometimes available when larger quantities are purchased.

Fixed costs do not necessarily remain fixed. While many fixed costs do remain constant within the relevant range of activity, there are likely to be steps or changes in the fixed cost if activity extends beyond this range. For example, it may be possible to operate with one salaried supervisor at a certain level of activity, but once this activity level is exceeded more supervisors are required and there is a resulting step in the fixed cost. This is known as step cost behaviour.

A lot of costs are actually semi-fixed (or semi-variable or mixed). The increasing labour cost described above has a flat fixed rate and a variable bonus element and a telephone bill will have a fixed cost for rental and a variable cost depending on the number of calls made. Other cost patterns include step costs (supervisor, as described above, and rent, where accommodation requirements increase as output levels get higher) and patterns appropriate to certain items (such as where a bulk purchase discount applies retrospectively to all units purchased or where a discount applies only to units purchased in excess of a certain quantity).

(b) A directly variable cost is a cost which increases or decreases in direct proportion to the level of activity. Production labour has traditionally been regarded as a directly variable cost. Any of the following factors or circumstances could make this treatment inappropriate.

(i) *The existence of guaranteed daily or weekly wages.* These are payable regardless of the level of activity. Production labour would then be a fixed or a semi-variable cost.

(ii) *Negotiated permanent manning levels.* This would mean that employees would still be paid even if there was no work available in a slack period.

(iii) *Differential bonus or piecework rates.* These would cause the labour cost per unit to increase for higher levels of output.

(iv) *A high degree of mechanisation.* This could mean that the labour input has little effect on the volume of output.

26   BUILDING COMPANY

First we need to calculate the fixed costs for the period using the high-low method.

	Units	Profit
		£'000
High - March	30	250
Low - June	16	40
	14	210
Variable cost per unit (£210,000/14)		£15,000

	£'000
Taking March as an example	
Sales (30 × £30,000)	900
Profit	250
Total costs	650
Variable costs (30 × £15,000)	450
Fixed costs	200

Fixed costs for the six months = 6 × £200,000 = £1,200,000.

We now need to calculate the breakeven point as follows.

	£'000
Per unit	
Selling price	30
Variable cost	15
Contribution	15

Breakeven point is where total contribution = fixed costs. Breakeven point is therefore where £15,000N – £1,200,000, where N is the breakeven quantity of units.

N = £(1,200,000/15,000) = 80 units

Breakeven sales revenue = 80 × £30,000 = £2,400,000

Breakeven chart

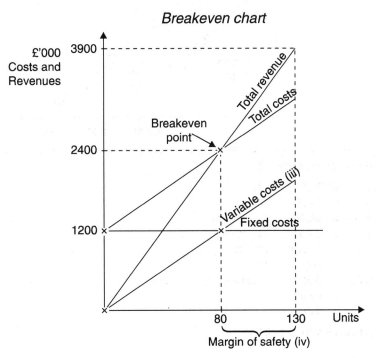

Note that at 80 units, the variable cost is 80 × £15,000 = £1,200,000.

27   **WALLOP LTD**

(a)
	Hake	_Pane_
Hours per unit		
Labour	8 hrs	6 hrs
Machining	5 hrs	8 hrs

The linear programming problem may be formulated as follows.

Let   x be the number of hakes produced per month
        y be the number of panes produced per month.

The objective is to maximise $16x + 20y$ subject to the following constraints.

$8x + 6y$	$\leq$	9,600	(labour hours)
$5x + 8y$	$\leq$	8,125	(machine hours)
x	$\leq$	1,000	(demand)
x, y	$\geq$	0	

(b)

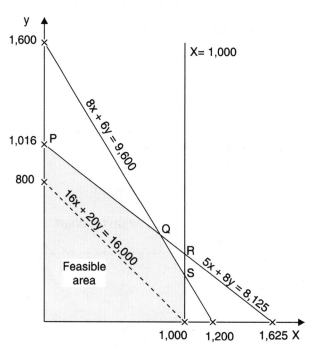

Using an iso-contribution line $16x + 20y = 16,000$ to obtain the gradient, we can see that the optimal solution is at point Q.

$5x + 8y$	=	8,125	(1)
$8x + 6y$	=	9,600	(2)
$40x + 64y$	=	65,000	(3) ((1) × 8)
$40x + 30y$	=	48,000	(4) ((2) × 5)
$34y$	=	17,000	(5) ((3) − (4))
y	=	500	(6)
$8x + 3,000$	=	9,600	(substituting (6) in (2))
$8x$	=	6,600	
x	=	825	

The optimal solution is as follows.

	Contribution
	£
825 units of hake (× £16)	13,200
500 units of pane (× £20)	10,000
Total monthly contribution	23,200

28   CHALK AND CHEESE

(a)   *Chalk Ltd*

$C = 2q^2 + 40q + 80$

$\dfrac{dC}{dq} = 4q + 40 = $ marginal cost (MC)

Revenue (R) = 200q

$\dfrac{dR}{dq} = 200 = $ marginal revenue (MR)

Profit is maximised where MC = MR:

$$4q + 40 = 200$$
$$q = 40$$

Profits at q = 40 are as follows.

	Chalk Ltd £	Cheese Ltd £
Revenue	8,000	14,400
Less costs	4,880	14,800 *
Weekly profit/(loss)	3,120	(400)

* $2q^2 + 280q + 400$ including the costs of purchases from Chalk Ltd which total 200q.

(b)   *Cheese Ltd*

$C = 2q^2 + 280q + 400$

$\dfrac{dC}{dq} = 4q + 280$

$R = 1,000q - 16q^2$

$\dfrac{dR}{dq} = 1,000 - 32q$

MC = MR where

$$4q + 280 = 1,000 - 32q$$
$$36q = 720$$
$$q = 20$$

Profits at q = 20 are as follows.

	Chalk Ltd £	Cheese Ltd £
Revenue	4,000	13,600
Less costs	1,680	6,800 *
Weekly profit	2,320	6,800

* $2q^2 + 280q + 400$

(c)   *Chalk and Cheese Ltd*

Total costs

	$2q^2$	+	40q	+	80
	$2q^2$	+	80q	+	400
C =	$4q^2$	+	120q	+	480

$\dfrac{dC}{dq} = 8q + 120$

$R = 1,000q - 16q^2$

$\dfrac{dR}{dq} = 1,000 - 32q$

MR = MC when

$$1,000 - 32q = 8q + 120$$
$$880 = 40q$$
$$q = 22$$

	£
Revenue	14,256
Less costs	5,056
Weekly profit	9,200

29 REED JUICES LTD

$$EOQ = \sqrt{\frac{2C_oD}{C_H}} = \sqrt{\frac{2 \times 32 \times 25,000}{4 + (15\% \text{ of } 16)}} = \sqrt{250,000} = 500 \text{ litres}$$

	800 litres per order		*500 litres per order*	
	£		£	
Holding costs	$(\frac{800}{2} \times £6.40)$	2,560	$(\frac{500}{2} \times £6.40)$	1,600
Ordering costs	$(\frac{25,000}{800} \times £32)$	1,000	$(\frac{25,000}{500} \times £32)$	1,600
Total annual costs		3,560		3,200

The annual saving would be £(3,560 − 3,200) = £360.

30 DAISY HOOF LTD

(a)

Year	Cash flow	Discount factor	Present value
	£	16%	£
0	(50,000)	1.000	(50,000)
1	18,000	0.862	15,516
2	25,000	0.743	18,575
3	15,000	0.641	9,615
4	12,000	0.552	6,624
		NPV	330

(b) The IRR is a little above 16%. Try 18%.

Year	Cash flow	Discount factor	Present value
	£	18%	£
0	(50,000)	1.000	(50,000)
1	18,000	0.848	15,264
2	25,000	0.718	17,950
3	15,000	0.609	9,135
4	12,000	0.516	6,192
		NPV	(1,459)

Using interpolation, the IRR approximately equals

$$16\% + \left[\frac{330}{(330 + 1,459)} \times (18 - 16) \right]\%$$

= 16.4%.

Lecturers' question bank

1   DATA PROCESSING AND COMPUTERS

Computers are used for the purpose of processing data for a wide range of applications.

(a)   What do you understand by the term *data processing*?

(b)   Identify and describe *five* basic data processing activities, illustrating each one with a practical example from a computerised weekly payroll system.

(c)   What are the advantages of using a computer to process data?

2   OVERHEAD ABSORPTION RATES (14 marks)   *25 mins*

One of the directors of Company X has been looking at the budgets that have been prepared recently and shows concern at the production costs budget. The overhead absorption rate, based on a percentage on direct wages, has increased from 200% to 300%.

Required

(a)   Explain how overhead absorption rates are calculated and used.   (4 marks)

(b)   Explain what factors may have caused the above increase.   (4 marks)

(c)   Explain the circumstances that could make this increase acceptable.   (6 marks)

3   RENT AND RATES

(a)   Suggest possible apportionment methods for the following overhead cost items.

(i)   Rent and rates
(ii)   Supervisors salaries
(iii)   Canteen costs
(iv)   Machine depreciation

(b)   Calculate under- or over-absorption of overhead from the following information.

	Machine department	Finishing department
Budgeted labour hours	2,200	4,000
Budgeted overhead costs	£11,000	£16,000
Actual labour hours	2,350	3,900
Actual overhead costs	£11,250	£16,720

(c)   Show the accounting entries for the above information.

4   REMUNERATION SCHEMES

The following information is available.

Normal working day	8 hours
Guaranteed rate of pay (on time basis)	£5.50 per hour
Standard time allowed to produce one unit	3 minutes
Piecework price	£0.10 per standard minute
Premium bonus	75% of time saved, in addition to hourly pay

Required

For daily production levels of 80, 120 and 210 units, calculate earnings based on the following remuneration methods.

(a)   Piecework, where earnings are guaranteed at 80% of time-based pay
(b)   Premium bonus system

5 SANDY BOTTOM PILINGS LTD (14 marks) *25 mins*

On 2 February 20X2 Sandy Bottom Pilings Limited began work on the construction of a telephone exchange building for a contracted price of £1,125,000 with a promised date of completion of 1 May 20X3. The budgeted cost of the contract was £900,000.

The financial accounting year of Sandy Bottom Pilings Ltd ends on 30 November 20X2 and on that date the cost accounts relating to the contract showed the following balances.

	£'000
Materials issued to site	242
Materials returned from site	21
Wages paid	102
Plant on site:	
Plant owned, at cost	144
Hired plant charges	108
Supervision	16
Sundry expenses	18
Head office costs	95

£3,000 is owed in wages.

Depreciation on plant is 12½% per annum on cost.

Materials on site at 30 November were valued at £36,000.

Value of work certified up to 30 November 20X2	£600,000
Cost of work completed but not yet certified	£60,000
Cash received for work certified	£495,000

It is expected that the contract will be completed on time without any foreseeable difficulties.

Required

Prepare the contract account up to 30 November 20X2 showing the amount to be included in the company's profit and loss account.

6 FACTORY A (14 marks) *25 mins*

In Factory A, the standard processing loss in a single production process is 15%. The scrap from the process, which has a sales value of 20p per kilogram, is delivered immediately to a dealer who has an arrangement with the company to purchase for cash whatever scrap is produced.

In Period 9, 26,000 kg of basic raw material was input to the process and 23,200 kilograms of the end product was made. The costs of production were as follows.

Raw material	80p per kg
Labour	£12,090
Overhead	100% of labour costs

There was no opening or closing stock.

Required

Prepare the necessary accounts to show the result of the process.

7 FACTORY B (14 marks) *25 mins*

In Factory B, a product called Golden Grime is made by passing input units through three consecutive and distinct processes. At each processing stage, extra materials are added to the product, and direct labour and overhead costs incurred.

Work in progress at the beginning of period 4 consisted of 12,000 units which had just completed the first process and were about to be input to the second process. The cost of these units up to this point was made up as follows.

	£
Direct materials	9,300
Direct labour	4,500
Overhead	3,000

16,800

During period 4, these units were input to process 2, when additional raw materials were added at cost of £8,400 and labour costs of £3,600 incurred. Production overhead is applied to cost at the rate of 160% of labour costs; actual overhead incurred during period 4 was £6,200.

During the period, 9,600 units of output were completed and transferred to process 3. Of the remaining units, it was estimated by the works engineer that half were 75% complete and the other half were 50% complete with regard to extra materials and conversion costs (that is, labour and production overhead).

Required

Write up the process 2 account for period 4, showing clearly the cost of raw material transferred to process 3 and the value of closing work in progress in period 3. Explain your treatment of production overhead.

8   ROSEBOWL HOTEL (14 marks)   *25 mins*

The Rosebowl Hotel has 80 rooms and these are all either double or twin-bedded rooms offered for either holiday accommodation or for private hire for conferences and company gatherings.

In addition the hotel has a recreation area offering swimming pool, sauna and so on. This area is for the use of all residents with some days being available for paying outside customers.

The restaurant is highly regarded and widely recommended. This is used by the guests and is also open to the general public.

Required

Discuss the accounting information that might be used in this organisation, concentrating on the cost information that might be needed for management control and pricing of services.

9   CRITICISE A GRAPH

The figure below purports to show the profits of four divisions within a firm during the period from 20X0 to 20X5.

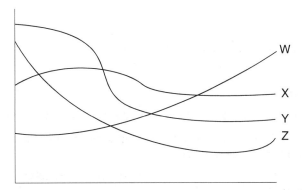

Required

(a)   Criticise the graph by outlining a series of rules for correct graphical presentation.

(b)   Suggest briefly some alternative methods of presenting these data.

10   COMPONENTS (14 marks)   *25 mins*

An item of electronic equipment uses 100 special components. From previous tests, the components are known to have a maximum life expectancy of 1,000 days. An estimate of the life expectancy of the 100 components has been prepared as follows.

Elapsed time	Number in working order
Days	
0	100
100	98
200	95
300	90
400	84
500	76
600	66
700	54
800	40
900	22
1,000	0

Required

(a) Graph these data, and from the graph, calculate the following.

    (i)   The median working life

    (ii)   The quartiles for the working life   (10 marks)

(b) Prepare from the data a frequency distribution of the expected working life of a component and calculate the mean expected life from your distribution.   (4 marks)

11 PRICE RELATIVES

A company wishes to construct a price index for three commodities, A, B and C. The prices in 20X0 were £2, £3 and £5 respectively and quantities consumed in the same period were 5,000, 6,000 and 3,000 respectively. The prices for 20X1 and 20X2 are given as percentages of 20X0 prices.

	20X1	20X2
A	100	110
B	108	115
C	90	100

Required

Construct a price index using 20X0 as a base year.

12 PERRY WINKLE LTD

The directors and senior managers of Perry Winkle Ltd have met to consider three subjects.

There is a proposal to move the head office of the company from London to Liverpool, and the current state of opinion appears to be as follows.

	In favour	Opposed	Undecided	Total
Executive directors	4	1	2	7
Non-executive directors	2	3	3	8
Senior managers	7	12	2	21
	13	16	7	36

Required

Calculate the probability that a person at the meeting, selected at random, will be as follows.

(a) An executive director in favour of the proposal

(b) Opposed to the proposal

(c) Either a senior manager or undecided about the proposal

13 CLAM

The company manufactures and sells a single product, the Clam. Estimated sales, costs and selling prices for the coming year are as follows.

Sales Units	Probability	Selling price per unit £	Probability
10,000	0.4	8.00	0.3
15,000	0.4	7.50	0.6
20,000	0.2	7.00	0.1

Variable cost per unit £	Probability	Fixed costs for the year £	Probability
5.00	0.1	12,000	0.4
5.50	0.2	15,000	0.6
5.80	0.5		
6.00	0.2		

The outcome for each item (selling price, sales, variable and fixed costs) is in no way dependent on the outcome of any other item.

Required

(a) Calculate the expected annual profit.
(b) Calculate the worst possible result for the coming year and the probability that this will occur.

14 BAGS OF SUGAR

A random sample of 100 bags of sugar taken from a particular supermarket's shelves has been classified by weight into the following frequency distribution.

Weight Kg	Number of bags of sugar
0.94 and < 0.95	8
0.95 and < 0.96	15
0.96 and < 0.97	22
0.97 and < 0.98	17
0.98 and < 0.99	10
0.99 and < 1.00	8
1.00 and < 1.01	7
1.01 and < 1.02	6
1.02 and < 1.03	4
1.03 and < 1.04	3
	100

Required

(a) Calculate the mean and standard deviation of the sample.

(b) Place confidence limits on the mean value of the weight of all bags of sugar at the following levels.

(i) The 95% confidence level
(ii) The 99% confidence level

15 DELIVERY DATES

A company, X Ltd, which promises delivery dates to its customers, has estimated from experience that only 70% of orders are delivered on time and 30% are late. In a recent sample of 60 orders in March 20X2, it was found that only 14 were late.

Required

(a) Test the claim, at a 5% level of significance, that the proportion of orders delivered late in March 20X2.

(b) Determine the level of significance at which the claim would be justified, based on the sample results.

16 FORMULATE

(a) Hitech produces and sells three products, HTO1, HTO2 and HTO3.

The following details of prices and product costs have been extracted from Hitech's cost accounting records.

	Product		
	HTO1	HTO2	HTO3
	£	£	£
Price per unit	150	200	220
Costs per unit			
Direct labour at £4/hr	100	120	132
Direct material at £20/kg	20	40	40

Direct labour is regarded as a variable product cost.

An estimate of the relationship between overhead costs and production of the three products has been made. Expressed in weekly terms this is as follows.

$$Y = 4,000 + 0.5x_1 + 0.7x_2 + 0.8x_3$$

where
Y = total overhead cost per week
x_1 = HTO1, weekly direct labour hours
x_2 = HTO2, weekly direct labour hours
x_3 = HTO3, weekly direct labour hours

The company operates a 46 week year.

Required

Compute the contribution per unit for each of HTO1, HTO2 and HTO3.

(b) The material used by Hitech is also used in a wide variety of other applications and is in limited supply. As business conditions improve in general, there will be pressure for the price of this material to rise, but strong competition in Hitech's sector of the market would make it unlikely that increased material costs can be passed on to customers in higher product prices. Hitech can obtain 20,000 kg at current prices.

Further, the number of available direct labour hours is estimated at no more that 257,600 hours for the next year.

Demand for each product over the year is forecast to be as follows.

HTO1	16,000 units
HTO2	10,000 units
HTO3	6,000 units

Required

Formulate a linear programme from the above data in order to obtain the annual production and sales plan which will maximise Hitech's contribution and profit. You are not required to solve the problem.

*List of key terms
& formulae to
learn and index*

These are the terms which we have identified throughout the text as being KEY TERMS and the formulae that you must learn. You should make sure that you can define what these terms mean and that you are able to reproduce the formulae correctly; go back to the pages highlighted here if you need to check.

BPP PUBLISHING

BPP PUBLISHING